D0816894

THE COMPLETE
Blackpowder Handbook
4th EDITION

By Sam Fadala

©2001 by
Krause Publications

All rights reserved.
No part of this publication may be reproduced or transmitted in any form or by any means,
electronic or mechanical, including photocopy, recording or any information storage and retrieval system, without
permission in writing from the author, except by a reviewer who may quote brief passages in a critical article or
review to be printed in a magazine or newspaper or electronically transmitted on radio or television.

Published by

krause
publications

700 East State St., Iola, WI 54990-0001
715-445-2214
www.krause.com

Please, call or write us for our free catalog of antiques and collectibles publications.
To place an order or receive our free catalog, call 800-258-0929. For editorial comment and further information,
use our regular business telephone at (715) 445-2214

Library of Congress Catalog Number: 2001091062
ISBN: 0-87349-294-3

Printed in the United States of America

DEDICATION

For Dad and Mom — two faithful friends.

ABOUT THE COVERS

Dixie Gun Works

Dixie Gun Works founder Turner E. Kirkland was not doing well as a traveling jewelry salesman. It was 1954, and the department stores he sold to were not providing him with a decent living.

Fortunately he had a hobby that was making him a little spending money: selling old guns and parts out of the back of his car's trunk.

When he returned home in April 1954 to discover that nearly all the gun parts he had advertised were sold, he turned a Model T garage into the first Dixie Gun Works site.

Today, Dixie Gun Works is one of the best-known names in supplying muzzleloading arms, parts and accessories worldwide. Kirkland's first 12-page pocket catalog of 1954 has become a 736-page wish book of more than 10,000 items sold to blackpowder shooters, hunters, collectors and re-enactment participants. The current 46,000-square-foot facility in Union City, Tenn., includes a 5,000-square-foot showroom that displays nearly 2,000 antique guns offered for sale.

This American company is proud of its many achievements, including the first replica large-scale firing cannon, the first production-made replica muzzleloading rifle, the first production replica flintlock, first production replica percussion gun and many others.

Kirkland died in 1997, but Dixie Gun Works lives on as a testament to his hard work and his foresight to realize that many thousands of Americans would one day embrace the fun and inhale the white smoke of blackpowder arms. Sometimes doing things "the old way" really is the best way!

> **Cover Guns:** From the top are the Dixie Gun Works Sharps rifle in 45-90 caliber, a Dixie Jaeger flintlock rifle in 54 caliber and a Dixie LeMat Confederate revolver in 44 caliber with a single 20-gauge barrel below the main barrel.

GOEX

GOEX, one of the oldest names in blackpowder, traces its history back to 1912. That is when a Pennsylvania plant owned by E.I. Du Pont de Nemours began producing its first blackpowder.

Within three years, the Belin Plant became the nation's second-largest producer of blackpowder. Production remained steady as its workers provided millions of pounds of military blackpowder for both world wars, as well as the Korean and Vietnam conflicts.

The increased use of other explosives reduced the need for blackpowder, prompting Du Pont to withdraw from the manufacture of blackpowder in the early 1970s. The Belin Plant eventually became part of GOEX Inc. GOEX retained most of the Du Pont employees and used their expertise to improve the new company. Soon GOEX powders were shipping to both commercial and government markets.

GOEX moved to the former headquarters of the Louisiana Army Ammunition Plant in Doyline, La., in 1997. Today, this facility is the sole blackpowder manufacturing facility in North America.

GOEX offers a full line of powder granulations, including Fg, FFg, FFFg, FFFFg, Cartridge and Cannon grain sizes for blackpowder rifles, shotguns and handguns.

Although the company makes traditional products, it also makes a new propellant that is attracting much attention from muzzleloader users. ClearShot, a non-corrosive propellant that does not contain ascorbic acids or perchlorates, is now available. ClearShot does not draw moisture like traditional blackpowder, has an indefinite shelf life and provides consistent velocity with low pressure — just like blackpowder. And it cleans up with water! It also has Class B DOT shipping and storing status — just like smokeless powder.

TABLE OF CONTENTS

INTRODUCTION

The world of blackpowder shooting has evolved in guns, ignition, bullets, powders, maintenance, and other important areas since the Third Edition of this book left the printing house. This Fourth Edition of *The Complete Blackpowder Handbook* reflects these important changes, with a two-fold goal: promoting great *success* in firing muzzleloaders and blackpowder cartridge arms *safely*. After all, these guns require more input and attention than cartridge-shooters, which demand only the feeding of prepared round after round, while muzzleloaders are a handloading proposition for each and every shot. Meanwhile, the blackpowder cartridge resides in a separate world unto itself, demanding exacting bullets, lubes, powders, and special handling to realize accuracy potential.

The Guns

Modern in-line ignition muzzleloaders, as well as the unique Outer-Line® design from Markesbery, have caught up with the popular non-replica. Sales are so brisk among the breed that there is little doubt of its continued march to leadership. The reason is clear and simple. The vast majority of frontloaders find their way into the big game hunting field, especially for special "primitive" seasons in which modern arms are not allowed. The average shooter harbors little interest in the amazingly colorful history of muzzleloading on the eastern seaboard or Far West. The exploits of Dan'l Boone, Davy Crockett, Jed Smith and Old Gabe (Jim Bridger) sell very few guns.

Today's hunter is looking for the most familiar firearm possible, while adhering to game department rules. This is why Remington's Model 700 MS, Ruger's 77/50, and the Savage muzzleloader thrive. While there has been a backlash against what may be considered too much advancement, such as Colorado's on-again, off-again ban of in-line muzzleloaders for special blackpowder-only hunts, modern muzzleloaders have weathered all storms and are here to stay. How far will technology carry them? We cannot say. We do know, however, that continued research and development is inevitable. After all, we now have a modern muzzleloader designed to safely shoot smokeless powder, the 50-caliber Savage Model 10 ML. Technology is an iron steed galloping into the future, spurred by curiosity, testing, and an unquenchable desire to invent.

Systems Muzzleloaders

Multiple barrels on one frame are not a new idea, but in the world of muzzleloading, it is a highly workable one. Citing but one example of this trend, there is the Markesbery Outer-Line® offering calibers 36, 45, 50 and 54, as well as a 12-gauge shotgun barrel, all on one frame. Sights go with the barrel, so there is no need to recalibrate as barrels are swapped, plus interchangeability is accomplished in scant minutes.

Ignition

Standard percussion caps in typical sizes, such as No. 10 and No. 11, are better than ever, yet two other sources of setting off black-powder charges in the breeches of a muzzleloader have gained considerable ground. These are the large English musket cap, also known as the tophat, and modern primers: small rifle, small pistol, plus No. 209 shotgun sizes prevailing. The idea itself is not new. The late 19th century saw devices that held primers instead of percussion caps. They replaced the standard nipple, screwing directly into its tapped and threaded seat. Many modern muzzleloaders follow the same path. An example is the Thompson/Center Encore, known as the 209/50 Magnum, 209 for its use of the shotgun primer for ignition, 50 for 50 caliber, Magnum because the rifle is engineered to take three Pyrodex 50/50 Pellets for a 150-grain **volume** equivalent powder charge. Knight's Disc Rifle also relies on No. 209 shotshell primers. Ignition by other than a standard percussion cap is the wave of the future, while at the same time, newly designed nipples do a better-than-ever job of delivering fire from the source to the breech.

Bullets

Bullet makers have worn their pencils blunt coming up with various projectiles for muzzleloaders. Jacketed pistol bullets started the trend, with Nosler's Partition a perfect example of the breed, and now spitzers from Buffalo Bullet Co. and Northern Precision. Why? To take advantage of those select modern muzzleloaders built for heavy powder charges for increased velocity with consequently flatter trajectories. The 200-yard frontloader, for better or worse, is a reality, especially when shooting high-sectional-density bullets with good ballistic coefficients. How about a muzzleloader bullet (the Devel) made of tin and copper, no lead, no expansion, producing a shock wave created by fins? It's here. Polycarbonate tips, all-copper missiles, projectiles with attached gaskets, are only a few examples of new bullets for muzzleloaders. The future will see many more.

Powders

Pyrodex Pellets are like solid rocket fuel. No measure necessary, no funnel, no powder can — simply drop the appropriate pellet or pellets in the bore, seat a bullet correctly on top of them and fire away. The pellet now comes in many different sizes and volume equivalent charges. Goex has Clear Shot, a clean-burning blackpowder substitute. High-grade Swiss Black Powder from that country has reached our shores. Wano from Germany is here. Elephant from Brazil has been recast into an even better powder in recent times. Meanwhile, hovering on the horizon is a propellant that behaves like blackpowder, can be loaded by volume, not weight, makes smoke (probably), is entirely safe in muzzleloaders, and yet is absolutely non-corrosive. This powder does not yet exist, but the midnight oil is burning in R&D labs right now.

Maintenance

Shooting blackpowder guns is so interesting that no dedicated arms lover could possibly turn away from this great sport within the sport. Along with the fun of making smoke comes the special hunt, where only frontstuffers are allowed. Why then isn't every marksman in the land in possession of at least one old-style firearm? Cleaning after shooting is the problem. It just seems like too much bother. That reason grows thinner as chemists work toward better and better solvents to quickly attack blackpowder fouling.

The 10-minute Pyrodex cleanup is already here, partially due to modern solvents, and as we await the invention of a non-corrosive muzzleloader propellant, more and better solvents continue to hit the street. Furthermore, most in-line designs allow removal of the breech plug so the guns can be cleaned from the breech, just like modern bolt-action rifles. Up to the elbows in blackpowder soot and a bucket of hot water is a thing of the past, with the future promising even easier after-shooting maintenance, as well as products designed to cut fouling on the range or in the hunting field to reduce left-over products, an example being any of the "all-day" lubes.

Accouterments

New guns require new accessories, and the marketplace is replete with them. Even companies known for superior traditional items, such as Cash Manufacturing, are in the game, as proved by its TDC Original Straight Line 209 Primer Dispenser, created especially to retain and dispense shotgun primers, proving that where there is a need, it will be fulfilled. Traditions blackpowder company offers a set of lightweight, compact shooting tools, including a short starter and a flask, while T/C has a long line of modernized blackpowder accouterments. Special tools also are provided with in-line rifles to speed up after-shooting maintenance.

Buckskinning

All this talk about modern muzzleloaders and sky-high advancements in the blackpowder world would seem to ring a death knell for the more historical aspects of shooting old-style guns. Not true. Rendezvous are stronger than ever, as a search on the Internet will instantly reveal. Old-time tents resting in a pristine valley are available east to west and north to south. The crackling of frontloaders going off is heard from border to border, coast to coast. For these

"doings," in-liners and similar high-tech guns and gear are as out of place as a tuxedo at a football game. Emulators of old times want to look the part, and they do, by the rules. Dressing in out-of-period duds delivers a keep-out ticket every time. While guns are less managed at these events than clothing and general gear, modern muzzleloaders will not be found on the firing range as a rule. The booshway (leader of the event) would probably frown on it. On the other hand, true replicas of Pennsylvania/Kentucky long rifles and Hawken plains rifles are not required. Lyman's Great Plains Rifle, as one example, has been generally welcomed because it embodies the spirit, if not screw-for-screw authenticity, of the "real thing" out of the past. So shooting the old way with traditional-style guns is far from extinct. This species of blackpowder shooting, with its special games and events, is not on any endangered list at this time.

Future Blackpowder-Only Hunts

Every state allows muzzleloaders for hunting. Most have special blackpowder-only "primitive" seasons. Hunts are often set up so modern guns are not welcomed. While frontloaders possess sufficient power to down any animal on the planet, given proper caliber, bullet, and load, they do not have the extreme range normally associated with high-intensity cartridges. A 7mm Magnum, for example, can launch a projectile three miles. A 50-caliber muzzleloader has far less range potential, making it a safer proposition in certain areas. Muzzleloaders are also desirable where certain game management goals must be met, especially where deer and other wild animals are in the process of destroying their own habitat, which may be in farm or ranch areas sensitive to long-range arms. Admittedly, there is another good reason for blackpowder-only hunts: more hunter participation with less impact on the game population. The 200-yard muzzleloader goes somewhat against this proposal; however, it remains a one-shot affair that demands deliberate reloading from the "front end." Therefore, the blackpowder hunter has a greater challenge in filling game tags, and is welcomed in areas where game departments want to put more hunters into the field, while at the same time reducing the success rate. Because of this, smokepole hunters are often given special seasons, such as elk or deer rut or migration times. More "primitive" hunts are a certainty for the future.

Why Shoot Blackpowder?

So why do it? Why go backwards? Because taking up the smokepole is not a rearward step at all. Blackpowder shooting never died out in America, as gun magazines such as *The American Rifleman* prove, carrying muzzleloader stories from inception to the present. Smokeless powder cartridges supplanted sootburners, but the old-time guns were too worthwhile to say die. In the meanwhile, an entirely new blackpowder niche has been created by the modern muzzleloader. Many who give the nod to the beautiful long rifles of yesteryear, and their pistol and shotgun mates, have to admit at the same time that the new guns stand on their own as interesting and also challenging, especially when carried on open-season hunts in which cartridge-shooting guns are allowed in the field at the same time. They are also well-crafted of superior design with super materials, and just plain fun to shoot.

Getting the Most from It

Myths and misconceptions are addressed throughout this Fourth Edition, providing the reader with a solid base of information to use. Getting started right is broached, along with choosing the best guns for special purposes. Safety is always the byword. Maintaining guns and gear in top shape is also laid out for the reader. And a lot more.

Sam Fadala, Wyoming

Anyone who doubths the power of a blackpowder rifle need only look at this photo. Author's brother Nick Fadala was behind the camera when this buffalo bull charge the pair. It was all caught on film. Fadala's first 54-caliber round ball took out the right hemisphere of the brain. The bull reared back and over, but got up, requiring a second shot. It pays to use readyloads in the field.

Chapter 1

IN THE BEGINNING

THE FIRST missiles to fly from the hands of man were probably stones tossed at wild beasts threatening the sanctity of the cave. David slew Goliath with what? A rock propelled at "high velocity" through the aid of a sling. Rocks found their way into battle much later when catapults launched large ones toward the enemy and his castle walls. But it was the bow that changed the destiny of man. Sticks sharpened in the flames of night fires became spears, thrust or thrown by hand. Although unproved, for it appears to exist in the same time frame as the bow, the atlatl probably supplanted the human arm in sending a spear-like dart away with multiplied force. When the bow came along, it far exceeded the atlatl in distance, delivered energy/penetration, and most of all, accuracy. The bow reigned for many centuries. The Ice Man, a 5,300-year old mummy found frozen in the Italian Alps, had with him a longbow with angled three-feathered shafts. An extremely similar bow fired deadly arrows from the hands of English archers in the battles of Agincourt and Crecy. The crossbow was proficient. The saying, "It struck like a bolt out of the blue" had nothing to do with lightning. This bolt, painted black or blue, was from a crossbow aimed high to rain its missiles down from the sky upon the enemy, but the crossbow was slow-loading and difficult to manage in the field.

No one knows when the first cloud of smoke from a blackpowder charge rose into the sky, but that moment in history marked the decline of the bow. We have no proof of who invented gunpowder (for that was its first name) or from where it came. China? India? Greece? We are certain, however, that the first real "engines of war" to use the propellant were created in Europe a very long time ago. These weapons were called "handguns." They were simply tubes held by hand, as opposed to cannons or other stationary weapons. They burned only small charges of powder and were probably of little consequence on the battlefield, mainly used to make smoke and noise, frightening more than harming the enemy. Because shooting history is shrouded in clouds of doubt, we know very little about these early guns. Examples from the Middle Ages, however, prove that advancement in firearms technology was well under way at that time in history. The firearm was now a viable tool, although clearly less effective in some regards than the bow. George Washington understood this fact. He toyed with the idea of arming his soldiers with archery equipment. After all, bows had more range and accuracy than smoothbore muskets of the same era. Of course, this did not happen. The gun prevailed and continued to advance in design and function.

First came the fuel. Gunpowder was nothing more than a mechanical mixture, not a compound, of three basic ingredients, as the forthcoming chapter on the topic relates. Furthermore, although simple in components, its pyrotechnic nature was, and amazingly still is, considerably involved and far from completely understood. India, China, Greece — there is no doubt that these countries had something that went boom in prehistory days. By the 11th century, there was some form of real gunpowder, probably weak in combustion, and certainly not employed as a propellant to fire bullets, rocks, arrows, or anything else. Smoke? Sure. Fire? Yes. Thunderous noise? You bet. But no references to smoke, fire, and noise in the very early times leads us to believe that a missile was propelled. In

The world of blackpowder shooting has changed immensely over time. Today, a rifle like this in-line Ruger Model 77/50 in 50-caliber is extremely popular with big game hunters. Coming from Ruger it is, of course, made of the finest materials and construction.

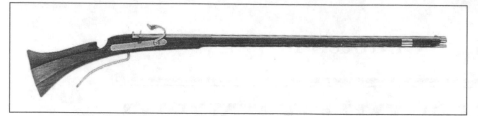

The matchlock was an early attempt to make a shoulder-held firearm that would shoot on demand. This is Dixie Gun Works' version of an English matchlock, probably the type that was first used in the New World. It's a smoothbore in 72 caliber.

short, the gunpowder that existed in the 11th century, and earlier, was not used in guns, because there were no guns.

There were few to no real guns in the 13th or 14th centuries, either, but incendiaries were quite popular for warfare. These combustibles were responsible for historical mayhem, because we think of gunpowder as belonging in guns. But this was not the case at the time. Long-ago notes pertaining to fire, smoke, and noise on the battlefield had to do with incendiaries. References to fire are clear enough. A ball of combustible stuff ignited would certainly provide the fire that historians spoke of, but these flaming objects could be tossed by a catapult. They would make plenty of smoke. The boom that came later could have been from an exploding missile. How long would it take the ancient warrior to realize that since gunpowder exploded, it could be harnessed within some sort of encasement, a type of shell that, launched at the enemy, would fragment into deadly shrapnel? Even if it did not explode into flying pieces of debris, it would flare up viciously. Because facts are missing, references to fire, smoke, and thunder do not prove that guns were on those ancient battlefields.

Another figure steps into the picture. Roger Bacon, the English friar, was a student at Oxford, and later a lecturer at that impressive institution of higher learning. This remarkable scholar wrote about explosives in various papers. We're talking about the middle 1200s,

which makes Bacon's observations very interesting. We don't know, unfortunately, if his original works were tampered with or left intact. Sometimes chapters were added to certain writings long after the original author passed on. However, we do have an interesting documented note from Bacon. He definitely knew about gunpowder, and what's more, he knew about it in the 1200s. He understood that the chemical mixture "blew up." Here is what he said in a treatise that Blackmore (mentioned below) pins down as written between 1266 and 1268:

"There is a child's toy of sound and fire made in various parts of the world with powders of saltpeters, sulfur, and charcoal of hazelwood. The powder is enclosed in an instrument of parchment the size of a finger, and since this can make such a noise that it seriously distresses the ears of men if one is taken unawares, and the terrible flash is also very alarming, if an instrument

of large size were used no one could stand the terror of the noise and the flash. If the instrument were made of solid materials, the violence of the explosion would be much greater."

The "firecracker" Bacon described, if larger and placed in a stronger container, could be used to improve the explosive quality of the powder. Furthermore, listen to Bacon's drift — the "instrument of larger size made of solid materials." The end result could be a grenade of sorts, even a bomb or exploding cannonball. But we don't hear Bacon talking about a gun. He's making note of gunpowder, obviously used in a rather innocuous manner to make noise, a little smoke, and a flash of fire. Interestingly, the three major ingredients that comprise blackpowder today, and for centuries earlier, were already noted in Bacon's time as saltpeter, sulfur, and charcoal.

We're forced to make assumptions when pieces of a puzzle are missing, as they are in shooting history. We do not know when the atlatl came about, or the bow. We will never know who made the first gun, either, or how it was built. Records indicate bamboo tubes were used to hold gunpowder. Later, these tubes were made of heavy paper. Did they shoot projectiles? Perhaps not at first. They may have been hand grenades containing hard objects that acted as shrapnel. But there

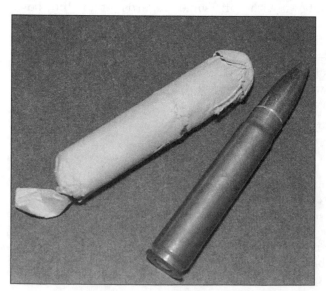

On the left is an original American Civil War paper cartridge, still containing bullet and powder. It's compared with a modern metallic cartridge for reference.

The evolution of muzzleloaders is now at the modern muzzleloader stage, with rifles like the Markesbery Outer-Line®, which in 50-caliber took this fine Kentucky whitetail buck.

is more to the story. Further references suggest that these tubes had one end open, the other end blocked. Some scholars believe they propelled arrows. Just as we like to think of the atlatl as a device that preceded the spear, without proof, and the bow logically coming after the atlatl, it's natural to consider these early tubes as throwing a missile that was common to man: an arrow. Records indicate that this is true, but we cannot fully rely on the data, for they came from an unscientific era of superstition.

So the path from blackpowder to guns is winding and thorny. Looking again at paper and/or bamboo tubes, we learn that one at least had a name. Howard L. Blackmore refers to the "lotus" and similar unnamed weapons in his book, *Guns And Rifles of the World*. He says, "The 'lotus' was a reinforced cylinder container on the end of a wooden stick. It was loaded with all sorts of powder and ejected fire, smoke, poison and iron arrows a foot long." Notice that the arrows Blackmore mentions were made of iron, rather than wood or other lighter material. It seems that the makers of the lotus and other "powder tubes" found that gunpowder had force enough to launch fairly heavy objects. Blackmore refers to another weapon as follows: "Another gun, without a name, consisted of a copper tube 3 feet long with a straight wooden handle which shot one arrow at a time a distance of 200-300 paces." This well-known researcher also points out that the arrow-throwing "gun" used gunpowder made of the three basic ingredients that still constitute blackpowder to this day: saltpeter, sulfur, charcoal, plus non-performing additives. The Chinese powder included superfluous materials in the mixture, based, one can

Guns of the 1800s were becoming more reliable. This 1763 Charleville from the Navy Arms Co. is a good replica of an 18th century shoulder arm.

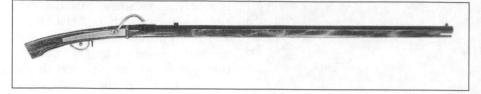

This matchlock shoulder arm is Japanese, coming from a village near Kyoto known for arms making. It's of 17th to 18th century design, smoothbore, and offered in 50 caliber by Dixie Gun Works.

The Kentucky rifle followed on the heels of the European Jaeger to become a true American breed, accurate and reliable. This magnificent rifle was built by modern gunmaker Mark Silver—it's an Augusta/Lockbridge County Virginia rifle circa 1775-1785.

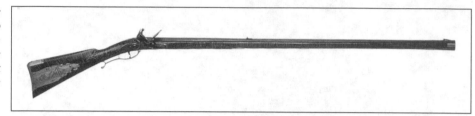

readily assume, on some absolutely non-scientific reasoning. In Blackmore's words: "The ingredients of this powder are worthy of note. They were the chemicals of gunpowder — saltpeter, sulfur, charcoal — plus white arsenic, stone coal, various bitter substances, four kinds of ginger and *human sperm* "(Italics his)." It's easy to see that shooting was as much alchemy as science to the ancient Chinese. They had the elements of gunpowder all right, but their additives were ludicrous.

These early tubes, or handguns, plugged on one end, open on the other, constitute a gun barrel.

After all, the muzzleloader barrel is little more than a tube with an open and a closed end, refined, of course, with precision construction and high-grade materials. These devices can be called guns, but they probably did not shoot bullets for quite some time, firing arrows and other missiles instead. Never to be left out of the story is the fact that the early guns were inferior to the bow, which probably retarded their advancement, explaining why guns did not take over the military field for a very long time. A perfect example of this fact was the guns carried into Japan in the late 1500s and early

1600s, which were no match against the bow in the hands of that country's admired trained archers. In the same period, ship's cannons were formidable, but hand-held arms carried by English, Dutch, and Spanish sailors were no match for Japanese bows. Our own Native Americans were also exceedingly deadly with their bows. Tennessee sharpshooters that literally sliced the British to pieces in the open field with their accurate muzzle-loading long rifles were themselves turned into human porcupines when they went up against Native American archers in the forest. The latter

There were dozens if not hundreds of different blackpowder arms offered over the years in many different styles and designs. The Sharps was one that made great impact.

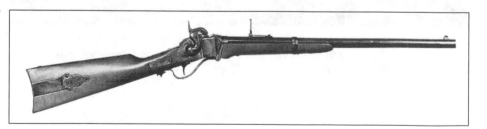

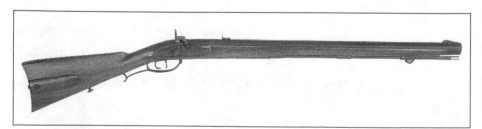

The original Jaeger rifle came to America very early, landing on the eastern seaboard. This one is from Dixie Gun Works in a percussion version for shooters who want to try the style, but not as a flintlock. The Jaeger preceded the American long rifle.

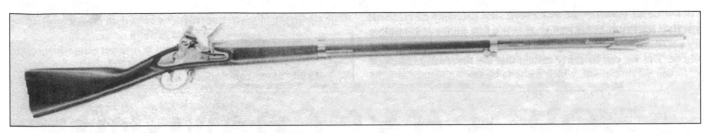

This Dixie Gun Works replica of a U.S. 1816 flintlock smoothbore musket gives a good idea of early firearms that were, on the whole, quite effective. Made until 1844, this musket even saw service in the Civil War when the 69-caliber longarm was converted to percussion ignition.

could put an arrow on target quickly and from just about any posture, even leaning around a tree. And it didn't take long to reload those bows!

Finally, however, the world did have a real gun. As with the ball patch, Europe deserves credit for producing the first true shooting machine. As to who really invented this gun, or precisely what it was, we can never be certain. After all, along with mistakes and bad scholarship, plus misplaced and lost documents, as well as other pitfalls of gun history, we also had the pre-

tenders to deal with. I refer to at least two figures who are often credited with early gunpowder and shooting, Mark the Greek (also known as Marcus Graecus) and Black Berthold (also known as Berthold Schwarz). Chances are, these experts never existed at all! They were made up by somebody writing "history." Such tomfoolery muddied the streams of firearms research.

But once the first true guns came into use, they were continually developed and improved upon. Many wonderful firearms were born in the era of blackpowder, long

before smokeless propellants prevailed. Some of these fine arms are covered in chapters of this book. They include matchlocks, wheel locks, flintlocks, and percussion systems. There were immensely interesting guns carried by early American soldiers, explorers, pioneers and hunters. These firearms were a far cry from the little bamboo and paper sticks of the distant past. They were so good that many never died. We are still shooting them today with great joy and interest.

Chapter 2

HOW A HAT CHANGED AMERICA AND AMERICAN SHOOTING

THE QUEST for the west began back east because that's where the European immigrants started life in America. They were from England in the beginning, but soon many countries contributed to the human wealth that would become the melting pot called the United States. Early on, German and Dutch craftsmen were extremely instrumental in building a unique American long rifle developed by vastly changing the German Jaeger, or hunting rifle. The Kentucky rifle was born, truly in Pennsylvania, its name derived, we are told, from a popular song of the day. The fantastic Kentucky/Pennsylvania long rifle was the epitome of the Golden Age of American arms. Travels by riflemen along the eastern seaboard into what we call the Midwest today were significant, with names like Dan'l Boone and Davy Crockett making permanent history. But it was another time and place that brought about the muzzleloader that influenced the blackpowder guns we shoot today, not the Pennsylvania/Kentucky piece.

It all happened because of a hat. More truthfully, it was American enterprise and politics that brought explorers into what was to be known, in capital letters, as the Far West. Hot fashion called for beaver top hats, similar to the style associated with President Abraham Lincoln — a fashion dating to the

1400s. Western American streams were thick with beavers, and so the era known as the Fur Trade came about in the middle 1800s, creating two developments we adhere to in our modern devotion to muzzleloading — the plains rifle and the rendezvous. Along with desiring beaver hides to make hats, Thomas Jefferson's political interest was an American presence in the Far West, where French and English trappers, traders, and explorers were gaining a significant foothold. Jefferson commissioned Lewis and Clark to embark upon their long

journey to study the environs west of the Mississippi, lay out routes for future pioneer migration, and establish who the land truly belonged to: not foreigners, but Americans. These developments brought about the invention of the rugged plains rifle, and when blackpowder boomed again, beginning in the late 1950s, it was this Hawken-type rifle that most pleased the modern shooter and hunter. Replica cap 'n' ball handguns truly got the ball rolling, but the trend would have leveled off on a modest plain of general interest

Informal gatherings of local clubs can also emulate rendezvous times. This was a silhouette match, patched round ball only, 12 different stations.

On the rendezvous trail to the shooting range, a sign tells the shooters what they must do—just keep on smiling. That's exactly what most attendees of the modern rendezvous do.

accuracy came with the invention of rifling. After all, that is where the gun we call rifle got its name: from the spiral grooves within the bore. Where did they come from? Rifling (never spelled riflings) was another European invention, perhaps of German origin, possibly Austrian birth. Some sources say Gaspard Kollner of Vienna, late in the 15th century, got the idea. Others credit Augustus Kotter of Nuremberg for inventing rifling in 1520. Yet another researcher mixes the two names, coming up with a "Gaspard Koller" of Nuremberg. No matter, really, but it is interesting that early rifling may have had nothing to do with spinning a projectile. Originators of the no-spin theory can produce old-time guns with straight, not spiral, rifling. The idea? To aid cleaning, they say. Smoothbores are much easier to clean than rifled arms, no matter how the grooves are cut. Shooters of the past figured that out, too. However, straight-groove rifling did exist. Why is open to question.

Regardless of theories, the European rifle was the forerunner of the long-barreled beauty of early America called the Pennsylvania long rifle. Leather-stocking lads such as Daniel Boone fought with this gun and hunted with it. British troops felt its sting on American soil. Trailblazers of the Eastern Seaboard cut many new paths into the frontier with their accurate rifles in hand. Various sources list different major calibers for the Pennsylvania long rifle, but the 45 prevailed. That assessment is based on three decades of studying original guns in museums, at gun shows, and in collections.

A super marksman could take the little 45 — 45 caliber is small when shooting a round ball — and bring home the bacon with it, usually in the form of eastern white-tailed deer and wild turkeys. Of course, 45-caliber was also ample for warfare. But when the initial shove west became a push in the early 1800s, a new breed of adven-

without the rifle, because America is a nation of riflemen. So the comparatively short, stout, big-bore hunting shoulder arm fondly known as the Hawken became king a century later. When it appeared again in revised form, it was ready to please space-age shooters interested in big-game hunting as well as target shooting and competition, the latter often taking place during

a re-enactment of the original Fur Trade gathering called the rendezvous.

But before talking about the Fur Trade, its rendezvous and rifle, let's walk to the valley for a moment to ponder a more distant past.

Roots

The greatest impact in long-range shooting and vastly improved

Three rendezvous shooters head down the trail to make smoke on the targets.

interesting explorers of American history. This is not an east/west prejudice, for the fur hunters of the Rocky Mountains were Eastern boys to begin with, a wild and crazy bunch of characters willing to risk all for a big time and free life. They thrived in the vast unexplored territory filled with truly large game: elk, grizzlies, and the heaviest four-footed animal on the continent, the American bison or buffalo. They staked claim to the American west for Americans, winning respect with their plains rifles. A great many never returned to their Eastern homes, falling prey to grizzly bears, bitter winters, rushing streams of icy water, and run-ins with "Bug's Boys," the intrepid Blackfoot Indians.

One highly historical figure and a second man whose contribution is seldom taught in grade school, played significant roles in westward expansion and the mountain man movement. They were Thomas Jefferson and John Colter.

turer answered the call. He relied on the long arm of the hour — at first — as well as a hodgepodge of different guns. These men were the original buckskinners and their rifles were wrong for the job at hand. While we think of Daniel Boone softly treading the forest floors of the East, we see Jim Bridger riding his horse over the rugged mountain passes of the West. Boone was often afoot and could carry only so much gear. Bridger was on horseback, often with pack animals to tote his supplies. The lean, long, and rather lightweight Pennsylvania rifle was out of place in the West. Thus the plains rifle was born: shorter for horseback, larger caliber for animals larger than deer, capable of burning heavy doses of blackpowder to gain reasonable range and power. Shots were longer out West and at bigger animals. The mother of invention, necessity, struck again. The trapper had his rifle.

Those who took trails west in search of beaver were called mountain men, and in spirit, if not replication, we most often carry their rifle today. The name "Hawken," which in reality fits only those rifles built by the Hawken brothers,

became generic in modern times. And why not? In general design, it is a prime blackpowder rifle for hunting. But we can't ignore the men who carried the rifle in the 19th century. They were the most

There is special attraction in the tipi of the plains. These, at rendezvous, are just as handsome as the originals. They also provide excellent shelter.

Jack Tripp makes bows of interest to buckskinners. Here he appears in his traditional outfit with a rack of fine bows.

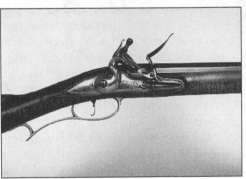

The Kentucky rifle preceded the Mountain Man era. It was superseded for rough work by the plains rifle. This is a look at an extremely fine long rifle built by modern gunmaker Mark Silver, one of the finest talents in the country.

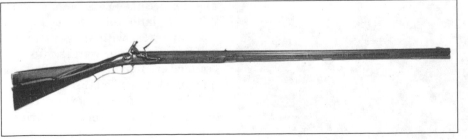

As explained in *Powder River*, a 1938 book written by Struthers Burt, Jefferson was far-sighted, the Seward of his time, for like Seward, who saw Alaska as more than a huge ice cube, Jefferson knew that the "other half" of America, the West, was worth having. "Seward's Folly," the purchase of Alaska, haunted the man to his grave. Jefferson was more fortunate. Jefferson got the ball rolling by dispatching the great Lewis and Clark Expedition. He saw to it that the men were well-supplied to carry out their duties. The surface goal was to go west until reaching the Pacific Ocean. The underlying goal was to study the flora, fauna and geography of the Far West

When rifling came along to stabilize bullets in flight, shooting became an entirely different game. The flintlock long rifle fired here is built with a barrel designed and produced for accuracy.

Knives played a strong role in the original mountain man adventure in the Far West. At today's modern rendezvous, the knife remains one of the principal parts of the costume.

while making their presence known to French and English trappers. Lewis and Clark were the head of a spear aimed at the unknown. That spear penetrated the entire breadth of Western America.

This is where John Colter enters the picture. The expedition's spirit of adventure was on the wane by August 1806, but not John Colter's, who made the acquaintance of two trappers, Forest Hancock and Joseph Dickson, on the Yellowstone River. These men had gone farther west than any American at that time, except for Lewis and Clark. Colter asked Lewis and Clark if they would honorably discharge him from their employ so he could join Hancock and Dickson in a trapping venture. He got what now seems a rather remarkable response from his commanders. The Lewis and Clark journals contain the following quote under August 14 and 15 entries: "The offer [to Colter by Hancock and Dickson] was a very advantageous one, and, as he [Colter] had always performed his duty, and his services might be dispensed with, we agreed that he might go, provided none of the rest would ask or expect a similar indulgence. To this they cheerfully answered that they wished Colter every success and would not apply for liberty to separate before we reached St. Louis." Lewis and Clark supplied Colter, as well as his new partners, with gunpowder, lead, and a "variety of articles which might be useful to him, and he left us the next day." August 16, 1806, was the beginning of Colter's adventure. He spent seven years of his life, from 1803 to 1810, exploring the Far West. He discovered in 1872 what we call Western Wyoming, including the land that was to become Yellowstone Park. When he later told about the Yellowstone area, with its geysers and scalding, gushing waters, he was branded a liar. People called his "imagined" land Colter's Hell.

John Colter's fascinating story is too long to relate here, but briefly, when asked by Manuel Lisa to

Homer L. Dangler was one of the first five blackpowder shooters to spur interest in the rendezvous, state of Ohio, requiring flintlock rifles and buckskins. This was in 1957 and the gathering is still going strong. Dangler is kneeling on the far right.

drum up a little fur-trade business, John walked an estimated 500 miles in wintertime visiting various Indian camps in search of traders. He traveled on "webs," which we call snowshoes, carrying provisions in a backpack. Rifle in hand, Colter covered an immense territory, which is now part of Montana and Wyoming, making it back to Manuel Lisa's trading post by spring. Obviously, the natives of the region would have killed Colter had he not been a special man. Colter explored, drew maps, and made perhaps the most exciting "run for your life" in American history. At the time of the run, John had a

The rendezvous is definitely for women, too.

The rendezvous is alive again, with white tents and tipis showing in the valley.

grizzly, "Old Ephraim." Here was an animal that could "shoot back." He was sometimes known as the "white bear," winning battles with many men in spite of their firesticks. Rifles that served well in the East were less than perfect west of the Mississippi. The Pennsylvania long rifle was handsome, light in the hand, swift to the shoulder, and accurate, but no match for the bear "that walks like a man." A 45-caliber round ball at only133 grains was a pesky fly against the flak jacket of hide and muscle worn by the grizzly.

The Plains Rifle

It is impossible to neatly categorize rifles that went west with the first explorers. There were small bores and military muskets, some noted as larger than 50 caliber in the Journals of Lewis and Clark. There also were smoothbores, shotguns, and various sidearms, mainly single-shot pistols. Most were flintlocks. Many were inaccurate and unreliable. A new breed of rifle was needed to serve the needs of the mountain man.

The new rifle was generally 50 caliber or larger, the bigger bore firing a larger round ball. The barrel was in turn heavier and wider across the flats than the Pennsylva-

partner named John Potts. The two encountered a party of Blackfoot Indians. Potts resisted and was immediately killed. Having a sense of humor, as Burt puts it, the Indians stripped Colter of his clothing, gave him a 100-yard head start, and told him to run for it. Cactus is not confined to the low desert, and the Indians saw to it that Colter's path of escape took him through plenty of the spiny plants. Feet filled with needles, John continued to run. He was fast, and he stayed ahead for a long while. However, one of his pursuers was faster, catching up to the white man. Colter turned on a dime. His chaser stumbled and broke his lance. John picked it up, killing the warrior with his own weapon. He survived by reaching the Madison River, diving in, and coming up in a beaver dam, where he found both air to breathe and a hidden sanctuary.

The mountain man found a different world out west. The black bear of the East was represented, but so was his larger deadly cousin, the grizzly. You didn't drop a grizzly with a peashooter. You needed a stout rifle to do the job. Some camps had such a rifle, a special grizzly bear gun. I saw one in a museum. It was huge of bore, massive of barrel,

capable of throwing a tremendous hunk of lead at good muzzle velocity. There were deer, too, the familiar white-tailed variety often referred to as the "common deer," along with mule deer, which were called blacktails. There was an even larger deer out West—the wapiti or elk, as well as western moose. The mountain man also encountered vast herds of bison with herd bulls ranging as high as 3,000 pounds on the hoof. The real terror, though, was the

The original rendezvous was a trade event. The tradition lives on. This is trader's row at a modern rendezvous.

The modern-day rendezvous is a family affair. Here, a father and son follow the trail to the shooting range, doing something together that is enjoyable for both.

nia long arm. Greater barrel-wall thickness was necessary for strength and the octagonal barrel of a plains rifle could be more than an inch across the flats, perhaps 1 1/8 inches. The big barrel demanded a stock to match, with a wrist thick enough to withstand the recoil of heavy powder charges. Accuracy was sufficient, if not on par, across the board, with the eastern rifle. The sturdy, rugged plains rifle was not that handsome, with its shorter, heavier barrel, but it managed well across the saddle, and that counted for more than beauty when lives were at stake.

While barrels in the 44-inch and even longer realm were common on Pennsylvania/Kentucky rifles, the plains rifle wore a tube of about 34 to 36 inches. Since they were made one at a time by hand, variation, not mass-production standardization, was the rule. One plains rifle could have a 33-inch barrel, another a 36-inch barrel. Along with the larger barrel and bigger stock came more weight, generally about 10 to 11 pounds, some original Hawkens tipping the scale at 15 pounds. The style was plain, although a few were embellished with carving and inlays. The half-stock design with iron furniture and no patch box lent the charm of a potato sack. Straight-grip stocks prevailed, but a few late Hawkens had pistol grips. Most wore fixed, open iron sights; a rare few sported peep sights. There were flintlock plains rifles, but most were percussion.

So here is the plains rifle: rela-

tively short barrel and overall length, stout, half-stock design, percussion ignition, rugged, accurate for big-game hunting, very reliable, a loose stereotype with many exceptions, such as the full-stock J&S Hawken rifle pictured on page 27 of John Baird's *Hawken Rifles* book. Caliber 53 is considered average, but others were common, including 55 and even 60 caliber. Furthermore, rifles could be freshed out, which simply means rebored to a larger caliber because of a worn or pitted bore. Therefore, a plains rifle starting out 50 or 53 caliber could end up 55 caliber or larger. The plains rifle was touted as "flat-shooting" to 150 yards, which it was not. No rifle, including the 220 Swift, shoots flat to 150 yards. However, the term was applied because it could be sighted in for about 100 yards with heavy powder charges and a patched round ball, and a practiced rifleman using a bit of "Arkansas elevation" could hit a target regularly at 200 yards.

The Hawken Rifle Today

Sam and Jake Hawken made superb plains rifles, so good that the name became generic. The famous name now marks an entire genre of firearms, including muzzleloaders that look as much like a Hawken as a Weatherby resembles an AK-47. Today's "Hawken" may have a barrel under 20 inches, or it might be 36 inches. It can be mass-produced or handmade.

The Mountain Men

The mountain men were trappers, but of course due to Jefferson's plan with the Lewis and Clark Expedition, beaver trapping in the Far West was for more than pelts. It created an American presence in a land not yet entirely secured. The mountain men set up housekeeping with permanent camps in the Rockies. They were the most outrageous, courageous, devil-may-care group to make tracks in North America. They won the West, not with a repeater, but with a plains rifle.

They were sent forth by two American businessmen, William H. Ashley and Andrew Henry. Ashley was the more enterprising, while Henry was a bit more adventuresome. How would they find their trappers? What do you do when you're looking for something in America? Advertise! And so the St. Louis papers of 1822 carried this ad:

To Enterprising Young Men

The subscriber wishes to engage ONE HUNDRED MEN, to ascend the river Missouri to its source, there to be employed for one, two or three years - For particulars, enquire of Major Andrew Henry, near the Lead Mines, in the County of Washington, (who will ascend with, and command the party) or to the subscriber at St. Louis.

Wm. H. Ashley

Free trappers, or Ashley Men, as they were called, did not receive fixed wages. They kept half of all furs in exchange for supplies and transportation to the mountains. The true mountain man was, as they put it in those days, "on his own hook." He worked for himself without wages, although there was a company in the background to supply trade goods in a summer meeting that came to be known as the rendezvous. If not fearless, the free trapper certainly acted and reacted with reckless abandon. Life was balanced like a coin on its edge. Many mistakes could be made only once. There was no second chance. Reports filtered back to civilization concerning these wayward souls. A greenhorn at one summer rendezvous saw a card game played on the back of a dead man. The dearly departed was set up "on all fours" by his comrades, his stiff body serving as a playing surface. Life was a thread dangling among razor blades. During a skirmish, one mountain man was struck. "I'm hit," he cried out to his friends. They pretended not to hear him correctly, returning answers that offered no comfort whatsoever to the injured party.

"He says he hit one!"

"No, I said, 'I'm hit!'"

"Where'd you hit 'im?"

"No, it's me who's hit!"

Another time, a rabid wolf sprang into camp. The men knew the animal was crazed with hydrophobia and aware of the danger of being bitten. Instead of putting a round ball through the canine, or climbing a tree to get out of harm's way, sport ensued. "He's over here," one mountain man shouted, burying himself beneath his sleeping robes to ward off the bite of death. Shouts of "No, over here" continued. Two men were bitten. They wandered away from camp and were never seen again. It was a tough life, but just right for the fur trappers. Many of them returned to civilization only to find their old world dull. They went back to the mountains to face the dangers all over again. They were bold, foolhardy, had a pocketful of time, and no master to tell them how to spend it. Their marks in the land live to this day, scraped out trails that became highways from East to the West. Lewis and Clark, yes, but it was individual trappers who truly mapped the Far West. Their names still grace the land: Bridger National Forest, Henry's Fork of the Snake River, Mount Fitzpatrick, Jedediah Smith Wilderness Area, Jackson, Wyo. A mountain man museum/memorial resides in Pinedale, Wyo., a tribute to the taming of the West. It is housed in a large and beautiful building displaying treasures of the era. The superb Museum of the Fur Trade in Chadron, Neb., also praises the free trapper of the West.

This is the romance of the mountain man. It is no wonder that some

The modern-day rendezvous is a family affair, with a good time dressing up in period clothing and enjoying shooting events.

modern blackpowder shooters emulate him. Today, his dress, firearms, camping style, and his summer gathering time, the rendezvous, are copied by people who call themselves buckskinners. Some of these men and women live their daily lives, if not in every way, at least in spirit, as the mountain man did. The buckskinner is also a student of the fur trade, although he does not adhere to every nuance of the mountain man code. The fact is, mountain men were the same as any other group with much individual variation. Frederick Remington did more, perhaps, than any other painter to give us an image of the fur hunter; however, he was late. He painted only a reflection on the water, for the true picture had passed with the ripples of time. Bearded? Maybe, but shaving razors were found in mountain man kits. An Indian maiden was not used to facial hair. Long hair? Probably. Indian clothes? The mountain man adopted part of the Indian costume, but not all of it.

The Original Rendezvous

Ashley and Henry's St. Louis newspaper advertisement worked. William Ashley stayed behind attending to business details, while Maj. Andrew Henry led a party of free trappers into the West. In order to receive value for their beaver pelts, the trappers gathered at a pre-established point in summer for a rendezvous, the first taking place in 1825 when General Ashley met his free trappers on what is now known as Henry's Fork of the Green River not far from Daniel, Wyo., near Pinedale. The men trapped until freeze-up, taking refuge until spring. Now spring had come and gone, and here they were to trade their hard-earned furs for worldly goods. It was called a "shining time." Pelts went for dollar value, that is, inflated dollar value. The trappers needed galena (lead) for bullets, powder, butcher knives, clothing, maybe even a new rifle, precious smoking tobacco, sugar,

flour. Gewgaws — trinkets the Indian ladies admired — were important. One mountain man, the story goes, gave up $2,000 worth of pelts for the hand of a chief's daughter. She must have been a knockout.

How much could a free trapper earn, plunging his hands into the frigid boreal waters of the Far West? One thousand, perhaps two in a season with rheumatism at best, a Blackfoot arrow at worst. Actually, the pay itself was not so bad, since a worker of the period made about a buck and a half a day, but the trapper really didn't get money. He traded his catch to the company store for goods, and the goods were swapped at grossly inflated prices. Whisky worth 30 cents a gallon in St. Louis was cut with water and sold for $3 a pint at rendezvous. Tobacco, coffee, and sugar at 10 cents a pound back East went for $2 a pound. Gunpowder ran the same for English Diamond Grade, while American du Pont, considered better, traded for $12 a pound. Gewgaws carried a 2,000 percent markup. A cheap Indian trade rifle worth $10 back home fetched several times that price at rendezvous, while a fine Hawken rifle worth $40 in St. Louis commanded $80. But money was not the real issue with the mountain men. Lifestyle was. The entire season's effort evaporated in as little as one day, but the men had their goods and a fine time gambling at cards, talking with friends they had not seen for months, learning of the goings on back home, arguing, competing in shooting games, 'hawk tossin', knife throwing, bragging, fist fighting, and impressing the Indian women. The deal wasn't so bad. After all, there was great risk hauling loaded wagons across hostile country. The investors deserved their returns.

The Modern Rendezvous

Finally, the beaver hat slipped from fashion and the mountain men were no more. They were a

presence out West, turning furs into dollars. When an era is gone, it's gone. But it can be emulated, and that's what happened. The rendezvous was born again, credit going to the NMLRA (National Muzzle Loading Rifle Association). Once again, people met on common ground to trade goods, compete in shooting, knife throwing, and fire-starting contests, and to have a big time the old way. Rendezvous sprang up both East and West, and continue to this hour. The NMLRA continues to inform about these modern shining times in its magazine, Muzzle Blasts, with blackpowder clubs all over the world holding rendezvous of their own. Information concerning times and dates can be located on the Internet as well. The shooting contests are especially interesting, some off-hand at common black bull's eyes, others animated. Want to have fun? Try splitting a fired round ball on the blade of an ax imbedded in a vertically-oriented stump. On either side of the blade, balloons are set. If you split the ball well enough, the two pieces will break the two balloons. Or cut a wooden stake in the ground in half with bullets from your frontloader. Or ring a gong at several hundred yards.

In the valley, tipis stand as if they were a painted upon the landscape, while smoke rises from campfires everywhere, hovering in thin wisps on the air, catching and reflecting the natural light of day, and the man-made light of fire when the sun goes down. At dark, tiny sparks from flint 'n' steel striking together play at ground level, curls of smoke rising like miniature smoke signals. Standing on a hill, an observer is mesmerized by long tongues of flame licking at the dry wood of evening campfires. He hears the people talking and laughing, as well as music on the air from dulcimers and flutes. Stew is bubbling. It's time to join friends around the campfire before resting back on a buffalo robe.

Chapter 3

TAKING THE BLACKPOWDER TRAIL

BLACKPOWDER SHOOTING is more varied today than ever before. A hundred years ago, 200 years ago, even before that, the choices were far fewer than now. Muzzleloading pistols, revolvers, shotguns, and rifles abound. There are originals, which can still be located, as well as replicas of originals (custom or manufactured), smoothbore muskets, rifled muskets, non-replicas, modern muzzleloaders in a huge variety of sub-models, even ultra modern long guns, handguns, and shotguns, some built on the very actions belonging to contemporary cartridge shooters. Add to this array a host of blackpowder cartridge guns, revolvers, single-shot rifles, repeating rifles and a few shotguns. Each niche demands its own accouterments as well.

The fact is, blackpowder shooting is more involved than firing modern arms, a complication that results in fascination. I recall my own beginnings. The road was bumpy, with many detours. I got my hands on a few poorly designed guns of questionable manufacture. They didn't "go off" reliably, and a few were not entirely safe to shoot. I considered dropping out before becoming a dedicated player. Then I got lucky.

The late Charles J. Keim, then the University of Alaska professor and Dean of the College of Arts and Letters, invited me to his home to see and handle an original muzzleloader, as well as a custom replica flintlock long rifle built by Royland

Those who choose the flintlock path have a little more adjusting to do, such as getting used to a puff of smoke like this one from the pan powder.

Taking the blackpowder trail today means big game hunting, especially whitetail deer. This fine buck was secured with a 50-caliber modern muzzleloader at Deer Creek Outfitters in Sebree, Ky.

Many original firearms remain intact, but not always safe. This interesting old double-gun is one of those—intact, but not safe. It simply shows too much wear.

Southgate in his own special style.

Keim showed me the rifles. "Oh, this is what it's all about," I thought to myself. I recall sitting by his fireplace examining the workmanship of the guns. "This rifle belonged to my wife's grandfather," he said. He held in his hand a sleek half-stock plains rifle, a handsome original. The flickering rays of firelight playing over the metalwork and stock sent heliographic messages. A charm exuded from that fine muzzleloader that was lacking in the blackpowder guns I had been shooting. The other rifle was an example of fine 20th-century craftsmanship. I was entranced. "You can shoot them," Keim offered. I didn't want to risk the rifles at the range, but I did spend the next two hours conversing about the old days and guns. That was the real beginning of blackpowder shooting for me. The path ahead was not totally blazed, but at least I knew where I wanted to go. Unfortunately, a few traps lay enroute.

Initially, I fell into a pit of misinformation, where well-meaning authors enchanted by the smoke and flame from muzzleloaders attempted to relate facts about them that were not facts at all, but instead old wives' tales. Much advice was clothed in conjecture and voodoo. A man named John Baird, publisher of a little magazine called The Buckskin Report, came to the rescue. Baird took exception to my unkind remarks on the inefficiency of the patched round ball. Logic, plus what I'd been reading, suggested that the sphere of lead had to be worthless. Baird set me straight, and I was wise enough to take his comments to heart. A period of listening, learning, and discovering began — especially discovering. I began testing for myself, while reading older texts on muzzleloading recommended by Baird. When I doubted something that I heard or read, I took the concept to the shooting range, where firing and chronographing generally set the record straight. I was beginning to learn about blackpowder shooting, and it was gripping.

Starting out in muzzleloading is best accomplished, as many new ventures are, with the help of a knowledgeable veteran — the emphasis on knowledgeable. Just because some fellow has been busting percussion caps for 20 years doesn't mean he knows the score. But there are real experts as near as the local blackpowder club. These dyed-in-the-buckskin, downwind shooters learned through experience, and they're willing to pass on their knowledge. Taking advantage of that know-how with an open mind pays off. Nobody knows everything about shooting old-style guns, strange as that may

Taking the blackpowder trail means hunting, especially big game, and with regard to learning the quarry and its niche. Here the hunter studies a patch of lechugia recently attacked by javelina.

The blackpowder trail has led from handheld firesticks to the in-line muzzleloader, including accouterments, and even projectile innovations, such as this Devel bullet—no lead, made of copper and tin. It does not mushroom. Instead, fins up front set up a shock wave that in turn creates the wound channel.

seem. So watching how practiced shooters handle their firearms, and for that matter, which guns and gear they prefer, pays off. This step can save a lot of wasted time, not to mention dollars, by avoiding mistakes made by others. Adhering to all the safety measures that long-time blackpowder shooters are mindful of also makes sense, as does keeping a sharp eye out for "familiarity breeds contempt," meaning that doing something for a long time can lead to relaxing the rules, resulting in big trouble. So joining a blackpowder club, going to shoots and asking questions translates to learning. But personal reading, study, and hands-on experience can never be left out of the picture.

Realistic Expectations

There are four major reasons for

initial discontent with muzzleloading. First, accuracy can seem downright grim compared with modern arms. Initially, the newcomer is content with 4- to 6-inch groups at 100 yards because he's fascinated by the smoke and boom of the old front stoker. Later, these shotgun-style patterns become discouraging and the shooter gives up the sport.

He should not, because the well-constructed muzzleloader, properly fed, can achieve perfectly acceptable accuracy. Many currently made hunting rifles keep three bullets inside 1.0- to 1.5-inch groups at 100 yards from the bench, while special heavy benchrest slug guns make cloverleaf patterns at that distance and farther. Second, blackpowder power may seem lacking. In a way, this is true. Muzzleloaders do not shoot as far or as powerfully

as high-intensity, big-game cartridges of the 30-06 class and larger. In fact, however, there are magnum-type muzzleloaders today capable of 3,000 foot-pounds of muzzle energy. Third, firepower is lacking. Fast shooting, except for two quick repeat shots from double guns, is out of the picture. That's not all bad. Slowing down can be rewarding. Fourth, cleanup after shooting may appear burdensome — tubs of hot water, rotten egg smell, rubbing, scrubbing—what a mess! Who wants to bother? However, a look at the maintenance chapter is in order before deciding, because the after-shooting cleanup task is more easily accomplished than ever before, with modern chemicals to the rescue.

Learning the Blackpowder Pace

The 21st century is an exciting, interesting time. It is also fast-paced. Promises of the 20-hour work-week, echoed in the 1950s, never materialized. The 40-hour week is now considered short for many. Just driving to the job can be an Indy 500 experience. But we don't have to shoot blackpowder that way. Muzzleloading enjoys a slower pace. In order to have a good time, the newcomer must slow down and savor the moment. Even at rendezvous, where multiple shots are often necessary in compe-

Taking the blackpowder trail is upping the challenge. In weather like this, the hunter requires knowledge of weatherproofing his rifle, whereas the usual modern cartridge-shooter will fire on command even in the wet.

A muzzleloader like this one means slowing the pace, savoring the moment. There is no way to make it shoot rapidly, and perhaps that's just as well.

tition, everyone understands that the blackpowder gun is not a semi-auto. It takes a little time to pour the powder charge, seat bullet or shot charge, then cap or prime before another shot can be delivered. Learning to load with deliberation and care, making every missile count downrange, is the right — and safe — attitude. Experience and practice yield proficiency, with fairly fast second shots, even at game, a reality.

Range

Some shooters consistently ring gongs out to 500 yards, while the metallic silhouette contest is played by blackpowder cartridge fans who knock rams over at 500 meters — with iron-sighted rifles. They also whack metal cutouts of shaggies and other animals at 1,000 yards. But with round-ball rifles, a shot on big game at 125 yards is about maximum for most of us, with 200 yards the limit for modern magnum muzzleloaders firing shapely bullets in front of large powder charges.

Meanwhile, blackpowder shotgunners enjoy great success at normal shotgun ranges. The grand old man of the soot-burning scattergun, V.M. Starr, actually won contests against modern shotgun shooters. Of course, the blackpowder shotgun cannot deliver the long-range patterns associated with the latest modern guns, such as Winchester's Super-X2 with extra full choke, but they can shoot far enough to fill the game bag, as well as shattering clay pigeons out of the air routinely.

Sights

Open iron sights continue to prevail, especially on new muzzleload-

Blackpowder shooting follows many trails, including competition at buckskin gatherings. Here is Homer L. Dangler, the gunmaker, getting ready to participate in the competition.

Taking the blackpowder trail may mean learning how to effectively use a simple sight like this one. With practice, the shooter will be amazed at how well he can do with such a sight.

ers. In the old days, some great shooting was accomplished with this basic sight style. Iron sights are still effective through know-how and practice. They are also the law on many blackpowder-only hunts where scopes are forbidden. However, the advent and surging popularity of the modern muzzleloader brought with it sights to match, and now scopes are popular on muzzleloaders. Check local laws before going scoped, of course. The rules vary state to state and hunt to hunt.

Firepower

While rapid shooting is out of the question, fast reloading is possible, especially with "readyloads" — powder, patch and ball in a container, ready to go. It's a matter of practice. Also, a well-placed round ball from the proper distance, or a single conical, will drop a big game animal in its tracks. The rule when

hunting is: reload immediately after shooting at anything, even a rabbit. That rule paid off for me on an exciting hunt. I had no interest in shooting a confined bison, but I did want the blackpowder experience of dropping a shaggy with a muzzleloader. I found such a hunt in Nebraska. Those who say the American bison is a barnyard milk cow don't know what they are talking about. That fact is grimly proved by tourists in Yellowstone Park. It's a rare season when someone isn't hurt or killed by a buffalo. The largest quadruped on the continent, bigger than a moose, grizzly, polar or Kodiak bear, it can outrun the fastest human sprinter in the world. My bison was on the loose, entirely unfenced and totally capable of making mashed potatoes out of our hides. My brother and I hunted the bull on foot, me carrying Number 47, a

54-caliber round ball rifle, Nick armed with a motor-driven Nikon loaded with 35mm film.

To make a long story short, the bull came our way when we got close to him on the plains. Our plan was for me to signal when I was ready to shoot. Nick was to photograph the action. I recalled the advice given by the fellow running the hunt. He said, "Don't aim dead center between the eyes. The ball could bounce off." I held to one side. The round ball penetrated the skull, passing completely through the right hemisphere of the brain. The bull rose to full height, and then toppled over. The "reload after every shot" rule paid off. I popped a readyload, dumped the powder charge, followed by a ball, capping the rifle as the bull, minus half his control center, rose to his feet. A second shot was required to put him down for good.

Mixing the old with the new, the author strikes out on a hunt with his 54-caliber round ball custom rifle, No. 47.

Taking the blackpowder trail means big game hunting, sometimes with a modern muzzleloader, scoped. Even so, range considerations are vital. While a muzzleloader like this Outer-Line® delivers high power, it is not a 300 Magnum, nor was it intended to be.

Muzzleloader Characteristics

No one could have guessed that the main muzzleloader of the 21st century would look no more like a Hawken or Kentucky than Olive Oyl resembles a beauty queen. The non-replica, often called a Hawken although it does not look like one, continues to be popular, but the modern muzzleloader is the "in" rifle. The blackpowder fan need not make a choice, however. He can have it all.

Initially, I detested modern muzzleloaders. They seemed to fly in the face of everything good about shooting black powder: the history, doing things the old way, the out-and-out fun of learning the old guns and their mannerisms. In time, however, the upgrading of the modern muzzleloader lifted it to new heights. Now it resides in its own special arena.

While I still prefer my custom 54 caliber ball-shooter for a lot of my shooting, I find the new-style frontloader to be fascinating. Made of top-grade materials with innovative designs, they shoot with accuracy and power, and I carry them often, especially on general hunts where modern cartridge rifles are allowed. I feel no shame toting a single-shot blackpowder rifle, regardless of style, when other hunters are allowed to pack 7mm magnums in the same field.

But why limit our selves to one type of muzzleloader? How boring that would be. The real fun comes from shooting all kinds of charcoal burners — replicas, rifled muskets, customs, long, short, small bore, large bore, rifle, shotgun, pistol, revolver, the works. Purists believe that the whole thrust of blackpowder shooting is emulation of the past, especially

the guns. They have a right to feel that way, enjoying their traditional firearms. At the same time, thousands of marksmen wouldn't shoot blackpowder guns at all if they had to deal with long barrels, heavy weights, a lot of drop at comb, and other features associated with old-time rifles. These men and women find modern muzzleloaders ideal.

Then there are shooters like me, who appreciate all of the differences. One day, I might be on the trail with my custom longer-barreled Pennsylvania style rifle shooting patched round balls with fixed, open iron sights. The next day, I will be shooting a Markesbery Outer-Line® with scope.

Recoil and Muzzleloaders

Getting started in soot burning means dealing with a difference in

Many different muzzleloaders have come along over the years, including this interesting Iver Johnson over/under in 50-caliber with double hammers. Fortunately, anyone interested in buying a front loader no longer made can usually locate one through The Gun List or other firearms sales outlet, as well as advertising in Muzzle Blasts or other blackpowder publication.

A newcomer to muzzleloading will find long guns like this one truly long; however, he or she will also notice that these guns hang steady.

recoil. This is not a problem, but awareness is required. Since the blackpowder rifle is essentially hand-loaded for every shot, it's a simple matter of charging light for plinking, practice, and small game, going to full powder charges for the big stuff. In order to gain reasonable veloc-ity/energy, the full-charge load is required, regardless of phony advice to the contrary that has seen print. This fact is easily proved. While three Pyrodex 50/50 Pellets are admittedly more than necessary for most hunt-ing situations, especially white-tailed deer from tree stands where short-range is the rule, those guns allowed that much fuel do show a difference in delivered power.

For example, a 50-caliber rifle fired a 350-grain Buffalo Bullet at 1,459 feet per second (fps) with two pellets (a 100-grain-volume load), three pellets (150 grains) produced 1,730 fps. The difference is signifi-cant: 1,655 foot-pounds of muzzle energy for two pellets, 2,327 foot-pounds for three pellets.

Since it takes a lot of powder to make a big-game hunting load in a muzzleloader, it follows that recoil will be upped, because the weight of a powder charge is part of the for-mula for deriving recoil energy. The shooter must choose a rifle that fits, also taking time to adjust to more

Blackpowder guns with full-throttle loads can produce fairly heavy recoil because so much powder is burned often behind heavy projectiles. This 12-gauge shotgun was loaded with 1-1/2-ounces of shot in front of over 100 grains volume FFg blackpowder.

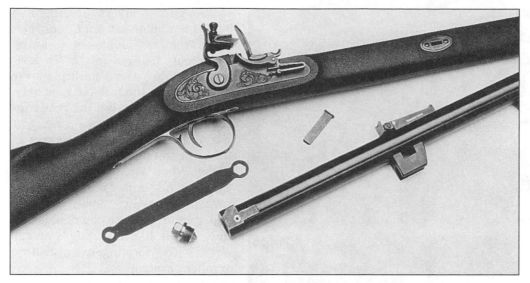

The Thompson/Center Firestorm is a flintlock by design, but with an entirely different character. It takes Pyrodex Pellets, has a removable breech plug, accepts powder charges up to 150-grains volume, and wears steel fiber optic sights.

drop at comb of stocks associated with old-style rifles. Modern muzzleloaders generally have recoil pads, while long guns of yesteryear often have crescent-style or rifle butt plates, as opposed to flatter shotgun styles.

Blackpowder Triggers

Good triggers are absolutely vital to successful shooting. Hard-to-pull triggers cause a shooter to pull off of target. Modern muzzleloaders generally have contemporary triggers, in some cases the same as found on cartridge rifles. Others may have double-set triggers, which are excellent, but can take some getting used to. This two-trigger setup consists of set and hair triggers, allowing the shooter to touch off the instant the sight picture is correct with the least disturbance of aim. When the set trigger is activated, the hair trigger is not only very light, often in the area of a half pound, but also crisp. So how does it work? The rear trigger is pulled fully rearward. Rarely, this is reversed, in which the front trigger is the set, the rear trigger the hair. There is an audible click when the trigger is set. It can also be felt. Now the front hair trigger is ready. Depending upon how it has been adjusted, it can be tripped with only a few ounces of pressure. Incidentally,

Shooters who take up the blackpowder sport find that guns loaded heavily do present some recoil. That in part is due to a large powder charge. The same guns can be loaded down for milder recoil when big power or flatter trajectory are not required.

Taking a step back on the blackpowder trail to flintlocks may include the patch box. This one on an old-time rifle is shown with spare flints in the hold.

The single trigger has its own advantages. There is no time taken in setting a trigger, and when properly designed and executed, single triggers are capable of light let-off and clean-breaking.

some gun makers distinguish between double-set and multiple-lever triggers, double-set meaning it can only be fired in the set position, while the multiple-lever design allows the front trigger to be pulled without having the rear trigger set. There is also a single-set trigger, one trigger only, which is set by pushing forward on it until it clicks. When set, the rifle "touches off" with just a few ounces of pressure, depending upon specific adjustment. As with the double-set, this type is like breaking a spider web with forefinger, providing excellent control.

George Larson, writing in a March 1949 issue of The American Rifleman magazine, said this of the double trigger: "The object of a set trigger is to allow a rifle or pistol to have a firing mechanism with a heavy engagement between the sear and the firing pin, for purposes of safety. Then, by the process of pulling or pushing the 'setting trigger,' a bar is cocked under heavy spring pressure and because of a leverage advantage that is gained it may be released by a light touch on the 'firing trigger.'" Mr. Larson continues: "Practically all set triggers have a provision whereby the gun can be fired by pulling the firing trigger without first having set the mechanism. Most of them also have an adjustment screw which controls the amount of contact surface at the crucial point of engagement." This set screw appears on many muzzleloaders. Warning: The double-set trigger should not be set too light, and should not be set at all until the rifle is in the firing position. Walking around with a trigger in the set position can be dangerous.

To Buckskin or Not to Buckskin

Getting started in muzzleloading means making a decision on the style of shooting a person prefers to engage in. Whether 'tis nobler to go forth in old-time clothing and live in a tipi, or stick to everything modern, must be decided. Buckskinning

At 200 yards, anything that moves is toast.

Encore. The most powerful, most versatile .50 cal. muzzleloader in the world.

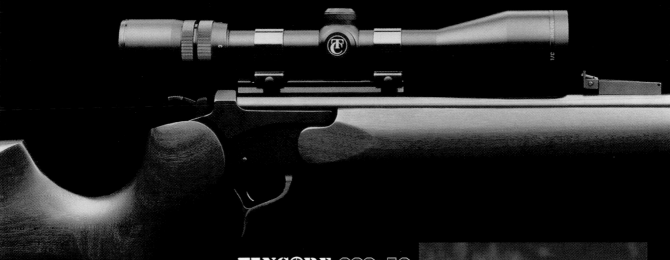

ENCORE 209x50 MAGNUM

- **Powerful.** Think of it as the artillery of black powder. Because the Encore 209x50 Magnum will bring down anything that's out there at 200 yards, with a muzzle energy equal to a 7mm Remington Mag.

- **Versatile.** You can also interchange with an array of centerfire barrels and 20 ga. shotgun barrels to create an Encore for all game, all year.

- **Reliable.** Forget misfires, even in wet weather. With a 209 shotshell primer in a sealed breech, 100% of the flame volume is delivered to the charge, 100% of the time.

- **Low Maintenance.** The Encore's closed breech design has no striker or breech area to clean. Just remove the breech plug for pass-through cleaning, like a bolt-action rifle.

- **Beautiful.** Its classic design and precision craftsmanship set the Encore 209x50 Magnum far ahead of the black powder pack, in looks and performance.

Come see the Encore, truly a gun for all seasons, only at your Thompson/Center Dealer.

THOMPSON/CENTER
Take your best shot.

Rochester, New Hampshire 03866 • 603-332-2333 • http://www.tcarms.com

Also Available From Krause Publications

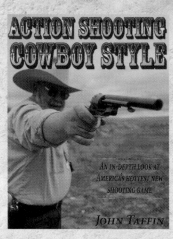

Action Shooting Cowboy Style
by John Taffin

Feel the rich gun leather and taste the smoke of America's fastest-growing shooting game. Every aspect is explained for shooters of all levels. Join the fun of cowboy-style shooting. Let John Taffin take you from the general store where he'll show you the latest in old western garb, to the firing line where some of the fastest guns around drop the hammer in search of a winning score.

Hardcover • 8-1/2 x 11 • 320 pages
300 b&w photos • 8-page color section
Item# COWAS • $39.95

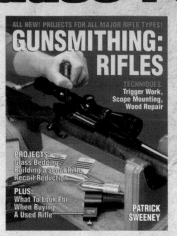

Gunsmithing: Rifles
by Patrick Sweeney

Anyone who owns a rifle will benefit from the information offered on these pages. Step-by-step gunsmithing projects for all types of rifles are presented and fully illustrated with outstanding photography. From improving accuracy to reducing recoil, this book will help every rifle owner put more bullets on target.

Softcover • 8-1/2 x 11 • 352 pages
700 b&w photos
Item# GRIF • $24.95

Reloading for Shotgunners
4th Edition
by Kurt D. Fackler and M.L. McPherson

The reloading guide every shotgunner should own. Shotshell, slug and buckshot basics plus advanced techniques for loading everything from field to high-performance target loads. The data section has the most comprehensive and current load data available organized by gauge, type and shot charge.

Softcover • 8-1/4 x 10-11/16 • 320 pages
600+ b&w photos
Item# RFS4 • $19.95

Black Powder Hobby Gunsmithing
by Sam Fadala and Dale Storey

Keep busy with projects for all levels of competence, from kitchen table through home workshop, all the way to the academic. Step-by-step tutorials on building from kits and a resource directory make the grade.

Softcover • 8-1/4 x 10-11/16 • 256 pages
440 b&w photos
Item# BHG • $18.95

The Gun Digest® Blackpowder Loading Manual
3rd Edition
by Sam Fadala

Worth its price just for the load data on 158 firearms alone. Sam Fadala crafts instructive articles and a loading tutorial into the must-have book blackpowder shooters have been craving. All-new information with expanded sections.

Softcover • 8-1/4 x 10-11/16 • 368 pages
390 b&w photos
Item# BPL3 • $19.95

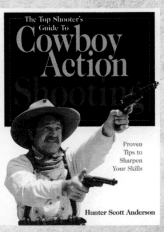

The Top Shooter's Guide to Cowboy Action Shooting
by Hunter Scott Anderson

Become a better cowboy action shooter. As a veteran of hundreds of these mock gun battles, Hunter Scott Anderson teaches shooters of all skill levels how to improve their shooting and their ranking among competitors. This book teaches you how to move effortlessly through a course of fire, while maintaining the accuracy needed to score well. This is the cowboy action-shooting book that will take you to the next level.

Softcover • 8-1/2 x11 • 216 pages
200 b&w photos
Item# TSCA • $21.95

To place a credit card order or for a FREE all-product catalog call

800-258-0929
Mention Offer GNB1

Mon.-Fri. 7 a.m. - 8 p.m. • Sat., 8 a.m. - 2 p.m., CST

Sales tax: CA, IA, IL, PA, TN, VA, WI residents please add appropriate sales tax.
Shipping: $4.00 1st book, $2.00 each additional. Non-US addresses $20.95 1st book, $5.95 each additional.
Satisfaction Guarantee: If for any reason you are not completely satisfied with your purchase, simply return it within 14 days of receipt and receive a full refund, less shipping charges.

krause publications
Offer GNB1, PO Box 5009
Iola WI 54945-5009
www.krausebooks.com

Taking the blackpowder trail may mean doing the rendezvous, dressing in the period and enjoying the many interesting shooting games.

is much more than blackpowder shooting — it's a way of life. The dedicated buckskinner is a lover of American history, a student of the past, devotee of an era. He knows not only the ways of the past; he also emulates them. He can start a fire with flint 'n' steel, make a capote, rig a tipi so that smoke curls up almost magically out of the center hole, and he may be able to thrive in the backwoods with 19th-century regalia about as handily as some of us get by with modern garments and gear. The best part of buckskinning, I think, is association with like-minded people. The modern rendezvous is a trade

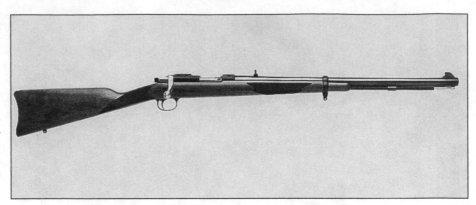

The shooter will have to decide how he or she wants to play the blackpowder game. Perhaps it will be with a familiar-looking, and handling, in-line muzzleloader, like this Ruger Model 77/50 with a totally modern trigger.

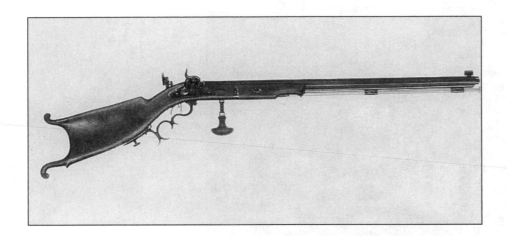

Taking the blackpowder trail may lead to serious target competition, which is why this Waadlt-lander rifle was invented and brought back as a replica by Dixie Gun Works. The rifle is still winning in competition.

Nobody could have guessed that the muzzleloader of the 21st century would not resemble a Kentucky rifle, nor a Hawken, not even a rifled musket, but rather a new creation known as the modern muzzleloader, looking something like this Markesbery Outer-Line®.

ground not only for a great deal of hand-made accouterments, but also ideas. Satisfaction lies in reliving a piece of the past, doing things in accord with the way they were done in early America. There is comradeship. There is fun.

So Many Side Trails

Blackpowder shooting has many side trails — shooting for shear enjoyment, as in plinking, informal target, skeet and trap; serious competition at local, national and international rendezvous games; club meetings; and of course hunting: small game, birds and big game, the latter being the number-one reason muzzleloaders are sold in America and Canada. Special blackpowder-only primitive hunts attract thousands, as well they should, since they offer some of the best opportunities for filling a tag, often in unique areas at opportune times of the year. Wise is the shooter who follows more than one of these trails.

Chapter 4

BLACKPOWDER GUNS

CLEARLY THE most important equipment decision the blackpowder shooter makes is choice of firearm, ideally plural. Going with one only is like having a single knife for all purposes, a situation no sportsman could possibly tolerate. A normal battery consists of handgun (pistol, revolver), shotgun and rifle, the latter chosen from many different niches. What do I want to do with the gun? That's the first logical question. Unfortunately, it is also limiting. We know that the vast majority of muzzleloaders are purchased for big game hunting, often for gaining access to seasons and areas limited to muzzleloaders. Someone who chooses on this basis alone is missing many of the most interesting shooting irons in existence, beginning with pistols and revolvers of soot-burning persuasion. He or she will also pass up shotguns, a sad mistake, because blackpowder shotguns are more fun than going to the circus. Also lost are small bores, since 50 caliber is far and away the most prevalent choice for deer and other big game hunting in North America.

The Revolver

The cap lock revolver is an iron-and-wood history book. These guns worked surprisingly well for old-time law officers as well as lawbreakers. They also served in the American Civil war in the hands of both Union and Confederate soldiers. In spite of the fact that many heroes and villains alike counted on cap 'n' ball revolvers to save their hides, or in some cases, wreak damage on someone else's person, the

The contrast between these two muzzleloaders is obvious. On the left is a custom long rifle. On the right is a modern muzzleloader.

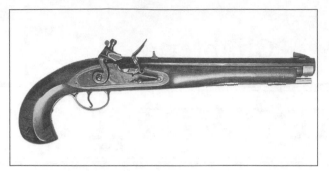

The single-shot pistol, like this flintlock model, made a significant impact upon history. Today, various companies continue to offer this interesting one-shot gun.

cap lock revolver today is best suited for plinking fun, taking small game, rendezvous shooting games, targets, and competition, not self-defense. There are too many more suitable sidearms available for anyone to rely on a cap lock six-shooter (or five-shooter for that matter) to save his bacon: semi-auto big bore pistols and powerful cartridge-bearing revolvers are better for that sort of duty. At the same time, especially following a training session, which is explained in the handgun chapter, the cap 'n' ball revolver can put its bullets into the bull's eye or fill the camp with edibles. Starting small, there's the 31-caliber revolver, a handsome little gentleman. For example, the Baby Dragoon, a 31-caliber wheel gun, shoots a little .319-inch, 50-grain ball at around 800 feet per second (fps) for a muzzle energy of 71 foot-pounds. This is sufficient for rabbits and other small edibles if you can hit 'em. The majority of 31s don't have target sights, so potting meat with them requires dedicated practice, but it can be accomplished. Going up a notch, the 36-caliber revolver shoots an 80-grain round ball at around 1,100 fps for a muzzle energy of 215 foot-pounds. Lots of good and bad guys were laid in the soil of Boot Hill by a 36-caliber ball. It's no powerhouse, but again can be mighty useful on the trail and in camp, as well as popping cans in front of a dirt bank.

The 44 is much stronger. The Ruger Old Army revolver, which is more 45 than 44, shoots a .457-inch, 143-grain round ball at up to 1,050 fps for a muzzle energy of 350 foot-pounds. As a matter of quick comparison, the 357 Magnum handgun cartridge with a 158-grain bullet at 1,300 fps gains close to 600 foot-pounds of muzzle energy, considerably more pop than the 44 cap lock. Yet most modern gunners no longer consider the 357 a powerhouse in light of the 44 Magnum and other big boys on the block. At the same time, the 9mm Luger is carried not only by police officers everywhere, but also the U.S. Army, and even with its 147-grain bullet moving at 1,000 fps, muzzle energy is only 326 foot-pounds, very similar to the blackpowder 44 revolver. With training, a handgunner wielding a 44 can put a lot of edible small game meat on the table. Big game has also been taken with this handgun, but only by experienced hunter-marksmen. Ballistically, the 44 blackpowder revolver is too small for big game and is disallowed in most areas, as it should be, but it's still a very interesting sidearm.

The replica blackpowder revolver is a lot of fun to shoot and a lot cheaper to collect than original cap 'n' ball wheel guns. There are dozens of copycats on the market today, such as Colt's current 1861 Navy, CVA's 1860 Army, Dixie's Spiller & Burr, Euroarms' Rogers & Spencer, and the interesting Le Mat from the Navy Arms Co. All of these guns and many others are entirely collectible for anyone satisfied with replicas, while small- caliber revolvers are adequate for small game, with the 44 good for small game, too, as well as varmints, or even deer with an expert behind the sights. Putting bullets consistently on target with these guns is nothing short of surprising once a shooter learns how to handle them, and takes the time to practice regularly.

The Pistol

The blackpowder pistol is generally a single shot, but there are a few double-barrels offered, too. Replicas in flint or percussion are ideal for the fun of owning and pure enjoyment of shooting, mainly plinking. Some blackpowder matches have pistol events that call for flintlocks or cap locks with primitive sights. If that's your game, go for it. But if you like clustering holes on the target, or putting a rabbit in the pot with a head shot, buy a pistol with sights. When CVA decided to offer a Hawken-style single-shot pistol, a decision was made to provide it with adjustable sights. While these sights do not replicate originals, they do promote bullet placement. Traditions' Trapper Pistol, also 50 caliber in either percussion or flintlock, also wears an adjustable rear sight, but its style leans more to the primitive. The same company's Buckhunter Pro pistol comes from an entirely different world. It's a modern muzzleloader, single-shot, with fold-down rear sight. As with revolvers, collectors can buy replica pistols to own and enjoy without

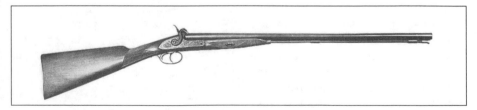

A blackpowder double-barrel shotgun like this one from Dixie Gun Works provides a fast-pointing gun with good ballistics.

breaking the piggy bank. There are many: Traditions' William Parker percussion, Navy Arms Co.'s Harper's Ferry flintlock, Dixie's LePage Percussion Dueling Pistol, and Pedersoli's Mang In Graz. Blackpowder pistols are fun to own, shoot and show. Buckskinners use them to complete their rendezvous outfits, because trappers of the Far West often carried one tucked in a belt for more than show. They were deadly at close range.

There are also blackpowder single-shot pistols that carry sufficient power for big game, provided the shooter is an expert with both gun and hunting skills. Lyman's 54-caliber Plains Pistol is one. It shoots a .530-inch, 225-grain round ball at around 925 fps for a muzzle energy close to 430 foot-pounds. The muzzle energy is not exciting, but at close range with good ball placement, the big 54-caliber hunk of lead does good work. Navy Arms Co. has a 58-caliber Harper's Ferry Pistol that is even stronger. I've gotten as high as 800 fps with a 500-grain Minie from this gun, for around 750 foot pounds of energy. Up close, that's big-game power. Thompson/Center's Scout pistol, calibers 50 or 54, is truly a blackpowder big game one-hander. Near the muzzle, it carries the punch of a 30-30 rifle. This pistol has been supplanted by the T/C Encore 209/50 Magnum, the main difference being ignition with a No. 209 shotgun primer in a break-open design. With 15-inch barrel and an allowable 110-grains volume FFg or Pyrodex RS equivalent powder charge, the Encore is big-game worthy.

The Blackpowder Cartridge Revolver

Partly due to the skyrocketing popularity of Cowboy Action Shooting, a game emulating the shooting style of old-time good and bad guys of the wild west, the blackpowder cartridge revolver is widely available once again, mainly in replica form. Examples are many, including the single-action Colt from various sources, including Colt. Many

Here are three muzzleloaders, all very different. On the left is a Whitworth rifled musket. A custom long rifle rests in the center. On the right is a Prairie River bullpup, an extremely unique modern muzzleloader.

of the replicas are not only handsome, but reliable and good shooting, one being the Bisley Colt from Navy Arms, a model tested with great satisfaction.

The Shotgun

The blackpowder shotgun is purely a joy to shoot at clay birds or the real ones, and unlike handguns or rifles, this soot-burner develops fairly close to modern performance. The most popular gauge, to no one's surprise, is the 12, but 10s can be located. Smaller gauges are also good, but 12s and 10s carry good powder and shot charges. No way can any of these soot-burners equal today's big 3 1/2-inch 12 gauge shotshell and similar hot loads, but the

main difference is range, not efficiency. Within its range, the old-time scattergun is absolutely deadly on everything from dove to geese. Some of these handle steel shot, making them legal for waterfowl. Bismuth shot has also come into its own, and is a legal non-toxic alternative to steel for those guns not steel-shot capable. While there are still a few fowlers (blackpowder flintlock shotguns) around, percussions lead the way by leagues. Double-barrels are especially handy for that fast second shot, but on the scene now are several modern muzzleloader shotguns. One example is Knight's 12 gauge, designed to handle up to 2 ounces of shot in front of heavy powder charges. This gun

Blackpowder guns can accomplish a wide range of applications, from plinking to taking a handsome whitetail buck like this one, dropped with a 54-caliber front loader and a 640-grain Parker Hydra-Con bullet.

comes with a screw-in, extra-full choke meant for wild turkeys, but entirely suitable for waterfowl and calling/dispatching of coyotes and similar-sized varmints.

But no amount of describing in words can convey the feeling of sending a cargo of shot into the sky amidst a cloud of blue smoke. That experience requires doing, not telling.

The Rifle

This brings us to the blackpowder firearm of great diversity.

Originals

Muzzleloaders, as with all good guns, were built to last lifetimes, and so it is that we still have originals in shooting order to this hour. They are not impossible to find, and some are a bargain. Originals must be completely checked out by a competent blackpowder gunsmith before shooting. This means debreeching, looking for possible dangerous wear or damage, and also checking to see that the rifle was not left loaded many years ago, as some are found to be. Naturally, truly collectible originals are not to see the field. They are too valuable. But there remain working guns from the past in shooting condition. On a trip to New Jersey, I was priv-ileged to see a huge collection of muzzleloaders, most of them for sale. My companion purchased one that looked almost new, in spite of its hundred-year-old vintage. Price: $300. A real bargain. It shot great.

The Replica

While there are non-collectible originals in good shooting shape, they're decidedly too few to satisfy the number of blackpowder enthusiasts enjoying the sport today. That is where replicas come in. Here is a rifle that closely resembles the real thing, but it isn't. Rather, it's built of modern materials and ready for action. A few replicas are screw-for-screw. It's difficult to tell them from the original. Most are not exact copies, however. Some closely copy the old-time rifle without concern for minute details. Others are in the spirit, definitely not clones of real guns from the past, but working just like them. Certain plains rifles have this effect. They do not look anything like originals, yet they have short, stout barrels, side locks, and other features that make then handle like the real thing. These rifles are generally accepted at rendezvous and are highly enjoyed by shooters who want to do things the old way, but not

Author's custom muzzleloader was patterned after an original.

The CVA HunterBolt™ 209 Magnum in-line modern muzzleloader is typical of the breed today. It's available in calibers 45 or 50 with 209 shotgun primer ignition.

down to the last detail. There remain quite a number of true replicas on the market, including rifled muskets of many descriptions.

The Non-Replica Rifle

The non-replica muzzleloading rifle occupied the number-one seat in popularity until very recently. Arguably, there are still more non-replicas offered than in-liners, but the gap is closing so fast that it's time to concede the lead. Non-replicas were designed for practicality. They could be built more easily than true replicas, and they suited most shooters because they were not exacting copies, meaning their stocks were straighter; they often wore recoil pads in place of steel butt plates, barrels were shorter, and all-in-all they carried lighter in the hand, many taking slings, which were not found on Hawkens and most other rifles of the pre-20th century. The non-replica loaded just like an original muzzleloader, one shot at a time from the front, and it was entirely adequate in the hunting field and on the target range. The vast majority are now well-made and offered in calibers ranging from 32 to 58, with 50 prevailing.

The Rifled Musket

When the smoothbore musket earned rifling without changing its military-like design, it became the "rifled musket," in the main a rugged, worthy firearm. While the military style tends to keep some shooters away, the truth is, certain rifled muskets make great hunting rifles. Those with quicker twist, such as the Navy Arms Whitworth and the same company's Volunteer, shoot long conical lead bullets at velocities sufficient to make these guns extremely big game worthy.

The Volunteer, for example, is allowed 130 grains of volume FFg or Pyrodex RS powder behind bullets in the 500-grain class, making it as much a 200-yard proposition in the big game field as the modern muzzleloader. Under certain conditions, these replica guns are nearly ideal, especially in tough terrain where ruggedness and reliability are called for. Anyone doubting the authority of a rifled musket need only consult the chronograph, which showed the Volunteer gaining 1,514 fps with a 490-grain bullet for a muzzle energy close to 2,500 foot-pounds. More importantly, that bullet delivered more than 1,800 foot-pounds of energy out to 100 yards—accurately.

The Modern Muzzleloader

There's nothing new about the modern muzzleloader concept. Decades ago, inventive gunmakers created non-original, modern-like front loaders. In-line ignition is hardly new, either, going back to the 1700s. The modern muzzleloader of the hour is more sophisticated by millennia than its predecessor. Most incorporate a list of special criteria, such as in-line ignition, removable breech plug, modern trigger, modern stock style, overall dimensions, recoil pads, sling swivels, adjustable

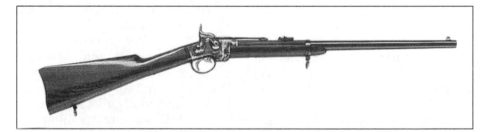

Every whim of the blackpowder shooter is catered to nowadays. If he or she wants a Civil War firearm, many are available, such as this Smith Artillery Carbine replica in 50 caliber. The barrel is only 21 inches long, with an overall length of only 39 inches.

Today, the blackpowder shooter has a world of options to choose from, all the way from originals and replicas to a modern muzzleloader like this Markesbery Outer-Line®.

One of the finest muzzleloader types of all is the custom. Shown here is No. 47, the author's 54-caliber round ball rifle built by Dennis Mulford.

sights, scope-readiness, modern safety and fast rifling twist.

In-line ignition and direct ignition are two different things. Underhammers and sidehammers (mule ear locks) of the past used direct ignition. Fire from underhammers and sidehammers flies directly from the percussion cap into the breech. In both cases, the nipple is screwed directly into the breech. In-line ignition differs in that fire from the percussion cap goes directly into the breech from the back. The percussion cap is, as the name implies, in a direct line with the breech. The cap rests, as it were, behind the powder charge, just as the primer in a cartridge lies behind the powder charge. The Outer-Line® from Markesbery is unique in that the nipple or optional primer-device rests at a 45-degree angle to the breech, but ignition flame still darts directly into the powder charge.

A distinct advantage of modern muzzleloaders is breech cleaning, the majority having removable breech plugs. The plug screws out, which opens the passageway into the bore. In this manner, a shooter can come home with a fired rifle, unscrew the breech plug, and clean the gun from the back end, just as he would his modern bolt-action rifle.

Modern muzzleloader triggers are generally the same design as those found on today's bolt-action big game rifle. Sometimes they are the very same. Most are adjustable. The modern muzzleloader resembles a modern rifle in stock design and lines, making feel and handling very familiar to shooters. Drop at comb, for example, follows the contemporary rifle, not the long tom of yesteryear.

Overall dimensions follow today's rifles: not muzzle-heavy, nor overly heavy, nor long-barreled. The modern muzzleloader picks up, carries, and comes to the shoulder like rifles already familiar to today's shooters. For those who simply want to shoot blackpowder with no regard for history, this feature can be very important.

Recoil pads are common on modern muzzleloaders. They do absorb some thrust-back, and they are, once again, familiar-feeling.

Sling swivels are very much a part of modern muzzleloader makeup. Old-style rifles, such as the Hawken, did not employ slings as we know them, although military muskets did. Carrying a muzzleloader in hand all day on a hunt can be taxing. The sling removes some of the burden.

Modern muzzleloaders have sights as found on contemporary rifles, often the same exact models. Adjustable open irons are common. Peep sights are also available from several companies, such as Lyman and Williams. These guns are also scope-ready with receivers drilled and tapped for mounts. While scopes are not legal on all blackpowder primitive hunts, they are widely allowed. They're also ideal for target work or testing a rifle's potential accuracy.

Modern safeties are found on the majority of modern muzzleloaders, as opposed to the hammer system with half-cock notch. Some have more than one safety.

The vast majority of modern muzzleloaders have a comparatively rapid rate of twist, as opposed to round ball rifles. A modern 50-caliber muzzleloader may have a 1:28 twist, while a 50-caliber ball-shooter carries a 1:66 twist. Therefore, modern muzzleloaders are meant to shoot conicals. See the chapter on twist for more on the subject.

Systems Rifles

An interesting concept, again not new, is providing several barrels on one frame. One of the better exam-

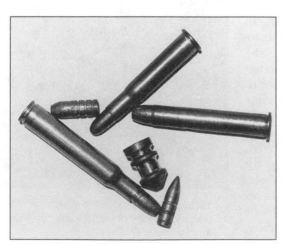

Cast bullets date into the distant past, and are just as viable today. The 30-30 cartridge, top, and 38-55 both came factory-loaded with an optional cast bullet at one time. The 30-06, below, shows that modern smokeless powder rounds can also play the cast bullet game. The three very different looking unseated bullets are all cast.

ples of the idea is Markesbery's Outer-Line® rifle, with interchangeable barrels in 36, 45, 50, and 54 calibers, along with a 12-gauge shotgun.

The Custom Muzzleloader

There are modern gun makers who create long arms (and pistols) just as handsome as their forebears made, with one drawback: price. A thousand dollars buys a fairly plain custom long rifle. Price can escalate many fold from that point, depending on quality and quantity of extras. Every dedicated blackpowder devotee deserves at least one custom in his career.

The Cartridge Rifle

Not a muzzleloader at all, but still a blackpowder rifle, there are two general styles: lever action and single-shot. Original lever guns are soaring at the moment, for the same reason blackpowder cartridge handguns are so popular: Cowboy Action Shooting. Models 1866, 1873, and 1892 are especially big. Tested was a Model 1892 chambered for the 45 Colt. It looked good and shot well. The single shot design is back for another reason: the blackpowder silhouette game, where competitors fire on metal cutouts at long range. The two most popular models are from buffalo-hunting days, the Remington rolling block sold through Navy Arms Co. and the Sharps from C. Sharps of Big Timber, Mont. The former is 45-70 Government MT caliber, the latter in many old-time blackpowder cartridge chamberings, including the 45-120 Sharps. Hunters are also finding that the blackpowder cartridge, loaded with blackpowder or Pyrodex, makes for an interesting hunting tool.

That's a look at blackpowder guns. There are also dozens of discontinued models for sale through *Gun List* and other publications, as well as gun shows everywhere.

Blackpowder single-shot cartridge rifles like this Sharps from Dixie Gun Works have gained great popularity.

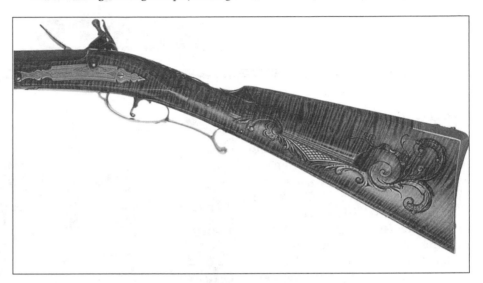

The top of the mountain in blackpowder guns as far as art and beauty go is a custom made by a master, in this case Mark Silver. This remarkable piece is Silver's rendition of an 18th century long rifle.

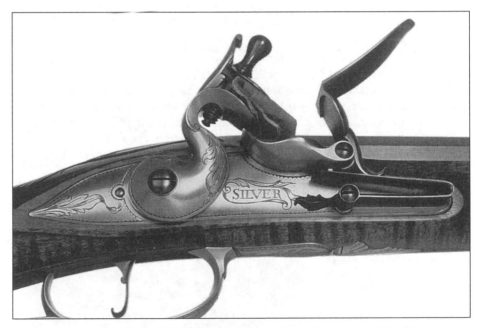

There is nothing quite like a custom muzzleloader, especially when the work is executed by a master like Mark Silver, who built this 62-caliber Virginia long rifle.

Chapter 5

GREAT BLACKPOWDER HUNTS

NORTH AMERICA is loaded with some of the finest hunts any outdoorsman could ask for—muzzleloader-only seasons, meaning no cartridge guns allowed, sometimes known as primitive hunts, which they are not. Primitive means spear or old-time archery tackle. There is nothing primitive about the Kentucky/Pennsylvania or Hawken rifles. On the other hand, the most up-to-date magnum single-shot muzzleloader is miles behind today's centerfire cartridge-shooting rifles. Regardless of super powder charges and high-profile bullets, the front loader is no 7mm Magnum. Thank goodness, for if charcoal burners were on par with high-velocity cartridges, the fabulous muzzleloader-only hunts of America and Canada would be as defunct as spats and knickers. The beauty of these hunts lies in two

There are great blackpowder hunts not only in America, but also Canada, as this photograph of Marty Atkinson proves. Marty took this high-ranking record class caribou with his Knight 50-caliber muzzleloader in the Northwest Territories of Canada.

areas: time of year and location. Many seasons are held during rut or migration when cartridge-shooting riflemen are not allowed to participate, and they often take place in areas closed to general seasons.

But there's more. While these hunts are immensely popular, it often is easier to be successful at drawing a license in tag lotteries than when trying to be selected for general firearms seasons, because fewer names are in the hat for the blackpowder-only hunts.

Taking advantage of these special hunts requires mastering the muzzleloader, the main purpose of this book, but it also means knowing where the hunts are, when they take place, plus the rules and regulations governing the adventure. Since these change, the Fourth Edition has taken a new approach — listing each state's game department with address, phone, and web site, rather than relating current firearms laws and special hunts, as the Third Edition did. The resource for seasons and laws is the official state proclamation, obtained via

Donald Scott took this handsome whitetail buck at 40-yards on his own property in Wisconsin, proving that great black-powder hunts can happen in your own back yard in America. He used a Thompson/Center 50-caliber Hawken with a 370-grain T/C Maxi bullets and 90-grains volume FFg black powder.

The author enjoys a hunt at Deer Creek Outfitters in Sebree, Ky. with a comfortable lodge and tree stands set up on private property.

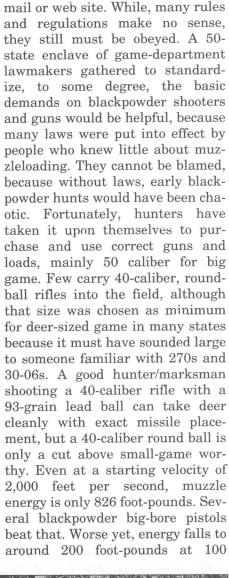

Forrest Rhodes of Wyoming does it again with his Knight muzzleloader, taking this fine black bear. His usual rifle is a Knight 50-caliber. He often shoots a 250-grain Barnes saboted copper bullet in the rifle with a heavy dose of Pyrodex.

mail or web site. While, many rules and regulations make no sense, they still must be obeyed. A 50-state enclave of game-department lawmakers gathered to standardize, to some degree, the basic demands on blackpowder shooters and guns would be helpful, because many laws were put into effect by people who knew little about muzzleloading. They cannot be blamed, because without laws, early blackpowder hunts would have been chaotic. Fortunately, hunters have taken it upon themselves to purchase and use correct guns and loads, mainly 50 caliber for big game. Few carry 40-caliber, round-ball rifles into the field, although that size was chosen as minimum for deer-sized game in many states because it must have sounded large to someone familiar with 270s and 30-06s. A good hunter/marksman shooting a 40-caliber rifle with a 93-grain lead ball can take deer cleanly with exact missile placement, but a 40-caliber round ball is only a cut above small-game worthy. Even at a starting velocity of 2,000 feet per second, muzzle energy is only 826 foot-pounds. Several blackpowder big-bore pistols beat that. Worse yet, energy falls to around 200 foot-pounds at 100

John Costes did not have to leave his home state of New Hampshire to take this very fine whitetail buck with a 50-caliber muzzleloader shooting 100 grains volume Pyrodex RS with a 210-grain saboted bullet, range about 85-yards. The buck weighed 207 pounds field dressed.

facturers voicing ridiculous claims for their charcoal burners. Game department personnel who believe these fanciful boasts have every right to ask, "If these muzzleloaders are that good, why should we offer special seasons for them?" But are modern muzzleloaders provably more effective than non-replicas, replicas or other blackpowder guns? Are they more accurate? Do they shoot farther? The chapter about these guns answers these questions. Meanwhile, many rules pertaining to cartridge guns also affect muzzleloaders. For example, while game departments across the nation impose few restrictions on blackpowder shotguns, non-toxic shot laws still pertain. The soot-burning scattergun loaded with lead shot in an area regulated non-toxic is in violation of the law.

The muzzleloader sportsman must learn the laws of the state he intends to hunt: Are blackpowder arms allowed for specific small and large game animals? For example, muzzleloaders are not legal on certain state bison hunts. Are there caliber or powder charge (weight) restrictions? Are sabots and modern pistol bullets allowed? Do terminal energy restrictions apply? Are scope sights allowed during special muzzleloader-only seasons? Are peep sights admissible? What about front loaders during regular

yards, less than the punch delivered by a 38 Special at the muzzle. A 40-caliber conical is a different story. A 410-grain, 40-caliber elongated bullet at 1,300 fps gathers a muzzle energy of 1,539 foot-pounds, with more than 1,200 foot-pounds remaining at 100 yards. The 45 caliber is not much better in round ball, but strong as a conical. Meanwhile, round balls in the 50- and 54-caliber class are deadly on big game when hunters get close for one well-placed shot.

State-by-State Blackpowder Restrictions

Ballistics rules were not the only ones made by game departments. High-technology front loaders forced new few questions: Should these guns be allowed at all on special primitive hunts? Are super muzzleloaders, some capable of tak-

ing a deer at 200 yards, right for blackpowder-only seasons? What about scope sights? Part of the problem lies with inflated advertisements from overzealous manu-

Great blackpowder hunts exist all over the United States now. Bryce Warwaller took this fine buck with one shot from a Traditions 50-caliber muzzleloader and 100 grains volume Pyrodex RS with a 225-grain boat-tail bullet. The mule deer scored over 170 Boone & Crockett points.

Hunting lodges are more popular than ever, and they've been in business for at least 100 years in America. The guides at Kentucky's Deer Creek Outfitters in Sebree do the work. The hunter has the enjoyment.

big game seasons? And what rules apply to modern muzzleloaders? Remember, there are a few flintlock-only hunts in which even old-time style percussion guns are not admissible, let alone in-liners. Also, are there any special restrictions on muzzleloader features, such as barrel length or number of barrels allowed?

Using the information below, a sportsman can obtain solid information about special blackpowder-only hunts, where and when they are held, and what regulations apply. The web sites are particularly useful. For example, calling up Georgia's web site resulted in a wealth of information, including current Georgia hunting regulations, license requirements, license fees, how to obtain a hunting license via phone, mail, or Internet, plus muzzleloader firearm laws, such as: 44-caliber minimum, no scopes, no blackpowder handguns during the state's special Primitive Weapons Season. Also: game management, current news releases, a video pertaining to hunting opportunities, and much more.

Alabama Division of Game & Fish
64 Union St.
Montgomery, AL 36130-1456
334-242-3465
http://www.dcnr.state.al.us/agfd

Alaska Department of Fish & Game
POB 25526
Juneau, AK 99802-5526
907-465-5999
http://www.state.ak.us/local/

Dan Coats took this nice pronghorn buck with a flintlock rifle that he built himself. He used a 54-caliber round ball with 90 grains volume GOEX FFg blackpowder, taking the shot from only 40 yards.

Arizona Game & Fish Department
2221 W. Greenway Road
Phoenix, AZ 85023
602-942-3000
http://www.gf.state.az.us/we/come.html

Arkansas Game & Fish Commission
No. 2 Natural Resources Drive
Little Rock, AR 72205
1-800-364-GAME
http://www.agfc.state.ar.us

California Department of Fish & Game
1416 Ninth St.
Sacramento, CA 95814
916-445-0045
http://www.dfg.ca.gov

Colorado Department of Natural Resources
6060 Broadway
Denver, CO 80216
303-297-1192
http://www.dnr.state.co.us/wildlife/

Connecticut Department of Environmental Protection
79 Elm St.
Hartford, CT 06106-5127
860-424-3000
http://dep.state.ct.us/burnatr/wildlife/wdhome.htm

Delaware Department of Natural Resources and Environmental Control
POB 1401
Dover, DE 19903
302-739-4431
http://www.dnrec.state.de.us/fw/fwwel.htm

Florida Game & Freshwater Fish Commission
620 South Meridian St.
Tallahassee, FL 32399-1600
904-488-3831
http://www..state.fl.us/fwc/

Georgia Department of Natural Resources
205 Butler St. SE
Atlanta, GA 30334
770-918-6416
http://www.ganet.org/dnr/wild/

Hawaii Department of Land & Natural Resources
1151 Punchbowl St.
Honolulu, HI 96813
808-548-4000
http://www.hawaii.gov/dnr/welcome.html

Idaho Fish & Game Department
600 South Walnut St.
Boise, ID 83707
208-334-3700
http://www.state.id.us/fishgame/fishgame.html

Illinois Department of Natural Resources
524 South Second St.
Springfield, IL 62701
217-782-6302
http://dnr.state.il.us/

Indiana Department of Natural Resources
402 West Washington St.
Indianapolis, IN 46204
317-232-4020
http://www.state.in.us/dnr/

Iowa Department of Natural Resources
Wallace State Office Building
East Ninth and Grand Ave.
Des Moines, IA 50319
515-281-4367
http://www.state.ia.us/government/dnr/index.html

Kansas Department of Wildlife & Parks
512 SE 25th Ave.
Pratt, KS 67124-8174
316-672-5911
http://www.kdwp.state.ks.us/

Kentucky Department of Fish & Wildlife Resources
1 Game Farm Road
Frankfort, KY 40601
502-564-3400
http://www.state.ky.us/agencies/fw/kdfwr.htm

Louisiana Department of Wildlife and Fisheries
POB 98000
Baton Rouge, LA 70798-9000
504-765-2800
http://www.wlf.state.la.us

Maine Department of Inland Fisheries & Wildlife
284 State St. Station
*41 House Station *
Augusta, ME 04333
207-287-8000
http://www.state.me.us./itw/homepage.htm

Maryland Department of Natural Resources
Tawes State Office Building
580 Taylor Ave.
Annapolis, MD 21401
301-974-3990
http://www.dnr.state.md.us/

Massachusetts Department of Fisheries

Wildlife & Environmental Law Enforcement
251 Causeway St.
Suite 400
Boston, MA 02114-2104
617-626-1591
http://www.state.ma.us/dfwele/dpt_toc.htm

Michigan Department of Natural Resources
POB 30028
Lansing, MI 48909
517-373-9400
http://www.dnr.state.mi.us/

Minnesota Department of Natural Resources
Division of Fish & Wildlife
500 Lafayette Road
St. Paul, MN 55155-4001
612-296-6157
http://www.dnr.state.mn.us/

Mississippi Department of Wildlife, Fisheries and Parks
POB 45
Jackson, MS 39205
601-362-9212
http://www.mdwfp.com/

Missouri Department of Conservation
POB 180
Jefferson City, MO 65102
314-751-4115
http://www.conservation.state.mo.us/

Montana Department of Fish & Wildlife
1420 East Sixth
Helena, MT 59620
http://www.fwp.mt.gov

Nebraska Game & Fish Commission
2200 North 33rd St.
Lincoln, NE 68503
402-471-0641
http://www.ngp.ngpc.state.ne.us/gp
.html

Nevada Department of Wildlife
POB 10678
Reno, NV 89520
702-789-0500
PAGE UNDER CONSTRUCTION

New Hampshire Fish & Game Department
2 Hazen Drive
Concord, NH 03301
603-271-3211
http://www.wildlife.state.nh.us

New Jersey Division of Fish, Game & Wildlife
401 East State St. CN402
Trenton, NJ 08625
609-292-2965
http://www.state.nj.us/dep/fgw

New Mexico Game & Fish Department
POB 21152
Santa Fe, NM 87505
505-827-7911
http://www.gmfish.state.nm.us

New York State Department of Environmental Conservation
50 Wolf Road
Albany, NY 12233
518-457-6367
http://www.dec.state.ny.us/
website/dfwmr/index.html

North Carolina Department of Environmental, Health, and Natural Resources
Archdal Building
512 North Salisbury St.
Raleigh, NC 27604-1188
919-733-3391
http://www.enr.state.nc.us/

North Dakota State Game & Fish Department
100 North Bismarck Expressway

Bismarck, ND 58501-5095
701-328-6300
http://www.state.nd.us/gnf

Ohio Department of Natural Resources
1952 Belcher Drive
Columbus, OH 43224
614-265-6565
http://www.dnr.state.oh.us/odnr/
wildlife/index.htm

Oklahoma Department of Wildlife Conservation
POB 53465
Oklahoma City, OK 73105
405-521-3856
http://www.wildlifedepartment.com/

Oregon Department of Fish & Wildlife
POB 59
Portland, OR 97207
503-872-5268
http://www.dfw.state.or.us

Pennsylvania Department of Conservation and Natural Resources
POB 8767
Harrisburg, PA 17105-8767
717-787-2869
http://www.pgc.state.pa.us

Rhode Island Department of Environmental Management
22 Hayes St.
Providence, RI 02908
401-277-2774
http://www.state.ri.us/dem/

South Carolina Department of Natural Resources
POB 167
Columbia, SC 29202
803-734-3888
http://www.dnr.state.sc.us/

South Dakota Game, Fish & Parks
523 East Capitol Ave.
Pierre, SD 57501-3182
605-773-3394
http://www.state.sd.us/gfp/gfp.html

Tennessee Wildlife Resources Agency
POB 40747
Nashville, TN 37204
615-781-6500
http://www.state.tn.us/twra/

Texas Parks & Wildlife
4200 Smith School Road
Austin, TX 78744
512-3809-4800
http://www.tpwd.state.tx.us/

Utah State Department of Natural Resources
1594 West North Temple
Salt Lake City, UT 84114
801-538-7200
http://www.nr.stateut.us/dwr/dwr.
hym

Vermont Agency of Natural Resources
103 South Main St.
Waterbury, VT 05671-0501
802-241-3701
http://www.anr.state.vt.us/

Virginia Department of Game & Inland Fisheries
4010 Broad St.
Richmond, VA 23230
804-367-1000
http://www.state.va.us/~dgif/index.
htm

Washington Department of Fish & Wildlife
600 Capitol Way North
Olympia, WA 98501-1091
360-902-2200
http://www.wa.gov/wdfw

West Virginia Department of Natural Resources
1900 Kanawha Boulevard East
Charleston, WV 25305
304-558-2771
http://www.dnr.state.wv.us/

Wisconsin Department of Natural Resources
POB 7921
Madison, WI 53707
608-266-2621
http://www.dnr.state.wi.us/

Wyoming Game & Fish Department
5400 Bishop Boulevard
Cheyenne, WY 82006
307-777-4600
http://www.gf.state.wy.us

Chapter 6

OUTFITTING THE BLACKPOWDER SHOOTER

THE WILL of the people cannot be denied. American and Canadian blackpowder shooters have their eyes cast upon the modern. Yet the interest in old guns and old ways continues, with thousands of shooters enjoying not only the firearm styles of yesteryear — mainly Hawken plains rifles and Kentucky long toms — but also the accouterments that attended these great guns, from powder horns to over-the-shoulder shooting bags. Outfitting the blackpowder shooter takes three avenues: old-time, modern, and a healthy mix of old and new. For example, powder horns remain as viable today as they were in the past. They serve to safely contain muzzleloader propellants used in either modern or old-time guns, so a powder horn in a modern muzzleloader kit is not at all out of place. Likewise, there are many other good tools of yesteryear, such as the nipple pick, charger, and old-time shooting bag. Today, that bag may be made of nylon, Polarfleece®, or other modern material, but again, the fine leather example works just as well for a bolt-action in-liner or replica Hawken.

Powder horns were used long ago and still remain popular today.

Accouterments of Old

Whether spelled accoutrements or accouterments, they were the same — the tools of the trade — those indispensables required for loading, shooting, and maintaining the muzzleloader. Buckskinners, those dedicated blackpowder enthusiasts who dress 19th century and play the role of the mountain man, must know what their heroes carried on those long trails into the Far West in order to copy them. These accessories are either purchased ready-to-go, or handmade by the man or woman interested in tipi times. The mountain man's goal was survival. His rifle was his lifeline. He counted on it to deter both two- and four-legged dangers, as well as putting meat in camp. Conditions prevented perfect maintenance, and it was common for a gun to fail after days, even months, without thorough cleaning and attention. But the trailblazer did have his kit and the items he carried were put into play daily. What were they? Charles Hanson, in his fine book, *The Plains Rifle*, quotes a 19th-century writer and adventurer named Ruskin, who listed mountain man Bill Williams' 1840 outfit. Williams was a well-known trapper. His memory still lives in the northern Arizona town of Williams. Here is what he carried:

"In the shoulder-belt, which sustained his powder horn and bullet-pouch, were fastened the various instruments essential to one pursuing his mode of life. An awl [for sewing], with deer-horn handle, and the point defended by a case of cherry-wood carved by his own hand, hung at the back of the belt,

The shooting bag of old has never been replaced. Beautiful examples are made by October Country and other companies. However, joining these are modern shooting bags like this one from Thompson/Center.

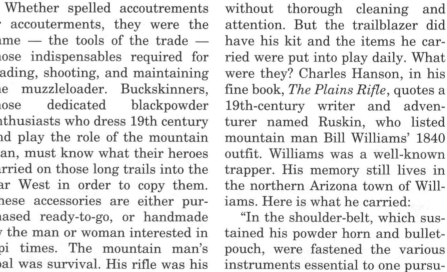

side by side with a worm for cleaning the rifle; and under this was a squat and quaint-looking bullet mould, the handles guarded by strips of buckskin to save his fingers from burning when running balls, having for its companion a little bottle made from the point of an antelope's horn scraped transparent, which contained the 'medicine' used in baiting the traps."

The mountain man's guns, pistol as well as rifle, fired lead balls often cast by firelight. Lead was brought into the mountains at rendezvous times. Of course, there was blackpowder, the fuel that propelled those round balls from the muzzle. In turn, blackpowder had to be carried in something, which turned out to be, as Ruskin reported, a horn. The horn was used to prime flintlocks that might be on the trail, but mainly it supplied fuel for the caplock plains rifles. Flintlocks needed flints, while percussion rifles and pistols required percussion caps.

Although initially designed to clear the touchhole of the flintlock, another little tool was handy — the vent pick, nothing more than a bit of wire, but extremely important in maintaining a clear passage from the flash of powder in the pan into the waiting charge in the breech. When this same tool, essentially,

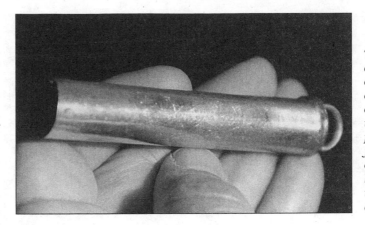

This charger is copied after an original. As a charger, it holds only one specific volumetric load of powder. But it's fast, and because of blackpowder's burning characteristics, produces accurate loads.

was used to clear the channel in the nipple, it became a nipple pick.

Whether flintlock or percussion, the round-ball rifle required a cloth patch, which did not create a gas seal in the bore, as wrongly believed for ages, but performed numerous vital duties, as described later.

Some shooters carried a charger, which was and still is nothing more than a simple, non-adjustable but effective powder measure made of brass, iron, horn, antler, bone or other material. The man who made the rifle also supplied a charger. It was his job to determine how much powder the rifle or pistol required for good shooting, and to then make a tool that held that much fuel by volume. The shooter simply poured powder from a horn into the charger and the right amount was measured

out. The gunsmith usually sighted the rifle for his customer, the charger supposedly gauged for an optimum amount of powder to provide both power and accuracy. As for the paper cartridge, supposedly employed by the mountain men, Hanson suggests little evidence of its existence during that period.

Sometimes the shooter practiced the dubious art of double-charging, which was dumping two scoops instead of one down the bore (not recommended) from the charger. Since guns were not chronographed, shooters did not know the law of diminishing returns, as described later. They concluded that more recoil and smoke always meant increased power, which was not necessarily so. Some historians say pre-cut patches were used. Others dis-

This exacting copy of an original charger is regulated for 75-grains volume. It is simple, but it also provides accuracy.

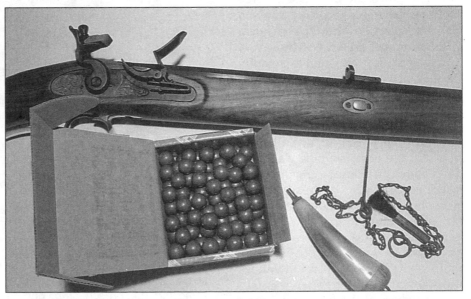

A few particulars for shooting the flintlock: round ball, and a fine pan prime and pick/brush combination on a chain handmade by William Knight.

Knives were very much a part of the mountain man's game. These fine blades were on trade row of a modern day rendezvous.

agree. Patch knives found among the gear of mountain men indicate that at least these men placed a hunk of material over the muzzle, followed by a ball, which was bumped downward past the crown of the muzzle with the snub portion of the short starter. The excess patch material resting above the ball was sliced away with the knife, after which the patched ball was seated on top of the powder charge in the breech. However, Ned Roberts had evidence that at least some old-time shooters used pre-cut patches.

The worm, a corkscrew affair, was run down the bore with coarse cloth attached, called tow, to swab out blackpowder fouling. The worm also could be used to withdraw a stuck patch. We don't usually employ a worm and tow for cleaning today, but the mountain men were not known for the fastidious rifle maintenance that modern shooters perform. If a ball was stuck in the bore, a screw was used to retrieve it. Picture an ordinary wood screw with the head cut off and the shank threaded to fit the tip of a ramrod and you have a screw that would cut into and hold the stuck lead ball for retrieval.

In spite of these maintenance tools, tough conditions often won out, with the bore of the mountain man's rifle becoming pitted. When the bore

was too eroded to shoot well, it was freshed out, meaning bored to a larger caliber, its rifling re-cut.

The old-time kit included a hunting bag, also called shooting pouch, erroneously referred to today as a "possibles bag." The bag, or pouch, was normally slung over the shoulder via a strap, and was a repository for the vital instruments of shooting, from spare lead balls to cap containers for the percussion rifle, extra flints for the flintlock, nipple wrench, and other neces-

sary tools. Vent or nipple picks, small screwdrivers, combination tools, and other devices were also found in original shooting pouches. However, to give an exact account of the early hunting kit is impossible. A straight starter might be included. This short version of the ramrod was used to start the patched ball down the bore a short distance. Not every kit had one. Today, we call it a short starter.

Along with the shooting bag or pouch, some historians claim there

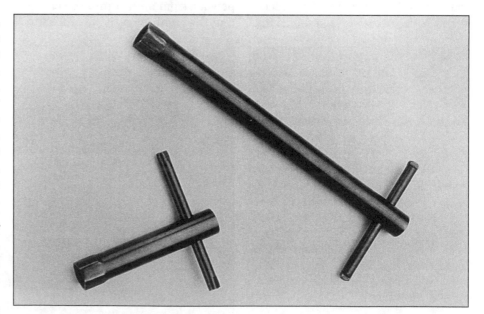

In-line guns, especially bolt-action models, demanded a new tool for removing the breech plug, one that could reach in. Thompson/Center came up with Breech Plug Wrenches to do the job, one with an especially long shank.

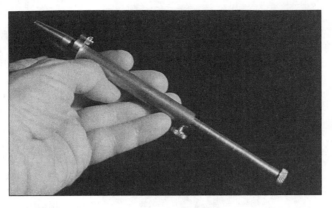

This is an adjustable powder measure. The funnel portion swings out of the way to admit powder into the body, and the slide is placed on the desired volume and set in place with the screw.

This Thompson/Center flask serves the same purpose as flasks of yester-year; however, it's made of high-tech materials with a transparent reservoir.

was a "possibles bag." In theory, the name alludes to the chance of finding almost anything in it. Or so the tale goes. The possibles bag was considered a larger pouch, and in it could found a bit of tobacco, spare gunpowder, flints, patching materials, a fire-steel for starting the well-known flint 'n' steel flame, and, according to Hanson's *The Plains Rifle*, this bag might also have a "fire-bag," which was a combination of fire-steel and tinder, sometimes carried on the mountain man's belt. In short, the possible bag was a catchall. Some students of the Far West don't buy into the possibles bag story. They think possibles simply meant an array of gear, regardless of how or where it was carried.

Along with the regular powder horn, which might hold about a pound of powder, the flintlock carrier could have a much smaller priming horn. Some historians argue that the old-time shooter didn't have time to fool with a priming horn. He simply poured a little powder from his regular horn into the pan. Perhaps this is true, but there is strong evidence that priming horns were used to disperse fine-grain powder into the pan. A little cap box served as container for percussion caps. There were cappers, too. These stored caps as well as dispensing them directly onto the nipple of the firearm. The in-line capper held caps in a row, while the magazine capper, a larger-capacity accouterment, held many percussion caps in a body section, gravity-feeding one cap at a time through a spring-loaded opening. Luckily, both styles remain available to modern shooters, including a handsome magazine capper from the Tedd Cash Co.

Modern Accouterments

While most of the gear invented before the telephone and flying machine works perfectly well in modern muzzleloaders, there are many tools that were created expressly for the high-tech firearm, both for shooting and maintenance.

The Savage Model 10ML Muzzleloader, capable of shooting smokeless as well as blackpowder, is a perfect example of an in-line front loader requiring special tools. The Savage rifle has a special breech-plug wrench 10 3/4 inches long, a specifically-designed decapper, which is also used as a handle for increasing leverage on the breech-plug wrench, and an absolutely unique module that holds a No. 209 shotgun primer.

The module is inserted into the chamber of the rifle and the bolt closed down to lock the module in place. After firing, the module is withdrawn by pulling back on the bolt handle. The module is pulled out of the chamber area just as if it were a cartridge. It's an ingenious design, but definitely requires the special tools supplied.

After the module is drawn free of the chamber, it's inserted into a special pocket in the decapper body to hold it in place, and an extension integral to the decapper is used to force out the spent primer. The Savage rifle is loaded from the muzzle, just like any other front loader, but with the option of blackpowder or Pyrodex metered out by volume only, or a specific safe smokeless

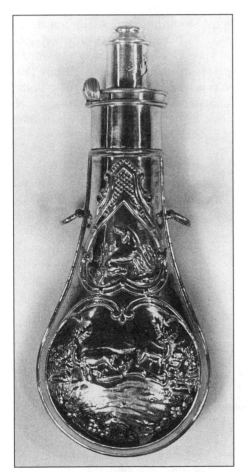

Flasks could be so ornate that they are collectible. This is a replica of a fine flask, offered by Dixie Gun Works.

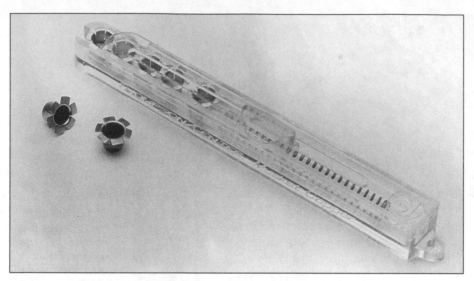

This in-line Musket Capper from Thompson/Center does an old job with new materials. It contains and delivers musket caps to the cone of the nipple from a transparent body.

powder charge prepared by exact weight only. Because this rifle is smokeless-powder capable, another tool comes into play, a bullet/powder scale to provide a specific charge weighed to the tenth of one grain or closer. The long, heavy-duty breech-plug wrench (with the decapper through the hole in the back of the tool for leverage) is used to withdraw the breech plug, thereby providing access to the back of the bore for cleaning like any modern bolt-action rifle.

While it's impossible to list every specific tool supplied with each individual modern muzzleloader, it is clear that these new guns demand special tools for safe and efficient operation. For example, Remington's Model 700 ML muzzleloader has a rain guard that fits into the action to prevent moisture from entering the breech area. A similar device is found on the Austin & Halleck modern in-line bolt-action muzzleloader. Since breech plugs are removable for cleaning from the back end, the in-line muzzleloader is provided with a tool for the job. Markesbery has a 4&1 Tool T-handle that screws into the ramrod for ease of loading and cleaning. It also contains a bullet jag, bullet starter, and nipple pick. There are many modern accouterments that function like old-timers, but with space-age design and modern material construction. This list of accessories deals with such accouterments. They will no doubt change in time as to name, exact style, and construction, as well as availability. However, there will be similar replacements that do the same work, so describing them is important. Here they are:

Short Starters

While still available in traditional style and construction, there are many modern short starters on the market, such as Thompson/Center's Compact Hunters Short Starter, weighing scant ounces. It has a solid aluminum shaft with concave loading tip, along with a palm-shaped knob made of all-but-indestructible polymer material. Traditions offers a Hunter Bullet Starter and Ramrod Extension of high-tech construction. The Hunter Bullet Starter from the Buffalo Bullet Co. is specially designed to seat conicals and sabots. It protects a soft lead nose from deformation.

Powder Flasks

Small powder flasks perfect for fitting into compact shooting bags are available, such as the T/C Blackened Flask in solid brass. Several companies now have clear powder flasks made of polycarbonates. Keeping with the trend, they are both compact and very lightweight. There's the Traditions Hunter Flask & Powder Measure set. The measure is standard in shape and function, but the flask is cylindrical with a special easy-operating valve. An interesting flask-like tool from Traditions is called the Pyrodex Pellet Dispenser. It holds 18 50/50-size pellets, dispensing two at a time when its button is pushed.

Powder Measures

Modern transparent powder measures, such as the U-View from T/C, have swing-out funnels and

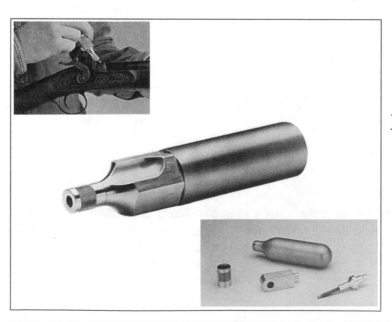

The Thompson/Center Silent Ball Discharger works with CO2 power, forcing a projectile from the bore.

locking shafts. One glance shows the level of powder in the measure. Extremely light in weight, they're also rugged and long lasting.

Quick Loaders (Pre-Loaders)

Ready loaders, also known as quick-loaders or pre-loaders, now come in many modern designs, such as the 4-in-1 from CVA with a Lexan transparent body instantly revealing its status: loaded or not loaded. It has a shirt-pocket clip, a palm saver, integral bullet starter, and the powder compartment is graduated in grains of volume. Snap caps on either end allow instant access to bullet or powder. Now there are even quick-loaders designed for the Pyrodex Pellet, an example being the Traditions Super Magnum Pellet Quick Loader. It holds three 50/50 Pyrodex Pellets on one end and a bullet compartment on the other. The covers double as cappers, holding one No. 11 or one Musket-size cap.

Cappers

In-line cappers as well as magazine cappers remain available in familiar brass construction, but there are also cappers made of con-

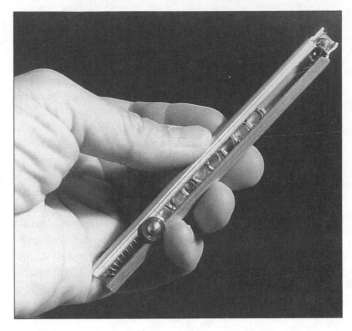

This Tedd Cash in-line cupper is typical of all products from this company, well-designed and well-made. It holds musket caps.

temporary materials, such as the U-View from T/C, which is designed to hold No. 209 shotgun primers. While the Tedd Cash Co. continues to build high-class traditional tools the old way, it surprises us with an in-line capper, made of brass, but containing and dealing out No. 209 shotgun primers.

Ramrods

The wooden ramrod is forever correct in traditional-type muzzleload-

ers, but modern blackpowder guns are more likely to have something on the order of the Hunter Super Rod as sold by Mountain State Muzzleloading Supplies and advertised as virtually unbreakable and non-abrasive. These are definitely not the ramrods Dan'l Boone poked through the pipes of his long tom.

Miscellaneous

The list goes on and on. There are various dischargers available,

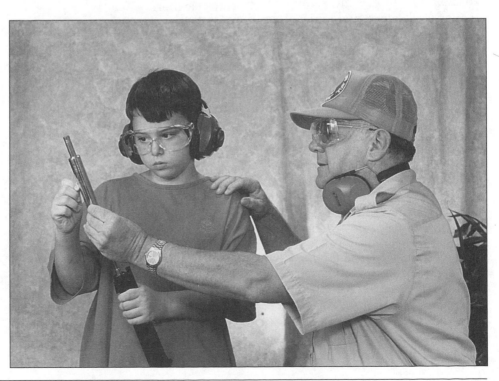

Starting this young shooter into the fascinating sport of blackpowder shooting the right way includes the use of the Kadooty loading rod, which offers an extremely safe loading procedure, along with mandatory hearing and eye protection.

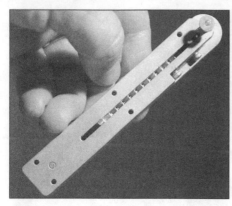

Modern muzzleloaders have brought on modern accouterments like this small rifle/small pistol primer "capper" from the Markesbery Muzzleloader for use with that company's nipple replacement that holds primers.

such as the T/C Magnum Silent Ball Discharger, which uses CO2 power to literally blow a load free after arriving in hunting camp, without having to fire the rifle. It's also good for removing charges that fail to ignite, or patches and projectiles seated accidentally without putting a powder charge down first. The EZ Unloader from Traditions functions in much the same way. There are nylon slings, special capper extractor tools, such as the one from CVA designed to remove fired No. 209 shotgun primers from in-line muzzleloaders, and many other modern muzzleloader accessories.

A Shooting Bag for Every Gun

A shooting bag for each individual blackpowder firearm is ideal. When the shooter heads for the target range or hunting field, he simply grabs the shooting iron in question, plus appropriate pouch to match that gun, and he has all the essentials required for that specific firearm, not only for shooting, but for general cleanup until reaching home for a more thorough job.

The Shooting Box

A blackpowder shooting box is vital. It's just like any other shooting kit, except for some of its contents. Along with the usual

screwdrivers, allen wrenches, targets, hearing and eye protection, the muzzleloader box includes special tools, such as nipple wrenches and nipple picks, plus the appropriate muzzleloader powder, projectiles, patching material, and so forth — a mini-warehouse of blackpowder stuff.

What's in a Shooting Bag?

Blackpowder shooting requires quite a few accessories, but many are small, fitting into a handy shooting bag. No two shooting bags will contain exactly the same items, but here's a list to serve as an example. All of these important tools are fully described in Chapter 7:

bullet bag
charger or powder measure
short starter
hornet nesting material
worm and screw
nipple wrench
combination tool and/
  or screwdriver
small tin box with pre-cut,
  pre-lubed patches
small (but ample) powder flask
priming horn
cleaning rag
solvent (in plastic eyewash bottle)
ready loads (2)
pipe cleaners
bristle bore brush
jag
capper
cap box (for percussion caps)
extra flints
cleaning patches
spare nipple
knife (which may attach to strap
  of shooting bag)

More Equipment

The following important items are not generally kept in the shooting bag, but they are important gear for the blackpowder shooter and should be owned and used:

wiping stick or loading rod
shot pouch or shot horn
cleaning kit
bullet molding outfit
patch cutter
shooting glasses

ear plugs
textbooks and notebooks
Tap-O-Cap
  (for making percussion caps)
holsters, scabbard, gun cases
clothing
  (buckskinning or standard)
knives and tomahawks

General Shooting Supplies

Some of these items are repeated because they are supplies directly involved in shooting, such as blackpowder, as well as items that should be kept on hand to replace worn or depleted necessaries.

flints
powder
percussion caps
cleaning patches and cloths
solvents and other chemicals
  (including lubes)
pre-cut shooting patches and
  patch material
extra nipples
extra ramrod
home-cast or commercial round
  balls
conicals
shotgun wads
shot
cleaning gear

Where do I buy it?

The Guns

Of course, the firearm is paramount to all shooting outfits. In Chapter 4, several different types of

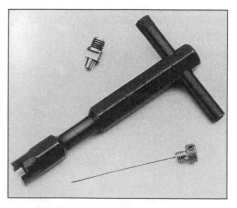

This Thompson/Center Deluxe Nipple wrench incorporates a nipple pick with very fine wire for clearing the flintlock vent or channel in a nipple.

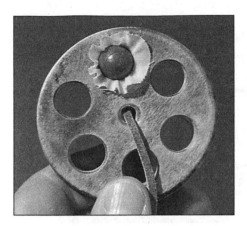

An old-fashioned way to carry round balls ready to go—simply rest the base of the ball on the muzzle and drive the patched ball past the muzzle with a short starter. William Knight made this one.

blackpowder guns were listed. This is about buying each one.

Buying Originals

The Gun List and Shotgun News, both papers dealing entirely with firearms and related gear, often have original blackpowder guns for sale. This is a good starting point. If nothing else, making contact with one person selling old-time guns generally branches into further contacts.

Buying Replicas, Non-Replicas, Modern Muzzleloaders

The selling world is full of all three types, from discount department stores to elite blackpowder shops.

Buying Cartridge Rifles

Versions of lever-action and single-shot rifles are easily located. Navy Arms Co., for example, continues to sell the Remington Rolling Block. Browning has brought out various blackpowder cartridge rifles, including a Winchester single-shot like the original John Browning invention, as well as Model 1892 and 1886 Winchesters, the latter in caliber 45-70 Government, a cartridge considered adequate for all American big game with the right load.

Buying Rifled Muskets

The rifled musket is a good purchase for shooters desiring a rugged hunting rifle. Some have target accuracy. The Whitworth does. All are dependable and powerful. Navy Arms Co. has a large supply.

Buying The Custom Rifle

The chapter on this rifle talks about its purchase. It's a matter of ordering first-hand. After all, it's a custom — one at a time unlike the one made before it, or the one to follow. The positive side: custom muzzleloaders made by real craftsmen are a joy to own and shoot. The negative side: they can demand a heavy roll of cabbage.

Buying the Handgun

A simple decision: What's it for? Rendezvous means a single-shot muzzleloading pistol. Plinking: Anything goes. Big game, big-bore pistol, especially a modern muzzleloader capable of handling big powder charges. For sale just about everywhere.

Buying the Blackpowder Shotgun

Choke: That is the deciding point. Cylinder-bore guns are good for close range. Choked guns are better for everything else. If waterfowl are included, steel shot capability is necessary, or the shooter must go for Bismuth. There are enough blackpowder shotgun choices to meet demands, including modern in-liners capable of big powder and shot

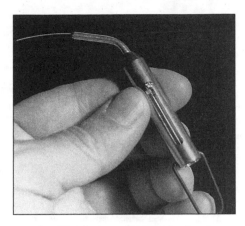

The CVA In-Line/Sidelock Combo Nipple Pick consists of a thin, strong wire encased in a solid brass handle. It flicks out like a snake's tongue to clear the vent of a nipple, and works with flintlocks, too.

charges, such as Knight's 12 gauge. Dixie Gun Works and Mountain State Muzzleloading carry a number of shotguns.

Buying The Blackpowder Knife and Hawk

Not a shooting instrument, but a knife, at least a jackknife, belongs in every kit. Traditions sells several, including a trade model. Big catalogs have even more, including replicas pleasing to buckskinners. The larger catalogs also have tomahawks. Navy Arms Company carries hawks, as does Dixie. Carl P. Russell's Firearms, Traps & Tools of the Mountain Man has good information on knives of that era, including trade knives, which were for trading, as the name implies, but also associated with a specific trade, or line of work. It's a book worth consulting for anyone interested in the cutting-edge side of muzzleloading.

Chapter 7

USING BLACKPOWDER ACCOUTERMENTS

THE LAST chapter talked about a number of vital tools necessary for successful muzzleloading, but nothing was said about function. That's the goal of this chapter: understanding what each accouterment does.

The Powder Horn

Horn played a significant role in ancient times, and it's still not defunct in the 21st century. That's because horn has amazing properties, in spite of its inauspicious origin: adornment and armament on the heads of bovines and other animals. Although Vikings never wore helmets with horns protruding from the sides — that's fictional — other employments were real, including drinking vessels and instruments to trumpet into the air. Shooters soon learned that horn was almost perfect for carrying propellant, too. It had all the right properties, and still does. It can be boiled to soften, then shaped with pleasing or functional lines. The small end turns into a beautiful spout. More importantly, it's non-sparking, which lends a lot of comfort to the muzzleloader shooter. A powder horn, stoppered properly, is essentially waterproof, another glowing quality, considering what moisture does to blackpowder. Horn is tough stuff. It takes a terrific blow to break it, which is ideal in the hunting field or on the shooting range. While not fireproof, a powder horn will not blow up should a spark or ash come in contact with it. It takes sustained flame to do that. Buckskinners like the powder horn for its authenticity, but modern muzzleloader fans can rely on one, too. WARNING: Never pour powder directly from a powder horn into the muzzle of a gun. A lingering spark from a previous firing could set off the entire cargo of the powder horn.

Priming Horn

A regular powder horn holds various amounts of powder, from a few ounces up. It's great for storing and dispensing muzzleloader powder, but too large to serve as a priming tool. A miniature powder horn serves here, usually spring-loaded with a small spout. Although scholars disagree about its wide use in the past, there is no argument that this little fellow is just right for priming the pan of any flintlock, be it rifle, pistol, or fowler (shotgun). The spout is pressed down on the hard surface of the flintlock pan, thus depressing the spring, which provides a trickle of FFFFg powder, just the right amount for ignition in the right spot, which is the outside of the pan, rather than up against the touchhole, the object being a clear channel from pan to main charge in the breech.

Priming Tool

This little metal flask serves the same purpose as a priming horn, containing and dispensing fine-grain powder into a flintlock pan.

Have some powder horns! Horns can be worked into many different shapes.

Making the use of accouterments easier all the time is the goal of many blackpowder companies. This CVA Muzzleloader Accessory Outfit comes in 50- or 54-caliber with appropriate bullets plus various accessories.

Of course part of a shooter's working supplies includes propellants. Today, the blackpowder fan is blessed with many different choices.

The Adjustable Powder Measure

As a reminder, a grain of weight is 1/7,000th of a pound. In other words, there are 7,000 grains of weight in a pound, or 437.5 grains of weight in 1 ounce. The name itself is somewhat unfortunate, since sometimes a single piece of powder is referred to as a grain. For our purposes, however, a grain is always weight, while a single piece of powder is a kernel.

Today, there are many different types of adjustable powder measures. Some copy the past; others are of modern design and materials, but they all do the same thing: They meter out a specific volume of propellant, usually by adjusting a sliding rod. The adjustable powder measure has graduated markings on the body or barrel segment, often running up to 120 grains of volume. It works supremely well for blackpowder or blackpowder substitutes, which are intended for volumetric loads, rather than weighed charges. It is not intended for smokeless powder. The Savage Model 10ML, which does allow smokeless, is loaded only with carefully weighed charges of Alliant 2400, Hodgdon H-4227, or other specified (only) smokeless powders. For blackpowder and proper substitutes, such as Pyrodex or Clear Shot, the adjustable measure is absolutely accurate, because weighing such powders to the tenth of one grain, as with smokeless, will not promote accuracy, as explained later. In use, the measure is first set for the correct volumetric amount of powder. It is then slightly overfilled with a few taps to settle the charge. If there is a swing-out funnel, it is rotated to align with the body of the measure, topping off the charge by swiping away a few granules of powder. "Grains weight" is a term used to describe a proper blackpowder/blackpowder substitute charge. A measure set for "100" often drops a charge of FFg blackpowder weigh-

ing close to 100 grains. Meanwhile, the same powder measure set at "100" will provide 71.5 grains weight of Pyrodex RS, which is exactly what it should do because Pyrodex is loaded by volume, not weight. Since Pyrodex is less dense than blackpowder, an equal volume weighs less but provides as much or more energy, as proven by chronograph tests.

The Charger

A charger is a non-adjustable powder measure. It works perfectly for one, and only one, volumetric charge. Often, the charger is no more than a metal tube, but it can also be made from a drilled-out antler tip or other non-sparking material. The tube is cut to a specific length to throw a specific volumet-

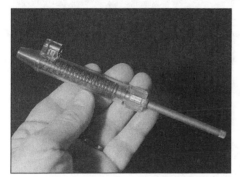

This modern Thompson/Center adjustable measure has a transparent body. It continues to function, however, just like older adjustable powder measures.

A charger is not adjustable. It's sized for one charge only. But this powder measure from CVA is adjustable, and offered in 90- or 120-grain maximum volumes.

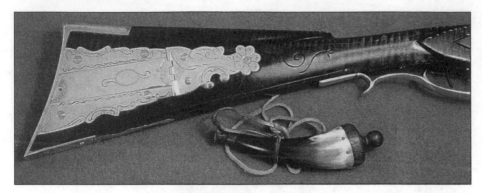

The exquisite work of gunmaker K.L. Shelton with his finely appointed Kentucky rifle is augmented by the handsome powder horn. Powder horns go way back in history, but their use still makes sense.

ric powder charge, or the piece of antler is drilled to a specific depth, also to provide a certain volume of powder. Powder is poured into the charger to measure the load. Then the load is poured into the muzzle of the blackpowder gun.

The Flask

A generous reader provided an original hard-leather shotgun shot flask, adjustable to throw either 1 1/4 ounces or 1 1/2 ounces of shot. After more than 100 years, it worked perfectly. Metal flasks are more common, but some flasks are even made of cloth. A metering device determines the amount of powder or shot thrown from the flask, generally through a spout that directs the powder or shot into the muzzle of a rifle, pistol, or shotgun, or the cylinder chamber of a cap-and-ball revolver. Or the flask may come with different spouts (tubes). The end of the spout is blocked with a fingertip. Then the flask lever is activated, allowing powder or shot to flow into the spout. When the lever is returned, it again blocks powder or shot from flowing out of the body of the flask. Flasks with screw-in spouts are adjusted for charge simply by changing the spout: longer spouts for more powder, shorter ones for less powder.

An excellent use for a small powder flask — there are many of these available — is carrying extra powder for the hunting field. These compact flasks hold more than enough fuel for any big game hunt or most small game outings, and they fit ideally into a shooting bag. Powder from the flask is poured into an adjustable powder measure or charger for the right load: perhaps as simple as a tube (spout) varying in length to provide different powder charges. I carry a small powder flask in my big-game shooting bag. Though compact, it holds enough powder for several shots from a big game rifle or shotgun, and a number of shots for a small-game gun.

The Readyloader

A readyloader is a handy tool for quick repeat shots. It's also good for safely containing a pre-measured volumetric powder charge in one compartment, along with the bullet in another compartment, and sometimes a percussion cap or primer as well. There are many different types available. While not a specific readyloader, plastic 35 mm film containers can be used for pre-measured shot and volumetric powder charges. The shooter simply pops the top on the powder container, squeezes the upper end to make a pouring trough, then drops the charge down the bore, followed by the same procedure with the shot container. Film containers are also useful for test loads with pre-measured powder charges. Since these plastic containers are non-sparking and essentially watertight, they are safe for carrying powder.

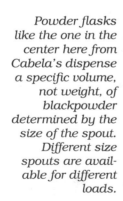

Powder flasks like the one in the center here from Cabela's dispense a specific volume, not weight, of blackpowder determined by the size of the spout. Different size spouts are available for different loads.

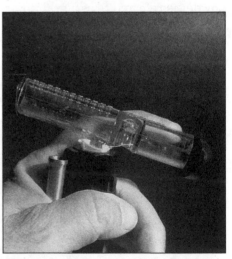

This readyloader, or quickloader, has a built-in nub that serves to start a bullet downbore. This feature allows fast loading without the use of a short starter. In effect, the loader itself is a short starter.

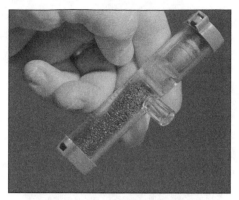

Here is a ready load packed with powder and bullet and ready to go into action.

The Ramrod

Simple, but vital, the ramrod rests in thimbles below the barrel, ready for action especially in the field, a loading rod preferred for the range. Ramrods for modern muzzleloaders are generally made of high-tech materials. Wood matches the older-style firearm. The ramrod seats a projectile firmly upon the powder charge in the breech with no air gap. It's also used as a cleaning rod in camp or field, with its threaded tip accepting a variety of accessories: worms, screws, jags, and other maintenance tools. Wooden ramrods work well and are correct for old-style guns. These rods should be straight grain. Wavy-grain rods are not as strong, and may tend to warp. Steel rods are not harmful to the bore as long as a muzzle protector is used. Because the muzzle protector aligns the rod in the center of the bore, it does not scrape against the rifling.

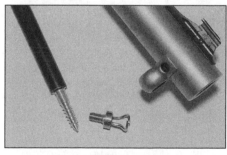

This ramrod has a removable tip cap. With cap removed, tools, such as a screw, shown here, can be installed.

The Loading/ Cleaning Rod

The loading/cleaning rod is ideal on the range for firmly delivering bullets onto powder charges. It serves also as a cleaning rod. Longer than a ramrod, strong and designed to hold many cleaning implements, the rod is a necessary maintenance tool and many different types are available. Ox-Yoke Originals, as well as Michael's of Oregon, offer the shooter a number of excellent loading/cleaning rods, some with muzzle protectors that slide on the shaft of the rod.

The Wiping Stick

Normally made of wood, the wiping stick was the forerunner of the loading/cleaning rod. It still works well, and fits into a primitive-style camp perfectly.

Palm Protector

Now offered in many different styles made of wood or high-tech materials, the palm protector does just that: it either slips over the end of the ramrod, or is part of a short starter, and it protects the hand while seating bullets.

The Short Starter

Round balls that closely match bore size are more accurate than undersized lead spheres requiring thick patches to take up the windage (space between ball and sides of bore). This is where a short starter comes into play. It usually has a stub stem and a main stem, the stub used to initially drive the patched ball just below the crown of the muzzle, the longer stem going to work to drive the patched ball a few inches deeper into the bore, ready for ramrod or loading rod to seat it fully on the powder charge. Lead conical bullets that fit closely to the bore, such as Maxi balls, also require a short starter to get them going. It's not smart to attempt seating a tightly fitted projectile downbore only with a wooden ramrod that might break. The short starter should be used first.

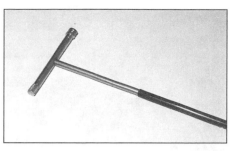

As part of the innovation associated with modern muzzleloaders, Markesbery developed a T-handle that fits on the end of the Outer-Line® rifle's regular ramrod for a better grip and delivery of reasonably firm pressure.

Bullet Starters

Essentially a short starter, these are specialized tools designed to seat conicals and bullets in sabots. Buffalo Bullet Co.'s Universal Bullet Starter is a good example. It protects the nose of the projectile from deformation.

The Vent Pick

Al though little more than a piece of fine wire, the vent pick, also called nipple pick, is ideal for clearing fouling from the touchhole of a flintlock, as well as cap debris from the channel of a nipple. If properly sized, it also can be used to block the touchhole of a flintlock during the loading process. This prevents powder from packing into that area and causing a fuse condition rather than a clear avenue from pan flame to breech.

The Nipple Wrench

Simply a wrench used to install or remove the nipple of a caplock firearm, the nipple wrench is an indis-

A loading rod is not a ramrod. It is longer and may have a handle up top, as does this Rugged Range Rod from the Thompson/Center Co.

This is a copy of an original vent pick with brush.

pensable tool. It must fit properly or it may damage the body of a nipple.

Pipe Cleaners

Found at most grocery stores, pipe cleaners are intended to clean smoking pipes, but this length of wire with fuzzy cloth wrapping also makes an ideal muzzleloading tool, acting somewhat like a nipple or vent pick, but with the ability to hold solvent. It's great for swabbing out flintlock touchholes, nipple vents, or picking up fouling from just about any hard-to-reach spot on a firearm.

The Capper

As explained in the previous chapter, there are two kinds of cap-

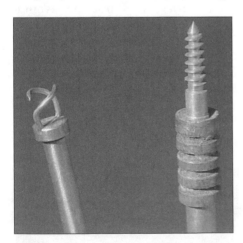

The screw and worm are simple tools, but extremely functional in spite of their vintage. The screw pulls a stuck ball. The worm retrieves a lost patch from the bore.

pers: in-line and magazine. Both serve the same purpose: to contain percussion caps and to dispense them onto the cone of the nipple. There are cappers that hold small rifle or small pistol primers, No. 209 shotgun primers and the large English musket caps. All of these cappers are handy. They are also a safe way of holding and delivering caps or primers. They make sense and should be used.

The Screw

A screw attached to the end of a loading/cleaning rod or ramrod drives into a stuck projectile downbore so it can be withdrawn out of the muzzle. Ideally, a bore protector should be used so that the screw is centered, rather than striking the rifling. The Kadooty loading tool includes a special knocker that provides extra impetus in pulling a stuck ball free. It works as a sliding hammer.

The Kadooty

Deserving its own special mention, this unique loading tool serves many purposes. A major function is delivering the same pressure upon the powder charge for each shot, which creates uniformity, always welcome in any form of shooting. Along with being a loading rod with repeatability, the Kadooty is also a cleaning rod, and it can be used to pull stuck bullets or sabots. The knocker, acting as a sliding hammer, makes withdrawing these objects effortless. It's good for pistols, revolvers, and shotguns as well as rifles, and it's built to last lifetimes. It comes in a handy haversack.

Jags

So small yet so vital, the jag screws into the tip of ramrod or loading rod to hold a cleaning patch. They come in various sizes and shapes, usually with concave noses so they can be used to drive soft lead round balls and conicals down the bore with minimal deformation. Certain breech shapes demand specific jags for proper fit.

Chris Pace of the company demonstrates his Kadooty to an interested group of shooters at a deer hunting lodge in Wisconsin.

Others may stick in the bore.

The Worm

While the screw is used to drive into and hold a projectile or sabot, the worm — also with a threaded shaft to fit on the end of ramrods and loading/cleaning rods — has wires or arms intended to grab a stuck cleaning or shooting patch.

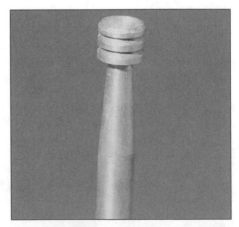

The jag is a small tool, but its job is big—retaining a cleaning patch run downbore so that it can be brought back upbore. This is a typical jag.

Blackpowder accouterments can be mixed for ease of operation. Here a traditional shooting bag from October Country combines with compact, lightweight implements from Traditions, including powder flask, powder measure, capper, short starter and bullet starter.

It's not intended for withdrawing a stuck bullet.

The Fusil

This term brings confusion. Sometimes a fusil described a type of muzzleloading firearm. The fusil noted here is the one mentioned by Ned Roberts in his writings: a threaded metallic body that takes the place of a nipple. Instead of holding a percussion cap, it retains a modern primer. A good example of a fusil is Markesbery's smartly designed 400 SRP

This is a mix of old and new, a handsome traditional shooting bag from October Country along with compact accouterments from Traditions. Also showing, the Devel bullet—no lead at all—made to create a wound channel with fins that set up a shock wave.

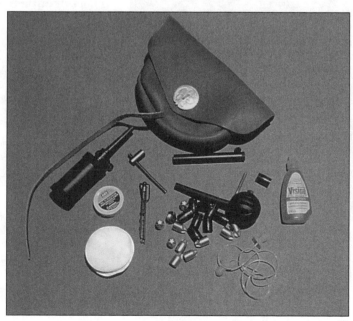

Magnum Ignition System. It replaces the nipple of the Markesbery Outer-Line® rifle, and it takes a small rifle primer rather than a percussion cap. It's fitted in place with an allen wrench that fits directly into the body of the SRP with cover removed. Fusils are not necessary for most dry-weather shooting, but they can be priceless in wet conditions, making a muzzleloader fire, rather than going f-t-t-t-t! Memory calls up the image of a huge bull elk only 12 paces away, stepped off afterward to verify the distance. When the trigger was pulled, the sights were lined up perfectly on the neck. Only instead of a healthy boom, the rifle provided nothing more than a tiny pop as the percussion cap was struck. Damp weather did it. While there is no guarantee, odds are a fusil with primer would have ensured ignition.

Kap Kover

The Kap Kover has been around for a long time. It fits over the top of the nipple, acting as a gasket to keep water out. It's also a safety device. The firearm will not go off until the Kap Kover is removed.

The Shooting Bag

Discussed in Chapter 6, this is one of the handiest tools a shooter can own, especially when set up to

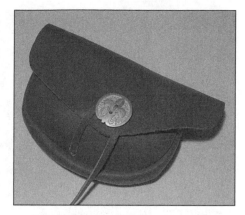

This fine shooting bag from October Country is small, but large enough to hold sufficient supplies for one firearm, including extra nipples or flints, little tools, compact powder flask, and so forth.

serve an individual firearm, as previously noted. Even a small bag, such as the excellent Courier from October Country, holds ample supplies for a hunter. The Courier is only four by six, but there isn't a muzzleloader it won't serve.

Ball Bag

The tanned scrotum of a bull buffalo or other super-sized bovine served to contain round bullets for the old-time hunter. Now the ball bag is made, usually, of tanned leather, but it serves the same purpose: containing any type of blackpowder bullet.

The Flash Cup

One of the neatest little gadgets, the flash cup fits on the nipple seat and is held in place by the nipple

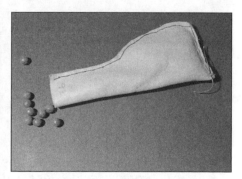

A homemade ball bag like this one works well in protecting projectiles carried in the shooting bag.

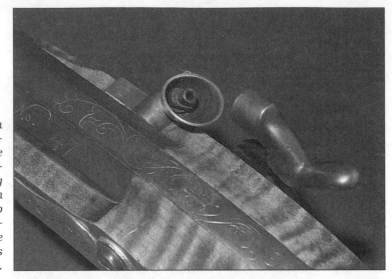

The flash cup surrounds the nipple, preventing flame from the fired cap from damaging the wood in this area.

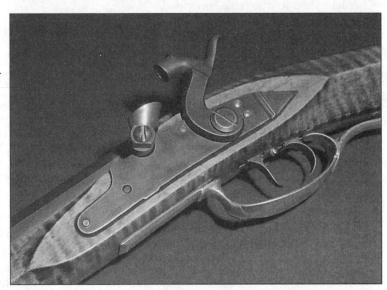

This is a side view of the flash cup, which surrounds the nipple so that flame from the percussion cap does not damage the wood in this area.

itself. It diverts flame and cap debris from wooden parts of the stock that could be burned or marred. The Tedd Cash Co. has excellent flash cups in different sizes. They're authentic, and if anything, they add to the beauty of a rifle, rather than taking away from it.

General Cleaning Gear

This catch-all section includes the already mentioned loading/cleaning rod and other maintenance instruments, as well as patches, solvents, old toothbrushes, pipe cleaners and more, including bore brushes, which are ideal for squirreling gunk out of rifling grooves. Bore brushes are ideal for getting down into the grooves of the rifling and removing fouling. Cleaning equipment also includes everything from rags and toothbrushes to pipe cleaners.

New blackpowder accessories constantly fly from the fertile minds of blackpowder shooters in companies everywhere. Some are born of commercial interest. Others come from the drawing boards of grassroots shooters with good ideas. Most are highly workable, with a few fanciful, outlandish, and scarcely workable items here and there. But one thing is certain: Making the blackpowder gun shoot right requires special tools, as does maintaining it in top shape.

This fine long rifle built by Royland Southgate is shown with a handmade knife with bear jaw handle, far left, a large capacity powder horn, a shooting bag from October Country behind the powder horn, and three handmade items: one to hold patched round ball, a horn container, and a flintlock pan charge, all built by the talented hand of William Knight.

This neat little device is a bore light. Turned on and dropped into the muzzleloader it helps a shooter visually check bore condition. Naturally, it is not used with guns that have removable breech plugs, which allow a clear view all the way through the bore. From CVA.

Chapter 8

SAFETY MANAGEMENT

THE ONLY good shooting is safe shooting. Having served as an expert witness on a dozen gun accident cases, I've seen firsthand what can happen when firearms are treated with less than full-attention respect. Sometimes shooters become too comfortable with their firearms. They forget simple rules of basic loading, handling, and aiming. The result can be disastrous. True accidents occur in any walk of life. They are unavoidable, like a boulder falling upon a highway that no one could predict. But most accidents are preventable with planning and active alertness. Blackpowder shooting is a safe sport when practiced safely. Odds of a mishap are lower than being struck by lightning or bitten by a snake. But there are rules and they must be followed, such as fooling around with "unloaded" guns, as Mark Twain, creator of *Huckleberry Finn*, warned when he wrote: "Never meddle with old unloaded firearms; they are the most deadly and unerring things that have ever been created by man. You don't have to have a rest; you don't have to have any sights on the gun; you don't have to take aim, even. You just pick out a relative and bang away at him. A youth, who can't hit a cathedral at 30 yards with a cannon in three-quarters of an hour, can take up an old empty musket and bag his grandmother every time, at a hundred."

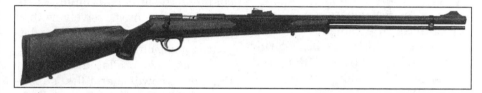

Maximum range for muzzleloaders has been extended with rifles like this CVA Fire-Bolt™ Ultra Mag in calibers 45 or 50. This rifle can push a bullet heavy enough to have good momentum, which helps retain velocity/energy downrange.

Safety includes carrying a side-arm secured, as this custom holster provides for a blackpowder cartridge revolver, fully protecting all but the grips.

MAXIMUM LOADS

USE BLACK POWDER ONLY AND NOTHING ELSE

The following loads are the maximum combinations of propellant and projectile for the Cougar In-line rifle. DO NOT EXCEED!

50 cal	240 gr Sabot	110 grs 2Fg
	335 gr Sabot	100 grs 2Fg
	50 cal Maxi (#504617)	100 grs 2Fg
	50 cal Plains (#508656)	100 grs 2Fg
	.495 RB	110 grs 2Fg
54 cal	300 gr Sabot	110 grs 2Fg
	335 gr Sabot	110 grs 2Fg
	54 cal Plains (#548657)	100 grs 2Fg
	.530 RB	120 grs 2Fg

Although the 36-caliber round ball does a great job, there are times when more bullet weight may be desired. That's where the Buffalo Bullet Company's 36-caliber 125-grain conical comes in.

When working with a double-barrel muzzleloader, it's wise to make some sort of mark to show that a barrel has been loaded. In this case, a card wad was inserted into the loaded barrel so that it would not receive two charges.

Extreme Range

Muzzleloaders have a much shorter extreme range than cartridge guns, in general. A 32-caliber squirrel rifle won't shoot as far as a 22 Long Rifle. A box of this rimfire fodder warned: "Range 1-1/4 Miles." Another box admonished: "Range One Mile — Be Careful!" A 30-06 with a 180-grain boat tail bullet at 2,800 feet per second, which is entirely achievable with a good handload, will travel about three miles when the muzzle is pointed upward at about 35 to 45 degrees. I know of no definitive tests with 50-caliber muzzleloaders, the most popular size used by blackpowder hunters, but I would risk a guess that half that distance would be the maximum, even with some of the higher profile bullets now available, let alone the low-profile round ball. Extreme range factors played a big role in allowing muzzleloaders in hunting areas sensitive to extreme range conditions. Nevertheless, the front loader marksman must never send a missile away without being certain of a backstop, be it target range butts, a hillside, or forest of trees.

In the Wrong Hands

"Keep out of Reach of Children." Guns in the hands of unsupervised kids can spell trouble. Add powder and percussion caps to this one.

The Short-Started Load

Not only was his rifle extremely overloaded, but the young man had also short-started the load, which means failing to seat the bullet, be it a patched round ball or conical, firmly upon the powder charge. This condition can destroy a barrel, as tests prove. In the case of the above short-start, however, a serious injury was sustained. No one has proved beyond a doubt why short-started loads can cause trouble. There are at least two theories, both grounded only in speculation. Theory One suggests that a short-started load allows the powder charge to form as a "trough," in the barrel, in other words laid out along the bottom. Now, rather than a compacted charge in the form of a column burning somewhat progressively with a normal-looking curve, the charge detonates, going off all at once. Perhaps.

Theory Two is related to the fact that blackpowder and its substitutes do not transform from solid to gas nearly as completely as smokeless powder. After combustion, about half of the charge remains in solid form. These solids are partially expelled from the bore. They act in a way like a projectile. If part of the blackpowder charge is indeed a projectile, then the unseated bullet in front of it becomes a bore obstruction very much like a barrel clogged with mud that blows up because the mud is a bore obstruction. The difficulty in arriving at a good answer for short-started problems lies in the fact that results do not repeat in tests.

A barrel may remain intact without bulge, ring, or rupture following several short-starts, suddenly coming apart with the 10th one. Regardless of the exact scientific reason that a short-started load sometimes ruins a barrel, short starting must be avoided at all times. This fact was known many years ago. Here is what Ezekiel Baker said in *Remarks on Rifle Guns*, first published in 1835:

Every rifleman should mark his ramrod at the muzzle end of the barrel, when loaded, which will shew him when the ball is close [firmly down] on the powder. After firing a few rounds, the filth from the powder will clog the bottom of the barrel, and prevent the ball from going close on the powder: in this case, a little pressing with the rammer will be required to get the ball into the right place. More accidents happen from a neglect of this precaution than can be imagined: if the ball be not rammed close on the powder, the intervening air will frequently cause the barrel to burst.

Copper Pipe Tests and Short-Started Loads

The following tests are not to be attempted by the reader under any conditions. They could prove extremely dangerous. The tests were conducted under strict safety conditions with a substantial barrier between shooter and copper pipe instruments. Copper pipes sized to accept 54-caliber patched round balls and conicals were seated in cans of molten lead, the lead hardening to form a breech. A drilled hole where pipe closely met lead breech served as a touchhole, into which was inserted a fuse for ignition. The goal was testing for specific ruptures or bulges when using specific loads. Amazingly, the thin copper pipes withstood modest loads of blackpowder with single projectiles. However, when short-started with what would be normal loads for a 54-caliber muzzle-

A capper, like this Redi-Capper from Hornady Manufacturing Co., retains and delivers conventional and musket percussion caps without the shooter forcing either on by hand.

loader, every pipe was destroyed or damaged. In all cases, a bulge or rupture occurred where the base of the short-started projectile rested within the pipe. Light loads produced the "walnut" spoken of in old-time literature, which is a bulge. Heavier loads split the pipes open. No wonder Elisha Lewis, in his 1885 book The American Sportsman, warned: "We are consequently forced to adhere to the ancient doctrine of explosion, and still believe that a fowling-piece is more apt to burst with a wad or a ball far up the barrel than if pushed home upon the shot or powder." Lewis concluded: "This phenomenon we cannot account for." We cannot account for it either, in provable scientific terms. We just know that short-starting can cause a disaster.

Multiple Bullets

Although less seen today, suggestions for putting down more than one patched round ball on a powder charge did see print. It's a bad idea that can cause serious trouble. Should the second ball not be seated right on top of the first one, this condition is surely a barrel obstruction. In one test firearm loaded with two patched balls, one seated so it was not touching the other, the barrel was ruptured at the base of the off-seated bullet. Furthermore, accuracy goes south with multiple projectiles. Simply stated: don't do it!

Bore Obstructions

As with any other firearm, the bore of the muzzleloader or blackpowder cartridge gun must be clear of any obstruction. An obstruction can cause the barrel to burst, resulting in serious injury or worse.

Duplex Loads

There is no good reason for making duplex loads. Tests with small amounts of bulk shotgun powder, supposedly useful for producing more velocity with black powder and easier after-shooting cleanup, showed absolutely no improvement

in velocity on the chronograph, nor was the bore easier to clean after shooting. The practice of putting down small amounts of blackpowder when using Pyrodex is useless. Pyrodex in its latest formulas ignites readily. While a trace of blackpowder is a part of one end of each Pyrodex Pellet, loading the pellet with the black powder base away from the source of ignition never caused a single misfire or hangfire.

Smokeless Powder

Although the Savage Model 10ML is a muzzleloader capable of shooting smokeless powder, it does so only because of its specific design, using special super steel modules inserted into the breech-like bullets. Smokeless powder will

destroy muzzleloaders. Nothing more need be added to this basic, but profoundly important warning. This means no smokeless powder in any amount for any reason.

Dirty Bores and Pressure

Pressures rise with a very dirty bore for at least three reasons. First, a caked-up bore is actually smaller in volume than when clean. The smaller the area for expanding powder gases to work in, the higher the pressure. This is why we see higher pressures with small-bore muzzleloaders, compared to big-bore muzzleloaders using the same powder and charge. For example, Lyman's tests with a 32-caliber rifle and 70 grains volume Elephant Brand FFg blackpowder produced 17,700 psi (pounds per

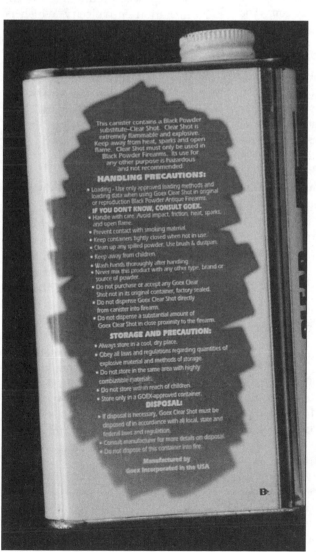

Simply reading information can promote shooting safety. The back of this GOEX Clear Shot can offers many important pointers to safe handling.

square inch) pressure, while the exact same powder and 70-grain volume charge in a 54-caliber rifle showed only 6,200 psi (both guns shooting patched round balls). Another negative is friction or drag. Built up fouling creates greater friction in the bore, which can raise pressures. But the biggest problem concerning a dirty bore is short-starting. Seating a projectile firmly upon the powder charge in the breech section of the barrel can be a problem when the bore is dirty.

Overloading

In this era of magnum muzzleloaders, using big powder charges to boost velocity, and therefore trajectory and downrange authority, is popular. However, each firearm has a maximum load imperative, which is set by the manufacturer. That limit is never to be exceeded for any reason. Too much powder can also violate the law of diminishing returns, which means there will be more smoke and recoil with an insignificant velocity/energy increase. Sometimes an overload can actually result in lower velocity because blackpowder does not go from a solid to a gaseous state with the efficiency of smokeless powder. The extra powder spends part of its energy essentially pushing its unburned portion from the bore, known as ejecta. Ejecta is the total mass fired from the bore, including bullet, patch or sabot, and also unburned powder, as well as fouling.

The rule is: Do not let fouling build up.

Managing Short Starter, Loading Rod and Ramrod

There should be no hurrying with blackpowder shooting. That's what the sport is all about — taking time out from a busy world to do something in a more deliberate and slow-paced manner. Patched round balls require the use of a short-starter to introduce them to the bore, followed by a ramrod or loading rod to seat the round bullet fully upon the powder charge. While some conicals can be intro-

duced to the bore without a short starter, the loading rod or ramrod must again be used for full seating. Short starters, loading rods, and ramrods are not merely tools; they are also safety devices. Instructions about pinching the ramrod between forefinger and thumb sound good — should the gun go off, the ramrod will slide between the fingers harmlessly — but are just a spoonful of pabulum. After all, the short starter was just used with palm pressure. True safety with short starter, loading rod and ramrod means full certainty that the gun is not capped or pan-charged during the loading procedure.

Ramrod/Loading Rod Pressure

Consistent pressure on the loading rod or ramrod produces low standard deviations in velocity, which is good. However, blackpowder is percussion sensitive, which means a charge could be set off with a blow, and it's also conceivable that very high pressure might do the same thing. Firm seating of projectiles is necessary. Putting full weight on the rod, however, is unwise, uncalled for, and could be dangerous.

Half-cock Notch When Loading

It's a good idea, with muzzleloaders that have exposed hammers, to place the hammer in the half-cock position when loading. A hammer fully down upon the cone of the nipple can impede the escape of air from the bore during the bullet seating process. With the hammer on half-cock, air in the bore is more easily expelled through the powder charge and out of the nipple vent. When air is trapped in the bore, it may force the seated bullet back up the bore a short distance, producing a short-started condition.

Blackpowder Pressures

Old wives' tales persist in the world of muzzleloading. One suggests that overloads of blackpowder are not a problem, because excess

propellant "just blows out of the muzzle." This is absolutely false. Another states that blackpowder can never achieve more than 25,000 psi. This, too, is entirely wrong. In the late 19th century, two Englishman, Captain Noble and his partner, Mr. Abel, generated 100,000 psi with blackpowder under laboratory conditions. The U.S. Navy repeated these findings in a similar time frame.

Pressures and Conicals

Proof is extremely difficult to come by in blackpowder tests, even with careful chronographing. The more mass in front of a powder charge, the greater the pressure generated. That's what physics says. This does not mean that conicals are dangerous in muzzleloaders. They are not. It simply means: follow the rules. Never exceed the manufacturer's maximum loads, paying attention not only to powder type and charge, but also recommended bullets.

Proofing

Proofing is the process of securing a firearm safely and firing it remotely with heavy powder charges to see if the gun is safe. While popular with gunmakers of the past, it's not what we want to do with our personal muzzleloaders and blackpowder breechloaders, which are made of modern steel. Overloads can cause unseen damage later, resulting in gun failure.

The Double-Barrel Gun

Be it shotgun or double-barrel rifle, a fired barrel must never be reloaded while the unfired barrel remains capped. The loaded barrel could somehow go off with disastrous results. Always remove the percussion cap from the loaded barrel before attempting to reload the fired barrel, and at all times direct the muzzles of both barrels well away from the face.

Load Shift

Recoil from shooting one barrel of a double-barrel gun can cause the load in the other barrel to move forward, creating a separated charge/projectile shotgun in either a double-barrel shotgun or rifle. After firing one barrel, and before reloading that barrel, it's wise to ensure that the load is still firmly seated in the unfired barrel.

The Shotgun Wad Column

Safety-wise, the smart way to handle a wad column is ensuring that it remains fully seated in the breech where it belongs, and that it's a proper wad not made of leftovers found around the house, such as newspapers or rags. Ballistic Products Corp., Dixie, CVA, Mountain States Muzzleloading, and other companies offer both traditional and modern wads.

Restricted Wad Column

The wad column must be free to move up the bore when it's smacked by expanding gases from the powder charge, because a restricted wad column can raise pressures. It takes more energy to put an object into motion than to keep it going, so if that object, in this case a wad column, cannot freely get under way, it becomes a sort of bore obstruction.

Nipples

There are so few poorly made or designed nipples on the market that this safety warning is almost outdated. However, suffice it that a proper nipple has a flat base with a pinhole. A nipple with a wide-open channel from cone to base may allow some gas to escape, although the laws of physics tell us that gas will escape in greater volume through a larger hole, in this case bore to muzzle, than a smaller hole, such as that in a nipple.

Cap Debris

Safety glasses prevent eye damage from percussion cap debris.

The Patch

While not a true gas-sealing gasket, the patch is vital for holding the round ball down firmly upon the powder charge, among other duties. Because of this, the patch is a safety feature of the load and must be made of properly strong material, not rags.

Granulations

While the latest tests from Lyman indicate perhaps a bit less difference in pressure generated by one granulation over another, the fact remains that kernel size, and to some degree shape, have much to do with burning rate. For safety, the granulation recommended by the gunmaker with regard to a maximum charge should be used.

Loading Pyrodex by Volume

Loading Pyrodex by volume with an adjustable measure or charger is the correct way.

The Capper for Safety

Convenience in carrying and dispensing caps, and now primers for muzzleloaders as well, is on the side of cappers. Cappers play a role in safety, too, keeping percussion caps and primers contained where they are unlikely to go off from any outside source, or find their way into the wrong hands, especially curious children. Cappers also avoid seating a cap or primer with fingers.

Powder Measure and Charger Safety

Powder measures and chargers preclude pouring powder directly from a powder horn or can into the muzzle of a recently fired gun, where a lingering spark in the bore might set off the entire cargo of propellant. These tools also measure out a correct volumetric powder charge for a safe load.

Blackpowder is Not Simply Black Powder

Spelling blackpowder as one word instead of two is taking liberty with the language, but the point is: just because a powder is black in color does not make it blackpowder.

There are many smokeless powders that are dark in color.

Blackpowder Storage and Management

Blackpowder and all blackpowder substitutes should be kept in a dry location away from any source of heat, flame, or sparks, for obvious reasons: Dampness can ruin the powder, and any source of ignition can set it off. All powder must be kept in its original container, which not only marks it carefully as to exactly what powder it is, but keeps it at least somewhat safe from moisture, sparks and other invading negatives. While not as dangerous as some other products we use today, such as gasoline, blackpowder is explosive. Accidents in its manufacture persist, and a number of early-day mills blew sky high from an internal spark or zap of static electricity. Drying blackpowder in open trays was abandoned in the 1820s for the process of using rotating wooden drums containing graphite to somewhat dissipate charges of electricity.

Smoking and Powder

Obviously, a hot ash from a cigarette, cigar, or pipe dropped into an open can of any kind of propellant will set off the whole can, a very serious mishap. Immediately after use, the lid of any powder can should be replaced.

Let the Experts Make It

Phil Sharpe, a gun writer of years past, warned that "Homemade black powder is extremely dangerous both to make and to use!" He was right. Concocting black powder is best left to the experts in a proper plant.

Lead Management

Lead fumes can be dangerous to breathe. Therefore, casting projectiles in a close area is considered poor practice. It's also unwise to cast bullets anywhere that water may invade the molten lead, which can make it spatter widely.

Hearing protection is obviously vital.

Casting Bullets

Protective clothing and the proper location make casting bullets a safe proposition, as the chapter on the subject concludes. Conversely, wearing sandals or slippers and short pants is asking for trouble.

Big Game & Muzzleloaders

More than ever, muzzleloaders are extremely capable of dropping big game on the spot; however, these are single-shot guns, with the exception of a few doubles, and the hunter must be aware of that limitation when facing a dangerous animal. Ideally, hunters of big bears and other dangerous beasts should have a backup nearby.

The Blackpowder Cannon

Rules for firing blackpowder cannons are many and stringent, all for good reason. They are not toys. These days, cannonballs may be as large as bowling balls — in fact, sometimes they are bowling balls with tremendous power and range. Cannonballs have been known to travel for a mile or more, thereby requiring safe backstops, as all projectiles do.

Muzzleloader Condition

Any broken tool has danger potential, even a screwdriver with a chipped bit that could slip and nick a hand. All guns, muzzleloaders included, must be in safe working order at all times. Anything less is asking for trouble. For example, a worn half-cock notch could cause the hammer to fall forward, firing the gun at the wrong time. If the hammer falls from thumb pressure, the half-cock notch is worn and must be repaired before shooting. Few are sold today, but in the past, a variety of wall-hangers found their way onto the market. They were junk then. They still are, and should never be fired.

Gunsmithing

As with making blackpowder, gunsmithing is best left to the experts for any job having to do with a function that could be dangerous. Meanwhile, worn out guns should be scrapped, rather than taking on stopgap repairs.

Eye and Ear Protection

Every owner's manual of late carries strong warnings about eye and ear protection: shooting glasses and earplugs or muffs. Such warnings do not appear on bullet or powder containers, nor should they, because these are components, not part of the mechanical functioning of the gun.

It Can Happen

In the interest of helping the reader understand how a terribly unfortunate accident can occur, the following is a real-life case. It was reported in Muzzleloader Magazine for November/December 2000. It occurred during a Mountain Man run, which is a rendezvous contest that includes moving rapidly from one challenge to the next. The match included a fire-building stage. One contestant entered the fire-making area where he was to use flint and steel to get a blaze going. He had forgotten to remove his powder horn. No one noticed. He gathered his tinder in a pile and began striking flint to steel for sparks. An errant spark found its way into his unplugged powder

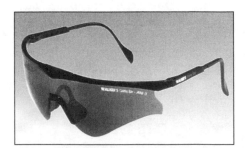

Eye protection is offered in many different types of glasses, including Walker's Game Ear All Sports Glasses, advertised with polycarbonate lenses 20 times stronger than glass.

The muzzle of the gun is always pointed in a safe direction, whether capping, uncapping, no matter what the task may be.

horn. A terrible cloud of smoke rose over the fire-building area as the powder in the horn ignited. The horn did not explode, but the flame flashed from its contents. Because of his position on the ground in trying to start the fire, the powder horn was directly beneath his face when the spark entered. The reporter of the story ran to the scene of the accident. Here is what he found: "His face was burnt red and raw and not a single eyelash or eyebrow hair remained on his countenance. Part of his hair along the front of his forehead had shriveled back with the sudden heat rushing up and around his focused face." An ambulance was called to rush the man to the hospital. The moral of the story is to always cap or plug any container that holds any powder at all.

Rules of the Road

The Ten Commandments of shooting safety apply to blackpowder guns as well as cartridge arms, and must be adhered to rigidly, along with the many specific safety regulations pointed out in this chapter.

Ten Commandments of Shooting Safety
(Modified for Blackpowder Guns)

Always keep the muzzle pointed in a safe direction, and never at anything you do not intend to shoot. Keep the muzzle away from yourself and others when loading.

Unload and secure guns that are not in use. Never store a muzzleloader that has a charge in it.

Never rely on a gun's safety. Treat all guns at all times as if they were loaded. Make certain that the half-cock notch on any blackpowder gun is functioning properly.

Be certain of your target and what lies beyond it.

Use correct ammunition. Never use smokeless powder in a muzzleloader that is not built for smokeless powder. Never exceed the manufac-

turer's maximum powder charge.

If the gun fails to fire, handle with care. With a muzzleloader, wait for a few moments, continuing to maintain the muzzle safely pointed downrange. Try to fire with a new cap or pan powder charge. Do not pull the load for several minutes.

Always wear eye and ear protection when shooting.

Be sure the barrel is clear of obstructions before shooting. With a muzzleloader, also check to see that it is not already loaded, in which case two charges would be seated in one barrel.

Do not modify or alter a gun. If there is any question concerning the safe functioning of a firearm, have it checked by a professional gunsmith.

Learn the mechanical operation of your firearm. This is especially important with muzzleloaders, which require more hands-on attention than cartridge guns.

Chapter 9

REPLICAS AND IN-THE-SPIRIT GUNS

ONE DICTIONARY definition for replica is: "any very close reproduction or copy; facsimile." That works for our purposes, but it doesn't go far enough. Replica guns can be screw-for-screw, as with certain revolvers that were so well duplicated that it took an expert to tell the difference between an original and a newly made gun. Most replicas fit the above definition, however: a close copy. Thirdly, there are in-the-spirit guns that function very much like the real thing, but do not reproduce it.

Replicas serve at least two important functions. They allow a shooter to relive the past, firing guns just like the old-timers carried. They're also great for collecting, where the original is either extremely difficult to locate, very expensive, or both. Serious collectors won't want replicas in their holdings, but for the rest of us, they work just fine. In-the-spirit muzzleloaders and blackpowder firearms serve only the first purpose. Study, history, shooting enjoyment, filling a niche in a collection: Replicas serve all of these functions.

Who Makes Them?

Replicas are made in both the United States and abroad by many different arms manufacturers. In America, Colt has long been known for its close copies of original revolvers. The Navy Arms Co., spurred by the special interests of its president, Val Forgett, brought forth many replicas of pistols, revolvers, and rifles over the years. The guns men-

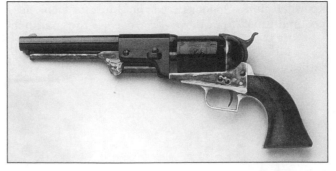

A number of in-the-spirit muzzleloading rifles remain strong today in both flintlock and percussion. They are important especially to rendezvous, where equipment must emulate the 19th century.

Early in the return of blackpowder guns in the general marketplace, replicas of cap and ball revolvers made a great impact. This one is the handsome Colt 1st Model Dragoon in 44 caliber.

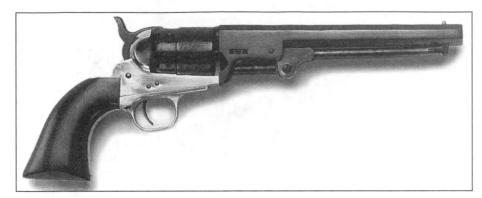
This CVA replica of a Colt Model 1851 Navy may not be a screw-for-screw replica, but it is extremely close to the original, and it shoots the same way, not only in loading and handling, but also ballistics.

tioned below are currently available; however, many fine replicas no longer featured in catalogs can be located at gun shows, newspaper classified ads, and especially in *The Gun List* and similar publications.

The Pistols

The Murdock Scottish Highlanders Pistol from Dixie Gun Works is an exact copy of an Alexander Murdock flintlock smoothbore in 52 caliber, with bright-finish steel frame and buttstock shaped like a ram's horn. The barrel is tapered round. The same company also offers a Scottish Watch Pistol in 58 caliber, also a flintlock, as well as a LePage Dueling Pistol, 45 caliber, with interesting French-style vertical ribbing on the European walnut grip. Navy Arms continues to sell a reproduction of the 1805 Harpers Ferry Pistol in 58 caliber with a browned, rifled barrel. Most of these pistols fired modest powder charges, but because of the caliber and bullet heft, they were quite effective up close, especially as boarding pistols when sailors from one ship swarmed upon the deck of another ship at sea. A more powerful single-shot pistol in near-replica form is Lyman's Plains Pistol, 50 or 54, with a 1:30 rate of twist. Many replica pistols are enjoyable to own, study, and shoot, while models such as the pepperbox fill gaps in a collection when the real thing cannot be located at an acceptable price.

Cap 'n' Ball Revolvers

Soldiers on both sides of the War Between the States carried many different revolvers, including the interesting Starr, favored by some Union officers, and again available as a copy from the Navy Arms Co. The Spiller and Burr, originally produced in Atlanta, also is back. So is the Rogers and Spencer Army Model. All are very nicely manufactured for the enjoyment of today's cap 'n' ball revolver enthusiasts. Continuing in the lead, however, are the two most-used Civil War revolvers: Remington's Model of 1858 and Colt's Model 1860 Army. Colt has resurrected many of its blackpowder revolvers, including the Colt Paterson of 1842 Holster Model, gold inlaid and hand engraved. The huge Colt Walker is also in the lineup, along with many others, such as the Trapper of 1862 and the 1851 Navy. A revolver, yes, but not a sidearm, the Remington Revolving Carbine, 44 caliber with 18-inch barrel, is back. Fewer than a thousand were manufactured between 1866 and 1879.

Muskets

British soldiers brought their 18th century Brown Bess Muskets, bored 75 caliber, to America to subdue the Colonists. The same rifle in replication is offered to today's shooter who wants to relive a piece of shooting history, or do a re-enactment of the past. Replica muskets continue in force with multiple examples from many companies. The Navy Arms Co. offers examples from both Confederate and Union sides, such as the Zouave 58 caliber (Union) and the 1841 Mississippi in both 54 and 58 (Confederate). The accurate Whitworth musket, used in 19th-century target competition and a favorite of Confederate snipers, continues to be made and serves as a rugged piece well-suited to the hunting field and target range.

Pennsylvania Long Rifle

Custom gunsmiths replicate this famous piece from the Golden Age of American firearms. Good ones are as accurate as they are handsome and historical. There are also in-the-spirit Kentuckies that follow the general lines of the original, but with no attempt to copy them. Shooting these rifles is definitely an old-time experience regardless of their overall appearance. Some shooters add a Kentucky-style pistol, making a set of two: long gun and sidearm. Distinguishing between replica and in-the-spirit Kentucky long rifles is no big trick, and the commercial models are far less expensive than the customs. Mountain State Muzzleloading Supplies Co.'s Golden Classic and Silver Classic long rifles are styled to serve the

The interesting Navy Arms LeMat revolver, with its large caliber underbarrel, is a replica cap and ball revolver.

buckskinner as well as hunter/shooter interested in the Pennsylvania traditional style.

The Plains Rifles

The Ithaca Hawken was about as close to a replica as a shooter could ask. It was patterned closely after an original plains rifle that supposedly belonged to Kit Carson, as I recall. Later, Navy Arms Co. took the rifle over; however, it does not appear in the current catalog. Lyman's Great Plains Rifle is still available, however, in 50 and 54 caliber, both as a flintlock or percussion gun. Here is a rifle that fully generates the spirit of old, although it is not an exacting replica. It comes in left-hand or right-hand models with a 32-inch barrel rifled a turn in 60 inches for round-ball stabilization. The Great Plains Hunter version of this rifle carries a 1:32 twist rate for conicals, giving the hunter the option of an old-style rifle that shoots popular elongated bullets. Pedersoli's Tryon Percussion Rifle, 45, 50, or 54 calibers, 32-inch barrel with 1:66 rate of twist in the 54, is a fairly close copy of the original plains rifle. Austin & Halleck's Mountain Rifle does a great job of bringing the plains rifle back to life. This 50-caliber half-stock comes in flint or percussion in 1:66 twist for ball, but with a 1:28 option for conicals. Although

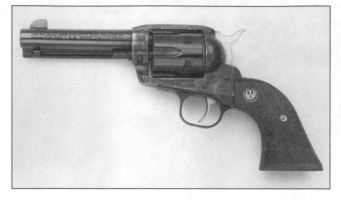

Ruger's Vaquero revolver has found high favor with Cowboy Action Shooters. While it is not a replica of a 19th century piece, it loads and handles the same, and is available in 19th century calibers. This one is chambered for the 45 Colt.

not historical, it is the choice of many modern downwind shooters.

The Mowrey Rifle

Mountain States Muzzleloading Supplies continues to sell the unique Mowrey rifle of Ethan Allen design, a replica of the 1835 half-stock rifle, offered on calibers 50 and 54, 32-inch barrel, 1:66 rate of twist for patched round balls. The lock has very few moving parts, and it is this simplicity that makes the Mowrey special.

Backwoods One-Man-Shop Rifles

They were called Dutch, but really they were German. The mistake came when these industrious people found their way into Pennsylvania. When asked of their origin, they said Deutch — German — but it sounded like Dutch, and that's

what stuck: Pennsylvania Dutch. Among the group were fine arms makers who began to ply their trade in the New World. Gunmaking in other parts of the country often focused on simpler and more practical rifles, because dollars were few, yet a decent rifle was still required. Sometimes called Poor Boy rifles, few are spotted these days, but there's one that's been around for a long time: Dixie Gun Works' Mountain Rifle in finished and kit choices. Percussion or flintlock, left- or right-hand, the Mountain Rifle is available in 32 as well as 50 calibers. It's a true long tom with a barrel measuring a full 41 1/4 inches. The 32 is ideal for small game and wild turkey hunting, firing a 45-grain patched round ball at more than 2,000 fps muzzle velocity with only 30 grains volume of FFFg blackpowder.

Blackpowder cartridge revolvers have not been left out of the picture. This copy of a Colt Bisley is a perfect example.

Rifled musket replicas abound. This one is from the Navy Arms Co. It's a faithful copy of the Enfield rifled musket of 1861, and it fires a heavy 58-caliber conical bullet.

The Sharps rifle is sold through various companies today. This one is an engraved model from Dixie Gun Works.

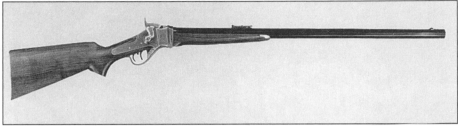

Ancients

Dixie Gun Works also offers two long guns from a distant past. The Dixie Japanese Tanegashima Match-lock, named for the Japanese island where the first matchlock came ashore in an auspicious manner via a Portuguese shipwreck. It's said that this incident brought firearms to Japan. The replica sold by Dixie is patterned after one from Kunitomo, a village near Kyoto. It's 53 inches long with a 41 1/2-inch, octagonal browned barrel, 50 caliber, with only a 7-inch length of pull (distance from butt to trigger). Dixie calls for a 45-grain FFg powder charge with a .490-inch patched round ball. The other ancient rifle is also a matchlock, the English model. This predecessor of the flintlock came to America, Dixie notes, in the 1600s to 1800s. It's 57 inches long in 72 caliber with a 44-inch Getz custom barrel. Dixie calls for 70 grains of FFg with a .715-inch patched round ball for this smoothbore rifle.

Blackpowder Cartridge Revolvers

There is no lack of blackpowder cartridge revolvers on the market today, with most of them in replica style. Cowboy Action Shooting has ignited a fire under these trustworthy handguns of yesteryear and a wealth of well-made imports copying Colts have come into the country. This includes the Bisley flat-top model (also known as the Frontier Target Model) manufactured from 1894 to 1913. It has an adjustable rear sight for windage, a spring-loaded front sight and the unique Bisley-style grip. Of course, the famous Model 1873 Peacemaker is represented in full force. Calibers are 38 Special, 44-40 Winchester and 45 Colt, also referred to as the 45 "Long" Colt, although there never really was a cartridge of that name. Navy Arms offers a reproduction of the Colt 1873 with the claim that parts will fit original Colt First and Second Generation single-action revolvers. It comes in 44-40 Winchester, 45 Colt, and also 357 Magnum. But that's not all. There's also the Smith & Wesson Schofield revolver, a break-top revolver in calibers 44-40 or 45 Colt.

Blackpowder Cartridge Single-Shot Rifles

Long before the now-popular blackpowder cartridge silhouette game played a role, there were many single-shot blackpowder cartridge rifles available, mainly in the tradition of Sharps and Remington models. The list has grown. The Springfield Trapdoor Rifle of 1873 is on the scene, caliber 45-70 Government, along with long-range Rolling Blocks, same caliber, but also offered in 40-65, which came along to satisfy silhouette shooters who wanted to knock metallic rams over at 500 meters, but with a cartridge of modest recoil. There is even a Baby Rolling Block, 20-inch barrel, calibers 44-40 Winchester or 45 Colt. Browning's Model 1885 Single Shot in 40-65 Winchester or 45-70 Government is a copy of the famous original. The same company has a Model 1885 BPCR (Black Powder Cartridge Rifle) with Vernier tang sight for long-range shooting.

This Remington No. 1 Rolling Block Mid Range Rifle from the Remington Arms Co. is a replica of the original. It comes in a 45-70 Government chambering.

Rifles like the Lyman Great Plains, as well as others, are in-the-spirit. While not exact replicas of past muzzleloaders, they look like them and definitely load and shoot the same.

Blackpowder Cartridge Repeaters

It's as if the past has come alive. Dozens of different repeating blackpowder cartridge rifles are back in modern manufacture. They include many Winchesters, such as Oliver Winchester's Model 1866 Yellow Boy, an improvement on the Henry repeater, as well as the famous Model of 1873, noted for One of One Thousand fame with an old Jimmy Stewart feature film in its honor. Tested was a Navy Arms version of the Model 1892 Winchester, selected in 45 Colt chambering to match a Bisley Colt 45 revolver. The rifle/revolver combination proved interesting and enjoyable to shoot. For the most part, these lever-action repeaters are chambered for the 44-40 Winchester cartridge; however, as referred to above with regard to the Model 1892, the 45 Colt has also been chambered in these replicas. Not to be forgotten are Browning's modern-made replicas of past blackpowder cartridge rifles, including the Model 1886 and Model 1892. Remington Arms has come forth with a rifle that it made in the 19th century. It's the rolling block. Remington's 21st century version from its Custom Shop is very much a copy of the original. It comes as a No. 1 Rolling Block Mid-Range Sporter or a No. 1 Rolling Block Silhouette Rifle with optional Vernier-type tang sight. An American walnut stock, satin blue metal finish, buckhorn rear sight and 30-inch round barrel of carbon steel are standard appointments. Options include a half-round, half-octagonal barrel; original Remington rear tang sight; front globe sight with spirit level; single set trigger; semi-fancy American walnut stock with steel Schnabel forend and steel butt plate; plus a case-colored receiver. The Silhouette model meets all requirements for the sport. It has a heavy 30-inch barrel chambered for the 45-70 Government cartridge, with button rifling (1:18 twist) for sta-

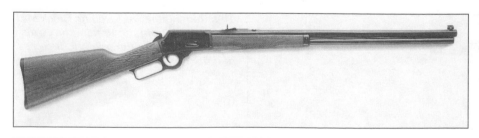

The lever-action rifle of the 19th century has made a huge impact in modern times, especially for Cowboy Action Shooting. This Marlin Model 1894 Cowboy is a copy of the original in most details.

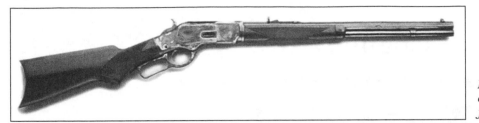

Left: The 1873 Winchester is available once again. The one illustrated here is from the Navy Arms Co.

Right: Marlin's handsome 1894 is back.

bilizing long-range conicals such as Lyman's special LRHP bullets (Long Range High Performance).

Blackpowder Shotguns

The double-barrel blackpowder shotgun of the hour is close enough in replication at least to deserve an in-the-spirit ranking. It certainly loads like and shoots like the original. It also enjoys ballistics on par with the old-time scattergun. In short, the experience is the same as if the gun were sold in a gun store of the 1800s. Flintlock fowlers have come and gone. These come closer, perhaps, in replication than single-shot and double guns. The 12-gauge, single-shot Pedersoli shotgun, cylinder bore, is a faithful reproduction of an English smoothbore. It's billed as one of the best guns in that manufacturer's lineup, with a lock that "resembles the workings of an expensive clock." A half-stock in European walnut with a checkered wrist, this one comes as a 54-caliber rifle as well with 1:66 twist for round-ball shooting.

So Many More

Replicas abound today, in spite of a lack of Hawken design among plains rifles. There's the Harpers Ferry rifle, Springfield Musket, Enfield Musket, Smith Carbine, percussion Sharps in various models, 1766 Charleville Musket, Waadtlander Target Rifle of Swiss origin, Bristlen Morges Target Rifle, and the list goes on. A blackpowder fan interested in replicas needs only to gather up a batch of catalogs and browse to find one suitable for his wishes and requirements.

The double-barrel blackpowder shotgun may not exactly replicate its predecessor of the 19th century, but it loads and shoots just like one, and it looks very much the part. This is a Navy Arms 12-gauge T&T with full and full chokes.

Chapter 10

NON-REPLICAS

KING OF the road for years, the non-replica blackpowder gun remains extremely popular, but definitely threatened by the modern muzzleloader. There were shouts of joy from dedicated, long-time buckskinners and traditional loyalists when announcements came that Hawken rifles were returning, newly manufactured of top-grade materials, ready to hit the target range and hunting field. The jubilee ended with groans of disappointment when the promised Hawken rifles reached the gun store. They no more resembled the "real thing" than daisies look like petunias. Soon, however, the management decision proved right. While lovers of the mountain-man era and the plains rifle sat dejected over the new guns, thousands of others reveled in them. This is just what they wanted: not a real Hawken at all, but a modified version with shorter barrel and, for them, much more familiar handling characteristics. Non-replica rifles, most of them loosely patterned after brothers Sam and Jake Hawken's 19th-century original, were a big hit.

The Guns That Never Went Away

While it's all but impossible for non-enthusiasts to understand, firearms are far more than shooting instruments to millions of Americans. Guns embody amazingly interesting history, as well as mechanical brilliance of design and function. They are also works of art, as proven by the fact that so many were embellished over the years with everything from stock carvings to gold and silver inlays. That is why blackpowder guns, both muzzleloaders and their cartridge-shooting brothers, never died away after the obviously more efficient smokeless-powder repeater came along. Originals continued to find their way into game country, putting meat on the table as certainly as they did before the invention of the telephone. Clubs and loosely organized shooting groups met to compare, enjoy, and shoot the firearms of yesteryear. There was the NMLRA, National Muzzle-Loading Rifle Association, dedicated to blackpowder shooters all over the United States and Canada. Gun magazines, especially *The American Rifleman*, continued to print stories about firearms long out of manufacture, many of them charcoal burners. Catalogs from the 1940s and 1950s, such as *The Shooter's Bible*, continued to sell blackpowder guns, albeit some of them were more suited to plinking than serious shooting. Two men of foresight, Turner Kirkland and Val Forgett, believed that if they pumped oxygen into the still-breathing, but not-too-lively blackpowder sport, it would flourish once again, and they were right. In truth, replicas (mainly revolvers) paved the way, but North Americans are hunters. They wanted the challenge of taking game with front loaders, and the non-replica was up to the task: reliable and not too expensive.

The 21st Century Non-Replica

Non-replica blackpowder guns exist in several categories: muzzleloading rifles, pistols, and shotguns, plus blackpowder cartridge-shooters.

Muzzleloading Non-Replica Rifles

Certainly, the modern muzzleloader is a non-replica, but it's so far removed from the field that it deserves, and has, its own chapter. Non-replica rifles here refers to models like the Thompson/Center Hawken, a perfect example of the breed. If not another one were made forevermore, this rifle is so successful that there would remain enough to go around for the rest of the century. In calibers 50 and 54, the T/C Hawken is available in both percussion and flintlock. It resembles the plains rifle of the Fur Trade era, but does not copy one. While weighing a solid 8 1/2 pounds, it is not as heavy as the original of the same name, nor at 45 1/4 inches is it as long. The octagonal barrel is 28 inches long,

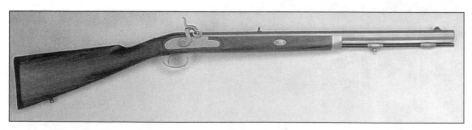

This is a typical non-replica muzzleloading rifle, the Lyman Deerstalker in stainless steel. It carries the half-stock lines of the original Hawken, but is much lighter and shorter.

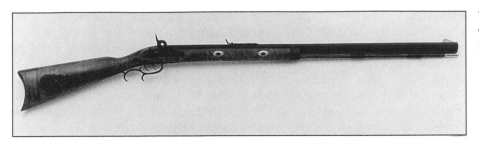

This CVA Mountain Rifle definitely embodies the old-time spirit, but it copies no gun of the past exactly, and is therefore a non-replica.

blued rather than traditionally browned, and 15/16 inch across the flats for the 50, 1 inch for the 54. Twist is 1:48, like Sam and Jake's Hawken rifles. The breech is hooked, meaning the barrel comes free with the removal of a single key in an escutcheon. The rear sight is adjustable for both windage and elevation, unlike its predecessor, which wore mainly fixed sights. The walnut stock bears resemblance to the 19th-century rifle, but with less drop at the comb. Double-set triggers are adjustable for an extremely light, crisp pull. The furniture is brass: thimbles, fore end cap, butt plate, and patch box, which is functional, not simply decorative. The lock is blued.

The breed is not difficult to distinguish. One glance at Traditions' Hawken Woodsman places it in the non-replica class with its 50 or 54 caliber 28-inch barrel, half-stock design, double-set triggers and other appointments. Rate of twist is 1:48, but the Woodsman also can be ordered in 1:66 for ball shooting. Lyman's Deerstalker shouts non-traditional with considerably less drop in the stock, compared to the original. The 50-caliber Deerstalker also has a much shorter barrel with a 1:48 twist rate, single trigger, and sling-swivel studs so the hunter does not have to pack the rifle in hand. CVA's St. Louis Hawken in 50 or 54 caliber is another non-replica that meets all of the criteria. Its 28-inch 1:48 twist barrel is a 44-inch rifle that weighs 8 pounds. Furniture is brass, including a patch box, but barrel and lock are blued. Double-set triggers and fully adjustable rear sight complete the package.

Navy Arms Co. at this time offers three non-replica Hawkens: a Hawken Rifle, Hawken Hunter Rifle, and Hawken Hunter Carbine, each one on the same theme in either 50 or 54 caliber with double-set triggers, but differently styled. All are half stock, as in the original. The Hawken Rifle has an engraved, color-case-hardened lock, blued 28-inch, octagonal barrel, and measures 45 inches overall. The 8 1/2-pound rifle has a brass butt plate and patch box mounted in a walnut stock, and a 1:48 rate of twist. The Hunter Rifle has blued hardware all around, no patch box, the same 28-inch barrel and weighs 7 pounds, 12 ounces. The Hunter Carbine has a 22 1/2-inch barrel and weighs a full pound less than the Hunter Rifle. Both have sling swivels.

Modernized Non-Replica Muzzleloading Rifles

These rifles lie between standard non-replicas and modern muzzleloaders, showing features of both. It's impossible to say where this trend will go. Perhaps most non-replicas, including the Hawken breed, will embody modern muzzleloader features in the future. The Traditions Hawken Magnum Percussion Rifle offers a good starting point for describing this cross-rifle style. It looks like many other non-replica Hawkens, with 28-inch barrel and double-set triggers, two keys, a nice wooden half stock, all furniture blued except for the two escutcheons, and a fully adjustable, fiber-optic rear sight (all but glowing when struck by light). Its rate of twist is 1:32 (for conicals). Moreover, the rifle is designed to shoot

Pyrodex Pellets with line of ignition striking the rearward portion of the breech. This magnum does not allow the use of three 50/50 Pyrodex Pellet charges as often associated with the title, however. Traditions Hawken Magnum Percussion Rifle is called a magnum because it takes the larger English musket cap, but it is allowed only two 50/50 Pellets for a 100-grain charge. No so the Thunder Magnum from the same company. It's even more indicative of the trend than the Hawken model. The hooked breech allows barrel removal, which is normal enough, but the Thunder Magnum also has a breech plug that can be screwed out for cleaning from the back end, rather than the muzzle. It uses the big musket cap with fire directed at the base of the breech, and this time, three Pyrodex 50/50 Pellets are allowed in the 50-caliber fire-breather for a full 150-grain volumetric powder charge. The Thunder Magnum also has a unique thumb-activated safety at the rear of the lock plate. Thompson/Center's Black Mountain Magnum is another modernized non-replica. The breech is designed for either loose powder or three 50-grain Pyrodex Pellets (150 grains total), with a twist of 1:28 in the 50, 1:38 in the 54 to stabilize conicals. Ignition is with musket caps, and sights are fiber optic.

Non-Hawken Non-Replicas

Colt's 50-caliber musket follows the lines of the original Model 1861, but it is a non-replica all the same. The original was 58 caliber. It's also designed to shoot conicals with a rapid rate of twist, and its sights are strictly modern. CVA's Bobcat rifle falls in the same class, a half stock in 50 or 54 caliber, but without Hawken lines. The Thompson/Center Pennsylvania Hunter is another non-replica, non-Hawken, again half-stock, caliber 50, choice of 28-inch standard barrel length or 21-inch carbine, 45 inches long for the first, only 38 inches long for the second. The longer-barreled model weighs 7 1/2 pounds, while the carbine runs only 6 1/2 pounds. Available in both flint and percussion, this rifle has a 1:66 twist rate for ball shooting. The sights are fully adjustable, and it has a single trigger. Originally, the rifle was designed, as T/C states, "for the hunter who prefers, or is required by regulations, to use a flintlock with a patched round ball."

The Non-Replica Handgun

Not to be confused with the modern muzzleloader pistol, the non-replica handgun rests quietly in its own niche. Sometimes it resembles a sidearm of the past, as in the interesting Traditions Crockett Pistol with 10-inch blued barrel and single trigger (32 caliber, 1:16 rate of twist). Then again, it may not look at all like an original. For example, the Traditions Pioneer Pistol embodies classic styling, but replicates no gun of the past. CVA's Kentucky and Hawken Pistols also meet the criteria for non-replica handguns. While at first glance they look old-time, comparing either with copies of originals, such as Colt's 1860 Army, clearly proves that they are not replicas. There have been a number of non-replica handguns in the past that were designed to serve shooters who simply want to enjoy firing side arms without concern for heritage. Lyman's Plains Pistol is one. It's not a true copy of a Hawken pistol, but it shoots fine, looks enough like the real thing to raise no eyebrows at rendezvous, and is very much at home in the camp or on the trail. Ruger's Old Army is another non-replica copying no handgun of the past, somewhat resembling a cross between a Remington 1858

Civil War revolver and a Ruger single-action. This well-built handgun comes in one of four ways, all 45 caliber. Two have adjustable sights (one blued, the other stainless steel). There are also two fixed-sight models: one blued, the other stainless. One thing is certain: Non-replica handguns are not going away. We can expect more of them in the future.

The Non-Replica Shotgun

Arguably, the admired double-barrel muzzleloading shotgun found in so many catalogs today falls into the non-replica class, but it so closely embodies the spirit of yesteryear,

that it falls into another category. Currently, there are very few non-replica shotguns on the market. Thompson/Center's New Englander, for example, does not appear in that company's catalog as this is written. Other non-replica shotguns have also been dismissed. But CVA's Trapper and Gobbler shotguns do fill the bill. The Trapper is a 12 gauge with chrome-lined barrel for lead, Bismuth, or steel shot. It's a single-barrel weighing only 6 pounds with blued 28-inch barrel. The hardwood stock follows the English straight-grip tradition. The Gobbler is also a 12 gauge with hardwood stock.

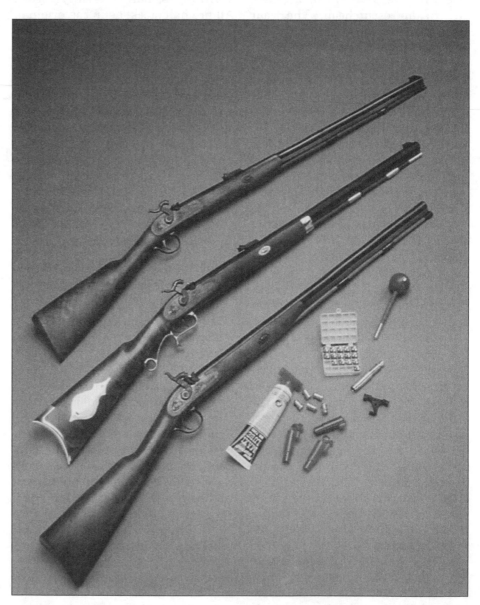

Thompson/Center's non-replica muzzleloaders have remained highly popular over the years.

The non-replica muzzleloader, like this Bobcat Rifle from CVA, continues to demand a good share of the blackpowder shooting market. The Bobcat is easy to handle and it weighs only 6 pounds in the synthetic stock version, calibers 50 or 54.

The Non-Replica Black Powder Cartridge Gun

Most blackpowder cartridge guns are copycats. The vast array of handguns definitely looks back to old-time heritage. Likewise for rifles in both single-shot and lever-action repeaters.

Many More

There are many other muzzleloaders of non-replica design, such as the Kodiak Express Double Barrel Rifle sold through Cabela's. This rifle copies no past model exactly, but comes from the world of dangerous game hunting, especially Africa, India, and Asia, where wild animals lurk that can "shoot back." The Kodiak is listed in calibers 50, 54, 58, and 72. It has a twist rate of 1:48, and weighs a bit under 9 1/2 pounds. It's a percussion rifle with double hammers, and is said to be regulated to deliver bullets from each barrel into a pattern at 75 yards. October Country has a big-bore rifle that has a definite link with the past, but when all of its particulars are included, it moves into the non-replica realm, in spite of its 19th-century lines. This is the Great American Sporting rifle, caliber 69, capable of handling a strong powder charge behind a big patched round ball. It can be ordered with a muzzle brake and express rear sights, three-blade or Ashley Ghost Ring Hunting Sight Set.

Non-replicas will be around for a long time to come, but they will not occupy the status held in the past because modern muzzleloaders are moving rapidly into the top spot. These guns will not die out, however, because they can be produced for a very reasonable market price, as CVA proves with its Bobcat Rifle at well under $125 with a synthetic stock, or only a little beyond that mark with walnut stock. The special Youth Hunter model is under $140. Furthermore, the non-replica continues to fill the bill for thousands of big game hunters who want to take advantage of the many special blackpowder-only hunts offered across the country, but are not interested in shooting the guns of the old-timers.

Chapter 11

THE MODERN MUZZLELOADER

DEDICATED BLACKPOWDER fans took to the modern muzzleloader like porpoises to sand dunes. There was something wrong. Wasn't the whole idea of the sport going back to old times, old ways — and old-style guns? The newfangled front loader violated all three. It did not represent old time, old days of shooting, or old-style guns. Regardless, it was just right for thousands, now millions, who were interested in shooting blackpowder in the most expedient way. Success was not instantaneous. Some of the earliest guns on the market failed to please, as proven by their demise. But when better ones came along, they blazed a trail wide and deep that is now a major highway. A hunt in Kentucky, camp of 12, saw 12 modern muzzleloaders, all but one loaded with Pyrodex Pellets. Another lodge in Wisconsin had a population of 21 hunters. Only three carried older-style guns, and two of these were non-replicas. Wherever regulations call for charcoal burners, it's a sure bet that the modern muzzleloader will be well represented, showing more prominence all the time. Although promoted on the basis of power and range, the fact is that modern muzzleloaders have no inherent ballistic authority or effective distance over any other style. The real reason for their popularity lies in another arena — overall design, special appointments, and allowable powder charges capable of launching conical bullets at veloci-

ties that provide 200-yard trajectory patterns with game-taking effect. The theme of the modern muzzleloader is: "Come as close as possible to a cartridge-shooting firearm while still qualifying as a muzzleloader."

In Their Own Niche

Many who initially balked at the very thought of, let alone sight of, a modern muzzleloader had to change their minds. These were, after all, good guns: accurate, powerful, well-designed, made of the best materials — and most of all, interesting. While never lending that great feeling of going afield as great grandfather did, there was,

after all, a place for modern muzzleloaders. The vast majority of modern muzzleloader enthusiasts latched onto the new-style gun for one reason: to take part in a special blackpowder-only "primitive" hunt with a rifle that was as close to not being a charcoal burner as possible while still qualifying. For the rest of us, modern muzzleloaders were perfect for the general hunt where the field was filled with long-range repeating rifles. There was no shame carrying a scoped in-liner when the hunter on the next hill held a bolt-action magnum repeater. The new guns promised highly reliable ignition, easy loading, familiar feel and handling, the

The Thompson/Center Encore is a modern muzzleloader with a break-open action. It takes a 209 shotgun primer for ignition and handles as high as 150 grains volume blackpowder.

Mark VanCleave left his home in Indiana for a six-day hunt in Alberta, Canada, with Alberta Trophy Hunters outfitters. In six days, six hunters took six bears. Mark used a modern muzzleloader, the Thompson/Center Scout, 54-caliber, shooting a 435-grain Maxi-Hunter bullet with 80 grains volume Pyrodex RS. The fine bear scored over 18 inches.

same sights found on cartridge-shooters, likewise triggers and safeties, easier after-shooting cleanup, and, where allowed by the rules, scope sights.

What They Are

Modern muzzleloaders are rifles, pistols, and shotguns that load as other muzzleloaders do, one shot at a time from the front, while looking and handling like contemporary cartridge and shotshell shooters. The best way to understand the breed and get the most from these updated fire breathers is to look at each criterion one at a time, which we will do here.

Where They Are and Where They Are Going

Modern muzzleloader development is on a high-speed rail directed toward the creation of a firearm meeting regulations set down by game departments, while at the same time having as few old-time attributes as possible. It was inevitable from the start because inventors cannot leave anything alone. That's why we have cellular telephones instead of the Pony Express. It's not all good. Having been in the hunting field with partners carrying cell phones that had to be answered every little while is the downside of that otherwise excellent development. Some game-department officials feel the same about modern muzzleloaders. "We gave blackpowder hunters special hunts in special places during special times of the year because they were handicapped, and now they're looking for every way possible to remove the handicap." The compound bow met with the same criticism. When bowhunters were given unique opportunities to take to the field with longbows and recurves, the wheel-and-pulley bow came along with let-off, which allowed the archer to hold back only a fraction of the bow's actual draw weight. The compound bow also used sights, trigger releases and other high-tech appointments.

Nevertheless, progress is an avalanche. You can stand back and watch it, but you can't stop it. The trend will continue. After all, the industry finally came up with a muzzleloader that shoots smokeless powder! Will game departments eventually limit muzzleloaders that go too far? Some have already tried, as witnessed by Colorado's on-again, off-again sanction against in-line muzzleloaders. No matter. The new guns will leave the drawing board for the manufacturing plant all the same.

In-Line Ignition

With only a few exceptions, modern muzzleloaders have in-line ignition. There is nothing at all new about directing the flame from a percussion cap into the main charge in the breech. The under-hammer, or understriker, does exactly that. A hole drilled in the bottom barrel flat is threaded to accept a nipple. A nipple screwed into the resulting nipple seat sent a flash of flame from a percussion cap directly into the waiting powder charge above it. The sidehammer, also called a mule-ear lock, did precisely the same thing, except that the tapped hole rested on a side barrel flat with the hammer striking from the horizontal. Again, fire from a percussion cap darted directly into the waiting powder charge. While these two styles are not popular today, both continue to exist. They worked well long before the invention of steel-belted radials, and they continue to function that way today because in essence the nipple has become part of the breech section of the rifle or pistol. So, understriker and mule-ear locks were around a long time ago, but surely in-line ignition is new. Yes, about as new as the flintlock. In fact, the Paczelt flintlock embodied in-line ignition, as author Doc Carlson reported in his article, "The In-Line Muzzle Loader," which appeared in the 1996 *Gun Digest*. The rifle can be seen in the Tower of London collection. The touchhole of the rifle is directly in line with the powder charge — as much an in-line rifle as any made today. This 57-caliber fowler with 33 1/2-inch smoothbore barrel is dated 1738. Carlson also discovered, through the experts at the Tower of London, that although gun maker Stanislas Paczelt's name appears on this in-line flinter, it is improbable that he invented the design because "weapons of a very similar design by other makers and of earlier dating are known."

Variations on the in-line theme are several. The chapter explaining firearms function goes into greater detail; however, suffice for now that a spring-loaded plunger could be aligned behind a breech plug to act as a striker. Trip the trigger and the plunger flies forward, its striker whacking a percussion cap, if not a modern primer. The primer is detonated and flame darts directly into the powder charge in a straight line (it's an in-line system). Bolt-actions also work, somewhat in the same manner. This is why rifles like Ruger's Model 77 muzzleloader, Remington's Model 700, and the Savage Model 10ML look just like their smokeless-powder cartridge counterparts: because they are very similar. The major change is that the first two have a striker setup, while the Savage retains its bolt face with extractor, relying on an inserted module that holds a No. 209 shotgun primer for ignition. Thompson/Center's Scout in both rifle and pistol form do not employ a striker. Rather, it relied on an exposed hammer for ignition. But the result was the same: Fire from a percussion cap directly lined up with the powder charge in the breech.

The Outer-Line®

Sufficiently unique to merit its own patent, the Markesbery Outer-Line® rifle is not an in-line design. Colorado's game department conceded this point when that state outlawed in-line muzzleloaders from special primitive hunts. The Markesbery rifle was brought forth and studied. Sure enough, although the flame of ignition from a percussion cap, small rifle primer, or small pistol primer entered the main charge in the breech in a straight line, that line was on a 45 degree angle. Therefore, it was not an in-line rifle, since in-line required ignition on the same plane as the powder charge. Was the Outer-Line®, or for that matter its many in-line brothers, a true muzzleloader? Yes. The Outer-Line® is a true muzzleloader, as are all in-line muzzleloaders, including the Savage bolt-action model that is especially built to handle smokeless as well as blackpowder. Every criterion is met. Each one loads from the muzzle only, just like the flintlock Paczelt of the 1700s noted earlier. None uses a cartridge. Shoot them once and reloading is required.

The world of muzzleloaders was set on its ear with the advent of the Savage Model 10ML, which was the first and only muzzleloader guaranteed safe by the manufacturer to handle smokeless powder (with specific charges only). Brad Arrowsmith made a 200-yard shot on this fine buck with his Savage Model 10ML prepared with an MMP high-pressure sabot, 44 grains weight of Vihtavouri N110 smokeless powder, and a 250-grain Hornady .451-inch XTP bullet. Sight is BSA Red Dot, not a scope.

Except for the Savage, all in-line muzzleloaders are designed only for blackpowder or a safe blackpowder substitute. Yes, the in-line rifle or pistol is a muzzleloader.

Bullets for Modern Muzzleloaders

The modern muzzleloader is a conical shooter by virtue of its rifling twist (conicals and twist are handled in their own chapters). Currently there are two diverse types of twist that concern muzzleloaders: one for stabilizing the patched round ball, the other for maintaining a conical on its axis in flight. Neither is a fast twist compared with most cartridges. The 30-06 Springfield, for example, does well with a 1:10 rate of twist, whereas twist in the 1:20 to 1:32 domain stabilize a range of blackpowder elongated bullets. Round bullets (patched lead balls, in other words) require very little twist for proper rotation on their axes. A 50-caliber ball shooter gets by splendidly with a 1:66 rate of twist. My own Mulford custom 54-caliber long rifle shoots accurately to at least 200 yards — as far as the rifle was tested — with a 1:79 rate of twist. Faster rates of twist with round balls may find them "stripping the bore" or "tripping over the rifling," as some old-timers called it. Because they are conical-shooters, modern muzzleloaders go with a shallow depth of groove, rather than the deeper grooves/taller lands associated with guns designed for round balls. Although it's been shown that super-deep grooves are not necessary for ball-shooters, taller lands are the norm to gain a good purchase on the patched round bullet.

Whereas lead conicals, sometimes with wooden or iron plugs, were the only elongated bullets fired in muzzleloaders of the past (the number of various styles was staggering) there are many different ones designed for modern muz-

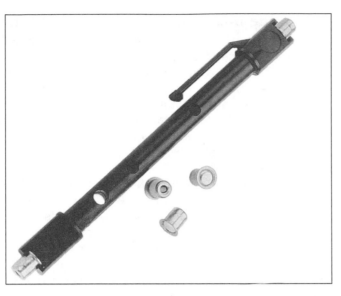

A number of new tools came on the scene as the modern muzzleloader continued to gain prominence. This one was created by Thompson/Center for that company's Encore rifle, but it works extremely well across the board. It's a capper, but not for percussion caps. Rather, it contains and dispenses No. 209 shotgun primers.

zleloaders. The jacketed pistol bullet in a sabot (sah-bow) is one. As so often is the case in shooting, there is nothing new about sabots, the word originally meaning a wooden shoe shaped from a single piece of wood and worn by certain European peasants. The word later took on the meaning of a bushing associated with an undersized projectile to bring it up to bore size. That holds today. Remington's Accelerator ammunition in 30-30 Winchester, 308 Winchester, and 30-06 Springfield employed plastic sabots of 30-caliber dimension containing 22-caliber bullets fired at very high velocity. Sabots are used in modern muzzleloaders to hold at least five kinds of bullets: lead pistol bullets, jacketed pistol bullets, solid copper bullets, lead rifle bullets, and jacketed rifle bullets. The latter two may have good sectional density and ballistic coefficient, meaning they hang on to their initial velocity very well for fairly flat trajectories and long-range energy. All-lead conicals are also highly popular and effective for modern muzzleloaders.

Modern Muzzleloader Ballistics and the Magnum Muzzleloader

The ballistic force of a muzzleloader is entirely related to the barrel. In a sense, a muzzleloader is nothing more than a barrel with a plug in one end to hold powder and a means to ignite that powder. Therefore, any thought of a modern muzzleloader having one shred of advantage over any other kind of muzzleloader, even a flintlock, is out of the question. Given a flintlock with a strongly made barrel of modern steel and a rate of twist suited to conical shooting, it will perform exactly the same as the hottest modern muzzleloader on the market. At the same time, modern muzzleloaders do pack the mail because they are designed with barrels engineered for heavy powder charges in front of heavy bullets. The magnum modern muzzleloader is especially suited to big power because it's built to take super doses, up to 150 grains volume as this is written, or three Pyrodex 50/50 Pellets in a 50 caliber. Important: All modern muzzleloaders are not allowed this much powder! Each manufacturer provides a gun's obligatory maximum charge, which must never be exceeded.

Gonic's Model 93 muzzleloading rifle is capable of firing a special 465-grain bullet for a muzzle energy rated at 2,650 foot-pounds. The 50-caliber CVA Eclipse 209 Magnum is built to take three Pyrodex 50/50 pellets for an equivalent 150 grains volume with a jacketed pistol bullet. Thompson/Center's 50-caliber Black Mountain Magnum is also allowed three Pyrodex 50/50 Pellets for a 150-grain charge behind a jacketed pistol bullet with sabot.

But do these heavy charges truly pay off? Ballistically they do, having not yet reached the limit dictated by the law of diminishing returns, discussed later. For example, a 54-caliber Markesbery Outer-Line® rifle launched a 325-grain Markesbery Beast Buster bullet at 1,992 fps muzzle velocity with a 150-grain charge of Pyrodex for a muzzle energy of 2, 864 footpounds. At the same time, all

Ignition sources include the modern primer. This 400 SRP screw-in unit replaces the nipple on this Markesbery muzzleloader. It takes a small rifle or small pistol primer.

This is a view of the Markesbery 400 SRP nipple replacement with a small rifle primer in place.

thoughts of modern muzzleloaders matching the punch of high-velocity big game cartridges of 30-06 and stronger is but a fable to be told. The 54 caliber just mentioned is sufficiently powerful to take any game in North America under the right conditions, and still it is no 30-06, let alone a 7mm Remington Magnum. Handloaded, a 30-06 with 180-grain bullet at 2,800 fps muzzle velocity earns more than 3,100 foot-pounds of muzzle energy. A 7mm Remington Magnum can be handloaded, using IMR 7828 powder, to drive a 160-grain bullet at 3,200 fps for a muzzle energy topping 3,600 foot-pounds. Furthermore, the high sectional density/ballistic coefficient of modern cartridge bullets enables them to retain higher energy downrange than the usual blackpowder bullet. Nonetheless, the modern muzzleloader in magnum persuasion is one powerful shooting machine.

Shape Means a Lot

Modern muzzleloaders are loved because of their shape. No, not the way they look, but rather the familiar way they handle. Anyone used to shooting a Remington Model 700, for example, or Ruger Model 77, or Savage Model 110, should be quite at home with one of these rifles in its muzzleloader form. After all, shape (dimensions) is essentially identical between the cartridge-shooting version and the muzzleloader. Not muzzle heavy, with modest drop at comb, some with cheek pieces, pistol grips common, and so forth. The modern muzzleloader clan offers familiarity. In other words, a Markesbery rifle with thumbhole stock feels nothing like a replica Hawken or Kentucky rifle. That's the whole point of the modern muzzleloader design from overall length to balance.

Appointments

The modern muzzleloader has the same general appointments found on contemporary cartridge guns. Here is a short list: recoil pad, modern trigger, modern safety, sling swivels, scope-readiness, standard adjustable open sights, and optional peep sights.

Waterproofing

The modern muzzleloader generally is a little easier to waterproof than traditional guns. This does not mean they are rainproof, because they are not. However, some even have shrouds that can be installed to thwart moisture, while others are designed to close up like a vault. An example of the first is the Remington's Model 700 ML, while the Thompson/Center Encore muzzleloader is a good example of the second. Once its action — it certainly can't be called a lock — is snapped shut, it takes a pretty good downpour to get to the No. 209 primer within.

Removable Breech Plug

The modern muzzleloader has a removable breech plug for cleaning from the "back end," just like a bolt-action rifle. Whereas the bolt on the cartridge rifle is withdrawn so a cleaning rod can progress downbore, the breech plug is taken out of the muzzleloader barrel for the same reason. This makes cleaning faster and easier, and perhaps more thorough, than going from the muzzle.

Materials

Modern muzzleloaders are made of space-age materials, including

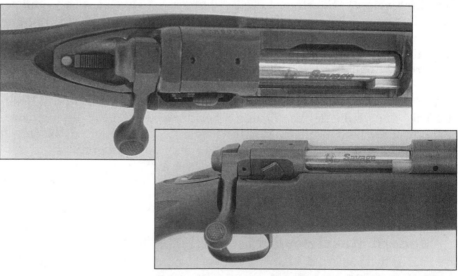

The only muzzleloader allowed smokeless powder is the Savage Model 10ML as this book goes to press. Smokeless powder in any other front loader could destroy the firearm and cause bodily harm to the shooter or persons nearby. The reason the Savage 10ML handles smokeless is its bolt design with locking lugs intact.

Remington used its bolt-action Model 700 rifle in modified form to make the 700ML muzzleloader. The bolt, shown here, was modified into a striker system.

high-quality steel, along with various synthetics for stocks. The Remington Model 700 MLS is a good example of this fact with its barrel of 416 stainless steel and fiberglass-reinforced synthetic stock.

More About Sights

Modern muzzleloaders normally come drilled and tapped for scope mounts, as already stated. More importantly, scopes work well on these guns because stocks are generally designed for them. The eye lines up with the ocular of the scope naturally. Many states now allow scope sights during special muzzleloader-only big game hunts, Other states do not. Regulations must be carefully checked.

Design and Manufacture

While there were a few cheaply made and not-so-cleverly designed modern muzzleloaders in the past, the usual firearm today is extremely well-made from the best materials with a myriad of clever ideas too numerous to include here. Among those clever ideas are the rain shroud, the break-open feature of the Thompson/Center Encore and CVA's 3-way ignition for No. 209 shotgun primers, No. 11 percussion caps, and English musket caps.

The Systems Muzzleloader

The Thompson/Center Encore is a systems rifle, changing its nature in seconds from cartridge rifle, to shotgun, to muzzleloader. Cartridge choices are many, from 223 Remington to 300 Winchester Magnum, with the good old 30-06 in there along with the old but still excellent 45-70 Government. The shotgun is 20 gauge in rifled-slug barrel or with ventilated rib. Then comes the muzzleloader: the 50-caliber 209x50 Magnum, capable of handling three 50/50 Pyrodex Pellets for a 150-grain volume charge. Markesbery's Outer-Line® is a systems rifle in another way: all muzzleloader. Choices are 36, 45, 50, or 54 caliber. The beauty of both of these systems guns is the fact that sights go with the barrel. For example, my own Markesbery has a 50-caliber scoped barrel for regular-season hunts when others are toting high-power repeaters, while a 54-caliber barrel with Williams aperture sight is ready for elk and other timberland animals.

Modern Muzzleloader Ignition

It's no surprise that modern muzzleloaders have looked to hotter and hotter igniters as part of their total reliability claim. The No. 209 shotgun primer is standard with many guns, such as Knight's Disc rifle and Gonic's Magnum, while other rifles, such as CVA's FireBolt™, offers its three-way Ignition system: No. 209 primer,

The Thompson/Center Encore 50-caliber muzzleloader provides a closed action that thwarts general moisture from invading the No. 209 primer within.

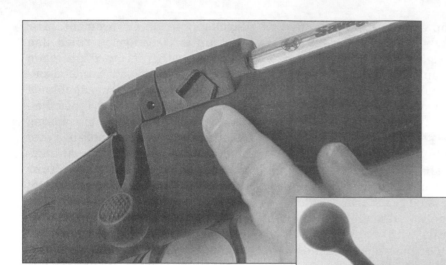

This is the bolt release on the Savage Model 10ML muzzle-loader. Removing the bolt allows access to the breech plug, which in turn is removed to clean from the breech end.

English musket cap, or No. 11 percussion cap. The latter, by the way, is far from obsolete. In dry conditions with direct-ignition front loaders, this old-style cap, especially the ones offered today from RWS, CCI, Remington, and others, is highly reliable.

Tools

As part of clever design tactics, there are tools to match. The Savage Model 10ML comes with a special steel tool for removing the breech plug. There's a hole in the tool that holds the No. 209 module in place for removal of a spent primer, and another tool with an incorporated pin that drives the primer out of its place in the module. At the same time, that second tool fits into the first one to act as a handle for increased leverage in removing the breech plug.

The Modern Muzzleloading Pistol

The Thompson/Center Scout is a strong horse capable of going up against any big game with the right shooter at the trigger, but it has been effectively replaced with a systems single-shot blackpowder muzzleloading pistol, the Encore. While the Encore Pistol is available with barrels chambered for a host of cartridges, including the 223 Remington, 7mm-08 Remington, 454 Casull, even the 30-06 and 45-70 Government, it also has a 15-inch 209x50 muzzleloading pistol barrel with adjustable sights and ramrod. This 50-caliber pistol is capable of shooting a heavy bullet at good velocities. It's a modern in-line muzzleloading pistol all the way. So is the Buckhunter Pro™ from Traditions, an in-line with adjustable

The Markesbery Outer-Line® is a true systems rifle. The barrel, shown removed from the buttstock/receiver, can be replaced with another of a different caliber.

Popular today is use of a modern primer in place of a percussion cap. The Savage Model 10ML muzzleloader uses an ignition module to retain the primer. It fits into a removable breech plug, shown.

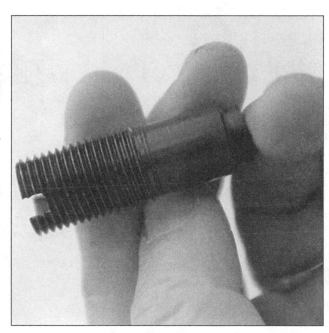

The removable breech plug is an important part of most in-line muzzleloaders, allowing cleaning from the breech end, rather than the muzzle. However, it is wise to apply an anti-seize lube, such as Kleen Bore High Tech Lubricant, before replacing the breech plug to promote removal next time the gun is fired.

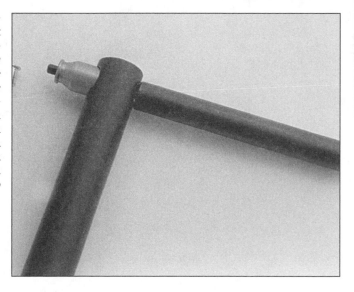

The modern muzzleloader has brought with it many innovations, including special tools like the decapper for the Model 10ML muzzleloader. The ignition module is held in place in the breech plug wrench, and a decapping pin is run into the model to expel the spent No. 209 primer.

folding sights. This is a 50-caliber pistol with exposed hammer and conical-shooting rifling twist. Gun manufacturers prove to us every year that they simply cannot abide standing still, so these pistols may not remain in the lineup for a long time, but if they go, something very much like them will fill the gap. The good news is longevity. Guns last a long time, showing up used, but not abused.

The Modern Muzzleloading Shotgun

Knight's 12 gauge is a definitive example of this breed, with all appointments regularly associated with in-line modern muzzleloaders. It's a single-barrel with a screw-in, extra-full choke intended for wild turkey hunting, but perfectly at home in the duck blind or goose pit. This one really packs a wallop with 2-ounce maximum shot charges capable of dropping a big gobbler with one shot as sure as sunsets and taxes. Whether more modern muzzleloading shotguns will come along or not is up to the whim of arms makers and the people who buy guns.

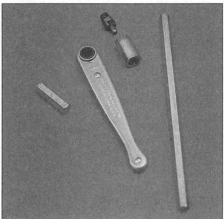

Mountain State Muzzleloading has come up with a number of interesting and workable muzzleloader tools over the years. This is the company's Ratchet Rench. It's a nipple wrench that ratchets a nipple in or out, and it comes with a long bar that can reach into those bolt-action muzzleloaders, as well as a short bar for sidelocks.

Here is the Ratchet Rench from Mountain State Muzzleloading in action, the long stem reaching a nipple in a bolt-action muzzleloader.

The modern muzzleloader, regardless of its specific design, shoots no farther, has no greater accuracy potential or special magic over any other load-from-the-front gun. However, it does have the blessing of its makers, who currently invest more time and effort into its design and manufacture than any specific old-time blackpowder arms. Love it or hate it, one thing is certain: The modern muzzleloader is here to stay. It pleases thousands who simply want to do blackpowder in the most expedient manner, both during and after shooting.

The bolt of the Savage Model 10ML is the heart of the rifle's strength, along with a unique ignition module that is seated into the chamber of the rifle like a cartridge.

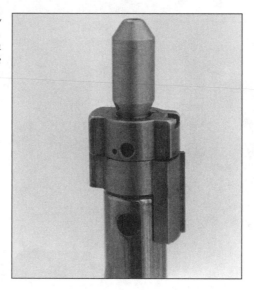

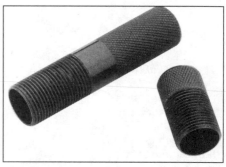

The modern muzzleloader has created a whole new line of accouterments, such as these Breech Thread Protectors from Thompson/Center, screwed in place of the breech plug for bore cleaning.

Chapter 12

CUSTOM BLACKPOWDER GUNS

THEY TOOK up where the original "Dutch" gunmakers left off, carrying the torch of tradition boldly into the 20th century, and now the 21st. Their names are unknown to the vast majority of modern marksmen, but those who make blackpowder guns a lifestyle recognize each man (for there were no women) who took up the trade after the one-man (or one gunsmith plus apprentice) arms-making shop passed into history. When America was brand new, every rifle, every pistol, every shotgun was a custom, if custom means handmade one at a time, for that is how firearms were made during the Golden Age of Firearms in America. Meticulous, highly skilled, but most of all dedicated to their profession, gunmakers of the 18th and 19th century created some of the finest examples of any era. They were works of art, but much more than that; they were reliable and accurate. They had to be. Lives depended on their continued good performance. The Pennsylvania/Kentucky rifle, especially, was so stylish, so interesting, so accurate and historical that firearms enthusiasts could not let it pass into obscurity. So a new gunmaker came upon the scene, prepared to keep the breed alive.

Wonderful craftsmen living in the mountains, not the Rockies, but the chains east of the Mississippi, took up the trade, albeit for these men it was more love than lucre. They were mostly regular folks who farmed for a living, bringing game and fish into the kitchens of their wives, women who were taught by their mothers to turn squirrels, rabbits, and upland birds into meals fit for royalty. Whenever duties allowed, however, they were in their shops. Arguably, these gunsmiths were better with their hands than any other tradesman in the region. Along with hand-making a beautiful and accurate long gun, they fixed almost anything that required mending, because they were master ironworkers, blacksmiths, furriers, and toolmakers who could also install inlays and carve beautiful lines in wood, as well as engrave metal. Today, we look upon their work as we do fine handmade automobiles of the era, true classics in every sense, with near-perfect workmanship and beauty that no firearm in history before or since has been able to match.

The pre-history of these artists in wood and metal goes, of course, back to the Old Country, when firearms of the 17th century reached a high point in excellence. But it was a unique American influence that made the Pennsylvania long rifle the joy that it was to behold and to shoot. In the very early 1700s, immigrants mainly from Germany and environs reached the shores of America, settling, a great number of them, in Pennsylvania. After their passing, the men who kept gunmaking alive were from various ethnic backgrounds. They were from the east, but no longer confined to Pennsylvania. Homer Dangler, for example, was a Michigan man known for building exact copies of original rifles of the masters, his just as fine as theirs. John Newcomer was another master of the middle area, that time between the original arms makers and the smiths making custom blackpowder guns today. Their rifles boasted every fine appointment familiar to originals of Early America: the wonderful wood carving, the inlays, the engraving, the patch boxes, fine stock finish and swamped barrels (smaller in the middle than either breech or muzzle ends). They learned the trade from their fathers and grandfathers. Hacker Martin, one of the best of this middle time, picked up the fine art of making long rifles from his grandfather, who in turn learned from one of the masters in the region.

So it was that the Roaring '20s brought with it not only wild times, but also supremely fine, new custom-made long guns of Pennsylvania heritage. Men such as Red Farris and his friends knew how to organize, which is what they did with the eventual creation of the National Muzzle-Loading Rifle Association (NMLRA). Other names rose like cream to the top during this revival. Joe Kindig wrote a fine book entitled *Thoughts on the Kentucky Rifle in its Golden Age* that spurred interest. William Large got into it through barrel making, creating some of the finest of his time or any other. Large lived a long life, his barrels winning

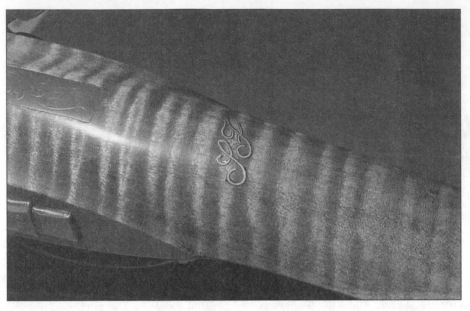

The author's custom rifle bears his initials in wire inlay.

try was an infant, but also those who followed in the early 20th century. For many years, I have carried a masterpiece built by modern gunmaker Dennis Mulford. It is a rifle patterned after an original that started life as a long rifle of Kentucky parentage, later modified with bobbed barrel — cut to 34 inches — and a larger, 54-caliber bore. It is rather plain as Mulford masterpieces go, but with wire inlay and other embellishments, any master of old would have been proud to call it his own work. Who are they, these masterful blackpowder custom smiths of the day? A short list at the end of this chapter credits a few of the best in the land, with apologies to the masters left out because of a lack of space.

The Custom Blackpowder Gun—What is It?

Most of them are muzzleloaders, the vast majority rifles, with Kentucky/Pennsylvania styles in the lead. However, there are a number of fine single-shot blackpowder custom cartridge rifles made these days. Winchester single-shot actions work well here, as do Sharps, with

matches from coast to coast. He was also a helpful soul. After reading a piece I wrote on the subject of cleaning muzzleloaders with water, Large sent a letter. "Never touch water to a muzzleloader barrel," he wrote, going on to explain that he had made hundreds of barrels, and having lived the better part of a century at that time figured out one thing for sure: solvent was good enough for removing blackpowder fouling and water was not needed. While men like Hacker Martin could make a firearm in all its separate parts, others found that buying components was the way to go. Along with Large and other barrel makers, locksmiths came to the fore, perhaps the best known being Bud and Dottie Siler. While men dominated early 20th century blackpowder unmaking, there were a few women who played a significant role as well. A lady named Mary Owensby, for example, was known for her ability to rifle a barrel the old-fashioned way: by hand with a rifling guide. While the process looks crude, it obviously produced wonderful results, as small target groups prove to this day.

The third part of the story is written today. Following those original gunmakers coming fresh to the New World came the artists in wood

and metal, such as Hacker Martin and Homer Dangler. Following their tracks along the trail of blackpowder gunmaking were the men (once again, women are generally lacking in the field) who continue to build, right now in the 21st century, fine arms of the Golden Age. The best of their work is a match not only for the German artisans who landed in America when the coun-

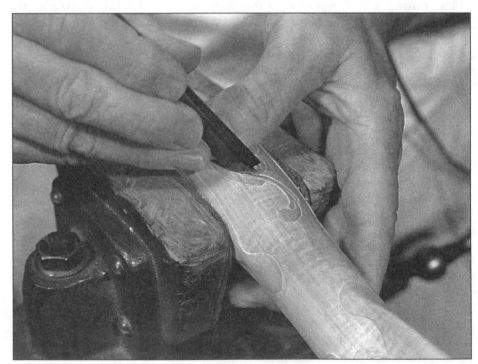

The talented hands of Homer L. Dangler at work turning a piece of wood into a piece of art.

There is so much interest in making muzzleloaders these days that traders' row at some rendezvous will have a display of barrels and other parts for sale.

Remington's Rolling Block well represented because the action is so easy to locate. Mine came from the Navy Arms Co. While a few refinements were made, the action overall was excellent as it arrived, the trigger surprisingly good, requiring no further touch-up at all. After fitting it to an appropriate stock and adding a good set of sights, the resulting 45-70 Government custom rifle was ready for long-range shooting at metallic silhouettes, big game or just plain enjoyable firing at various targets in the distance in front of safe backstops. The main criterion of custom is that it truly is made one at a time by an expert craftsman. Just because a gun is homemade does not make it a custom. In fact, a goodly amount of junk comes from the hands of wannabes who do not have the talent to make true custom firearms. A custom rifle or pistol is unique unto itself, but it must also exhibit excellence of manufacture.

A true custom has no screw-for-screw clone anywhere in the world, although this is not to say that it has no cousins. Of course it does. The work of individual gunmakers is often easier to spot than the paintings of famous artists. It

requires no heavy knowledge of art to tell a Picasso from a Dali, and the same holds true for many gunmakers whose style stands out as their own. Interestingly, a custom firearm is not perfect, not in the sense of machine duplication. For example, it's possible to program a computer-operated machine to engrave nearly flawless lines. The machine will not err. The lines will repeat, repeat and repeat. The work on a custom gun will reveal the human hand, and that is what makes it so superior over the assembly-line product. In a way, the work exhibits its own kind of perfection, from talented human fingers, but also a touch of imperfection that makes it one of a kind, although it may take a magnifying glass to discover that slight waver of the engraving tool. The true custom shows tight wood-to-metal fit, clean lines all around, a correct interpretation of a classic design, super clean wood and metal finish, and a touch of personality. If the firearm is intended to replicate an original from the past, then it should do so faithfully. Homer Dangler and other custom smiths of the 1920s were extremely good at repli-

cation, building rifles that closely duplicated originals from the past, sometimes as far back as the 1700s.

Replicating the Past

Replica custom rifles do not always follow on the most ornate examples of the past. Sometimes they're plain and downright simple. For example, there are replicas of what some called "poor boy" rifles: hardworking muzzleloaders fully capable of doing a day's work putting food on the table, or for that matter cutting a round hole in a black bull's-eye. However, these long guns were not pretty. To beautify one of that clan would be trespassing on the goal of the replica: making a new gun that copies an old one. A wonderful example is a particular long rifle built by Frank House to be carried by the hero in a film called *The Patriot*. House decided on replicating a John Thomas rifle featured in *Rifles of Colonial America*, another volume by the dedicated arms historian George Shumway. The resulting flintlock rifle is beyond beautiful. It is a true work of art and extraordinary talent.

The Non-Replica Custom

Many custom guns of the day follow nothing from the past, but they are still customs in every sense. For example, there are slug guns: super-heavy front loaders fired from the bench only with the single goal to produce ultra-tight groups. These rifles are not intended as duplicates of any past firearm, but they are still custom-made guns. Likewise, consider special custom guns from some of today's masters who prefer inventing their own styles. Therefore, an excellent custom muzzleloader need not be a replica.

The Professional Custom Blackpowder Gunmaker

Blackpowder gunmakers need not be in the game full-time to be professionals, although many do

Unbelievably, what looks like fine line drawing is actually silver wire inlay on this custom 16-gauge fowler circa 1762 built by Mark Silver. Touches like this one render fine custom muzzleloaders collectible in their own time frame.

make a living in this art form, most of them zeroing in on a particular style of the past, or a significant specialty that sets them aside from all other gunmakers. A good example of the first is Allen Martin, who was interviewed by Muzzle Blasts magazine's Eric Bye. Martin pointed out that he was recognized as the leading contemporary builder of Lehigh County rifles of Allentown origin. Dixon's Gunmaker's Fair, an event held annually to honor the finest old-time traditional arms currently handmade, honored Martin with best of show overall. "It was almost covered with ribbons," Martin remarked. He began handcrafting muzzleloaders as a teen on his home farm, and by age 30 had a following of true believers, some of them returning for second, third, and fourth rifles. From a family of 13 children, Martin learned a good work ethic early on. Along with the dedication to build the best rifles he is capable of, he credits Paul Alison, Jr., who taught him many of the basics. He relies mostly on hand tools: rasps, files, sculpturing gouges, and planes, with all metal polishing done by hand. While not a competitive target shooter, Martin admits that hunting is an important part of his life, his favorite being the Pennsylvania flintlock-only season. He builds guns for collectors, who rarely if ever shoot them, for hunters who always shoot them, and devotees of the rendezvous. Of course, blackpowder custom gun builders are as individual

as any artisans in the land; however, Martin's devotion to perfection and his undying interest in creating the finest firearms of old-time style are typical of the clan.

Ordering a Custom Blackpowder Gun

Of course, the buyer must know what he wants the firearm for. If it's collecting, he will very likely want a piece representative of one of the "schools" of the past, of which their were many. Counties in Pennsylvania often name these schools: Lancaster, Lehigh, Clarion. If it's hunting, then style falls back in favor of handling, power, and range. Muzzleloader or cartridge rifle? Andrew Fautheree

(see gunsmith list at end of chapter) is known for his blackpowder cartridge rifles as well as front loaders. Competing in contests demands the ultimate accuracy, but also fine handling qualities and allegiance to the past with a firearm matching a given period in time. Once the rifle's intended use is established, it's time for riflemaker and future owner to get together on the details. Most difficult for the buyer to understand is the builder's inertia when it comes to making a firearm that the builder does not support. I discovered this fact prior to ordering my oft-mentioned Mulford custom long rifle, No. 47 by name. I wanted a piece as close to a Hawken half-stock plains rifle as the gunmaker could build, a tough piece capable of rugged times in the field. I put my plan on the table. Mulford balked. He didn't make Hawkens. They were interesting and historical, but compared with the long rifles of the east, a cousin to a fence post. A compromise was struck: a rifle that began life as a long arm, but ended it with a shorter barrel, larger bore, and conversion from flint to percussion with a drum-and-nipple conversion. I'm glad I listened to the gunmaker. Had I

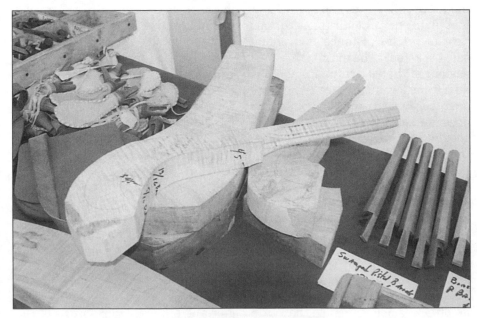

Here is a semi-formed pistol stock for the gunmaker.

Parts and more parts for the builder of muzzleloader firearms.

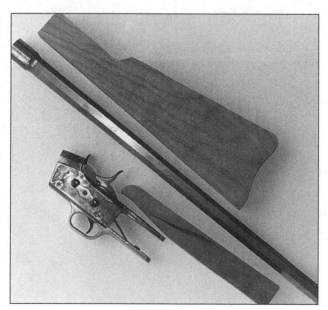

The principal parts of a Remington Rolling Block action from the Navy Arms Co. include two-piece stock, action, and barrel.

never fired the resulting rifle, I still would have gotten my money's worth alone in the joy of owning it. As it was, the rifle did go afield, taking deer, antelope, elk, and other game. The path to success was straight and clean: get close, put one 54-caliber lead ball right on the money and fetch a tag from the pocket. A .535-inch lead round ball wrapped in a .013-inch thick, pure Irish-linen patch left the muzzle at 1,970 fps on average for 1, 983 foot-pounds of muzzle energy. Of course, that rating dropped dramatically over distance, but I found if I stayed inside of 125 yards, I could count on one-shot kills on deer and antelope, with 75-yards a better distance for elk. Accuracy was supremely good: as tight as 2 inches center-to-center with iron sights when conditions were just right and the shooter was doing his part. I got a call from the gunmaker one day. He wanted my permission to build more rifles with the same general makeup as No. 47. That was OK with mc. Mine would still be a true custom, one-of-a-kind with hand-drawn octagonal barrel and of course touches that were unique.

Digging for Dollars

True custom blackpowder guns — pistol, muzzleloader, cartridge-shooter — when done properly by a real master, demand dollars. It has to be that way. There is too much time and energy involved to give these guns away. They're an awful lot more than a steel barrel attached to a piece of wood. Each true custom embodies hours of intensive labor. Furthermore, talent deserves its reward, and the better smiths of the day are extremely talented. Why should they sell their wares for pennies? Also, a custom blackpowder gun is an investment. It lasts forever, and gives far more enjoyment than it costs. Break it down by the month over many years of ownership, and a top-grade rifle or pistol turns out to be a true bargain.

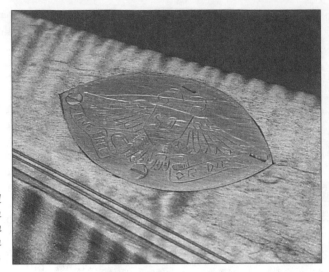

Dennis Mulford selected an inscription for the author's custom rifle, appearing here on an inlay.

Where to Find the Master Gunmaker

Rendezvous and competitive shoots are good places to start looking, because a firearm can be seen firsthand and perhaps even fired if the owner doesn't mind. But the majority of contacts come not from rendezvous or shooting events, but through advertising. Such is America. Two excellent sources for locating a gunmaker are Muzzle Blasts magazine and Muzzleloader magazine. Gun List is a third. Sometimes fine blackpowder firearms are also displayed in Blackpowder Hunting magazine, another excellent periodical dealing strictly with the sport. *Gun Digest* and *Shooter's Bible* are also good sources, as is Shotgun News and many other periodicals. References are also worthwhile. At the close of this chapter, several smiths are listed. Each is a master in his own right. Fortunately, the field is replete with gun builders of tremendous talent and all-around ability.

The Contract

After checking through periodicals and other avenues, it's best to either get a real look at a gunmaker's work, or at the very least a brochure. Once a decision is made, a contract is drawn up. Normally, the smith initially requires about half of the agreed-upon price of the gun. Final payment is made after the firearm is finished. Also vital is agreeing on a time of delivery. A six-month wait is short. A year is entirely normal. A year and a half can be lived with. Both gunmaker and client must agree on a delivery date. There are also appointments to consider beyond the style (school) of gun. Wood prices today are high. An especially fine blank now may cost what an entire rifle once cost. Along with wood choice, decisions must be made concerning patch box, type of lock, particular barrel choice (there are many different ones), inlays, carvings, sights, type of finish, trigger system, caliber, barrel length, and more. Gunsmiths have a whole list of particulars from which to choose.

What You're Paying For

No matter how deep the well, it's always nice to know why you're dipping into it. So how much effort, really, goes into building a fine blackpowder custom rifle? The following is not intended as a short course in gun building, but only a quick look at a few of the basics. The smith may prepare a drawing of the gun's profile at a reasonable charge. The drawing is nothing more than an outline, but it's useful in providing an overall look before work is under way. The arts search is easier now, with many excellent sources of everything from barrels to embellishments. A custom smith will have his favorite parts houses. Some gunmakers prepare their own barrels. Others buy them from specialists. Either way, a barrel must be cut to length, the muzzle crowned, dovetail slots cut for sights and underlugs fitted by the smith. The lock may require some assembly and a certain amount of tuning. The stock begins as a blank, nothing more than a hunk of wood. It must be shaped into a gunstock with filing and more filing, sanding and more sanding. Inletting is required for the barrel, lock, and other appointments. The barrel must fit perfectly into its channel, the lock into its mortise. Furniture, such as patch boxes and butt plates, is introduced into the wood with a marriage that must be perfect. Drilling the ramrod channel can be a challenge. If the hole goes astray, the stock blank becomes a candidate for knife handles or even firewood. Trigger positioning

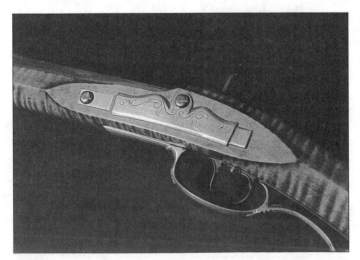

The custom muzzleloader will have touches here and there that set it apart, even if it's only a little engraving on a side plate.

demands room for function without sloppiness. The upper-tang screw hole is drilled, the butt plate fitted, the vent hole drilled in the side of a flintlock's barrel flat. Drum and nipple may be fitted to a percussion rifle, the trigger guard installed, upper and lower tangs crafted, carving and inlays done. Metalwork may be engraved, the stock stained, metal polished, barrel browned, stock finished. From wood and metal, a firearm is born, but it is special only when created by a specialist. For those willing to give this game a try, there are videos on gunmaking, such as those from Homer Dangler: No. 1, Building the Kentucky Rifle; No. 2, Carving the Kentucky Rifle. (see address below).

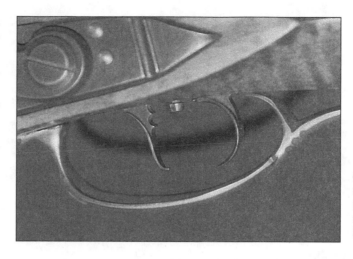

On the author's custom rifle, even the triggers are special, with a little embellishment of design.

Short List of Contemporary Blackpowder Gunmakers

The following short list of contemporary gunmakers is supplied for the reader's convenience. Brochures displaying the particular artisan's specialties normally are available.

K.L. Shelton Custom Kentucky Rifles
36831 S. Wind Crest
Tucson, AZ 85739
520-818-1756
klshelton@uswest.net (Email)

G.L. Jones Fine Custom Rifles
POB 325
Tremonton, UT 84337
435-257-2825
GLJRifles@aol..com (Email)

Caywood Gunmakers
18 King's Hill Estates
Berryville, AR 72616
870-423-4741
http://www.caywoodguns.com ((Website)

Allen Martin, Gunmaker
POB 80
Swengel, PA 17880
570-922-4281
ramrod@sunlink.net (Email)

Ron Ehlert Custom Muzzle-Loading Gunmaker
1066 New Sheboss Road
Duck River, TN 38454
931-285-2622
flintloc@usit.net (Email)

Dick Micka, Gunmaker
38756 French Gulch Road
Baker City, OR 97814
gunmaker@eoni.com (Email)

Mark Silver, Gunmaker
Route 2 – Box 382
Chassell, MI 49916
906-523-4014

Ronald Scott, Gunmaker
1370 Linn Road
Eagle Point, OR 97524
ronsguns@internetcds.com (Email)
http://wwwhome.cdsnet.net/ ~ronsguns/ (Website)

Homer L. Dangler, Gunmaker
2870 Lee Marie Drive
Adrian, MI 49221
517-266-1997
(May through December)
863-382-1018
(January through April)

J.L. (Jack) Brooks, Gunmaker
800 West Oxford
Englewood, CO 80110
303-789-4029

Judson O. Brennan, Gunmaker
POB 1165
Delta Junction, AK 99737
907-895-5153
907-895-5404 (Fax)

Andrew Fautheree, Gunmaker
POB 4607
Pagosa Springs, CO 81157-4607
970-731-5003

After a while, a person runs out of adjectives to describe the kind of work accomplished by the best of today's custom gun makers. This is a prime example. Mark Silver's superb carving on a fine piece of wood, the rifle a 54-caliber with 45-inch barrel circa the 1800s, York County Pennsylvania.

http://www.black-powder.com
(Website)

Tom McCann, Gunmaker
14 Walton Drive
New Hope, PA 18938
215-862-2728

Jerry Kirklin, Gunmaker
1772 Bates
Birmingham, MI 48009

Eric Kettenburg, Gunmaker
POB 99
New Albany, PA 18833
570-363-2071

Earl Williams, Gunmaker
1001 Obes Branch Road
Sevierville, TN 37876
423-453-3552

James Klein, Gunstocker
319 Locust Street
Marshall, IL 49068
616-781-5428

Jack's Stock Shop
890 CR 400
Corinth, MS 38834
662-286-6266

Anthony Palyszeski, Gunmaker
POB 32 Tarentum, PA 15084
724-727-2714
    Check it Out

The Annual Gunmaker's Fair
    Dixon Muzzleloading Shop,
    Inc.
9952 Kunkels Mill Road
Kempton, PA 19529
610-756-6271

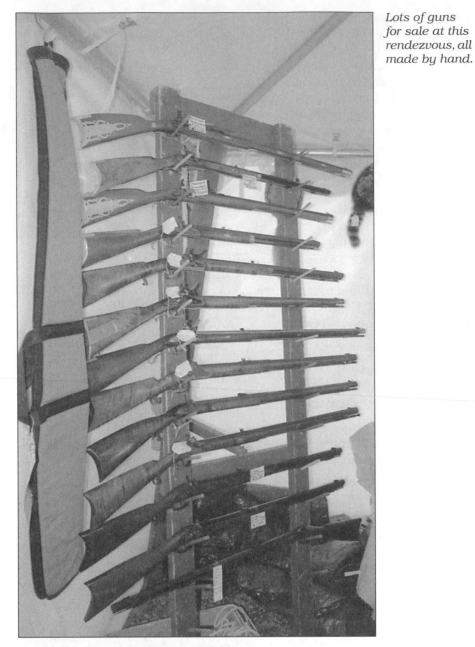

Lots of guns for sale at this rendezvous, all made by hand.

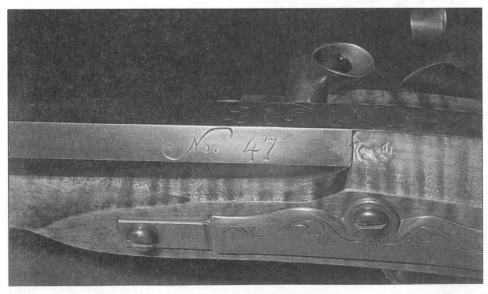

Custom means personal. The author's 54-caliber ball-shooter is the only rifle Dennis Mulford made that bears the number 47.

Chapter 13

JUST FOR SHOW AND TELL

THERE ARE two ways to collect blackpowder guns, be they muzzle-loading rifles, pistols, shotguns, cap 'n' ball revolvers, or cartridge handguns and long guns. The first is finding originals. While not offered at every gun show, originals do show up now and then, as well as in The Gun List newspaper, as well as Shotgun News and similar periodicals. Now and then, originals find their way into the classified section of gun magazines as well. There are also collectors who have large, sometimes very large, holdings, some for sale, others offered in trade. Certain originals are in outer space, dollar-wise, costing in the thousands. Others go for little, if any, more than new firearms on the current market. The first have what is called collector value for rarity, historical significance, and uniqueness. Rare guns do not always command big bucks. After all, there were junkers made in the past. They were worth little when they came off the assembly line and they have retained every bit of that value. Then there are the good rare guns, in the class of Winchester's

One-of-One-Thousand series, for example. Few were made and the ones that were came from the hands of fine craftsmen. Historical significance also plays a role. An original Volcanic, for example, may not be the most interesting firearm ever made, but it certainly had its place in firearms progress. An original Whitworth carried by a Confederate sniper would fit into the historical niche as well. Then there is uniqueness. Usually, this trait is combined with rarity, such as specific firearms that bore unusual features. Consider in-line flintlock rifles, or for that matter, breech loading flintlocks, for example.

The television series, "Saga of the Gun," clearly demonstrates why we collect firearms. They are highly interesting on their own, but each significant gun also speaks of change in society. In some ways, the history of North America can be told in firearms. Pilgrims landing upon eastern shores, pioneers making their way in the New World, westward expansion, the American Civil War, wars and conflicts to follow, all had an impact on the

growth of the country. Firearms also meant business, from one-man gun shops to huge factories providing work for many thousands of people over the years. In short, to hold a gun collection of any size represents a history book in iron and wood. Large collections, such as found at the Buffalo Bill Historical Society in Cody, Wyo., offer a feast for any observer. Such displays will draw interest from those who never held a firearm, as well as from enthusiasts who have shot guns for years, or from scholars who may have enjoyed rich careers in the adventurous business of locating, collecting, identifying, and categorizing important arms from the ages. The Tower of London collection, for example, employs full-time experts who are capable of relating English history from longbow to the guns of modern warfare. It is this house that holds the interesting in-line flintlock rifle, for example, only one of numerous amazing firearms from the past.

Guns are interesting not only for their historical significance, but as engines of genius. Many of the most

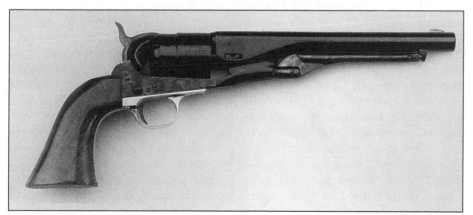

Another good replica for collecting is the 1860 Army, because of the role that it played in the American Civil War. This replica is from the Navy Arms Co.

inventive people in the world were designers of firearms. Mannlicher of Austria was one. His list of firearms inventions includes designs that were decades ahead of his time. In the United States, there was John Browning, who had a hand in the invention of firearms that changed the world.

First Steps

Putting a library together is a prime first step on the road to gun collecting. There are dozens of books on the subject of firearms. Every year, *Gun Digest* presents a long list of books pertaining to the collecting of firearms. This is a good bibliography to start from, containing many books that show excellent scholarship. It is called "The Arms Library," and it includes a large section called "Collectors," with numerous titles showing, such as *Military Small Arms of the 20th Century*, 7th Edition, a DBI/Krause book by well-known expert Ian V. Hogg. *A History of the Colt Revolver* is an important title for anyone interested in that company's handguns from 1836 to 1940. This 711-page text, compiled by Charles T. Haven and Frank A. Belden, contains information from the inception of the first Colts to U.S. patents associated with the company, some of Colt design, others from the hands of various inventors. Another title along the same lines is *The Winchester Book* by George Madis. This volume spans 543 pages. Part I, "The Forerunners," goes into the Hunt Repeater, Jennings and Smith-Jennings, Smith & Wesson, New Haven Arms, and the famous Henry rifle. Part II runs through the lever-action Winchesters beginning with the Model of 1866, ending with the Model of 1895. Part III goes into Winchester bolt-actions, while IV deals with slide-action models.

Books of this thorough nature teach the newcomer enough to help him decide which line of collection might interest him. At the same time, they serve as treasures of information for dedicated expert

Books like the extensive Standard Catalog of Firearms *from the publishers of* The Gun List *newspaper help collectors with both identification and values.*

collectors and for those who are fascinated with the progress of firearms manufacture and its impact upon societies. Along with books on the subject, *Gun Digest* also lists magazines that can be helpful, such as The American Rifleman. Another important source of study is the *Blue Book*, a compilation of firearms with approximate stated values. *Flayderman's Guide to American Antique Firearms* is another book of gun values. It includes information on numerous companies, such as Sharps, Winchester, Remington, Browning, and a gang of other manufacturers most of us never even heard of. The library is a good starting point for a search of books and magazines pertaining to collecting. A run on the computer, with Books in Print helping, reveals numerous titles that can be obtained through interlibrary loan, usually for a nominal fee. Books can be called in from just about anywhere, and waiting time is normally modest. The Internet is another source of study. What to pay for a firearm, after locating one for a collection, makes Flayderman's and other guides invaluable. *The Standard Catalog of Firearms* from Krause Publications (the publishers of the Gun List newspaper)

is another worthy shopping tool, as is Gun List itself, along with Gun Week, Shotgun News, and similar publications. It's not a simple matter of worth, but rather what a gun is worth in a given condition. For example, a specific firearm may be worth $1,000 in excellent condition, but only half that in fair or poor condition. The buyer must decide what he wants his collection to reflect: good-looking guns in prime shape, or simply examples of guns for purposes of filling in a missing link in lineage, or piece of history. Usually, shooting is of no consequence to a collector, with the exception of certain devotees of collectible guns who want to experience the workings of the firearm as well as its design idiosyncrasies or historical niche.

Condition

It is impossible to pigeonhole each separate category from excellent to poor. Nor is the percentage value perfect, with the exception of 100 percent, which indicates a firearm in brand new condition, regardless of its vintage. All indicators include some judgment value. However, the categories are extremely important to a collector because they are close enough to present an excellent picture of the firearm in question without seeing it first-hand. Standards, therefore, are vital to collecting, or for that matter purchasing a firearm for a functional purpose, such as target shooting or hunting.

There are different grading systems, but first, what is a modern firearm, and what is an antique?

Modern or Antique?

In the context and buying firearms for collecting, the two terms carry important meaning. A modern firearm may, in fact, come from a distant era. A good example is the Colt revolver. Some models have continued in the same form for over a hundred years. The Model 1873 Colt revolver, for example, came to the public of shooters in the 19th century, but Colt continues to offer that same firearm today. Is it antique or modern? It's modern. Antique more accurately applies to firearms that are no longer in manufacture, and in fact most have not been for a significant period. Consider an antique lamp. If the exact model has not been made for 100 years, it definitely is an antique, even if it has been replicated in recent times. These criteria have to be generalized, because there are so many exceptions. However, the collector should think of an antique firearm in terms of an original Hawken or Kentucky rifle, although both are still around in newly made examples.

Grading Systems

NIB

NIB stands for new in the box, meaning that the original box is supplied with the gun. This category pertains to manufactured arms, since custom or handmade guns never had boxes. A firearm in NIB is essentially the same as brand new, with no marks or signs of use.

Excellent

This category refers to a firearm that probably will not have with it the original box. However, in spite of some use, the gun appears to be entirely intact in all regards. It may be referred to as 100 percent factory as well, meaning that no additions or deletions can be found. In fact, alterations will disqualify a firearm from an excellent rating. As for cosmetics, an excellent firearm need not retain 100 percent of its original finish. Modern firearms must show 95 percent of their original finish, while antique guns require only 80 percent of their original finish to qualify. The excellent firearm is in perfect working condition, all inner parts intact and functioning. Even antiques must show with clean sharp rifling, if the arm is rifled.

Very Good

Very good condition is a high ranking. The firearm must be in prime working order to quality, with modern arms retaining at least 85 percent of their original finish. Antiques may retain as little as 25 percent of their original finish, but they must also be in excellent mechanical condition. Bores must be in good shape, and there must be no evidence of repairs. Perhaps evidence is a giveaway word here, as there are probably some professionally repaired firearms of the past that don't show it.

Good

The first criterion here is working order. A gun in good condition must be in safe shooting condition. Modern firearms retain about 60 percent of their original finish, at least, while antiques in this category may be fairly devoid of finish. Guns in good condition may show some refinishing. While modern arms in good condition must show at least fairly good bores, antiques rated as good need not require clean bores. They are, after all, for collecting and not shooting.

Fair

Fair is obviously a low rating, but the gun must be intact and not broken to merit even this status. Evidence of repair is acceptable. Modern guns in fair condition must retain about 25 percent minimum finish, while antiques can be essentially devoid of original finish. Modern guns in fair condition must have shootable bores, rather than pitted ones.

Poor

Poor means an inoperable firearm, its only value for a collection if it is a particularly interesting gun important for its uniqueness of design or rarity. These guns must be considered dangerous to shoot.

*Collectors rely on books to show them the way to the most interesting firearms of yesterday. This one is dedicated to its title—*Winchester Rarities, *with calendars, displays, sporting goods, and other collectibles. It comes from Krause Publications, publishers of* The Gun List.

Collecting the real thing can be highly expensive. A replica fills a gap with a lot less expense. It will never take the place of an original, but it's a lot better than no gun at all. This well-executed Army LeMat from the Navy Arms Co. is a good example of a collectible replica.

Modern arms in this category may have no original finish, while antiques rarely show any original finish at all. The bores of these guns are dark and often pitted. Guns in poor condition may show considerable reworking, sometimes of very low quality.

Blackpowder Guns

Essentially, the rules that apply to collection in general fit blackpowder muzzleloaders and cartridge guns as well. Obviously, originals with important historical background are highly valuable. A prime example is the military version of the Colt Walker. This big sixgun of the 19th century weighed in at 4 pounds, 9 ounces, and was meant not for holstering on the hip so much as to be carried on a horse. The Walker cap 'n' ball revolver was a specialty to begin with, rare even during its days of manufacture. Not many were made, so it holds not only historical value, but also rarity. Should a military Walker be located in excellent condition today, the price tag could exceed $50,000. One in poor condition might fetch $20,000. The civilian model of the Walker, which was numbered from 1001 to 1100, is worth only a little less than the coveted military version: as high as $45,000 for one ranked excellent, down to around $18,000 for the same gun in poor shape. Naturally, these prices are approximations. There could be a collector out there so desirous of the Walker that he'd be willing to lay out dollars above and beyond the normally assessed value.

Blackpowder guns are also valued for their special appointments, such as high-grade engraving. Certain Winchester factory lever-action rifles were highly embellished with gold and silver inlays, as well as superlative engraving. Interestingly, the finest engravers of today are at least as good as the best of yesteryear, but that takes nothing away from the fine specialty guns of the past. Serial numbers can greatly add to the value of an old-time gun, with low numbers carrying the most weight. Matching serial numbers also count. Imagine a pair of Colt revolvers with serial numbers in sequence. Models also make a big difference. There were many special models offered over the years. Often, these were special guns because of embellishments or specific features. There were various Winchester blackpowder cartridge rifles, for example, that came in various sub-models with longer or shorter barrels than ordinary, special sights, as well as a number of minor differences compared with the standard model.

The Manufacturer

It's no surprise that firearms from better-known manufacturers noted for excellence carry bigger price tags than guns from the minor leagues. This holds true of small shops as well as large plants. Certainly, an original Hawken carries value based on its makers alone. A Hawken carried by Jim Bridger, Kit Carson, or other famous mountain man is especially coveted. Many middle guns, those created espe-

cially in the early 1900s after the original smiths passed on, are sought after. A rifle properly numbered with the name Royland Southgate, for example, is well worth $1,200 or more in spite of its rather plain style. Southgate made rifles of high quality, known for accuracy, and carefully numbered in sequence, at least most of them. His rifles are highly recognizable and definitely valued as collectors.

Very Old

Matchlocks, wheellocks, very early flintlocks, flintlocks with in-line ignition, breech-loading flinters, all guns of the distant past hold some interest for collecting if for no other reason than their vintage. Of course they are rare, and most of them have found their way into museums such as the Remington Collection in Cody, Wyo. Sometimes, however, an old gun surfaces in the strangest place, tucked in between the boards of an old barn being torn down, or buried in the earth. Usually, condition is deplorable, and value is low because of it, but that does not take away from the attraction these chunks of rusted metal and marred wood hold. Very old guns hold deep interest for historians, and books have been written to include them, two being *Guns and Rifles of the World* by Howard L. Blackmore, Viking Press, New York, 1965 and *The Flintlock: Its Origin and Development* by Torsten Link (translated from the Swedish by Urquhart and Hayward). Link's book begins with the snaphaunce. *Remington, "America's Oldest Gun-*

maker," by Roy Marcot and published by Remington Arms, deals with old guns in this country from that famous manufacturer, beginning with 1816 muzzleloaders. It's a fascinating story, and a book any collector would want to see.

Named for a Song

The famous long rifle born in Pennsylvania was named for a song about Kentucky. It, and its companion pistol, command tremendous interest because these guns belong in that special time frame known as the Golden Age of American Firearms. There are numerous books on this subject, as proved by a library search or a look on the Internet. An especially good one is Russell Harriger's *Longrifles of Pennsylvania*, Volume I, Jefferson, Clarion & Elk Counties published by George Shumway. Col. Harriger attacked his subject with scholarly interest and effort, explaining the guns and gunsmiths of these Pennsylvania counties. The book is packed with photographs of rifles and gunsmiths, plus old-time shops and other interesting illustrations. It also carries a multitude of solid references, a history of the wonderful Pennsylvania long guns and the gunsmiths who made them. Interesting business records belonging to the gunsmiths themselves show not only the work they were commissioned to do, but charges made for their labors. *The*

Kentucky Rifle by Capt. John G.W. Dillin, printed in 1924 by The National Rifle Association, is another good book on the Kentucky rifle, as is *The Pennsylvania-Kentucky Rifle* by Henry J. Kauffman, published by Stackpole Books.

Conflicts

While we may wish firearms were confined only to target ranges and hunting fields, the fact is, they have found their way onto battlefields the world over. Many of these guns were blackpowder shooters of muzzleloader or cartridge persuasion. In our own American Civil War, snipers on the Confederate side used English Whitworth muzzleloaders to fire upon their brothers in blue. Before that, the American Revolutionary War saw the use of muzzleloaders as explained by Harold L. Peterson in *The Book of the Continental Soldier*. This book deals with the smoothbore musket of the period, as well as uniforms and equipment. Peterson details not only the firearms, but also how they were employed.

Guns of the Mountain Men

Serious students of the mountain-man era know that many firearms were carried west of the Mississippi River in the early 1800s. Of course, the plains rifle captures the imagination, the

Hawken being the epitome of the breed. Many books have been written on this period of time, some dealing strongly with equipment in general, such as *Firearms, Traps, & Tools of the Mountain Men* by Carl P. Russell, University of New Mexico press. Russell includes knives, tomahawks, traps, and of course the guns, not only the Hawkens, but others as well. *The Plains Rifle* by Charles E. Hanson, Jr., published by the Gun Room Press in 1960, continues to hold an honored place in the library of any collector of mountain-man guns. Hanson includes early trade guns, Leman flintlocks, and of course the rifles of Sam and Jake Hawken. Books strictly on Hawkens are also available, such as John Baird's *Hawken Rifles, The Mountain Man's Choice*, The Gun Room Press, 1976. Baird also wrote *Fifteen Years in the Hawken Lode*, published in the same year by the same press.

Catch-All Collecting

Quite a number of collectors worry not about vintage, history, special examples, or any other specific traits. They simply enjoy collecting guns designed to shoot blackpowder in cartridges or muzzleloaders. There are many books dealing with guns in general, including those of pre-smokeless powder days. *Guns and Rifles of the World* by Howard L. Blackmore is

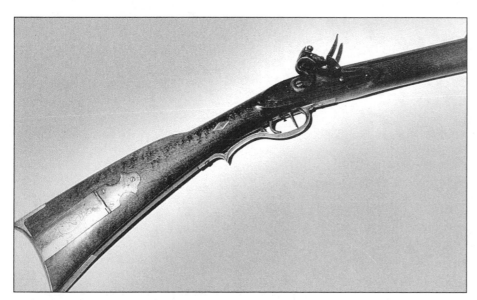

Collecting originals provides the most valuable and most interesting holdings; however, originals can be expensive and quite often too valuable to shoot.

While nothing matches an original for collection, filling a gap with a well-made replica like this Rogers and Spencer revolver from Navy Arms is a lot better than no gun at all. The history is still there, too. We know, for example, that this gun was made toward the end of the war in Utica, N. Y.

a perfect example from Viking Press. This book begins with the handgun, then covers the matchlock, wheellock, flintlock, to percussion systems of various types (such as the pill, disk and patch, tube, tape and cap), to breechloaders, multi-shot guns, right into air, steam, and electric guns. The photos in this text are excellent, revealing features of firearms we might think of as fictional if not for their very existence. How about an air gun from Germany, circa 1600? *Famous Guns from the Smithsonian Collection* published by Arco Publishing Co., 1966, is another good title that deals with "the story of firearm patents between the years 1836 and 1880," with drawings and photographs for illustration.

Fortunately, gun collecting began a very long time ago. That is why we have examples of arms from such a distant past. And even if we do not wish to collect guns ourselves, we can enjoy them in museums and the holdings of others.

Chapter 14

THE PYROTECHNICS OF BLACKPOWDER

ONE OF the most fascinating aspects of blackpowder is its pyrotechnic complexity in light of the fact that it's only a physical mixture, not a chemical compound, of three basic ingredients. Professor F.A. Williams, physicist in propellants and fuels, put it this way: Blackpowder's "burning mechanics remain poorly understood because of their complexity." In this enlightened time with DNA testing and e-mail, our research tools still prove too blunt to penetrate the core of blackpowder's characteristics. Not to say that we're ignorant of its major traits, but this simple propellant composed of saltpeter, charcoal, and sulfur — for centuries known simply as "gunpowder"

because there was no smokeless powder to contrast with — defies full understanding. We don't even have a handle on where it came from: perhaps Greece, India, or China. Consider the Gentoo Code of warfare, dating before Christianity. It states:

"The magistrate shall not make war with any deceitful machine, or with poisoned weapons, or with cannons or guns, or any kind of firearms, nor shall he slay in war any person born an eunuch, nor any person who, putting his arms together, supplicates for quarter, nor any person who has no means of escape."

The meaning of "fire-arms" here is uncertain, but surely there was

some form of flame involved — flame generated from gunpowder? A small piece of ancient writing by Quintus Curtius suggests that Alexander the Great encountered "fire-weapons" in India. Likewise, many ancient Chinese and Indian terms refer to fire generated by a substance.

English writer Henry Wilkinson theorized that blackpowder was discovered when a cooking fire was built upon ground impregnated with niter. The ancient chef preparing his culinary coals suddenly found himself in the midst of a mild explosion. In 275 A.D., Roman Julius Africanus mentions "shooting powder" in his memoirs. The history goes on and on, including speculation blended with ancient records. Chapter 2, "The Invention of Gunpowder," in that great arms book, *The Gun and Its Development* by W.W. Greener, 9th Edition, is packed with information concerning the advent of gunpowder. It includes the story of Berthold Schwarz, the German monk of Friburg who supposedly experimented with blackpowder based upon the writings of Roger Bacon, an English scientist of the late 1200s. Schwarz is sometimes credited with inventing true gunpowder, based on improvements over Bacon's data. Theories of blackpowder invention are all interesting, each entirely without proof. But one thing is certain: once the propellant gained prominence, it was made in many countries with various brands differing widely in performance.

WANO blackpowder from Germany has been made for many decades. It's a high-grade propellant available in various formulations, including the familiar FFg and FFFg shown here.

The author found Swiss Black Powder to be a highly developed product with hard kernel structure and good uniformity among granulations.

Sportsmen recognized this fact, praising some powders, cursing others. Greener taught that "the shape of the grain [kernel] affects materially the combustion of the powder, the sharper diamond-shaped grains [kernels] burning more rapidly than the rounded ones." Greener presented illustrations in his book that showed how diverse the various blackpowders of his day truly were. There was very fine kernel configuration in a French powder, a little more coarse shape in an American example, with a German powder showing very coarse. He also mentioned Hall's mixed-grain powder. A small sampling of different brands includes Hazard's Kentucky Rifle & Sea Shooting Powder, Loflin & Rand's Orange Extra, Lightning, Ducking, du Pont Diamond Grain, Eagle Sporting, Eagle Duck, Eagle Rifle, Oriental in America, Curtis & Harvey Diamond Grain, Col. Hawker's Duck Powder, Pigoo, Wilks and Laurence's from England. There were many others. Although all of these powders contained the same essential ingredients, they differed by precise amounts of each product in the mixture, and by exact burn rate and composition (how the ingredients mixed together), plus granulation or kernel size, and other properties. The manufacturing process itself promoted differences from brand to brand, and while saltpeter, sulfur, and charcoal made up these different powders, the exact nature of each part often varied.

The Chemistry of Blackpowder

The basic ingredients of blackpowder have not changed through time. They remain saltpeter, charcoal, and sulfur. Saltpeter is potassium nitrate, KNO_3, the oxidizer of blackpowder. It may be thought of as the energy-maker. Sodium nitrate was also used as an oxidizer for blackpowder. KNO_3 has a melting point of 633 degrees Fahrenheit, but the ignition point of blackpowder, depending on the source, is noted as 572 to 662 degrees F. Charcoal, a form of carbon, is considered the "body" of blackpowder, but it's

more than that because different charcoals affect burn rate and combustion properties, which would not be the case if charcoal were simply a medium to contain saltpeter and sulfur. Over the years, specific woods, especially willows, have been sought after for high-grade blackpowder charcoal. The third ingredient, sulfur, can be considered a binding agent for saltpeter and charcoal, serving to maintain the integrity of the powder. We do know that alterations in sulfur content can change performance, suggesting that sulfur promotes both ignition and combustion. Mixture ratios of the three main ingredients changed over the years. A circa-1350 English gunpowder shows 66.6 percent saltpeter, 22.3 percent charcoal and 11.1 percent sulfur, while a circa-1650 French powder ran 75.6/13.6/10.8. A popular mixture in the distant past holds today: 75/15/10.

One gram of blackpowder yields 718 calories of heat, 270 cubic centimeters of permanent gas, and roughly a half-gram of solid residues, proving that transformation is inefficient compared with smokeless powder (more on that below). Some gases of combustion are: CO_2, CO, N_2, H_2S, H_2, K_2CO_3, K_2SO_4, and K_2S, along with carbon dioxide, carbon monoxide, nitrogen, hydrogen sulfide, hydrogen, potassium carbonate, potassium sulfate, and potassium monosulfide. In one test,

WANO blackpowder from Germany comes in standard formulations like these: Fg, FFg, FFFg, and FFFFg. It's been made since the early 1700s in Germany.

Just because a powder is black does not mean that it is blackpowder, and that is why the spelling convention is changed in this book from black powder to blackpowder. The powder on the bottom is definitely black, but it is not blackpowder and must never be used in a muzzleloader.

82 grains weight of FFg blackpowder left 42 grains of solids after combustion.

The factor of remaining solids is related not only to powder efficiency, but also muzzleloader cleanup. Obviously, a lot of the powder charge is left behind after combustion, requiring removal from the bore of the gun. Granulation also determines how blackpowder behaves (more on granulation below). Blackpowder is surface-burning; therefore, particle size and shape are in part responsible for the rate of combustion. The kernels are polyhedral, which refers to many-sided or many-faced. The shape of the powder charge is always cylindrical in the breech of the muzzleloader when the charge is properly loaded (no air space between powder and bullet). When seated correctly downbore, load density is always 100 percent because there is no air space between powder and projectile. Both of these factors, the shape of the powder charge and load density, occur also in the blackpowder cartridge when the charge takes up all case space. Kernel dimension also relates to generated pressure in the gun, with finer kernels yielding somewhat higher pressure per same charge compared with kernels of large dimensions. This is logical based on the fact that blackpowder is surface-burning, and that kernel size alters that burning surface. Because of this fact, FFg blackpowder is normally recommended over finer granulations in big-bore muzzleloaders, while finer granulations are more at home in smaller-bored guns. FFFFg is considered pan powder for flintlocks.

Loading by "Grains Volume"

Because of the nature of blackpowder, including its inefficiency compared with smokeless as discussed below, volumetric loading is required. Never figure a charge by weight with a bullet/powder scale.

An important term describing the blackpowder charge is "grains volume," indicating that a powder measure was set for a specific charge noted in grains, most measures seen today running up to a scale of 120. Yet the charge was not weighed. It is, therefore, in grains volume, not grains weight. A charge of 100 grains volume FFg blackpowder may indeed go 100 grains in weight, but other granulations will not identically match this condition because of variations in density. This is profoundly true of Pyrodex, which is far less dense than blackpowder. When the powder measure is set for 100, Pyrodex does not come even close to 100 grains of weight. For RS, it's 71.5 grains of weight per 100 grains of volume, according to recent tests. Pyrodex is always loaded just like blackpowder, in grains volume, not grains weight. One charger sized for a specific volume of blackpowder or Pyrodex works for both. One adjustable powder measure set on a specific unit, such as 50, 60, or 100, also works for both Pyrodex and blackpowder.

Granulations

Granulation is highly important to blackpowder pyrotechnics, not to suggest that kernel shape and size is unimportant in smokeless powder combustion, because it is highly vital there, too. Granulating blackpowder

DuPont blackpowder was made in America and well-distributed. Today, GOEX has taken its place.

Another good blackpowder comes into America from Brazil. Elephant brand has been made since 1866. It comes in numerous granulations today.

was much more consistent in burn rate, also offering the advantage of greater powder integrity, although the kernels were of somewhat irregular size. A mix of odd-shaped and odd-sized chunks and hunks would never burn as regularly as granulated blackpowder. Also, when the powder was properly made into rather hard kernels, it had a tendency to remain that way, rather

This powder measure set at 100 dropped a charge just short of 103 grains weight FFg blackpowder. If it were left at the 100 setting, a charge of Pyrodex RS would run around 70 grains weight.

than breaking down. Again, this was important to burn rate and stability, but also to storage. Furthermore, granules thwarted moisture better than a dust-like powder, partly because the kernels could be coated. All blackpowder is hygroscopic — with a "g," meaning that it tends to attract moisture. A hardened kernel would absorb less moisture than a broken down mass of powder with flour-like consistency. Also, granulated powder was easier to transport, especially onto a battlefield.

Barrel Length and Blackpowder

There is no such thing as a perfect correlation between barrel length and muzzle velocities. The oft-quoted 25 feet per second per inch of barrel is off-the-wall information. Blackpowder guns, as with any other firearm, gain or lose velocity per length of bore; however, there's a balance point between how long a barrel is and carrying convenience with modern muzzleloaders, while replicas should adhere to original dimensions. A 36-inch barrel on an in-line front loader is as ludicrous as a 24-inch barrel on a Kentucky rifle.

In one chronograph series conducted by Lyman for test purposes, a 50-caliber muzzleloader with a 22-inch barrel earned a muzzle velocity of 1,362 fps with a 370-grain bullet in front of 100 grains volume Goex FFg

WANO blackpowder comes in various granulations, including a special F series, such as 7FA.

blackpowder. The same bullet and powder charge in a 32-inch barrel got 1,503 fps. On one hand, a difference of 141 fps is significant. On the other hand, the hunter perched in a tree stand with the 22-inch barrel rifle would consider the velocity loss compensated for by ease of handling. Powder granulations make a difference, too. Staying with the same 50-caliber rifle, same bullet, but Goex FFFg blackpowder, velocity in the 22-inch barrel is 1,488 fps, but only 1,551 fps in the longer barrel. Here, the shorter tube definitely wins the compromise between short and handy VS velocity, with a loss of only 63 fps. Guns can vary widely, so the above must be considered true for the two test rifles only, and not across the board for all guns.

Be sure to follow the gun maker's recommendations on powder type and maximum load at all times.

The Blackpowder Burning Curve

Often printed is the erroneous notion that blackpowder simply explodes, that it does not burn progressively in the bore as other propellants do. Blackpowder's burning curve does show a sharp spike at ignition, but then the curve smoothes out. This is why short-starting proves a problem, because the powder charge is no longer formed into a column with 100 per-

The precautions on the back of a can of Elephant brand black-powder contains many useful warnings, even how to pick up spilled blackpowder with a "brush and dustpan only."

cent loading density, but lies in a trough along the bottom of the bore. While blackpowder does not go boom in one fell swoop, it ignites rapidly when confined properly in the breech of a muzzleloader or a cartridge case. Therefore, while blackpowder does ignite readily in the firearm, it does not explode.

Blackpowder Pressure

Pressure is often used as a dirty word in shooting. However, without pressure behind the bullet, it would sit like a lump in the breech, going nowhere. On the other hand, blackpowder pressure can get way out of control, as one shooter learned when the entire left-hand flat of the barrel blew out from an overload, causing serious injury. A blackpowder dictum from the old days went: "Blackpowder cannot be overloaded, because it is impossible for a charge to exceed 25,000 psi (pounds per square inch) pressure." How wrong! Pressures exceeding 100,000 psi were generated in 19th-century tests conducted by two Englishmen, Able and Nobel. The U.S. Navy, interested in blackpow-

der because it was, and still is, the detonator for the big guns on battleships (hence the huge cloud of smoke), found similar pressures. In short, muzzleloaders can be overloaded, especially because they are not confined by a cartridge case. The entire length of the bore, minus the seated bullet, can hold powder. Maximum powder charges dictated by arms manufacturers for their firearms must never be exceeded. Also, short-starting, explained earlier, must be considered a dangerous practice. Damage from most short-started loads normally occurs at the base of the unseated projectile, where a lump (walnut) is formed in the barrel. However, short-started guns have also suffered ruptured barrels.

Blackpowder Fouling

Since blackpowder fails to convert from solid to gas much beyond the 50 percent level during combustion, much residue is left behind in the bore. Today's special lubrications help in reducing such fouling; however, there is no substitute for swabbing a bore clean when it becomes caked. Two bad things happen with a badly fouled bore. The first is a combination of increased drag and reduced volume for powder to expand in, resulting in higher pressures. The second is the possibility of short-starting a bullet because gunk in the bore prevents full seating of the projectile down on the powder charge. Recall that a short-start can act as a bore obstruction as well as causing the powder charge to burn erratically in the process of expelling the ejecta (sum total of powder and bullet) from the bore.

Ramrod Pressure and Black Powder

Tests show that blackpowder is sensitive to compacted pressure as the charge rests downbore in the breech of the muzzleloader. Varying ramrod pressure changes compaction of the powder, which alters uniformity from one shot to the

next. Meanwhile, uniformity is vital to all good shooting. A chronograph with standard deviation capability shows that consistent ramrod pressure makes for shot-to-shot uniformity. The Kadooty loading tool was invented expressly for uniform ramrod pressure. The Kadooty verified that constant ramrod pressure resulted in a low standard deviation from the mean velocity. When working up test loads, I use a spring-loaded device that slips over the end of the loading rod, providing 35 pounds of bullet seating pressure for every shot. Warning: leaning heavily on the ramrod could prove dangerous, crushing the blackpowder charge in the breech, because blackpowder is impact sensitive. I found that a consistent 35-pound force on the loading rod was sufficient to compact the powder charge.

The Bore Obstruction and Black Powder

Bore obstructions of any kind can destroy a barrel. The blackpowder firearm is no exception. The situation may be compounded with a muzzleloader because the powder

Chemical engineering is ongoing to find a powder that burns cleaner in the muzzleloader as well as blackpowder cartridge. GOEX's Clear Shot, while not non-corrosive, is a clean-burning powder.

Swiss Black Powder is a highly refined propellant that comes in various granulations, including a unique 1F called Shuetzen Powder.

charge is not converted from solid to gas efficiently. Therefore, solids in the charge become part of the projectile, in a sense, which are partially expelled from the bore, the remainder left behind as fouling. A bore clogged with mud or snow may explode due to the elasticity of the air that rests between the projectile and the bore obstruction. Perhaps.

Spikes

A spike is an upsurge of pressure that rises from a normal burning curve. Blackpowder ignites readily, as stated earlier. That's why it remains in use for detonating huge smokeless powder charges on battleships, which was also mentioned. But there is a difference between the original spike at ignition and spikes that occur downbore, the latter possibly causing trouble. This phenomenon is open to study, but it's safe to conclude that any type of bore obstruction may alter the normal burning curve of the powder charge and therefore safety dictates a clear bore at all times.

Blackpowder and Ambient Temperatures

Anyone who loads a good deal of smokeless powder cartridge ammo knows that maximum charges with no signs of pressure problems on a cold day can cause heavily cratered primers, head stamp engraving by the bolt face and even blown primers on a hot day. On the other hand, very cold conditions may reduce the potency of a load. But blackpowder remains vigorous in cold temperatures.

Blackpowder Pressures and Bore Size

Bore size affects all guns. A prime example is the 17 Remington, one of the most enjoyable cartridges of the day, capable of shooting tiny 25-grain bullets at well over 4,000 fps muzzle velocity. Due to the diminutive bore, slight changes in powder charge can increase pressures markedly. This factor has been known for a very long time. A 19th-century naval report on blackpowder translated from the French notes: "In similar guns charged with the same powder, the maximum pressure is proportional to the caliber." We see this in our blackpowder loads in three ways: velocity per powder charge, velocity per bore diameter, and pressure per bore diameter.

For example, a 50-caliber rifle firing a 177-grain round ball with 80 grains of GOEX FFg blackpowder gains 1,573 fps at just over 6,000 pounds per square inch of pressure. Half that charge (40 grains of GOEX FFg) in a 32-caliber rifle produces almost 1,900 fps muzzle velocity with about 8,000 psi, using a 45-grain round ball.

Blackpowder Limits

There is a certain limit in the work that any fuel can perform, including blackpowder, with power representing the gas produced minus the energy consumed in pushing solids (and the bullet) in the bore, and minus heat loss. A firearm can be studied as a heat engine. Depending upon the specific firearm and load, the barrel may absorb 25 percent of the heat generated from the powder charge. This represents lost "power" in terms of work applied to a projectile. Efficient cooling of the big barrel walls of the muzzleloader is greatest when the ratio between powder-load weight and interior bore surface is small. For example, a modest powder charge in a big bore allows faster barrel-wall cooling than a heavy charge in a smaller bore size (less volume and reduced bore-wall contact).

Blackpowder and Obturation

Inertia, the condition of an object at rest tending to remain at rest, detains initial bullet movement in the bore This condition can be overstated, but bullet obturation is a reality, meaning the powerful gases strike the base of the projectile, causing it to slightly widen. It is this principle that allows accuracy with a Maxi-Ball. Although the Maxi-Ball has a solid base, it is slightly enlarged in the bore because of obturation. If this did not occur, contact between the bullet's shank and rifling would be limited. Pressures with blackpowder are quickly raised. In one test, 2,200 psi was reached in less than 0.1 (one-tenth) millisecond after ignition of the powder charge, showing that indeed there was instantaneous force on the projectile. Hot flame may also cause partial destruction of a conical's base, especially the skirt of a Minie. The same hot gases can also eat up a round ball patch. The first condition requires reducing the powder charge or getting a mold with a thicker skirt. The second calls for protecting the patch with a couple layers of hornet nesting material, which prevents burnout. Of course, round ball obturation helps the missile gain a purchase on the lands of the rifling in spite of patch deterioration.

Patch Destruction

Blackpowder can cause burned-out patches, also called blown patches, as opposed to cut patches, which are sliced by the rifling, not harmed by burning powder flame.

Here's how to check for patch cutting: Load no powder downbore. Seat a patched ball into the empty breech. Do not force the patched ball all the way to the bottom of the breech, which can cause extraction difficulty. Withdraw the patched ball with a screw on the end of a loading rod. The patch should be intact. If it is cut by the rifling, there are two cures. First, shoot more. Patch material flying through the bore laps the lands smoother. Second, have a gunsmith lap the bore with rouge to smooth sharp edges.

The Smoke

We love it, all that smoke generated by blackpowder because it does not convert readily from solid to gas. But this smoke sends a message. It says: "Clean the gun." Failure to do so can ruin a muzzleloader. For target shooting, lighter charges of FFFg make bore swabbing easier, since the smaller kernels are a little better consumed.

When Inefficiency Pays Off

Because blackpowder is inefficient compared with smokeless, it can be loaded perfectly well by volume, making it simple to manage. Grab a pre-set charger or adjustable powder measure correctly set and either works well. Reports of carefully measured blackpowder charges making significantly better groups on the target range are exaggerated. The most sensitive chronograph in the world cannot detect, for example, any significant difference between 60, 60.5, or 61.0 grains of blackpowder in the most popular big-bore muzzleloader of the hour, the 50 caliber. Volumetric loads, therefore, are safe and accurate, as simple shooting tests on the range and thorough chronographing prove.

Blackpowder and Recoil

While blackpowder inefficiency allows the unencumbered volumetric loading process, it does cause a small problem with recoil, because the weight of a powder charge is part of the recoil formula. Small charges of smokeless powder get a lot of work done, as indicated in the comparison between a 30-30 cartridge and 50- caliber muzzleloader. The 30-30 gets 2,000 fps with less than 30 grains of smokeless powder, while the muzzleloader needs about 110 grains of blackpowder to achieve the same muzzle velocity. Since blackpowder big bores demand a lot of powder for hunting loads, recoil is the result. Yet, it's manageable. Lightweight 12- and 10-gauge shotguns with heavy shot and powder charges, however, do say hello with a tap on the shoulder.

Storing Blackpowder

Kept in a cool place away from any source of flame or contamination, blackpowder lasts a very long time in sealed containers. Chronograph tests with well-stored, 19th-century powder reveals full velocity, proving retained potency. But blackpowder abused by heat and high humidity can deteriorate. Proper storage is demanded for safety, with heat a major enemy. Potassium sulfide rapidly heated or brought into contact with powerful oxidizers may explode. Also, potassium sulfite, when heated to a point of decomposition, emits sulfur dioxide, which can corrode metals, such as gun barrels and locks. Furthermore, the purity of potassium nitrate is suspect as powder deteriorates. Potassium nitrate and sulfur may convert to potassium sulfide, sulfite, and sulfate, which may reduce power or etch metal.

Roughly half of a blackpowder charge remains in solid form after ignition.

"Keep your powder dry" was, and still is, good advice. Place a little blackpowder on the ground. Pour water over it. The powder is destroyed. Oxygen is no friend of blackpowder either, hence the warning about well-sealed containers. As blackpowder breaks down, it becomes more hygroscopic, attracting even more moisture than usual, partly because of degraded kernel integrity.

Impact Sensitive

It's safe to say that blackpowder is impact sensitive. It may detonate if struck by a hard object, which would be an act of foolishness in the first place. Moreover, super pressure on a ramrod or loading rod is unwise. Such pressure is entirely unneeded, does nothing good, and possibly causes something bad to happen: ignition. Putting full body weight on the loading rod or ramrod is hereby listed as dangerous. Why some shooters also get a kick out of whacking the ramrod downbore on either powder or seated bullet is hard to figure. It will do nothing for the powder charge, and deforming the nose of a projectile, especially a round ball, makes no sense. Yet some whack away all the same as part of some ritual, not a sound, proved loading technique. There are two key words here: "impact sensitive" and "ignition."

A Few More Facts

F Sizes

Elephant Brand Black Powder offers a FFFFFg (5F) blackpowder, smaller in kernel size that the usual FFFFg (4F) pan powder used in flintlock. FFFg (3F) is an ideal great kernel size for smallbore rifles and pistols as well as cap 'n' ball revolvers, plus light target/plinking loads in any muzzleloading rifle. FFg (2F) is the workhorse for big-game power in 45-caliber and larger rifles, as well as shotguns. It's also appropriate for big-bore pistols. Fg (1F) works in 12-gauge shotguns, is even more appropriate in the 10-bore and

is excellent in the blackpowder cartridge, but Fg does not yield good velocity in muzzleloaders of 45 to 58 caliber. German Wano, along with the standard F numbers, also has 4FA and 7FA unglazed powders. Swiss offers a 1 1/2 Fg powder. Cannon grade and other granulations are not included here, since they are not normally employed in blackpowder shooting, while Pyrodex has its own chapter, with an explanation of its kernel sizes.

Corning

The corning process was an important step in the development of a truly successful blackpowder that could be formed into specific granulation kernel sizes, which in turn allowed soldiers and hunters to carry powder into the field safely. When stored properly, corned powder also lasted indefinitely. It was prepared wet, and then turned into kernels (granulated), unlike the previous serpentine powder, which was ground dry. The following is for the reader's reference only. In fact, various powder companies have always insisted upon their own kernel sizes. At this very hour, kernel sizes still vary among different brands.

Square Mesh Screen

It's impossible to provide one set of "go" and "no go" mesh sizes for all companies, because one manufacturer's FFg slightly differs in kernel size from another's. Therefore, the following is for general reference only.

Mesh screen is a fast way to sort out various kernel sizes. For example, if powder gets caught in a

.0376-inch mesh, it would classify as FFg. Of course, there's a runover, because the high end of FFFg is also .0376-inch size. So it's not precise, but the square mesh screen gives a general idea of kernel dimensions.

Glazing

Glazing means tumbling the powder, usually with graphite, in the final phase of manufacture, a process possibly dated back to the 1500s. Powder so treated was supposed to be more spark-resistant, although the process was not embraced by all manufacturers.

Propellants and Explosives

In general, there are three major classes of propellants/explosives. Certain substances have the property of "going off" on their own. They are, in other words, explosive by nature. We know that magnesium and water react chemically, for example, while Greener notes picric acid and its alkaline salts as explosive, along with fulminates of silver and mercury. Fulminates made percussion caps a reality as an "explosive salt of fulminic acid containing the monovalent negative radical CNO." Fulminic acid in turn is "an unstable isomer of cyanic acid, known chiefly in the form of highly explosive, shock-sensitive salts used as detonators." The only germane part of all that science talk, for our purposes, rests in the words "shock-sensitive." This stuff goes off when whacked. Place a little bit inside a tiny metal cup, then slip the cup over the cone of a nipple. Strike the cup with a blow, as

Square Mesh Screen Granulation Sizes		
	Granulation Go	Granulation No-Go
Fg	.0689-inch	.0582-inch
FFg	.0582-inch	.0376-inch
FFFg	.0376-inch	.0170-inch
FFFFg	.017-inch	.0111-inch

from a gun's hammer, and the fulminate erupts in flame, that flame directed to a main charge of powder in a breech, and boom! The gun goes off. So that's the first class of explosive/propellant substance.

The second class includes substances that do not "go off" on their own, but when joined in combination, produce considerable energy through combustion. This class includes chlorate of potassium plus sugar, or how about saltpeter and sulfur mixed with charcoal?

The third class is composed of chemical compounds such as nitroglycerine and nitrocellulose. All three classes pertain to shooting: the first with percussion caps and primers, the second includes blackpowder itself, and the third includes smokeless powder.

Smokeless Powders

Important: Just because a powder is black in color does not make it blackpowder. Many smokeless powders are black in color. No matter how many times, or how loudly, the fact is preached from coast to coast, someone will use smokeless powder in a muzzleloader with devastating results. The least effect is destroying a firearm, while the worst is a badly injured shooter. Smokeless powder is absolutely forbidden in any muzzleloader with the exception, as this is written, of only one rifle, the Savage Model 10ML, which uses an entirely different system in order to safely handle a smokeless propellant. That system includes locking lugs on the bolt of the rifle, along with a module of super-strength steel that is inserted into the chamber just like a cartridge. Why is smokeless powder so deadly in all other muzzleloaders? It's an entirely different type of propellant from blackpowder with completely different burning characteristics, including considerably more generation of energy compared to blackpowder. Two major smokeless powders dominate: single base and double base. The first consists mainly of nitrocellulose. The second, double base, is

Part of muzzleloader shooting fun is definitely the smoke. This is proven at Cowboy Action Shooting matches, where spectators always show more interest when the cartridge guns are loaded with blackpowder instead of smokeless. Here, a woman at rendezvous fires at a target with the telltale puff of smoke up front.

also mainly nitrocellulose, but contains a degree of nitroglycerine as well. While blackpowder converts from solid to gaseous state at roughly a 50 percent level of efficiency, smokeless converts at a much higher rate. This is why blackpowder hunting charges are often quite heavy, with several in-line magnum muzzleloaders allowed as high as 150-grains volume, while smokeless powder charges are far

smaller. A good contrast was touched on earlier: a 50-caliber muzzleloader compared with a 30-30 cartridge. Both can achieve around 2,000 fps muzzle velocity, the muzzleloader with a 177-grain patched round ball, the 30-30 Winchester with a 170-grain bullet. The difference lies in the powder charge. In order for the muzzleloader to gain 2,000 fps, something on the order of 110 grains volume FFg blackpowder is required, while the 30-30 achieves that velocity, and more, with less than 30 grains of smokeless powder. No special savvy is required to figure out that smokeless in this comparison generated a lot more energy per charge than blackpowder.

Many Powders from the Past

It's important to recognize at least some of the propellants that have come along over the years, not only from the aspect of historical interest, but to generate this warning: Never use any of the older powders in a muzzleloader. Fortunately, few of the following powders will ever be located at all, but that's not true of all of them.

Brown Powder

Under-oxidized wood, rather than full charcoal, was used for brown powder, which had a sulfur content of only 3 percent. That's why it turned out brown instead of black. Certain records depict brown powder as powerful as early smokeless. Odds of locating brown powder are small, thankfully, for it is entirely inappropriate in any firearm today.

Schultze Powder

Composed of "light fibrous woods similar to those used for making black gunpowder charcoal," according to W.W. Greener, this powder surfaced around 1867 and has no place in muzzleloaders or any other type of firearm. It's mentioned only for historical interest.

King's Semi-Smokeless

Patent papers prove that King's Semi-Smokeless was a modified blackpowder. It achieved identical velocities as GOEX FFg in a test rifle under strict test conditions. Should King's Semi-Smokeless be encountered today, it should be avoided entirely. It's very old and could be contaminated or deteriorated, thereby causing damage to a firearm and/or its shooter.

Dense Powder

Gun Week newspaper, December 22, 1978, cited Dense Powder as "a modern smokeless powder, frequently combined with nitroglycerine, that gives ballistic results identical to those obtained with blackpowder." Dense Powder must be avoided under any and all conditions. It could blow a muzzleloader to smithereens.

Ballistite Powder

The same issue of Gun Week newspaper stated that "Ballistite powder, also known as Nobel powder, was the first of the modern smokeless powders. First made in 1887, it consists of 40 percent nitroglycerine and 60 percent nitrocellulose." This stuff will blow your muzzleloader beyond smithereens.

Bulk Powder

Once again, Gun Week gets the credit for information on Bulk Powder, noted as obsolete smokeless powder with a nitrocellulose base. This powder could turn a muzzleloader into shrapnel.

Du Pont Bulk Smokeless

To this day, some older shooters continue to advise using this powder mixed with blackpowder to reduce fouling and improve velocity. Under strict test conditions, Du Pont Bulk Smokeless was mixed at 10 percent and 15 percent with 100 grains volume FFg. It neither produced any increased velocity at all, nor did it make after-shooting cleaning easier. It must never be used in a muzzleloader. Du Pont Bulk Powder was marketed from 1893 into the 1960s. Here is a warning that came with the powder: "Warning: While it [Bulk Smokeless] is intended for volumetric loading by drams it is not suitable for use as a replacement for blackpowder in the older guns." This powder was never intended for use in a muzzleloader.

Amberite, Axite, Cannonite, Chilworth, Coopall's Powder, Empire, Cordite, Empire

These are all old-time smokeless powders containing nitrocellulose. They've been gone for a long time, with the exception of British Cordite, which is unique in that it comes as solid strings of powder, looking like spaghetti. Any of these powders could destroy a muzzleloader as well as injuring the shooter.

The fascinating world of muzzleloader propellants goes on with a comparison of various powders, including imported brands, as well as a look at Pyrodex and the highly successful Pyrodex Pellet.

Chapter 15

PYRODEX AND PYRODEX PELLETS

THE NORMAL course of American enterprise includes a deep search for that better mousetrap, the one the world has been waiting for. It's no surprise, then, that pyrotechnic experts continue looking for a substitute blackpowder that makes smoke, works safely in muzzleloaders, and loads by volume, while at the same time providing the non-corrosive traits of smokeless powder. To date, the journey has been futile. However, along the way, an excellent propellant surfaced: Pyrodex as a "loose" powder and the amazingly successful Pyrodex Pellet.

In one camp of 12 hunters, 11 guns were loaded with Pyrodex Pellets, only one stoked up with standard powder. That's not unusual. It's typical because the pellet is handy to carry, requires no powder measure, loads quickly with ease, and packs plenty of power.

Pyrodex is called a replica blackpowder, but it's actually a unique propellant in its own right. The pellet version is even more special and significant.

There are three main advantages of Pyrodex over standard blackpowder. First, cleaning between shots with Pyrodex is not necessary for a reasonable number of shots. This does not imply in any way that Pyrodex can be loaded indefinitely into a firearm without swabbing the bore. After all, that is not possible with any powder, including smokeless. Even smokeless eventually cakes up the bore.

Second, Pyrodex provides more shots per pound than blackpowder because it is less dense, but embodies similar energy per volume. Set a powder measure at 100 and it will throw very close to 100-grains weight FFg blackpowder. However, with the same measure at the same 100 setting, Pyrodex RS comes out at 70.5 grains weight. That figure may vary slightly with different lots (runs) of the powder, but holds well across the board. Because of this factor, a can of Pyrodex weighing a pound, which is 7,000 grains weight, provides more shots than a can of blackpowder: 70 shots for blackpowder, 99 for Pyrodex. Third, Pyrodex provides at least as much energy as blackpowder per volumetric load and greater energy per weight, so while getting more shots out of a can, those shots remain at full velocity.

Never has the Hodgdon Powder Co., home of Pyrodex, suggested that Pyrodex is non-corrosive, or that guns need not be cleaned after shooting just as if they had been loaded with blackpowder. However, like blackpowder, Pyrodex does not "eat up" bores on its own. It is hygroscopic, tending to attract moisture, but not significantly so. Also, when stored properly, Pyrodex remains totally viable indefinitely. Pyrodex is classified as a flammable Class B solid propellant, while blackpowder is listed as a Class A explosive. This is not to suggest that blackpowder cannot be shipped via a common carrier, as

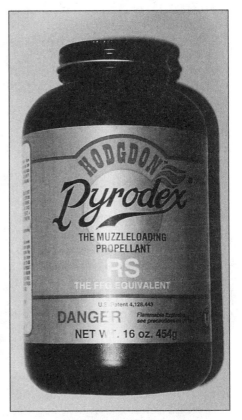

Pyrodex RS is the workhorse of the line, matching up with FFg. It's at home in big bore muzzleloaders, blackpowder cartridges, shotguns, as well as smallbores with certain loads.

can Pyrodex. While Pyrodex is entirely suitable for muzzleloaders, it is also excellent in the blackpowder cartridge. As with any propellant, getting the most from Pyrodex comes from understanding its nature, its specific properties and how it behaves in blackpowder guns.

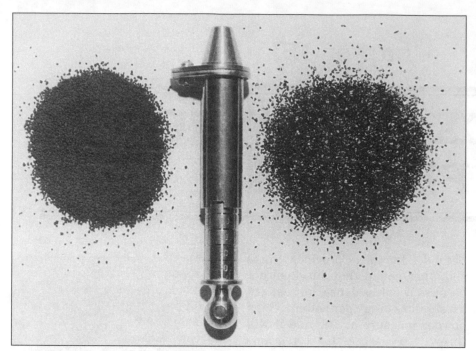
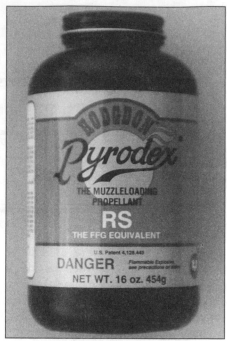

Pyrodex is loaded volume for volume with blackpowder, not by weight. The charge on the left is Pyrodex RS, the charge on the right is FFg, both thrown from the same measure with the same setting.

Pyrodex in RS, which stands for Rifle/Shotgun, serves similarly to FFg blackpowder by volume, not weight.

Formulations

Pyrodex has not remained exactly the same from inception to present, as proven by the fact that the powder has been awarded several U.S. patents on different formulations. Because Hodgdon Powder Co. continued research on Pyrodex over the years, today's formula is not exactly the same as lots from the past. Early Pyrodex did have ignition problems in flintlocks. Today's Pyrodex ignites more readily than earlier samples. Tests show this to be the case not only with standard Pyrodex, but also with the Pyrodex Pellet when it is employed as intended by the company: in firearms with some form of direct ignition. This includes in-line muzzleloaders, the Markesbery Outer-Line® and newly designed systems incorporated in certain non-replica muzzleloaders, such as the Traditions Thunder™ Magnum rifle, a sidelock with the nipple located to deliver fire from a musket cap directly into the breech of the rifle. The Thunder™ Magnum 50-caliber rifle is designed to take as many as three 50/50 Pyrodex Pellets for a total of 150 grains volume, with tests proving that sure ignition and full power with pellets are achieved.

After Shooting

Touched on above, Hodgdon Powder Co. never suggested that Pyrodex was non-corrosive. To the contrary, the company always recommended cleaning guns thoroughly after shooting. Conversely, the tale about Pyrodex etching bores (eating into the metal) is entirely false. Careful testing of this unsubstantiated notion revealed that neither blackpowder nor Pyrodex "ate up" gun barrels with proper cleaning after shooting. The results of this study are included in a section on Corrosion Tests. Standard cleaning procedures work perfectly with Pyrodex, including the water method, solvent-only method, or combination of water and solvent, as explained in the chapter on maintenance.

Prepping the Bore

Also called dressing or fouling the bore, the concept is not new, the goal being to maintain a blackpowder bore in as stable a condition as possible. The first shot fired on the range from a squeaky-clean bore is followed by consecutive shots from a fouled bore. Precisely the same results at the target cannot be expected when the bore differed between the first and consequent shots. Therefore, while cleaning between shots for a reasonable number of firings is not necessary with Pyrodex, and can actually raise standard deviations (precise velocities from one shot to the next), dressing the bore is wise for a target match. It is unnecessary for hunting, where group size is not as vital to success. The hunter should dry the bore of his gun completely before loading, but he need not fire a fouling shot. While older advice included firing four shots with Pyrodex to completely dress the bore, that rule has been altered. Shooting one time is normally sufficient. After continued firing, the bore should be swabbed clean, and then one more fouling shot fired before any attempt to create a tight group on a target. Before going for score, a single prep shot is also useful in clearing lingering oil, grease, or lube. Reminder: Ensure after firing a shot to dress the bore that the nipple vent is clear of cap debris. This is easily accomplished by poking with a nipple pick or pipe cleaner.

RS, RS Select, and P

Just as blackpowder comes in granulation sizes, normally designated by Fg numbers, such as FFg, Pyrodex also has differently sized kernels. The company dropped CTG, which stood for Cartridge. In spite of its popularity with blackpowder cartridge shooters, CTG — its kernel size larger than RS and advertised as an Fg replacement — was not a big seller. Furthermore, Hodgdon felt that RS worked so well in the blackpowder cartridge that CTG was not necessary.

RS stands for Rifle/Shotgun. It's the workhorse of the line, considered a substitute for FFg granulation in

Pyrodex P is billed as the FFFg equivalent and is used in the same volume, not weight, as FFFg. It is not, as some seem to believe, an FFFFg type of powder. While it does yield higher pressure per volume compared with RS or FFg, it is not dangerous in rifles when used in the proper amount.

blackpowder and excellent in all bore sizes from 32 to over 60 caliber. It also works admirably in blackpowder shotguns of all gauges, as well as blackpowder cartridges of all sizes.

RS Select Premium Muzzleloading Propellant, billed as "Specially Processed and Tested," is represented as a special RS, offering superb kernel-size uniformity. It was originally intended as a powder ideal for target shooting, where ultimate groups were important, but since has earned its way into the hunting field as well. Today, RS and RS Select have the largest kernel size in Pyrodex.

P stands for Pistol. It's considered a substitute for FFFg blackpowder, and is employed the same way. As the finest granulation of Pyrodex, it works well in cap 'n' ball revolvers and pistols, in keeping with its P title. But P is also very much at home in smallbore rifles, such as the 32 or 36, where it develops good velocity with small charges. It's also workable in larger-bore rifles for light practice or plinking loads.

Volumetric Loading with Pyrodex

Correctly loaded muzzleloaders always have 100 percent load density because the latter part of the bore becomes the breech of the gun. This section of the barrel can be thought of as doing the same job as a cartridge case: the reservoir for the powder charge. After seating a projectile fully upon a powder charge down in the breech of the muzzleloader, there is no air space left between that bullet and the charge, which is 100 percent load density. The same situation exists with blackpowder cartridges when they are loaded with a full case of propellant. Pyrodex must be loaded at 100 percent load density in the muzzleloader: zero air space between missile and charge. Likewise for blackpowder cartridge guns, where best accuracy is achieved when Pyrodex is treated to 100 percent load density (no air space in the case). When lighter loads are desired, air space in the blackpowder case

Pyrodex RS Select is an FFg equivalent when used in equal volumetric charges, not by weight. It is different from standard RS in performance, as proved by chronograph tests.

should be taken up with fillers or wads. After shooting, blackpowder cases employing Pyrodex must be cleaned, starting with soapy water, but finishing with a good workout in a tumbler, or at the least polishing the interior of the case with solvent and cotton swabs, drying cases completely before reloading.

Along with 100 percent load density, Pyrodex is always matched volume-for-volume with blackpowder, not weighed out to create a charge. This is so simple and effective that weighing would not only be incorrect, creating a charge greater than called for, but also useless in bettering accuracy. Since Pyrodex is indeed a blackpowder substitute, it should be loaded as such, meaning volumetric charges only. Careful range tests with charges weighed on a powder/bullet scale to a tenth of a grain (weighing 70.5 grains exactly for a 100-grains volume load) provided zero improvement in groups, nor did they improve upon standard deviation figures on the chronograph. The same adjustable powder measure or charger used for blackpowder is therefore the proper tool for throwing charges with Pyrodex.

Energy Yield

While Pyrodex shows 30 percent less density than blackpowder — 70.5 grains weight of RS when the powder measure is set for 100 grains volume — energy yield is at least on par with blackpowder. The latest tests with current formulations of Pyrodex prove this. For example, a 32-caliber squirrel rifle with 26-inch barrel achieved 2,072 fps with 40 grains volume GOEX FFFg black powder. The same rifle firing the same 45-grain round ball showed 2,039 fps with 40 grains volume Pyrodex P, virtually identical results.

A 50-caliber test rifle with a conical projectile (a 350-grain Buffalo Bullet), using 100 grains volume of GOEX FFg, showed a muzzle velocity of 1,440 fps, while Pyrodex RS got 1,480 fps.

A 54-caliber, 430-grain Thompson/Center Maxi bullet propelled by 100 grains volume charge of GOEX FFg produced 1,390 fps. The same 100-grain volumetric charge of RS (70.5 grains weight)

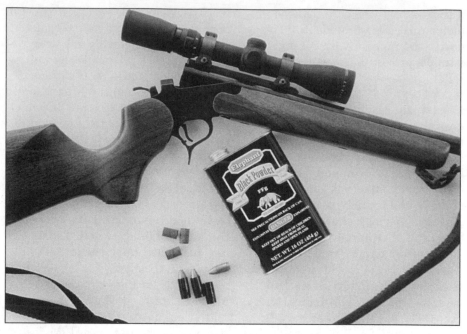

This Thompson/Center Encore 50-caliber rifle is allowed three 50/50 Pyrodex Pellets for a total charge of 150 grains volume.

fired the 430-grain bullet at 1,384 fps, statistically the same performance when both powders are loaded volume for volume.

Pressures

As with blackpowder, overloads with Pyrodex can be dangerous. Again, maximum charges as dictated by the gun manufacturer must be adhered to rigidly and without alteration. Pyrodex also obeys the

Law of Diminishing Returns: Adding powder beyond a certain level produces no worthwhile increase in velocity. Also, overloads may cause subtle damage in a firearm that can become apparent later.

Flintlocks

Today's formulation of Pyrodex works better than older examples, but most shooters of an old-time sparkmaker prefer staying with standard blackpowder, employing FFFFg for the ignition flash. This is a case of trial and error. Flintlock shooters interested in shooting Pyrodex are invited to test their personal firearms with Pyrodex at the range.

Ignition

The No. 11 percussion cap remains highly popular with muzzleloader shooters because it works extremely well. However, muzzleloader ignition today is not what it used to be. The No. 209 shotgun primer is popular because it provides a terrific flame for sure ignition. So does the "big top hat," known as the English musket cap, which is sometimes referred to as the U.S. musket cap. Tests with a

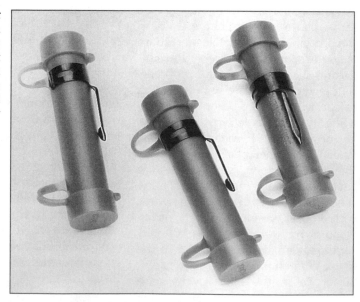

The Pyrodex Pellet has been so widely accepted that there are even speedloaders intended expressly for their use.

Markesbery Outer-Line® muzzleloader with No. 11 CCI caps provided 100 percent ignition with both Pyrodex RS and the Pyrodex Pellet under dry range conditions. In damp weather, the 400 SRP insert was installed in place of the standard nipple and small rifle primers were used in the Markesbery loaded with Pyrodex. Results were good.

Pyrodex Lube

Pyrodex is compatible with standard lubrications on the market, as well as solvents. However, the Hodgdon Powder Co. has developed a special product. It's called Pyrodex Lube and billed as a "patch or bullet lube and cleaner; all natural, biodegradable, environmentally safe." The back of the can bears instructions for use of this special lube. There is also the Pyrodex Patch containing this special lube.

The Pyrodex Pellet

The package arrived in good shape. I kept my promise, tucking it away in the gun safe for future unveiling. Some time later, Dean Barrett, vice president of the Hodgdon Powder Co., showed up at my Wyoming home. We sat at the dining room table with the mysterious unopened package resting between us. "Go ahead and open it," Barrett said. I did. And there they were: Pyrodex Pellets. While they had been laboratory tested extensively, no one had fired them in everyday rifles under everyday conditions. For the next three days, Barrett

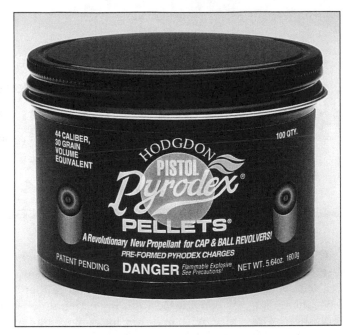

Pyrodex Pellets are offered in several different volumetric values and calibers. For example, this one is 44-caliber, each pellet equivalent to 30 grains volume.

and I did just that. At the conclusion of the visit, I had but one thing to tell the visiting inventor about his Pyrodex Pellet: "You have a winner." In the forthcoming comparison of various muzzleloader propellants, the pellet compares well with other fuels for front loaders. It is here to stay. Initially, the pellet came only as a 50/50, meaning it was sized for a 50-caliber muzzleloader and each pellet was valued at 50-grains volume equivalent Pyrodex RS charge per pellet. Shooters soon demanded a 54-caliber Pellet, which came along as a 60-grain volumetric equivalent charge per pellet named the 54/60: 54 caliber, 60 grains volume equivalent with Pyrodex RS. A 50/30 followed: 50 caliber once again, but 30 grains volume equivalent with Pyrodex RS, ideal for juggling with the 50/50. For example, an 80-grain volumetric charge could be gained with one 50/50 Pellet and one 50/30 Pellet. Pellets for the cap 'n' ball revolver are also available, with, inevitably, more pellets of various caliber/charge combinations on the way.

Pyrodex is a replica blackpowder, as well as a unique propellant on its own. It makes smoke for those who like the old-time flavor of shooting muzzleloaders, which is almost all of us, and it serves well in blackpowder cartridge guns as well as muzzleloaders. The Pyrodex Pellet is in keeping with the high-powered trend created by the modern muzzleloader.

Chapter 16

THE AMAZING LEAD SPHERE

AMAZING BECAUSE the lead sphere works when it shouldn't. The round ball is called round because it is, and ball because it's a bullet, hence "spherical bullet." The term is entirely accurate, because there can also be a conical ball, and in military terms, ball ammunition means a jacketed bullet, ball standing for bullet. But aerodynamically, what could be worse than a round lead ball? Only some sort of disk. There is sectional density to consider, along with ballistic coefficient. Sectional density is the ratio of a bullet expressed in pounds to the square of its diameter. The result is a number expressed in fractions of an inch. Ballistic coefficient incorporates sectional density in its formula as the ratio of the bullet's sectional density to its coef-

ficient of form, also expressed as a number. For our sandlot purposes, a bullet that is "long for its caliber" is considered high in sectional density, with one that looks more like a rocket than a basketball assigned a high ballistic coefficient, abbreviated simply to "C." The round ball is terrible on both counts. Since ballistic coefficient includes sectional density, that figure only is given in these comparisons from *Lyman's Black Powder Handbook*:

45 Caliber Round Ball (.445-inch)
— Ballistic Coefficient = .063
50 Caliber Round Ball (.495-inch)
— Ballistic Coefficient = .070
54 Caliber Round Ball (.535-inch)
— Ballistic Coefficient = .075
45 Caliber Minie No. 445369
— Ballistic Coefficient = .151
50 Caliber Maxi No. 504617

— Ballistic Coefficient = .095
54 Caliber Minie No. 533476
— Ballistic Coefficient = .137

All these C figures are very low, including those belonging to conicals, especially when compared with modern bullets of spire point or spitzer profile, such as Hornady's racy 162-grain 7mm Boat Tail Spire Point with a C of .514. The round ball, especially, falls on its face by comparison. Because of a low C, even for standard conicals, bullet makers came up with shapely muzzleloader bullets represented by spitzers, such as Buffalo Bullet Co.'s SSB and Northern Precision's jacketed missiles. Each of these compares favorably with modern projectiles of similar caliber and weight, with high ballistic coefficient ratings. Lyman's 40- and

Swaged round balls are extremely uniform, as these from Hornady prove when weighed on a powder/bullet scale.

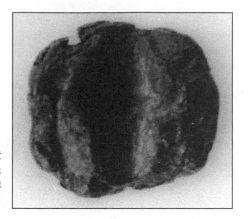

The lead sphere is amazing in what it can actually get done in the field, considering how poorly it shows on paper. The flattened lead ball on the right was taken from a big game animal—another one-shot affair.

45-caliber LRHP (Long Range High Performance) bullets for 40-65 Winchester and 45-70 silhouette shooters are examples of blackpowder cartridge bullets styled for longer-range shooting. Of course, pointed bullets shoot flatter than round balls, as well as popular blackpowder conicals, although the latter are so extremely effective that some hunters prefer flat-nosed lead bullets over pointed ones for big game. But that's another story.

Downrange

As the round ball grows in caliber, it improves its downrange effectiveness because of increased mass. However, even the fine 54-caliber lead pill that starts out at close to 2,000 fps loses more than 40 percent of its original velocity at 100 yards. A 54-caliber, 460-grain lead Buffalo Bullet sheds less that 25 percent of its starting velocity at the same distance. Woe to the smaller lead balls, such as the .350-inch size. Fired from a 36-caliber squirrel rifle at a muzzle velocity of more than 2,000 fps, this little ball is chugging along at less than 1,000 feet per second at 100 yards, with an energy rating of under 145 foot-pounds (although that's plenty for small game).

Bullets with a higher C rating, such as the pointed muzzleloader missiles of the hour, may lose about 15 percent of their initial speed out to 100 yards. All of this translates to sighting in 3 inches high at 100 yards and actually having a 200-yard-plus muzzleloader

requiring no holdover whatsoever on a deer-sized animal at the 200-yard mark. While this fact consternates certain game-management people, as well as traditional black-powder fans, it remains a reality all the same.

Penetration

On paper, the simple lead ball has no more chance of penetrating into the vital zones of a big game animal than a snowball has of a long life in the Sahara Desert. Now comes that word again — amazing — because round balls of larger caliber continue to shoot sufficiently flat to ensure chest cavity strikes at 100 to 125 yards. Moreover, they penetrate far better than they should. When a 54-caliber round ball was located on the off-side of a bull elk, I marveled. When another .535-inch round ball managed to travel the full breadth of a bull bison's chest, I took off my hat and scratched my head. How could it do that? But it did. The right way to hunt with a round ball is to get close. At close range, there is little it won't do. Make it large enough, and it'll put an elephant down, which is exactly what big lead balls accomplished in the hands of Africa's ivory hunters in the 19th century. Major Shakespear, author of *Wild Sports in India*, and mentioned again below, said of the round ball: "I have Minie bullet-moulds for my rifles, but so long as the spherical bullets go through and through large game, I do not see the use of running the risk of shaking the stock of the gun, and of extra recoil, by using heavier balls."

Round Ball Size and Weight

The round ball is the lightest projectile per caliber. Unlike the conical, it has no shank, and therefore cannot grow heavier than its circumference allows. A .490-inch lead pill, for example, can only weigh 177 grains in pure lead and no more, not ever, while a 50-caliber conical can weigh as much as it takes for the firearm's rate of twist to stabilize it. The aforementioned SSB (Special Saboted Bullet) from the Buffalo Bullet Co. weighs 375 or 435 grains, with the actual diameter .452 inches. I have on hand another true 45-caliber bullet that weighs 600 grains. Yet, a 45-caliber round ball in .440-inch diameter weighs only 128 grains. The little spitfire 32-caliber squirrel rifle, while deadly on wild turkeys and adequate for even larger quarry with placed shots, shoots a pill weighing less than 50 grains. Additionally, every round ball is smaller than the caliber of the gun that shoots it. It has less bearing surface than any other bullet, with only its sides touching the rifling, and then basically "by proxy," since the sphere itself is not engraved by the rifling. Rather it's the patch that takes up the windage (space) in the bore. It's also the patch that translates rotation from the rifling to the ball.

Round Ball Effectiveness

Let's go back to sectional density for a moment. It's worthwhile to compute a figure for a common 30-

caliber, 150-grain bullet. First divide 150 grains by 7,000 (to reduce to weight in pounds), arriving at .0214285. Now square the bullet diameter (.308-inch) for .094864. Then divide that figure into the first one for .2258865, which rounds off to .226.

Here's the payoff. A 500-grain, 45-caliber bullet, such as fired in the 45-70 Government cartridge (squat that it may appear) runs .341 for sectional density. Obviously, mass counts. Even the lowly round ball gathers strength as it increases in weight. This factor does not show that well with the kinetic energy (KE) formula used worldwide to determine power in foot-pounds of energy, but it does prove itself in the field. The reason the ball is feeble power-wise on paper is its velocity. There isn't enough of it to satisfy Newton's KE formula, especially downrange, where the lead pill loses so much velocity because of its poor ballistic coefficient rating. Blackpowder fans may curse KE, but it remains the only acceptable formula for determining delivered energy. When KE shows a 30-06 Springfield with a handloaded 180-grain bullet ahead of a well-loaded 54-caliber ball-shooting rifle, that's only because it's true, especially when downrange energy is the comparison gauge. The chronograph shows that 180-grain bullet at 2,800 fps for a muzzle energy of 3,134 foot-pounds, while the 54 pushing a 230-grain lead ball earns under 2,000 foot-pounds at the muzzle. It gets worse. At 100 yards, a 30 caliber 180-grain pointed bullet possesses about 2,700 foot-pounds of energy, while the 54 drops to under 700 foot-pounds!

Regardless of these facts, for they are facts, the silly round ball continues to claim the bacon regularly. That's because KE, while highly useful, does not tell the whole story of "killing power," nor does any other formula presented over the years. It's not possible. Mathematical figures are one thing. Action in the field is another. There are three ways to make a round ball work on big game. They are: get close, get close, and get close. At close range, the energy level, even when figured by KE, is pretty good.

Caliber is All to the Ball

While we blame gravity for raising havoc with a bullet, which it does, the atmosphere is a much greater enemy. As a projectile approaches the speed of sound, drag dramatically increases, escalating as a bullet flies faster and faster. We know that a high C rating is excellent for fighting the ravages of drag, and so the poor round ball gets knocked in the head again, because it does not enjoy a high ballistic coefficient. That's why it loses so much speed as it progresses downrange.

As touched on earlier, missile mass (best thought of simply as weight here) helps a ball overcome its inherently poor flight characteristics. High velocity would help, too, only it's not possible with muzzleloaders. Whereas 2,000 fps is considered fast for smokepoles, it's nothing compared to the 3,000- and even 4,000-fps speeds associated with high-intensity smokeless cartridges. So the only aid a round ball gets is going up in caliber.

As caliber increases, weight rises out of proportion. There's a handy formula proving this fact. It begins with computing the volume of a sphere. First, diameter is brought to the third power. The resulting figure is multiplied by .5236. That number is then multiplied times 2873.5, the weight of a cubic inch of pure lead. Computing for a 54-caliber round ball of .530-inch diameter, diameter to the third power is .148877; times .5236 (a constant) = .077952; times 2873.5 = 223.99, which rounds to 224 grains weight, the theoretical perfect weight of a .530-inch ball in pure lead.

A .535-inch round ball in pure lead weighs 230 grains. A .350-inch round ball weighs 65 grains. Double its diameter to .700 inch and weight does not double. It goes up almost eight times to 516 grains.

This formula is also valuable for testing round ball lead purity by comparing the actual weight of the cast ball against the theoretical perfect weight of that same size ball. If pure lead is used, the cast ball should match the formula right on the money. It's easy to test with a bullet/powder scale. If a .535-inch ball weighs 227 grains, it is not made of pure lead, but contains tin, antimony, or another element of lower atomic weight than lead. Of course, the true diameter of the ball is vital to this test. The best way to determine this is with a micrometer, because designated mold size may actually cast a bullet slightly smaller or larger.

Velocity and the Round Ball

While caliber is paramount to round ball performance, the low velocity trap must be bypassed. Certain old-time shooters reasoned that since the round ball loses speed so rapidly, why bother worrying about gaining good velocity in the first place? They also reasoned, and in this they were correct, that faster bullets shed more velocity proportionally than slower bullets. Beyond the speed of sound, the atmosphere does play havoc with a bullet. So why not go with smaller powder charges? The problem is, you cannot end up with something without starting out with something, and terminal velocity/energy is not improved by beginning with low velocity/energy. A faster round ball has advantages over a slower one. It does have more energy, and penetration requires energy. It also shoots flatter, making hits, even at only 100 yards, more certain.

Why Pure Lead?

The word "pure" associated with lead means, in reality, "almost pure." It's nearly impossible to come off with lead that is 100 percent free of any other metal. The chapter on bullet casting discusses how to render lead as pure as possible with equipment normally used by bullet casters. Pure lead is ideal for three important reasons. First, a round ball of pure lead will be at its heaviest, heavier than one containing other elements. Second, pure lead obturates in the bore better than a harder substance, and while the round ball does not make full contact with the rifling, it remains important that it fill out against the patch as much as possible for best guidance in the bore. Recall that a bullet at rest is predisposed to remain at rest, because of inertia, so when it's smacked with pressure from an ignited powder charge, it tends to foreshorten a little. Third, pure lead enjoys high molecular cohesion. In other words, it stays together, rather than fragmenting, and this becomes important to penetration in a big game animal, as pure lead balls make long wound channels.

Pure lead can be obtained. Lead can also be purified by the bullet caster. Another way to ensure pure lead round balls is by buying them. Speer, Hornady, and Buffalo Bullet Co. all start out with the purest lead available. This is easily proved again with a bullet scale by weighing a commercial round ball. Using the formula for the weight of a ball in pure lead, it's a simple matter of matching up. A Speer .535-inch round ball weighed on an RCBS electronic scale was 230 grains — right on the nose.

Choosing the Right Ball

Matching the gun to the game has been a common-sense approach since the Pilgrims waded ashore a couple hundred years ago. Likewise is matching bullets to game. While larger round balls always have more energy-retention capability over smaller ones, they are not appropriate for all shooting. Round balls in 32 and 36 caliber, for example, are right for small game such as wild turkeys, up to javelina-sized animals, with perfect bullet placement. Furthermore, economy is much in favor of small round balls for the obvious reason of lead con-

servation alone. It's possible to shoot the 32-squirrel rifle, for example, cheaper than the 22 rimfire, especially when caps are formed, using metal from beverage cans, with the Forster Tap-O-Cap tool. For just about everything else, there are the 50s and 54s. That includes rendezvous games, where larger lead pills usually have the advantage, be it a long-range game of hitting the gong or a short-range contest of striking the cutting edge of an ax to split the ball in two so it will hit double targets.

Round Ball Performance by Caliber

32-Caliber Round Ball

Weighing 45 grains in .310-inch diameter, this little pill can achieve more than 2,000 fps at the muzzle. Properly loaded, it'll drop the biggest gobbler in the woods with one shot, and without destroying too much white meat. It will also put cottontails, squirrels, and varmints in the bag at ranges up to 100 yards or so. As already noted, it's cheap to shoot. Only 10 grains of FFFg blackpowder drives the little 32 round ball at 22 Long Rifle muzzle velocity.

36-Caliber Round Ball

Weighing 65 grains in .350-inch diameter, the 36 lends a tad more confidence to the wild turkey hunter,

while also performing a bit better on larger varmints downrange. For rabbits and squirrels, both taken normally at close range, the 36 has nothing on the 32, and it does cost a little more to shoot. While the 32 gains 22 Long Rifle velocity with 10 grains of FFFg for 700 shots per pound of powder, it takes 15 grains of the same fuel to launch the 36 at about the same speed.

40-Caliber Round Ball

Game department personnel, having to come up with a minimum caliber for big game, often seized on the 40 as allowable. It probably sounded pretty large to shooters who considered 30 caliber as a big bore. The 40-caliber ball is fine for target shooting, but it only weighs 93 grains in .395-inch diameter, which is larger than necessary for small game and not heavy enough for big game (in spite of the tons of venison the little pill no doubt has taken over the ages). Rifles bored for the 40-caliber round ball are mild shooting and accurate, but ballistic facts put the 40 in a middle zone, as its lack of popularity shows. A 40-caliber Muskrat rifle with 36-inch barrel fired a .395-inch, 93-grain round ball at 1,993 fps with 50 grains volume FFFg blackpowder for a muzzle energy of 820 footpounds. At 100 yards, energy dropped to only 214 foot-pounds.

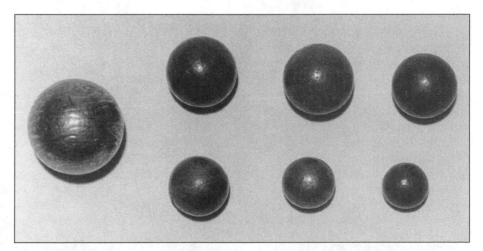

Size is all to the round ball, from the little 32-caliber round ball at the lower right, to the 75-caliber ball on the far left, going in weights from 45 grains to almost 500 grains.

45-Caliber Round Ball

Those who have had an opportunity to study numerous original Kentucky/Pennsylvania long rifles find that 45 caliber was highly popular in the Golden Age of American Firearms. Today, however, the 45-caliber round ball is leagues behind the 50 and 54 in popularity. A .445-inch round ball weighs 133 grains. Even when pushed at 2,000 fps muzzle velocity, remaining energy at 100 yards is only a little more than 300 foot-pounds.

50-Caliber Round Ball

A 50-caliber, .490-inch round ball weighs 177 grains in pure lead. Kicked off at almost 2,000 fps, muzzle energy is around 1,500 foot-pounds, with close to 500 foot-pounds remaining at 100 yards. The 50 is perfectly adequate for deer-sized game and it has dropped many elk and even moose from the guns of hunters willing to stalk close for that one perfect shot.

54-Caliber Round Ball

A 54-caliber round ball weighs 230 grains in .535-inch diameter. From my own Mulford No. 47 rifle, this lead globe leaves the bore at 1,970 fps, chronographed at that speed many times with a good dose of Pyrodex RS or FFg blackpowder. This puts muzzle energy very close to a ton, with retained energy of about 675 foot-pounds at 100 yards. The hunter willing to get close can rest assured of good performance on big game, including elk and moose with the 54 ball. The 54 produces good velocity with reasonable powder charges, while larger round balls require heavy doses of fuel to achieve decent muzzle velocities.

58-Caliber and Larger

There is no doubt that caliber 58 and larger round balls are deadly. Very large round balls put elephants down in Africa and Ceylon with regularity.

The simple ball of lead really works, with diameter determining its effectiveness. This point is well illustrated with a formula.

Let's pit a 50-caliber ball against a 60-caliber ball. We will use .500- and .600-inch diameter, respectively, to simplify the math. First cube each ball: The 50-caliber ball is .125, while the 60-caliber ball is .216. Now, divide .216 by .125 and the result is 1.728, rounded to 1.73. Theory holds that the 60-caliber ball has the potential of gaining 1.73 times the energy of a 50-caliber ball. This is not a law. It's only a game, but it does have some degree of application.

Suppose both 50- and 60-caliber balls are fired at 2,000 fps muzzle velocity. The result is 2,877 foot-pounds of energy for the 60-caliber ball, which weighs 325 grains in pure lead, and 1,670 foot-pounds for the 50-caliber ball, which weighs 188 grains in pure lead. To prove the mathematical point, multiply 1,670 (the energy of the 50-caliber ball) by 1.73, which should provide the energy of the 60-caliber ball if the latter is truly 1.73 times more potent. The figure is 2,889, only 2 foot-pounds from the actual energy rating of 2,887 foot-pounds. This shows that the potential kinetic energy of the 60-caliber ball, which is only .10-inch greater in diameter than the 50-caliber, is about 1.73 times superior. But recall that it takes a lot of fuel to drive a big ball fast, so the 2,000 fps rating given both 50- and 60-caliber round balls above is more theory than practice. In one chronograph test, a 62-caliber round ball achieved only 1,600 fps at the muzzle with a very large powder charge.

Great blackpowder whitetail hunts take place over much of the USA and Canada. Dallas Hudson got this excellent whitetail buck, scoring just under 140 Boone & Crockett points, in Iowa with his 54-caliber Pennsylvania style rifle that he built himself. One round ball in front of 100 grains volume FFg blackpowder took the buck at 35 yards.

Regardless of this, bigger is ballistically stronger when it comes to round balls, as Major Shakespear, Captain Forsyth, and Sir Samuel Baker, three British hunters of the 19th century, knew. All three proved their belief on very large game. Baker, known for his exploration of the Nile and elephant hunting in Ceylon, had this to say about the round ball, even for pachyderms:

"I strongly vote against conical balls for dangerous game; they make too neat a wound, and are very apt to glance on striking a bone. . . . In giving an opinion against conical balls for dangerous game, I do so from practical proofs of their inferiority. I had at one time a two-groove single rifle, weighing 21 lbs., carrying a 3 oz. belted ball, with a charge of 12 drachms powder. This was a kind of "devil stopper," and never failed in flooring a charging elephant, although, if not struck in the brain, he might recover his legs. I had a conical mould made for this rifle, the ball of which weighed 4 oz., but instead of rendering it more invincible, it entirely destroyed its efficacy, and brought me into such scrapes that I at length gave up the conical ball as useless."

Baker stayed with his convictions. He continued hunting with the round ball, especially in 19th-century Ceylon, even for elephants and water buffalo. He was known to shoot the latter from ranges of 300 yards or more with the round ball. How could the lead sphere be so effective at long range, especially on such heavy animals? Ball size was the answer. Baker's rifles were truly big bores — beyond what we consider big bore. His 12-bore guns, meaning twelve round balls to make a pound, were his small bores. He relied on 4-bore for bigger animals, four rounds to the pound, with each round weighing 1750 grains. Today, we think of the 458 Winchester as an elephant cartridge, which it is, but this big boy normally drives a bullet of "only" 500 grains weight. The old-time hunter of dangerous game realized that the only way his blackpowder rifles were going to make the grade was going to big bores shooting heavy projectiles. Even then, however, powder charges were not ignored. Big bores of the old-timers swallowed a great deal of propellant.

October Country, well-known for superb blackpowder accouterments, especially its high quality leather goods, has come up with a few guns designed to please traditionalists. Along with a Northwest Trade Gun, flintlock 20 gauge, and a J.P. Henry 54-caliber rifle, is the Great America Sporting Rifle in 69 caliber. This gun is billed as "the most powerful traditional muzzleloader rifle manufactured today." The rifle is built along the lines suggested by Capt. James Forsyth, a lieutenant when he authored his well-received book, *The Sporting Rifle and Its Projectiles*, in the 19th century. Rifling twist is 1:104, which is very slow and strictly intended for the round ball. The barrel is 1 1/4 inches across the flats at the octagonal portion and 1 1/8 inches across at the round muzzle end. It has a five-step, adjustable rear sight and fires its big round ball at 1,700 fps for a muzzle energy of more than 3,000 foot-pounds.

The Wind and the Round Ball

Bullets drift in two ways. There's drift associated with rifling twist. Right-hand twist barrels drift bullets a little to the right, left-hand twist sends them a little to the left. Then there is the wind, which plays a much larger role in moving a bullet off its path. Two major factors are at work here: the shape of the projectile and its velocity. First, spitzer and spire-point bullets slow down less rapidly than blunt-nosed bullets, which is extremely important to the second factor: time of flight. The round ball suffers on both counts. Its shape is hardly the best for retaining initial velocity, so it takes longer to fly from muzzle to target, which gives the wind more time to push on it. While bullet mass (momentum) is very important to sustaining velocity, bullet speed has a surprising effect on wind drift. This is easily proved by comparing a 220 Swift with its little 50-grain bullet against a 45-70 with a 500-grain bullet. The Swift's bullet at 4,000 fps muzzle velocity drifts 8 1/2 inches at 200 yards in a 20-mph crosswind. In the same wind, the big 500-grain bullet at 1,300 fps muzzle velocity goes off course by more than 2 feet at 200 yards. Round balls really suffer in the wind, especially the smaller ones when the wind hums at around 30 mph, as it can do on the plains. In such a wind, a 65-grain, 36-caliber round ball starting at around 1,800 fps muzzle velocity would drift by about 4 feet — not at 200, but at only 100 yards. Even if the crosswind dropped to a mild 10 mph, the little pill would drift off course by a foot.

A bigger ball is a little bit better. Using the same 1,800 fps starting speed for comparison with the 36-caliber ball, a 30-mph crosswind would move a 230-grain, .535-inch round ball two feet off course at 100 yards in a 30-mph wind. That mild 10-mph breeze shoves the 54 all over by about 10 inches at 100 yards. It takes a lot of practice to shoot the round ball effectively in the wind.

Brush Busting

Over the years, bullets designed to buck the brush pleased hunters to no end. The only problem was the fact that they didn't work. Flat-nosed bullets get bullied aside by brush. So do round-nose missiles. Even with the hardy 458 Winchester poking a 500-grain round nose bullet into the brush is inviting deflection. In one demonstration, firing a 270 Winchester with 130-grain bullet and a 45-70 with a 405-grain bullet, the 270's bullets reached the target more frequently than the 45-70's. Round balls fired through the same screen of brush found an even harder time getting to the target. In short, no bullet bucks the brush like a bulldozer, while round balls are especially poor.

Long Range with Round Balls

S.W. Baker was an honest man. Even if he were not, his claims for long-range hits on big game with round-ball rifles stand, because he did not always hunt alone. He hit water buffalo in Ceylon out to 300 yards, according to reports. Baker was highly practiced, shooting at more animals in a week than the average North American hunter would in several seasons. He also had some miserable failures in long-range gunning, in spite of huge lumps of lead fired from the tunnel-like muzzles of his big-bore rifles. Shooting far with blackpowder is done all the time, especially on silhouettes at ranges of 1,000 yards or more. However, hunting is another matter. The hunter owes it to his game to make clean kills, and when muzzleloader hunting, that means getting close. A 100-yard shot is normally plenty far. The mountain man, because of familiarity with his plains rifle, probably made some 200-yard shots. Joe Rose was applauded for dropping a buck antelope at rendezvous at the paced-off distance of 125 paces. The archaic pace was 2 yards, not 1. A step was 1 yard, with two steps equaling one pace. Mountain man Joe Rose may have dropped the buck at 200 yards. No one will ever know. What we do know is that 200 yards is too far to shoot at game with a round ball.

Trajectory

The reason I limit myself to 125 yards with the round ball on deer-sized game, and consider 75 yards far enough for elk, is the practical trajectory of the round ball (as well as conicals traveling in the 1,500 fps-arena). The conical hangs on to its starting velocity considerably better than the round ball. The conical starts at 1,500 fps, while the ball takes off at around 2,000 fps, which puts the two on equal ground: Either will drop a half-foot below line of sight at 125 yards when sighted in for 75 yards. Even when sighted dead on at 100 yards, both drop a few inches at 125. Magnum muzzleloaders of the day have extended that range to 200 yards when firing conicals like the Buffalo Bullet SSB Spitzer at around 1,800 fps muzzle velocity.

It's an old story, and well-worn, but it fits the round ball so well that it bears retelling. The bumblebee cannot fly. Scientifically speaking, the little bugger has far too little wing surface to lift its carcass into the sky. But the bumblebee does not know it can't fly, so it continues buzzing all over the place. Likewise, the round ball is no good for much of anything. It's sectional density and ballistic coefficient stink. But the round ball simply doesn't know that it's no good, so it continues printing tight groups on paper, delighting shooters at rendezvous, ringing gongs 500 yards in the distance, and when properly centered and used at modest range, the old lead sphere brings home the bacon today just as it did when Dan'l Boone walked the forest floors of a new America.

Chapter 17

CONICALS FOR MUZZLELOADERS AND CARTRIDGE GUNS

IF NOT hundreds, than at least many dozens of different conicals existed in the 19th century. There may not be that many today, but that's not for lack of trying. Never does a week go by without another conical surfacing somewhere, be it for muzzleloading rifles, pistols, cap 'n' ball revolvers, or blackpowder cartridge guns.

In keeping with long-standing tradition, today's conicals are as unique as they were more than a hundred years ago. Every company seems to have its own idea concerning the best-possible elongated bullet for front loaders and blackpowder cartridge guns. Conicals are especially popular with shooters of in-line guns because they have great mass per caliber with decent sectional density and ballistic coefficient. In summary, they hit hard and shoot flat enough to make the 200-yard muzzleloader a reality, whether we like it or not, provided that the firearm is allowed big powder charges that drive bullets at good starting velocities. Most of today's blackpowder conicals fall somewhere between the round ball and modern jacketed high-profile bullets in terms of ballistic coefficient. Whereas diameter is all to the ball, that's not so for the conical. A perfect example is 45 caliber, a ball weighing perhaps 133 grains, whereas a 45-caliber conical may weigh 500 grains or

more. This factor, however, does not preclude large-caliber conicals, such as the 58, a common size for rifled muskets.

Conical Categories

Categories for blackpowder bullets include the Minies, named for the French Army Captain; Maxis, better known as Maxi-Balls, associated with the Thompson/Center Co.; what we'll call standard lead bullets; pistol bullets with sabots; all-copper conicals; high ballistic coeffient blackpowder bullets; and long-range conicals for blackpowder cartridge guns. Each type differs dramatically in design.

Capt. Minie's Conical

Imagination is important here. On the cinema screen of the mind, soldiers fight in the heat of battle, shooting blackpowder muzzleloaders as rapidly as they can reload, their guns soon fouling so badly that another missile cannot be run downbore. The answer: an undersized bullet, except for one problem — it will not engage the rifling for accuracy. The cure: Create an undersized bullet with a hollow base forming a skirt. Expanding gases from the exploded powder charge rush into the hollow base, flaring the skirt, which in turn engages the rifling in the bore. The Minie was born.

However, it may not have

belonged to the venerable French captain after all. Numerous inventors laid claim to the idea. It's not unusual, as we know from the Nobel prize each year, for inventors countries apart to come up with the same idea at about the same time. Another Frenchman, Delvigne, is sometimes credited with a hollow-base bullet before Minie. However, samples of his bullet, brought out in 1828, point to a round ball, not a conical. This undersized lead sphere rammed home readily. Imbedded in the nose was a wedge-like piece. By power-stroking the ramrod, the wedge was driven into the soft projectile, widening it out, something like pounding a wedge into the handle of an ax head to tighten it in place. The hollow-base bullet of French Army Capt. C.E. Minie shows up in the 1840s. But there's another problem. W.W. Greener, well-known gunner of his era and author of still highly regarded writings on the subject of firearms, also claims invention of a hollow-base projectile. Furthermore, the English courts are satisfied that Greener was right, for they granted him a government settlement based upon his claims. If the court could have proved that Minie was the inventor, and not Greener, it would never have laid out cash along with the glory.

The history is interesting, but not as important as the concept, for it lives on today in undersized lead

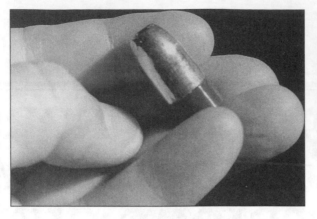

Big Bore Express started attaching plastic gas seals to bullet bases and the concept caught on. The sabot is eliminated with gas seal bases, and the bullet is close to bore size.

Here is a Minie ball, a lead bullet with a hollow base forming a skirt that flares out under pressure to create a seal.

bullets with hollow bases. Minie-type bullets worked in the American Civil War with a 500-grain, 58-caliber lead slugger, a terrible killer partially responsible for 600,000 casualties on the battlefield — and the Minie is still working today. Buffalo Bullet Co. offers a 58-caliber, 525-grain hollow-point, hollow-base bullet of pure lead. The company rightfully claims that this big slug "delivers awesome shock power." Lyman provides a number of excellent molds for hollow-base bullets as well, with a list worth noting. There's a 425-grain, 54 Minie-type bullet, along with six 58-caliber, hollow-base bullets, one called the Parker-Hale at 566 grains weight, and a 69-caliber tipping the scales at 730 grains. Hornady's Great Plains Bullet has a tapered hollow base, along with a hollow-point for expansion, and it comes in 45, 50, or 54 sizes at 285, 385, and 435 grains weight. Generally, the Minie is about a caliber undersized for easier loading, not only in a fouled bore, but in a clean one as well.

The Maxi-Ball

The Maxi-Ball functions on an entirely different principle than the Minie. Rather than a hollow base, the Maxi's base is flat. Rather than undersized, the Maxi is quite close to bore size. It is intended to engrave as it's seated, meaning the shank of the bullet is indented by the lands of the rifling. When the bullet is driven upbore as the gun is fired, it does slightly fill out at the base due to obturation. This factor is not nearly as important with the Maxi as it is with the Minie, the latter of which would be like shooting a smoothbore if not for the skirt expanding to meet the rifling.

While the Maxi is not intended for speedy reloading shot after shot, it loads quite readily in a clean to moderately fouled bore. Today's better lubes make Maxi loading easier than ever. There are numerous Maxi-type bullets available today. Buffalo Bullet Co. offers flat-based bullets in various weights per caliber to satisfy different rates of twist. Thompson/Center's Original Maxi-

Ball lineup is especially strong with pre-lubed bullets, ready to load, in calibers 45 through 58, with weights of 240 to 555 grains. I took the largest black bear of my hunting career with a 370-grain, 50-caliber Maxi-Ball that penetrated completely in the 6-foot, 7-inch-tall bruin. Lyman offers two Maxi molds, one in 45 caliber at 245 grains, the other 50 caliber at 370 grains.

Standard Lead Conical Bullet

Many pages could be filled with examples of standard lead conical bullets, because the breed has been around for a very long time. Most of these bullets are cast in home workshops with molds from numerous companies. Rapine makes good molds for standard lead conicals, as does NEI with some excellent choices. Dixie sells a Bore Rider Bullet Mold that produces a 40- or 45-caliber bullet of standard style. RCBS does, too. So does Lyman. But what is it? As the name implies, this lead bullet is exactly what we would expect to find for the 30-30 Winchester, 30-06 Springfield, 270 Winchester, and just about any other metallic cartridge. But this bullet also works great in some muzzleloaders. For example, Lyman has a Whitworth bullet mold that produces a 45-caliber, flat-nosed bullet of 475 grains made expressly for the rifle of the same name as made by Parker-Hale. These are flat-based bullets with fairly long shanks, usually with grease grooves to retain

Conicals have come in numerous styles over the years. These are but two: a boat-tail based bullet, left, for easier seating in a sabot, and a bullet that resembles the Minie, but it has a solid base.

lubrication (a few have slightly concave bases). While fired mostly in blackpowder cartridge rifles, standard conicals work in muzzleloaders as well, such as the Volunteer and Whitworth. Most standard conicals are round-nosed, with some flat-nosed, but there are spitzers, too. For example, Lyman's Spitzer Mold Blocks are offered in 40 or 45 calibers: the 40 is available in 385-grain weight, with the 45 in 480 grains.

Longer bullets in this style retain original velocity well. A 50-caliber, standard-style lead conical weighing 430 grains and starting at 1,600 fps from a muzzleloader is still doing 1,300 fps at 100 yards. That's good carry-up. A number of great standard lead bullet molds are also available for Sharps, Remington Rolling Blocks, and other single-shot blackpowder rifles that really allow these arms to reach out and touch a target at great distances.

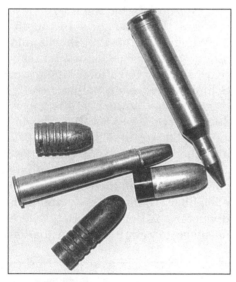

There have been many different conicals over the years. Here are just a few: on the bottom a 45-caliber bullet for the Whitworth rifled musket; to its upper right a 50-caliber Big Bore Express copper conical for the muzzleloading rifle. Just above that bullet, a jacketed projectile for the 32-40 Winchester. Above the 32-40 rests a 50-caliber lead conical for the muzzleloading rifle. At the upper right, for comparison, is a 7mm Remington Magnum loaded with a jacketed 162-grain bullet.

Pistol Bullets in Sabots

Most of these bullets were actually intended originally for big-bore revolvers in calibers 44 and 45. Jacketed hollow-points, or with exposed lead tips, along with some pure lead bullets, these missiles made sense in blackpowder rifles (and a few pistols) because they were designed to upset (mushroom) at handgun velocities. That made them extremely effective on deer-sized game when zipped out of muzzleloaders often at speeds considerably higher than cartridge revolvers attained. For example, a 44 Magnum, well-loaded, can push a 240-grain bullet out of the muzzle at 1,400 fps with a 7 1/2-inch barrel. Load that same bullet in a 50-caliber muzzleloader — a Knight MK-85, for example — and 1,700 fps is easily achieved. But how can a 44-caliber bullet fit the bore of a 50- caliber rifle? It can't. That's where the sabot — that plastic cup noted earlier — comes into play. It's the sabot that measures 50 caliber, with the smaller bullet fitting inside of it.

There are multitudes of jacketed pistol bullets offered in sabots, including a very good one from Nosler. It's called the Partition-HG™ and rather than 44 caliber, the bul-

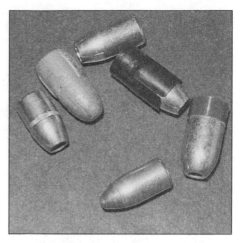

There were many different types of conicals in the 19th century, including examples with fins, like the one shown here.

let measures 45 caliber (.452-inch diameter). Weighing 260 grains, and being one of the company's famous Partition styles, the HG drops bucks in their tracks, especially from in-line magnum muzzleloaders allowed three Pyrodex 50/50 Pellets for a charge equaling 150 grains volume. The front end of the bullet opens, but penetration is ensured by the retained weight of the shank section, since the bullet cannot mushroom beyond the metal wall separating the forward portion from the back. There are dozens of differ-

The American bison is the largest animal on the North American continent, bigger than a Kodiak bear or a moose. Contrary to false notion, people are injured or killed annually by "buffalo." This old bull was dropped with one 600-grain Parker Non-Expanding bullet in South Dakota. This particular conical is known for super penetration.

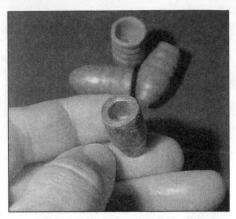

The skirt on this Minie-type lead conical is thicker for more reliable obturation in the bore of the muzzleloader, rather than flaring out widely.

ent pistol bullet/sabot combinations from a number of fine companies, such as the Thompson/Center Break-O-Way Sabot. This is a 240-grain, XTP soft-nosed bullet contained in a two-piece sabot with a "doughnut" for a base. The sabot breaks away into three parts — two halves plus the doughnut — and the bullet spins its way to the target.

Copper Conicals

The Barnes Expander-MZ Muzzleloader bullet, made of solid copper (not an alloy, with no lead whatsoever), turned out to be a big hit with hunters. All-copper bullets are not new. Germany had such bullets in the 1940s, if not earlier. Barnes came along with the all-copper bullet with a huge open nose (hollow-point) to ensure expansion, with the bullet retaining most of its original weight to enhance penetration. The bullet is loaded in sabots. It measures .451 inch. Barnes calls it "the first non-lead projectile designed specifically for use in muzzleloading rifles," designed to upset (mushroom) at impact speeds from 1,000 to 1,900 fps. In this way, the bullet would work on deer-sized game especially at close range — as often encountered from tree stands — out to normal muzzleloading distances.

Tests in Sam's Bullet Box — more about the box later — showed

the Expander-MZ retaining just about all of its original 300-grain weight at an impact velocity of 1,500 fps. Markesbery Muzzle Loaders, Inc. offers the same bullet, called the Beast Buster. There is also a T.C.P. (Total Copper Plated) bullet from the Buffalo Bullet Co., also fitted into sabots, and advertised as follows: "The T.C.P. bullet has a thin coat of copper plating to assure maximum expansion at all muzzleloader velocities."

High C Muzzleloader Bullets for Longer Ranges

Recall that C is an abbreviation for ballistic coefficient, a rating that scores a bullet's ability to buck the atmosphere. Compared with streamlined, modern jacketed bullets, blackpowder conicals always had a comparatively low C rating. As pointed out earlier, this is not always a black mark against the bullet. Hunters who stalk for close shots, or who frequent thickets and woods where chances at game at over 100 yards are rare, do not need spitzer or spire-point bullets. However, in response to a desire for longer-range shooting, spitzer-pointed bullets are on the march. Two mentioned earlier are the Buffalo Bullet Co.'s SSB (Special Saboted Bullet) and jacketed spitzer bullets from Northern Precision Co. Oddly, the C-rating of a bullet actually increases with lower velocities, because bullets at higher velocity suffer more from the ravages of the atmosphere. Sierra, therefore, gives C data with regard to velocities. For example, the company's 300-grain, 45-caliber bullet earns a ballistic coefficient of .206 for velocities of 1,900 fps and up. The same bullet has a C-rating of .211 for velocities from 1,601 to 1,899 fps, and .245 for velocities of 1,600 fps or lower.

Muzzleloader velocities for sharp-pointed bullets weighing 300 grains and up rarely exceed 1,800 fps. For example, when the 375-grain SSB was tested in a 50-caliber Thompson/Center 209/50 Mag-

num Encore with three Pyrodex Pellets equaling 150 grains volume RS, it achieved 1,800 fps. That bullet carries a C of .296, while its sister SSB at 435 grains weight goes .342. Like it or not, the 200-yard muzzleloader is here. Bullets of high-C character ensure a sight-in of 3 inches high at 100 yards for a dead-on hold at 200 yards on a deer-sized target (when the chest cavity is at least a foot square).

Long-Range Conicals for Blackpowder Cartridge Rifles

Lyman came to the fore with bullets especially designed to please blackpowder-cartridge silhouette shooters, who fire at metallic cutouts at terrific distances. The bullets were named LRHP, meaning Long Range High Performance. There are two 400-grain examples for the 40-65 Winchester and other 40-caliber blackpowder cartridges and two bullets for the 45-70 Government that also shoot in the 45-90 Winchester, 45-120 Sharps and other 45-caliber blackpowder cartridges. The 40-caliber, 400-grain Schmitzer carries a ballistic coefficient of .352, while the 40-caliber, 400-grain Snover goes .435. The 45-caliber, 500-grain Schmitzer is .372 and the 45-caliber, 535-grain Postell is .402. The 40-caliber bullets run .409-inch diameter, while the 45-caliber bullets go .459-inch diameter. All four bullets were designed to retain sufficient ballis-

Lead bullets like these have high molecular cohesion, which means they tend to stay together as a unit instead of fragmenting, which promotes penetration, even for small missiles like the 36-caliber Maxi Ball on the left.

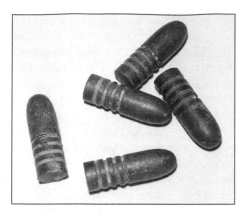

These bullets are standard conicals. They're going to see action in a 45-caliber Whitworth rifled musket muzzleloader.

tic force at long range to knock over the ram silhouette. With shoulder strikes, these long-range blackpowder cartridge bullets can be counted on to take big game cleanly.

Conical Effectiveness

A solid lead conical bullet striking the chest cavity of a deer-sized animal can whistle through without telling effect. Even though the animal may not travel far, it could still be lost. This is why bullet manufacturers have come up with hollow-point designs, which help. At closer ranges, especially from tree stands, pistol-type bullets that expand rapidly take deer cleanly and on the spot. The longer-range, all-lead bullets under the same circumstances should be directed into the scapular region of the animal, not the "boiler room." When a big lead bullet strikes this shoulder region, the animal drops like a sack of spuds. On elk, moose, and other large animals, which offer a great deal more resistance to a projectile, the big lead bullet is especially appreciated, but still does its best work when driven into the shoulder region. This strike will usually drop elk and moose in their tracks.

What They Really Shoot

Surveys of what blackpowder hunters really shoot in their big game rifles are interesting. Here are a few samples:

Black bear, 250-grain Barnes saboted bullet, 150 grains volume Pyrodex RS powder, Knight 50-caliber rifle.

Elk, 300-grain Hornady saboted bullet "charged with Pyrodex," no specific amount given, Knight 50-caliber rifle.

Whitetail buck, 355-grain conical lead bullet, 90 grains volume Pyrodex RS, Thompson/Center 50-caliber White Mountain Carbine.

Pronghorn antelope, 215-grain round ball, 90 grains GOEX FFg blackpowder, long rifle, name of rifle and exact caliber not supplied.

Whitetail buck, 300-grain Barnes bullet, two 50/50 Pyrodex Pellets (100 grains volume), Knight Disc 50-caliber rifle.

Caribou, 240-grain jacketed pistol bullet, 110 grains volume Pyrodex RS, Knight 50-caliber rifle.

Elk, 300-grain Barnes bullet, 100 grains volume Pyrodex RS, Remington Model 700ML 50-caliber muzzleloader.

Black bear, 430-grain Maxi-Ball, 90 grains volume GOEX FFg blackpowder, Thompson/Center Fire Hawk 54-caliber rifle.

Whitetail buck, 300-grain Barnes bullet, two 50/50 Pyrodex Pellets (100 grains volume), CVA FireBolt rifle.

Musk ox, 325-grain Barnes bullet, 110 grains volume Pyrodex RS Select, 54-caliber Knight Predator rifle.

Whitetail buck, 250-grain Nosler, three Pyrodex 50/50 Pellets (150 grains volume), Thompson/Center Encore 50-caliber rifle.

Whitetail buck, 240-grain Sierra hollow-point bullet in sabot, two Pyrodex 50/50 Pellets (100 grains volume), Markesbery 50-caliber rifle.

Black bear, 435-grain T/C Maxi Hunter bullet, 80 grains volume Pyrodex RS, T/C Scout 50-caliber rifle.

Whitetail buck, 300-grain Barnes bullet, 120 grains GOEX FFg blackpowder, Markesbery 50-caliber rifle.

Grizzly, 325-grain Barnes bullet, 110 grains Pyrodex RS, Remington Model 700 ML 50-caliber rifle.

Black bear, 385-grain Remington lead conical, 110 grains Pyrodex RS, Remington Model 700 ML 50-caliber rifle.

Whitetail buck, 370-grain Maxi-Ball, 90 grains volume GOEX FFg blackpowder, T/C 50-caliber Hawken rifle.

Obviously, the 50 caliber is far-and-away king with the above hunters, with a couple 54s in the group. Only one hunter reported using a patched round ball, another finger pointing to an obvious trend toward conicals for blackpowder hunting. In-line modern muzzleloaders prevailed.

How Far was Far?

The buffalo hunters of the 19th century were known for long-range shooting. Chances are good that

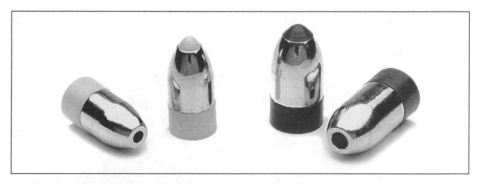

Conicals for muzzleloaders changed dramatically over the years, from bullets of the Minie type to jacketed projectiles like these shown here from CVA, the company's PowerBelt™ Bullet with AeroTip™ and hollow-point. A polymer tip covers the hollow-point cavity. No sabot is required. The snap-on base creates the seal.

There is nothing new about sabots. They were around in the distant past, and are still with us. They have even been used with centerfire cartridges like this 30-30. Remington Accelerator like this used a sabot around a smaller caliber bullet, in this case a 22-caliber missile fired from a 30-caliber bore.

these reports are accurate. They had the rifles, and the conical bullets, to do the job. Their rifles were mainly single-shot Sharps and Remingtons chambered for various blackpowder cartridges. While the 45-120 Sharps is often named the favorite of these "buffalo runners," as they were called, that seems improbable in light of the fact that the 45-120 did not gain popularity until the end of the bison-shooting era. The standard lead bullet, according to the definition laid down in this chapter, was most likely the missile of choice among these hunters. Such bullets had pretty good ballistic coefficients, and were capable of good penetration on this largest quadruped in North America, which is bigger than a moose and much heavier

The SSB from Buffalo Bullet Co. is a conical with Spitzer profile and hollow point—made of pure lead. It fits into a sabot.

than an elk. How far did the buff runners shoot at shaggies? Very far, we think, because bison are dangerous beasts, as proven by the records. Teddy Roosevelt lost a hunting partner when a big bull turned on horse and rider, lifting both into the air, a horn penetrating the hunter's thigh. Considering that many of their rifles were scoped, and that these shooters had lots of practice, a range of 300 yards or more is not far-fetched.

Wind Drift

We know that the wind drifts a round ball way off course. The blackpowder conical is also prone to wind drift as all bullets are, no matter the caliber, shape or starting velocity. It's surprising, however, to find how badly most blackpowder conicals do in the wind. Partly, this is due to time of flight. The fastest conicals leave the muzzle at something in the area of 2,200 fps. Most start out slower by a good margin. The wind, therefore, has more time to act upon the missile than a super-speed bullet. Maxi-Balls and Minies don't drift as far off the path as round balls, but the difference is minimal. A 50-caliber, .490-inch round ball starting at 2,000 fps muzzle velocity is pushed aside 18 inches in 100 yards by a 20-mph crosswind. A 50-caliber Maxi-Ball beginning its journey at 1,500 fps drifts about 16 inches off the line of sight at the same distance in the same wind.

Higher ballistic coefficient (C) bullets fare much better. A 435-grain Special Saboted Bullet of .342 C drifts a third as badly as the Maxi-Ball in a 20-mph crosswind. Lyman's 45-Caliber Postell at .402 moves sideways even less. All shooters have to learn how to "dope the wind" if they expect to put bullets in the black. This means guesswork, especially in the hunting field, but with practice and experience, shooters can get pretty good at figuring how far to hold off target so the bullet drifts back into the line of sight. At the shooting range, wind flags help by showing direction and to some degree speed. A flag standing directly out sideways suggests a wind in, roughly, the 30-mph zone.

Conicals and Pressure

There's nothing tricky about figuring the maximum load for any conical blackpowder projectile. It is the maximum powder charge with that bullet allowed by the maker of the firearm. If a shooter has the least doubt about a maximum charge with a specific conical, he must contact the gun manufacturer, which is a simple matter of dialing a phone, sending a fax, or calling up an e-mail address. More on pressure coming up next.

Powders and Conicals

Dedicated blackpowder cartridge shooters lean toward larger-granulation powders. Whether it has been clearly proven that larger kernels make for better accuracy is open to question. Swiss Black Powder, distributed by Petro-Explo (see list of websites for home page) is offered in a 1 1/2Gg Schuetzen granulation that works well in blackpowder cartridges, while some silhouette shooters like Fg for long-range work with single-shot blackpwoder rifles. Across the board, however, FFg and RS granulations are by far the most popular in 50-caliber muzzleloaders designed to shoot conical bullets. As for conicals raising pressures compared with round balls, *Lyman's Black Powder Handbook*, Second Edition, deals with this in its

The use of jacketed conical bullets came upon the blackpowder scene with modern muzzleloaders. Because they were designed to open up reliably at handgun velocities, these bullets did quite well at blackpowder rifle ranges. This is a PTX Power Tip Express Sabot from Thompson/Center. It employs a polycarbonate tip to facilitate expansion.

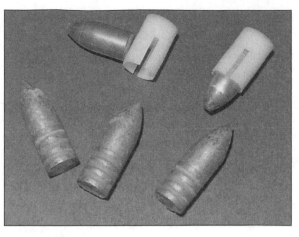

Bullets of higher ballistic coefficient are now available for muzzleloaders and blackpowder cartridge guns. The Northern Precision Spitzers, above, and Lyman LRHP bullets are good examples.

numerous pressure-tested readings. For example, a 50-caliber round ball in front of 120 grains volume GOEX FFg black powder generates 11,500 PSI pressure with a .490-inch round ball and 1:60 rate of twist. However, a 50-caliber, 385-grain lead conical shows a pressure of 19,700 PSI from a 1:32 twist bore, with the same powder brand, granulation, and charge. There is more pressure for the conical in this specific test, but both loads are safe, which is the important factor.

Twist and Conicals

Simply stated, round balls require very little RPS (revolutions per second) to keep them spinning on their axes, while conicals demand more RPS for stabilization. This situation is well taken care of by arms manufac-

There is no end in sight for blackpowder conicals, including solid copper bullets in sabots, like these.

turers who learned (it took a while) that the 1:48 rate of twist was not perfect for every muzzleloader in the world just because Sam and Jake Hawken made rifles that way in the 19th century. Testing for conical bullet stabilization is easy. Shoot at a paper target, preferably set up at 150 to 200 yards. Group size does not matter as long as there are some holes in the target. If all of the holes are round, the conical has been stabilized. If any of the holes are elongated — the shape of a bullet striking sideways — then the conical was tumbling. Sometimes the hole will simply be irregular, rather than round, indicating yawing, which also indicates negative stabilization. A shorter conical of less sectional density may solve the problem. If not, the rifling is probably for a round ball.

Conicals in the Revolver

Many different conical bullets are available for the cap 'n' ball revolver, especially from bullet molds, but also commercially, as in the Buffalo Bullet Co.'s 36-, 44-, and 45- caliber, round-nose pre-lubed examples. The 36 at .375-inch diameter weighs 124 grains. The 44 at .451-inch diameter weighs 180 grains, while the 45 at .457-inch for the Ruger Old Army revolver gains 10 more grains for a 190-grain lead bullet.

The Blackpowder Slug Gun

Bullets for blackpowder slug guns, noted briefly in the forthcoming accu-

racy chapter, are quite special and not at all common. None are for sale commercially at this time. These super-heavy bench rifles are carefully loaded with strict uniformity. They are known as the 40-rod guns, because they were counted on for tight groups at that distance — 220 yards. Ned Roberts mentions the 40-rod gun in his book, *The Muzzle-Loading Cap Lock Rifle*, on page 92: "In times past, many remarkably small groups have been made at 40 rods rest shooting with the most accurate muzzle-loading target rifle, equipped with false muzzle and telescopic sight, using various calibers of cylindro-conoidal bullets. Even at 60 to 100 rods [one rod equals 5.5 yards or 5.03 meters], these rifles and bullets when handled by expert rest shots would make groups that very few of our modern high power rifles today can equal." Bullets for these bench rest slug guns were often cast in two parts fitted together with a soft base section and harder nose section.

The Future

The future of pistol bullets in sabots requires no crystal ball to read. Likewise new conicals, all-lead, all-copper, jacketed: Anything is possible. The trend is clear. CVA's Power-Belt™ Bullet is but one sample of the many possibilities available to the bullet designer. It's an all-lead bullet, but with a fitted plastic base rather than a sabot. The base acts as a gas seal, but the bullet itself is engraved by the rifling. Or how about a jacketed 350-grain bullet from Northern

Marty Atkinson does it again. This dedicated blackpowder hunter took this record class—well over 150-points Boone & Crockett whitetail—at over 150 yards with his 50-caliber Knight rifle shooting a saboted conical bullet.

Here are round balls, along with conicals for comparison, retrieved from game animals. From left they are (top row): .40-caliber round ball/antelope, .50-caliber round ball/mule deer, 50-caliber round ball/antelope, 50-caliber round ball/elk; (bottom row) 54-caliber round ball/mule deer, 54-caliber round ball/mule deer, 54-caliber round ball, elk, 50-caliber 370-grain Maxi ball/zebra.

Precision with boat-tail base for easy loading into a sabot? This one isn't even off the drawing board yet, but it will be in the future. Bullet designers are always working on new ideas. That's how the Buffalo Bullet Ball-et came about. It's an unlikely projectile, sort of a round ball with a shank. Why it groups the way it does defies even its inventor, but many fine clusters have been created by this very different black powder conical/round ball combination. Meanwhile, just about every bullet workable in the revolver becomes a candidate for the muzzleloading rifle with a sabot to guide it in the bore.

Conical bullets like these from CVA continue to flow from companies. These Power Belts have attached plastic cups that act as gas seals. No sabot is required.

The Devel bullet, far left, is an entirely new concept in blackpowder projectiles. Made of tin and copper, it does not expand. Rather, the fins create the shock wave. On the right is a Nosler 45-caliber 260-grain bullet for comparison. Both bullets were retrieved from Sam's Bullet Box prepared with especially tough media.

Chapter 18

THE CLOTH PATCH
(And Paper Patched Conical)

LOVE OF tradition is admirable, especially if tradition means keeping the best and changing the rest. However, casting a blind eye on new facts is taking tradition too far. That's what happened with the bit of cloth that surrounds the round ball in the front loader's breech. Traditionalists bucked like rodeo bulls when word came down, after testing, that the cloth patch was not a gasket. One fellow roared, "Everybody knows that the patch was used to seal gas behind the round ball!" Perhaps it was originally intended to accomplish that trick, but no piece of common cloth, regardless of toughness or close weave, made an infallible barrier against hot gases from a burning powder charge. But why let evidence get in the way of romance? Those who sputtered when told that patches were not gaskets never changed their minds. Others took the news too far, wondering if the cloth patch was good for anything. The upshot of the whole thing is this: Cloth patches are not true gaskets that seal gases from a powder charge under combustion, but they remain highly important in shooting the lead round ball. Wise downwind shooters take this to heart, learning all they can about the management and values of the ancient patch. So if the patch is not a true gasket, then what good is it? And while we're at it, how about paper patched conicals? How can wrapping bullets with paper make them work better? But first, a little history.

Where Did They Come From?

As with blackpowder, a sole inventor of a ball patch is impossible to name. American shooters, always known for their love of accuracy, are often credited with the invention of the cloth patch, a Yankee marksman coming up with the idea. John G. Dillin, author of that fine collectible book, *The Kentucky Rifle*, published in 1924, wrote, "Here in America, balls were cast smaller than the bore and were enveloped in a 'patch' of leather or cloth to prevent contact with the barrel. The patch enabled Americans to load faster, and to fire longer without cleaning, and to outshoot all others of that time. It was the distinguishing difference between the American rifle and those of Europe." Dillin was right. Americans were known for their sharp shooting. However, the idea of wrapping a piece of cloth, sometimes leather, around a lead ball to take up windage in the bore came from Europe, and it was one of man's better shooting ideas. Dillin believed that the patch was a "mas-

ter stroke," as he put it, and "the last link forged in the chain of evolution which brought forth a distinctly American rifle." However, there is strong evidence that American shooters were not first with the patch. An interesting book titled *Espingarda Perfeyta* (The Perfect Gun) came along in 1718. The Portuguese author, J. Joav, wrote at that time, "Others made barrels with rifling inside, some with more, and others with less rifling, all of them deep and twisted in the form of a spiral. These were loaded by putting the bullet in a little piece of leather of a thin glove, folded only once, dipped in oil, and thus it was pushed down to the bottom in such a manner that the bullet may not lose its roundness." Here was a patched round ball if ever there was one, but no surprise. European shooters also invented jacketed bullets before the days of smokeless powder.

We know that muzzleloader accuracy was always bettered, and still is, by shooting a projectile closely matching bore size, which promotes a good relationship between the bullet and the rifling. The problem,

This is the type of rifle often associated with the cloth ball patch. It's a Lyman Great Plains with slow twist. Note special sights, Lyman 57GPR aperture rear and No. 17AEU up front.

THE CLOTH PATCH (And Paper Patched Conical) **133**

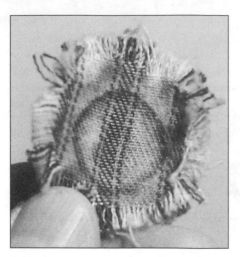

Here is a typical ball patch picked up downrange. No cross whatsoever. But there is a black circle where the ball rested.

especially on a battlefield, was getting a bore-sized missile to seat readily. Imagine those Tennessee sharpshooters at the Battle of New Orleans shooting once or twice, and then having to hammer a round ball down the muzzle to shoot again as the bore fouled. Hunters, as well as target shooters, would also find it troublesome to ram home a bore-sized round bullet after a few shots, and we know there was plenty of hunting as well as competitive shooting in the old days. The patch, be it cloth or leather, allowed the use of an undersized lead sphere. It worked in days of yore, and it works now, with stout cloth, not leather. Obturation is undoubtedly somewhat helpful, the round bullet flattening out slightly for a better purchase on rifling lands. The cloth patch forced between ball and bore transfers rotational value. Someone is going to ask: "Why wouldn't a well-fitted round ball, without a patch, shoot accurately, obturating to engage the rifling?" Naked lead balls, as long as they remain down on the powder charge, work. They were used eons ago.

William Cotton Oswell was one of the first professional ivory hunters to kill African elephants for profit. His method was hot-galloping his horse after pachyderms, getting close, then letting go with a big-bore

front loader. The more shots he got, the more ivory, and so he was known to carry a smoothbore for easy loading. Shoot, reach into a pouch for a fistful of coarse black-powder, drop the haphazard charge down the bore, roll an undersized ball literally down the bore, secure ignition, and blast away. Accuracy was akin to wishful thinking, but at 20 paces, Oswell's patchless lead balls found the mark regularly.

This sort of sloppy loading worked for the old ivory hunter, but it is all wrong for us, and can prove dangerous as well as highly inaccurate. Patched round balls performed several duties as described below, along with improved accuracy. We cannot tolerate bushel-sized groups at 50 or 100 yards. We demand close clusters on the target. So did our North American ancestors. And they got it with rifled bores and round balls wrapped in cloth patches. In theory, an absolutely perfect round ball must fly true. It need not rotate on its axis. Nice try, but no cigar. Round balls, in the first place, are not perfect. Spinning not only keeps a ball rotating through the air on its axis, but also averages flaws on that common axis. Well-cast round balls are not lopsided. Swaged round balls from Speer and Hornady are even more homogenous. However, it takes very little imperfection to throw a missile off course. That's why spinning is paramount to accuracy, even with the most precise round balls available.

The Cloth Patch is Not a Gasket

In spite of outrage from traditionalists, the cloth patch lost its claim to gasket fame in three ways. First, Ed Yard gave the lie to the gasket theory in his 1980 *Gun Digest* article, "The Round Patched Ball And Why They Used It:"

"The inherent inefficiency of the patch as a bore seal was the big factor... of the loss [in pressure]," wrote Yard. "So we find that no patch really seals," wrote the man who

studied patches with a pressure gun. "Based on the test information presented here and the tabulated data appended, the major function and the practical effect of the cloth patch on a round lead ball in the American rifle is to spin a loose-fitting and easily loaded ball to attain real accuracy. It does not really seal the bore," Yard concluded.

Second, I put a chronograph to work on the problem, seeing what would happen to velocity if a naked round ball was fired across the screens. This was for test purposes only, since an unpatched ball can ride up the bore, creating a dangerous short-started condition. This little investigation was not a real experiment. It was not sufficiently precise for that. But it was a worthwhile demonstration that proved fairly convincing. Velocity with a well-fitted ball and no patch was virtually the same as velocity with a patched ball. If the patch was serving as a gasket, its use would have increased velocity. Badly undersized round balls were aided in muzzle velocity by patching, but further testing convinced that this was due more to delaying the ball downbore for obturation than an actual gas seal.

Third, a high-speed camera stopped the action at the rifle's muzzle as the gun went off. There was something rather curious about the results. The 16mm movies, for that is what they were, clearly showed that the patched round ball was not the first thing to emerge from the muzzle. No, first out was a jet of smoke. Obviously, gas had gone through the cloth patch, preceding the patched ball in exiting the bore. If the patch were a true gasket, the projectile would have exited the muzzle first, perhaps with a little evidence of blow by, but certainly not with a definite blow of smoke out front. This is what we see with modern bullets coming from the muzzle: the bullet first, and then evidence of gas behind it. If a gasket, as stated in the dictionary, is: "A ring, disk, or plate of packing to make a joint or closure watertight or gastight," then the cloth patch is not a gasket, because it does not make the bore gastight.

The Amazing Properties of the Cloth Patch

Having put aside what a cloth patch does not do — serving as a true gasket to seal the bore — here comes the wonderful things the cloth patch does do. Warning: Under no circumstances should round balls be fired without a patch. That was done only for test purposes under controlled conditions.

Accuracy and the Ball Patch

Accuracy is a prime and important reason to use the patch. I tested unpatched balls that fit tightly to the bore and they proved fairly accurate. However, they were miserable to load; they did not outshoot the patched ball; and they could have proven dangerous if an unpatched ball migrated upbore, creating a gap between powder charge and projectile. A well-fitted bare lead ball engraves, making contact with the rifling in the bore, which in turn causes rotation. The patch, however, does this same work without the lead ball touching the rifling lands at all. Normally, the round ball emerges from the muzzle with nary a mark on it. Best accuracy is still earned by shooting a ball fairly close to bore size, rather than two or three calibers under. While strong well-lubed patches do a great service, they should not be counted on to fill a great void between the lead sphere and the bore. Range shooting proves this. Firing a 54-caliber ball, either .530-inch or .535-inch diameter, from the oft-mentioned accurate Mulford custom rifle, coupled with pure Irish linen .013-inch thick patches provided fine groups. Going to a .526-inch ball with a thicker patch blew patterns wide open.

The Ball Patch and Safety

The broken record plays again — that infernal short-started load — but the story must be told. It is the cloth patch wrapped around the lead ball that retains it firmly down in the bore upon the powder charge where it belongs, so that a gap between powder and projectile does not develop. Never fire an unpatched ball in a muzzleloader.

Consistent Pressure on the Powder Charge

If it's true, as we believe, that blackpowder functions better when reasonably compressed, then the patch serves another important function. It not only retains the round ball down in the breech for safety reasons, but maintains a constant and specific pressure on the powder charge. Using the Kadooty or other method of ensuring the same pressure on the powder charge every time a round ball is seated, the patch finishes the job by maintaining that pressure. After seating patched round balls, rifles were tested later to see if they were still located exactly where they were when first pushed downbore, or if they had migrated forward toward the muzzle. A marked ramrod proved every time that the seated, patched balls had remained in place.

Uniformity of Powder Charge Pressure and Standard Deviation

Standard deviation, a term that will find its way into the book more than once, is a measure of variance that for our purposes serves to show uniformity in a load. Top-grade chronographs, such as the Oehler Model 35P Proof unit used for this work, automatically provide standard deviation figures in feet per second. Tests with varying ramrod pressures showed higher standard deviation figures than when ramrod pressure was consistent.

The Patch as a Go-Between

"Do you think patches on round balls and sabots with conicals really spin either one?" The question came from a knowledgeable person and he was serious. The answer is yes in both cases. Anyone who thinks otherwise need only shoot either type of projectile from a smoothbore, comparing accuracy for both in a rifled barrel. In the past, there were round balls that did not take patches. How-

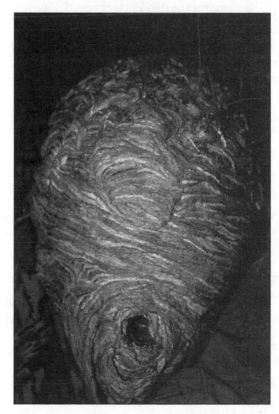

This fine hornet nest, which was blown down in a wind and abandoned by its residents, will provide plenty of patch-saving layers to place between the powder charge and the patched round ball.

ever, these spheres were bore-size, engraving when run downbore in the gun, then obturating in the bore when fired. This point is a first cousin to accuracy; however, it's worth noting that tests show the patched round balls fired from rifled barrels do rotate in flight.

No Bore Leading

This particular advantage of the patch could easily be overstated, because with muzzleloader bullets at normal blackpowder velocities there is little leading in the first place. One reason is because the round ball has no shank and very little of it makes contact with the bore, even if it were not patched. Nevertheless, the lead round ball never touches the bore when it is patched, and therefore cannot cause leading at any level.

The Patch as a Reservoir for Lube, Solvent, and Modern Chemicals

The cloth patch holds lubrication perfectly for loading ease. It also retains various solvents, from saliva to the most advanced chemicals of the day, which in turn keeps fouling soft, thereby allowing more shots in a row before bore swabbing is necessary. Today's commercial products are both lube and solvent, as in Ox-Yoke's Wonder Lube.

The Art of Reading Patches

Recovering patches after shooting is no problem. Usually, the spent patch is found on the ground not far in front of the muzzle of the rifle or pistol, often within 10 or 20 paces. It's a simple matter of looking, picking up, then reading. The patch is vital to safe and accurate round ball shooting, but it must remain fairly intact to accomplish all of its intended functions. The patch has two enemies. The first is the rifling itself, specifically the lands. The second comes from the blast-furnace fire produced by the burning powder charge. The first

Hornet nest leaves placed between the powder charge and patched ball save the patch from burnout.

problem results in a cut patch. The second problem results in what is called a blown patch. Checking for cut or blown patches makes sense, while looking for that artist's conception of the perfect black cross in the center of a spent patch is a waste of time. It will not be there. In spite of so many drawings in shooting manuals and articles, I have yet to spot the magical cross on picked up patches. A dark place indicating contact with bore fire is the norm.

The Cut Patch

The raised portion of the rifling (the lands rather than grooves) can cause a cut patch. Since the patch suffered the ravages of traveling the bore at possibly 2,000-fps speed, cutting may not always stand out clearly. Is the patch cut or burned? That's the question, and there's a safe test to determine if it was cut. It goes like this. Warning: Use only an unloaded firearm for this test.

Run a patched ball downbore without a powder charge in the firearm.

Do not seat the ball firmly into the breech. Use the ramrod as a gauge to determine when the patched ball is about an inch from the breech (bottom of the bore). If a patched ball is run firmly down into the empty breech, it may get hung up there.

After the patched ball is seated in the empty bore, attach a screw to the end of a loading rod, such as the Kadooty. Use a muzzle protector with a screw.

Gain a purchase on the patched ball with the screw, pulling it all the

way out of the muzzle of the gun.

First, study the ball itself. It should be free of engraving. If the ball itself is marred by the rifling, that may indicate that the ball is too large for the bore. This condition is rare and occurs mainly with odd-sized bores. Next, study the patch. It may very well show marks from contact with the lands, but it should not be sliced. If it is, the culprit is sharp lands, since there was no exploding powder charge to harm it, nor a high-speed dash in the bore. There are two possible remedies for sharp lands. The first is lapping the bore with cleaning patches dressed with rouge or lapping compound, which can be ordered from a gun store. The second remedy is to keep on shooting. Patches flying through the bore at high speed will burnish the lands smooth in time.

The Blown Patch

This condition is indicated by holes in the patch, often in a circle, indicating where hot gas rushed through the rifling grooves, burning the cloth patch itself. Sometimes a blown patch simply seems tattered, especially at the edges, without neat little holes in it. Either way, a blown patch is easily remedied. A reader in his 70s reported many years ago that his grandfather cured blown patches with hornet-nesting material. That's right, the stuff hornets produce to make nests. The gray paper-like nesting material (not to be confused with the mud nests of mud daubers) is odd. It burns up readily when touched with a match, but downbore, it works like asbestos. It's easy to use, too. After pouring the appropriate powder charge downbore, two or three thin sheets of hornet-nesting material follow, seated right on top of the powder charge using a ramrod or loading rod with a jag on the end. Sometimes the off-end of a ramrod works, too. Then the patched ball is loaded normally. The hornet-nesting material forms a barrier between the powder charge and the patch, yet it is so thin that it does not disrupt the work of the patch at all. I have yet to pick up a blown patch that was protected by hornet-nesting material.

Make certain that the dome-shaped nest of the bald-faced hornet has been abandoned before trying to collect this prize from a tree, or you will certainly be stung repeatedly by these fierce insects. Winter is the best time to collect them.

Torn or blown patches do not always destroy accuracy, strange as that may seem. Apparently, enough of the patch remains intact that its work continues full force. However, in some cases accuracy was definitely improved by lapping a bore, or shooting it smooth, to round off sharp lands, or by safeguarding the patch with hornet-nesting material. This seems especially true when patches are both cut and blown, which is entirely possible. If a rifle or pistol that shoots round balls continues to shoot inaccurately after cut or blown patch problems are corrected, then obviously there is another gremlin at work, possibly a badly undersized ball, a damaged bore, especially the crown of the muzzle, and in rarer cases these days, an ill-made barrel.

Patches and Bore Wear

Lucky is the shooter who gets to wear a barrel out from firing so many patched round balls through it. We should all have that problem. There is no doubt that cloth patches do burnish the bore. How many shots are required to destroy the accuracy of the barrel is up for

grabs. That would depend upon many factors, including the steel used to make the barrel, as well as lubes, and patch material. There is no way to prevent bore lapping as the cloth patch rips through at two grand or so. However, it'll be a while before a rifle becomes a smoothbore.

Patch Materials

The important work a patch does is clear, but it cannot accomplish its duties if made of flimsy material from the ragbag. Commercial patches are readily available, and made from strong, close-weave cloth. Denim has been used successfully. It's sold in various thicknesses in fabric stores, but pillow or mattress ticking is more reliable.

This is an extreme example of a blown patch.

Pure Irish linen, also found in fabric shops, is extremely good. It's very strong as well as reliably consistent in thickness. Commercial patches are ready to go, but Irish linen or ticking must be washed thoroughly to get rid of sizing, which is a starch-like substance impregnating the cloth to improve its appearance in the store. Sizing may lay down a coating in the bore of the muzzleloader. The cloth is washed normally, either by hand or in a washing machine, and then rinsed completely and allowed to dry. Now the material is ready to be cut into patches.

Patch Configuration and Size

Patches come round just because. Square patches work just as well as round ones. Therefore, if a shooter wishes to simply cut appropriately-sized square patches from washed, rinsed, and dried ticking or Irish linen, that's fine. On the other hand, round patches are the rule, just because history says so, and they do look nicer. These can also be cut by hand, especially with a template. An ideal template is the top off a bottle. Bottles come in so many sizes that there is bound to be one just right for the desired patch diameter. For example, the cap from a salad dressing bottle proved perfectly sized for a 50- or 54-caliber round ball. Removed from the bottle, the cap is placed directly on the cloth, a lead pencil used to trace around it, and there's a perfectly marked circle to cut out with sharp scissors. Pre-cut, pre-lubed patches are handy in the hunting field or on the shooting range. They keep well, clean and uncontaminated, in sealable sandwich bags or hinged metal cans for throat lozenges. Another way to make nice patches is with a patch cutter. One kind is essentially a punch with a sharp circle edge. The cloth patch material is placed on a hard wood surface, and hammer blows on top of the cutter whack out patch after patch. Another patch cutter uses sharp rotating blades to cut patches from cloth. Both types are sold by Dixie Gun Works. As for size, a correct patch totally covers the round ball so that no part of the ball contacts the rifling.

Paper Patching for Conical Bullets

A shooter owned a special English rifle, but could not find the correct bullet to fit the bore, although he had located brass from which he could form proper cases. He solved the problem by patching slightly undersized jacketed bullets so that they did make full contact with the rifling. Once patched, the bullets worked perfectly in this unique rifle. Much more prominent, however, is paper patching for lead conical bullets, especially for blackpowder cartridge rifles. The paper patch serves at least three functions. It acts as a bearing surface for the rifling, very much like a cloth ball patch goes between round ball and rifling. Instead of the rifling biting into the shank of the conical lead bullet, it engraves the paper around it. The paper patch is also wrapped under the base of the bullet, which can save the important bullet base from damage. We know that damaged conical bases can harm accuracy. The paper patch also prevents bore leading, since the paper, not the bullet itself, makes contact with the rifling.

Paper patching conical bullets is not a panacea. It does not improve accuracy or function in all cases. But when it does work, it works admirably.

Various means of paper-patching bullets are available. Randolph S. Wright describes an excellent process in his information booklet, *The Paper Patched Bullet*, printed by Montana Armory. The author shows how to determine the correct length of a patch for a given projectile by wrapping the bullet with a strip of paper that rolls tightly around it three times, then cutting through all three layers with a sharp tool, such as an X-Acto knife blade. When the paper is unrolled, it has three slits. Measuring between the two farthest-apart slits, then subtracting 1/32-inch from this measurement, provides the correct length of the bullet patch, which can be adjusted later if necessary so that the patch laps around the projectile exactly twice, but no more than twice. The paper patch should be shaped like a rhomboid parallelogram. This par-

ticular shape allows the ends to match up at an angle to the bullet. The ends of the rhomboid parallelogram are cut at about a 30- to 35-degree angle. The bullet is wrapped with a double thickness of paper patching, since the patch is cut to go around the bullet almost, but not quite, two times. This means that the ends of the paper patch do not rest exactly one above the other. Naturally, the ends cannot touch, because one end is wrapped underneath, so the two ends themselves never meet. The ends do not match up exactly, a slight space existing between them when the paper patch is cut to the correct length. This also means that the two ends of the paper patch never overlap, which is important. Also, the wrap of the paper patch must be in the opposite direction of the rifling twist. In this manner, the rotation of the projectile in the bore will not unroll the paper patch, as it might if the patch were rolled in the same direction as the rifling twist.

The process of wrapping a bullet with a paper patch is not involved, but it does take practice. The parallelogram-shaped paper patch is started with one corner located about where the bullet shank begins to taper toward the nose of the projectile. A good thickness is about .0025-inch, which increases 45-caliber bullet diameter by one caliber. A paper thickness of .0025-inch increases a 45-caliber bullet diameter by .01 inch (one caliber), because the paper goes around the bullet twice, and that increases "both sides" of the bullet shank by .05-inch. As Wright points out, this turns a .448-inch bullet into a .458-inch diameter after paper-patching. Correct paper patching material is 100 percent rag or cotton content, which is essentially high-

Finding a blown-down hornet nest is good luck for the shooter who likes patched round balls. A few leaves of hornet nest between powder charge and patched ball saves the patch from burnout.

grade stationery that can be purchased at an office-supply house or Montana Armory.

Well-practiced paper patch wrappers use the dry method of wrapping. This is best because the paper falls away after it works, whereas wet-patched paper may stick to the bullet downrange, possibly compromising accuracy. Excess paper extending downward at the base of flat-based bullet can be "tucked inward" to cover most of the projectile's base. Excess paper at the base of a hollow-base bullet can be twisted and pushed into the cavity. This is a quick look at the fascinating world of paper-patching lead bullets for use in blackpowder cartridge rifles. Those interested in more information should read carefully into Wright's manuscript, which is only 19 pages long.

Simple that it is, the cloth patch surrounding the round ball performs many important functions. Paper-patching conical bullets can also improve performance.

Chapter 19

CHEMICALS FOR BLACKPOWDER SHOOTING

MARKSMEN FROM the days of pre-science had many colorful tales to tell about hard-kicking guns and long shots, as well as "facts" concerning chemicals used in firearm maintenance and shooting. Bear grease was known to cure everything from lumbago to arthritis. Possum fat was perfect for restoring leather. Cooking grease was great for lubing patches. But whale oil topped 'em all. It was ideal for everything. One shooter wrote that whale oil penetrated so completely that if a bore were filled with it at night, the rifle leaned against the wall muzzle up, by morning oil would be leaking right through the sides of the barrel. Amazing stuff, that whale oil, and of course it truly was, lighting the lamps of Early America, and yes, lubricating patches and preserving wood and metal. But seep through the sides of a gun barrel? Uh, I don't think so! And how about the story of a round-ball rifle that simply would not shoot straight with a specific patch lube because that lube wasn't properly "balanced, whatever that meant. Having tried patch lubes from saliva to the latest modern formulas, the odds of lube alone causing round ball inaccuracy are small, albeit lube is important.

Scarcely any time goes by before another homemade lube or solvent is touted as a miracle worker. The reason liquids found under the kitchen sink reduce blackpowder fouling is simply the fact that darn near any water-like substance will

do that. This chapter is not intended to throw rocks at old-time lubes and solvents. Those who enjoy playing the whole game the old way have every right to go with bear grease and possum fat, but first, how about those modern chemicals?

Space Age Blackpowder Chemicals

New chemicals for blackpowder guns made shooting more enjoyable by reducing clean-up time, plus less between-shot bore wipes during a shooting match or plinking session. These products work because they are lab-created and lab-tested.

Chemical engineers know a great deal about gun care and shooting products and their most recent concoctions prove it.

Lubricants—What They Do

Everyone who drives a car knows that lubricants are absolutely essen-

tial in keeping the engine running. The fact comes home especially hard to those of us who had an oil pump suddenly fail and — wham! The car grinds to a halt, the engine "seized up." Friction is the culprit, the act of one thing contacting another through motion and the drag created. In a muzzleloader, friction can make seating a patched ball or conical an exercise in arm power. That's one place where lubricants are used. They work as a go-between, creating a buffer of sorts between two surfaces, thereby reducing the "grab" that these surfaces have for each other.

Above, the idea of a rifle's accuracy hinging almost entirely on lube was attacked. However, there's no doubt that without the right lubricant, accuracy can go down the drain. This is perhaps more true of the blackpowder cartridge gun than the muzzleloader. There is also lube to consider for

Whale oil was fine in its day, but the 21st century blackpowder shooter has better chemicals to rely on.

Today's shooting chemicals protect as well as lubricate and clean the bore.

the workings of the firearm: the lock, for example. When tumbler parts go truly dry, they may "gall," which refers to freezing up or refusing to move. Blackpowder lubes function to reduce friction, just like other lubricants, but at the same time, they should also work at reducing blackpowder fouling from "cake" to sludge. Cake can be thought of as "baked on" fouling, while sludge refers to fouling that's been, for lack of a better term, "softened." In the state of cake, fouling is difficult to remove from the bore, although a bristle brush will scratch a lot of it from rifling grooves. Dry swabbing, however, is not the avenue to a squeaky clean bore: That requires turning cake to sludge so it can be cleared from the bore by flushing with liquids, water or solvent, or cleaning patches soaked with either. Blackpowder fouling breaks down in plain water, so for cleaning only, even between shots at the range, water is workable. But water does not perform the double-duty of a modern lubricant, lacking the ability to truly curb friction. In short, modern shooting lubricants for muzzleloaders create a slick medium between the patched ball and bore, or conical and bore, while also serving as a cleaning agent. A good blackpowder lube also promotes repeat shots,

while making later cleanup easier by attacking fouling right there on the range or in the field during the shooting process.

Lubricant as a Metal Protector

While a lubricant is not necessarily intended to safeguard metal from ferric oxide, otherwise known as rust, as a true metal preserver is meant to do, lube does serve the important function of creating a barrier between metal and the atmosphere. It keeps moisture from reaching metal, at least to some degree, and it also acts as a shield against oxygen. Since moisture plus oxygen can attack metal, this service of the lubricant is highly valuable. Recall that one function of the cloth patch is to retain lubrication. A lubed patch is vital to reducing friction so the ball can be seated, but it also leaves a film of lubrication in the bore when that treated patch is run home on top of the powder charge. This coating remains in the bore as the firearm is carried in the field.

True Metal Preservers

The work of a true metal preserver is not reduction of friction. That is where this product differs from a lube. Nor is a metal preserver called upon to break down blackpowder fouling. Its job is precisely what the name implies: to safeguard metal from damage caused by moisture and oxygen. Fortunately, chemists have arrived at metal preservers that truly do more than sewing-machine or fishing-reel oils, which remain useful in creating a thin barrier between metal and the atmosphere, but do not actually bond with that metal. Considerable experience over the years with Accragard from the Jonad Corp. bears convincing evidence that metal preservers do work. Rusty Duck Protective Gun Lube is an example of a metal preserver. It penetrates well, while remaining fluid at 50 degrees below zero Fahrenheit. Shooter's Choice Rust Pre-

vent is another metal preservative with lubricating qualities, noted for displacing moisture. Rusty Duck Vapor Inhibitor Protection (V.I.P.) is formulated especially for firearms that will be cased. Cases can trap rust-causing moisture. Birchwood Casey's Sheath® is noted as "Polarized for maximum gun protection, repels dust."

Gun Oils

Gun oils were always good; now they're even better. Hoppe's has a special No. 9 lubricating oil noted for water-displacement qualities. Thompson/Center's No. 13 Gun Oil is noted for superior penetration. Birchwood Casey company has a Synthetic Gun Oil advertised as protecting "up to 10 times better than ordinary petroleum," with promised performance from 50 below zero to 300 degrees F.

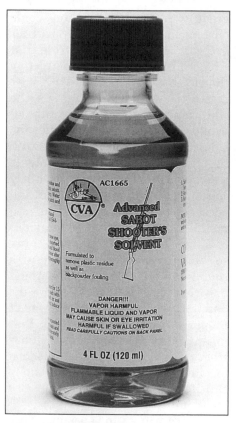

Blackpowder companies have long worked toward the best possible modern chemicals to help shooters enjoy the great sport. This product is especially formulated to attack plastic residue and blackpowder fouling.

Paste lubes like these are workable on ball patches, but essential for conicals, where a liquid would not stick to the base of the bullet.

Butch's Gun Oil from Lyman is another modern-day product engineered to work in conjunction with the same company's Butch's Bore Shine. Its strong point is withstanding intense heat in the bore, plus fighting corrosion.

Anti-Seize Lubricants for Removable Breech Plugs and Nipples

Continued firing may cause sufficient buildup of fouling on nipple threads to lock it into its nipple seat, making removal difficult. A little anti-seize lubricant normally prevents this problem. A slight trace of lube is touched onto the lower threads of the nipple. When the nipple is installed in its nipple seat, this lubricant disperses onto the rest of the threads. Breech plugs are another story. They can become fiercely locked in place from prolonged firing, or even a few shots with magnum-type charges. Anti-seize lubricants are available at hardware stores, but there are also special products, such as Birchwood Casey Choke Tube Lube, originally intended for shotgun screw-in chokes, but also workable for breech plugs. Kleen Bore TW25B is noted as a "high-tech lubricant," but is also considered a good anti-seize product. Another good product is Thompson/Center's All-Purpose Anti-Seize Super Lube, "a hardworking, synthetic-based lube containing Teflon, which seals the threads of muzzleloading breech plugs." Before installing the removable breech plug back into the mod-

ern muzzleloader, the threads are treated with one of the anti-seize lubes. Rusty Duck Polymer Anti-Seizing Gun Grease is recommended specifically for nipples and breech plugs.

Shoot-All-Day Lubes

There are many products on the market today formulated for multiple shots before the bore requires swabbing. When used properly, these "all-day" lubes are excellent. The operative word is "properly." As soon as any muzzleloader bore balks at the seating of a projectile, no matter what kind of lube is used, it's time to swab that bore out with solvent. This common-sense approach, coupled with the many fine lubes on the market today, makes for safe repeat shooting. Lube 103 is an all-natural product promising that it "eliminates fouling from black powder," while also getting rid of "rotten egg stink." Thompson/Center's Bore Butter Natural Lube 1000 Plus™, in original scent or fresh pine, boasts that a Thompson/Center New Englander rifle "had 1,015 shots fired through it. During that time, it never had a patch put through it. It was never cleaned; not even once!" There you have it. Coupled with the common-sense warning about cleaning any bore, regardless of lube, when that bore shows a need for swabbing, Bore Butter is excellent for repeat shots. Likewise is Ox-Yoke's Liquid Wonder Spray Lubricant, which, as the name states, comes in a spray bottle.

Pyrodex Lube is another good one, especially for breaking down Pyrodex fouling. All-day lubes work especially well with target loads, less well with big hunting charges, which makes sense, as the heavier charge leaves far more fouling.

Lubrication Types

There are four basic types of lube for blackpowder guns: liquids, greases, pastes, and creams. The last two are essentially the same, although pastes may be a little thicker. Liquid patch lubes were long considered the only viable type. But that has changed. Now there are good patch lubes in all types. For example, rubbing one of the all-day lubes well into the patch is good. Liquids still are excellent, too, such as Ol' Griz from Dixie Gun Works. Any lube

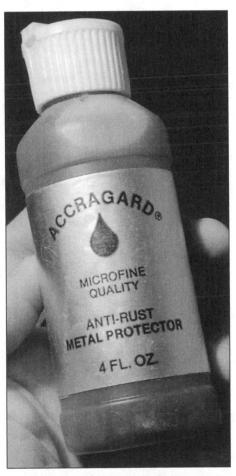

Special metal protectors came about to prevent rust and consequent damage to bores and other metallic parts of firearms.

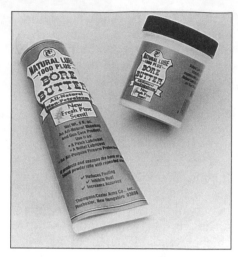

Paste lubes have gained considerable ground in blackpowder shooting. These are noted for reducing blackpowder fouling during shooting to make after-shooting cleanup easier.

compatible with the cloth patch is useful as long as it attacks the many salts left behind by blackpowder combustion. But this is not true of lubes for conicals. Liquids are no good. It takes a cream, grease, or paste to stick to the base of an elongated bullet, with the base a good place to apply a dab. Thompson/Center's Maxi Ball® and Maxi-Hunter® bullets are offered pre-lubed, their grease grooves neatly filled with Natural Lube 1000+ Bore Butter, which holds well in place during proper storage and loading. Liquid lubes are also no good with sabots, whereas a dab of grease, paste, or cream directly into the base of the plastic sabot works well in keeping fouling under control and also ensures an easier job of after-shooting cleanup.

The Spit Patch (Saliva)

Always available, and at no cost, is a ready supply of liquid lube that will allow the seating of a patched round ball. The shooter plops a ball patch into his mouth, then transfers it to the muzzle, followed by a round ball. It works. For plinking and even target work, shooters continue to use this old method of ball-patch lubing. But

there are drawbacks to the spit patch. Saliva dries out quickly, especially in a hot bore, but this really isn't much of a problem. The ball still flies through the bore just fine. If tradition beckons, then a shooter should go ahead and use a spit patch, but at the range only where the gun will be fired, then taken home for a cleaning. The spit patch is not for hunting, where a charge may rest downbore for quite some time.

Whale Oil

The sperm whale contributed immeasurably to early America. Whaling-ship crews made a living at the trade of taking leviathans from the sea, while the vessel's owners accrued an even larger bounty. Along with lighting homes, whale oil was popular with shooters. It served the duty of a lubricant, curtailing friction between patched round bullets and bores. It did not dry out. A lubed patch stayed that way. Whale oil did not cake onto bores when blasted by the hot gases of powder charges, hence no sludge. Sperm whale oil is a rust preventative, a polarized compound that combines with surface oxide films on steel to form a barrier against moisture and oxygen. It's sticky enough to stay put, rather than rolling off, metal. At the same time, it's not an animal fat, but rather an oily wax something like jojoba. It has the same property as honey, which, when found in ancient tombs, remained viable. Whale oil lasts indefinitely, too, holding up in both hot and cold weather. Along with patch lube duties and rust prevention, whale oil serves the sportsman as a leather preserver.

Great as it was, and is, however, whale oil is not an end-all for blackpowder shooting. Its main fault is that it fails entirely to break down blackpowder fouling in the bore. Residue just keeps building. Shooters interested in repeating history are welcome to use whale oil. But modern shooting chemicals are better.

Whale oil was one of America's most important products for many years. This original container boasts 100 percent pure sperm whale oil good for many different requirements.

Synthetic Whale Oil

When honest-to-goodness whale oil became hard to locate, someone came up with synthetic whale oil. It works about the same as whale oil, according to testing. Like whale oil, is not ideal for blackpowder shooting, especially with so many good modern chemicals available.

Water-Soluble Oil

Long, long ago, mixing water-soluble oil with water was sometimes called moose milk, because the mixture looks like milk — where the moose came in is anybody's guess. Later, some shooters added a dash of dish detergent to the mix. This is a cheap solvent that does a fairly decent job of breaking down blackpowder fouling — and why not? It's mainly water, and water eats up blackpowder fouling. It also works as a patch lube, since it is a liquid, and conversely is useless for lubing

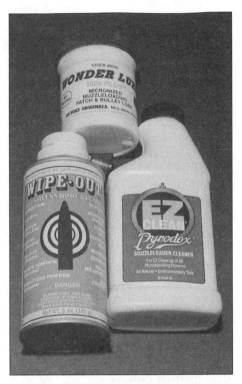

Modern chemicals for blackpowder shooting have come far. They're a lot better than under-the-sink remedies.

conicals. Typical of modern vs. old, a commercial Moose Milk came along from Winchester Sutler Co., and it was better than the original. For those who have to try it, water-soluble oil is mixed with water in a 10/90 ratio (10 percent oil, 90 percent water). Some recipes call for as much as 25 percent oil.

Shortening, Sheep Tallow, and Bear Fat

Be if vegetable oil or animal fat, it can go rancid; therefore, lubing up a bunch of patches with any of these products for the long term is unwise. Of course, they work as lubricants, being slick, but they don't break down blackpowder fouling. Modern greases, creams, and pastes are better. Once again, for those who wish to use shortening, sheep tallow, or bear fat, it's simple enough. They all melt readily and soak fully into ball patches. These fats are slick and therefore they serve as lubricants. They are also easy to use: just melt, soak patch, blot patch on paper towel — done.

Petroleum Jelly

It's cheap, easy to find, slick and does not dry out. Petroleum jelly is a good lubricant. It even stays put in the base of a conical or sabot. But once again, we're dealing with a product that may leave traces of itself in the bore after shooting, and it has no power against breaking down blackpowder fouling. Good advice goes like this: Forget it.

Cooking Oils

While peanut oil, olive oil, and similar natural agents of the clan lubricate a patch, they do not cut blackpowder fouling.

Waxes

Beeswax and candle wax can build up in the bore. They don't touch fouling. They make a patch stiffer than a good gun barrel. While useful for many other applications, they're no good for black-powder guns.

Isopropyl Alcohol

Isopropyl alcohol cuts blackpowder fouling and can be used as a solvent. It works quite well, but not as good as the modern commercial solvents explained below.

Commercial Solvents

The big difference between solvents and lubes is duty: Today's commercial lubes are designed to cut fouling as well as thwart friction during shooting. But as good as these lubes are, they were never intended to clear the bore of black-powder fouling after shooting, or get rid of external film or soot that has invaded working parts. Attacking blackpowder fouling is the work of solvents, and there are many super products today.

Proving a solvent's worth is simple. Dirty guns are cleaned with A, B, and C brands. The one most liked by the individual shooter will show itself. Or, he or she may like them all. There are so many good ones, like Rusty Duck Black Off, which gives the one-two knockout punch to dirty bores quickly. Hodg-

don's Spit Patch continues to punish blackpowder fouling. So do solvents from Ox-Yoke such as Competition Bore Cleaner and Concentrated Bore Cleaner. Hoppe's No. 9 Plus solvent is formulated for blackpowder cleanup, as is T/C's No. 13 Bore Cleaner, as well as Venco's Black Powder Gel. Space prevents naming all the good solvents.

Products that Attack Plastic Fouling

Common sense alone tells us that a piece of plastic racing through a gun bore at 1,500 to 2,500 fps is going to leave a little bit of itself behind in the form of fouling on lands and in grooves. Plastic wash from pistols, rifles, and shotguns is not a problem, however, because once again chemistry has come to the fore with several products to loosen and remove plastic wash left behind by sabots and one-piece shotgun wads are fired in the blackpowder shotgun has not studied the situation very closely. A few good solvents for plastic wash are

Rusty Duck is known for coming up with a number of shooting chemicals, such as these, each one formulated to clean and protect firearms, including black-powder guns.

Butch's Bore Shine is another product useful in clearing plastic fouling produced by sabots or one-piece plastic shotgun wads from the bore.

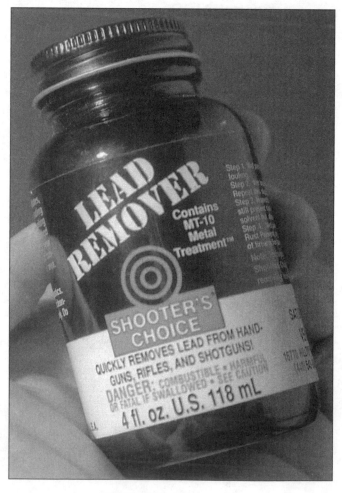

While the muzzleloader is not very prone to leading due to the round ball being patched and relatively low velocity for all-lead conicals, blackpowder cartridge guns can pick up a little lead in the bore and there are chemicals to aid that problem. This is one.

Butch's Bore Shine from Lyman, Wipe-Out from the Paul Co. of Paola, Kansas, and Venco's Shooter's Choice. The Ox-Yoke Co., recognizing the fact that plastic fouling is reality, came up with Accuracy Restorer™. It is especially designed to clear plastic residue from the bore.

Bore Leading

Muzzleloaders shooting conicals seldom show bore leading because of bullet speed, which is, compared with modern cartridges, on the slow side. Fast-shooting lead missiles, such as Buffalo Bullet Co.'s 302-grain, 50-caliber Lead Saboted Boat Tail Bullets, ride in plastic sabots. There are formulas especially for lead removal. In addition, the plastic fouling products listed above all claim to remove lead from the bore. Severely leaded guns — an example that comes to mind is an original Colt six-gun whose owner failed to

become familiar with a cleaning rod — may require the attention of a gunsmith, who will have special tools to get the lead out.

Copper Fouling

Although copper fouling is essentially non-existent in muzzleloaders and blackpowder single-shot cartridge rifles firing lead bullets, it can show up in lever-action blackpowder repeaters shooting jacketed bullets, as well as revolvers shooting a lot of speedy jacketed bullets. When it does, accuracy can fly away like a quail bursting from the grass. The products mentioned above for removing plastic fouling are also good for copper. A telltale blue patch lets the shooter know that copper is present in the bore and under attack. Another product designed to remove copper (as well as lead) fouling is Ox-Yoke's Accuracy Restorer™.

The Blackpowder Cartridge

Blackpowder cartridge handguns shooting lead bullets require special lubes. But blackpowder cartridge rifles are even more demanding. There are many good lubricants on the market, such as SPG Lubricant sold through Dixie Gun Works or Wonder Lube Sticks Premium Bullet Lubricant from Ox-Yoke. Lyman sells Silver Star Cowboy Action Shooting Lead Bullets made of a hard alloy and pre-lubed with that company's well-known formula.

A Few Other Chemicals

There are a number of special firearms chemicals useful to blackpowder shooters, such as Birchwood Casey's Cleaner-Degreaser billed as "Specially formulated to remove dirt, fouling, grease and oil." It's a metal cleaner that comes in handy for the outside of barrels, locks, and actions. It comes in a spray can or standard container.

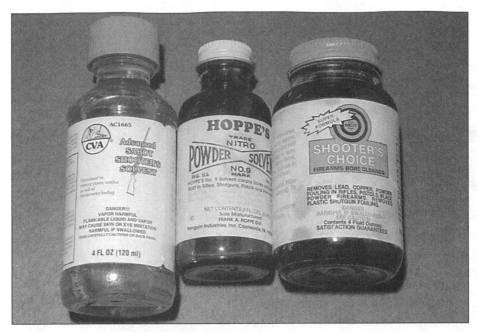

There are many solvents available to attack muzzleloader fouling, but also blackpowder cartridge guns using smokeless powder.

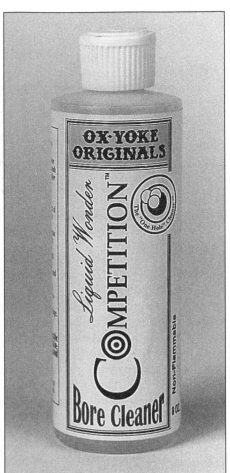

Ox-Yoke Originals company offers several chemicals in the interest of promoting easy after-shooting blackpowder cleanup, including Liquid Wonder Competition, a modern bore cleaner.

Brand Names

Brand names may come and go, but that's only because companies are working even more diligently to supply the blackpowder shooter with the best chemical helpers of all time. On the other hand, many of the brands mentioned here will be around for a long time, perhaps in upgraded formulas. In recent times, these chemicals have made muzzleloading and blackpowder cartridge shooting a lot more fun with a lot less toil after shooting.

New chemicals continue to come from blackpowder companies. This is Hodgdon's EZ Clean. Although it bears the Pyrodex name, EZ Clean works on all blackpowder guns.

Chapter 20

LOADING PROCEDURES FOR SUCCESS

THERE IS no such thing as one and only one right loading method for blackpowder guns. This is proven over and over by shooters who do things their own way, but safely and reliably. At one shooting match, during a timed event for flintlock smoothbore muzzleloaders, a contestant did very well with his musket without paying the least attention to the condition of the touchhole. After several shots, it seemed impossible that the fellow could get that gun to go off one more time, but he did. He knew his firearm and how to manage it. That's fine, but day after day, the successful blackpowder shooter goes by the book, learning a sound routine and sticking to it faithfully.

Before Loading

Pre-shooting preparation is essential to loading and shooting success.

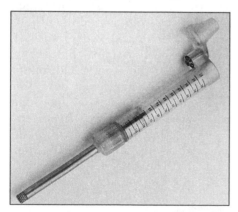

This U-View powder measure from Thompson/Center performs the same function as the old-time adjustable measure, only it's made of modern materials with a transparent reservoir.

Most points are obvious. A clogged touchhole in a flinter, likewise the vent in a nipple or channel in an in-line muzzleloader, has to spell doom before the shooter so much as thinks about putting powder charge and bullet downbore. A filthy bore can destroy all chance of a proper load, and in some cases can be dangerous, especially when the bullet fails to seat properly upon the powder charge, resulting in a short-start condition. Leftover preserving oils and grease can thwart the flame of ignition. Inconsistency during the loading procedure also can spell doom. More on that in Chapter 23, the chapter about accuracy.

Steps for Loading the Percussion Rifle or Pistol

The muzzleloading pistol is functionally a "short muzzleloading rifle," and therefore it is treated to the same loading procedures. Protecting the patch from burnout is not required for target loads, but may prove useful for heavy hunting loads in big bore pistols, such as the Thompson/Center Encore.

Step 1: Clearing all Channels

The simple pipe cleaner, found in the smoking section of stores everywhere, works wonders in sopping up oil or grease from any ignition channel: the touchhole of the flintlock, vent in the nipple, or fire lane of the in-line muzzleloader. After pipe cleaner probing, percussion caps may be fired on the nipple to

After the round ball has been seated beyond the crown of the muzzle with the stub end of the short starter, the longer stem on the starter goes to work driving the patched ball further downbore.

ensure a dry passage into the breech. The same is true of primers with No. 209 shotgun or small rifle/pistol ignition systems.

A simple test for verifying a clear channel is conducted with the muzzle of the gun pointed at a lightweight object on the ground, a bit of paper, cleaning patch, twig, small leaf or anything that will readily move. The muzzle of the unloaded rifle or pistol is pointed at the object on the ground, within a couple inches of it. Standard percussion caps, such as the No. 11, musket caps, and of course No. 209 or small rifle/pistol primers all have sufficient force to push a light object

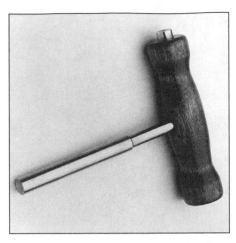

An important tool in proper loading of round balls or conicals in a muzzleloader is the short starter. This one is from Thompson/Center. It has a T-handle for improving applied force from the shooter's hand.

Showing the short starter with the longer stem fully inserted into the muzzle to deliver a patched round ball partway downbore. Follow-up with a ramrod or loading rod will properly seat the projectile down firmly upon the powder charge in the breech.

away. If the leaf, patch, paper, whatever, fails to jump when the rifle or pistol is fired, this indicates a blockage in the flash channel, the bore, or both, which must be cleared.

Another trick is played by ear, listening to the sound an unloaded gun makes when a cap or primer is detonated. A hollow-sounding thump indicates a clear passage, while a sharp crack signifies trapped gases and a blockage. The gun must be cleared before attempting to load it. Usual procedures — pipe cleaner, cleaning patches, bristle bore brush — work. After these measures have been done, another cap is fired from the unloaded gun, again aimed at a light object on the ground.

The process of clearing oil or grease to get a clear fire channel from cap or primer to powder charge in the breech is a Catch-22 proposition, because exploding caps on a nipple can cause a deposit of cap fouling or debris. While most percussion caps today are non-corrosive, they still expel a certain amount of residue. Also, while unlikely, it is possible for tiny shrapnel from the body of the cap to clog the nipple vent, and sometimes the entire top of the cap body will remain fixed to the cone of the nipple. Running a pipe cleaner briefly into the vent of the nipple after firing a clearing cap is therefore a good plan. Use a twisting motion to scrape the channel and pick up any cap debris. This little step can save a great deal of consternation during a shooting match or at that moment of truth when a big game animal is in the sights. Tests indicate that residual cap deposits are more likely

to occur when popping percussion caps to dry the nipple than during actual shooting. This is because the loaded rifle has minor blowback to help clear the nipple vent, while the unloaded rifle has no blowback.•

Step 2: Dropping The Powder Charge and Ball Patch Protection

Now that it has a clear fire channel for ignition, the pistol or rifle is brought to half-cock if it has an exposed hammer; if not, then the safety is placed in the on position with the bolt (if the rifle has one), in the open position. Hammer guns especially demand this step because a hammer nose down flat upon the cone of the nipple can trap air in the bore. When the load is seated, that air pressure tends to force the projectile, patched ball or conical, forward toward the muzzle, creating an air gap: the old devil separated charge or short-started load. With the hammer eared back on half-cock, trapped air is expelled from the bore through the nipple vent as the charge is seated.

Now a proper charge of the right powder is dropped downbore. On top of that charge goes the aforementioned patch protector in the form of a couple sheets of hornet-nesting material, especially for a heavy hunting charge. This is accomplished with the off-end of the loading rod or ramrod, or with a jag. No protector is required for a sabot, of course, nor for most lead conicals, or a light powder charge in the ball-shooting pistol or rifle. In lieu of hornet-nesting material, an Ox-Yoke Wonder Wad does the trick. The idea

Modern blackpowder companies continue to modify standard loading tools, such as this Universal Hollow Point Bullet Starter from CVA with special inserts to better match conical nose configurations.

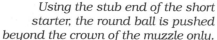

A round ball is settled upon a patch situated on the muzzle after a powder charge has been delivered downbore on an uncapped or unprimed muzzleloader.

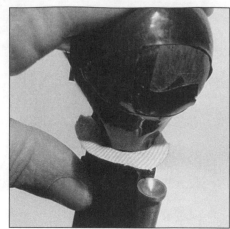

Using the stub end of the short starter, the round ball is pushed beyond the crown of the muzzle only.

is to create a firewall between the powder charge and the cloth patch. Proving a need for a patch buffer is simple: Pick up fired patches downrange and check for damage. Proving a patch buffer works is equally simple: Pick up fired patches downrange and check for damage. At this point, the rifle or pistol has a powder charge down in the breech.

Step 3: Seating a Patched Ball or Conical

In either case — round bullet or conical — a short starter is essential to driving the projectile a short distance beyond the muzzle. First, the stub end goes to work, then the longer rod. Even with the undersized Minie, using the short starter is a good idea. For a round ball, a patch of proper size and thickness is centered over the bore, and a ball of proper dimension is carefully laid down in its middle. Then the short starter goes to work. A conical demands clean centering for best accuracy. There are tools to accomplish this, one being the Thompson/Center Tru-Starter™. More about proper round ball size/patch matching and conical-centering in the accuracy chapter. At this point, the projectile is only partially seated. Now the loading rod or ramrod comes into play, driving the missile fully down upon the powder charge. At this point, the rifle or pistol is loaded with powder charge and projectile.

Pre-Shooting Bore Prep

Ensuring the best possible consis-

tency from one shot to the next requires similar bore condition. Dressing the bore, or firing a fouling shot, was noted and will be again in the accuracy chapter. Here, we're concerned with mopping up any excess lube from a patch or conical that may be deposited in the bore. This is accomplished with a cleaning patch on the end of the loading rod or ramrod. But wait a minute! Isn't this dangerous? After all, there's a powder charge and a projectile lodged in the breech of the rifle or pistol. Only a little thought is required to realize that a moment ago, a ramrod or loading rod was pushed by hand downbore, driving a bullet ahead of it to be seated on the powder charge. So this step carries no more danger than the essential bullet-seating step just performed. Naturally, the firearm is never capped or primed at this point. Furthermore, the muzzle is always aimed away from yourself and others at all times. The clean patch mops up excess lube in the bore, giving the rifling a uniformly dry bore from shot to shot.

Seating Pressure

As part of Step 3, whether seating a conical or a patched ball, it is important to maintain the same pressure upon the powder charge for consistency. This translates to accuracy. There are three ways to accomplish this. The first is feel. With practice, a shooter can do a pretty good job of maintaining about the same pressure on the powder charge. The second is with a special

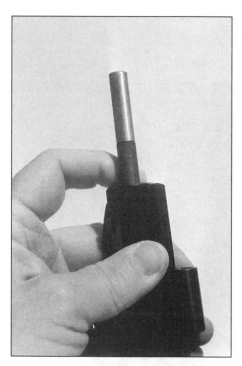

A ramrod or loading rod is employed to seat the patched round ball fully downbore. The ramrod can be marked where muzzle and rod meet to provide a witness point showing when the load is fully seated. The mark can also be used to determine if a gun is truly unloaded. Even if it is deemed fully unloaded, however, by using the mark on the rod, the gun must be treated as if it were loaded for safety reasons.

06-21-02
19.951
96.61

This shooter, using a special loading rod with a top handle for extra surface (rather than the tip of a ramrod) pushes the patched ball downbore with very little effort.

Using his special loading rod with top handle, the shooter has now fully seated his patched round ball down upon the powder charge where it belongs.

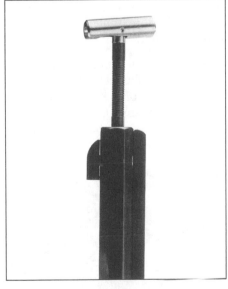

One way to turn a ramrod into a loading rod is with an extension, such as this Thompson/Center Power Handle for the company's Rugged Rod. Markesbery has a T-Handle that serves the same purpose, fitting the Outer-Line® rifle's regular ramrod.

tool that fits over the end of the ramrod. This tool is spring-loaded, the spring collapsing at a specific pressure, such as 35 pounds. This is not a commercial device at the moment. The third is the Kadooty, which is designed to deliver the same pressure upon the powder charge every time. Varying pressure on the ramrod or loading rod causes a rise in standard deviation, which translates to a different velocity for each shot fired. Furthermore, blackpowder is known to burn more consistently when consistently compacted. Warning: Never lean body weight on a ramrod or loading rod.

Pile-Driving the Seated Bullet

If a projectile has been firmly seated down upon the powder charge to the correct depth, there is no reason to slam the tip of the loading rod repeatedly against the projectile. On the other hand, although nose damage (especially to a round ball) does nothing for accuracy, if there is any question about bullet seating, then judiciously pile-driving is better than chancing a separated charge/projectile (short-start).

How to Employ Lubricant

Modern patch lubes are so good that kitchen-cabinet products are unnecessary, although anyone wishing to use them is welcome. Pastes especially rub into patches completely, using only the fingers as applicators. There are also spray lubes and liquids. The conical projectile requires a paste, cream, or grease lube that sticks to it, preferably a little dab on the base. Likewise the sabot, with the same bit of lube applied in the same place. The elongated missile is simply lubed and rammed home without a patch. The sabot/pistol bullet is treated likewise.

Modern lubes do not damage the powder charge when used properly. Left downbore indefinitely can be another matter, but that's improper procedure.

Step 4: Ignition

Using a seating device — these are now available for No. 209 shotgun primers and musket caps as well as standard percussion caps — the cap or primer is set in place. This means on the cone of a nipple for caps or some sort of seat for primers, or in the case of the Savage Model 10ML, a No. 209 primer is installed in the end of a percussion module. At this point, the rifle or pistol carries a powder charge, plus a seated missile, and is now ready for firing. While there is considerable talk about significant variations in muzzle velocity depending on the type of cap or primer used for ignition, extensive chronographing fails to support the theory. There are differences in velocity with various igniters, but they are not significant. After all, the means of ignition plays a small, if any, role in transferring energy to the bullet. That's the job of the powder charge. There are also only minor differences among various brands of caps or primers. See Chapter 28 on ignition for details. The percussion rifle or pistol is now ready to fire.

Steps for Loading the Flintlock Rifle and Pistol

As with the percussion muzzle-

The Kadooty can be used with a cap and ball revolver as well as rifle to create uniform pressure on the bullet.

loading rifle and percussion muzzleloading pistol, the flintlock pistol is also a short version of the flintlock rifle, and therefore is treated here in the same section.

Step 1: Clearing all Channels

While it's the habit of some flintlock shooters to fire off a pan of FFFFg prior to loading, the logic is questionable. Adding blackpowder fouling to the touchhole does nothing for clearing it out. Otherwise, the same pre-shooting rules apply to the flinter. The goals are a clean bore and a clear touchhole as an avenue for flame from the pan to the powder charge in the breech.

Step 2: Block the Touchhole

While this step is overlooked by successful flintlock shooters, the method remains recommended because it works more often than not. The idea is simple: Blocking the touchhole allows the passage to remain clear of powder from the main charge when that charge is loaded, then followed by a projectile forced on top of it. The unblocked touchhole may allow the invasion of powder from the main charge, sometimes filling it full. The touch-

hole then becomes a fuse. The flash from the pan powder must burn its way through the powder in the touchhole before it can reach the breech to set off the powder charge. This is not all bad, but it does constitute a delay as opposed to the flame of ignition darting through a clear touchhole directly into the powder charge. Blocking the touchhole is simple. A pipe cleaner does the trick. A nipple pick or vent pick also works if there's one that fits. A friend who collects original Kentucky/Pennsylvania long rifles believes that some old-time shooters used to block the touchholes of their flintlock rifles. His surmise comes from finding quills (feathers) in some original shooting bags. The quills have squeezed-down ends that just happen to fit the touchhole perfectly. It's pure conjecture, but perhaps the quills were used to block the touchhole. And maybe they were not.

Step 3: Clean the Frizzen Face

The job of the frizzen is to supply tiny hot curls of metal that fall into the pan, igniting the powder there. Friction between the flint, fondly known as the "rock," and the face of

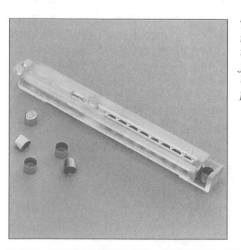

The standard percussion cap remains entirely workable, and this in-line modern-style capper from Thompson/Center, called the U-View, is built to hold and dispense these caps.

After the muzzleloader is charged, with a projectile seated downbore, it can be (always) pointed in a safe direction and capped for firing.

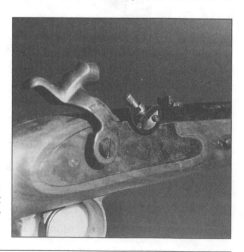

This modern Thompson/Center flask uses the same funnel system to determine the amount of powder by volume in a charge.

the frizzen creates this shower of ignition. However, friction-reducing grease, grime or other substance on the face of the frizzen reduces its ability to produce those hot curls of metal to ignite the fine-grain powder waiting in the pan. Solvent works great for cleaning the frizzen. Afterward, it simply dries.

Step 4: The Powder Charge

Steps 2 and 3 can be reversed of course, as long as the touchhole is blocked and the face of the frizzen is clean. The correct powder charge is up next. There is no difference between dropping a powder charge down the muzzle of a percussion arm or a flintlock.

Step 5: Priming the Pan

The touchhole block remains in place. Powder and bullet rest firmly downbore upon the powder charge. Time to remove the touchhole block and prime the pan with FFFFg or FFFFFg fine-kernel powder. The pipe cleaner or vent/nipple pick is withdrawn. Advice about twisting the pipe cleaner to draw powder from the breech into the touchhole must be ignored. That defeats the purpose of the touchhole block. Specific amounts of pan powder vary with the size of the pan, as well as the specific design of the flintlock. However, most flintlocks respond better to less, rather than more, pan powder. Half a pan, up to two-thirds, is enough, with care to introduce the powder to the outside of the pan, rather than pushed up against the touchhole. It's difficult to verify, but it seems that when the pan is completely full of powder, there is more tendency to "blow-out," where there's a big puff of smoke, but no snake-tongue flick of fire darting through the touchhole. By retaining the powder on the outside of the pan, with a little free space between the powder and the touchhole, there is a greater chance for the resulting flame to find its way through the touchhole and into the breech. Those of us who carry our flintlock rifles tilted a little so that priming powder remains to the outside of the pan seem to have pretty good luck with ignition.

One afternoon, an editor friend from Chicago who was visiting me at my Wyoming home found himself alongside as I loaded a 36-caliber flintlock squirrel rifle in pursuit of cottontail rabbits. He asked, "Can you really get that thing to go off reliably?" The Hatfield flinter fired a couple dozen times in a row that day without a hang fire or misfire. Perhaps it would have done likewise without blocking the touchhole or cleaning the face of the frizzen, or with a pan full of FFFFg powder, rather than only half resting to the outer portion of the pan, but maybe not, too.

Step 6: Shooting

The flintlock is ready to fire, with

Robert Rez drops a load into his smoothbore flintlock muzzleloader during a contest.

Rez enters a patched round ball into the muzzle.

He uses his short starter to drive the patched round ball further into the muzzle.

Rez now uses his ramrod to fully seat the patched ball downbore.

He drops FFFFg powder into the pan of his flintlock.

He now raises his flintlock smoothbore musket and fires at the target.

the hammer cocked and the shooter prepared to squeeze the trigger with hold-steady confidence. That's what it takes with the flintlock rifle: the ability to concentrate, maintaining the sight picture beyond the puff in the pan all the way to the boom!

Touchhole Location and Touchhole Liners

Ideally, the touchhole should be installed as high on the barrel flat as practical so pan powder cannot sift into it. Also, because of the obvious invasion of flame after flame, the touchhole can eventually become scored and essentially burned out. The fix for this problem is a touchhole liner, which can be installed by a gunsmith. The new liner returns the touchhole to a smooth interior surface conducive to flame travel.

Frizzen Replacement

The face of the frizzen will eventually scar up from multiple attacks from "the rock." When this happens, it's curtains for reliable ignition. Recall that it's the face of the frizzen, not the flint, that produces those hot curls of metal that ignite the pan powder. Cure? Easy. Replace a bad frizzen with a new one.

Fine FFFFg pan powder is presented to the outside of the pan only with a pan primer.

A first step in loading any gun is to know that it is unloaded. The ramrod of this shotgun is dropped downbore, falling to the bottom of an empty barrel.

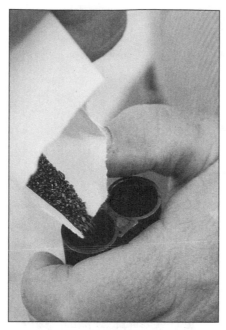

A pre-measured powder charge is dropped downbore in this 12-gauge shotgun.

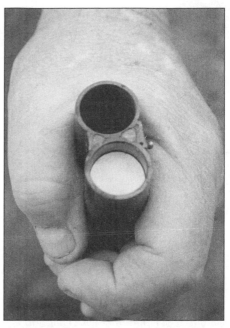

An over-powder card wad installed after the powder charge is dropped.

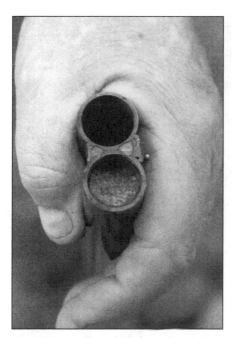

Following the over-powder wad a cushion fiber wad is installed in the bore.

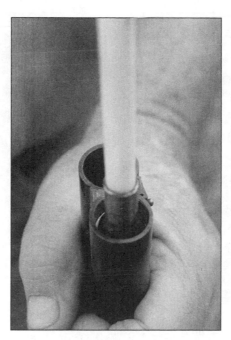

The broad tip of the ramrod is used to push the over-powder wad and the cushion fiber wad to the bottom of the bore on the powder charge. The rod is used later to seat an over-shot wad.

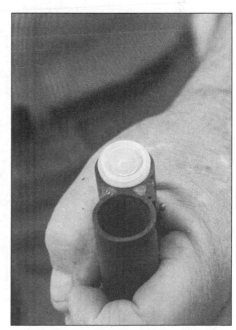

Before the one-piece CVA plastic shot wad is installed in the bore, a special sealing wad goes down firmly upon the powder charge.

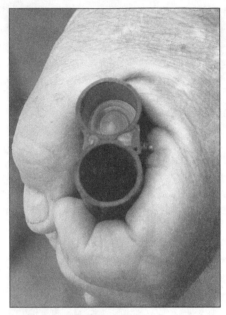

The over-powder CVA sealing wad is pushed partway down the bore, as shown here. It will be delivered fully upon the powder charge with the ramrod.

The CVA one-piece plastic wad can be run downbore upon the over-powder sealer wad. It is shown here loaded with shot first to illustrate how the shot column rests within the wad.

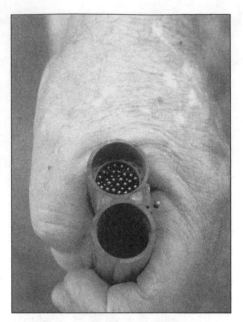

The CVA one-piece plastic wad, filled with shot, gets a ride to the bottom of the bore to be fully seated upon the sealer wad, which in turn is fully seated upon the powder charge. The ramrod tip is used to push the wad to the bottom of the bore.

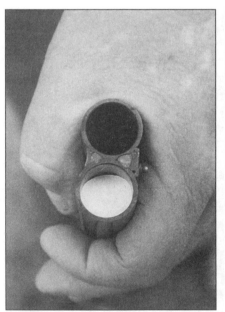

Following the shot charge, an over-shot wad is inserted into the muzzle.

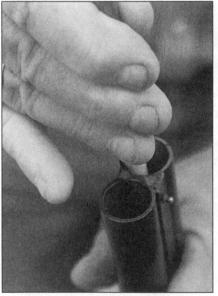

Shown here is the ramrod fully seating the over-shot wad firmly upon the shot column. The same thin over-shot wad is used with standard wad columns or the one-piece plastic wad. Note how high the ramrod rides now from the muzzle, showing that this bore is loaded.

After both barrels of the double-barrel blackpowder shotgun are properly loaded, the nipples may be capped, the gun always pointing in a safe direction.

Flint Quality

Cheap flints are too expensive. They cost a shooter missed opportunities in the game field, and last place in shooting matches. Always buy new flints for matches and special hunts if there is any question about the condition of an existing flint. That 's good economy.

Matching Flint to Frizzen

The edge of the flint must make full contact with the face of the frizzen for best results. This is easy to accomplish by first loosening the jaws of the hammer, which in certain literature will be referred to as the cock, allowing the hammer to come forward slowly until the flint makes contact with the frizzen. Since the frizzen is loose in the jaws of the hammer, it can be moved so that it makes full contact with the frizzen, and when it does, the jaws of the hammer are tightened to lock the flint in place.

Flintlock Reliability

If flintlocks were as uncertain, unreliable, and as cantankerous as often portrayed in print these days, the early American settler would have starved to death. Beyond hunting for food and self-defense, wars were fought with flintlocks, with devastating results. The Battle of New Orleans in January 1815 saw 7,000 trained British troops under General Packenham, transported from Jamaica, duke it out with the Colonials. General Jackson had 5,000 men ready to meet the attack, including a handful of "Tennessee sharpshooters," as they were called. Assumptions about the Americans firing from behind rocks and trees are unfounded. After all, Americans were transplanted Englishmen, many of them, and so they stood in rank and file just like the enemy, blazing away with their flintlock rifles. When the smoke cleared, literally, the British had lost 700 dead, with 1,400 wounded and 500 taken prisoner. The American loss was eight killed and 13 wounded. Were flintlocks in the hands of those Tennessee riflemen reliable or not? Two

reasons British soldiers failed in this battle were their smoothbore muskets — rock-tossers compared with the American long rifles — and the terrific bravery of the Redcoats who continued to march forward and die rather than retreat. After all, they were among the finest soldiers in the world and they had their pride.

Steps for Loading the Percussion Shotgun

There are a few fowlers around today, and they can be loaded the same as caplock scatterguns, with the exception of handling the idiosyncrasies of the flintlock. Mainly, however, it's the percussion shotgun that rules the roost these days: great fun to shoot, effective on game as well as targets, easy to load and no real trouble to clean up afterwards with its smooth bores (no rifling to catch and hold soot).

Step 1: Preliminaries

The general preliminary rules laid down above continue to apply. Start with a clean gun, fire caps to ensure a good path for ignition fire into the breech, use only the right powder in the right amount, and of course use a safe, allowable shot charge and wad column. Now the gun is clean, caps are fired on nipples and the game is afoot.

Step 2: The Powder Charge

A proper powder charge drops into the bore(s). Great caution is exercised with the double-barrel gun to ensure that each barrel receives only one charge. It's never a mistake to slip an over-powder wad into the muzzle of the charged barrel just to mark it so that bore will not get a second charge.

Step 3: The Wad Column

There is no one perfect wad column. A reader wrote, "My White muzzleloading shotgun with choke tubes makes wonderful patterns with old-fashioned card wads, but not very good patterns with plastic wads." Another shooter remarked that his Navy Arms T&T 12 gauge, choked full and full, made fine patterns with one-piece plastic wads.

The chapter on the blackpowder shotgun goes into more detail on wad options and columns. For now, however, the important maneuver is seating wads properly, whichever kind they may be. Seat them firmly upon the powder charge, but never jammed into place so movement is restricted when it comes time to shoot. Restricted wad columns can raise pressures dramatically. Wads intended for blackpowder shotguns are widely available from Ballistic Products Inc., Circle Fly, Dixie, CVA, Ox-Yoke, and many other sources.

Seating the wad column is accomplished with a ramrod or loading rod with a large, flat-faced jag. Hammers are eared back into the half-cock position so air can escape through the powder charge and out the nipple vent. Hammer noses down on nipple cones can block air passage, allowing air pressure in the bore to force the wads toward the muzzle, leaving a gap between the powder charge and the wad column/shot charge. Warning: After firing one barrel of a double-barrel shotgun, it's OK to shoot the other barrel right away. However, if the shotgun is to be carried around, it pays to ensure that the

This adjustable measure from CVA is calibrated for shot charges.

After ensuring that the cap and ball revolver is entirely unloaded, caps are installed on the nipples and fired to clear out lingering oils.

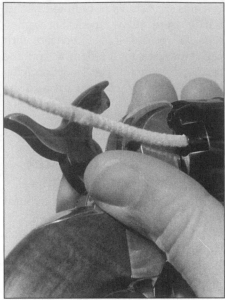

Following firing caps to clear nipple channels, a pipe cleaner is run into each nipple to remove any possible cap debris.

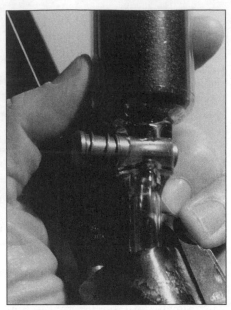

Using a modern powder measure, a proper charge is dropped into the chamber of the cap 'n' ball revolver.

A specially treated wad can be placed on top of the powder charge in the chamber of the blackpowder cap and ball revolver.

wad column/powder charge in the unfired barrel has remained seated.

Steps for Loading the Blackpowder Cap and Ball Revolver

Step 1: Preliminaries

It's the same old song: The gun must be clean, with all nipple vents clear and the barrel entirely free of any obstruction or fouling. If grease or oil is in the bore, cylinder chambers or nipple vents can cause a misfire or hang fire. A lack of lubrication on moving parts can cause a revolver to lock up.

Step 2: Clearing Nipple Vents

Same as ever, using pipe cleaners followed by a cap fired on each nipple of the unloaded gun to dry leftover metal preservers or lubes. As before, use a pipe cleaner after firing caps to remove any cap debris that may be left behind.

Step 3: Charging the Cylinder Chambers

Each cylinder chamber receives the correct amount of the right powder at this point, using a flask, charger, or adjustable powder measure. Safety notches on the Remington Model 1858 revolver serve to misalign the hammer nose with the nipples. With the hammer nose locked into a safety notch, all six chambers could be loaded. Some Colts of the period had a pin between each chamber and a notch in the hammer nose to affect the same safety condition.

Step 4: Seating the Bullet

A round or conical bullet is seated firmly upon the powder charge using the loading rod that rests beneath the barrel. This underlever puts plenty of pressure on the bullet, making excessive force unnecessary. A dab of grease or lube is now placed on top of each fully seated bullet as it rests in the cylinder chamber. This is done to prevent chain firing — when all the chambers fire at once — and to keep fouling soft. Option: a lubed wad can be located between the bullet and powder charge, also to prevent chain firing. While over-bullet lube or grease is recommended mainly to prevent chain firing, it is actually vital to the con-

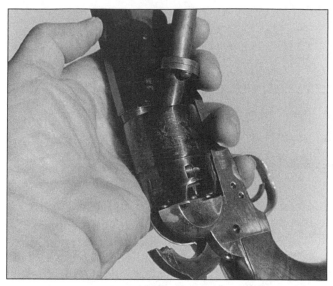

After clearing nipple channels a proper powder charge can be installed in each cylinder chamber. An adjustable powder measure is used here.

Following the charging of each cylinder chamber, a treated felt wad can be run down upon the powder charge, acting as a buffer between bullet and powder, also known to prevent chainfiring.

tinued functioning of the revolver. Shooting without grease or lube will eventually lead to the gun's moving parts no longer moving.

Step 5: Capping

Using a capper, each nipple of the percussion revolver receives a percussion cap, usually a No. 10 or No. 11, depending upon the exact dimensions of the nipple cone. Now the revolver is ready to fire.

Maintenance for Surefire Ignition

All aspects of firearm maintenance are vital to continued surefire ignition, especially the cleaning after shooting. But there's more to maintenance than bore scrubbing. For example, the Savage Model 10ML muzzleloader has a unique removable vent liner located in the forward portion of the breech plug. The liner is removed for proper cleaning of the rifle. When it shows wear, it is replaced. The same is true for the percussion module on the Savage rifle, which requires routine cleaning, but also needs replacing when worn. Failure to maintain a blackpowder gun is asking for misfires and hang fires. Conversely, proper maintenance, along with correct loading procedures, ensures reliable ignition.

At this point, powder rests in each cylinder chamber, plus a treated wad on top of the charge. Now a bullet is rested upon the mouth of chamber and then delivered down into the chamber by working the loading lever.

The cap and ball revolver is now loaded with powder, wad, and bullet in each cylinder chamber. At this time the nipples may be capped using a capper like the in-line model shown here. The revolver is now ready to fire, with all safety precautions in full force.

Chapter 21

OPTIMUM LOADS

ACCURACY WITHOUT consistency is like H2 without the 0 — it won't wash. The optimum load is first cousin to consistency. It's a matched load: matched to the shooting task at hand, be it small game, big game, knocking a metal ram over at 500 meters, or punching a hole in a paper target. So much has changed in loads over the past half-decade that old data is almost useless. For example, modern muzzleloaders like Gonic's magnum are allowed three Pyrodex 50/50 Pellets, each Pellet worth 50 grains volume equivalent to FFg black powder, generally speaking. That's a total of 150 grains volume, a pretty big charge. Behind heavy conical bullets, the three-pellet load produces a heap of energy. But is it an optimum load? Specifically, it's a big-game recipe, certainly far too heavy for informal target shooting and plinking, or teaching a newcomer how to handle a muzzleloader. And entirely overkill for smaller animals at closer range. But it may be perfect for moose.

One Gun, Many Loads

Among the many wonders of old-time blackpowder muzzleloaders and cartridge guns, including the shear enjoyment aspect of shooting them, is their versatility, especially the front loaders. While it's entirely possible to make up mild ammo for blackpowder cartridges like the 45-70, they must be put together at the loading bench, even if that bench is at the shooting range. The muzzleloader, on the other hand, is ready at all times for a wide range of loads, each one put down by hand just prior to firing the gun.

The oft-mentioned Mulford No. 47 54-caliber long rifle is a perfect example of this versatility. It chews the X-ring out of the 25-yard off-hand target with patched round balls and 60 or 70 grains volume FFg blackpowder or Pyrodex RS. Next day, that same rifle might be in the field for big game with 120 grains volume FFg or RS behind the same patched round ball. Both loads are accurate in the 1:79 rate of twist. While the lighter charge is perfect for most target work, it will never be found in No. 47 when big game is on the agenda.

Optimum vs. Maximum

There is nothing wrong with a maximum powder charge. Maximum means the top safe load allowed by the manufacturer of the firearm. Optimum is a different story. It's defined here as that charge of powder that produces the best ballistic results with allowable and safe pressures. Optimum is a carefully chosen word. While a full max load may be ideal under certain conditions — perhaps knocking over a metallic silhouette target at long range or putting a moose in the pot — an optimum load may be

Chronographs are now available in many price ranges, including good ones like this ProChrono.

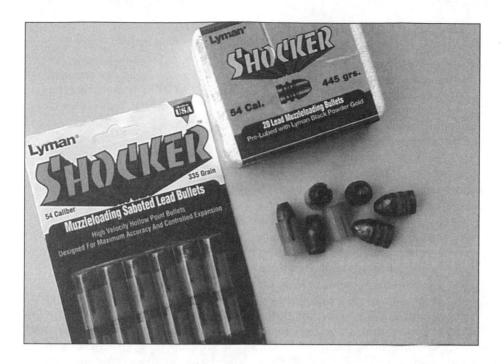

Matching bullets to powder and powder charge, as well as rate of twist, promotes the optimum load. These 54-caliber Lyman bullets proved accurate in a Markesbery Outer-Line® rifle with its 1:26 rate of twist. A good charge was 120 grains volume Swiss FFg blackpowder.

one of less powder for target work, or deer taken from a tree stand only a few yards away. The optimum load also pays attention to the law of diminishing returns. There are times when a maximum charge is little more than a waste of good powder, rewarding the shooter with a bigger bump on the shoulder than necessary, along with more soot in the bore and smoke in the air.

The Law of Diminishing Returns

It's for real. There is often a point at which adding more powder provides very little increase in velocity with a specific bullet, whether round or conical. A perfect example is a 58-caliber rifle with 150 grains of RS powder. Out of a 26-inch barrel, the rifle launched a 625-grain Shiloh Minie at 1,400 fps

with this powder load. Dropping all the way down to 130 grains volume RS, the same bullet lost only 100 fps. While the additional 20 grains did produce higher muzzle velocity, the increase was not worth the additional recoil. This particular rifle's optimum charge was 130 grains RS, not 150 grains, though the rifle was allowed that charge by the manufacturer. More importantly, groups with the 130-grain charge were better than groups with the 150-grain charge. That is the clincher.

In more severe cases of this law, velocity may actually go down when more powder is added to the charge. That's because blackpowder and equivalents do not convert from solid to gas nearly as efficiently as smokeless powder, so in effect, the powder charge itself becomes part of the mass that the expanding gases are pushing. This uses up a little of its energy, not to shove on the base of the bullet, but to work on the solids left over from combustion.

The Efficient Load

Handloaders of smokeless powder cartridges often read of the efficient case vs. the inefficient case, and it's true. For example, the

An optimum load also means using the correct powder charge, including granulation. This demonstration visually proves how vast a difference there can be in granulation kernel sizes, with FFg on the left and FFFFFg on the right.

7mm-08 Remington is more efficient than the 7mm Remington Magnum. With the right handloads, the smaller cartridge drives a 140-grain bullet at around 2,900 fps. Depending upon the powder used, the larger cartridge pushes the same 140-grain bullet at 3,200 to 3,300 fps, sometimes faster. But what about the powder charge? The little 7mm-08 does its magic with less than 50 grains of powder, while the magnum uses 20 grains more fuel to gain its 300 to 400 fps advantage. The prize for efficiency goes to the 7mm-08, which is a fine cartridge. However, the shooter who feels a need for more foot-pounds of delivered energy chooses the 7mm Remington Magnum over its little brother, in spite of the fact that the larger cartridge is less efficient. A similar condition exists with the muzzleloader. For example, a particular in-line 50-caliber magnum muzzleloader allowed three 50/50 Pyrodex Pellets for a total of 150 grains volume gained 1,459 fps with a 350-grain Buffalo Bullet. Three Pellets pushed velocity to 1,730 fps. It took a third more fuel to gain 271 fps. Not efficient! But wait a minute. Energy for two Pellets was 1,655 foot-pounds, while energy for the three-pellet

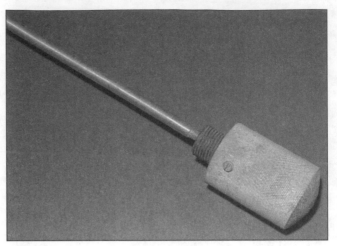

While not nearly as versatile as the Kadooty, this little pressure regulator works fairly well in maintaining a constant pressure upon the bullet, and therefore the powder charge. Here it is shown in place on the end of a loading rod with the handle of the loading rod removed.

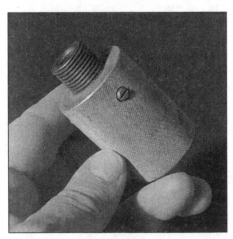

This is a small homemade pressure regulator, a spring-loaded device that goes on the end of a ramrod or loading rod to promote load consistency. It's spring-loaded, the spring collapsing at a specific pressure.

load was 2,327 foot-pounds. A hunter feeling a need for the extra energy might opt for the heavier load, in spite of it being less efficient than the lighter load. If it's a bear, the additional energy may well be worth the extra recoil.

The Chronograph

The only means of determining when the law of diminishing returns has entered the picture is with a chronograph. Anything else is guessing. Fortunately, chronographs are now affordable. Any serious shooter can own one. It's a simple process. Starting from well below the allowable maximum charge, each different load is chronographed. When the machine shows that additional powder has not provided a significant increase in velocity, the law of diminishing returns has been reached.

Steps for Building the Optimum Load

Step 1: Never exceed the manufacturer's maximum charge. Gunmakers are responsible for setting the safety limits for their firearms. Today, many muzzleloaders are allowed as high as 150 grains volume blackpowder, Pyrodex, or Clean Shot, or three 50/50 Pyrodex Pellets, which is the same equivalent charge. This does not mean that it is now all right to load any muzzleloader with that much propellant. Each gun must be considered individually.

Step 2: As with handloading metallic cartridges, starting below maximum is always recommended, working up in 5- to 10-grain increments toward the maximum allowable charge. Blackpowder and other proper muzzleloader propellants are far too inefficient to benefit from 1 grain. That's why 5- to 10-grain workups are suggested. One additional grain of volume will not register on a chronograph.

Step 3: The only powders allowed for building the optimum load in a muzzleloader are blackpowder, Pyrodex, and Clean Shot at this time. Others may come along in time, and no doubt will. The only muzzleloader in the world allowed smokeless powder is the Savage Model 10ML. It, too, has maximum ratings, of course, that are not to be exceeded. Working up from below is again recommended.

Step 4: Pay attention to recommended powder granulation when working up an optimum load. Kernel size, as clearly shown earlier, can make a significant difference in performance, mainly with velocity, but also accuracy.

Step 5: Prepare safe test loads of bullet and powder charge. For example, a particular muzzleloading rifle may allow a maximum of 120 grains FFg blackpowder or equivalent with a round ball. That's easy. The ball will always be the same. Only the powder brand and charge will vary. Conicals are another matter. Individual rifles will usually prefer some conicals more than others. The Savage Model 10ML did OK with 44-caliber pistol bullets in sabots, but 45-caliber bullets in sabots were more accurate in the test rifle.

Step 6: Test for accuracy. This means keeping records. It's unlikely that a shooter will remember exactly what happened with each tested load. Shooting from the bench and keeping records of groups provides solid data to use.

Step 7: Stick with your best loads as optimum, with one powder brand, one granulation and one bullet all forming a chain of success. Trying other loads to see how they go is fine. However, the whole idea of building the optimum load is having something to go back to that always produces.

If the shooter always adheres stringently to the maximum allowable powder charge allowed in a specific firearm, there is no need to be concerned about problems with an optimum load. Also, one gun may have several optimum loads. An in-line 54-caliber magnum muzzleloader allowed 150 grains volume FFFg blackpowder gave best accuracy with 130 grains FFFg, with minimal loss of velocity over the full maximum allowable charge. That load was considered optimum for elk in the timber. However, the same rifle with the same powder charge drove a lighter bullet at higher velocity. So this rifle had two optimum

loads, at least, and both were accurate. No load is worthwhile if it cannot be counted on for accuracy.

Old Information

Old data can be fascinating, and some of it is right on the money. Unfortunately, the latter is not always the case. A quotation from a magazine states: "To start somewhere, lay a ball on the palm of your hand and pour powder over it until it is quite covered. Set your measure for this amount. It should be within 10 grains of the proper charge for that ball and rifle, if you poured the powder over the ball with care to just cover it." This is not a slam against the author of those words. He probably got the idea from another source, as we all have done. Anyone wishing to experiment for himself is welcome to lay a round ball in the palm of his hand, covering it with powder. Is the hand flat or cupped? A flat palm could produce a whale of a powder charge, while a ball cupped into the palm might produce a light charge. Optimum, according to one dictionary, means "The condition or degree producing the best result." Covering a ball in the hand with powder is not the way to achieve the optimum.

New Information

Just as old information can be troublesome, new information must be sought out. Who would have believed that the 21st century would

While sabots seldom come apart, it still pays to check out spent examples picked up downrange, as these were, to see just what they look like.

find several million blackpowder shooters in the field? There are many blackpowder companies, as the Directory in this book proves. Furthermore, several major gun houses have joined the muzzleloader game, including Remington, Savage, and Ruger. What was right and prudent in the past for guns of old may not stand today. So in looking toward that optimum load, new data must be observed. Powders have changed. Into the country comes Wano from Germany and Swiss from that country, along with Elephant from Brazil. Clean Shot from Goex is on the market. Hodgdon includes a Pyrodex Pellet in its lineup.

Optimum Loads with Pyrodex

The basic rule is "load by volume." When Pyrodex is loaded by volume, it conforms perfectly to muzzleloading rules. From its unveiling at the 1976 NRA Convention in Indianapolis, Pyrodex has continued to improve, so that today in either loose or pellet form, it provides optimum results when loaded intelligently by the rules.

Optimum Loads and Igniters

The world of blackpowder shoot-

MMP—Muzzleload Magnum Products Co.—answered the call for sabots that would stand up to large powder charges allowed in many modern muzzleloaders. Their response was a special sabot designed to withstand higher pressures. These come in color codes. For example, there is a black sabot especially designed for bullets of .451-inch to .452-inch diameter with up to 150-grain volume maximum. MMP warns not to exceed whatever the maximum charge is as provided by the individual gunmaker. Having the correct sabot is part of creating an optimum load.

Pouring powder over a round ball in the hand will not suggest an optimum load.

ing made another abrupt turn when it embraced means of ignition other than the standard percussion cap, normally found in size No. 11. The top hat, or English musket cap, found its way onto various firearms because of its larger flame output. Primers were used with muzzleloaders before cars were popular, so there is nothing really new there — except for the fact that now there are so many different systems that use small rifle or small pistol primers, as Chapter 28 on ignition reveals. But what about primers and optimum loads? Optimum loads are fired with everything from No. 11 percussion caps to No. 209 shotshell primers. The only way igniters play a role in optimum loads is through surefire ignition. Some systems call for more fire than others, especially if the avenue from spark to main charge in the breech is long, or circuitous, or both.

Kernel Size and the Optimum Load

This area is not as clearly defined as it once was. Tests have shown some interesting results, for example, with FFg granulation in smaller calibers. A little 32-caliber squirrel rifle with a 26-inch barrel got more than 2,100 fps with a .310-inch round ball and 50 grains volume GOEX FFg blackpowder, with a pressure rating slightly less than 10,000 psi (pounds per square inch).The same grains volume GOEX FFFg gained a hundred fps with 500 psi more pressure. Obviously, the way to find the optimum

powder granulation and charge here has to be shooting for accuracy. Certainly the differences in velocity and pressure aren't enough to make that determination. Another test, this time with a 50-caliber in-line magnum muzzleloader with a 150-grain load of FFFg, gained 200 fps when compared with the same volume of FFg. That is quite a significant increase in bullet speed and according to the manufacturer, entirely safe.

Quick Review of Finding the Optimum Load

Step 1: Projectile

Twist and bore dimensions dictate the right bullet — one that is stable and accurate, while at the same time effective when big game is part of the picture. An MK-85 50-caliber modern muzzleloader with 1:28-inch rate of twist gets a conical. A 50-caliber Navy Arms Ithaca Hawken with 1:66-inch rate of twist is a ball shooter. Saboted pistol bullets in 44 and 45 caliber shot well in the Knight, while another test muzzleloader did far better with saboted 45-caliber pistol bullets. The 50-caliber Navy Arms Ithaca Hawken shot well with both .490-inch and 495-inch round balls.

Step 2: Try the Gunmaker's Suggested Loads

It's unlikely that a company will suggest a bullet of another brand as best. On the other hand, most run tests and oftentimes do have a han-

dle on optimum loads for their particular guns. They're worth a try, if only to get started.

Step 3: Accuracy First

A powerful bullet singing in the wind near a big game animal is not nearly as effective as a slightly weaker missile that finds the mark. It's accuracy first. Ideally, a big game hunting rifle will provide good accuracy with power, but the first goal in seeking the optimum load is making groups off the bench that engender great confidence. There's nothing like knowing that the firearm is sufficiently accurate to place its bullets right where they belong.

Step 4: The Accuracy/Power Compromise

Target shooters require only that bullets reach their destination with sufficient force to punch a hole in a sheet of paper, unless the target is a silhouette that requires knocking down. Hunters have a different goal: to deliver the most impact, but accurately. Sometimes a compromise is ideal: good authority, but with accuracy. A particular 54-caliber conical shooter proved very powerful with a particular bullet, but not very accurate. Another bullet loaded up with less authority, but good accuracy. It was the right compromise, promising good projectile placement with enough force to get the job done.

Step 5: Juggle Components Safely

The combinations are mathemati-

This photograph attempts to show some of the many different orifices in the bases of nipples. Don't be fooled by the one at the top—it is not a straight-through design.

cally astronomical. It's all but impossible to match a bullet with every possible powder and powder charge, as well as other particulars, such as lubes and sabots (see accuracy chapter for more on lube and sabot choices). While means of ignition seldom makes or breaks accuracy, small differences can occur. Then there are round ball sizes and patch choices. A lot of time can be spent at the range, juggling components to make the best load — as long as it's all done with safety in mind, never going beyond maximum ratings.

When asked by a newscaster where in the world all those bullets went that were manufactured in America, one spokesman said, "Most of them end up in dirt banks." How true. Testing for an optimum load means putting plenty of projectiles into dirt banks. It's both educational and enjoyable, especially when that one "pet load" emerges — that near-perfect combination of all components in the load chain.

Chapter 22

BALLISTICS

BUCKSKINNING IS hot. A quick look at the Internet proves the fact, with rendezvous listed coast to coast. But by far the number one reason for buying a muzzleloader today is hunting, especially deer. Blackpowder-only "primitive" hunts are carried out in most states. They're often held during particularly good times of the season, with some hunts in areas closed to metallic cartridge firearms. Regardless of where we are going with muzzleloaders, including the most up-to-date versions, hunting with the charcoal burner remains interesting and challenging. Even though high-tech bullets are driven by magnum powder charges, it's still one shot at a time. That is true even for the most far-reaching smokepole loads with the hot, high-intensity cartridges of the day, which include new powerhouse rounds that drive deadly bullets at terrific velocities.

The muzzleloader hunter's intent may be to take advantage of a special hunt with a modern muzzleloader, or step back in time with a flintlock. Either way, one fact remains constant: Ballistics play a big role in success. Ballistics for target shooters also are important, especially when the task is knocking a metallic silhouette over at long range, or delivering a projectile on target with sufficiently flat trajectory to take some of the guesswork out of Arkansas elevation and Kentucky windage. The concern of this chapter, however, is hunting power. Every hunter, whether in the field with a primitive bow or a space-age scoped rifle, owes his quarry a fair shake. For the front loader fan, that means delivering proper energy where it will do the most good. He also wants to fill a tag, as he should. That's why game departments issue hunting permits — to harvest game. As much as that word grates on the nerves of some folks, the hunt is a harvest of a renewable resource — take some, leave some for the future. Along with success in the game field, understanding muzzleloader ballistics is part of enjoying the shooting experience.

Ballistic Basics

Projectiles in motion: That's the name of the game in two parts. There are interior ballistics — what happens inside the bore of the gun — and external ballistics — how the projectile, be it a round ball, modern jacketed bullet, or shot pellet, behaves from muzzle to final destination. Internal ballistics is the more elusive study of the two branches. What happens to Minie

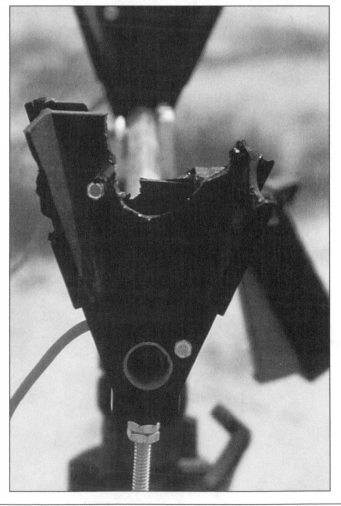

Several screens were sacrificed as the author studied downrange chronographing to determine velocities.

skirts in the bore, how patches fare in the fire of combustion, compacted vs. loosely packed powder charges, varying ramrod pressure vs. uniform pressure on the powder charge: These and other occurrences within the bore of the firearm fall under internal ballistics. Topics such as bullet energy at the muzzle and downrange, trajectory, and how projectiles behave in various media fall under the banner of external ballistics. All data were derived through chronographing with an Oehler Model 35P Proof Chronograph — nothing extrapolated and no educated guesses. The 35P provides highest velocity in the string, lowest velocity, average velocity, extreme spread, and standard deviation from the mean velocity, all with the push of a button. All energy figures were derived by Newton's formula, noted as KE for kinetic energy.

Calculating Power

Newton's KE formula is the only one used by ammo factories and bullet-making companies the world over. Final figures may be expressed differently, depending upon the country, but all results interchange, be it in foot-pounds or the metric system. Foot-pound is a unit denoting the amount of energy required to lift 1 pound of weight one foot off the ground with earth's gravitational force. Not everyone is happy about how foot-pounds of energy come about in Newton's formula. That's because the math squares velocity. Shooters who believe that bullet weight is worth as much as its speed in terms of final effect balk at this. The late Elmer Keith, popular firearms author, made his fame on the basis of bullet weight for effect. I sat in Keith's Idaho living room one afternoon, along with gun maker Frank Wells, as Keith applauded Wells' fine work on my custom 7mm Remington Magnum. Keith allowed that the Big 7 was a pretty good deer cartridge, "as long as the heavy bullet were chosen." Certain muzzle-

Ballistic potency naturally increases with bullet velocity as larger powder charges have been allowed by certain manufacturers for specific firearms. Because of these higher powder charges, special sabots were in order. MMP—Muzzleload Magnum Products—answered the call with tough sabots that can withstand maximum powder charges. Shown here is a bullet speeding away from its MMP sabot. Note that the petals of the sabot, while wide open to release the bullet, are not rolled back.

loader fans also balk at Newton's formula, which favors fast bullets — something muzzleloaders are not known for. Regardless, Newton's KE prevails everywhere.

It goes like this: First, the velocity of the bullet is squared, then divided by 7,000 to reduce from pounds to grains (there are 7,000 grains weight in one pound). The resulting number then is divided again by 64.32, a constant for gravity going back to Galileo's studies. The product of these divisions then is multiplied by the weight of the projectile. Given a 50-caliber round ball rifle firing a 177-grain bullet at 2,000 fps muzzle velocity, 2,000 is squared to get 4,000,000. Divide that by 7,000 for 571.42857, then divide that again by 64.32 for 8.8841506, which is foot-pounds for one grain of bullet. Now multiply times 177 grains (the weight of the round ball) for a final figure of 1572.4946, which is rounded off to 1,572 foot-pounds of energy. Is this KE idea so bad? A 30-06 Springfield with a factory 180-grain bullet at 2,700 fps earns 2,914 foot-pounds.

Bullet weight, while not gaining the advantage of squaring, also certainly comes into play. The 458 Winchester with a 500-grain bullet at 2,100 fps earns almost 4,900 foot-pounds of energy, in spite of its slower bullet speed compared to the 30-06. Furthermore, when muzzle-

loaders get really large, they, too, fare well with the KE formula. William Moore's 19th-century custom fire-breather proves this. Awesome is an overworked word today, but if it ever applied, Moore's rifle would be the place. This monster 2-bore fired a round ball. Since 2-bore means two round balls to the pound, each missile weighed 1/2 pound, or 3,500 grains. Burning a heap of powder behind this lead bowling ball pushed muzzle velocity to 1,500 fps — not very fast. But wait for the energy: 17,000 foot-pounds. That's more pasta at the muzzle than the 50-caliber machine gun round normally earns.

Outlandish Claims

There's no doubt that many of today's muzzleloaders are allowed stout powder charges with big bullets. The Savage Model 10ML, the only front loader allowed smokeless powder at this time, is capable of shoving a 300-grain bullet at 2,215 fps for 3,240 foot-pounds of muzzle energy. That's more steam than the factory 30-06 round achieves with a 180-grain bullet at 2,700 fps. Even when handloaded, the '06 gains only 100 fps on that figure for 3,134 foot-pounds. However, that's like reading the first page of a book and deciding its worth. Downrange, the ballistically efficient 30-caliber bullet surpasses the muzzleloader in delivered energy. Boasts of muzzleloaders having 7mm Magnum power are even less accurate. The 30-caliber magnum clan, such as the 300 Winchester Magnum or 300 Weatherby Magnum, makes the comparison even less plausible. Two-bores and 4-bores of the distant past were definitely, at close range, on par with most of the metallic cartridges fired today. But those behemoths are not the norm. The most popular muzzleloader caliber today is 50, with 54s represented and 45s gaining some ground with quick-twist rifling for conicals.

In-the-Field Experiences

Actual in-the-field experiences tell a great deal about muzzleloader authority. Those of us who still enjoy hunting with the round ball know that if we close the gap, get close, and put a 54-caliber lead pill on the money, a big game tag is as good as canceled. Shooting into gelatin blocks or Sam's Bullet Box, two devices among many (stacked wet newspapers also work), reveal a lot about bullet performance on the "real thing," but they do not take the place of putting deer, elk, moose, bears, or other game on the ground.

Two extremes: the little 17 Remington on the left with a tiny 25-grain bullet at over 4,000 feet per second muzzle velocity, the 45-70 Government on the right with heavy bullet.

Range tests are static. Field experiences are dynamic. Animals of varying sizes at close to far distances, at rest, running, tenacious, not so tough — it all makes a difference in firearm effectiveness. Nonetheless, tests in media are important, sometimes carrying amazing reliability.

Another Energy Theory: Pounds-Feet

Elmer Keith, mentioned above, and some of his dedicated readers came up with a formula more suited to their liking. These big-bullet guys did not cheat velocity. They simply placed it on equal ground with bullet weight. Their theory revolved around momentum, which is the product of mass times velocity. In physics, mass is the measure of inertia for a given body, established as a quotient of the weight of the body divided by the acceleration due to gravity. On the moon, with its gravity being 1/6 that of earth, a pound of lead weighs 1/6 pound, but the mass of the object is the same on the moon or earth. For present purposes, weight times velocity works fine for momentum. The fun part lies in comparisons. How about a 17 Remington with 25-grain bullet at 4,100 fps muzzle velocity, a 30-06 Springfield with a 180-grain bullet at 2,700 fps, a 230-grain, 54-caliber round ball at 2,000 fps, and a 50-caliber, 375-grain Buffalo SSB Bullet at 1,800 fps? The 17 Remington with a 25-grain bullet at 4,100 fps muzzle velocity earns a momentum figure of 102,500, divided by 10,000 for an easier work number, which is 10.25, rounded off to 10 pounds-feet. The 30-06 goes 49 pounds-feet. The 54-caliber round-ball rifle shows 46 pounds-feet, and the 50-caliber with 375-grain bullet comes up with 68 pounds-feet. The 54-caliber round ball at the muzzle, of course, just about equals the 30-06, while the 50-caliber conical whips it by around 28 percent at the muzzle. Believe it? Some do. Ballisticians don't.

KE in the Real World

While not perfect, KE is good enough as a gauge for telling the

shooter what to expect from his muzzleloader out where the big game animal is touched. Figures for a couple magnum muzzleloaders are presented below in KE terms. Pounds-feet, while showing a shred of merit, works no better, if as well, as KE, nor do other cooked-up formulas. In pounds-feet, the little 17 Remington showed poorly, with a score of only 10 points. Yet, that giant killer, in the hands of a good marksman, can take deer-sized game cleanly. One Montana resident has a record of seven antelope with seven shots from his 17 Remington, proving nothing, except that he's a good shot who gets inside 150 yards (he says) before taking a poke with the sub-caliber spitfire. Personally, I'd put my money on a stoutly loaded black-powder rifle at that distance, and at 100 yards, I'd bet on my 54 ball-shooter. KE does not leave bullet mass hanging in the breeze. Nor does the formula rely solely on velocity. A good example is a 3,000-pound automobile moving only 30 miles an hour, or 44 fps. That car would deliver 91,000 foot-pounds of energy despite the slow speed.

The Magnum Muzzleloader

A new force to be reckoned with, the modern muzzleloader that can use heavy powder charges with big bullets shows well no matter how it is assessed, including the standard KE formula. Tests with two examples proved how powerful they truly are. The first was a 50-caliber Savage Model 10ML, rated high for power due to its ability as the only muzzleloader in the world safe for use with smokeless powder. The second rifle was a Markesbery 54-caliber, well-built to safely stand up to heavy loads. A 300-grain conical bullet left the bore of the Savage rifle at 2,244 fps in front of 44.5-grains-Vihtavouri N110 powder for a muzzle energy of 3,355 foot-pounds. At 100 yards, the Hornady .452-inch XTP bullet churns along at around 1,830 fps for a remaining energy of

Muzzleloader power is provided in one, and only one, front loader by the use of smokeless powder. That rifle is the Savage Model 10ML, which uses a No. 209 primer (said to provide over ten times the flame of a No. 11 percussion cap), along with an ignition module. Shown here with a 300-grain Spitzer sabot bullet from Northern Precision. The use of smokeless powder in any other muzzleloader could destroy the firearm and badly harm the shooter and bystanders.

2,231 foot-pounds. Considering that some game departments believe 500-foot pounds at 100 yards lethal for deer, the full ton of power provided by this muzzleloader definitely walks the magnum trail. The 54 Markesbery, allowed 150-grains volume muzzleloader propellant, was actually tested with "only" 120 grains volume Goex FFg and a 510-grain Buffalo Bullet for a muzzle velocity of 1,517 fps and a muzzle energy of 2,607 foot-pounds. Here is where the big bullet-lads shake their heads, pleading that a 54-caliber, 510-grain bullet is formidable on its own account. After all, before it even starts expansion, it's well over a half-inch in diameter. While we can't buy into the pounds-feet theory, one thing is certain: There isn't a bull moose in Moosedom that will stand up to just one well-placed shot with that 54-caliber rifle. Lyman's test with two Pyrodex Pellets equaling 120-grains volume showed the same 510-grain bullet at 1,570 fps for an energy figure close to 2,800 foot-pounds. The rifle in question wears a Williams aperture sight, making it fast-aiming in woods and brush. The two rifles above, along with several others, such as the Thompson/Center Encore and CVA Firebolt™ 209 Ultra Mag, are examples of the modern muzzleloader magnum clan.

The Bullet Packs the Mail

The bullet is the only product of firearm, powder, lubes, patches, solvents, or any other aspect of a gun that delivers the goods. Because of medium velocities, muzzleloader bullets are both manageable and a problem. They're manageable because they do not have to meet the rigors of 3,000+ fps speeds. Bullets from high-intensity cartridges fly so fast that it can become fairly tricky to keep jackets and cores together (if that's the goal). The slower-moving muzzleloader missile is far less likely to come apart on impact. Furthermore, all-lead projectiles behave better than might be expected on big game. The molecular cohesion mentioned elsewhere works wonders in holding the lead missile together as a unit, which maintains mass, which in turn promotes penetration and a deep wound channel. Lead also upsets well in round ball form, although not always as a conical, depending on what it hits: the rib cage of a 150-pound deer, or a bull elk or moose

weighing several times that with much heavier bone structure. Here's the unmanageable part: Bullets designed for higher impact can fly right through a game animal when fired at lower muzzleloader velocities. And those heavy lead slugs, so great for penetration on really big animals, likewise penetrate deer or antelope like a hot poker through a sheet of onion-skin paper, spending most of their energy on the hill behind the beast, rather than in the quarry. The upshot of this whole business of proper projectiles for hunting muzzleloaders is to use pure lead round balls of significant size for large game, jacketed or lead bullets designed originally for handguns that open up readily at muzzleloader velocities, and big lead conicals that smash through and through, anchoring large animals on the spot with proper placement — a subject coming up immediately.

Round Ball Placement

Bullet placement is not everything. Anyone would rather drive a lesser projectile through the rib cage, rather than nicking the tail with a big bullet, but the right one still counts for a great deal. The best is the right bullet delivered to the right spot. When it comes to the round ball, that spot is the chest area. Round balls tend to upset (mushroom) readily. My own collection includes tortilla-shaped lead spheres recovered from various big game animals up to bull bison. On the other hand, counting on the lead globe to smash both shoulders of a bull elk may be asking for too much. Within round ball range, wild animals taken full in the boiler room seldom go far.

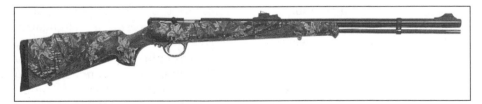

Power is achieved in this CVA Eclipse Magnum In-Line Muzzleloader by combining heavy bullets with an allowed 150-grain volume powder charge for good muzzle velocity.

Using the right bullet with the right powder charge puts the muzzleloader in the big game league even for an animal the size of a moose. This bull was dropped with a 54-caliber 640-grain Parker Hydra-Con bullet.

Lead Conical Placement

The big lead conical, such as the 510-grain, 54-caliber chunk of pure lead mentioned above for the Markesbery 54-caliber rifle, should be directed a little forward of the chest region. A case in point is the javelina, certainly one of the smallest of the big game animals hunted regularly. This one is a 20-yard shot with a 58-caliber musket driving a 500-grain pure lead Minie with 100 grains volume FFg blackpowder. Boom! The boar looks up, moves not one inch, remains planted on the spot. The hunter reloads. Boom! The boar walks in a tight circle, whirls around once, and drops. Those big lead bullets simply whistled through the target.

Handgun Bullet Placement from Muzzleloading Rifles

Handgun bullets from muzzleloading rifles behave more like round balls in big game than heavy lead conicals. Most are designed to readily open at modest arrival velocities and therefore do a fine job on big game with the chest strike. A case in point was a big whitetail buck at 50 yards. Boom! A 50-caliber muzzleloader sent a Nosler 260-grain jacketed Partition bullet on its way. The buck is chest-centered. It makes one leap and plops down onto the Kentucky forest floor. Another example: an elk standing at 75 yards. Boom! A 50-caliber muzzleloader sent a 240-grain Sierra handgun bullet on target. The elk whirls, dashes into the trees and drops inside of 25 yards.

Energy Delivered Downrange

Suffice it to say that round balls, even the big ones, lose about half of their punch only 100 yards from the muzzle. So getting close is the ticket. Up close, round balls are deadly. Handgun bullets carry a modest ballistic coefficient, but get to 100 yards with reasonable remaining steam. Blunt-nosed lead conicals shed speed faster than pointed bullets, but the longer ones do quite well downrange. Spitzer-shaped conicals retain their original velocity/energy better as the distance from muzzle to target increases. For the majority of tree-stand hunting, racy bullets with high ballistic coefficients are of little value, while round balls and blunt conicals doing the job magnificently. But for those who feel a need to have a 200-yard front loader, shapely missiles are the ticket.

Muzzleloader Powders and Ballistics

Rather than fewer muzzleloader powders in the 21st century, there are more choices than in the recent past. Goex is well-known for its regular blackpowder offered in Cannon Grade for blackpowder cannons; Fg for muskets and the 10-gauge shotgun; FFg for big bore rifles or pistols; FFFg for smallbore rifles, pistols, and revolvers; FFFFg as pan powder for priming; and Cartridge Grade for cartridges, as well as big-bore muzzleloading rifles and pistols. The company also makes Clear Shot in FFg and FFFg granulations. Clear Shot is not another ascorbic acid propellant, nor does it contain perchlorates. It's noted as clean burning and non-hygroscopic with an indefinite shelf life. While it is non-corrosive in the sense of damaging the bore (it will not), Clear Shot does require cleanup after shooting. Water is fine, as well as solvents, or a combination of water and solvents. Clear Shot can be shipped and stored with the same regulations governing smokeless powder. Goex also imports KIK Blackpowder from Slovenia, once the northern part of Yugoslavia before the name changes came in. Mick Fahringer, president of Goex, says: "This is another good blackpowder, nothing special. It works like any other blackpowder and it costs a little less. The company is about 150 years old."

WANO Schwarzpulver GmbH Black Powder comes out of Germany and is distributed in this country by Luna Tech Inc. (see Directory). It comes in many granulations, including FA grades, which are unglazed in kernel sizes 2FA, 4FA, and 7FA, the latter a 40-mesh powder on par with FFFFg. WANO also comes in FFFg and FFg granulations. It's noted for strict control of kernel size, especially in FFFg and FFg. Two more excellent blackpowders come in from Brazil and Switzerland: Elephant Black Powder from Brazil and Swiss Black Powder from Switzerland. Both are sold in the United States through Petro-Explo Inc. (see Directory). Elephant is offered in many different granulations, beginning with a FFFFFg (5F), super fine. There is also FFFFg, FFFg, FFg, and Fg. This is another very old company founded in 1866. Swiss Black Powder dates back to 1853. It's another high-grade propellant with high-energy output, and it's available in Fg, FFg, FFFg, FFFFg, and a special 1 1/2 Fg Schuetzen granulation.

Pyrodex is a blackpowder substitute that's been on the market since the 1970s with constant improvement. Today it's offered in P for pistol, RS for rifle/shotgun, RS Select, especially high-grade, and the Pyrodex Pellet, a solid propellant.

Muzzleloader propellants have always varied from brand to brand and they still do. Quality of components plays a role, including even the exact type of wood used to make the charcoal for blackpowder, as well as the origin of the saltpeter. Manufacturing methods also differ, along with the numerous specific granulations, as proved by the list above. These differences do result in a range of ballistic performances. However, and as usual, a perfect attribution of exact ballistic results per powder is not only difficult to prove, but perhaps impossible. This fact is easily shown in chronographing, when a specific powder in a specific test rifle provides higher velocity than another powder, yet when those two powders are evaluated in another test firearm, the results do not match. The powder that gave a little less velocity in Rifle A, for example, may provide more velocity in Rifle B. Everyone in the testing business would prefer clean, always-the-same results, but the real world does not work that way. When the chief engineer at the Lyman Co. compiled his huge data bank of muzzleloader performance, these hard-to-explain differences cropped up regularly. For example, in one test rifle, Goex FFg achieved 1,551 fps with 120 grains volume and a 350-grain bullet. In the same test rifle, 120 grains of Elephant Brand FFg got 1,508 fps — quite close to the same considering normal extraneous variables in testing. However, the difference remains hard chronograph-generated fact. Then to muddy the waters further, the same test rifle and same bullet, got lower instead of higher velocity with Elephant FFFg: 1,498 fps with the same 120-grain charge and same 350-grain bullet. In another rifle, Elephant FFFg got higher velocity than Elephant FFg, which we would expect of the finer granulation.

Shooters who are extremely concerned about the exact ballistics of their favorite muzzleloading firearms or blackpowder cartridge guns simply must gain access to a chronograph, then test different powders with different loads and various bullets to learn what each combination provides in velocity/energy.

Beyond Velocity

Velocity is definitely a deciding factor in delivered energy. However, accuracy is another high priority factor to be considered. Most shooters would gladly surrender a hundred fps for much improved bullet clustering, and wisely so. Col. Townsend Whelen, well-known shooter/writer of his day, said it all with his oft-quoted remark, "Only accurate rifles are interesting." Ditto for pistols and revolvers, as well as effective patterning in shotguns. The fun is in the testing. It is not difficult work. The shooter heads for the range with safe components: different powders and granulations, a variety of missiles, and he shoots, and shoots, and shoots a little more. Eventually, with good record keeping, the most accurate load chain surfaces. The reward is great. Naturally, bullet energy, especially where big-game hunting is the goal, must be considered. In that case, a slightly larger group with considerably more power is better than a slightly smaller group size with a lot less delivered energy.

While knockdown power does not truly mean bowling a big game animal over, many shooters rely on a flat-nosed bullet like these from Parker Productions to deliver a wallop.

Muzzleloader Bore Size and Ballistics

Smaller bores generate more pressure per powder charge than larger bores because of the volume of gas dispersion. A 32-caliber rifle firing a 45-grain round ball with 70 grains volume Elephant Brand FFg blackpowder produced 17,700 psi (pounds per square inch) pressure. However, a 50-caliber rifle shooting a 177-grain round ball with the same exact powder and charge (Elephant FFg, 70-grains volume) generated only 6,100 psi: quite a difference. A 12-gauge muzzleloading shotgun produced 1,200 fps muzzle velocity with a 1-ounce shot charge and 102 grains Elephant FFg blackpowder, with a psi rating of only 2,200. Incidentally, the only reason a 102-grain charge was used rather than a 100-grain charge had nothing to do with ballistics, but rather the fact that 102 grains volume equals 3 3/4 drams equivalent. When we get into truly large-bore rifles, large powder charges are vital to velocity development.

The Zephyr™ rifle from the Pacific Rifle Co. comes in calibers 62, 72, and 8 bore. This well-made under-hammer long gun is designed with slow-twist rifling to shoot round balls in these sizes with good velocity and trajectory by allowing heavy powder charges. It's ballistic law. Another big boy is October Country's Great American Sporting Rifle at 72 caliber, or the same company's Heavy Rifle, which fires an .820-inch round ball weighing 830 grains or a .989-inch round ball weighing 1,455 grains. Jim Craig dropped a 550-pound African lion with his October Country 8 bore. His charge: 300 grains of FFg blackpowder. "The ball penetrated the entire length of his body," Craig reported, "and exited through his hindquarters."

Pyrodex and Clear Shot Ballistics

Pyrodex yields more energy per weight than blackpowder, but when used volume-for-volume with blackpowder (the only correct way to employ Pyrodex), ballistic results are

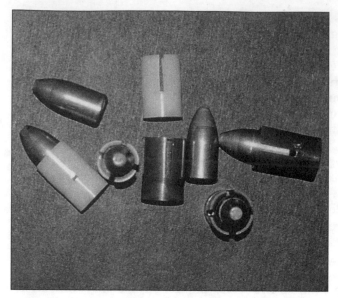

Northern Precision has been offering Spitzer-shaped bullets for muzzleloaders for some time. These jacketed bullets fit into sabots.

similar. A 50-caliber rifle shooting a 177-grain round ball got 1,900 fps with 120 grains volume Pyrodex RS (70.5 grains weight), while the same rifle earned about 75 fps less muzzle velocity with Goex or Elephant FFg: very similar results. Clear Shot from Goex comes in with similar figures.

Muzzleloader Powders and Recoil

Recoil is part of the ballistics game because it is produced by the energy of the load. "Kick" is the price paid for power. There is no escaping this law of physics, Newton's Third, that every action will have an opposite and equal reaction. The reason the firearm doesn't fly back as fast as the missile flies forward is weight: The gun weighs a lot more than the bullet or shot charge. Newton's Third is working all the time. A person steps into a boat. He tosses a line to a partner on the shore. The boat moves away from the shore in the opposite direction of the thrown rope. A rocket in space could not steer without Newton's Third. Certainly there is no air out there to "push on," but air is not the factor. When the gun goes bang, the bullet flies downrange and the firearm comes back at the shooter. Part of the recoil formula is the actual weight of the powder charge. Since blackpowder and its mates are not as efficient as smokeless, it takes

more fuel to produce decent ballistics. Therefore muzzleloaders generate a bit of kick (recoil), especially in the big bores that require considerable propellant for decent velocity. Here are some comparisons:

Rifle A: 30-06 firing a 180-grain bullet with 55 grains weight of powder. Rifle weight, 9 pounds.

Rifle B: 54 caliber firing a 230-grain ball in front of 120 grains weight of powder. Rifle weight, 9 pounds.

Rifle C: 54 caliber firing a 460-grain conical in front of 150 grains of powder. Rifle weight, 10 pounds.

Free Recoil of Rifle A = 20 foot-pounds

Free Recoil of Rifle B = 36 foot-pounds

Free Recoil of Rifle C = 70 foot-pounds

Formula for computing free recoil energy:

RE = recoil energy

G = gravitational constant of 32.2 ft/sec/sec.

W = weight of the gun in pounds

bw = bullet weight in grains

bv = bullet velocity in fps

cw = weight of the powder charge in grains

C = the constant of 4,700 fps, also known sometimes as the "velocity of the charge."

There are other formulas for computing recoil that will give slightly different results, but the above comparisons are sound. Muzzle velocity for the 30-06 was entered as 2,700 fps; muzzle velocity for the 54 ball-shooter was called 1,975 fps; and the initial takeoff for the 54 conical-shooter was gauged at 1,700 fps. None of the generated recoil figures are that hard to manage, especially when compared with a real kicker, such as the 460 Weatherby Magnum firing a 500-grain bullet with 120 grains of powder at 2,700 fps muzzle velocity from a 10-pound rifle with a recoil energy of 116 foot-pounds.

The round nose bullets resting on their sides are Parker Production company's Hydra-Shock with hydraulic action.

Blackpowder Handgun Power

Ballistic performance favors the rifle in this chapter, and the handgun has its own chapter. Briefly, however, here's what can be expected from a blackpowder sidearm. The 44-caliber revolver produces 38 Special ballistics, while a pistol on the order of Thompson/Center's Encore in 50 caliber can challenge a 30-30 rifle at close range. The blackpowder cartridge is on the mild side when loaded with blackpowder, with a 45 Colt developing around 300 to 350 foot-pounds of energy. The same cartridge in a modern revolver, such as a Ruger, can be loaded with smokeless powder to much higher energy levels comparable to a 44 Magnum. A Hornady reloading manual shows the 45 Colt with a 300-grain XTP-MAG bullet at 1,300 fps muzzle velocity for over a half-ton of muzzle energy. This load is allowed only in Ruger or Thompson/Center guns.

Muzzleloading Shotgun Ballistics

The muzzleloading shotgun gains something in the domain of 1,000 fps with heavy shot charges, such as 1 1/2 ounces, and around 1,200 fps with 1-ounce charges. It cannot compete with the modern shotshell, but within range limitations, and when choked properly for a good pattern, the soot-burning scattergun fills the game bag remarkably well.

Blackpowder Shotshell Ballistics

The blackpowder breech-loading shotgun is limited by the shotshell case capacity itself. Once again, good patterns make for effectiveness, and just as great grandpa fed his family with blackpowder shotgun shells doing the work, the same ammunition can be counted on today within reasonable ranges.

Blackpowder Cartridge Rifle Ballistics

Unlike the muzzleloader, the blackpowder cartridge rifle is limited by the capacity of its metallic case. However, the big bores provide plenty of big game authority. While the 44-40 Winchester scoots a 200-grain bullet away at about 1,200 fps for a muzzle energy under 650 foot-pounds, the Sharps 45-120 cartridge loaded with 110 grains volume Fg comes in at close to 1,500 fps muzzle velocity for well over a ton of muzzle energy.

Muzzleloader and blackpowder cartridge ballistics are an integral part of the sport. Not only are they needed for discovering firearm performance — which is important on the target range and vital in the big-game hunting arena — but also for the shear enjoyment of interesting facts.

One of the more powerful pistols of recent times is the Thompson/Center Scout, which has been replaced by the company's Encore. The Scout is an in-line pistol, calibers 50 and 54, capable of handling a heavy powder charge with good bullets.

Chapter 23

ACCURACY OR NOTHING AT ALL

Colonel Whelen was right when he said, "Only accurate rifles are interesting." The same applies to every other firearm, including muzzleloaders and blackpowder cartridge guns. There are ways to milk the most accuracy from blackpowder front loaders or cartridge guns. First, what can be expected from regular, off-the-shelf firearms? Monster slug gunoefficients resting on the bench like railroad ties with barrels stuck on them make superlative groups, but they're extremely specialized. The guns of interest here are carried at rendezvous, in the hunting field, or a special shoot, such as one of the National Muzzle Loading Rifle Association (NMLRA) events: National Black Powder Cartridge Shoot, National Spring Shoot, Family Shoot, National Championship

Shoot, National Turkey Shoot and many others. Regardless of the marksmanship's task, accuracy is essential, even if the game is nothing more than putting holes in soda cans on the side of a dirt hill. Bucket-size groups kill the sport. At first it's fun to load the old way, handling firearm styles and types of the past, with clouds of smoke hanging on the air. But the honeymoon ship soon crashes on a rocky shore called "can't hit nothing."

I wanted to find out what a couple ball-shooting rifles could do at 100 yards off the bench if they were scoped. A gunsmith drilled and tapped the barrels for mounting a Bausch & Lomb 6x-24x scope. With open sights, the rifles rarely grouped under 2 inches, and usually 3 inches or more, even under

ideal range conditions. Three patched round balls punched holes slightly under an inch center-to-center the first time out. Next time, too. And the time after that.

Points of Consistency

No guns shoot their best groups with haphazard loads or handling tactics. Here are five consistency pointers for muzzleloaders and blackpowder cartridge firearms:

The powder charge must be consistent for every shot, not only same brand and granulation, but also the amount for every load.

Ramrod pressure must be consistent.

Ignition must be consistent.

Patches must be consistent.

Bore condition must be consistent.

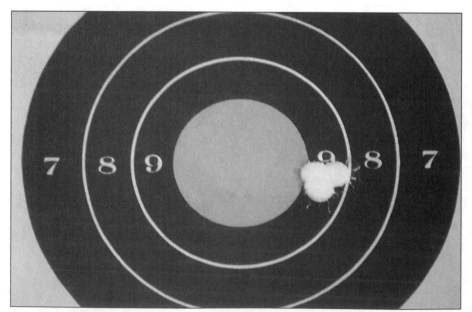

Groups like this one will not happen all the time; however, once the right load was found with the right bullet, a Markesbery 50-caliber muzzleloader made this three-shot group at 50 yards.

The rules of accuracy dictate that the sprue of the round ball faces outward toward the muzzle when loaded. This is a good idea, not so much because the ball will not shoot if the sprue faces down toward the breech, but as another means of observing consistency.

Powder Charge

The right way to load blackpowder, Pyrodex, and Clear Shot is by volume with a charger or adjustable powder measure. However, haphazard dumping is not the way to employ a charger or an adjustable measure. A routine is much better, such as: fill charger or measure to slightly over full; tap the barrel of the charger or measure a specific number of times, such as six, eight, or 10; if using a measure with a swing-out funnel, swing the funnel back in place to swipe off the few kernels of powder resting above the barrel of the measure. The charger can be leveled a little, too, as with a Popsicle stick. This sort of routine establishes consistency. Now we also have special mechanical blackpowder measures, such as Lyman's 55 Classic Black Powder Measure. Warning: Never meter out blackpowder loads in a standard mechanical measure. The friction and/or static electricity normally associated with these measures could cause the powder to explode! Lyman's 55 Classic Black Powder Measure is designed especially for blackpowder, although it will also throw smoke-less powder charges safely. The internal metering bars rotate in a non-sparking brass sleeve. The powder reservoir, which holds a pound, is made of non-static aluminum.

Ramrod Pressure

A reader cooked up a neat device for maintaining consistent ramrod pressure upon the bullet/powder charge downbore. Mr. French's ramrod pressure tool had an aluminum body with a ramrod-size hole in its center. Inside was a spring with a metal button on the end. The tool was fitted over the end of the ramrod via the hole. Pushing down on the tool in turn pushed down on the ramrod, the spring collapsing at 40-pounds pressure. A commercial device that does the same job is the Kadooty. It delivers the same pressure upon the bullet/powder charge for every load. For fieldwork, plinking, informal target shooting, and general hunting, applying the same pressure upon the load "by feel" is acceptable. But when testing a rifle for accuracy, or loading up in camp before a morning's hunt, a tool such as the Kadooty is much more reliable. Test-shooting rifles with both varying and consistent pressure on the ramrod show that standard deviation is lower (better) with consistent ramrod pressure. Variation in muzzle velocity is lower when ramrod pressure upon the bullet/powder charge is consistent.

Consistent Ignition

Best accuracy results from consistent ignition. This is not necessarily a matter of the igniter. Percussion caps these days are quite uniform in output. Modern primers are also uniform in the amount of "fire" they put out. Inconsistencies can arise, however, if the channel from the igniter to the main powder charge in the breech is more a winding road than straight. In such cases, after a couple shots, delayed ignition is experienced. Anything that retards the flame of ignition is potentially harmful to accuracy. Fortunately, this problem is not common. The flintlock deserves a high-quality flint in good shape for consistent ignition.

The Round Ball Patch

Patch quality can make a difference in accuracy. This is usually a minor factor. However, patches that

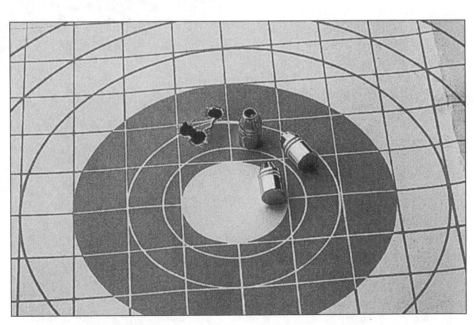

Markesbery's claim for accuracy is a realistic 1.5-inch three-shot group at 100-yards, which is more than tight enough for any big game hunting. This three-shot group, which falls into that 1.5-inch domain, was made with a Markesbery rifle, 1:26 rate of twist, and the company's 300-grain Beast Buster copper bullet, range 100 yards.

Today, the standard percussion cap, which is still highly popular and effective, upper left-hand corner, has been joined by the musket cap, right, and modern primer, both No. 209 shotgun and small rifle or small pistol.

fail due to cutting or blowout must be considered non-uniform in function. As discussed in Chapter 18, it's easy to detect blown or cut patches. Picked up downrange, the fired patch should be intact, small holes notwithstanding. Blown patches can be cured with hornet-nesting material, as previously described.

Bore Condition

While patch quality is a minor accuracy factor, bore condition is major, beginning with damage at the muzzle. The crown of the muzzle can be important to bullet flight. If it's bunged up, bullets can go astray. Also, a filthy bore does nothing but threaten accuracy. The rifling must be clean and in good condition for best accuracy. It's as simple as that.

Accuracy with Volumetric Loads

There is nothing wrong with achieving the closest possible powder charge weight from shot to shot; however, anyone can test accuracy with volumetric loads vs. scale-weighed charges. It's as simple as shooting sample groups from the bench with both types. Careful tests conducted multiple times proved volumetric loads with black-

The Kadooty is designed to deliver the same pressure upon the seated projectile time after time for consistency, which is the hallmark of top-grade accuracy.

measure. Velocity also remains essentially the same between loads by volume and loads by scale. This is why half-grain increments are of no value in blackpowder shooting, in spite of "pet loads" often given that way. Any time a shooter insists that his 50-caliber muzzleloader is more accurate with 60.5-grains volume blackpowder over 60.0-grains, that person has not tested his theory very carefully.

Accuracy with Chargers and Adjustable Powder Measures

Recall that a charger is a simple metal tube, cut-off piece of antler, or other device that provides one and only one volumetric charge, while the adjustable powder measure is capable of throwing various volumetric charges of powder. Here is what happened with an adjustable powder measure set at 100 for Goex FFg blackpowder, which weighs out very close to 100 grains for a 100-grain volume setting. Ten charges carefully thrown with the measure set at 100, using a strict routine, showed a low of 99.2 grains and a high of 101.7 grains. Compared with the accuracy provided by a powder/bullet scale, that seems crude; however, since blackpowder is not as efficient as smokeless, shooting results with this sort of variation prove accurate. Accuracy is born of consistency, and powder chargers and measures are both capable of producing consistent loads.

Powder Brand/ Granulation, Charge, Bore Dimension, and Rifling Twist

All four of these factors are linked for several reasons. Muzzleloader propellants vary from brand to brand. It is wrong to go strictly by how much velocity a specific powder provides in a certain gun compared with another brand of powder. That does not necessarily determine how good one powder is over another. Other factors, such as kernel unifor-

The Kadooty is used here at the gun range for testing purposes to ensure that each load receives the same amount of pressure upon the bullet, and therefore on the powder charge for best accuracy.

powder, Pyrodex, and Clear Shot are just as accurate as scale-weighed charges with the same powders. Haphazard or sloppy use of a charger or adjustable powder measure nullifies this fact, of course, while a solid routine with either charger or powder measure proves as accurate as scale-weighed loads every time. It takes a little shooting to prove the point. One or two tries won't usually do it. However, even then it becomes clear that scale-weighed loads are no more accurate than volumetric loads. Human error sometimes will make a group smaller or larger than another, but the problem isn't

normally linked to the method of forming the charge.

Blackpowder and replica propellants are simply not efficient enough to gain anything by weighing charges. Another quick test is with a chronograph that shows standard deviation, which does not change between scale-weighed loads and volumetric loads. Since standard deviation describes variance, it's a good test to prove the accuracy of volumetric loads. A standard deviation of 12 fps, for example, with a scale-weighed charge will be followed by a very similar standard deviation of a charge created with a charger or mity, apply. Furthermore, there is a matter of velocity per pressure. One powder may provide a little less velocity than another, load for load, but with a good velocity/pressure ratio. Finally, minor firearms variations may favor one propellant over another for accuracy. This seems to hold somewhat true for blackpowder cartridges, when a larger kernel shows a little accuracy improvement over a smaller kernel, but that factor has not been tested to full satisfaction at this time. Factors other than granulation may be at work.

Along with powder brand and bore size, the actual powder charge plays a role in accuracy in part because of generated pressures, as discussed below. Too-light charges prove inaccurate, while too-heavy charges also fail to provide good bullet grouping. Along with ballistic factors, the size of the powder charge determines how manageable the firearm is to shoot.

Bore size determines pressure, as we know from pressure-gun readings. For example, a 36-caliber squirrel rifle firing a 65-grain round ball in front of 50 grains volume Goex FFg blackpowder showed a psi rating of 11,200 in a pressure gun. The same Goex FFg charge in a 50-caliber rifle, pushing a 177-grain round ball, generated only 2,900 psi. Granulations also make a difference in pressure. Example: 50-caliber rifle, 177-grain round ball, 70 grains volume FFg Elephant Black Powder, 6,100 psi; 70 grains FFFg Elephant Black Powder, 8,300 psi. So what does pressure have to do with accuracy? Recall bullet obturation or upset in the bore. If a charge fails to provide sufficient pressure to force the pro-

jectile into the lands for guidance, accuracy will suffer. This is why shooters report poor groups with very light powder charges in some guns. On the other end of the spectrum, super heavy charges may "blow" a group wide open, sometimes because of actual damage to the base of a conical, which hampers its "steering" ability.

Rifling twist also plays an integrated role along with the other three criteria above. The bullet, round or conical, must be stabilized for proper flight from muzzle to target. The unstable round ball, failing to rotate on its axis, does not equalize minor discrepancies in its construction, and therefore cannot fly as true as a round ball that is spinning properly. A conical that fails to spin on its axis is in worse shape, because it will tumble in flight, doing what's called keyholing, and likely will strike the target sideways instead of point first. Since it is up to rifling to provide rps (revolutions per second) of a projectile, then twist is very much linked with accuracy. Rapid twist does nothing for the lead sphere, as proved by the fine rifles coming from October Country with super slow twist in big bores. This is the way it should be, for as the round ball grows in mass, it requires less rps to keep it on track. That's why a little 32-caliber squirrel rifle may have a 1:40 rate of twist for a round ball, while an 8-bore goes with one turn in more than 100 inches. The conical-shooter, on the other hand, must provide a sufficient rate of twist to rotate the elongated bullet on its axis for accuracy.

Altering the Powder Charge

The many factors that govern pressure and velocity hinge greatly

The Minie ball at the top shows a flared skirt, indicating that the powder charge was too strong for the thickness of the skirt, or the skirt too thin for the powder charge. Either way, ideal accuracy is unlikely.

upon the size of the powder charge. For example, if a rifle shoots inaccurately with a small powder charge, the obvious cure is going up, albeit never beyond the maximum charge allowed by the manufacturer. When a big powder charge simply "blows" the group, the obvious cure is reducing the charge. Most shooters seem to know these facts well, for any day at the range will find them going up and down in powder charge to find that most accurate load.

Bullet Precision

Benchrest shooters who are concerned with minute degrees of accuracy go only with the most precise bullets available. There is no other way. Spinning reveals concentricity. Bullets that wobble are out. Weighing discovers too-light or too-heavy missiles that will not fly perfectly into the group. Bullet quality may not be quite as crucial to big-game hunters as it is to benchrest shooters, but don't tell that to the hunters. Most hunters want the most accurate projectile possible. Fortunately, these are available in many forms. Anyone who has cast round or conical bullets knows how amazingly precise they can be, with good lead and careful management of the right tools. Swaged round

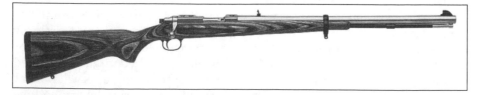

Matching the correct bullet to rifling twist is vital to accuracy. This Ruger K77/50 50-caliber in-Line muzzleloader carries a comparatively fast rate of twist for stabilizing conicals, and stabilization must occur for a bullet to shoot accurately.

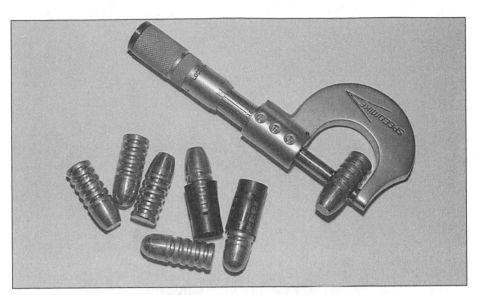

There is no such thing as top accuracy with poor bullets. These Parker Productions all miked out on the money, lending a lot of confidence that they would group at the range, which they did.

balls from Speer and Hornady are superb. Ten .535-inch Hornady round balls randomly selected from a box of 100 averaged 231.6 grains weight, the heaviest going 231.9, the lightest 231.2. That is only 0.7 grain variation. Seven-tenths of one grain is a tiny percent of the ball's weight. Apply the formula for obtaining the exact weight of a round bullet in pure lead: diameter to the third power times .5236 times 2,873.5, the .535-inch ball should go 230 grains weight. And it does, because the Hornady 54-caliber lead sphere micrometers out at a bit over .535-inch diameter. Cast projectiles, when accomplished properly with good lead and procedures, are also remarkably precise. Lyman-molded .395-inch round balls, cast with purified lead as described in Chapter 24, varied only 0.8 grain from lightest to heaviest. A run of .520-inch round balls showed an extreme spread of only 0.5 grain — one-half of one grain. That's not a lot when it takes 7,000 grains to make a pound.

Conicals and Base Lube

Old wives' tales are a curse to any branch of shooting, especially muzzleloading, where so many continue to thrive. Therefore, when tests are not conclusive, it's best to say so. However, considerable shooting with base-lubricated conical bullets, shank-lubricated bullets, and base-lubricated with very little lube on the shank, continues to show shank-lubed in last place. Groups seem best when the base of the bullet is treated to a dab of lube, with a touch on the shank OK, but not entirely necessary.

Lube, Sabots, and Accuracy

A dab of lube on the base of the sabot only promotes repeat shooting. That it makes for better accuracy is doubtful, but possible. More shooting is required before that one can be answered.

Lead Conical Alignment in the Bore

While lubing the base only of a conical may not be as much a boon to accuracy as suggested, one thing is certain: Seat a conical cockeyed and it will not shoot straight. Positively the best conical accuracy comes from bullets that are seated perpendicular to the bore: square, in other words, not titled off to the Jones' eastern pasture. This factor was recognized by Thompson/Center, so the company brought out a

little miracle worker than weighs less than an ounce in tough plastic. It's called the True-Starter™, built in two parts, with a hollow body and a plunger running through its center. T/C warns that the Tru-Starter™ must never be used with a primed firearm. It's advertised as good for patched round balls as well as conicals, but patched balls cannot go down tilted. Conicals can, and this is where the T/C tool pays off. First, the plunger is pulled outward, evacuating the body of the starter. Then a pre-lubed conical is inserted into the unit point-upward, its base protruding slightly from the bottom of the device. The base of the bullet is centered on the crown of the muzzle, with the bottom of the Tru-Starter™ flush and even with the muzzle. The bullet is now aligned with the bore. A rap on the top of the plunger with the palm of the hand drives the conical into the bore, its point slightly below the crown of the muzzle. Now a short-starter pushes the projectile deeper into the bore, followed by a ramrod or loading rod to seat the conical fully and centered upon the powder charge.

Lead and Copper Fouling

Neither of these gremlins harms muzzleloader accuracy very much, but both can be present in blackpowder cartridge guns, especially rifles that are sometimes loaded with smokeless powder, which is allowable with the proper safe charges. Lead or copper fouling in the bore can compromise accuracy. As one gunsmith put it when a customer walked in with a rifle that had gone sour: "The first thing I'm going to do is work on getting any copper fouling or lead out of the bore, so you can go home and do that or pay me to do it." Many guns that used to shoot fine, but don't anymore, only need a good copper/lead removal to get back on track. See Chapter 19 for the right chemicals.

Breaking in a New Gun

A break-in period is not always necessary, but some guns require a few bullets through the bore before they deliver their best accuracy. Or the bore can be lapped to take the sharp edges off the lands. Shooting the firearm is more fun than lapping the bore.

Bullets that Fit the Bore

Across the board, bullets that "rattle around" in the bore are the least accurate, while those that more closely meet bore diameter provide the best groups. This is true of both round ball guns and conical-shooters. Ideally, however, the round-ball rifle, especially, should be tried with the smaller ball and good stout patch. If it shoots well with the smaller ball, all the better, for that leaves the gate open to go to a larger ball if accuracy should slip, as broached next. Some guns, however, insist upon full-size bullets at the start. Testers of the Savage Model 10ML learned that 45-caliber bullets in sabots provided better accuracy in that particular rifle than 44-caliber bullets in sabots.

Normal Bore Wear

After-shooting maintenance ensures a long life for blackpowder guns. However, shooting also creates wear. Lucky is the man or woman who shoots a barrel out, because that's what the gun was bought for — to shoot. However, when accuracy drops, there are a few remedies to bring it back, at least for awhile. One is going to a larger bullet. This is very simple with muzzleloaders. For example, if a rifle has been shooting .490-inch round balls, going to a .495-inch round ball can restore group size. Sometimes a thicker patch helps, but not as much as the larger ball. Larger-diameter conicals are also a possibility. So are larger lead or jacketed pistol bullets in sabots. When all remedies fail, there is re-boring or re-barreling. The old-timers, often hard put to do their firearms justice with proper cleaning after shooting, were said to have gun barrels "freshed-out," which

If undue force is required to seat a round ball downbore, it's best to examine patch thickness and exact round ball diameter. A tight ball/patch fit with a round ball that matches fairly closely to the bore does promote accuracy, but having to exert a great deal of pressure on the loading rod to seat the ball is not called for.

meant reboring to a larger caliber, then re-rifling. The same can be accomplished today, especially by top-grade barrelmaking establishments such as Morrison Precision (see Directory), where some of the most accurate barrels in the world are made by hand.

Sabots and Accuracy

The oft-mentioned Savage Model 10ML, the only muzzleloader in the world as this is written that is safe to shoot with smokeless powder, taught a lesson about sabots. Regular sabots, hit hard by smokeless powder gases, often failed. The problem was cured when Muzzleload Magnum Products brought out its High Pressure "Semi-Hemi" sabots (see Directory). Sabots have a big job to do, containing the real projectile in its mad dash up the bore without burning out or breaking up. Just as it can pay off to pick

up a few spent ball patches downrange, the same goes for sabots. Accuracy may improve dramatically if a failed sabot is found and replaced with a tougher model.

Component Consistency

Murphy's Law says that if a fine product comes out, one that works perfectly, it will be removed from manufacture as soon as the company finds out how much you like it. Components do change in time, although blackpowder shooters are fortunate in the fact that changes so far are for the better, as with the latest sabots. Nevertheless, the shooter must keep a weather eye open for component changes that in turn alter consistency. Maybe that's why a shooter returned to the fabric shop and bought up a lifetime supply of pure Irish linen that measured .013-inch thickness no matter which part of the cloth was tested.

Dressing the Bore for Accuracy

Touched on earlier, dressing the bore is a stabilization tactic. Ideally, a bore should be the same from shot to shot, but that is not possible. Heat alone creates changes. However, especially with Pyrodex, firing a "fouling shot" before attempting to create a tight group pays off.

Oily Bores and Accuracy

Oily bores can make bullets do bad things. For serious bullet grouping, a quick swipe of the bore after loading prevents the problem, and, as stated before, poses no more threat than putting the projectile down upon the powder charge, which was just accomplished.

Accuracy and Damaged Bullets

Range tests indicate that round balls with frontal damage tend to fly off the mark, while conicals similarly affected do better. On the other hand, the base of the conical seems to do the most "steering," for when it's hurt, bullets fly wide of the mark. These statements are generalizations. However, one thing is certain: damaged bullets do not help accuracy, so all projectiles should be safeguarded from harm.

Accuracy and Ignition

Igniters from the major companies, such as CCI, RWS, Winchester, Federal, Remington and others, are extremely uniform in the "fire" they put out, be they percussion caps or modern primers. Accuracy problems because of ignition are more likely to come from a problem with the firearm, either a circuitous route from igniter to main charge of powder in the breech, some form of obstruction along the way, or other mechanical factor, right down to the power of the mainspring to deliver the proper hammer blow to set the igniter off every time. Flintlock ignition problems often fall upon a failure to follow a structured loading procedure, a low-quality flint, a worn flint, or a frizzen that

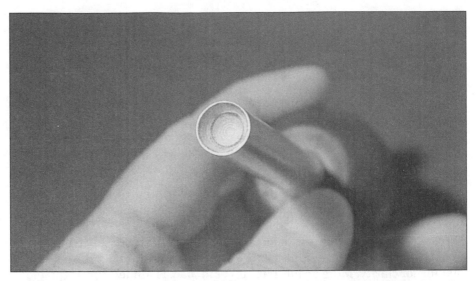

While nose damage with conicals may cause minimal bullet deflection if not too severe, still it's a good idea to maintain the bullet's integrity in all ways. This is the end of a short starter from Parker Productions. The interior wooden sleeve prevents nose damage to conicals.

is either dirty or worn out. Nipples can also make a difference in ignition, and therefore a variation in group size on the target. With musket caps and No. 209 shotgun primers so popular now, along with the best regular percussion caps ever, accuracy problems due to a failure in setting off the main charge in the breech are fewer and fewer. See Chapter 28 for more on ignition.

Accuracy and Sights

The big B&L scope mounted on the two muzzleloaders mentioned at the beginning of the chapter proved what those guns were capable of groupwise at 100 yards from the bench. Sights do make a difference. Certain special muzzleloader-only hunts forbid scopes, and so it is up to the shooter to get the best iron sights on his hunting rifle and learn how to use them. Practicing the proper sight picture with major concentration on the front sight helps, and where apertures are allowed, some shooters may find them ideal. A 54-caliber Markesbery Outer-Line® destined for black timber elk country got a Williams aperture sight, and putting bullets in the black with it is no big trick. Surprisingly, ordinary open sights, especially the so-called "fixed" versions, are entirely adequate for good shoot-

The author's custom 54-caliber ball-shooting rifle has an excellent open rear sight with two aiming points: a smaller deep notch, and a larger upper notch. By lining up the front sight in the first, the rifle is on for closer shooting, while the second is on at longer range.

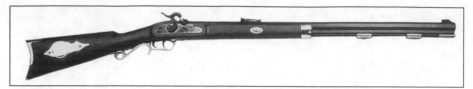

The Thompson/Center Cleland Match Hawken comes in 40 caliber. It is intended "for serious target shooters," according to the manufacturer. The 1:48 rate of twist in 40-caliber promises accuracy with a patched round ball. The rifle wears a precision adjustable rear sight with click adjustments.

ing, especially on big game. The open iron sights on No. 47, once on target, ensure meat in the pot. Because of the longer barrels of older-style muzzleloaders, sight radius — distance from rear to front sight — is also long, making for clarity. More about that in Chapter 29 on sights.

Accuracy and Targets

Why do we expect good groups from any gun when we cannot truly pick a specific aim point on the target? But we do. Fortunately, target makers know that in order to hit it, shooters have to see it, and so better targets have come along steadily over time, well-designed with the human eye and gun sights in mind. A whole series from Outers proves the point perfectly, each target carefully designed to give the shooter a precise aim point for the kind of sights that the firearm has.

The Eyes Have It

An eye checkup now and then is a fine plan. If groups out of that favorite front loader have expanded over time, maybe it's not a problem with a worn bore or failing components.

Body Stable

Just as eyes must be keen to best see the target and produce good groups, the body in general has to be in decent condition. That's why many Olympic-quality shooters have a workout regimen.

Shooting Bench Tactics

Sitting uncomfortably at the shooting bench and achieving the best groups are as possible as finding a hundred-dollar bill stuck to the bottom of your shoe. Proper form is with feet planted solidly on the ground, backside firmly on the bench, and if necessary, on a pad of some sort, angled to see the target through the sights without making a pretzel out of the body. The rifle's forearm usually is settled firmly on a rest, as is the butt of the rifle. A skid pad is under the right elbow for a right-handed shooter (more comfortable than the elbow sliding on a wooden bench top), and there's another pad between the shoulder and rifle butt. At the bench, sitting solidly, the body takes full recoil. A shooting pad helps absorb recoil.

Accuracy is so multi-faceted that no single chapter in any book can do every tiny fragment of the discipline full justice, but laid down here are some of the principles. The soot burners we have today are highly accurate, especially because they wear good barrels. But it doesn't end there. Sights are good, too, and give a little credit to the contemporary marksman with his knowledge of guns and his interest in shooting them better and better.

Old Information

Science wore swaddling clothes when blackpowder shooting was the only show in town. Data was often gathered by the light of the moon, stirred in a caldron with newt's toes, and sent forth as gospel. Not all old-time information was bogus, by any means; it's just that so much of it does nothing to promote accuracy, the present topic. Unfortunately, some of the most colorful tales survived, finding their way into the 20th century, when the embers of blackpowder shooting burst once again into flame. Sophisticated shooters who scoffed at daydream data for modern-style guns soaked up blackpowder "rules of thumb" like a rag in a rainstorm. They went around placing round balls in the palms of their hands, covering them with powder to come up with an "accurate load." Gun-store clerks who had never seen a muzzleloader before were instant experts, handing out false doctrine at no charge. One representative of a gun company was overheard telling a shooter that he could load all the powder he wanted in a muzzleloader as long as he used a conical, but watch out for those round balls! Dangerous counsel. But why let facts get in the way of a good story? Regardless of the source of information, the shooter is invited to test for himself, respecting all laws and rules of safety and gunmaker's maximum loads, to see which facts work in his firearms, especially where accuracy is concerned.

Shooting with cross-sticks is popular for blackpowder single-shot cartridge games. This local club match also allowed a chair.

Chapter 24

RUNNING BALL

SOME OLD-TIMERS called it "running ball." To us, it's the science/art of casting lead projectiles, round or conical, for all manner of blackpowder guns: muzzleloading pistols and rifles, cap 'n' ball revolvers, blackpowder cartridge guns, even big lead spheres for shotguns. There are three major reasons for casting lead bullets: economy, creating missiles for special guns, and pure enjoyment. First, while commercial round balls, swaged or cast, are a bargain, picking up lead, preparing it for bullets, and making projectiles ourselves saves money. For example, shooting the 32-caliber squirrel rifle for fewer pennies than 22 Long Rifle ammo is a reality through bullet casting. Second,

finding bullets for some guns is next to impossible. For example, I have an old-time flintlock in caliber 42. Perhaps a company offers .425-inch round balls. However, I've not come across any. Home casting put that long gun back on the range. Third, making lead projectiles is a hobby in its own right, a calming enterprise that combines fun with relaxation. It's a safe operation, too, when the rules are followed, and as with any other undertaking, can be dangerous if the rules are not obeyed. And one thing more: satisfaction. A certain amount of pride in manufacture accompanies cast bullets that punch close holes in the paper, or put game meat on the table. Know-how and experience,

along with a careful attitude, equals extremely accurate and effective "homemade" projectiles. Bullet casting is part of a shooter's testament to self-reliance, as well as his or her education. Did I already say it's also fun?

Once Upon a Time

The image of a mountain man huddled by his fire on a cold night in the Old West after plunging his hands in icy streams in his role as beaver trapper, plays clearly on the cinema of the imagination. I see him casting round bullets from what was called galena, "lead ore," according to the *Oxford English Dictionary*. What we call a possibles bag included the raw lead, along with a mold. There might

Getting ready to cast bullets—the area is well sheltered from any invasion of rain or snow, and the table is clean and clear. Ingots of lead stand out in front, with all other tools and supplies nearby.

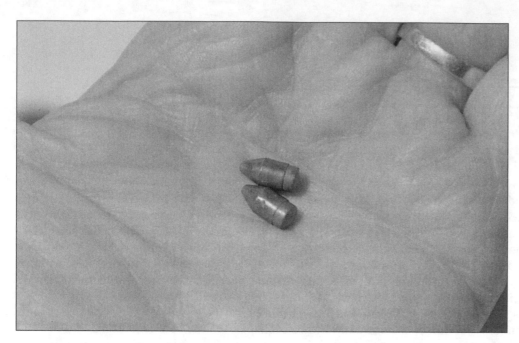

How small can they go? These cast bullets are only 22 caliber.

also be a bellows for super oxygenating the fire to red-hot melting nuggets. Unlike the Lone Ranger — who could not have cast his silver bullets by campfire as he was shown to do — the Mountain Man was entirely capable of making good lead spheres on the trail because of lead's comparatively low melting point. Lead melts at 327.4 degrees Celsius (621 degrees Fahrenheit). Silver melts at 961.9 degrees C (1,763 degrees F), with a casting temperature over 1,000 degrees C, a little high for an ordinary wood fire.

At any rate, shooters made their own bullets prior to commercial production because they had to. They continued to make their own bullets after commercial production because they wanted to, right up to the present. After the mountain men went home (those who survived their adventures west of the Mississippi), their trails were followed by the buffalo hunters, or "buffalo runners," as they seemed to prefer. These men (if there were lady buff' runners, they failed to make the history books) cast bullets for their Remington and Sharps blackpowder cartridge rifles. Hunters were known to look for, and

find, lead bullets in bison carcasses. These they recast into new projectiles. In *The Great Buffalo Hunt* by Wayne Gard, the author quoted the words of a runner named Hanna, who said, "We used the softest lead that we could buy. When a bullet hit a buffalo, it would flatten out like a one-cent piece and tear a big hole in the animal. Generally it would stop on the opposite side against the hide, and the skinner would be able to save the lead and remold it. As lead was high, we reloaded all our shells. After we had killed all the boys could skin in a day, we would go to our shack and reload ammunition for the next day."

The Tools

Molds

The practice of casting bullets from molten lead poured into molds never died. Today, thousands of shooters make their own lead projectiles. There are several companies offering molds in dozens of different configurations and calibers, not only for muzzleloaders and other blackpowder guns, but for modern arms as well, including slugs for shotgun shells. A glance

into Lyman's catalog shows conical molds from 22 through 69 caliber, with round ball molds running 36 to 75 caliber. Dixie Gun Works offers round ball molds in a basic design without sprue cutters in .310-inch to .850-inch diameters in increments of .001 inch. Dixie also has molds for the 45-70, 50-70, and a host of projectiles from the Civil War era, such as the 52-caliber Sharps and Colt Root 56-caliber rifle. Rapine has special molds for Cowboy Action Shooting for the 38-40 Winchester, 44-40 Winchester, and 45 Colt.

These are single-cavity molds, but double-cavity molds are also available. Prices vary widely for molds, $20 to $30 being common, $35 for the special LeMat Mold, a three-cavity model that casts a .451-inch conical bullet, plus two .285-inch round ball cavities for buckshot (between No. 1 and No. 2 size). The extra special Whitworth mold runs just a little more: close to $240, but it creates a 575-grain hexagonal bullet that goes 1 3/8-inches in length. An English gunsmith prepares these molds for Dixie. There are many other specialty molds, including Sharps,

The furnace is set for melting lead and a mold is rested on the heating plate to warm it up for casting.

Waadtlander, Tryon Creedmoor, and a number of Minie and Maxi designs. Lee has its REAL molds in bullet weights from 200 to 380 grains. Rapine also offers a long list of molds, as does the NEI Co. Lyman's Parker Rifle Bullet mold produces a 565-grain shallow-cavity base Minie ball for 58-caliber muskets with 1:48 twist. Lyman's Spitzer Mold Blocks make 40- and 45-caliber, high ballistic coefficient bullets, while the Bore Rider® Bullet Mold builds 40- and 45-caliber conicals at 405- and 500-grain weights. RCBS also has a fine line of bullet molds in various sizes.

Mold Handles

Some mold handles are integral to the mold block itself, such as the Kentucky Style Brass Molds from Dixie Gun Works. The authentic scissors-style handle contains a sprue cutter. Other mold blocks require separate handles, which save the bullet caster a few bucks, since the handles transfer to different blocks.

Bullet Sizing Dies

Various bullet-sizing dies are available, such as those from RCBS, which are precision-manufactured to hold a +/- .002-inch diameter variance with hand-polished interiors. Various bullet-sizing dies "true up" cast lead bullets, where necessary. The lead bullet is forced through the die, reducing its diameter slightly to conform to the exact interior dimensions of the unit.

Basic Melting Pot

The simple melting pot is ideal for smaller amounts of lead, and of course is essential at the campfire, where there is no electrical plug-in for a furnace. Lyman's basic melting pot holds 10 pounds of lead.

Basic Plug-In Melting Pot

This electric lead melting pot has no temperature-control gauge, but it does offer the convenience of plugging into an outlet in a spot that has good ventilation, along with shelter from any form of moisture, especially rain.

Furnace

The Lee Production Furnace is a good example of a furnace because it incorporates temperature control. The RCBS Pro-Melt Furnace is for high-temperature casting. It has an industrial-grade thermostat coupled to a remote sensor on the bottom of the reservoir. This 800-watt unit holds 22 pounds of lead, which is especially handy when making tin/lead alloy blackpowder cartridge bullets. Lyman's Mag 20 Electric furnace is another heavy-duty, 800-watt unit with bottom-pour valve system designed for casting a great many excellent projectiles each session. Lyman also has a Magdipper Casting Furnace that uses a ladle, as well as a Mini-Mag Furnace with 10-pound capacity. These various "lead-melters" offer a variety of price levels to choose.

Dipper/Ladle

While the terms are sometimes interchanged, a dipper has a partially closed bowl, while a ladle is more spoon-like. The dipper also has a pouring spout. Lyman's cast-iron, long-stem dipper has a wooden handle and holds about a half-ounce of molten lead. While this capacity is good for making extremely heavy bullets, it is has another important trait: forcing molten lead deeply into the cavity mold for a complete fill-up, which thwarts air pockets.

Casting Thermometer

Lyman's casting thermometer ranges from 200 to 1,000 degrees, ideal for testing the temperature of molten lead in a pot, and also useful for checking the actual temperature of molten lead in a furnace.

Ingot Mold

Sort of like a Jell-O mold, ingots accept molten lead that hardens into a specific rectangular shape for storage. Lyman's 1-pound ingot mold has a 30-degree drift, so cooled lead ingots are easily removed.

Spoon

A large kitchen tablespoon is useful in skimming dross (foreign materials) from the surface of molten lead in a pot or furnace. It must be used with gloves at all times.

Gloves, Eye Protection, Clothing

Gloves and goggles are obvious safety devices for casting bullets. Gloves protect hands, while goggles ensure against a splash of molten lead. Less obvious is clothing: shoes (not open sandals), long pants (not shorts) and shirts that cover the arms.

Molder's Hammer

Although not entirely necessary because a hardwood dowel also does the job, a molder's hammer has a head of nylon or other material that will not damage a mold. It's useful in knocking the hinged sprue plate aside so the finished bullet can be set free. A molder's hammer may also have a pick end with a sharp point for freeing a stuck bullet. Having to use the pick end usually spoils the bullet, but it was stuck and had to be freed, so no big loss.

Bullet Casting Kit

Lyman's Master Casting Kit offers a good way to get started in bullet making. It includes the *Lyman Cast Bullet Handbook*, a title that is packed with information on bullet making.

Bullet/Powder Scale

A bullet/powder scale is important for weighing finished cast bullets to the tenth of a grain for testing purposes. Weighing finished bullets instantly ferrets out the light ones with air pockets.

Supplies

Blackpowder cartridge bullets require special lubes, such as Black Powder Gold™ Bullet Lube, which is formulated for blackpowder cartridges and popular with silhouette shooters. Paraffin is also useful when preparing lead for casting. It can be purchased at grocery stores. There are also commercial lead-purifiers, such as Leadex, which is formulated to separate dirt and other impurities from molten lead. However, it will not remove tin, antimony, zinc, or bismuth. Therefore, for pure lead bullets, Leadex is good for starters, but the steps for preparing lead should be followed for round balls and conicals fired in muzzleloaders. Lead for blackpowder cartridge guns is prepared as an alloy, usually of lead and tin, making a harder projectile.

Bits of lead are added to the furnace. When all the lead is melted, the cleaning process will begin as described in the text.

Another helper in casting is Rapine Mold Prep, which lubricates and protects the hinge, while also aiding as a release agent. Paper patching, mentioned earlier, is more easily accomplished with commercial products, such as Trucal® Paper-Patch from Dixie Gun Works. The same company offers precut cartridge papers. There is also the Trucal® Paper Patch Dressing Kit containing paper patch material, a neoprene rolling pad, tail snips, burnishing tool, X-Acto knife, 35-degree angle template, along with operational instructions.

Lead for Bullet Casting

If scientists set out to create a near-perfect element for making round or conical bullets for muzzleloaders, they would be hard pressed to come up with anything better than lead, noted as Pb in the Periodic Chart of Elements from its other name, plumbum. Lead is soft; it is heavy; and as noted earlier, lead melts at 327.4 degrees C or 621 degrees F. Lead is also relatively easy to purify, not to the 100 percent level, but close enough for high-quality bullets. Because it has great mass, lead bullets retain their initial velocity/energy well, compared with other metals. Imagine a bullet made of aluminum, for example. Even with a super shape, it would lose velocity/energy rapidly. Because of high molecular cohesion, lead "hangs together" well, rather than fragmenting. This is why we find a lead round ball flattened out, but essentially intact, on the off-side of a big-game carcass.

Lead is right for blackpowder cartridge bullets, too, because it readily accepts other metals to produce an alloy. An alloy is a mixture of two or more metals. Blackpowder breechloaders do well with tin/lead alloys, such as one part tin, 30 parts lead (1:30 ratio), one part tin to 20 parts lead (1:20 ratio), or one part tin in 16 parts lead (1:16 ratio). Alloy bullets, being harder than pure lead projectiles, fare well from the blast furnace of hot gases created by powder combustion. Lead, along with being relatively easy to liquefy, also forms well in a mold. Air pockets are minimal when molten lead is at a proper temperature, and the bullet maker does the job right, ensuring a full flow of liquid metal into the mold.

How to Purify Lead for Bullet Casting

The process of fluxing combines various metals within the lead, which is important when creating an alloy, such as tin and lead, antimony and lead, or both of these

At this point, the lead has been cleaned and is now hot enough to cast into bullets.

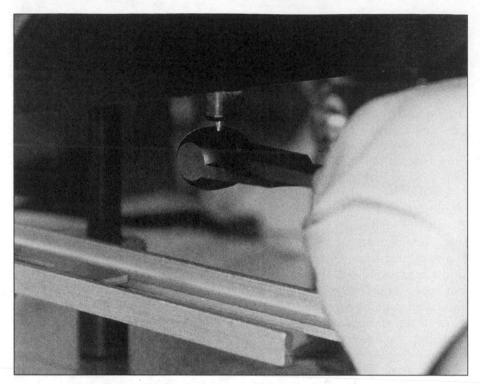

Using the bottom pour spout, molten lead is introduced into the mold.

metals added to lead. Purifying lead for making round or conical bullets is another matter, however. The idea now is taking out everything but the lead, which is impossible; however, nearly pure lead can be obtained.

The first step is melting the lead supply in a pot or furnace. Although lead turns from solid to liquid state at only 621 degrees F, lead for purifying should be heated to about 800 degrees F by setting the temperature gauge on the furnace, or checking with a thermometer for pot-melted lead. Temperature at this level will not melt harder metals within the lead, but it will promote their release. Since these metals are lighter than lead, they naturally flow to the top of the pot or furnace, which is perfect, because on the surface, they can be skimmed away using the large tablespoon listed above. The spoon, held in gloved hand for protection, skims off the dross (floating impurities) on the surface of the lead. Dross is set aside in a metal container. It can be very hot, and will burn a workbench top.

At this point, a fluxing agent is added, in spite of the fact that this is not truly a fluxing operation. One way to accomplish this step is with a small chunk of paraffin (wax), about the size of a thumbnail, dropped directly into the molten lead (gloves always on to protect hands). The paraffin will make considerable smoke, which can be subdued with a lighted match. Caution is the byword here, with flames rising above the molten lead. A long-handled ladle can be used now, or the same spoon as above, as long as it has a long shank. Even gloved hands must remain clear of the molten lead. The flames can also cause a burn to the face, so it's vital that the caster keep his body back from the molten lead at all times, rather than leaning over the pot or furnace. Furthermore, while casting is always conducted with plenty of ventilation, there is no reason to breathe in the fumes coming from molten lead, which now has a flame above it. In place of paraffin, commercial caster's flux may be used, following the directions on the container exactly. At this point, most impurities in the lead have been skimmed away with the spoon or ladle. There will be minute traces of tin, antimony, or other heavier metals within the lead, but not enough to cause harm. The lead is now ready to cast muzzleloader bullets. For blackpowder cartridge bullets, the addition of tin in the proper amount is called for, fluxing this time to combine tin with lead into an alloy. Also, lead containing tin flows better into the mold cavity, filling it fully with no air pockets, Dave Scovill, editor of Rifle Magazine and expert bullet caster, points out.

A round or conical bullet of pure lead is important for muzzleloaders because it upsets well in the bore — obturation once again. Even the round ball surrounded by a patch obturates to some degree, important for pressing into the patch, which in turn translates the rotational value of the rifling to the ball to spin it. A Minie, or any bullet with a hollow base, obviously must expand or the shank will not engage the rifling, in which case there is no rotation. Maxi bullets also shoot best in pure lead, because they engrave well when seated, and they also obturate nicely. So pure lead is best for both of these muzzleloader bullets to take up some windage in the bore. Lead alloy, however, is generally right for blackpowder cartridge guns. Alloys are best made by starting with pure lead. Molded into 1-pound ingots, it's easy to get the 1:20 ratio mentioned above. One pound of tin is joined by 20 one-pound ingots, creating about the usual capacity of major furnaces. Or a half-pound of tin joins 10 one-pound ingots. For a 1:30 ratio, a half-pound of tin is fluxed into 15 one-pound ingots. Any ratio is possible, including the 1:16 some blackpowder cartridge shooters prefer. A source of tin can be found in the Yellow Pages of the phone book under metals, oftentimes sold in handy 1-pound units.

Casting Temperatures

Experimenting with various lead temperatures is important. Larger

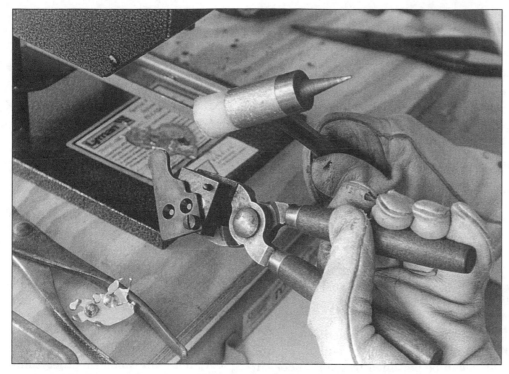

A few seconds after molten lead is poured into the mold, the sprue plate is forced to the side using a molder's hammer (or wooden dowel). The mold can now be opened to drop the formed bullet.

projectile molds may require a little hotter temperature than smaller bullet molds. The type of mold also makes a difference, with aluminum blocks heating up faster than cast-iron blocks. The good news is that if a bullet comes out badly, it is set aside and then returned to the pot for recasting. Also, conicals may require a little higher lead temperature than round balls, especially when they have grease grooves that must be fully formed. When lead is too hot, a frosty-looking bullet is produced, rather than one with proper smooth skin. Lead that is too cold makes an incomplete or wrinkled bullet. For example, using a Lyman mold for 500-grain, 45-caliber bullets, a lead temperature of 850 degrees F made good bullets. The goal is a fully formed bullet, free of air pockets, with a smooth, silver-shiny surface. The projectile must also weigh right on the money. A perfect bullet will not fall from the mold every time, but creating 50 to 100 good bullets in a session is not hard to accomplish.

The Process of Turning Molten Lead Into Bullets

Purified lead brought to the right operating temperature is now ready to flow into the mold like water, quickly hardening into the shape of the mold's interior cavity. A ladle, dipper, or pour spout on a furnace introduces the molten lead into the mold. Allowing lead to fully flow into the mold cavity works best. Molds go way back in time. The Ice Man, a mummified bowhunter's body found in the Italian Alps, was judged at 5,300 years old. He had with him a copper ax that was formed in a mold. At one time, even soapstone was used, but soft molds do not produce perfect missiles because as they heat up, cavity dimensions change (just as telephone lines grows longer in summer and shorter in winter due to temperature variation). Furthermore, today's shooters and hunters expect a great deal from their muzzleloaders and blackpowder-cartridge guns. While an imperfect bullet, as long as it was sufficiently accurate to take game, may have pleased a 19th century or earlier outdoorsman, it is not acceptable today. Fortunately, contemporary iron and aluminum molds make projectiles of extremely close tolerances.

As with all other aspects of shooting, making bullets requires consistency. The end result is a round or conical bullet possessing great uniformity. Singly, the bullet must be precise. Collectively, all bullets in the run must fit into the group, varying very little from one projectile to the next. This sort of reliability is not difficult to come by when bullets are cast correctly from purified lead or proper alloy at the right temperature in good molds. Of course, visual inspection alone won't prove the worth of a bullet, and spinners from the world of bench rest shooting are set aside as well. The bullet must be weighed to ensure gyroscopic perfection in order to spin on its axis — in other words, no lopsided bullets because of air pockets. Rotation helps distribute discrepancies, but even rapid spinning on its axis will not overcome a bad bullet. It will not group if it has air pockets, or traces of heavier metals running through it haphazardly, rather than homogeneously as is the case with a well-produced alloy missile.

Sources of Lead

Lead purchased from a plumbing-supply house or builder's mart can be expensive. That is why blackpowder shooters spend time searching for plumbum in many different places. Old buildings sometimes give up lead that is associated with pipes. Telephone cable sheathing is supposed to be 98% percent pure, so it makes a great source of bullet lead when it can be found and bargained for. Tire weights are chiefly lead, but they must be melted down and purified to remove other metals. Lead seals from moneybags and other sources, such as on railroad-car doors, is also almost pure. However, even if lead is purchased, bullet casting is still a bargain. A pound makes about 40 50-caliber round balls or 30 54-caliber spheres. Big bullets require more product, of course, but even a 500-grain conical goes 14 to the pound. Smallbores are much more economical to cast. The little 32-caliber squirrel rifle shoots 45-grain bullets at 155 to the pound. That's a good return for a pound of galena.

Be Safe

As with all aspects of shooting, there is only one way to cast bullets: the safe way. Accidents can

happen. They are part of life. Also, equipment can be faulty. If a product, be it a gun or a car tire, fails through faulty design or other problem, that's not the user's fault. Casting is safer, statistically, than taking a bath, but a person can slip in the tub, and a bullet maker can burn a hole in his toe.

Safety Rules for Casting Bullets

Cast bullets only in good ventilation. Lead fumes can be harmful. The NRA conducted tests with a Mine Safety Appliance Company device hanging directly over molten lead to detect lead dust and fumes. Only trace amounts were discovered. However, concerning lead pollution, the NRA concluded that "A maker and user of bullets possibly can be poisoned by lead, under sufficiently extraordinary exposure. This can hardly exist for the individual casting bullets on a scale for his own use, with reasonable ventilation and sanitation." Always cast bullets in a well-ventilated area only, never in closed quarters.

Along with casting bullets in a safe environment of good ventila-

tion, ensure that the source of heat does not produce carbon monoxide. Melting lead with a camp stove, for example, requires good ventilation. Carbon monoxide is a colorless, odorless, tasteless gas, and therefore can be very difficult to detect. Headaches, nausea, and dizziness may be signs of impending carbon monoxide poisoning.

Molten lead must never be exposed to water. Bullet casting on a porch is all right if there is a good roof overhead. Should it begin to rain, all bullet casting must come to a halt. Water landing in molten lead can create a tremendous rush of steam capable of blowing lead right out of the pot or furnace and into the air.

Bullets must be cast in a fire-safe area, preferably with a cement floor, not over wood or other combustible materials. Spilled molten lead is obviously very hot, perhaps 850 degrees Fahrenheit or hotter.

Only cast bullets in a private area where there is no human traffic, especially children who could run into the pot or furnace, spilling its molten contents.

Safety glasses are a must for all bullet casting.

Long pants, never shorts, are imperative when casting bullets. Hot lead may still burn a clothed leg, but having a barrier between molten metal and skin is extremely important.

Shoes, not moccasins or sandals, are worn to protect the feet from molten lead.

A long-sleeved shirt, not short-sleeved, offers a little barrier between hot lead and flesh. Again, a little protection is far better than none at all.

Gloves are absolutely essential at all times.

Casting bullets for hours on end is a mistake. Casting demands full attention and a tired person is not always fully attentive. Also, there's no point hovering over the pot or furnace. Stand back. Give it some room. The human body can take on lead through fumes, and once it

The new bullet, in this instance a round ball, is carefully dropped on a surface that will not cause damage.

Cast bullets are easily tested for uniformity using a bullet/powder scale, such as this electronic from RCBS. Bullets that do not weigh out with the rest are melted down and recast.

does, getting rid of it can be slow. There is also a cumulative effect, as with carbon monoxide.

Do not touch freshly made bullets. They are very hot.

Closing Tips

Competitive shooters, such as those involved in blackpowder cartridge silhouette shooting, may wish to purchase pure lead, which is available with a rating of more than 99 percent free of other metals.

While paraffin has been known to serve as a fluxing agent for making blackpowder bullets for competition, the shooter may wish to purchase a commercial product. Follow the product's instructions.

When making alloy bullets, rely on a fairly hot product, somewhere in the 800 degree F range.

Ensure that as lead alloy is used up, the pot or furnace receives the proper ratio of tin to lead for good blackpowder cartridge bullets.

Even though lead has been purified for making muzzleloader bullets, not blackpowder cartridge projectiles, skimming the surface of the molten lead from time to time during the casting process is worthwhile.

Iron molds are more rugged than aluminum molds. They take longer to heat up, but also make more bullets before getting too hot. Aluminum molds heat up fast, and make good bullets quickly. Aluminum molds can also last indefinitely with proper treatment. They cool down quickly when overheated, so bullet casting can continue. Both types are worthy choices.

Multiple-cavity molds create more bullets faster than single-cavity molds, but the latter are fine for most bullet making.

Molds must be properly broken in if they are to make good bullets and last a long time. Break-in instructions come with the mold, as well as the rules for proper care.

To heat the mold, dip the end of an aluminum mold block into molten lead. Rest an iron mold on the warming plate if the furnace has one. Another way is to simply begin pouring lead to form bullets (this may result in a few imperfect bullets, but it will warm the iron mold).

Managing the dipper or ladle begins with filling it quite full of molten lead from the pot or furnace. With one continuous motion, put the spout up against the chamfered hole in the mold. Hold the spout in place

firmly, and then tip the mold downward so molten lead flows freely into the mold. Hold the dipper for a second, allowing the mold cavity to fill fully. This practice helps avoid air pockets in the finished product.

If a fin appears around the base of the bullet, this indicates that the sprue plate has probably warped. Lubricating the sprue plate joint can usually prevent this problem. A machinist may be able to fix a warped sprue plate, or it may have to be replaced with a new one.

Go gently with the molder's hammer or hardwood dowel in knocking the sprue plate aside.

Drop freshly cast bullets onto soft surfaces, such as piece of cardboard or lint-free cloth, not a metal plate.

Along with weighing cast bullets on a powder/bullet scale, consider checking their diameters with a micrometer to see that they are coming out the right size.

There are several good books on casting bullets, each one bringing the shooter closer to perfecting this hobby within a hobby.

What to Expect

Near perfection is not too much to ask in a cast bullet, round or con-

Proving that cast bullets remain absolutely viable today, Oregon Trail's Laser-Cast projectiles have proven highly accurate in Cowboy Action Shooting firearms.

ical, for the muzzleloader or blackpowder cartridge gun. Home-cast bullets should be as good as commercial lead projectiles of the same caliber and type: absolutely uniform and accurate. If cast bullets are not top-rate, the causes are probably impure lead, the wrong casting temperature, sometimes the technique, such as failing to truly fill the mold cavity with molten lead. Millions of cast bullets are prepared every year by shooters enjoying every phase of the operation, including what could be the best part: walking up to a target with a close group, or game to grace the table taken with a projectile made by the blackpowder marksman/hunter himself.

Chapter 25

HOW BLACKPOWDER GUNS WORK

FOR THE pure enjoyment of knowing, as well as understanding the basic functions of blackpowder guns, a number of firearm types are dissected, mildly, in this chapter. This is not a gunsmithing book. The workings of principle parts described here do not in any way suggest tinkering. A trip to the gunsmith is cheaper than ruining a firearm, or worse, having a mishap caused by "messing around" with the workings of a gun. There are more blackpowder gun types now than in the 20th century, 19th, 18th, or any other time in history. Still available on a small scale are matchlocks and wheel locks. Flintlocks are well-represented with examples from many different companies. All manner of percussion locks continue. They include front-action lock, back-action lock, front-action side hammer lock, back-action side hammer lock, under hammer lock, drum and nipple, along with plunger-system in-line muzzleloaders, bolt-action models made on the same basic design as their smokeless powder cartridge cousins, even an Outer-Line® that has its own patent because it stands alone in specific design. There are also blackpowder revolvers, as well as shotguns, a few flintlocks and many caplocks. Blackpowder cartridge guns are well-represented in single-shot rifles, lever-action repeaters, and revolvers of various backgrounds.

Simplified Concept

Simplified, the muzzleloading rifle or pistol is essentially a barrel with a plug on one end, plus some means of getting fire to a main charge down in the breech area, which is just forward of the sealed end of the metal tube. The barrel, in turn, is attached to some form of stock plus a mechanism for firing — call it a trigger — incorporated to put the gun into a firing mode. A powder charge is dropped from the muzzle down into the breech area, followed by a round or conical bullet, or a wad column/shot charge. Because the breech end is closed, when the charge of powder is set off, expanding gases push against the projectile, bullet or shot, forcing it up the barrel, out of the muzzle, and on its way toward the target. The reason significant gas does not jet out of the "wrong end" — in other words through the touchhole or nipple vent — is a basic law about pressure seeking an exit from the larger orifice rather than the smaller one. Otherwise, flame would shoot out like a blowtorch through the nipple vent or touchhole, which it does not on a sound firearm in good working order. Nipples blown from nipple seats are invariably caused by short-starting, obstructions, a totally filthy bore, or other problems, such as the wrong powder, but not by design of the

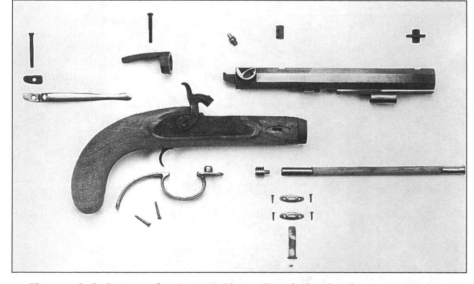

This exploded view of a Lyman Plains Pistol clearly shows its working parts—a lock, still attached to the stock of the gun, with mainspring power to deliver a hammer blow, a barrel with breech plug blocking one end, a bolster with nipple seat to contain the nipple, which in turn will hold the percussion cap, two escutcheons, one key or barrel wedge to hold stock and barrel together, and so forth.

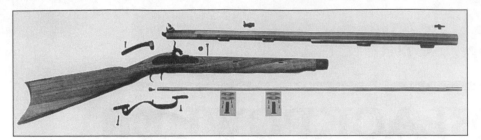

This is a breakdown of the Lyman Great Plains rifle, typical of a half-stock plains rifle of yesteryear. It has a hooked breech, which means that the breech plug interlocks with the upper tang when it is in place. Then the barrel can be lifted free of the stock for cleaning by removing the two keys (wedges) that hold stock and barrel together.

muzzleloader. So, the barrel is closed off on the "back end" with a well-fitted breech plug screwed in place and then an avenue of ignition is provided via a flintlock's touchhole or caplock's nipple vent. Breech plugs are so important to safe functioning that they are specially fitted to completely seal the breech end of the barrel.

Choose Your Expert

A sit-down debate among expert firearms historians would be interesting, but also somewhat futile. To say there were a hundred different lock styles and gun designs over the years would be a gross understatement. Think of something wild and you can bet a gun designer in the past not only thought about it, but created examples of the idea. In-line flintlocks, flintlock repeaters, breech-loading flintlocks, a flintlock with two locks (one well forward of the other in case the gun exploded) — the possibilities are almost endless. This is not a gun history book, and so the blackpowder firearm types listed below are provided for two reasons only: general understanding, and a basic knowledge of how blackpowder guns work.

Firestick/Hand Gun

The *baston-a-feu*, or firestick, was essentially a hand-held cannon — little more than a metal tube that held powder down in its base, along with a projectile. Firesticks were common in the Netherlands in the 15th and 16th centuries, some functioning as clubs or battleaxes as well as guns. Shoot, then try to whack the enemy with the metal tube. Some even had attached hatchets. One of them measured 2 feet long and encompassed a touchhole at the topmost part of the breech section. Ignition was accomplished with a handheld "slow match," a sort of smoking rope, presented to the touchhole. It worked for the reason stated above: closed on one end with a small orifice to admit fire for ignition, with major gas exiting through the larger exit, the bore of the tube. While the firestick probably had minor battle advantage as projectile-shooter, the flame and noise alone would tend to demoralize the enemy. But imagine having to aim the firestick held under the arm or on the shoulder like a bazooka, then having to ignite the charge with a piece of smoking rope.

Matchlock

The matchlock probably followed the firestick. The progression seems logical, since the major difference between a firestick and a matchlock gun is the addition of a device secur-

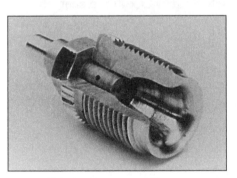

Part of the workings of a percussion muzzleloader is the nipple itself, which is designed to retain a percussion cap (sometimes a primer), which is detonated on the cone, fire progressing into the main charge in the breech. Here is the Thompson/Center Flame Thrower Breech Plug with nipple inserted into the plug itself, in a cutaway to show how the two parts work together to promote surefire ignition.

The hammer nose will come down not only to strike and detonate the percussion cap, but also to direct cap debris away from the shooter. Note, too, the cleanout screw in the side of the bolster.

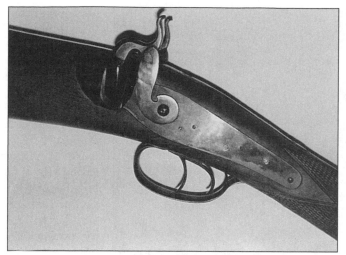

This is a back action lock. The mainspring is behind the hammer, or in this case, hammers, since this is an over/under double-barrel muzzleloading rifle.

ing the match, rather than the match behind hand-held. The exact date of invention is difficult to pin down, but a German manuscript from the 1500s describes a matchlock. Specifically, the slow match was held in a serpentine, so-called because it was built in a snake-like backward S-shape. The serpentine, also categorized as a cock, pivoted on an axis, its most forward part delivering flame from the burning match, while its lower portion served as a trigger. When the lower section of the serpentine was pulled rearward, the upper section pivoted forward, delivering fire to a touchhole. There were many variations of the matchlock, including one that foretold of the future flintlock, with a type of flash pan situated to deliver flame into the touchhole. Obviously, the matchlock had a very slow "lock time," which is the time required from trigger pull to the gun "going off." This meant a shooter had to observe follow-through: pull the trigger, then hold very still until the gun fired, maintaining the muzzle in the general direction he wanted the projectile to take.

Wheel Lock

Following the matchlock in its various designs and styles, the wheel lock came along. It may have come about in 16th-century Germany. The idea for wheel lock ignition actually dated back to prehistoric times: Sparks were created when flint came into swift contact with a spark-making object. A device that somehow

attached to the gun, lined up to deliver sparks into a pan and sent flame into the main charge in the breech would be much better than a slow match. An example known as the Monk's Gun, dating back to the very early 1500s, was spark-fired. Although not a true wheel lock, the Monk's Gun had a serpentine. Instead of holding a slow match, it had jaws that gripped a piece of flint or pyrite for spark ignition. The gun had a sort of plunger connected to the serpentine. By drawing the plunger with a thumb or forefinger ring, a roughened steel bar scraped against the pyrite or flint, creating sparks that in turn flew into a touchhole located immediately in front of the serpentine's jaws.

The Monk's Gun was not a true wheel lock, but was definitely its parent. Nuremberg 1515 is a place and date given for creation of a gun with a wheel rather than a serpentine.

Wheel equaled wheel lock. It was an integral part of the lock system, functioning much like a clock mechanism. A key or spanner wound a spring, just like a clock. Firing the wheel lock required first opening the flash pan lid to expose ignition powder. The cock, securing pyrites in its jaws, is then placed in contact with the wheel. When the trigger is pulled, the spring uncoils, whirling the wheel round and round rapidly against the pyrites, creating not a spark, but a shower of sparks. Numerous improvements turned the wheel lock into an ignition system of high merit and reliability. Instead of a slow match — and slow was a good word for it — or a few sparks from a modified matchlock, sparks rained down upon the powder in the pan, almost certain to ignite it.

Snaphaunce

The snaphaunce, also snaphance, is treated here as a flintlock. Dedicated historians will require much greater depth, but for present purposes, this particular lock style is pretty close to the flintlock in function. Howard Blackmore, respected firearms historian, put the snaphance in the same chapter as the flintlock. The name stems from a Dutch of Flemish word, snaphaan, "snapping hen."

The Flintlock

Wheel locks were intricate, difficult to produce and costly. Going back to the matchlock was out of

This is a sidelock, but it is also a front-action type.

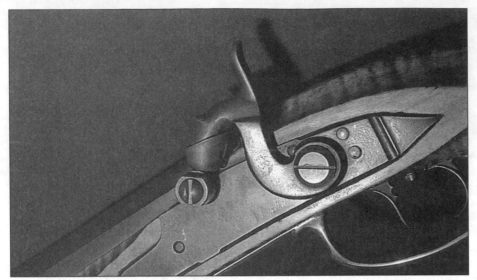

Here is a good look at the drum and nipple system explained in the text. The cleanout screw is prominently shown. It's easy to see how the drum and nipple replaced the touchhole of the flintlock.

the question; however, something simpler and more economical was required to serve the average shooter. The flintlock fulfilled that need perfectly and remained the most important lock type in the world for a very long time.

Again, there was a cock or hammer. Again, the cock had jaws. This time, a simple flint, well-beveled, was tightened in the jaws and held firmly in place. There were hundreds of variations, even breechloaders and in-line flintlocks; however, the standard flintlock became a lock plate incorporating functional parts. The hammer or cock pivoted on the lock plate. The tang or comb section of the hammer contained jaws. The jaws held a

flint via a jaw screw going through a top jaw into the lower jaw, pinching the two parts together like a little vice. In order to contain the flint under pressure, a flint pad was used, usually a piece of soft tanned leather. Thin sheets of lead were used for flint pads on some old-time muskets.

When the trigger was pulled, the spring-powered hammer traveled in an arc. This brought the carefully sharpened, beveled edge of the flint in contact with a spark maker, a metal piece called a frizzen (also known as a frizzle, battery, steel, or hen). A simple screwdriver was the only tool needed to loosen the jaws of the hammer, relocate the flint to meet squarely with the frizzen,

then retighten the jaws to pinch the flint in place. The frizzen, also on a pivot pin, was driven forward by the falling flint, thus delivering a shower of sparks into the pan. A frizzen spring, also known as a feather spring, located on the exterior of the lock plate, provided the energy to fully force the frizzen forward, uncovering the pan, also called flash pan. The fine-grain powder in the pan flamed up instantly from curls of hot metal scraped from the face of the frizzen by the flint. Flame from ignited pan powder then darted through the touchhole and into the powder charge in the breech.

The In-Line Flintlock Rifle

Doc Carlson, in his fine article, "The In-Line Muzzle-Loader in History," *Gun Digest*, described the function of the Paczelt rifle and its trapdoor frizzen as an ingenious flintlock system that "could be used to build a modern percussion in-line rifle." It is, however, a flintlock, whose flint-holding jaws dart forward under spring tension to strike a frizzen, which pivots upward to expose the pan. The touchhole, however, lies in line with the bore, not on the side of the barrel.

The Breech-Loading Flintlock Rifle

Since there were also matchlock and wheel lock breechloaders, it's no surprise that there were also breech-loading flintlock firearms. A

This is a good example of a sidelock. It's on the side of the stock, as the name implies. It's not a back action, because the mainspring isn't located behind the hammer. It also has a bolster—the clump of integral metal that holds the nipple seat, which in turn takes the nipple. This model also has a cleanout screw on the side of the bolster.

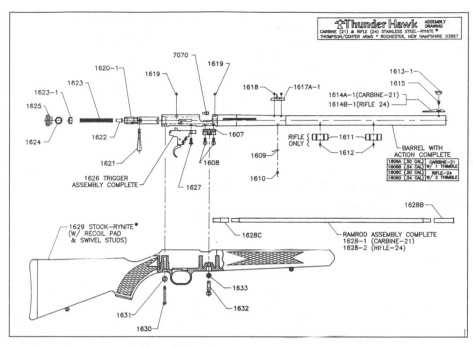

This schematic of a Thompson/Center modern muzzleloader, the Thunder Hawk, provides a clear understanding of the rifle's function.

number of examples still exist, some from the 1600s. Essentially, the trick was accomplished with a breech that lifted out so the gun could be loaded from "the back." Then the section of barrel was locked back in place and the gun was primed for firing.

The Lock of the Flintlock

The flintlock's lock contains a lock plate, which is seen from the outside. It covers the workings of the lock, which all rest inside. There's a tumbler in the lock, a metal piece that does "tumble" or rotate when the hammer is activated. The tumbler has built-in notches. These notches are engaged by a sear, which operates with a sear spring. When the sear spring is depressed, the nose of the sear disengages from the notches in the tumbler. The nose of the sear falls into a half-cock notch, which is deep. This is the position the firearm is placed in during inactivity. It is not a safety, as we might find today with cross-bolts on some rifles, or the safety bar on a revolver which, when functioning properly, will not allow the gun to go off should it be dropped. However, the half-cock notch, when fully engaged by the nose of the sear, will not allow the hammer to fall forward. The full-cock notch is entirely different. Now the hammer is in its most rearward position. When the trigger is pulled, the nose of the sear disengages from the full-cock notch in the tumbler so the hammer can fly forward. In the case of the flintlock, this brings the flint, held in the hammer's jaws, into contact with the frizzen. A mainspring powers the hammer. The lock may also have a bridle, which is a piece that spans over both the tumbler and the sear, providing solid pivot points for both tumbler and sear.

There may also be a fly in the tumbler, also known as a detent. The fly serves an important function with double-set triggers by preventing the sear nose from falling into the half-cock notch when the gun is fired. In effect, the fly is an override device, causing the nose of the sear to override the half-cock notch in the tumbler. The fly allows the firearm to be brought into battery (firing position) without the sear hanging up in the half-cock notch. The workings of the lock may also contain a stirrup that rests between the tumbler and spring tip, reducing friction at this contact point. While the interior workings of the lock sound intricate, they're actually extremely reliable. The flintlock itself was reliable, not to the extent of later percussion models, but far more trustworthy than sometimes credited, or should that be discredited? Naturally, quality of the lock made a big difference, but if the flintlock failed to go off at that moment of truth when a pioneer took aim at game or foe, the country never would have been settled. There is more than one way to load flintlock firearm so it will "go off" almost all the time. See Chapter 20 for details.

The break-open design of the Thompson/Center Encore is entirely different from others. It offers a true systems firearm with numerous barrel options, including a 50-caliber muzzleloader, as shown here. No. 209 shotgun primers load directly into the back of the breech plug.

This modern muzzleloader bolt-action design does not retain locking lugs. The breech is closed with a breech plug, while the bolt becomes a striker.

In-Line Percussion System

The distinguishing feature here is exactly what the name describes: Fire from the source of ignition is introduced on the same plane as the bore of the gun. An in-line muzzleloader may have a plunger that strikes a percussion cap or modern primer, or it may have an exposed hammer. Bolt-action models are widespread. Typically, there is a screw-in breech plug with a channel running through it. A standard percussion cap, musket cap, small rifle primer, small pistol primer, or No. 209 shotgun primer rests on the "back end" of the breech plug. When the igniter is set off with a thump from a plunger or hammer nose, fire darts through the channel and directly into the waiting powder charge in front of it. The Thompson/Center Encore proves that many different designs can be incorporated into the in-line niche. This is a break-open rifle. Opened, a No. 209 shotgun primer is lodged into a special slot at the rear of the breech plug. Closed, the Encore is ready for firing. After shooting, it is broken open again to remove the spent primer. Now the rifle can be loaded again, from the muzzle, of course, because it is a true muzzleloader.

Drum and Nipple

Converting flintlock to caplock was accomplished with a drum and nipple setup. The drum and nipple system also stands on its own as another percussion system. A cylindrical metal piece with a channel running through it is screwed into a side barrel flat, its outfacing end sealed with a cleanout screw. Tapped into this metal cylinder is a nipple seat. Fire from the percussion cap flies downward into the drum, making a left-hand turn (for a right-hand lock) into the breech. In spite of percussion-cap flame diversion into the breech, the drum and nipple system provides excellent ignition.

Front-Action Percussion Lock

This is the standard lock of the day, a sidehammer model, because the hammer is mounted on the side of the lock. The name front-action applies because the mainspring is in front of the hammer, rather than behind it.

Back-Action Percussion Lock

This lock has the mainspring behind the hammer. It's easy to identify because the hammer, mounted on the side, is forward on the lock plate.

Back-Action Sidehammer Percussion Lock

In this system, the hammer cocks out to the side of the firearm. That's why it's sometimes called a "mule ear" lock. A nipple is seated in the side barrel flat for direct ignition into the breech.

Underhammer Percussion System

It is difficult to call this one a lock because it is so simple in design. The trigger guard can actually serve as the mainspring. The nipple here is seated on a lower barrel flat for direct ignition into the breech.

The escutcheon is a plate through which the key, also called wedge, fits to join barrel and stock together.

The contrast between these two shotguns clearly shows how different the muzzleloader system is from the modern. Above, the Navy Arms T&T side by side contains powder, wads, and shot packed in by hand. Below, the Winchester Super-X semi-automatic shotgun shoots shells as rapidly as the trigger is pulled.

The Markesbery Outer-Line® Rifle

This uniquely designed, well-made systems rifle with interchangeable barrels has an exposed hammer. It is not an in-line system, because fire from a No. 11 percussion cap or a small rifle/small pistol primer does not enter the powder charge on the same plane as the barrel. Instead, flame arrives from above the powder charge on a 45-degree angle. While not an in-line, the Outer-Line® has direct ignition because fire from the igniter goes directly into the main charge in the breech, albeit not on the same plane as the bore of the rifle.

The Savage Model 10ML

Although more smokeless-powder muzzleloaders may enter the market, as this is written, the only muzzleloader allowed the use of smokeless powder is the Savage Model 10ML. The use of smokeless powder in any other muzzleloader could cause the firearm to explode. Rather than removing the locking lugs of this bolt-action rifle, they are left in place and remain fully functional. This is why the Model 10ML can handle smokeless powder. The heart of the system is a "percussion module." The percussion module has a slightly acorn shape. The back of the module is built very much like the head of a rimless cartridge case, with an integral groove that is gripped by the rifle's extractor. In this way, the module is loaded into the chamber just like a cartridge. It is also extracted after firing just like a cartridge case. The back end of the module accepts a No. 209 shotgun primer. After the Model 10ML is loaded, from the muzzle just like any other muzzleloader, the primed module is inserted into the action and bolted home. Now it is held in the chamber by the bolt's big locking lugs. The firing pin of the bolt strikes the center of the primer, its fire darting through a breech plug channel into the main charge of powder in the breech on the same plane as the bore, so the Savage Model 10ML is an in-line muzzleloader.

The Package

Unlike the ancient firestick or hand gun, the blackpowder firearm is an entire package, normally built around a stock with a mortise or channel into which the barrel is fitted. The stock may have a forend cap, or metal piece, fitted over the foremost part. Barrel and stock may be joined by a key or keys, a flat metal piece running through a barrel lug. On the exterior of the stock,

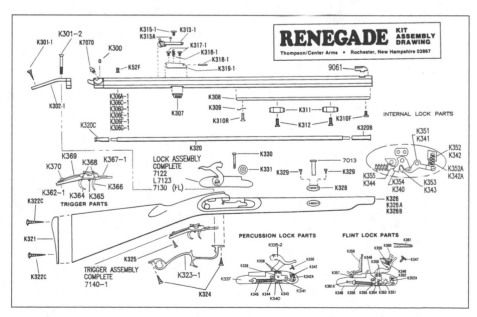

As opposed to the modern muzzleloader, this Thompson/Center non-replica Renegade rifle is constructed differently. Although basic function remains the same, the lock alone shows how different the two types of muzzleloaders are.

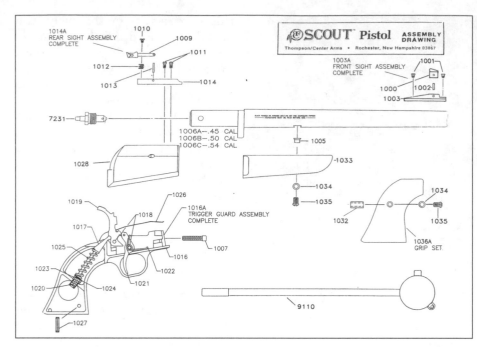

The Scout Pistol from Thompson/Center, a powerhouse one-hander, had very few moving parts, as this schematic proves.

the key goes through two escutcheons that are inletted in place, similar to keyholes. These two pieces of metal rest on either side of the forestock, the key passing through both of them. A mortise in the stock holds the lock. A lock plate covers the lock. A trigger lies on the underside of the stock, with a trigger guard to prevent accidental discharge. As we know, there are many types of blackpowder guns, so the generalizations here are open to a great deal of specific differences. See Chapters 9-12 for details.

The Shotgun

Flintlock shotguns are called fowlers or fowling pieces. A good example is the Trade Fowler offered by Mountain State Muzzleloading Co. The caplock muzzleloading shotgun is essentially one or two barrels with breech plugs and locks, quite similar in function to the caplock rifle.

The Pistol

The muzzle-loading pistol is, for present purposes, a "short rifle," its workings being the same as the muzzleloading caplock or flintlock long gun.

The Caplock Revolver

There were flintlock revolvers in days gone by, but they are of historical interest only now. The works of the blackpowder cap 'n' ball revolver are more involved than the percussion or flintlock rifle. Essentially, this gun is a frame with barrel, grips, loading lever, cylinder, and internal moving parts that revolve the cylinder into battery position. The frame is the body. There is, of course, a barrel attached to the forepart of the frame. The frame may or may not have a top strap, a piece between the rearmost of the barrel and the hammer. The famous 1860 Colt blackpowder revolver had no top strap. The equally famous Remington Model of 1858 did. Sometimes revolvers are called "wheel guns" because of the revolving cylinder containing chambers that align, one at a time, with the bore of the barrel. The word "revolver" says it all. The cylinder revolves on a pin at its center. It moves when the hammer is pulled back, which in turn activates a hand that rotates the cylinder. A cylinder bolt locks the cylinder in place, aligned so that one chamber is "looking" right

The Remington Rolling Block action, this one from the Navy Arms Co., functions as its name promises, with a rolling block of steel that rotates to block the breech. The hammer nose in turn drops into the block to lock it in place.

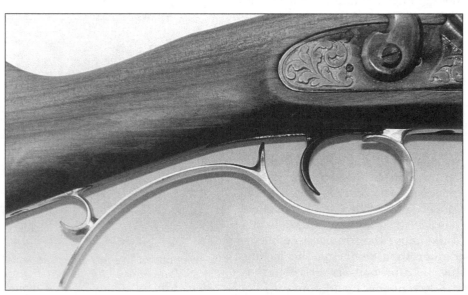

The single trigger dominates today. This one proved excellent from the factory.

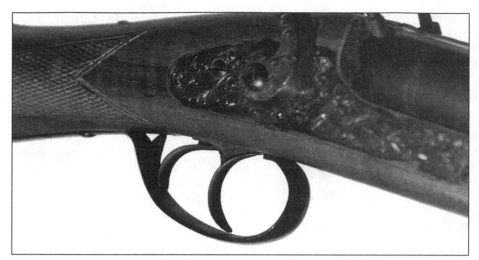

This gun has double triggers, but not double set triggers. The typical blackpowder double barrel muzzleloading shotgun used the two-trigger system for firing each barrel.

out of the barrel. There are springs and many other parts that allow the single-action blackpowder revolver to function. Chapter 20 explains how the caplock revolver is loaded and how it functions. This includes everything from loading powder into the cylinder chambers to forcing bullets into the same chambers with the use of the loading lever, to placing caps on nipples screwed into the back of the cylinder. Sights vary.

The Cartridge Revolver

The major difference between the cap 'n' ball revolver and the cartridge revolver is the cylinder, which holds cartridges instead of powder and ball. Of course, there are no percussion caps, since primers installed into the heads of the cartridges provide ignition. The hammer falls on a firing pin instead of a percussion cap.

The Single-Shot Cartridge Rifle

The Remington Rolling Block and the Sharps were two of the most famous single-shot blackpowder cartridge rifles of all time, and both continue manufacture to this day. Essentially, these rifles lock up with a block system, a very strong metal piece that slides into position behind the cartridge. On

the Sharps, the operation of a lever slides the block up or down. When the block is down, a cartridge can be inserted into the waiting chamber. When the block is in the up position, the chamber is locked off and the rifle is ready to fire. The Remington has a block, too, but it rolls into position, rather than "falling" down and rising back up. These two actions are both strong in principle and, when made of modern steel, can hold quite a bit of pressure. Remington Rolling Blocks were chambered for smokeless powder cartridges, such as the 7x57mm Mauser, while various modern falling block actions have been used to chamber many modern rounds, including magnums.

The Lever-Action Blackpowder Cartridge Rifle

Lever-action rifles, along with slide-action models, initially were developed for rapid fire of blackpowder cartridges. By 1895, they were chambered for smokeless powder rounds, with the advent of what we call today the 30-30 and the 25-35 Winchester rounds. Although various magazines can be employed, most lever-actions, such as the Model 1894 Winchester and its predecessors, carried a tube beneath the barrel, with cartridges fitting one behind the other. Work-

ing the lever downward expelled a fired round, with the comeback of the bolt re-cocking the hammer. A follower lifted another cartridge into line with the chamber and the upward thrust of the lever slammed the bolt forward, locking a new cartridge into the chamber, ready for firing.

Muzzleloader Triggers

A basic understanding of triggers can be valuable to the shooter, because the trigger is vital to the charcoal burner, serving mainly to trip a sear, which in turn activates a hammer, which in turn raps a percussion cap or causes flint and frizzen to produce a shower of sparks. An exception is the modern muzzleloader with modern-type trigger, which is a release-type mechanism instead of a trip-type mechanism. The following touches only on some of the more widespread trigger styles. As with all other aspects of firearms history, noting each trigger design would require a book of its own. After all, there were not only air guns in days of yore, but models of electric firearms as well. Lewis and Clark had a large-caliber air gun on their march across America. Leonardo da Vinci, the amazing inventor who lived from 1452 to 1519, laid out a plan for a gun working with steam.

The Single Trigger

The simplest is the single trigger pinned directly into the stock without a trigger plate, as found on old-time fowlers. There is no trigger adjustment in this design, and today it is seldom seen.

Single Trigger with Metal Trigger Plate

Simple, effective and popular, this type is mounted on a metal trigger plate, rather than pinned directly to the stock. The trigger plate acts as an anchor for a tang screw, also serving as a solid base for the trigger to pivot upon. The single trigger does have some travel before engaging the sear,

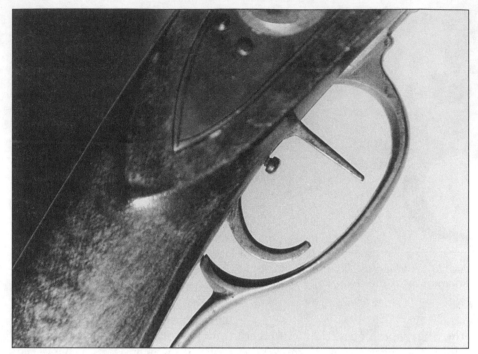

This original style double set trigger system remains extremely effective today in producing a light and crisp let-off. The screw in the center adjusts trigger sensitivity.

The Single-Lever, Double-Set Trigger

There are two triggers in this system. The rear trigger is the set; the front trigger is the hair. Incidentally, this can be reversed, as seen on the now-discontinued Thompson/Center Patriot pistol. Unset, the gun will not fire. When the trigger is set, trigger pull is very light. An adjustment screw between the triggers alters let-off. The deeper the screw is threaded upward, the lighter the trigger pull, sometimes measured in mere ounces. Caution: This type of trigger can be set too light for safety.

The Double-Lever, Double-Set Trigger

Similar to the single-lever, double-set trigger, the double-lever version can be fired either in the set or unset position. It is the most common type of trigger found on today's muzzleloaders, as well as on numerous originals. Caution: The adjustment screw can be set too light, making the gun dangerous.

The Modern Muzzleloader Trigger

This is the same trigger found on modern cartridge guns. It is normally adjustable, and as with any trigger, can be set too light for full safety. Trigger settings should be left to a competent gunsmith.

which is bothersome, but this can be corrected by installing a weak mousetrap-type spring on the trigger plate to hold the trigger against the sear.

The Single-Set Trigger

The single-set trigger offers a very light trigger pull with only one trigger, instead of two. While this type of trigger comes in various sub-styles, it demands precise adjustment for full benefit, and it must be set before the lock can be cocked. The more advanced single-set multiple-function trigger also has but one trigger; however, the gun can be fired in two modes, the trigger set by moving it forward until it clicks, or pulled without setting and the gun will fire. Setting the trigger provides a very light let-off, while for fast-action, the trigger need not be set.

Chapter 26

REAL GUN BALLISTICS

THIS CHAPTER deals with chronographed test results for a small sampling of actual muzzleloading rifles, pistols, and shotguns, along with cap and ball revolvers, plus blackpowder cartridge rifles and revolvers: all firearms for sale on the open market. Test barrels are essential, especially with their ability to read out pressures; however, having a few figures for over-the-counter firearms is also worthwhile, if only for comparison purposes. Select loads were tested for exact downrange velocities with an Oehler chronograph set up at 100 yards. The large shoot-through area of the skyscreens allowed for accurate readings. A few stray bullets did blow some screens to pieces, but that was considered a worthy sacrifice for information. Actual downrange chronographed figures closely matched computed data, although the former showed a little higher velocity than the latter in most cases because the tests were conducted at high elevation (more than a mile above sea level).

The author used his Oehler Model 33P Proof Chronograph to gather data for real gun ballistics in this chapter.

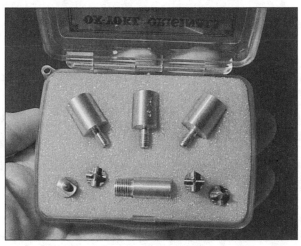

Along with real gun ballistics, the characteristics of the projectile must be included in the final effect of that bullet on game. This little kit from Ox-Yoke Originals alters the nose of a lead bullet, changing its performance at the target.

Chronograph runs were conducted mainly for verification of printed tables. In no way are the following figures offered as competitive. One firearm was not pitted against another. Certain guns show stronger ballistics than others due to specific bullets and powder charges employed, not because of any inferior trait associated with any other test gun. Of course, muzzleloaders allowed 150 grains volume produced higher velocities than guns held to smaller powder charges.

Value

A shooter looking at velocities and energies at the muzzle, and again at 100 yards, has a good idea concerning the performance of his own muzzleloaders and black powder cartridge guns, even if the model he has is slightly different from the gun tested. It's also valuable to see what blackpowder guns develop in Newtonian energy at the muzzle and again at 100 yards downrange, although downrange ballistics are not always important, as in the case of cap and ball revolvers best suited to close-

range shooting. However, as stated above, the most important aspect of shooting actual guns for chronograph results is satisfying curiosity. Experienced round-ball shooters know, for example, that if they get close enough to big game and place one good-sized lead sphere where it belongs, it's meat for dinner that night, regardless of velocity/energy figures. Still, it's fun to see what today's muzzleloaders and blackpowder cartridge guns can do. Also, in some cases, the lesser powder charges are preferable. A good example is the first rifle tested, a 32-caliber Dixie long gun, which provided excellent plinking and small-game ballistics with only 20 grains volume of powder. On the other hand, a moose or elk hunter will want to go with full-throttle loads. All full-power loads tested were in accord with the manufacturer's maximum allowable charges.

Note: See *The Gun Digest Black Powder Loading Manual*, Third Edition, for more ballistic information, as well as the *Lyman Black Powder Handbook, Second Edition*.

All Powder Charges Below in Grains Volume Only, Never by Weight
(Powder charge listed in grains in left column)

CODE:
fps = feet per second
mv = muzzle velocity
f-p = foot-pounds
me = muzzle energy

Muzzleloading Rifles

32-caliber Dixie Tennessee Mountain Rifle
41 1/4-inch barrel
.310-inch 45-grain round ball
Goex FFFg powder

10 grains	1,263 fps mv	170 f-p me	100 yards:	720 fps/55 f-p
20 grains	1,776 fps mv	336 f-p me	100 yards:	852 fps/77 f-p
30 grains	2,081 fps mv	462 f-p me	100 yards:	936 fps/93 f-p
40 grains	2,225 fps mv	495 f-p me	100 yards:	960 fps/96 f-p

36-caliber Cabela's Blue Ridge Rifle
39-inch barrel
.350-inch, 65-grain round ball
Elephant FFFg powder

30 grains	1,764 fps mv	449 f-p me	100 yards:	1,112 fps/179 f-p
40 grains	1,966 fps mv	558 f-p me	100 yards:	1,219 fps/215 f-p
50 grains	2170 fps mv	680 f-p me	100 yards:	1,324 fps/253 f-p

36-caliber Cabela's Blue Ridge Rifle
39-inch barrel
125-grain Buffalo Bullet
Pyrodex RS

30 grains	1,233 fps mv	422 f-p me	100 yards:	963 fps/257 f-p
40 grains	1,381 fps mv	529 f-p me	100 yards:	1,057 fps/310 f-p
50 grains	1,509 fps mv	632 f-p me	100 yards:	1,140 fps/361 f-p

45-caliber J.P. McCoy Squirrel Rifle (Mountain State Muzzleloading)
42-inch barrel
.440-inch, 128-grain round ball
Pyrodex RS

40 grains	1,662 fps mv	785 f-p me	100 yards:	947 fps/255 f-p
60 grains	1,842 fps mv	965 f-p me	100 yards:	1,032 fps/303 f-p
100 grains	2,222 fps mv	1,404 f-p me	100-yards:	1,186 fps/400 f-p

45-caliber Gonic GA-87 Rifle
26-inch barrel
45-caliber 405-grain Gonic Bullet
Goex FFg powder

90 grains	1,489 fps mv	1,994 f-p me	100 yards:	1,269 fps/1,449 f-p
100 grains	1,542 fps mv	2,139 f-p me	100 yards:	1,312 fps/1,548 f-p
120 grains	1,591 fps mv	2,277 f-p me	100 yards:	1,354 fps/1,649 f-p

45-Caliber Navy Arms Volunteer Rifled Musket
32-inch barrel
45-caliber, 490-grain Lyman No. 457121 Bullet
Goex FFg powder

70 grains	1,164 fps mv	1,475 f-p me	100 yards:	1,013fps/1,117 f-p
90 grains	1,240 fps mv	1,240 f-p me	100 yards:	1,067 fps/1.239 f-p
130 grains	1,474 fps mv	2,365 f-p me	100 yards:	1,254 fps/1,711 f-p

50-caliber Lyman Great Plains Rifle
32-inch barrel
.490-inch 177-grain round ball
Pyrodex RS

60 grains	1,471 fps mv	850-f-p me	100 yards:	897 fps/316 f-p
90 grains	1,762 fps mv	1,221 f-p me	100 yards:	1,022 fps/411 f-p
100 grains	2,027 fps mv	1,615 f-p me	100 yards:	1,070 fps/450 f-p

50-caliber Markesbery Outer-Line® Muzzleloader
24-inch barrel
375-grain Buffalo SSB Spitzer Bullet

3 Pyrodex 50/50 Pellets (150 grains volume)	1,700 fps mv	2,407 f-p me	100 yards:	1,522 fps/1,929 f-p

Same rifle with 175-grain Devel Bullet

120 gr. Swiss FFFg	2,114 fps mv	1,737 f-p me	100 yards:	1,797 fps/1,255 f-p

54 Caliber Lyman Great Plains Rifle
32-inch barrel
.535-inch, 230-grain round ball
Pyrodex RS Select

80 grains	1,597 fps mv	1,303 f-p me	100 yards:	988fps/509f-p
100 grains	1,755 fps mv	1,573 f-p me	100 yards:	1,027 fps/539 f-p
120 grains	1,924 fps mv	1,891 f-p me	100 yards:	1,121 fps/642 f-p

54-caliber Thompson/Center Black Mountain Magnum
26-inch barrel
300-grain Hornady Power-Tip Express Bullet/sabot
Elephant FFg powder

60 grains	1,185 fps mv	936 f-p me	100 yards:	1,001 fps/668 f-p
90 grains	1,413 fps mv	1,330 f-p me	100 yards:	1,184 fps/934 f-p
120 grains	1,635 fps mv	1,781 f-p me	100 yards:	1,369 fps/1,249 f-p

58-Caliber Navy Arms Parker-Hale Musketoon
24-inch barrel
505-grain Buffalo Bullet
Pyrodex RS

70 grains	903 fps mv	915 f-p me	100 yards:	841 fps/793 f-p
100 grains	1,226 fps mv	1,686 f-p me	100 yards:	1,043 fps/1,220 f-p

62-Caliber Light American Sporting Rifle – October Country
28-inch barrel
62-caliber, 342-grain round ball
Goex FFg powder

200 grains	2,000 fps mv	3,038 f-p me	100 yards:	1,300fps/1,284 f-p

69-Caliber Great American Sporting Rifle – October Country
28-inch barrel
69-caliber, 473-grain round ball
Goex FFg powder

200 grains	1,750 fps mv	3,212 f-p me	100 yards:	1,208 fps/1,533 f-p

October Country 8-Bore Double Rifle
30-inch barrel
8-bore, .834-inch diameter, 873-grain round ball
Pyrodex RS Select

300 grains	1,610 fps mv	5,026 f-p me	100 yards:	1,144 fps/2,538 f-p

October Country 4-Bore Single-Barrel Rifle
30-inch barrel
4-bore, 1.052-inch diameter, 1,750-grain round ball
Goex Fg powder

400 grains	1,400 fps mv	7,618 f-p me	100 yards:	1,008 fps/3,949 f-p

Big Bore Blackpowder Pistols, Revolvers, and Shotguns

Traditions 50-Caliber Buckhunter Pro™ In-Line Pistol
12-inch barrel
.490-inch 177-grain round ball
Elephant FFFg powder

30 grains	1,117 fps mv	490 f-p me
40 grains	1,212 fps mv	577 f-p me

Thompson/Center Encore 50-Caliber Pistol
15-inch barrel
T/C 50-caliber, 370-grain Maxi-Ball
Goex FFg powder

100 grains	1,287 fps mv	1,361 f-p me

Navy Arms 36-Caliber 1861 Navy Revolver
7 1/2-inch barrel
.375-inch, 81-grain round ball
Pyrodex P

25 grains	949 fps mv	162 f-p me
30 grains	968 fps mv	169 f-p me

Colt 44-Caliber1860 Army Revolver
8-inch barrel
.451-inch, 138-grain round ball
Goex FFFg powder

25 grains	665 fps mv	136 f-p me
35 grains	904 fps mv	250 f-p me

Navy Arms Co. Colt Walker 44 Revolver
9-inch barrel
.454-inch, 141-grain round ball
Pyrodex P

55 grains	1,200 fps mv	451 f-p me

Ruger Old Army 45-Caliber Revolver
7 1/2-inch barrel
.457-inch, 143-grain round ball
Pyrodex P

40 grains	1,047 fps mv	348 f-p me

12-Gauge Navy Arms T&T Double-Barrel Shotgun
28-inch barrels
1 1/4 ounces of shot
Goex FFg powder

100 grains	1,113 fps mv

12-Gauge Knight Modern Muzzleloading Shotgun
26-inch barrel
1 3/4-ounces of shot
Pyrodex RS

120 grains	1,011 fps mv

12-Gauge Knight Modern Muzzleloading Shotgun
26-inch barrel
2 ounces of shot
Pyrodex RS

110 grains	966 fps mv

<u>Blackpowder Cartridge Guns</u>

Sharps 1874 Single-Shot Cartridge Rifle, 40-65 Winchester
32-inch barrel
390-grain bullet
Goex Cartridge powder

60 grains	1,293 fps mv	1,448 f-p me	100 yards:	1,114 fps/1,134 f-p

Marlin 1895 Lever-Action Repeater, 45-70 Government
22-inch barrel
405-grain Remington Bullet
Goex FFg powder

67 grains	1,231 fps mv	1,363 f-p me	100 yards:	1,083 fps/1,055 f-p

Navy Arms Model 1892 Lever-Action Rifle, 45 Colt
24-inch barrel

(Tested With Factory Ammo)

Federal Classic Pistol Cartridge, 225-grain Semi-Wadcutter Hollow-Point

984 fps mv	484 f-p me

Winchester 255-grain Lead Round Nose

912 fps mv

Winchester 225-grain Silvertip Hollow-Point

912 fps mv   471 f-p me

Hornady Frontier Cowboy Action Loads 255-grain Lead Round Nose

829 fps mv   389 f-p me

CCI Blazer 200-grain Jacketed Hollow-Point

1,123 fps mv   560 f-p me

Remington 225-grain Lead Semi-Wadcutter

1,094 fps mv   598 f-p me

Remington 250-grain Lead Round Nose

1,010 fps mv   566 f-p me

Cor Bon 200-grain Jacketed Hollow-Point

1,272 fps mv   719 f-p me

Navy Arms Colt Bisley 45 Colt

4 1/2-inch barrel

(Tested With Factory Ammo)

Federal Classic Pistol Cartridge 225-grain Semi-Wadcutter Hollow-Point

620 fps mv   192 f-p me

Winchester 255-grain Lead Round Nose

663 fps mv   249 f-p me

Winchester 225-grain Silvertip Hollow-Point

695 fps   241 f-p me

Hornady Frontier Cowboy Action Loads 255-grain Lead Round Nose

614 fps

CCI Blazer 200-grain Jacketed Hollow-Point

765 fps

Remington 225-grain Lead Semi-Wadcutter

750 fps

Remington 250-grain Lead Round Nose

687 fps

Chapter 27

UNDERSTANDING RIFLING TWIST

THERE IS no such thing as one correct twist for all bullets. The laws of physics make that impossible. However, romanticists insist that the 1:48 rate of twist was, and still is, perfect for all muzzleloaders. After all, Sam and Jake Hawken rifled their guns that way, or so we're told, proof notwithstanding. How could those great gunmakers be wrong? If the Hawken brothers did go with the 1:48 rate of twist for all of their guns, regardless of caliber, it was probably due to having only one rifling machine. Apparently, according to Ned Roberts, author of *The Muzzle-Loading Cap Lock Rifle*, 1:48 was a standard in the late 19th century. Roberts wrote: "It appears that the old-time riflesmith's 'standard' twist of rifling for round ball rifles was one turn in 48 inches." The author went on to say that some smiths preferred 1:60 and even slower twists.

Meanwhile, Capt. James Forsyth, well-respected English shooter, apparently understood the properties of rifling twist better than many of his peers, because he knew that no single rate of twist could possibly be correct for all calibers. His round-ball rifles carried super slow rifling twist, such as 1:112. Nonetheless, shooters who would laugh at the idea of rifling all modern guns with the same rate of twist buy into the idea that smokepoles somehow defy the laws of science. Going back to 1895, the 25-35 Winchester had a fast 1:8 rate of twist to stabilize long 117-grain, 25-caliber bullets. The 30-30, called the 30 W.C.F. (Winchester Center Fire) at the time, appeared in the same year, but it was built with a 1:12 rate of twist. Obviously, Winchester engineers knew something.

Speaking in general terms, bullets of low sectional density and ballistic coefficient require less rps (revolutions per second) to stabilize them in flight, than bullets of higher sectional density and ballistic coefficient. That's why the round ball requires very little spin to keep it on track, while conicals demand more rps for stability. As caliber increases, projectile mass also grows, requiring fewer rps to stabilize the missile. In other words, a bullet from a 32-caliber muzzleloader requires more rps to keep it revolving on its axis than a bullet from a 58-caliber rifle. So there it is: No single rate of twist can possibly be correct for all guns.

The reason ballistic coefficient is included in the story is due to streamlined projectiles of long length needing more rps than bullets of the same caliber and weight, but more blunt in profile. This was a consideration when the SSB came along, because though it was 45-caliber (fitted into sabots), it was long for its diameter. Comparing another 45-caliber bullet (a 285-grain hollow-base) from the same company, it's easy to see that it's much shorter for its diameter than the SSB. Because muzzleloader manufacturers finally got around to installing faster rates of twist for guns intended to shoot conicals, the SSB did all right in modern muzzleloaders. Going with an example from the modern world, there's the accurate Sierra 69-grain .224-inch diameter Match King bullet. This long-for-its-caliber bullet found its way into a 222 Remington rifle with 1:14 rate of twist. The bullet keyholed on its way to the target, hitting sideways instead of point-first. The same bullet from a Colt AR-15A2 rifle with a fast 1:7 rate of twist flew point-forward to the target, obviously stabilized.

Rifling Twist Range

Just as no single rate of twist is right for all bullets, no one twist is necessary to stabilize a given pro-

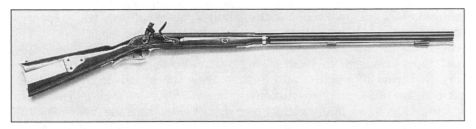

The model for this replica rifled musket in 54-caliber went on the trail with the Lewis & Clark Expedition. Its 1:66 rate of twist calls for a round ball.

When Markesbery Muzzleloader company picked up on a line of bullets, the conical was selected to match up with the rifle's 1:26 rate of twist, which is as fast as muzzleloaders go.

jectile. There is a range of acceptability. The 1:24 rate of twist on my own Markesbery muzzleloader stabilizes a wide variety of bullets, from the short Buffalo Bullet Ballet, to the aforementioned SSB Spitzer. While one rifling twist has a range of bullets it can stabilize, the same is true in reverse: one bullet can maintain its axis in flight from a range of rifling twist. The 32-caliber round ball can be stabilized with a 1:30 or a 1:50 rate of twist, depending in part upon the muzzle velocity imparted to the projectile (more on that later).

Comparing Smoothbores

Smoothbores, while more efficient and useful in the field than often credited, never produced the brand of accuracy sought after by serious marksmen, especially target shooters. There is also good reason to believe that soldiers armed with rifled guns were deadlier than those firing smoothbores, as the Battle of New Orleans suggests. The projectile fired from a smoothbore tends to take a line of flight dictated by its distribution of mass. One reasons for superb round-ball accuracy from a rifled gun is equalization of discrepancies on a common axis. No lead bullet is perfect. It is not 100 percent homogenous in its molecular distribution. Each round bullet is lopsided, if only by microscopic proportions. By spinning the ball, minute flaws in its structure revolve around a common line or axis. So instead of one side of the ball causing it to drift off course, the sides are constantly changing position, keeping the bullet on track. The lead globe can be extremely accurate because of this

factor: equalizing irregularities through spinning. Firing a round ball from a smoothbore shows this clearly. Although reasonable close-range, big-game type accuracy can be achieved, the rifled bore produces much tighter groups.

RPS: How it is Achieved

The number of revolutions per second is determined by two, and only two, factors. These are rate of twist and muzzle velocity. The operative word is rate of twist. Barrel length is not directly a part of the equation. The length of the barrel, in and of itself, does not dictate rate of twist. Unfortunately, twist is stated as the number of turns a bullet makes as it progresses through the bore. This presents the mistaken notion that a "turn in so many inches of barrel" determines how fast the bullet spins. This is not so. Again, only two factors determine how fast a bullet revolves on its action: rate of twist and exit velocity. Barrel length does matter! But as stated earlier, not directly. Barrel length only matters because longer barrels, up to a point, generate more muzzle velocity than shorter barrels. For example, if two 50-caliber rifles with exactly the same rate of twist — one with a two-inch barrel, another with a 42-inch barrel — could both somehow achieve the same muzzle velocity, bullets from either one would have the same rps. Barrel length then matters only in terms of muzzle velocity, not because of so many revolutions of the bullet in so many inches of barrel. If the two mythical 50-caliber guns above with the same rate of twist fired the same bullet, there

would be no difference in the stabilization of the projectile. Forevermore, think of rate of twist as a turn in so many inches, but not inches of barrel, but rather inches of flight.

Trigonometry

Although it's been done on paper, and rather convincingly, missile stabilization is not a matter of trigonometry. Tangents of angles, graphic triangles, and little line drawings tell nothing worthwhile about rifling twist. This statement will anger readers who have believed in an explanation of rifling twist based on trigonometry. I advise these people to consult a scientist who understands ballistics, or to bring this chapter to that scientist and see what he says about angles, tangents, triangles and such when missile stabilization and rate of twist are under discussion. Capt. James Forsyth, mentioned above, worked diligently on the mathematics of rifling twist in the 19th century. While his formulas are not of much interest today, his conclusions are. Forsyth concluded, along with Maj. Shakespear and Sir Samuel Baker, that the greater the missile grows in mass, the less rps required to stabilize it. He was right, proving his conclusions with rifles made up with very slow rates of twist to stabilize large-caliber lead spheres accurately to long range.

Stripping the Bore

Sometimes called "tripping over the rifling," stripping the bore meant that the bullet rode over the lands, rather than being guided by them. Like a train on a track, the bullet can only go where the rifling leads it. Also like a train on a track, the projectile can either stay on its "rails" or it can scoot over them and crash. When the projectile is no longer guided by the rifling — in 19th-century terminology "tripping over the rifling or "stripping the bore" — it spells disaster to accuracy. This condition can exist under various circumstances, especially with undersized bullets that do not obturate to meet the rifling. It's also a clue about accuracy with bullets that fit well to the bore.

Super Light Loads

There is a way to defy rate of twist to a modest degree. Considering a rifle with a comparatively fast rate of twist, a round ball may achieve a degree of accuracy by reducing the load, in turn lowering muzzle velocity. Since rps is a product of rate of twist and muzzle velocity, reducing muzzle velocity also cuts down rps and a ball that may have tripped over the rifling is now guided by the lands. Advice given that only light loads shoot accurately is wrong. In reality, when the ball was given too much speed in a rifle with a too fast rate of twist, it left the rifling and flew off course. The idea that only light loads are accurate is, therefore, false. Many factors are at work. If a bullet is damaged in the bore for any reason, accuracy suffers, but a fast bullet that is stabilized can shoot accurately. Ideally, rifling rate of twist and bullets should match.

Grooves and Lands

Another factor that can alter how a bullet behaves is depth of groove, which in turn produces the height of the land. A taller land may bite into a bullet, forcing it to spin in the bore in spite of a rate of twist normally too fast for the particular bullet. Much talk about tall lands being necessary for round-ball stabilization is not quite on the mark. Round-ball rifles with shallow grooves and modest land height shoot accurately when the rate of twist is correct. However, shallow grooves with corresponding shorter lands seem to be best for conicals, as taller lands doing little more than scar the projectile.

Round Ball Circumference and Twist

While angles and tangents are relatively meaningless in a discussion of bullet stabilization, it is true that the circumference of a bigger ball is rotating faster than the circumference of a smaller ball. In other words, the speed of a 60-caliber lead sphere on the outside of its surface is greater than the speed of a 50-caliber lead sphere on the outside of its surface when both missiles are driven at the same velocity from a bore with the same rate of twist. Taking the 1:66 rate of twist as an example, the ball makes a single revolution per 66 inches of travel. While the 60-caliber ball's circumference is moving faster than the 50-caliber ball's circumference, there is an equalization factor at

work because the diameter of the rifling changes in exactly the same proportion with the different calibers. So the faster surface movement of the outside of the 60-caliber ball moves over a longer path in the 1:66 rate of twist, compared with the 50-caliber ball in the same twist. It all comes out to dead equal. Do not be confused by the preceding: The number of turns in the bore for the 50-caliber ball and the 60-caliber ball are exactly the same in a 1:66 rate of twist barrel.

Here is a mental model that may help produce a picture of the situation. It deals with bolts and nuts. There are two bolts and nuts in this story. One bolt is 1/4-inch in diameter, the other 1/2-inch. Both have, of course, corresponding threaded nuts. Both have 20 threads to the inch, or in rifling talk, 20 turns to the inch. If either nut is moved down its respective bolt 1 inch, that nut will make 20 turns. That's the fact we're after in this model. In spite of the diameters of the two bolts being quite different, both are guided identically by their rate of twist. This holds true as long as the nut (or bullet) does not strip out. This model is important because it reveals several facts. First, no matter if the bolt is 1/4-inch long or 2 feet long, the rate of twist imparted to the nut has to stay the same. Second, the nut can be driven that inch in one minute, one second, or one millisecond, or any other period of time. If the nut is driven at different speeds, the revolutions per

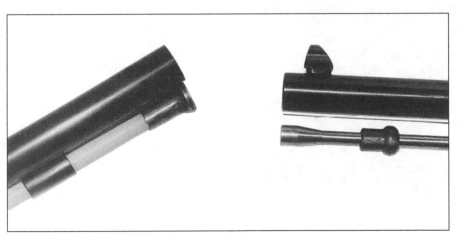

Understanding rifling twist becomes much simpler when comparing two muzzleloaders that are on different poles, a smoothbore on the left and a rifled musket on the right with a 1:20 rate of twist.

time must vary. This is important to our story, because we can see that rps will vary in accord with forward motion of the projectile as it is guided by the rifling.

Rifling Twist in Practice

Given that rps is related to rate of twist and exit velocity of the missile, how many revolutions per second are required to keep an elongated bullet flying point-on, or to maintain a round ball revolving on its axis? A projectile is like a free-moving gyroscope. In order to stabilize a gyroscope, you spin it. Can you spin it too much? There may be a point at which the gyroscope goes crazy when it is revolved too rapidly. However, it is clearly evident that when the gyroscope slows down below a specific spin rate it falls on its side. When a conical projectile is not given sufficient rps, it may wobble in flight or keyhole (tumble). Too little rps may also cause it to depart from its original intended line of flight. Consider two rifles, in this case real-life examples. Both are 54-caliber, one a ball-shooter, the other meant for conicals. The first has a rate of twist going one turn in 79 inches for the lead sphere, while the second runs 1:34. The rifle with 1:79 twist shoots a patched ball remarkably well, as proved with a 6-24x Bausch & Lomb scope and five-shot groups under an inch center-to-center at 100 yards from the muzzle.

The other 54-caliber rifle with a 1:34 rate of twist also will shoot a round ball, but only if velocity of the missile is held down. Otherwise, accuracy goes to pot. However, it shoots a 460-grain Buffalo Bullet well. Meanwhile, the rifle with the 1:79 twist will not stabilize the conical at all, as proved by targets with elongated holes in the paper. While a turn in 34 inches is slow for a modern cartridge that shoots long bullets, it is actually fast in blackpowder terms. That's because many elongated or conical blackpowder bullets have a comparatively low sectional density and low ballistic coefficient. On the other hand, longer blackpowder bullets, such as the SSB, shoot better with a rate of twist faster than 1:34, with all other elements, such as bore quality, being equal.

Super Fast Twist

It's interesting to see what happens with truly long bullets in modern guns, just to give an idea of how much rps can be required for stabilization. A bullet known as the VLD (Very Low Drag) is extremely long for its caliber. The 105-grain 6mm VLD bullet keyholed from rifles with 1:10 rates of twist. A special barrel had to be made to stabilize these handsome projectiles, It turned out to be 1:8. The 226 Barnes QT (Quick Twist) is another example of a cartridge demanding a fast twist. This 22-caliber wildcat

fires a 125-grain, .226-inch diameter missile that runs about 1 3/8 inches in length. Experimenters found that a twist of 1:5.5 was necessary to stabilize it. That's a full revolution of the bullet in only 5-1/2 inches of forward motion.

Variables That Affect Twist

Numerous cause-and-effect gremlins bend the laws of linear (Newtonian) physics, seeming to make liars of the most careful ballisticians. Guns perform differently due to what are known as extraneous variables, those little hidden gremlins so difficult to isolate and figure out. For example, we think of a 50-caliber barrel as being a 50-caliber barrel, and it is. But all 50-caliber barrels are not the same, not even in exact bore dimensions, let alone rifling configuration. Bullet fit to the bore, therefore, varies among different firearms of the same caliber. Furthermore, once we chisel a rule in granite, the block sometimes crumbles. We know, or think we know, that accuracy is usually improved when a round bullet fits the bore fairly closely, rather than an undersized sphere with a thick patch. However, it's no real surprise when a front loader creates a good group with undersized lead pills and heavy patches. So the rule bends a little. The Savage Model 10ML definitely proved more accurate with bullets closer to bore size, .451-inch

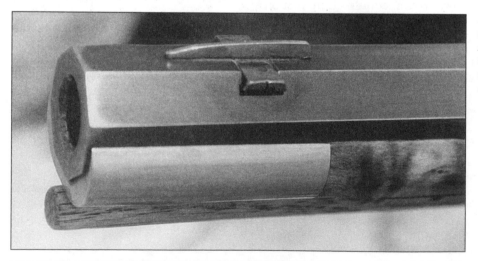

Barely visible at the crown of the muzzle the rifling groove can be seen. Although this is a round ball barrel with a very slow rate of twist, grooves were not made overly deep. The rifle shoots with excellent accuracy.

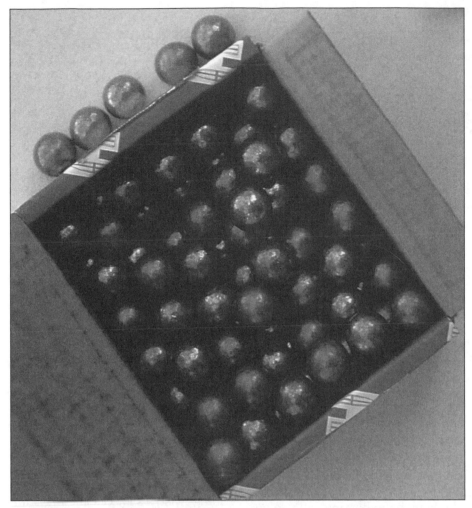

Understanding rifling twist guides the shooter to the proper projectile. These excellent swaged round balls from Hornady, for example, match up with slow rate of twist.

pays off, because guns can be so individual in performance. But starting with an appropriate missile is a big first step to success. Choose a few samples for range work. Before long, the right bullet/powder charge will surface.

Too Much Twist

One barrel maker put it this way: "Rifling twist is like money in the bank. You can't have too much of it." Under-spinning a bullet is more often the cause of trouble than spinning it too much, this veteran shooter contended. However, we do know that over-stabilization can occur, especially when we push a patched round ball down a quick-twist bore and expect it to shoot accurately. Another barrel maker had something different to say about twist. "You want just enough rotation to keep the bullet spinning on its axis, and no more. That's why we build bench-rest rifles with just enough twist to rotate the bullet for stability and no more." He also felt that too much spin ate up energy. Modern manufacturers know about rifling twist. That's why we find three general categories for muzzle-loaders: medium-fast for conicals, rates generally in the realm of 1:24 to 1:32; the middle-of-the-road 1:48 for short Minie bullets in rifled muskets; and truly slow spins for round balls, most 50s taking on a 1:66 rate of twist. Also, spin reduces bullet speed because it takes energy to rotate a missile.

Bullet Spin Downrange

Clearly, some knowledge is for its own sake, with little practical application. The fact that rotational velocity is retained, while forward velocity drops off rather quickly, is one of those nice-to-know facts that purchases very little. However, it is true that once the bullet is spinning merrily on its axis, it tends to remain on track for quite a distance. This is because of retained rotational velocity, while forward velocity drops off severely due to atmospheric hammering — in the

or .452-inch as opposed to .429-inch diameter. Sabots capable of withstanding higher pressures were also necessary for best results. There are also match-ups made in heaven, and sometimes we don't know why. For example, a particular test rifle put the Buffalo Bullet Co. Ball-et into tighter groups than other projectiles that seemed more suitable. That specific bullet shape "liked" the bore and the bore "liked" it. There is also bearing surface to consider. Bullets with long shanks have good bearing surface, and we believe this is important in rifling guidance. Then comes the patched round ball that barely engages the rifling and it creates fine groups. However, one aspect holds up day-in, day-out: the fact that slow-twist is best for the

round ball, while quicker twist is more suited to the conical.

Applying Twist Knowledge

Knowledge of rifling twist is useful for selecting an appropriate missile, as well as selecting the right powder charge for that twist rate. It also is a factor in other rifling considerations, such as groove depth, consequent land height, and projectile shape variations. In working toward the most accurate load possible in a blackpowder firearm, knowing rate of twist is vital. Slow is for ball, faster for conical. The popular in-line muzzleloader is a conical-shooter, but there remain quite a number of round-ball rifles, pistols, and revolvers on the market, too. As usual, personal testing

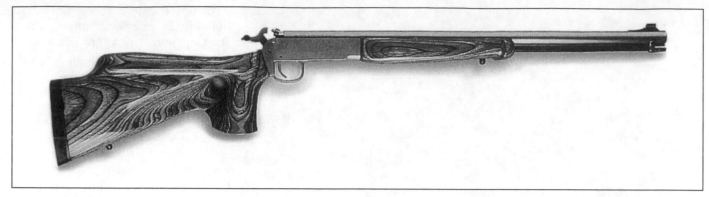

This Markesbery Outer-Line® modern muzzleloader has a 1:26 rate or twist, definitely a conical-shooter.

50-percent realm over the course of only 100 yards for the round ball. Over the same distance, rotational spin of the same round ball is reduced by only a few percent.

Handguns and Twist

Handguns require faster rates of twist per caliber than rifles, leading some to believe that barrel length is, after all, an important factor in achieving rps. Not so. The reason sidearms carry faster rates of twist per caliber is because of reduced exit velocity compared with rifles. Back to the same story: two 30-caliber barrels, one 30 inches long, the other 3 inches long, both with 1:10 rates of twist. Either would stabilize a 180-grain bullet if the velocity imparted by both barrels was high enough to create the right rps. The problem is that the usual handgun barrel is not long enough to generate high velocity, so it receives a faster rate of twist to generate more rps.

For example, the Browning 45-70 single-shot rifle has a 1:20 rate of twist, while the 45 Colt pistol has a 1:16 rate of twist. The rifle shoots a 45-caliber bullet in the 400- to 500-grain class, while the pistol fires a shorter bullet in the 200- to 250-grain domain. And in keeping with the fact that larger bullets require less rps than lighter ones, a smallbore ball-shooting rifle will have a faster rate of twist than a big bore ball-shooting rifle. A 36-caliber squirrel rifle may have a 1:40 rate of twist, because its .350-inch ball only weighs 65 grains, demanding higher rps to stabilize it, while a 50-caliber ball-shooting rifle carries a 1:66 rate of twist.

Blackpowder Cartridge Guns

Appropriately, blackpowder cartridge guns are built with varying rates of twist to match bullets. Just as the Whitworth muzzleloader is intended for long bullets of rather high sectional density, and so it has a 1:20 rate of twist, blackpowder cartridge rifles made to shoot longer bullets also have rates of twist to match. Conversely, certain blackpowder cartridge-shooting guns that fire shorter bullets have slower twist.

That's a brief walk in the woods of rifling twist, a subject sometimes tangled in the webs of "so many turns per inch," when the real factors are rate of twist and bullet exit velocity.

Chapter 28

IGNITION

THE BULL elk was 12 paces away. I know. I measured after the incident. I'm familiar with elk. I live in elk country. This was a grand bull, a royal six by six, not an imperial, but heavy, heavy beams with long tines. He was mine. Or should have been. Steve Pike called the mature wapiti into rock-tossing range. I raised my rifle, taking aim, centering the blade front sight squarely for a clean neck shot. But instead of the healthy roar of 120-grains volume powder going off with a .535-inch round ball making its way to the target, there was a Fttttt!, the loudest sound I'd heard in a long time. Rain had fallen for a few days, but not that day. Nonetheless, wetness on the trees invaded the nipple area and the cap failed to go off. My fault. I had forgotten my weatherproofing gear home, and home was a long distance away — a horseback ride for hours to a main road, with big time travel after that. I was disappointed for myself, but felt worse for Pike, who had worked hard to get that shot for me.

That would not happen today. My rifle would be weatherproofed to the garters, so that nothing short of a stream-dunking could cause ignition failure.

Ignition. A little word, but to the blackpowder shooter, the difference between success and failure. Not only is ignition crucial on the big-game hunt, but also when hunting small game, birds, and at rendezvous, or wherever shooting games and competitions are held. Without ignition, the muzzleloader is a doorstop, not a gun. Likewise for any blackpowder-cartridge firearm, but on that score we can rest. The metallic case holds the primer fast in a tight pocket, and for those concerned, a tiny trace of clear nail polish along the very edge of the primer, where it's seated in the head of the round, is sufficient to ward off any attack of snow or rain. Meanwhile, the bullet seals the front end of the cartridge, safeguarding the powder charge from the evils of wet. And so the concern in this chapter is the front loader,

plus cap 'n' ball revolver, not the blackpowder metallic package.

First Ignition

Fire was the first igniter in the form of a rope, punk, whatever may have been on hand; no one has all the details. The matchlock certainly relied on flame, or at least a smoldering hot ash of some sort. There were also heated irons, smoldering coals, slow matches, hot wires, and other sources of heat used to set off the fire stick of old. In a sense, fire remained an igniter throughout snaphaunce and flintlock history. The flash from the pan is, after all, a flame engendered by hot curls of metal scraped from the face of a frizzen by a flint. Recall that the wheel lock turned to pyrites and other sparkmakers for the initial burn that brought ignition to the waiting powder charge in the breech. Fine-grain powder was no doubt developed early in gun history to supply fire for ignition. Typically, FFFFg (4F) has been the finest-grain pan powder available over the counter, but Elephant brand has a finer grind yet — FFFFFg (5F). I'm not sure if FFFFFg is truly necessary; however, it certainly worked in a 42-caliber flintlock rifle that came from my mentor, the late Professor Charles Keim, Alaskan master guide who got me started on the charcoal-burning trail. There isn't much more to tell about fire as an igniter. Fine-grain blackpowder rests in the pan of the flintlock, creating a quick flame that darts through the flashhole into the main charge of powder in the breech. And that's about it.

Today's source of ignition comes from standard percussion caps, left, musket caps, center, and modern primers, both small rifle/pistol, or No. 209 shotgun primers, right. Thompson/Center Company offers devices to use regular percussion caps, musket caps, or No. 209 primers.

Good flints are vital to flintlock ignition. They're not expensive, nor hard to locate. However, going a few extra pesos for a little higher quality can pay off.

The Tube Lock

The tube lock is of interest here not because of any special mechanical function, but because of historical interest as a means of ignition. The tube lock itself was essentially a hammer gun. It's what the hammer hit that made it interesting: a small tube filled with fulminate of mercury, an impact-sensitive explosive. The falling hammer crushed the tube and the resulting explosion created a flash for ignition in the breech. The tube lock was patented by famous English gunmaker Joseph Manton in 1816, supposedly two years after the invention of the percussion cap.

The Pill Lock

The pill lock goes back in time even farther than the tube or percussion cap. It is considered the invention of Scottish clergyman the Rev. Alexander John Forsyth, who patented the device on April 11, 1807. This is noteworthy because Forsyth is credited by other historians as the inventor of the percussion cap, which may or may not be true. The pill itself was a tiny pellet filled with what literature calls simply "detonating powder." A hammer fell upon the pill, setting it off, which in turn exploded fire into the powder charge in the breech.

The Tape Primer

The tape primer has been credited to dentist Edward Maynard as an invention of 1845. Again, we are well out of sequence with the percussion cap of 1814, but it's well to get some of the minor (interesting and important) ignitions out of the way before talking about caps. Imagine a roll of toy caps. The tape primer was essentially two strips of tape with interspaced fulminate pods lodged in between the strips. The tape was fed over the top of the nipple mechanically by a ratchet arrangement. Each time the hammer was eared back, the tape advanced to offer a new priming pod under and in line with the falling hammer nose.

Disc Primers

Also out of sequence is the disk primer of 1852, an invention of Christian Sharps, whose name is hardly unfamiliar to blackpowder cartridge fans. These were tiny copper discs launched forward one at a time by the action of the hammer. The discs contained fulminate of mercury, making them explode when struck by the hammer nose. The sparks emanating from the exploded disk flew into the breech to ignite the powder therein.

The Percussion Cap

The exact origin remains a question mark, but the percussion cap is still with us because it works. Patents help, but not all great inventions were protected. As previously mentioned, the Rev. Forsyth is often credited with the percussion cap, but other sources disagree. Capt. Joshua Shaw of Philadelphia is noted in certain arms histories as father of the percussion cap, dating back to 1814. The claim holds water, but the concept of installing fulminate within a small metal container (cup) was ingenious. It changed shooting forever, because the modern primer is no more than another style of percussion cap. Fulminates are percussion-sensitive; thus the term "percussion" cap used to describe the device. Give fulminate a good whack and it explodes, producing flame. Once har-

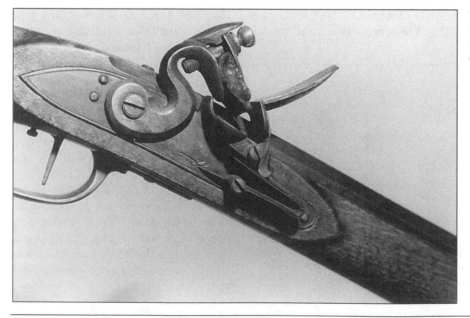

The bevel of the flint shown in this photograph aims directly toward the bed of the pan. It delivered a shower of sparks directly into the pan every time.

nessed within a container, its powers could be controlled and channeled. The idea was simple: When struck by the hammer of a firearm, the cap exploded, sending the flame of ignition into the breech of the firearm via a nipple. Fire had to proceed from the cone of the nipple, through its vent, and then into the main charge in the breech. But that's not all. A good cap had to be consistent, providing similar duration of flame from one to the next, plus emitting a spark lasting long enough to reach the powder charge every time. So a proper percussion cap was a precise detonator with specific repeatable and reliable properties.

The big push for years was the hot cap, "hot" referring to one that threw a powerful flame. But early hot caps were not always reliable. Those who tested the situation decided that a "cool" cap could be just as effective as a hot one. The ideal cap delivered just enough spark to bring about ignition, but not an excessive explosion. A cap that was more powerful than necessary caused pieces of its own body to fly in all directions, and the too-hot cap could all but "blow itself out." It went crack! on the nip-

There are two main types of percussion caps—standard, on the left, and musket size. Standards come in different sizes, the smaller the number, the smaller the cap, such as No. 10 vs. No. 11, the latter being larger. The musket cap is much larger, again, than a No. 11 or No. 12 standard percussion cap.

ple, but the flame seemed to spatter, for lack of a better term, rather than channeling under control through the vent and into the powder charge. Excessive cap debris also clogged the nipple, impeding the progress of flame when the next cap was fired. This situation could cause a misfire, or at least a hangfire. Today, the problem is rectified. We have hot caps that throw the same flame every time. Today's percussion caps are the best the world of muzzleloading has ever seen, providing a sustained spark, rather than a short-lived blast. This includes the CCI Magnum percussion cap, which is not to be confused with "hot" caps of the past. This cap provides consistent flame of good duration.

The Non-Corrosive Cap

At first glance, a non-corrosive cap coupled with blackpowder seems to make no sense. Why worry about a little soot from the cap when about half of the charge will soon become fouling anyway? But this is not the case. Non-corrosive caps are recommended. Before loading the front stuffer or percussion revolver, it's advisable to pop off a cap or two on nipples to clear lingering oil, ensuring a clear channel from the nipple cone into the breech. A corrosive cap can deposit "smudge" in the nipple vent, nipple seat, even the breech area. Then the firearm may not be fired for some time, especially on a hunt, where the sportsman may not fire his charcoal burner for some time. During this time, the corrosive elements from the cap are working

CCI, realizing the growing popularity of the musket cap, brought out its own, calling it the U.S. Musket Cap.

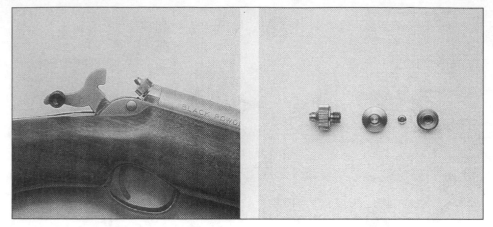

Over the years there have been numerous devices developed to shoot modern primers with muzzleloaders. The Markesbery 400 SRP Magnum Ignition System is a modern version. It takes small pistol or small rifle primers in a closed unit, which is especially good in damp weather.

against metal. The firearm will not likely be ruined by a little corrosion in and around the nipple, but the condition is best avoided anyway, especially with regard to perfect ignition. So the non-corrosive percussion cap does make sense after all.

The Waterproof Cap

Some caps withstand moisture better than others, right down to running water over them. This is an easy self-test. At the range, dampen a cap and see what happens to ignition. The most waterproof cap in the world will fail when soaked, meaning we should call them "water resistant," but these caps do tend to fire more reliably than non-waterproofed caps under the stress of high moisture. On a hunting trip especially, the so-called "lacquered" cap is worthy. How

to tell? Just dampen a few caps at the range and see what happens.

Cap Sizes and Construction

Percussion caps are not created equally in terms of output, duration of spark, consistency, and other particulars. They also come in various sizes. The No. 11 percussion cap is a standard today that fits most nipples, while a No.10 is better on some revolvers. A shooting friend complained, "Why don't they make more No. 10 caps? No. 11s just fall off the nipple." I suggested that he change nipples. The No. 11 is far more popular than the No. 10, and if it does not fit the cone of the nipple, accuse the nipple, not the cap. Minor variations in cap sizes from brand to brand have existed. For example, a No. 11

cap in Brand A may be identical in size to a No. 12 cap in Brand B. But manufacturers have listened and this situation is under correction. Measuring with a micrometer, a regular CCI No. 11 cap was 0.1775 inch. The CCI Magnum No. 11 cap measured 0.1775 inch. An RWS No. 11 cap was 0.177 inch across. A Remington No. 11 cap was 0.185 inch across. All are very similar in size, which has not always been the case.

Another percussion cap criterion is cup construction: ribbed or smooth. Both work equally well.

A more important cap body difference is malleability. Brittle caps tend to fragment upon firing, while more malleable caps smash against the cone of the nipple where they either fall off of their own accord or can be flicked away.

Modern primers are becoming more and more popular in muzzleloaders in both small pistol/ small rifle size, or the larger No. 209 shotgun primer.

Powder flasks like the one in the center here from Cabela's dispense a specific volume, not weight, of blackpowder determined by the size of the spout. Different size spouts are available for different loads.

The Musket Cap Now

The English musket cap — nicknamed the "tophat cap" and also now called the U.S. musket cap — originally served as its name implies, on muskets, and it still does. But this large cap has also come into its own for sidelocks and even modern muzzleloaders. That's because it truly does provide a terrific flame for ignition. It is not a "hot" cap in the negative sense of exploding on the cone of the nipple like a little bomb, but rather it puts out a long and sustained flame. Currently, these big caps are available from Germany in the RWS brand, or the United States from CCI, the latter measuring 0.240 inch across.

Modern Primers

Conversion nipples, sometimes referred to as fusils, have been available for many years. However, there are many rifles today that use modern primers as a regular part of the system, not as an add-on. For example, the Savage Model 10ML takes a No. 209 shotgun primer fitted on the end of its special percussion module. Fire from the hot No. 209 primer flies through the center of the module and into the powder in a straight line (in-line ignition). Likewise, the Thompson/Center break-open style Encore muzzleloader also uses No. 209 primers, not as an option, but as the firearm's means of ignition. The rifle is hinged open, revealing the back end of the removable breech plug, and a primer is installed directly into a pocket. There is even an extractor on this rifle to push out the fired primer. The Markesbery Outer-Line® muzzleloader has the 400 SRP unit, which screws directly into the nipple seat. While this may be considered an alternative ignition system, it's actually very much a part of the rifle's design and can be used exclusively. It takes small rifle or small pistol primers. While it's obvious that modern primers provide a terrific flame for ignition, it's equally true that under most conditions, standard percussion caps provide total reliability. As a demonstration of this fact, a Markesbery rifle was fired with No. 11 caps only for a period of three months. The rifle enjoyed 100 percent ignition with the caps. On the other hand, at the first sign of inclement weather, this rifle will be fired with small rifle or small pistol primers.

Working with the Percussion Cap

As already mentioned, an accepted practice of clearing the nipple of the firearm prior to loading is popping percussion caps on the cone of the nipple to dry things up. As also noted, bits of metal may end up within the vent (channel) of the nipple. This fouling within the nipple vent could prevent the clear passage of flame, causing a misfire or hangfire. That's why poking a pipe cleaner into the cone of the nipple after detonating dry-up caps is recommended to ensure that no cap debris remains behind. This step only takes a few seconds and can prevent an ignition problem.

Cap Holders and Dispensers (Cappers)

Seating devices are now available not only for popular regular-size percussion caps, but also for musket caps, No. 209 shotshell primers, and small pistol/small rifle primers. For example, Markesbery offers a special capper that holds small rifle or small pistol primers in line. This spring-loaded unit delivers one primer at a time into a loading gate, where it can then be pressed into the 400 SRP's primer seat. There are two general types of

The Thompson/Center Flame Thrower Nipple is designed for the large musket cap. The long lower shank section with vent helps distribute flame to the main powder charge in the breech.

There are replacement nipples to take different types of percussion caps. This nipple screws into a standard nipple seat, but the cone is sized to retain a musket cap.

cappers: in-line spring-loaded, where caps or primers are contained in a straight line, one behind the other; and gravity-fed magazine cappers. There are even special models available for individual guns, such as Ted Cash's superb magazine cappers for cap 'n' ball revolvers. The Knight Capper is designed for in-line rifles. All of these cappers work well. They are also considered safety devices, as well as tools providing a means of containing and dispensing caps and primers. That's because they eliminate placing caps or primers into position with the fingers.

Safely Evaluating Percussion Cap Performance

Percussion caps can be tested and evaluated by the shooter using a screw-barrel pistol, such as the 44-caliber Dixie Gun Works Derringer Liegi. Keep all parts of your body clear of the pistol in this test. Do not allow anyone else in the area when you are testing caps. The use of the pistol is entirely safe unless the shooter does something outrageously foolish. For the No. 11 size, unscrew the barrel from the pistol, exposing the breech. Place a percussion cap on the nipple. Fire the unloaded gun in a darkened area, such as the garage at night. A flame/spark will jet from the pistol.

The shooter can visually determine for himself the duration of the spark and its size, as well as the shape of the flame, whether long and slender, short and wide, or in between. Cap brands can be readily compared with this useful visual inspection method.

Types of Nipples

There are a staggering number of different nipple types, perhaps in the hundreds, considering 19th as well as 20th and 21st century styles. Differences in thread are several, including the 1/4-28, 6-75 and 6-1mm metrics, 12-28s and other thread dimensions. There are also numerous design variations. The Spitfire nipple from Mountain State Muzzleloading is credited with "more fire to powder" and "self cleaning" with a small fire channel of .031-inch diameter. It's made of stainless steel. There is also a Spitfire Musket Nipple in various sizes, including one to fit standard nipple seats, thereby offering musket cap ignition on a firearm originally designed to take No. 11 caps. The Hot Shot nipple by Uncle Mike's comes in numerous sizes, including a special Ruger Hex Head Nipple for the Old Army.

The Flame Thrower from Thompson/Center is yet another nipple design. Dixie Gun Works offers a

number of excellent nipples, including metric sizes. Dixie's list includes the Ampco Nipple in numerous sizes, noted as "a tough alloy with a tensile strength of 118,000 psi, tougher than most steels used in muzzleloader barrels." Dixie also has the interesting "Primer Nipple," which incorporates a "tiny removable coiled retainer spring" to hold a small rifle or small pistol primer. The spring is adjustable to the most convenient location for installing the primer. This otherwise standard nipple allows the use of modern primers in place of percussion caps. It's sized at 1/4 x 28 thread and is installed using a 1/4-inch, open-end wrench. Dixie also has nipple taps to clean up damaged threads or recut

Sometimes nothing works better than simply adding a new flint. These are from Thompson/Center. The company calls them Premium Agate Flints.

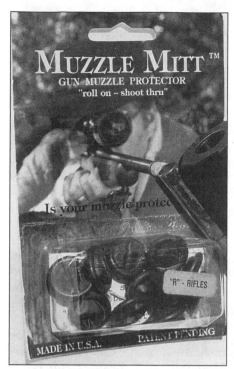

The Muzzle Mitt fits over the end of the barrel as a waterproofing measure.

them to a larger dimension. The company also has "substitutions for nipple taps not available," explained in the Dixie catalog this way: "The vast majority of old nipple seats are .250 or larger. Take one of our .250 hardened nipples and force it into the old threads. Then with the next size .255 force it into the threads. Continue using larger-size nipples until our hardened nipples have chased out the old threads and recut new ones. Use our T-nipple wrench for this heavy work."

The "Straight-Through" Nipple

The name is contrived, but there are still nipples that have a large orifice from base to cone, as opposed to nipples with flat bases and pinholes. Straight-through nipples should be replaced with flat-based types that have a pinhole in the base. Even though the laws of physics allow very little gas to escape through the small port in a nipple when that gas has a route through a much larger exit (the bore of the gun), these large-hole nipples can cause more blowback than flat-based nipples with a small orifice. Exception: There are some nipples today that appear to have an open channel from cone to base, but they do not. The base is actually flared; however, a look up into the nipple from the base reveals a narrow channel.

Priming Nipples

A nipple should never have to be primed by putting powder down into the cone. That is not its proper function. Such priming of the nipple could cause cap debris dispersion. The cap is the spark plug of the gun and the nipple is its guide. Nipples are designed to direct the flame of the cap right where it belongs. If this is not occurring with regularity, there is something wrong and priming the nipple is not the way to correct the problem. A different nipple may help. If the new nipple does not correct the problem, a gunsmith should check the gun for an irregularity.

Cap Safety

Only correctly threaded nipples are safe. An incorrect nipple could blow out of the nipple seat when firing the gun. The proper cap size also is required. Do not choose one that is loosely fit onto the cone of the nipple so that it can either fall off or

blow off, nor so tight that it must be forced on the nipple cone, which could cause it to fire as it's being seated. Furthermore, since percussion caps are sensitive to blows — after all, that is what makes them work — never strike them with anything. Percussion caps can also be set off by heat, so they must be stored them away from any such heat sources, such as stoves, heaters and heater vents. Caps must also be carried safely, in special cap boxes (as made by Tedd Cash) in their original containers, in cappers (in-line or magazine), or in some other sturdy holder where a blow won't set them off. Percussion caps must be stored where children cannot find them. Also, as noted earlier, make sure your caps fit the nipples of your guns. Forcing a percussion cap on a nipple is unwise for obvious reasons. Snug fit, yes, so the cap does not fall off the cone of the nipple when you're hunting. But an overly tight cap fit is asking for trouble. Use a capper, too. It keeps caps away from fingers. While a flash cup is mainly used to prevent the burning of wood around the lock of the gun, it can also be useful in containing cap debris. Tedd Cash Co. makes good ones.

Ignition and Accuracy

We know from modern cartridge firearms that ignition can affect accuracy. In some cases, going to a different primer can reduce group size. However, in the muzzleloader arena, caps and nipples are often wrongly blamed for ill accuracy. Usually, the cause is another factor. However, inconsistent ignition can damage accuracy in two ways. First, it's difficult for a marksman to make a good shot when he cannot rely on the gun firing when the trigger is pulled. Second, hangfires do nothing for accuracy, because the powder charge is not burning uniformly.

Ignition and Muzzle Velocity

Much overstatement has been voiced on variations in muzzle

velocity because of ignition. Hot caps do not guarantee higher velocity. As long as the powder charge is fully ignited — which is no big trick with blackpowder, considering how readily it ignites — velocity will be normal. After all, it is the powder charge that creates the energy to drive bullets and shot charges, not a cap or primer. The differences found with various igniters are usually attributable to normal variance, not the igniters themselves. In one test, three different brands of No. 11 caps were used. Total variation was 26 fps, absolutely insignificant in terms of the caps themselves. Toby Bridges, fellow writer and experimenter, ran a study of four different No. 209 primers to find out if one gave higher muzzle velocity than another. The primer brands were Remington, Winchester, Cheddite, and Federal. Muzzle velocities with a 175-grain Devel bullet ran 2,394 fps, 2,411 fps, 2,426 fps, and 2,423 fps in a Savage Model 10Ml rifle. The extreme spread from slowest to fastest velocity was only 29 fps, statistically insignificant in terms of testing the effect of the primers on velocity. Although muzzleloader powders, including Pyrodex and Clean Shot, are known for extremely low standard deviations

(often 10 fps or less), a 29-fps variation proves nothing about ignition differences.

Ignition Failure

There are many different reasons for ignition failure. They include bad caps, cap debris, poor firearm design, damp powder, the wrong nipple, poor touchhole location, a badly made lock (either percussion or flint), improper loading practices, burned out touchhole and so on (see Chapter 39 on troubleshooting the blackpowder gun for more details). When the firearm is OK, however, with proper nipple, breech plug, percussion cap, or modern primer, the culprit is generally moisture. Since blackpowder and replica propellants are hygroscopic, they can take on moisture from the atmosphere. Moreover, even primers can fail if they get wet.

Waterproofing Measures

The big game hunter, especially, must do everything possible to keep snow or rain out of the system. Fortunately, there are devices that help, from a simple covering of the lock with plastic food wrap, to specific tools, such as the Kap Kover, which has proven itself for years. Sold through Mountain State Muzzleloading, the Kap Kover incorpo-

rates a neoprene O-ring around the nipple to prevent water invasion into the powder charge. As the name promises, it also has a cover, which fits over the top of the nipple to keep the percussion cap dry. It also serves as a safety barrier between hammer nose and cap until removed for firing the gun.

The CVA Super Shot Nipple also has what the company calls a threaded "impact cover" to prevent cap dampening in foul weather.

A small toy balloon stretched over the muzzle keeps water out of the bore.

There is also a powder made to help keep pan powder dry. It's called Rain Coat and Mountain State Muzzleloading has it.

The Hangfire

The hangfire, also written as hang-fire or hang fire, means ignition delay. The gun does goes off, but not instantly. Pssttt—boom! That's the sound of a hangfire. Warning: Continue to safely aim the firearm downrange if it does not fire. The longest hangfire I am personally aware of is 1 1/2 minutes between trigger pull and firing.

The Misfire

The misfire sounds like this: Click! The gun does not fire at all

To ensure good ignition, the edge of the flint is mated solidly with the face of the frizzen.

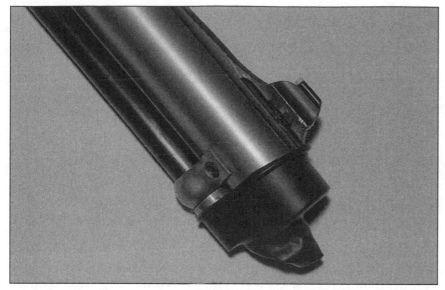

Weatherproofing means keeping water out of the bore. The Muzzle Mitt does just that by stretching over the muzzle like a small balloon.

after the trigger is pulled. Again, continue aiming in a safe direction after a click. It could be a hangfire instead of a misfire.

Flintlock Ignition

This subject was covered in the chapter on loading techniques.

The Flash in the Pan

There are many terms from the world of shooting used in today's language: He's a straight shooter, the idea missed the mark, he bought the plan lock, stock, and barrel. Something can also be a flash in the pan: a quick start, but no finish. In a flintlock rifle, a flash in the pan means the priming powder went poof! but ignition of the powder in the breech did not follow.

Poor ignition can spoil the day, be it a fun time plinking, informal target shooting with friends, rendez-vous games, Olympic competition or finalizing the end of a stalk with a Click! or Poof! instead of a big boom. Knowing the ways of percussion caps, primers, nipples, and other aspects of the ignition system, however, can prevent disappointment.

Chapter 29

SIGHTS FOR BLACKPOWDER GUNS

I SPENT the 18th year of my life in a little village (couldn't call it a town) named Patagonia, along the Arizona/Mexico border. Not far from the cluster of small houses tucked along dirt roadways (the place has changed) lived two silver miners. I doubt that they got a lot of pay dirt out of mother earth. But apparently they shoveled and panned enough to buy grub and gear, including plenty of 30-30 ammo, probably finding gold now and then, which at the time sold for $32 an ounce. One day, while hunting the diminutive Coues white-tailed deer of that beautiful area, I heard a shot. Investigating brought me alongside the old miners looking down at a fantastic buck, their Model 94 carbines tucked on crooked elbows. The magnificent rack was destined for the junk pile

behind their slab-board cabin, but when they offered the antlers, I turned them down. After all, they were not mine. That was a mistake in false pride, for the Boone & Crockett set should have been on display somewhere for sportsmen to enjoy. Later that day, as well as before and after, I did partake of a little shooting with the gentlemen. I enjoyed watching how they managed those stubby carbines. They were really good shots, and fast.

Both men assured me more than once that they "snapshot" only, never looking at their sights, claiming they didn't even know where the bead was when they pulled the trigger. I got the hang of snap shooting myself, becoming a fair hand at the game. I never paid the least attention to the sights — I thought. Until one day it came to me as I matured

in shooting knowledge. The only place a bullet could go was where the sights were aiming. There was no other option. The old gents, as well as the newcomer to the game, had that front sight nestled down in the rear open sight, the bead visually pasted right on the target. Had to be. We just weren't conscious of what we were doing. Hit a target without using the sights? Not hardly. It can't be done. Allowing that a rifle is regulated on target to begin with, where can the bullet go but where the sights are "looking"? Reversing the thought, haphazardly pointing the muzzle in the general direction of the target won't work because the bullet has to go where the sights are aiming. The old-timers and the kid shot fast, all right, but all three were aiming, if only unconsciously. Our guns were sighted close to the mark,

Many modern muzzleloaders are now outfitted with fiber optic sights like this one. Their only drawback is breakage and a sight hood for protection is a good idea.

Original sights on long rifles often rested very close to the top barrel flat. This one is set in a dovetail notch for drifting left or right. While it has a barleycorn effect from the side, this front sight provides a sharp, clean, and rather precise picture in the notch of an open rear sight.

too. Anything else would have brought a miss.

The concept of sights was born early in gun history. We don't know for sure who came up with them or when, but it's a good guess that shooters quickly learned how futile pointing a firearm was. True, many armies from Mongols to Britishers shot bows with good accuracy, and certainly without sights. The Japanese archer was also known as a remarkably good shot. Aim was perfected in various ways. The term "instinctive shooting" came along to describe the process of aiming effectively without sights. It's probably better explained as reflexive shooting, where coordination between hand, eye, and brain make it work. I have no doubt that guns were fired in a similar manner for some time. After all, fire sticks had no sights whatsoever. The British Brown Bess musket was fired effectively on the battlefield for years and to say it had real sights would be an exaggeration. However, precision of aim was never possible without refined sights. And so it was that sights of many different types were invented.

Ancient Fixed Iron Sights

An early form of sight was the true fixed set adoring both rifles and blackpowder pistols. The front sight was an immobile blob. The back sight was likewise, encompassing a slit. The front sight fit optically into a notch created by the slit in the rear sight, if a lump of metal with a cleft in it can be called a sight. And that was that. Precise aim was impossible with these sights because the shooter could not generate a clean, repeatable sight picture. But they were no doubt much better than pointing the muzzle of the gun in the general direction of the target and blasting away.

Improved Fixed Iron Sights

An updated form of fixed iron sight proved effective many years ago, and it still is. These sights qualify as fixed because they have no device to move them, such as a ladder underneath the rear sight to make it go up or down. My oft-mentioned Mulford No. 47 has fixed sights, and yet they are adjustable — in a way. The front sight, a blade, is dovetailed directly into the top barrel flat just behind the muzzle. The rear sight is a plain metal fixture with a V-slit, also attached in a dovetail notch. These sights lie very

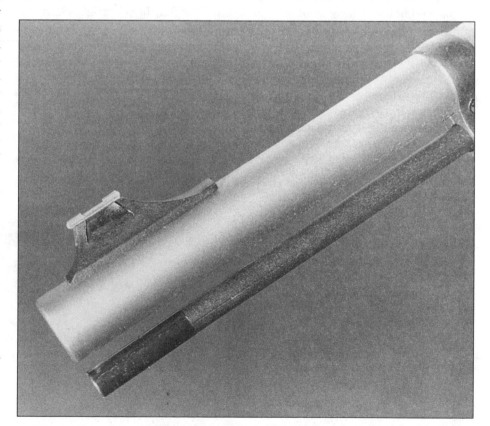

This fiber optic front sight provides a glow that offers a clear aim point in low light. However, this type of sight is more fragile than one made of metal.

The long-range rear sight on this Navy Arms replica of a Whitworth rifled musket elevates with a sliding open rear sight, as well as three ladder steps.

low on the barrel. They come into the line of sight instantly, and they do provide a clean sight picture. They're a far cry from the primitive fixed sight noted above and both front and rear sight are adjustable — but only by drifting or filing, explained below. I have another special rifle with fixed sights. It's a 42-caliber flintlock. When Royland Southgate originally built this rifle, he very carefully matched sights to performance. The round ball hits right on the money at about 75 yards and a touch low at 100 yards. For a 42-caliber round-ball rifle, this sort of sight-in is ideal. The little pill shouldn't be fired on deer-sized game at anything that resembles "far off," if it's used on big game at all. The Southgate rifle's sights do qualify as fixed irons, yet both front and rear sight can be moved by drifting or filing, as with No. 47.

To change the point of impact on the target, the front sight is drifted (moved) in its dovetail notch to the left to make the next bullet hit to the right, and to the right to make the next bullet hit to the left. The front sight is filed down to make the next shot strike higher on the target. To lower point of impact on the target, the front sight must be made taller, which is best accomplished by exchanging the sight for a higher one. In other words, the front sight is moved in the opposite direction of the desired point of impact on the target.

Since the fixed rear sight has no elevator bar to raise or lower it, this sight cannot be adjusted for vertical change of bullet impact on the target. However, it can be altered to change group point of impact horizontally, again by drifting, or sliding it in its dovetail notch with a punch (Lyman offers a great Gunsmith's Punch Set). Since the rear behaves the opposite of the front sight, it's drifted to the left to move point of impact left, to the right to move point of impact to the right. In other words, the rear sight is moved in the direction the shooter wants the next bullet to land. This design cannot move up or down, however, so elevation adjustments must be made with the front sight. So while these fixed sights truly are set in place, they are capable of adjustment.

Muzzleloaders are not left out of the aperture sight picture, as the 57R sight proves. It couples nicely with a 17AEU front sight, which has interchangeable pieces from post to peep hole.

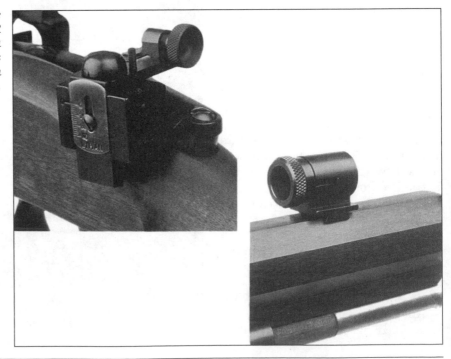

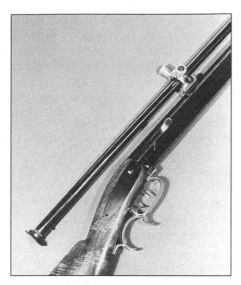

This is a tube sight.

Fixed Iron Sights on Cap 'n' Ball Revolvers

Original-style cap 'n' ball revolvers may have fixed sights that are rigidly in place. For example, the Remington Model 1858 blackpowder revolver has a barleycorn front sight integral to the front of the barrel. There is no dovetail notch in which to slide it. This sight is truly fixed in place. The only way to make the revolver hit to the right or left (horizontal adjustment) is by manipulating the front sight — bending it, hopefully without breaking it off in the process. The front sight is also responsible for vertical adjustment by filing it lower for the next bullet to strike higher on the target. If the revolver is already shooting too high, metal must be added to make it taller. A gunsmith can usually accomplish this task. If you want this revolver to shoot higher, the front sight must be filed lower. The "rear sight" on the Remington Civil War revolver is not a sight at all, but rather a groove in the top strap of the frame. Absolutely nothing can be done to change point of impact with it. The 1860 Civil War Colt revolver carried the same type of front sight found on the Remington revolver, but this time the "rear sight" was nothing more than a notch cut into the hammer nose. Cocking the hammer

back to fire brings the hammer nose into the view of the shooter, who aligns the notch with the front sight. While these fixed handgun sights are not target-shooting affairs, they work well enough for close range on large targets.

Buckhorn and Semi-Buckhorn Fixed Sights

Buckhorn and semi-buckhorn rear sights were quite popular for a long time. Sometimes they are adjustable, as with an elevator bar or ladder, but on many front loaders they are not. Many modern gun writers have declared the buckhorn rear sight all but useless, supposedly covering the whole target, making precise aiming impossible. In real life, however, these sights work well enough. They do tend to block out part of the target, but they also provide a decent aiming point and no one knows how much game was brought home with rifles bearing buckhorn sights. In design, the buckhorn sight is simply a rear sight with "horns." When these horns curl around almost to touch, that's the full buckhorn. When they do not project so far up (less curl), they're semi-buckhorns.

That's a little bit about the fixed iron sight found on some muzzleloaders. When set in dovetail notches, they allow windage (horizontal) adjustment. Elevation (vertical) adjustment is generally accomplished by filing the front sight down, installing a taller front sight, or having a gunsmith add metal to an existing fixed front sight.

Adjustable Iron Sights

The Ladder-Adjustable Open Sight

There are numerous ways to accomplish iron sight adjustment. One is the ladder or elevator bar, which rests beneath the back sight. The ladder has graduated notches cut into it. On the shortest notch, the rear sight rests lowest on the barrel and the firearm hits lowest. On the tallest notch of the ladder, the rear sight is elevated to its highest position and the rifle hits highest. The ladder-type rear sight is normally coupled with an ordinary non-adjustable front sight, but the front sight may rest in a dovetail notch, offering lateral movement through drifting. The ladder rear sight often rests in a dovetail notch. While elevation adjustment is accomplished with the previously described notch-in-ladder arrangement, bullet impact on the target horizontally comes by drifting either the rear sight or the front sight in its respective dovetail notch.

The Modern Adjustable Open Sight

There are many different types of adjustable open sights. The rear sights on many non-replica and modern muzzleloaders are fully adjustable in various ways. There may be elevation and windage screws, for example. When the elevation screw is turned downward, the rear sight is forced upward to make the next shot striker higher on the target. There may also be a screw adjustment that moves the

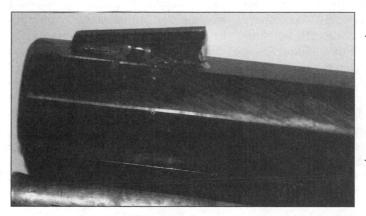

As simple as this front sight appears, it is highly effective, appearing to the eye as a post that rests in an open rear sight notch, or within the clear circle formed by a peep rear sight.

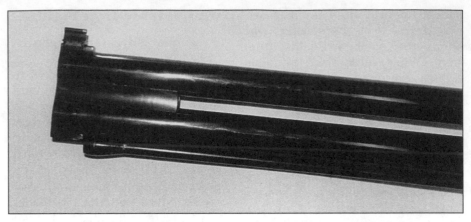

The front sight on this Iver Johnson over/under 50-caliber muzzleloader is a very fine gold bead, modern in design. A fine bead provides a definitive sighting point; however, a heavier bead is sometimes preferred for brush and timber shooting, where a finer bead may not show up as well.

rear sight left or right for windage changes. There are too many variations of the adjustable iron sight to treat them all here. However, the type is easily recognized because adjustment is in the rear sight, which can be moved up or down, left or right.

The Adjustable Receiver Sight

The term "receiver sight" is a misnomer on old-style muzzleloaders because they have no receiver. They have locks instead. However, the popular modern muzzleloader has a receiver. The Ruger Model 77/50, for example, has a true receiver. After all, the rifle is patterned directly after the cartridge shooter of the same bolt-action design. However, the name is accurate because it refers to a rear sight that mounts around the breech area. The receiver sight is also known as a peep or aperture sight. There are quite a few blackpowder guns drilled and tapped for receiver sights these days. A Markesbery systems muzzleloader with two barrels, 50 and 54, finds a Nikon scope on the 50-caliber barrel and a Williams adjustable receiver sight on the 54-caliber barrel. The latter is perfect for fast big-game shooting in woods and thickets because the object with the receiver or peep sight is to look through, not at the hole in the rear sight, focusing the front sight only on the target — very fast.

Shooters who insist on consciously trying to center the front sight in the center of the peephole have a terrible time until they stop fighting it. Just relax the face firmly on the cheek piece, and don't try to center the front sight at all. Simply look through the peephole, place the front sight on the target, maintain the sight picture, and squeeze the trigger. It works because the human eye automatically centers the front sight in the aperture where the greatest light is. In fact, the eye can do this unconsciously better than with conscious effort.

The micrometer-adjustable aperture sight provides extremely close and accurate movement, some having clicks that gauge only one-quarter minute of angle, which translates to about (not exactly) 1/4 inch at 100 yards. An example of this kind of aperture sight is Lyman's No. 57, which is offered for muzzleloaders. However, for hunting, receiver sights without micrometer adjustment capability are excellent. The Williams peep sight on the just-mentioned Markesbery 54-caliber Outer-Line® adjusts via screws, and it has precise markings to ensure return to the same location if the sight is removed for any reason. Of course, it readily adjusts for both windage and elevation, meaning the front sight remains fixed in place at all times. The same rule holds: Move

the peep left for left-hand bullet placement on the target, right for right-hand movement of the projectile. The sight picture is simple and clear — nothing more than a front bead optically laid upon a target.

The Front Bead

Personal preferences, along with individual eyesight, make front bead choice wide and varied. Choices are many. Lyman's current catalog lists eight different front sight beads with more than 50 options regarding height. There's a good reason for this. The front sight bead should match the rear sight, as well as the shooter's specific needs. Lyman's list, therefore, includes a No. 3 1/16-inch ivory bead, a No. 3 1/16-inch gold bead, a No. 28 3/32-inch ivory bead, a No. 28 3/32-inch gold bead, a No. 31 1/16-inch ivory bead, a No. 31 1/16-inch gold bead, a No. 37 3/32-inch ivory bead, and a No. 37 3/32-inch gold bead. The No. 3 and No. 28 front sights are identical, designed to be mounted into the barrel dovetail, while No. 31 and No. 37 are for ramp mounting. Heights run from 0.240 inch to 0.500 inch. These are beautiful front sights; moreover, the various heights make it possible to alter vertical bullet placement on the target.

Bushnell's Holo® Sight

Unique by design, the Bushnell Holo® Sight, short for holographic, gets on target super fast. The image perceived is of an illuminated aiming point suspended in space in front of the gun. The shooter can see the sight from varying distances behind the gun. Field of view is unlimited because there is no tube with lenses. Weaver-style mounts are used to attach the Holo® Sight to firearms.

Fiber-Optic Sights

Fiber-optic sights are remarkably clear in low light, although of course they must be struck by some light in order to show up brightly. An example of a fiber-optic sight for muzzleloaders is the Traditions

Fiber optic sights like this one pick up light well. They do not provide light, and are not workable in dark conditions, but they stand out well. This rear sight provides two glowing dots as guides to front sight alignment.

Tru-Glo, which comes as a set. The front sight is a ramp style with fixed blade. The rear sight is fully adjustable for windage and elevation. The sight picture shows as two green dots (rear sight) and a red front sight. While the Tru-Glo is quite rugged, no fiber-optic sight is as strong as a metal sight, which is its only major fault.

The Tube Sight

The tube sight may have been forerunner to the scope. Logically, it seems that someone came along to put optical lenses inside the tube, but proof is lacking. The tube sight looks like scope as it rests above the rifle barrel, but it has no glass in it. It is simply a long metal tube mounted full-length atop the rifle barrel. But more than just a piece of metal, the tube sight is adjustable, with some sort of aiming device contained within. Tube sights were effective because they isolated the view of the shooter for easier concentration on the target, as well as blocking out superfluous light, including glints from the sun's rays. A particular tube sight I studied incorporated an eye cup with a tiny hole — a peep sight, if you will. Mounted in the other end of the tube was a globe front sight, simply a round chunk of metal, hence "globe." This peep and globe sight resided in the shade all the time, providing a clean and effec-

tive sighting device. Since the tube sight contained no optical lenses, it is classified as an iron sight.

The Scope Sight

State laws on the use of telescopic sights on muzzleloaders carried during special blackpowder-only hunts vary widely. Some states are all for it. Others say no scopes for these hunts. Shooters reside in two distinct camps on the issue. Purists don't like them, preferring the greater challenge presented by old-time sights. They dislike scopes on Kentucky/Pennsylvania long rifles that did not originally wear glass sights. Aperture sights on these classic rifles are also disdained because historically the flintlock long guns of Daniel Boone's era were not fitted with scopes or aperture sights. However, peep sights are nothing new, some appearing hundreds of years ago on crossbows. A few Hawken rifles have been discovered with peep sights They were not common on plains rifles, but were used by at least some mountain men. Scopes definitely found their way onto single-shot breechloaders of the latter part of the 19th century, especially in the hands of the buffalo runners.

The other camp is filled with shooters who feel that the blackpowder challenge is tough enough with guns that demand front loading one shot at a time, with nothing even close to real long-range trajectory, and reloading a time-consuming procedure that precludes anything close to real "firepower." Some hunters believe that scopes are actually more sporting than iron sights. As one put it, "I can't understand why some states don't allow scopes on muzzleloaders. Don't they want hunters to make their best shot?" Appropriateness should prevail. Topping off a long rifle from the 1700s with a scope is not appropriate, while scoping a modern muzzleloader is, especially for those of us who feel that these guns reside in their own niche between old-time

front loaders and cartridge-shooting firearms chambered for high-intensity cartridges. The hunter capable and willing to get close requires no scope, of course, with close being under 100 yards (which is a lot farther than the average bowhunter would shoot).

What won't wash is denying scope sights because they are inventions of modern times. They are not. Riflescopes were born of terrestrial telescopes. Johann Lipperhey of Middleburg, Holland, a spectacle maker, came up with the first working model of a terrestrial telescope in 1608. It was crude and of little practical value until Galileo, the noted Italian astronomer, took the idea to new heights, creating a viable instrument. Because of his efforts, Galileo, not Lipperhey, is credited with the first true telescope. It was carried far and wide by explorers, finding its way into Jim Bridger's possibles during the fur-trade era. Bridger was known to climb vantage points for a study of the area via his telescope. As far as riflescopes go, Englishman William Ellis Metford had a practical model by 1824. A Metford scope sight was attached to an experimental rifle by Col. George Gibbs, a rifle shooter of the day. Gibbs' scope was said to be 8-power, which was an approximation. Regardless of the exact magnification, the Colonel's scope did work. Metford's claim was simple. He claimed that mounting one of his scopes on a rifle would improve the chances of putting bullets right on target, and he was willing to prove it to anyone.

Oddly, scopes did not catch on. It took years for hunters to gain trust in glass sights. Younger shooters may find it hard to believe, but even as late as the 1950s, some of our country's more proficient outdoorsmen claimed that scopes were gimmicks. It was after World War II that riflescopes gained a toehold in America. Even then, it was more a matter of tiptoeing into the shooting world, not racing headlong into broad use. Leaders of the hunting community began

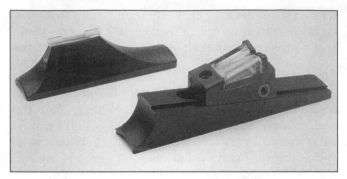

Fiber optic sights, like these Illuminator™ II Sight System examples from CVA, are now installed on muzzleloading rifles. The object is high "light gathering" ability; however, they do not generate light.

not only using scope sights, but also writing about them. Jack O'Connor, for example, extolled the virtues of the scope sight, stating that it was ideal for hunters who wanted to put bullets right where they belonged on big game. Elmer Keith, another famous gun writer, wrote the same, as did Col. Townsend Whelen, Paul Curtis, Stewart Edward White, and other respected shooters of the day. From distrust, the scope sight moved into the ranks of faithful use. It's no wonder that modern American shooters look to the glass sight even for their charcoal burners.

Which Scope?

Riflescopes on today's muzzleloaders are the same ones built for modern big game cartridge rifles. They offer high optical resolution, providing a good, clear sight picture. It is just as important to see well through a scope mounted on a front loader as it is to make the target out clearly when shooting a cartridge gun. Optical resolution especially pays off when the target is in the brush, or any other hideaway terrain, because the shooter can better see where to aim. The blackpowder scope must be ruggedly constructed so that lenses remain mounted within the tube following recoil. Reticles must be proper. The duplex is the most popular, with its heavy, easy-to-see crosswires coupled with thinner wires in the center for precise aiming. The scope also must be capable of precise adjustment. In short, the muzzleloader or blackpowder breechloader scope is the same one a hunter would choose for his 30-06 big game rifle.

What Power?

The brush and timber hunter is well equipped with a 2.5-power scope, or even less magnification. Conversely, the target shooter whose goal is tight clusters relies on high magnification. No serious modern benchrest match in the world was won with a low-power scope because benchrest shooters know that a super-magnified target allows the greatest precision of aim. If all hunting takes place in thickets for close-range white-tailed deer, a low-power scope is perfectly fine. For greater precision of bullet grouping, more magnification is needed, especially with modern muzzleloaders that are now truly capable of delivering big-game power at 200-plus yards.

The Variable-Power Scope

Today's variable is so good that it's the best all-around choice for big-game hunting with a modern cartridge gun, muzzleloader, or blackpowder breechloader, for those who wish to go with a scope. The once-upon-a-time negative features of variables are long cured. Today's variable is optically excellent, has superb reticles, and is capable of precise adjustment. I'm open-minded on most matters of guns and shooting, but find arguments in favor of fixed-power scopes weak. "I don't like big scopes." Variables may have been oversized at one time, but not now. Many are no larger than fixed power scopes. "I prefer 6X over any other magnification." Then leave your variable on 6X if you insist, but is 6X ideal for close-range, fast-action shooting? Is 6X

better than a higher magnification for exact bullet placement? The variable can do it all. Having taken up a serious interest in modern muzzleloaders for general hunts where any firearm is allowed, including 300 Magnums, I find the scope sight acceptable. I would not mount one on a classic long gun, nor half-stock plains rifle. Also, I remain confident with open sights and have no interest in giving them up. The aforementioned 54-caliber Markesbery with fire-breathing loads is well equipped with a peep sight, and will remain so. But when the muzzleloader is scoped, it will be with a variable, such as a 3X-9X, which has overshadowed the 2.5X-8x. The hunting rifle is carried with the scope set at 3X for a wide field of view — fast for close game on the move. Meanwhile, a bedded buck located with binoculars or spotting scope commands 9X for the best bullet placement. In-between settings are also useful. When hunting antelope, for example, there's no reason to leave the scope on 2.5X for a wide a field of view when 5X or 6X provides a common ground between field of view and magnification.

Scope Mounts

Modern muzzleloaders come drilled and tapped for scope mounts. It's a simple matter of buying the correct mounts to match the fire-

This is Bushnell's HOLOsight, a high-tech aiming device that presents the target aim point on a single plane.

The globe front sight is just that—a metal ball. This one is on the author's Navy Arms Whitworth rifled musket, and it creates a fine sight picture.

arm. The scope mount should be of high quality, however, for it's responsible for retaining the glass sight firmly locked in place. A scope mount that allows movement of the sight is no bargain at any price.

Older Eyes and Scopes

Young eyes have the ability to accommodate, focusing rapidly fore and aft. As eyes age, rapid focusing ability declines. At that point, a scope sight can be a real boon. Not only is the target magnified, but the scope's picture is on one flat, two-dimensional plane, demanding the eye to focus only on that plane — unlike iron sights, which require the shooter to focus on the rear sight, front sight, and target; or a peep sight, which demands focus on the front sight and target.

Front Sight Focus

A misunderstanding may arise concerning focus with iron sights. While it's true that the eye must see the back sight, front sight, and tar-get, sharp focus is not on all three. Sharp focus is on the front sight only. Front sight/target. Front sight/target. It's a rule worth repeating.

In some cases, simple open iron sights are entirely adequate, and even preferred. They are also appropriate. Sometimes, however, and on some guns, the aperture sight is better. And then there are firearms and situations best suited to the glass sight with its single plane of focus and magnification.

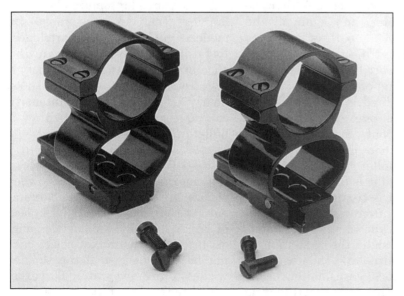

Scope mounts like these Universal series from CVA provide stability for the telescopic rifle sight. These particular mounts come in two styles: Low or See-Thru, blued or nickel finish. Shown is the See-Thru option for iron sight use.

Chapter 30

SIGHTING-IN AND HITTING THE TARGET

THE MOST accurate gun in the world with the finest sights is doomed without proper sight-in. Front loaders can be very accurate. The heavy, benchrest-type blackpowder rifle known as the slug gun has produced groups rivaling modern arms. How about a .734-inch center-to-center cluster recorded not at 100 yards, but 200 yards from the muzzle, and not for three shots, or even five, but 10 shots? Another slug gun printed a group that measured .505-inches center to center for five shots at 200 yards from the bench. Establishing faith in blackpowder accuracy is important, but the potential of any firearm can only be realized with good sights, distinguishable targets, careful gun management, and of course proper sight-in.

Trajectory

All bullets from all guns travel in an arc known as a parabola. Even the 220 Swift with its 4,000-fps capability does not "shoot flat," not even to a mere 100 yards. Blackpowder guns, with their considerably lower bullet speeds, arc even more from the line of sight. Getting close to game is part of the blackpowder challenge, as is putting round balls and conicals on target downrange, but neither can be performed without an understanding of bullet flight and proper sighting of the gun.

Line of Sight

Line of sight is produced by vision. The eye makes an absolutely straight "line" to the target. In the game field, line of sight continues to remains straight, but not necessarily horizontal, because a game animal may be standing uphill or downhill. On a target range, the line of sight should be horizontal if the range is correctly prepared — flat, in other words. A model of the line of sight has a baseline representing a horizontally flat line from muzzle to target. The line the bullet takes from muzzle to target is anything but flat. It runs along a curve that is called a parabola. The bullet takes off "nose up," aiming above the line of sight. This is called the line of departure, where the projectile leaves the baseline to rise on its journey to the target. It crosses the line of sight twice, once fairly close to the shooter, and again at the zero point. That path is known as the bullet's trajectory, with zero being the exact location of the bullet's striking of the target when properly sighted. A 50-caliber muzzleloader, as one example, fires a round ball that crosses the line of sight twice, once up close and again where the bullet strikes the target. So the base line is flat, but the path of the bullet is curved. Specifically, a round ball from a well-loaded 50-caliber blackpowder rifle crosses the line of sight the first time at about 13 yards, and then again at around 75 to 80 yards, falling below the line of sight after that. Sighting a gun includes both line of sight and parabola. Knowing the path a bullet takes along the line of sight, both above it and below it, allows appropriate holds for both close-range targets and those at the outer limit of the firearm.

Extreme Range

Few studies have been made to assess just how far a muzzleloader can shoot when the barrel's muzzle is elevated to 45 degrees. Clearly, bullets of higher ballistic coefficient shoot farther than those of more blunt profile. One thing is certain: No muzzleloader normally fired today on the range or hunting field will launch its missile as far as cartridges in the 7mm Magnum class (a distance of about three miles). Until careful testing has been published for all to see, suffice that extreme range for a muzzleloader is far less than extreme range for modern high-intensity cartridges. Regardless, every downwind shooter must be aware that though his front loader will not shoot nearly as far as a high-intensity cartridge gun, it will still throw a bullet quite some distance.

Long-Range Shooting

Long-range target blackpowder shooting is definitely in the bargain, with the emphasis on target. A piece of paper, metallic silhouette, gong, or any other inanimate object cannot be wounded, so if the shooter wishes to fire away at 1,000 yards, why not? In fact, 1,000-yard matches are nothing new in the smokepole business, going back at least to the 19th century, and continuing to this day. Rifled muskets were often employed to put bullets downrange all the way to 1,000 yards with acceptable accuracy. The Whitworth rifled musket is a perfect example of a muzzleloader capable of such far-away accuracy. That's why the Confederate snipers used them in the American Civil War. Naturally, muzzles were aimed skyward to the proper degree in order to land a bullet in the bull's-eye at long distance. However, as noted earlier, we have no rifle of any vintage that shoots "flat." Even the fastest current magnums require severe muzzle-up attitude to put a bullet on target at 1,000 yards. Another long-range shooting game practiced today by dedicated blackpowder shooters is the silueta, the Mexican name for this sport. It means silhouette shooting: firing at metallic cutouts at long range with single-shot blackpowder cartridge rifles. The sport is touched on in Chapter 50. Long-distance shooting at game animals, on the other hand, means 200 yards, although practiced riflemen with one of the accurate magnum muzzleloaders or a blackpowder cartridge rifle can probably extend this limit. The rest of us should get closer. It's true that 19th-century buffalo runners hit their targets at long range reliably. But they shot their rifles every day, learning trajectory by rote, many of them also relying on high-power riflescopes to aid bullet placement.

Today, modern adjustable rear sights like this one found on the Savage Model 10ML are quite popular. The scale on the side shown here allows a witness mark to be drawn connecting upper and lower lines so the shooter always knows that the sights have not moved.

Sighting In for One Distance Only

In target shooting, a firearm can be sighted-in specifically for long range, even 1,000 yards. Mid-range trajectory (how high a bullet rises between the muzzle and the bull's eye of the target) is of no consequence until the shooter wishes to fire on a closer target, at which time specific hold-under will be necessary, since the bullet is rising. Suppose a target shooter sights his musket for a 1,000 yards, and suppose this sighting puts his bullet several feet high in between the muzzle and that distance. No harm done. But for game shooting, sighting in for a practical distance is imperative. The hunter must learn how far to hold under and over the exact point he wishes to strike at distances other than the zero (sight-in distance) of the gun. Naturally, the firearm and its load dictate the exact zero point. Most muzzleloaders should be sighted to hit dead center at about 75 to 80 yards. The round ball or conical falls about 6 inches below the line of sight at 125 yards, which is far enough to shoot at most big game (modern magnum muzzleloaders and other guns firing high-ballistic coefficient bullets, such as Lyman's special long-range lead conicals for 40- and 45-caliber breechloaders, may be exceptions to this sight-in distance).

Conicals and round balls describe similar parabolas from muzzle to 125 yards for normal guns with normal loads. Faster-shooting pistol bullet/sabot combos shoot a bit flatter, as do missiles like the SSB. The round ball starts out faster than the conical (about 2,000 fps), but loses initial velocity rapidly. The conical begins its journey slower, generally in the 1,500-fps realm, but retains initial velocity better, resulting in a stand-off in trajectory. Either missile lands roughly a half-foot low at 125 yards — about as much variance as a hunter wants to accept on a big-game animal when chest strikes are required.

Sight Adjustment

The two terms used most often when discussing sight-in are windage and elevation. Windage is horizontal movement. When sights are adjusted to move bullet impact to the left or to the right, that is affecting a windage change. Elevation is a vertical movement. When sights are adjusted to move bullet impact either higher or lower on the target, that is affecting an elevation change. But before any sighting can be accomplished, a shooter must know how to adjust the sights on his firearm. This was touched on in the previous chapter, which explained how fixed sights were manipulated by drifting them left or right in their dovetail notches, if they are mounted in such notches. That takes care of windage. Fixed sights are adjusted for elevation by filing the front sight down, installing a taller front sight, or having a gunsmith make a front sight taller by welding metal on it. To review, the rear sight is moved in the direction the shooter wants the next bullet to hit, left for left, right for right. The front sight is moved in the opposite direction the shooter wants the next bullet to hit. A taller front sight makes the gun shoot lower. A shorter front sight makes the gun shoot higher.

Sights readily identify themselves in terms of adjustment. The ladder/dovetail rear sight, for example, is clearly altered in one of two ways. For elevation, the ladder (elevator

This modern adjustable rear sight is found on the Savage Model 10ML muzzleloader. Easy windage change is made by moving the sight in the direction the shooter wants the next shot to strike, left for left, right for right.

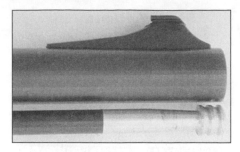

The rear sight is adjusted for windage first, but if need be this modern front sight can be drifted left or right.

bar) either raises or lowers the rear sight. For windage, the rear sight is moved to the right or to the left by drifting it in its dovetail notch. Other iron sights have different means of adjustment. Sometimes a set-screw holds part of the sight firmly in place, for example. Loosen the screw, move the sight appropriately, then retighten the screw. There are far too many variations to broach here, and most sights have obvious adjustment features.

Scopes are easy to adjust. Turret caps are removed, revealing arrows. For windage, the arrow may have an "R" for right. For elevation, the arrow may show an "Up." Some scopes vary this feature, but all clearly show windage and elevation directions. If the shooter wants the next bullet to hit to the right, he rotates the windage knob in the direction indicated by the "R." If he wants the next shot to hit to the left, he rotates the knob in the opposite direction of the arrow. For up/down (elevation) adjustment,

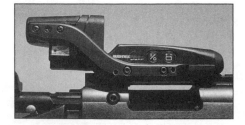

The HOLOsight from Bushnell is adjustable per directions for sighting in a firearm. Since it has no magnification, the HOLOsight is legal where scopes may not be for special blackpowder-only hunts.

the knob is rotated appropriately. Scopes offer calibrated adjustments. Sometimes the adjustments are marked off with lines, each line signifying a value at 100 yards. Directions with the scope give the values, or the values may be written underneath the scope turret cap. Sometimes adjustments are arranged in "clicks." Rotating the knob results in actual clicks that can be felt. A single click may be as precise as one-quarter minute-of-angle.

A minute of angle, sometimes written as MOA, is 1/60th of one degree. A circle has 360 degrees, or 21,600 minutes. Specifically, a minute of angle is valued at 1.047 inches at 100 yards. For practical shooting purposes, however, a minute of angle is considered 1 inch at 100 yards, 2 inches at 200 yards, 3 inches at 300 yards, and so forth. So in shooting, a quarter minute of angle is only 1/4 inch of movement at 100 yards, a very fine adjustment that is found on quite a number of riflescopes these days.

Sight Radius

Sight radius applies only to iron sights. Scope sights have one flat field, which totally eliminates the concept of sight radius. While sight radius is simply the distance between back sight and front sight, it's important in shooting because it has a lot to do with sight picture. The longer the barrel, the longer the sight radius, but sight radius is also adjusted by where the sights are located. A rear sight, for example, can be mounted well forward of the breech, which improves clarity for older eyes that have trouble focusing up close. Iron-sight shooters ordering a custom muzzleloader have the option of leaving the back sight off at delivery. The object is going to the range with a flat-based back sight that will rest firmly on the top barrel flat. The rifle is rested solidly on the bench. The shooter then slides the loose rear sight slowly back and forth along the barrel, while at the same time carefully checking for sight picture.

The perfect "sweet spot" is where the rear sight is placed just far enough from the front sight to afford the owner of the rifle the clearest possible picture. Then the sight is marked for position and the rifle is returned to the gunmaker, who fits the rear sight into a dovetail notch. A long sight radius is helpful as eyes "mature." On one long-barreled 42-caliber flintlock, for example, the distance between front and rear sight is exactly 28 inches. The rear sight on this rifle is a full 9 inches forward of the base of the breech, about 14 inches away from the eye.

How we See the Sight

We have stressed the importance of sight radius, especially mounting the rear sight so that it shows up at least somewhat clearly instead of a blur. However, this can be misleading. Proper use of iron sights means focusing on the front sight. The back sight is obviously important with regard to lining up on the target, but with emphasis on the front sight sharply focused on the target: front sight/target, front sight/target, that important shooting rule again. A scope requires little more than adjusting the ocular lens, the one closest to the eye, so that the image is clear. For the receiver sight, the main criterion for how we see the front sight is the size of the aperture or peephole. For hunting, a slightly larger aperture is preferred. It's easy to see through,

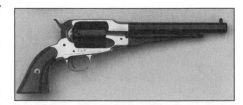

The front sight on this replica 1858 Remington can be filed down in order to raise point of impact on the target, but little else can be done with it. However, the front sight is designed to closely match ballistics, so its fixed station does not pose a problem.

This front sight can be drifted in its dovetail notch to change point of bullet impact on the target, moving the sight left to bring the next bullet over to the right, and vice versa.

plenty accurate, fast to put into play, and the somewhat larger orifice affords a nice, bright sight picture. With open iron sights, frame of reference is important. If the front sight optically fills the rear sight notch, a precise aiming point cannot be repeated time after time. There should be a little light showing on both sides of the front sight as it rests in the notch of the rear sight. In this way, a frame of reference is created. The shooter can tell when his or her sights are truly lined up. Some shooters prefer the so-called Patridge front sight, named for E.E. Patridge, one-time president of the U.S. Revolver Association. This front sight optically presents parallel sides, appearing

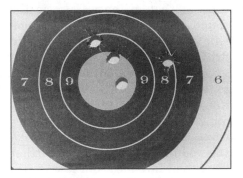

Sighting in requires proper knowledge of sight movement. The first bullet hole on the right prompted the shooter to move his sight so that the next shot would strike to the left, which is exactly what happened for the following three shots at 100-yards from the bench.

as a rectangle that fits into a rectangular or square notch in the rear sight. Shooters can align the Patridge sight readily, because light clearly is seen on both sides of the front sight as it rests in the rear sight notch. Also, it is easy to align the top of the front sight right across the top of the rear sight notch. This affords a very clear sight picture.

Sight Picture

The 6-o'clock sight picture is often used with the Patridge sight, which means resting the target optically right on top of the post-like front sight, like a pumpkin sitting on a square-topped board. That way the target is not covered up by the sights, further clarifying the aiming point. Of course, the gun is sighted in to print its bullet upward from the topmost of the front sight, so the bullet will strike the center of the bull's-eye. An option is sometimes called the hunting sight picture, where the front sight optically rests directly on the target. Any type of iron sight can be sighted in for this sort of picture, including the Patridge.

The globe front sight, which got its name many years ago, is a small metal ball. It remains in use today, and often is hooded to protect it from breakage. It is often sighted with the hold-on-target mode, rather than the 6-o'clock sight picture.

Projectiles in Flight

Aspects of blackpowder bullet performance were touched on, with mention of wind drift in Chapter 17, but this important subject requires another look here, because sighting in and consequent hitting of the target demand an understanding of projectiles in flight.

Bullet Drift

Bullet drift is not vital to blackpowder sight-in. Understanding wind drift, on the other hand, is very important in shooting blackpowder guns accurately. Bullet drift is the normal horizontal departure of a

This front sight can easily drift left or right in its dovetail notch for a change in windage.

bullet from the line of sight in the direction of rifling twist. Right-hand twist makes bullets rotate right, and bullets that rotate to the right tend to drift a bit off course to the right, in the direction of their spin. Left-hand rifling twist encourages bullets to drift left.

Wind Drift

Unlike bullet drift — which is a minor element of almost no consequence — wind drift is a prominent factor in sighting guns and shooting them accurately under field conditions. Also known as wind deflection, this is the condition of the bullet drifting left or right of the line of sight because of the power of the wind. All bullets drift in the wind, no matter how fast they are going or how much mass they possess. Furthermore, it takes very little wind to move the usual blackpowder bullet well off course. Time of flight is an important factor in wind drift. It's easy to see why. The longer it takes a bullet to go from muzzle to target, the more time wind has to act upon it. Super-fast bullets have a very short time of flight, which means the wind does not have as long to push on them. But time of flight is not the only criterion in wind drift. The mass of a bullet helps it maintain its path, as clearly shown by comparing the 220 Swift versus 30-06 Springfield, which reveals a lot about wind drift. The following figures are rounded off for easy reference.

> **220 Swift — 50-grain bullet —
> 4,000 fps MV
> Wind velocity: 20 mph
> Bullet drift at 100 yards = 1.75
> inches
> Bullet drift at 200 yards = 7.00
> inches**
>
> **30-06 Springfield — 180-grain
> boattail bullet — 2,700 fps MV
> Wind velocity: 20 mph
> Bullet drift at 100 yards = 1.25
> inches
> Bullet drift at 200 yards = 5.25
> inches**

The 220 Swift bullet covers the ground fast, but it's light. The 30-06 bullet starts out much slower than the Swift, but the bullet has better windbucking properties (higher ballistic coefficient), and so it wins the duel in bullet drift at both 100 yards and 200 yards in the same 20-mph wind. Next, two round balls are compared, 36-caliber versus 50-caliber.

> **36-caliber round ball — 65-
> grain bullet — 2,000 fps MV
> Wind velocity: 20 mph
> Bullet drift at 100 yards = 28
> inches
> Bullet drift at 200 yards = 113
> inches
> 50-caliber round ball — 182
> grains — 2,000 fps MV
> Wind velocity: 20 mph
> Bullet drift at
> 100 yards = 18.5 inches
> Bullet drift at
> 200 yards = 80 inches**

Clearly, the larger, heavier round ball, with its better ballistic properties, outshines the smaller round ball when it comes to wind deflection. At the same time, both round balls fly well off course in a 20-mph wind. Imagine what a powerful wind would do to these projectiles. The importance of wind drift cannot be overstated. Good marksmen know what it is, and they know what to do about it, at least to the best of their judgment

in applying Kentucky windage, as described below. Hefty blackpowder conicals do better in the breeze, but are still thrown off course considerably. A 50-caliber Maxi-Ball weighing 370 grains and moving at 1,500 fps MV drifts 16 inches at 100 yards in a 20-mph wind and 60 inches at 200 yards in the same wind. A 54-caliber, 400-grain conical starting at 1,500 fps MV drifts 11 inches off course at 100 yards in a 20-mph wind and 43 inches off the beam at 200 yards in the same wind. These conicals do better than round balls, but still suffer badly from wind deflection.

Kentucky Windage and Arkansas Elevation

Because the wind blows bullets off course, the shooter must figure out how to hold so that the projectile drifts back into the line of sight. While target shooters may have wind flags and coaches to help them "dope the wind," hunters must rely on Kentucky windage, a term describing estimations learned through experience. Bullets are not only bucked by the wind, but they also begin to drop as soon as they leave the muzzle. Initial drop is minute, while drop at long range is pronounced. Obviously, bullet drop is vital to sighting-in, and must be considered as we look at Arkansas elevation, which is also based on good guesswork in the hunting field. This differs from the target shooter, who knows exactly how far away the bull's eye is, can actually adjust his sights to match the distance.

The good shot applies both Kentucky windage and Arkansas elevation to overcome wind deflection and bullet drop. Nobody can guess the exact velocity of the wind under field conditions, or the precise distance from muzzle to target, but practiced shooters do a pretty good job. Applying Kentucky windage and Arkansas elevation becomes a habit for these shooters. They get a good feel for how far their bullet will blow off

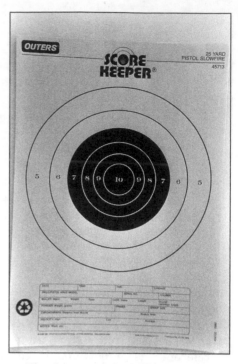

The long-standing black bull's eye on a white background remains highly effective, especially with iron sights.

course and how much that bullet will drop at a given guesstimated distance.

Kentucky windage simply means guessing, with a degree of accuracy, how far to hold off a target so that the bullet will be blown by the wind back onto the target by the time it arrives there.

One time I was hunting mule deer in a powerful wind. My chance came from only 80 yards or so. But even at that distance, I knew the round ball of my 54-caliber long rifle in that little hurricane would drift over as much as 3 feet. I applied a dose of Kentucky windage to the sight picture by aiming at an imaginary target suspended in mid-air 2 feet to the left of the buck's chest cavity. Even with that hold, the round bullet hit a bit farther back than intended, but it was still in the vitals and I had my deer. Without Kentucky windage, it'd been a miss.

Arkansas elevation means guesstimating the range or distance from muzzle to target and allowing for bullet drop. Hunters who work at getting close have very

This open notch rear sight will match up with a patridge type front sight for a clean picture. The six-o'clock hold is especially effective with this type of sight.

little trouble with Arkansas elevation because they need only hold right on and fire. Now that we have the 200-yard muzzleloader, however, field practice in Arkansas elevation is a worthy endeavor, as is carrying a compact rangefinder so the distance from a standing buck, bull, or boar is known, rather than guessed. The best way to manage Arkansas elevation is practice. One afternoon my brother and I were field testing the then-new Thompson/Center Encore 50-caliber magnum muzzleloader with 375-grain SSB Spitzer bullets with a heavy cargo of powder behind them. In a safe area, we selected targets, first firing on them with pure Arkansas elevation, then checking with a rangefinder to see just how closely we had called the distance of the shot. It was excellent practice and a learning situation. Reservations about the rifle and load being 200-yard worthy faded in the face of reality. From a sitting position using a walking staff for extra steadiness, every bullet fired landed inside a half-foot zone at a rangefinder-verified 200 yards.

Good Targets

If you can't see it, you can't hit it. If you cannot delineate the aiming point on your target clearly, sighting-in will be a problem and so will repeated good shooting afterward.

Fortunately, target makers caught on in the last decade or so, realizing that black bull's-eyes are excellent and viable, but not the only worthwhile aiming points. Many new targets have come along, including a whole series from Outers called Score Keeper® worth looking into. For sight-in and later verification of sight-in before going hunting, all of these Outer targets were worthy. The 100-yard No. 45762 smallbore rifle target is four-color: white background with orange and green rings outlined in black. The rings are 1 inch apart for easy vertical sight-in and horizontal grouping reference through a spotting scope from the bench. The very center of this target is a one-half inch orange ring within a green ring. A white cross runs through the target, defining the center point perfectly for scope-sight shooting. A larger 8-inch orange ring works great for iron sights. It's marked off by a one-inch wide green ring. This target provides clear aim points. No. 45716 is called a 100-Yard Rifle Precision Sighting-In target. Its

A specific aim point is necessary in order to realize the accuracy potential of a firearm. This target has a typical black bull's eye, but dead center is a conspicuous orange inner bull's eye.

When sighting in with an original style rear sight like this one, the front sight is rested in the notch so that its top comes even with the top of the rear sight.

white background contains five black bull's eyes, one in the center, four more on the corners. The same target is available in color as the No. 45761. Another similar target is Outers No. 45726 with red bull's eyes. The company's pistol targets are great for that purpose, but also highly useful for rifle shooting. The target must have a clearly defined aiming point so the shooter can line his sights up precisely every time. Also, some targets are better suited to the 6-o'clock sight picture, while others work well with the hunting sight picture.

Practical Sight-In Guide

Every big-bore muzzleloader can be sighted in for a flat 100 yards. Every smallbore muzzleloader can be sighted in for 50 yards. Such sight-in will suffice, but here is a simple and practical sight-in guide for various blackpowder guns that might help to develop a more refined sight-in. The following data are generalized, not specific. They're presented to give the shooter a good starting point only. From there he or she must refine the sight-in for the specific firearm in question with the exact bullet and powder charge loaded in the gun. Ideally, first sight-ins should start at only 13 yards for round ball guns or 25 yards for conical shooters, just to get on the paper.

Big Bore Rifle — Hunting Load

Rifle calibers 45 through 58, whether shooting a round ball or a conical, can be pre-sighted at 13 yards for starters. This normally puts the bullet back into the line of sight at about 75 to 80 yards, considering a round ball at about 2,000 fps and a conical at about 1,500 fps. Another good way to sight-in the big-bore hunting muzzleloader with hunting loads is to center your group an inch high at 50 yards. An accurate muzzleloader should shoot a fairly tight group at 50 yards, so determining where the center of that group is located is not difficult. Sighted to hit an inch high at 50 yards, the round ball or conical will hit an inch or so low at 100 yards and about a half-foot low at 125 yards.

Medium Round-Ball Rifle Calibers

Calibers in the 38 to 40 range, shooting round balls at around 2,000 fps, can be sighted dead-on at 50 yards. This puts the round ball an inch low at 75 yards, and 2 or 3 inches low at 100 yards.

Smallbore Rifle Calibers

Calibers 32 and 36, shooting round balls loaded to about 1,500 fps for small game, should be sighted dead-on at 50 yards, which is about as far as most hunters shoot at small game. By sighting dead-on at 25 yards, a 50-yard zero

is established. So sighted, these light missiles strike about an inch low at 75 yards, which is not enough to miss a small game animal. Loaded to shoot around 2,000 fps, the little 32 or 36 can be sighted dead-on at 75 yards, giving these smallbores a practical range of about 100 yards.

Modern Muzzleloaders with Pistol Bullets and Sabots

A 50- or 54-caliber modern muzzleloader firing a 44-caliber, 240-grain pistol bullet in a sabot with a muzzle velocity of 1,600 fps can be sighted-in to print the group 2 inches high at 50 yards. This puts the group about 1.5 inches high at 75 yards and on the money at 100 yards. From there, the bullet drops about 3 inches at 125 yards. While it's possible to hit out to 150 yards on big game with the 44-caliber bullet so loaded, the bullet does drop about 7 inches at that distance when the rifle is sighted in as suggested here. Bullet energy is down to around 775 foot-pounds at this range.

Magnum Muzzleloaders with Pistol Bullets and Sabots

Magnum muzzleloaders are now capable of pushing bullets in the 250-grain class at about 2,000 fps muzzle velocity. The Savage Model 10ML is an exception, driving this same bullet weight at more than 2,300 fps. This means that a sight-in dead on at 150 yards shows the bullet dropping only a couple inches at 200 yards, realizing the promised 200-yard effective muzzleloader range.

Magnum Muzzleloaders with High Ballistic Coefficient Bullets

Choosing the 375-grain SSB Spitzer from the Buffalo Bullet Co. as a representative of this group, a sight-in of two inches high at 100 yards puts this bullet back in the bull's eye at 200 yards. This is a

This Outers target has five aim points, which worked well for the sight-in of a modern scoped muzzleloader. Rather than walking up to tape over holes, a different bull's eye was fired on.

practical sight-in when the missile takes off at 1,700 to 1,800 fps. Furthermore, this bullet retains a velocity between 1,300 and 1,350 fps at 200 yards for energy delivery of 1,400 to 1,500 foot-pounds.

The Breechloader

The blackpowder cartridge rifle can usually be sighted in for 100 yards. Considering the 45-70 Government round, for example, with a 500-grain round-nose bullet at 1,200 fps, sighting to print the group 3 inches high at 50 yards will give a 100-yard zero. The bullet will fall about 6 inches below the line of sight at 125 yards, and 9 inches below line of sight at 150 yards. Firing high ballistic coefficient bullets (such as the 535-grain 45-caliber Postell with a .402 ballistic coefficient), the same 45-70 with the same muzzle velocity can be sighted in for 125 yards with an initial sight-in 3 inches high at 100 yards.

The Blackpowder Handgun

The cap 'n' ball revolver, as well as most muzzle-loading pistols, do well with a starting group at 25 yards that is about 1 inch high. This puts the bullet back on target at 50 yards. The same sight-in applies to the blackpowder cartridge handgun.

Don't Forget Protection

When sighting in, eye and ear protection are paramount to safety. Also, when shooting big bores with full-power loads, a pad between your shoulder and butt stock makes sense. Special shooting pads are available at gun shops. Never use a sandbag between your shoulder and the butt plate. This may cause the stock to break.

Sighting In Tips

Be sure your blackpowder gun has good iron sights. If it wears a scope, make certain that the mounts are correct and secure. Sighting in is impossible with improper iron sights, scopes, or scope mounts.

Make certain that your firearm is sound. Tighten all screws, including sight screws. Loose screws make consistency impossible.

Be certain of your load. An inaccurate load cannot be expected to print consistently in the same group on the target.

Use a benchrest for sight-in, and use it right. Make certain that both

Sighting in and shooting for groups requires targets that can be clearly made out. These from Hoppe's, held in place by a stand from the same company, provide colorful aim points that stand apart from the background.

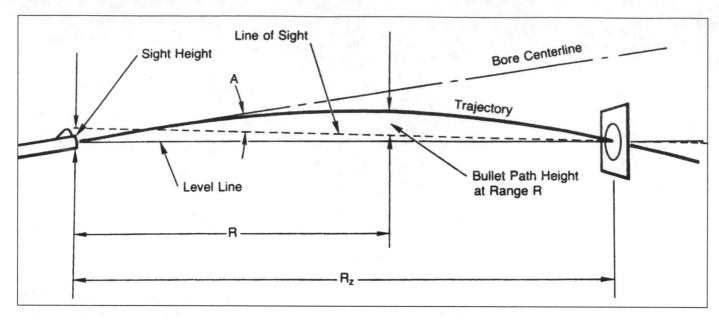

Labels in figure: Sight Height, Line of Sight, A, Bore Centerline, Trajectory, Level Line, Bullet Path Height at Range R, R, R$_z$

This schematic of a parabola shows the potential path of a bullet in flight. The shooter must know the trajectory of his firearm in order to sight-in to best advantage.

the forend of a rifle, plus toe of the stock, are well padded and secure on the bench top. A rifle should be set up so that it all but aims itself when properly resting on the bench. The shooter should be comfortable, both feet flat on the ground and spread apart for stability. The left hand for a right-handed shooter may grip the forestock if recoil is a problem. If not, it's better to rest the left hand flat on the bench. The right hand for a right-handed shooter controls aim, as well as the trigger.

Heavy-recoil rifles may skid the elbow across the surface of the bench. An old pillow under the arm saves the elbow from abrasion.

Only top-notch targets with well-defined aiming points are useful in sighting in.

Start close to get on the paper. Don't be frustrated by trying 100-yard shooting with an unsighted gun. Start out at only 10 to 15 yards. Adjust sights to hit dead center at this close range, then move the target out to 100 yards

Know your trajectory before trying to sight in. There is no point sighting in a big-game rifle with a full-power hunting load for only 50 yards when even a round-ball rifle deserves to be sighted dead-on at 75 to 100 yards.

Chapter 31

SHOOTING THE SMALLBORE MUZZLELOADING RIFLE

SMALLBORE MUZZLELOAD-ERS take a back seat today because most shooters get into the blackpowder game to take advantage of a special opportunity — the so-called "primitive hunt" when modern arms are not allowed. But squirrel rifles, as they were called in the old days, are superior not only for smaller game (squirrels, of course, and rabbits, the top small game animal on the continent), but also 'possum, armadillos, and a host of varmint animals, such as skunks and in some areas, porcupines. The smallbore is also a fine wild turkey caliber, putting Ben's bird down quickly without messing up too much succulent meat. Javelina are fair game, too, for the well-trained

marksman willing to get close for one perfect head shot. In fact, the head shot is the only right one on any small game, too, except turkeys, where a lead pill through the pinion (where wing joins body) does the trick. It's a shame that smallbore blackpowder rifles are overlooked, because along with "making meat," they are also wonderful for economical plinking and just plain fun shooting. They are all but recoilless and better on the target range than the lack of popularity at rendezvous and shooting matches suggest.

Smallbore by Definition

According to Capt. Dillin, in his fine book, *The Kentucky Rifle*, the

most popular smallbores of the shooting's golden era in Early America carried either 110 or 150 round balls to the pound. The first translates into 36 caliber (.350-inch lead sphere), while the second comes up 32 caliber (.310-inch pill). Ned Roberts, in his book The Muzzle-Loading Cap Lock Rifle, said: "The 100-to 220-to-the-pound gauge — 36 [about] to 28 calibers — were called 'squirrel rifles.'" As in the past, the two most popular smallbore calibers today remain 32 and 36. Arguably, other calibers qualify. Smaller-than-32-caliber rifles can be custom ordered, while calibers 38 up to 40 also offer decent economy, light recoil, and small-game-hunting abil-

The javelina of the Southwest and Mexico is about as large as a smallbore rifleman should tackle, and then only with perfect bullet placement.

ity. But the truth is, smaller-than-32s are darned hard to come by, and anything over 36-caliber is entirely unnecessary for small game and plinking. So 32 and 36 dominate the smallbore world, as they should.

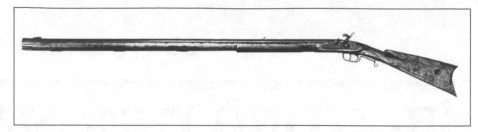

This Tennessee Mountain rifle from Dixie Gun Works in 32-caliber is capable of providing good economy with cast lead round balls and light, but sufficient, powder charges.

Versatility

Smallbores are overlooked in part because they are not considered versatile. "What would I do with one?" a shooter might ask. "Aren't they good only for small game?" Arguably, smallbores may be the most versatile front loader of all, wrong for big game, less than perfect for rendezvous shooting sports, but useful in many niches.

Small Game

When Markesbery elevated the Outer-Line® systems muzzleloader from drawing board to manufacture, the plan was calibers 54, 50, 45, and 36. Barrels in 36, however, are difficult to come by. That's because demands cry out for the 50, followed by the 54, with 45 coming into its own with regard to new bullet options and large allowable powder charges. But what a completion to the system the 36 would, and hopefully will be, in the near future. The rifle owner goes with a 50 or a 54, perhaps 45 if interest is mainly for deer-sized game. But swapping one of the bigger-bore barrels for the little 36 turns the rifle into a pussy cat with long claws: mild to shoot, but capable of putting fine meals in camp or on the home table. Big game seasons open. Big game seasons close. Meanwhile, many small-game hunts remain wide open with some form of small game generally available close to home, easy to get to, fun to go for, with no guide required. Cottontail rabbits live just about everywhere in North America, and also are well-represented in other countries, such as Australia. In some areas, the season on cottontails is open a half to a whole year. My home state, Wyoming, opens up for bunnies on September 1, and closes down at the end of February, the latter making for a wonderful winter hunt. In Arizona, there is no closed season on cottontails.

Tree squirrels are second only to the rabbit in small-game popularity. It's such a privilege to stalk bushytails that some hunters prefer Mr. Chatterbox to all other game.

Ben's Bird

Ben Franklin was right about the wild turkey being a fine choice for our national symbol, rather than the bald eagle, but luckily he lost out and we get to hunt this fine big game of upland birds. They're hunted with shotguns, including blackpowder guns in both traditional and modern in-line styles, plus some cartridge rifles, with the little 32- or 36-caliber lead pill also ideal. I've taken several birds with both calibers, finding both good. The challenge elevates a notch with smallbore muzzleloaders, but I've never lost an opportunity on a gobbler because I had a squirrel rifle in hand. A 32- or 36-caliber rifle will pot "Ben's bird" every time with solid ball placement. That's because of good ballistics for the challenge, as explained below.

Small Big Game

The javelina of the Southwest and Mexico weighs in the 25- to 35-pound class field dressed, sometimes quite a bit more, but not very often. That translates into an animal that goes in the 50-pound class on the hoof, which is about large enough for the squirrel rifle to tackle, and then only in the hands of a good shot dedicated to close stalking. Javelina are small, as big game goes, but a lot bigger than wild turkeys. Wild pigs, as they're fondly called, can be pretty tough little guys to bring down. But one well-placed head shot will kill a musk hog, for that's what these fine little animals truly are.

Economy Shooting

A 32-caliber squirrel rifle can be fired for fewer pennies per pop than a 22 rimfire, if the shooter casts his own ball (from scrap lead) and makes his own percussion caps (using the Forster Tap-O-Cap tool). The little 32-caliber patched ball achieves 22 Long Rifle muzzle velocity with only 10 grains of FFFg blackpowder — that's 700 shots for one pound of propellant. The larger 36-caliber smallbore costs a bit more to shoot, but it's not expensive either. The 36 demands a bit more lead: 65 grains per round ball instead of 45 grains, but it costs no more in percussion caps, and it only takes 15 grains of FFFg blackpowder or Pyrodex P to achieve 22 Long Rifle muzzle velocity.

Target Shooting

Smallbores are as accurate as the barrels that shoot them. Sub-caliber smokepoles in 32- and 36-caliber produce five-shot groups under an inch center-to-center at 50 yards regularly, and that's with iron sights. One reason they cluster so closely is ease of shooting. While there's no reason to jerk the trigger regardless of the gun — it will not reduce recoil — the squirrel rifle is a neat little pea shooter that promotes a steady hand and smooth trigger pull. These little pill-shooters are not ideal for serious long-range competition for the simple fact that a larger ball has a better chance of cutting the black (bull's-eye) when it hits in that area than a smaller ball. In other words, if a 32- or 36-caliber ball just misses the black, a 50-caliber ball would have counted as a bull. Also, the larger projectile drifts a bit less in the wind, which helps on the target range. Due to bullet diameter, the little pill is not as good as the big one for certain rendezvous games either, such as splitting the round ball on the ax. Again, it's a simple matter of size: the bigger ball provides a better opportunity than the smaller one. Nonetheless, the rifle shooter with a pleasant-shooting smallbore may just win the target match.

Plinking and Practice

Plinking and practice are enjoyable, both affording important shooting lessons for anyone willing to take either pastime seriously, which means setting targets up that make sense, and at varying ranges. Plinking games are fun, such as popping beverage cans placed inside a circle scratched on the ground to see who can scoot the most cans out of the arena. There's no pressure here, just enjoyment, and the smallbore makes it all the more so because it's so pleasant to shoot. There's considerable transfer

value from shooting the smallbore to mastering the big bore. If a marksman can manage to put little bullets on target with a smallbore, chances are he'll be do well when it comes to placing larger missiles on target with his big bore. Also, what is in effect a pair of negatives turns into positives, because smallbore bullets from squirrel rifles demand careful attention to the wind and range. Wind blows them off course readily, and they drop like loose change from an open pocket. These little challenges, however, can be turned from detriment to learning experience. Shooting out to 200 yards or more is especially interesting. On a calm day, once a shooter "gets the range," the small ball can knock over quite a number of targets, such as water-filled cans, or burst balloons filled with water.

Recoil and Noise

Blackpowder big bores are known to develop pretty fair recoil with heavy hunting charges because they demand a lot of powder to gain reasonable muzzle velocity, but smallbore blackpowder rifles don't develop enough kick to bruise a ripe tomato. Noise pollution is no problem either, especially with light loads in the well-mannered squirrel rifle. Even when shooting full-throttle loads, calibers 32 or 36 are com-

paratively quiet. This trait is also positive for the landowner who doesn't hear the roar of a cannon on his back forty when a small game hunter hikes his back forty. Smallbores prove the adage that bigger isn't always better. You don't need a baseball bat to down a gnat.

Children, Smaller Shooters, and Newcomers

The smallbore rifle is ideal for starting young marksmen on the road to blackpowder shooting. Lack of recoil or objectionable noise makes the 32 or 36 ideal. Furthermore, the newcomer learns the basics from a basic firearm design, loading his own ammunition right on the spot. While successful blackpowder shooting can require more know-how than fitting a prepared cartridge into the chamber and firing, it clearly shows how guns work — powder, projectile, and means of ignition.

Ballistics for Smallbores

Smallbore ballistics are ideal for many applications where big bores don't fit in. The 32-caliber squirrel rifle, for example, can be used on small game up to gobblers, with perfect head shots on javelina tossed in. Furthermore, power varies greatly with the charge, making the little 32 just as versatile as promised earlier in this chapter. Ten grains of pow-

This comparison between a 36-caliber (.350-inch diameter) round ball and a Buffalo Bullet Co. 125-grain conical visually shows the difference between the two.

der behind the 32-caliber round ball produces about 1,200 fps in a 24-inch barrel. I have found through chronographing that most brands of 22 Long Rifle ammo develop a muzzle velocity in that speed range, so that's enough power to bag a bunny or drop Mr. Bushytail from a tree limb. The chronograph shows about 1,650 fps with 20 grains of FFFg. Going up to 30 grains of FFFg produces a strong wild turkey load with the 45-grain ball departing the muzzle at 1,871 fps for an energy of 350 foot-pounds, again in the 24-inch barrel. At close range, the 30-grain charge equals the authority of the 22 Winchester Magnum Rimfire cartridge. Longer barrels produce even more muzzle velocity with this charge. The 41.5-inch barrel of the Dixie 32-caliber rifle delivers close to 2,100 fps with 30 grains of FFFg, creating about 440 foot-pounds. A 22 LR firing a 40-grain bullet at 1,250 fps earns 139 foot-pounds of muzzle energy. So at close ranges, the 32-caliber pill is stronger.

The 36 is excellent for pure enjoyment and it possesses useful ballistics. Its .350-inch round ball weighs 65 grains. In a Hatfield flintlock 36-caliber rifle with 39.5-inch barrel, 20 grains of FFFg delivered 1,471 fps. Thirty grains gave 1,799 fps, and 40 grains volume FFFg drove the patched ball at 2,023 fps for 591 foot-pounds of muzzle energy. The 32's super economy of 700 shots per pound of powder is not duplicated by the 36, and loads under 20 grains may not always deliver top accuracy, depending upon the rifling twist. Nor does the 36 enjoy flatness of trajectory with very light loads. However, 350 shots per pound is still economical shooting, and some 36s do shoot accurately with only 15 grains of fuel. The 36 ball "carries up" better than the 32, with greater terminal ballistics, and it bucks the breeze very slightly better. But all smallbore muzzleloaders are prey to wind.

Choosing 32 or 36

Either caliber means a lightweight rifle, because a heavy barrel is not necessary for a smallbore. The squirrel rifle can be long-barreled, but doesn't have to weigh much. The long-tom Hatfield noted above hefts under 7 pounds. Either the 32- or 36-caliber rifle with muzzle velocities in the 1,500 fps range can be sighted to print the group's center of impact an inch high at 25 yards. So sighted, the lead balls chew the X-ring out at 50 yards, clustering about two inches low at 75 yards, which is farther than most hunters shoot at small game with a charcoal-burner (or any other rifle). Most rabbit and squirrel shooting takes place no farther than 25 yards from the tip of the sportsman's boot. The squirrel rifle in either caliber is simple to manage on the range or in the field, and easy to take care of. Because modest powder charges are burned, heavy-duty caking and fouling common to the big-bore hunting rifle is not present in the squirrel rifle. Modern shoot-all-day lubes work well with smallbores. Many shots are fired in the field in succession without serious bore swabbing. They're both great, but the 32 wins for economy. It's a case of less being more. The 32-caliber, 45-grain round ball is large enough to get the job done with less shooting cost. Loaded up to snuff, the 32 is fine for game up to the size of wild turkeys, with javelina tossed in if the shot is perfect. The 32-caliber squirrel rifle edges its bigger 36-caliber brother, but when smallbore rifles are located, most will be caliber 36, which is also OK.

The Right Powder for Squirrel Rifles

FFFg blackpowder, Pyrodex P, and Clean Shot FFFg are proper squirrel-rifle propellants. Pyrodex P and Clean Shot are especially clean-burning. Swiss blackpowder, an especially well-made product, shows good velocity in both the 32 and 36, with easy after-shooting cleanup. Hodgdon Powder Co. tested P in smallbores, finding it ideal for either the 32 or 36. The small powder charges required in the squirrel rifle do not cause excessive pressure with the finer-granulated Pyrodex P powder. Swabbing between shots is unnecessary with Pyrodex, as shown in Chapter 15, and this powder can be used in the same volume, not weight, as FFFg blackpowder. Since Pyrodex is less dense than blackpowder, it offers more shots per pound. Meanwhile, FFg granulation is wrong in the smallbore. It yields low velocity. Pyrodex RS (Rifle/Shotgun) is also unwarranted in the squirrel rifle. On the other end of the spectrum, FFFFg is equally out of place in smallbores, being unnecessarily fine-grained for the main charge.

Smallbore Bullets

The least expensive way to shoot the smallbore is casting round balls, as described earlier. This is especially true when scrap lead can be found free or at small cost as explained above. Casting is a hobby in its own right, and the shooter may wish to run his own smallbore pills for the pure fun of it. However, the smallbore fan is also well-supplied with commercial round balls in both 32 and 36 calibers from several major companies. Commercial pills are excellent. Hornady offers a .310-inch for the 32. Thompson/Center had a nice 36-caliber Maxi-Ball® for a while, but it does not show in the current catalog. That bullet went a little over 100 grains weight. Currently, the Buffalo Bullet Co. has a 125-grain, 36-caliber bullet that flies at more than 1,900 fps, according to Lyman tests (from a 28-inch barrel). For the shooter who plinks and practices a great deal, casting is probably the best way to go, while the person who mainly hunts small game with his squirrel rifle may wish to buy a couple boxes of round balls at the beginning of each season and call it good. For those who choose casting, Lee has a .311-inch mold for the 32-caliber, plus a .313-inch round ball mold. Lyman also offers several smallbore molds.

Patches and Lubes

Matching patches to squirrel rifles is no problem. The .010-inch

Although the 36-caliber round ball does a great job, there are times when more bullet weight may be desired. That's where the Buffalo Bullet Co.'s 36-caliber 125-grain conical comes in.

thick patch is usually fine. However, this is not a suggestion across the board. The Hatfield 36-caliber rifle mentioned above did best with a .350-inch commercial round ball and a .017-inch thick patch. Clusters for five shots were under an inch at 50 yards from the bench on calm days.

Creating a Demand

As long as blackpowder shooters ignore the smallbore, companies will continue doing likewise. The demand has to come from us. There is a definite role for 32s and 36s on the blackpowder stage. At the same time, there are rifles available as this is written, and should they go out of production, a shooter may still be able to find a sample at a gun show or in The Gun List or Shotgun News. Traditions has a 32-caliber Crockett rifle patterned in long-gun style with a 32-inch barrel and 1:48 twist. The same company has a Deerhunter™ model in 32-caliber with a 24-inch barrel.

Markesbery has a 36-caliber barrel in its catalog. Dixie's Tennessee Mountain Rifle, finished or kit, comes in 32-caliber. Mountain State Muzzleloading Supplies Inc. has a J.P. McCoy Squirrel Rifle in 32-caliber, percussion or flintlock. If we shooters show more interest, a greater number of smallbores will appear, along with a wider selection of projectiles. In the meanwhile, however, we do have smallbore rifles on the market with round and conical bullets to match.

Chapter 32

THE BIG-BORE BLACKPOWDER GUN

BIG BORES for American and Canadian shooters are metallic cartridges intended for deer-sized and larger game. Handgun-wise, the 45 ACP and similar cartridges are also big bores to us. But a hunter in Africa would consider most of our big-bore hunting rifles small, and our powerful sidearms strong, but not ideal for stopping a charging rhino with a toothache. To these chaps, a 375 H&H Magnum is a "medium" cartridge, while the 416 Rigby is just approaching the big-bore realm. Big handgun cartridges such as the 454 Casull with a 300-grain bullet are baby cakes compared to medium rifle rounds on the Dark Continent developing two short tons of muzzle energy: 4,000 foot-pounds. Calibers 45 and up, shooting bullets in the 500-grain class, are big bores, with little peashooters like the 600 Nitro Express with

its 900-grain bullet truly qualifying for that status. In the world of blackpowder shooting in the United States and Mountie country, there's a little confusion on big-bore status. Because game managers were familiar with the North American concept of big bore, 40-caliber was considered pretty hefty. So the little 93-grain lead pill from a 40-caliber muzzleloader was deemed legal for big game in some states, and still is in spite of its low power.

Kinetic Energy Again

An Arizona hunter harvested a dozen deer in a row with a dozen shots from a 22-250 Remington rifle firing 50-grain bullets at 3,800 fps. A game warden saddled with the duty of dispatching car-struck deer on the highway counted on a 220 Swift for the job. He said he never needed more than one shot. Good

marksmen who take only proper shots do fine with 22-caliber centerfire rounds on deer-sized game, especially when loaded with the 60-grain Nosler Partition bullet in that caliber. That is all good, but bigger bullets are normally preferred for big game. Blackpowder guns especially demand larger projectiles because — unlike the two hotshot 22 centerfires noted above — truly high velocity is out of the question. Given top loads, the 22-250, for example, will push the 60-grain Nosler at 3,600 fps from the muzzle, while high velocity for a muzzleloader, even the new Savage Model 10ML, is normally under 2,500 fps muzzle velocity. Even round-ball guns shoot relatively heavy missiles, the 54 pushing a 230-grain lead pill, for example. The rule is: get close, put that lead ball in the boiler room and set the table for elk steaks.

Muzzleloader conicals go much heavier than round balls. Bullets in the 240-grain class are not considered large. Chunks of lead twice that heavy are common in calibers 50, 54, and 58. That is true also for blackpowder rifle cartridges, such as the never-die 45-70 Government. Drop 65 grains or a bit more FFg in that old-time case, topped off with a 500-grain lead projectile, and it will cleanly take big game within range. Handgun-wise, the blackpowder pistol is king for punch, especially on the order of the Thompson/Center Encore firing heavy bullets with stout powder charges. Blackpow-

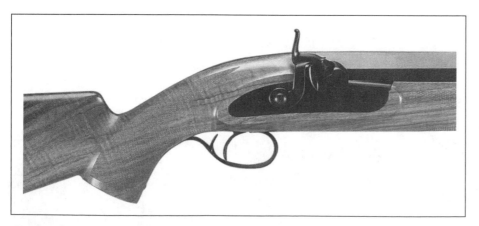

October Country's Heavy Rifle requires a stock to match the caliber, heavy with a strong wrist area. Note single trigger.

dcr handgun cartridges are not as strong, but a lot of game fell in the 19th century to 38-40s, 44-40s, 45 Colts, and similar rounds. Then there are the real beast-busters of the muzzleloader clan. The word may be overused today, but it fits like a half-inch nut on a half-inch bolt — awesome. Two-bores, 4s, 8s, even 10-bores firing round balls were sufficiently potent to drop pachyderms. The often-mentioned 2-bore William Moore rifle built by the London gunmaker of the same name fired that wicked 3,500-grain lead ball at 1,500 fps mv with 800 grains of blackpowder for an energy rating of more than 17,000 foot-pounds — making a 458 Winchester with 5,000 foot-pounds of energy look like a varmint round. And this is using kinetic energy as the gauge. No unfair advantage taken here. The blackpowder big bores below are subject to KE, not a momentum rule to favor them.

Knockdown Power

Speaking of unfair advantage, there are blackpowder shooters who declare that powerhouse modern cartridges are strong, all right, but that big-bore blackpowder guns have more of that long-lived buzzword, "knockdown power." A 7mm Magnum shoving a 160-grain bullet over 3,200 fps with a handload is OK, but for knockdown power, it pales against a 45-70, or for that matter a 50-caliber in-line magnum muzzleloader, according to these devotees. Sounds good, but what is this thing called knockdown power? Does a great big bullet, such as a 500-grain hunk of lead from a front loader, truly knock an animal right off its feet? It can look that way, and it doesn't

October Country makes only big-bore rifles with regard to the advice given by Captain Forsyth so long ago—very slow rate of twist for large-caliber round balls, and plenty of powder. This is the company's Light American Sporting Rifle. It's a hunting piece all the way, with Ashley Ghost Ring sight and plain black walnut stock, caliber 62. October Country bills the rifle as "light enough for a lady, big enough for an elk."

take a 500-grain bullet to create the illusion. I watched an antelope buck struck by a high-speed bullet from a 7mm Magnum fly right off its feet — at least I thought it did at the time. No such thing happened, although it looked that way. The animal uncoiled its "springs" after being hit, launching itself. There is conjecture, and then there are the laws of physics. I'll take the latter, and they say no animal is blown off its feet when struck with a bullet fired from a gun any of us would normally use for hunting. A book from 1903, Mechanics for Engineers, by Maurer, Roark, and Washa, refuted the knockdown-power argument. Here is how the authors told it: "The forward momentum of any bullet can be no greater than the rearward momentum of the recoiling gun from which it was fired — actually it is less due to loss of forward momentum in powder gas — [so] the bullet exerts on the object it hits no greater impulse [italics mine] than the gun exerts on the shooter." (Page 270)

The authors of Mechanics for Engineers vote "No way!" when it comes to knockdown power. A gun capable of truly tossing a big-game

animal through space would knock the shooter off his feet, too. The term "impulse" was used in the explanation above. It has a special meaning. A 5-pound bucket of sand lifted 1 foot high represents 5 foot-pounds of work. That same bucket can be set back down slowly or dropped to the floor —kaboom! If the bucket is dropped it picks up speed (and momentum), hitting harder than if it had been set down slowly. That harder hit from dropping the bucket is called impulse. This sort of understanding is important, because blackpowder shooters need to know what their guns cannot do, as well as what they can do. Thoughts of taking a 58-caliber musket with a 525-grain Minie ball and blowing a deer sideways through the air with knockdown power is total myth. On the other hand, there isn't a buck in the land that will stand up to that same Minie ball through both shoulders.

Stopping Power and Impulse

Bullets fired from anything resembling normal guns don't knock game down, but big bullets have certainly put a stop to the charge of the

October Country's 8-bore double rifle has an English walnut stock, 30-inch tapered barrels, checkered at wrist and forearm, three-blade express rear sight. At 8-bore, that's about 875 grains per round ball.

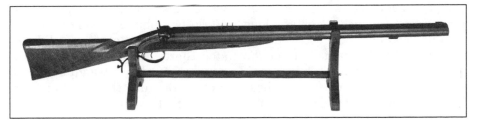

heaviest and toughest dangerous game in the world, from North America's coastal grizzly (brown bear) to Africa's rhino. The fellow counting on a 220 Swift to stop the charge of a Cape buffalo should have his will made out before he heads into the bush, because he's going to lose the jousting match. Better to whack the beast with a great big bullet going half the speed of the Swift or slower, perhaps a 458 Winchester with a 500-grain "solid" at 2,100 fps mv, or if the hunter can handle it, an even larger bone buster. While no right thinker would want to face a big angry beast with a blackpowder single-shot rifle with anything short of a super-size bullet, he would be better off with that rifled musket and a big lead bullet opposed to any hot rock 22 centerfire on the planet. No one is suggesting tackling dangerous game with a charcoal burner. The point is, big bullets, even from muzzleloaders, have their own brand of authority. Energy is energy is energy, but how it is delivered makes a difference in performance. Back to impulse for a moment. A blow from a two-pound hammer is capable of delivering a thousand pounds of force, yet that blow only drives a nail a short distance into soft pinewood. At the same time, a 38 Special with a mere 250-pounds of force may send a bullet through several inches of the same wood. Part of the reason for this is work versus time, or how long energy is applied. When an object is moved any distance (any object, including a bullet), time is consumed. It does not matter what the object is, or how it is moved. The hammer blow consumes only a tiny fragment of time. The 38 Special bullet applies its energy longer to the wood. This concept is all-important to energy delivery. Big bullets are capable of doing several things, including achieving deep penetration, which creates long wound channels as described in Chapter 42 on big-game hunting. So while big bullets don't knock animals down, their mass and shear diameter can be formidable, a point

to remember as calibers are presented below. A 50-caliber lead ball or conical, for example, ends its journey larger than many other bullets begin theirs.

Under 40 Caliber

Muzzleloaders less than 40 caliber are not big bores, especially when firing round balls weighing under 100 grains. In blackpowder cartridges, however, sub-40 conicals can do considerable work. The 38-55 Winchester is a good example. This was a popular cartridge in its time, toward the latter days of the 19th century and well into the 20th. Rowlands, author of Cache Lake Country, the story of contented cabin living in the North Woods, had an Indian friend who used the 38-55. It's a sure bet he took moose down regularly with the round, especially in a lever-action rifle capable of delivering fast second shots to go along with the first one. Even smaller numbers such as the 32-40 Winchester brought deer to the table. Hunters of the era carrying rifles on the order of the 32-40 may have realized that close was the only right shot. Some went so far as to employ the little 32-20 on deer, as did an old-timer in Wyoming who dragged his rifle out of the closet to show a couple of fellows who were toting considerably heavier artillery that day.

40 Caliber

Forty-caliber is included in the big-bore realm because it deserves to be, but not as a round ball. Even at 2,000 fps, the 93-grain, 40-caliber round ball is puny, carrying less than 250 foot-pounds to the target at only 100 yards. On the other hand, White offered a 40-caliber muzzleloader that fired what the company called a Superslug, which measured .409-inch. That 40-caliber bullet weighed 280 grains. But the company did not stop there, also offering a 40-caliber Superslug weighing 320 grains. Because these bullets carried decent sectional density, they

When the blackpowder cartridge came along, big bullets from large bores remained the only viable way to gain high power. This trend was, and still is, strong in the ever-popular 45-70 Government cartridge, bottom, continuing into the smokeless powder era with rounds like the 405 Winchester, top, a favorite of Teddy Roosevelt now offered by the Old Western Scrounger. The 30-06, center, represents a cartridge leaning away from a large bore and toward higher velocity.

managed to penetrate well on deer-sized game, although muzzle velocity was not very far above the speed of sound. But even at a modest 1,200 fps these 40-caliber bullets were good medicine at 100 yards for deer-sized game, and would work on bigger animals with well-placed shots.

The 40-caliber blackpowder cartridge was truly a horse of another hue, and it's interesting to see the old-time 40-65 Winchester chambered again in 21st-century single-shot blackpowder cartridge rifles intended for long-range silhouette shooting. The round is capable of knocking the metal targets over at long range, while delivering a little less push to the shooter's shoulder, which is important when numerous shots are fired in a match. The 40-65 was sufficiently popular to deserve special long-range bullets, with two versions provided by Lyman. They are both LRHP (Long Range High Performance) lead spitzers: the 400-

Big bullets always provided terrific potency, not only in times past, but today. The huge 50-140 Sharps, center, continues to provide a powerful package.

grain, .409-inch Schmitzer and 409-inch Snover in the same weight. Some old-time hunters preferred 40-caliber single-shot breechloaders above all others because they were pleasant to shoot, while at the same time delivering good penetration downrange. Certain buffalo runners counted on 40s for their work. For example, the 40-50 Sharps Bottleneck cartridge was offered by Sharps. The round didn't hold a heap of blackpowder, but it did push bullets in the 300-grain class at speed-of-sound muzzle velocities with powder charges ranging from only 45 to 50 grains weight. A 300-grain, 40-caliber bullet at around 1,100 fps in an accurate rifle is rifle is a worthy hunting combination. The 19th century saw many other 40s, such as the 40-70 Sharps Bottleneck round taking around 70 grains of fuel. While the 40-50 Sharps Bottleneck pushed a 277-grain bullet at a little under 1,200 fps, the 40-70 Sharps launched the identical projectile at about 1,400 fps. Going up another notch, there was the 40-90 Sharps Bottleneck firing a 300-plus-grain bullet at about 1,600 fps and a 400-grain bullet at about 1,400 fps. There were many

other 40s, too. Another worth mentioning, if only because of its popularity, is the 38-40 Winchester cartridge. It was used in both the rifle and the sidearm. This cartridge fired a 180-grain bullet at about 1,200 fps MV — nothing to get worked up about, but many hunters loved it, employing the rather small cartridge in a big way. Incidentally, as with other ammo of the period, the 38-40 was not 38 caliber. It belongs with the 40s, because it actually was 40 caliber.

44 Caliber

The 44-caliber, ball-shooting, muzzleloading rifle was no heavyweight, but somehow it got the job done for quite a number of shooters in its time. A particular mold tested in this caliber threw a round lead ball that went .435-inch diameter for a weight of 124 grains. Even at a muzzle velocity of 2,000 fps from a long-barreled flintlock rifle, muzzle energy was only 1,102 foot-pounds. At 100 yards, velocity was down to about 1,150 fps for a remaining energy of only 364 foot-pounds, sufficient to stop the charge of an angry field mouse, perhaps, but not powerful enough to

lend confidence for big game hunting. Because of this sad showing energy-wise, the 44-caliber ball-shooting rifle should be scrapped for big game, with the always-present exception of those deer hunters who get close and put the ball perfectly on the money.

Blackpowder lead conicals for 44-caliber muzzleloaders are not prevalent. However, dozens of 44-caliber bullets, most of them modern jacketed projectiles originally intended for cartridge revolvers such as the 44 Magnum abound in sabots, especially for modern muzzleloaders. The caliber is also prominent in cap 'n' ball revolvers, on the average delivering about 38 Special ballistics. Both Colt and Remington caplock revolvers of the Civil War era were 44-caliber, as was the more powerful Walker. As a blackpowder cartridge revolver, caliber 44 appeared especially as the 44-40 Winchester, with the round also chambered in lever-action repeating rifles. Power was on the low side, but repeat shots made the 44-40 deadlier than its ballistics. Good marksmen were deadly with the short-cased 44-40 on both man and beast. The 44-40 remains factory-loaded to this day, chambered in many newly manufactured handguns and rifles, which says something for it. Other 44-caliber blackpowder cartridges were less popular, but more powerful. The 44-60 Winchester was available in that company's single-shot rifle, along with the 44-60 Sharps Bottleneck, both pushing bullets of around 400 grains at about 1,250 fps. There were many other 44s, including the long 44-100 Remington Creedmoor and 44-100 Ballard. These rounds qualify as big bores. Jacketed 44-caliber bullets, .429-inch diameter, are widely used in sabots for muzzleloaders.

45 Caliber

The literature may not always agree, but 45 caliber was highly popular in the Kentucky/Pennsylvania long rifle, as existing examples of these rifles prove. A 45-caliber round ball is not exactly a

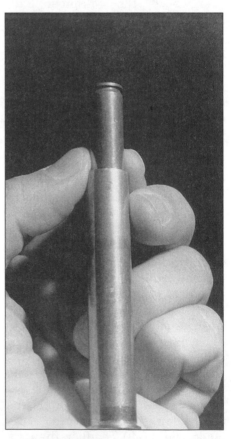

To give a perspective of 50-140-700 Sharps size, here is a 30-06 cartridge placed inside the big 50-caliber case.

Halloween pumpkin. In .445-inch diameter, it weighs only 133 grains, delivering less than 350 foot-pounds of energy at 100 yards, about like a 9mm Luger pistol at the muzzle. The 45 round ball makes a decent rendezvous caliber, and will harvest deer-size game at modest range with that oft-repeated ideal bullet placement. But that's about it. On the other hand, 45-caliber conicals can produce considerable power. In the Navy Arms Parker-Hale Volunteer rifled musket, a bullet in the 490- to 500-grain weight range leaves the muzzle at over 1,500 fps for a muzzle energy close to 2,500 foot-pounds. This long 45-caliber lead bullet carries the better part of a short ton in energy at 100 yards. There were many fine 45s among the blackpowder breechloaders of the 19th century, including the still-factory-loaded 45-70 Government cartridge, king of the modern blackpowder silhouette game. So many super 45s existed that the rest of this chapter would be not sufficient to list them. They include a whole line of Sharps rounds in that size, such as the 45-90-2.4 Sharps, 45-100-2.6 Sharps, 45-110-2 7/8 Sharps, and the historically interesting 45-120-3-1/4 Sharps, which propels a 500-grain missile at more than 1,600 fps with black-powder loads. While the 45-caliber round ball is on the anemic side, long-bullet 45s as conicals for muzzleloaders or bullets for blackpowder breechloaders are big bores to be reckoned with. The 45 Colt, along with the less popular but well-liked 45 Schofield, could be formidable. In blackpowder loadings, neither was terribly strong, but due to good-sized bullets in the 250-grain class, they got the job done. It's popular to call the 45 Colt a 45 "Long" Colt, but there never was any such thing. It's just 45 Colt. Chambered in the excellent Ruger Blackhawk revolver, the 45 Colt proves its potency with a 300-grain bullet at 1,300 fps MV, right on the heels of the 44 Remington

Magnum round. The 45-caliber bullets, such as the good ones from Hornady and Nosler, also are excellent in sabots for muzzleloaders.

50 Caliber

By the time the round ball reaches 50 caliber, it has true big-game potential: a .490-inch lead pill weighing in at 177 grains. At close to 2,000 fps, the 50-caliber lead sphere drops deer-sized animals in their tracks at up to 100 yards, with 125 yards an outside limit. Many an elk has also been brought down with 50-caliber round balls, both today and in the past. Getting close to these big animals, however, is essential for a clean harvest with a 50-caliber round ball, providing correct bullet placement directly into the boiler room. A 50-caliber ball retains sufficient velocity and energy at the 75-yard mark or closer to offer a good, long wound channel. One afternoon in Colorado, son Bill Fadala dropped a bull elk with his Ithaca 50-caliber caplock rifle. The bull was very close. The lead round ball passed through the breadth of the chest region, the big animal falling within mere yards. Fifty-caliber blackpowder conicals are provided in weights that range into the 600-grain category, such as the Parker Hydra-Con 650-grain bullet. Lead 50-caliber bullets can take any North American big game, grizzlies included, if and only if, the blackpowder hunter is backed up by a good shot with a powerhouse cartridge rifle. I have taken game with 50-caliber round balls and 50-caliber conicals. Inside 100 yards, deer-sized animals fall to the round bullet as quickly as the conical. At longer ranges, the conical, of course, wins the energy battle. The 50 caliber is by far the number-one choice today in muzzleloaders. That's because it works on all big game, especially deer with either ball or conical. Not only in the rifle, but also in a pistol like the Thompson/Center Encore, 50-caliber is a deadly dimension. The Encore can launch a 350-grain, 50-caliber bullet at muzzle velocities capable of providing close-range performance on par with a 30-30 rifle.

The 50-caliber blackpowder cartridges were capable of tall power. The 50-70 Sharps, for example, was well liked by buffalo runners of the late 19th century. The 50-70 can still be loaded today. Its bullet of more than 500 grains travels downrange at about 1,050 fps. The 50-90-2 1/2 Sharps is more potent, driving a 605-grain bullet out of the muzzle at close to 1,250 fps. The powerful 50-140-3 1/4 Sharps was the largest cartridge in that company's line, but historians say this big boy was late for buffalo hunting, arriving on the market at the close of that era. Regardless, the 50-140 Sharps remains capable of propelling a 605-grain bullet at about 1,500 fps for a muzzle energy over 3, 500 foot-pounds with a 700-grain lead bullet.

The 1/2-inch diameter bullet proved worthy in the past, and still is good in both round and conical form. Odds are, this caliber will dominate for many years to come in the world of blackpowder shooting. The majority of new muzzleloaders coming onto the market today are caliber 50.

52 and 53 Caliber

In days gone by, these calibers were represented in muzzleloaders; however, they are not popular today. The Allen Santa Fe Hawken

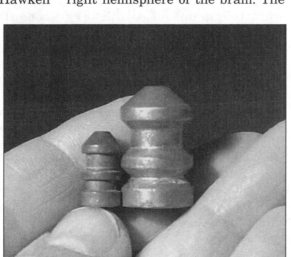

While conicals can carry far more weight per caliber than round balls, because they are elongated, big bore conicals continue to dominate in power over smaller calibers. The 36-caliber Maxi-Ball on the left is clearly outclassed for mass by the 50-caliber Maxi-Ball on the right.

was provided in 53 caliber, firing a round ball of .520-inch diameter that weighed 211 grains. It did well for a while, but currently this rifle is no longer available, except as found used.

54 Caliber

Overall, the 54-caliber round ball makes a lot of sense for hunters. At .530-inch or .535-inch diameters, the ball hefts well over 200 grains, yet reasonable muzzle velocity is easily achieved without going to huge doses of powder. This is not to say that larger round balls aren't more potent. They are, all the way up to the 2-bore. However, a 54-caliber round ball delivered from reasonable range is big-time deer medicine and at close range is worthy of elk-sized game. After all, this lead globe starts out well over a half-inch in diameter, and by the time it flattens out, large wound channels are the rule. The only animal charge I've faced occurred not in Africa, although there were a couple close calls with Cape buffalo. Rather, it was an American bison that came my way. Luckily, the event was recorded on film as proof. The bull was free-roaming on the range, but quite familiar with two-legged creatures, having little respect, apparently, for the breed. The shaggy came at a gallop, but met with a 54-caliber .535-inch 230-grain round ball, which penetrated the skull, taking out the right hemisphere of the brain. The

bull reared back like a rodeo horse, falling on its side and then, amazingly, he rose to his feet. A second 54-caliber round ball caught him in the chest, penetrating fully to the off-side and the bull stayed down this time. That round ball was recovered flat as a coin and marked by an impression made by a piece of rib punched all the way through the thick hide.

All of the above happened at under 20 yards. Had the bison been farther away, the results would not have been so dramatic. A 54 ball, .530-inch diameter, runs 224-grains weight, while one in .535-inch diameter weighs 230 grains. In well-made muzzleloaders, the 54-caliber lead sphere can be driven at around 2,000 fps for a muzzle energy not far from a short ton, or 2,000 foot-pounds. The problem, of course, is round-ball velocity loss, and this good muzzle energy looks more like 675 foot-pounds at only 100 yards. That's partly why a 125-yard limit is imposed on deer-size game with the 54-caliber round ball, 75 yards and under much preferred for elk-size animals. The other reason is trajectory. A drop of a half-foot at 125 yards is expected with the 54-caliber ball-shooting rifle sighted for 75 yards or so.

As a conical shooter, the 54 is shortchanged by American bullet makers. Even those companies that provide good lead conicals for this caliber don't follow through all the way. For example, the SSB Spitzer from Buffalo Bullet Co. is made only in 45 caliber at this time. It can be fired in a 54 with a 54-caliber sabot, but the bullet should be sized 52- or 53-caliber to make it fit right in the 54 with a proper sabot. Thompson/Center also makes fine 54-caliber conicals, but again provides nothing in the way of a bullet truly designed to fit a 54-caliber sabot. The same story repeats over and over. Northern Precision also makes excellent jacketed bullets in sabots for muzzleloaders, but again comes up short in caliber 54. An exception to the 54-caliber orphan

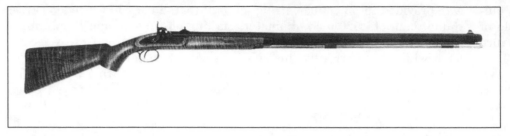

The Great American Sporting Rifle from October Country is another big bore ball-shooter with Forsyth super-slow rate of twist. Smallest caliber offered is 62, along with 66, 69, and 72. Although its style is basically English, every piece is made in America, hence the American title.

story is Parker Productions with several heavyweight lead conicals, such as the company's 500-grain Colorado Legal, which measure .546 inch across the driving band and .5415 inch diameter at the base. Another Parker Productions 54-caliber power bullet is the hollow-base 54 (shallow hollow base). This bullet on my scale weighs 550 grains and measures .545 inch across the driving band, .541 inch across the base.

A 54-caliber rifle firing conicals can be a true powerhouse capable of a big punch. The two Parker Production bullets just mentioned, especially from a rifle like the Markesbery, which is capable of safely digesting big powder charges, will penetrate the breadth of a bull moose. Knight's MK-85 modern muzzleloader in 54 caliber drives a Hornady 425-grain Great Plains Bullet faster than 1,500 fps, with a muzzle energy over 2,200 foot-pounds. The 460-grain, 54-caliber Buffalo Bullet leaves the muzzle at 1,400 fps, and this deep-penetrating bullet achieves over a ton of muzzle energy. In Sam's Bullet Box, the 460-grain, 54-caliber Buffalo Bullet penetrated all manner of media, as did Parker Productions bullets. Out of my Markesbery systems rifle with a 54-caliber barrel in place, Swiss Black Powder drove a 325-grain Beast Buster bullet at 2,100 fps MV for an energy level topping 3,000 foot-pounds. A 425-grain Buffalo Bullet lead conical left the muzzle of the same rifle at 1,800 fps for an energy rating topping 3,000 foot-pounds.

Tests are still in progress with other 54-caliber conicals, along with different powders and charges.

In the meanwhile, bullet companies might consider offering a few saboted projectiles properly-sized for 54-caliber, rather than stuffing undersized missiles into 54-caliber sabots. Understandably, caliber 50 gets the attention. After all, 50-caliber conicals can do it all. However, I know one hunter who plans to carry a 54-caliber rifle into moose and elk timberlands this coming season, pending the luck of the draw. That hunter is me.

56 Caliber

Bullets in this caliber have appeared over the years, but are so rare now as to play no part in the muzzleloader or blackpowder cartridge game.

58 Caliber

There is no doubt that the 58-caliber round ball is capable of deadly action; however, quite a charge of powder is required to gain velocity that will produce a decent trajectory. Lyman's tests show a 58-caliber round ball leaving the launching pad at 1,857 fps; however, that velocity was achieved with 160 grains of GOEX FFg blackpowder. Although no longer made, the Navy Arms Hawken Hunter, a well-built rifle, fired a 58-caliber round ball accurately. Even with 140 grains of GOEX FFg powder, however, velocity was only 1,550 fps at the muzzle with energy under 1,500 foot-pounds. Of course, with caliber alone having an effect on target impact, the big 58-caliber round ball is effective. For normal hunting purposes, however, the 54-caliber ball — which achieves good velocity with less powder — makes more sense. A major exception

would be the hunter who does not mind burning a lot of powder and disregards smoke and recoil in order to achieve close to 1,900 fps MV with the 58-caliber ball — yielding more than a short-ton of muzzle energy.

The 58-caliber conical is entirely a different story. The American Civil War saw 58-caliber rifles in action, and they were devastating. The Navy Arms Parker-Hale Musketoon in 58 caliber is allowed only 100 grains of Pyrodex RS with a 505-grain Buffalo Bullet. This produces a muzzle velocity just faster that the speed of sound — 1,200 fps — with a muzzle energy just under 1,700 foot-pounds. This is where KE figures fall a little shy of reality. In-the-field experience proves that a 58-caliber 505-grain bullet, although traveling rather slowly, is definitely game worthy at close range. Navy Arms' longer-barreled 1853 3-Band Enfield musket did better with the same 100-grain RS charge, turning up closer to 1,300 fps for a muzzle energy approaching a short ton. Thompson/Center's Big Boar rifle was tested in 58 caliber with a 560-grain Maxi-Hunter bullet at 1,350 fps loaded with 120 grains of FFg for a muzzle energy of 2,267 foot-pounds. Pistols in 58 caliber don't show much on paper, because this true big-bore, single-shot, one-hander fires its bullets too slowly to achieve high muzzle energies. However, a 58-caliber, 500-grain Minie at 800 fps, with only 750 foot-pounds of energy showing, has to be honored at close range, if due only to the heavy bullet. A 58-caliber Harper's Ferry throwing a 570-grain Minie at just under 700 fps earned only 650 foot-pounds of

Big bores mean big bullets, like the 75-caliber round ball compared here with a 32-caliber lead pill. Weight rises way out of proportion to diameter. The 32-caliber ball only weighs 45 grains, while the 75-caliber ball weighs closer to 500 grains.

muzzle energy — even less dramatic on paper, but once again shear projectile weight and diameter must be taken into account. In spite of low velocity and unimpressive energy, the big 58-caliber, single-shot pistol will drop a deer at close range.

60 Caliber

A 60-caliber round-ball test rifle that fired a 317-grain lead pill at 1,600 fps with a heavy dose of FFg blackpowder yielded a muzzle energy of only 1,800 foot-pounds — the word "only" used because a shooter might expect more from such a heavy bullet. Using even more powder, where allowed by the gunmaker, the 60 would prove quite powerful. Recoil was definitely well-represented with the load, but the allowable charge for the rifle was well under what other rifles would be capable of, as proved by the information below on October Country's arms, which are allowed big powder charges behind big round balls.

62 Caliber

Sufficient demand for a 62-caliber round ball rifle prompted October Country to bring one out in that size

with a very slow rate of twist, only a turn in 104 inches. Using super blackpowder charges, a muzzle velocity close to 2,000 fps was achieved with the 62-caliber Great American Sporting Rifle, as October Country calls its little toy. Muzzle energy is more than 4,000 foot-pounds with the 480-grain round bullet. Again, get ready for big-time recoil. However, considering the larger calibers coming up, October Country's 62 falls into the milder big-bore realm. Another company offering a 62-caliber ball-shooter is the Pacific Rifle Co., selling its Zephyr® underhammer model. This rifle, too, is allowed a good-sized powder charge for big-time energy.

69 Caliber

The 12-gauge shotgun is more like 72-caliber, but the round balls tested in a 12-gauge smoothbore measured .690-inch, and weighed 494 grains. Following allowable powder charges in a 12-gauge shotgun, velocity with this big ball was only 1,000 fps, with muzzle energy measuring an unexciting 1,100 foot-pounds. What would happen with this big lead globe in a rifle that was allowed more powder is simple to determine. Big power. Incidentally, although history shows that there were truly "buck and ball" loads with both round ball and shot in the same barrel, that particular manner of loading is not recommended here. There is no reason for it, and the final weight of the missile on the powder charge could be extremely high. A buck and ball load that is permissible, however, is loading a proper amount of shot in one barrel of a double-barrel shotgun, with one correct round ball in the other barrel. In this manner, a hunter in the brush could deliver a load of buckshot followed quickly by a single heavyweight projectile.

72 Caliber

The Pacific Rifle Co. Zephyr® underhammer also comes in 72 caliber, shooting a ball weighing in at

550 grains. October Country also has a 72-caliber round ball shooter. Given a .710-round ball in the 72, weight in pure lead goes 538 grains. Provided with a big powder charge to get the ball rolling at around 1,800 fps MV, energy tops 3,800 foot-pounds at the muzzle.

75 Caliber

The British Brown Bess Musket was a 75-caliber smoothbore. Firing a comparatively modest powder charge behind a ponderous round ball, it was effective for its purpose, but could never be considered in the same ballistic ball park with October Country and Zephyr® big bore ball-shooters.

The 10-Bore Rifle

Old-time data shows one 10-bore rifle shooting a 698-grain bullet in front of 5 drams of blackpowder. Since a dram is 27.34 grains weight, that's a powder charge of 136.7 grains weight. Because this weapon is noted as a "jungle gun," close-range work is assumed. This particular 10-bore produced only 1,316 fps muzzle velocity, but no doubt the big bullet made up for a muzzle energy rating of only 2,685 foot-pounds.

The 8-Bore Rifle

An old load for an 8-bore rifle was a 10-dram powder charge (273.4 grains of blackpowder) behind a 1,257-grain bullet for a muzzle velocity noted as a flat 1,500 fps. The chart showed a muzzle energy of 6,273 foot-pounds. My calculations say 6,282 foot-pounds. Close enough. Obviously, the 8-bore is some kind of powerful. The Zephyr® rifle is available in 8-bore, as is an 8-bore rifle from October Country. The latter is capable of handling as much as 300 grains of blackpowder for a muzzle velocity listed by the company as more than 1,400 fps with a round ball weighing more than 800 grains.

The 4-Bore Rifle

October Country's 4-bore double rifle weighs about 14 pounds.

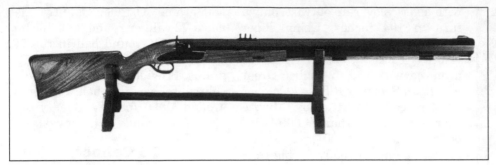

Here is the Heavy Rifle from October Country. It's a 4-bore, meaning four round balls to the pound, or 1,750 grains weight per ball. It has an English walnut stock with ebony nose cap, checkered at wrist and forestock, three blade express sights. The barrel tapers from 1 3/4-inches to 1 1/2-inches octagonal. English style breech plug with drip bar over the lock.

That's good, because it shoots a .989-inch round ball weighing 1,400-grains, according to company figures. Specifically, a .989-inch round ball would weigh 1,455 grains in pure lead (four balls to the pound would be 1,750 grains each). This load creates 1,400 fps MV, as well as 7,000 foot-pounds of energy.

The 2-Bore Rifle

Noted more than once, William Moore's 2-bore shoulder buster fired a half-pound spherical bullet that created 17,000 foot-pounds of muzzle energy.

Recoil and Big Bores

Whoever came up with the cliché about no free lunch was right. Big bores, especially the truly large ones loaded with plenty of powder, come back and say hello to the shooter. It could not be otherwise. Blackpowder guns require heavy doses of powder to achieve good velocity, and more powder means more recoil. Furthermore, part of the recoil formula is bullet weight, and big bores possess plenty of that. In the hunting field, recoil is much less noticed than on the bench. At the bench, wise shooters pad their shoulders.

Blackpowder big-bore rifles, pistol, and revolvers, in muzzleloader or cartridge form, are capable of delivering the cargo no matter how power is measured. A 670-grain Parker Productions 54-caliber Colorado Traditional Hunter bullet fired with a stout powder charge in a Markesbery muzzleloader all but destroyed the Sam's Bullet Box in one test. Not only was penetration high, but the impact literally blew out a side panel. That's the brand of authority possible with big-bore bullets from blackpowder guns.

Chapter 33

POWERS OF THE RIFLED MUSKET

MUSKETS WERE generally considered smoothbore military long guns. One American dictionary calls them an "archaic smoothbore," another "a smoothbore long-barreled firearm." The Oxford English Dictionary labels the musket an "early form of hand firearm." Origin of the word comes from "fledged arrow," fledged indicating an arrow with feathers. When the musket earned its rifling, it therefore became the "rifled musket." The "power" or value of this blackpowder muzzleloader lies in two distinct camps — power as in ballistic force, and power as in accuracy to deliver its message downrange, sometimes way downrange. For example, the Whitworth rifled musket, still with us today, is capable of hitting a target at 1,000 yards with groups close enough to count for something. Being military oriented, muskets had (and still have) another good quality — ruggedness meant to keep the rifle intact under trying conditions that might wreck a more delicate firearm. The word also applies to the Musketeers, as in the famous fictional "The Three Musketeers." The Musketeers are given the period from 1622 to 1786, when they served as the French Royal Body Guard. America had its Springfield Rifled Musket, now adding the word "rifled" to indicate that it was not a smoothbore. Today's rifled musket is mainly a replica that copies a real piece from the past. One exception is the Volunteer, which has been around for a long while. The Volunteer is a Whitworth without the specific particulars known to the breed. It's just as rugged, and shoots fine.

Rifled muskets are not what they appear to be. They look heavy and clumsy. They're generally neither. Not lightweights, these long guns have good balance and though the

The sights on this Whitworth rifled musket clearly indicate that its power is intended to continue well downrange.

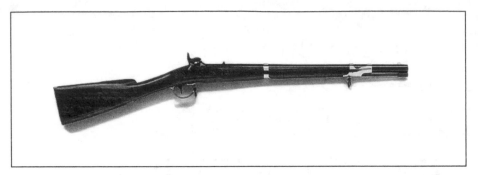

The J.P. Murray Carbine, this one a replica from the Navy Arms Co., shoots a heavy 58-caliber Minie ball.

world of blackpowder shooters never has quite figured it out, they make fine hunting front loaders. Why? As stated before, they are powerful, rugged, accurate and not that heavy to tote. The Volunteer has a 32-inch barrel. The Whitworth barrel is 36 inches long. These two are among the heavier rifled muskets at about 9 1/2 to 10 1/2 pounds, depending upon exact model, while the carbines run much lighter. The J.P. Murray 1862-1864 Cavalry Carbine, on the other hand, wears a 23-inch barrel and weighs only 7 pounds, 9 ounces. In 58 caliber, it's ideal for wild boar, or other hunting, in close quarters, delivering a terrific blow with bullets in the 500-grain class. All of these rifled muskets are of quality manufacture, accuracy and strength. Navy Arms allows a full 130 grains volume FFg or 130 grains RS for a muzzle velocity of about 1,500 fps with a 490- to 500-grain, 45-caliber projectile. That's more power than the 45-70 Government round, which drives similar bullets at 1,200 fps MV with blackpowder loads. The weight is a plus with heavy loads, while also providing stability in the field, unlike flyweights that are nice to carry, but flighty when it comes to pulling down on game, especially after a hunter has been hiking a while in the mountains and may be a little out of breath.

Sights

Original rifled muskets had a variety of different sights. How-ever, one thing is certain: The rifled musket of our interest has adjustable sights with windage and elevation variation built in. The Whitworth I personally shoot a good deal has a hooded globe front sight. The hood is essential, because the globe, a little round ball, rests on a stem and could be damaged in the field. That would render the rifle useless until a new front sight was put in place. The front sight pedestal is easily drifted for windage. The back sight is open with a shallow U-shaped notch. A clear sight picture is possible because the front globe does not optically fill the U-notch, leaving light on both sides for reference. The rear sight is adjusted for windage via a screw that attaches the sight plate firmly in place. Elevation adjustment is tremendous, with the rear sight sliding in a rail. The body of the sight has elevator notches so that as the rear sight is moved in the rail, it makes contact with the notches in three numbered slots marked 1, 2, and 3 (1 being the lowest elevation). Then for super long-range shooting, the sliding bar is pulled upward, putting a second notch into position. With the rear sight flipped up, the muzzle of the rifle can be severely raised for distant shots. In the raised position, the readings on the bar start at 5 and go all the way up to 10. Other rifled muskets have very different sights, of course, since the Whitworth is not only a military musket, but also a target rifle. The Dixie C.S. "Richmond" Musket, built originally when the Federal arsenal at Harper's Ferry was captured in April 1861 and moved to Confederate ordnance in Virginia, had a blade front sight with leaf-adjustable rear sight. The Zouave rifled musket had similar front sights, but the rear sight was, and still is, blued steel with two flip-ups. The J.P. Murray Artillery Carbine has a brass blade front sight with a dovetailed open rear sight.

Calibers

The Whitworth and the Volunteer are both 45 caliber, while many other muskets are 58 caliber, such as the well-known Zouave and the Navy Arms Musketoon, the latter with a short 24-inch barrel. Specifically, both the Whitworth and Volunteer have .451-inch bores.

Bullets

The regular rifled muskets, such as the Zouave, Musketoon, Mississippi Rifle of 1841, and many others, shoot Minie-type bullets, such as the 530-grain, .577-inch Minie from Lyman mold number 5777611. They also handle Thompson/Center Maxi-Balls in 58 caliber. Rate of twist for these rifles is 1:48, which works out all right for the rather short missiles they shoot. The Volunteer and Whitworth are entirely different. They both carry 1:20 twist and are therefore geared for long 45-caliber bullets that carry up well downrange. While the regular rifled muskets shoot Minies and similar projectiles, the Volunteer and Whitworth handle "standard lead conicals." Tests with Lyman's 490-grain, .457-inch bullet, mold number 457121, proved accurate in both of these rifles. While 58-caliber bullets are less streamlined with a lower ballistic coefficient, they pack a lot of weight with considerable penetration potential. Volunteer and Whitworth 45-caliber rifled muskets, on the other hand, shoots bullets that are as heavy as those fired in the 58-caliber muskets, sometimes 600 grains or more. As an example of this fact, the 58-caliber Dixie U.S. Model 1861 Springfield rifled musket (with 40-inch barrel, but only 8 pounds weight) normally shoots a Minie-type bullet that weighs 500 to 600 grains. The 45-caliber bullets, being about the same weight as the 58-caliber bullets, are much longer per diameter, resulting in higher sectional density. It has a blade front sight, and the rear sight is adjustable for windage only, accomplished by drifting the sight in its dovetail notch.

The Historical Zouave Rifled Musket

The rugged 58-caliber Zouave hunting rifle is imported by several companies, including Dixie and Navy Arms. It's bored 58-caliber and has a blade front sight with two flip-ups. Some imported rifles had different sights. The barrel is 32 1/2 inches long, and it weighs 9 pounds overall. Typically, the Zouave is another rugged rifled musket. In tests, it fired a 530-grain Lyman Minie (mold No. 577611) at 1,100 fps MV with 80 grains volume FFg blackpowder. One company gave the 80-grain volume load as maximum, even though it produces less than 6,000 psi pressure. Pyrodex provided a surprisingly low 3,400 psi with 80 grains volume RS and a 315-grain Lyman Minie for a muzzle velocity just over 1,200 fps. Another company allowed 100 grains volume blackpowder or Pyrodex. With that load, the Zoauve produced just shy of 1,400 fps mv with a pressure rating just over 5,000 psi. As always, the big bullet must be taken into account along with KE ballistic fig-

ures, because even with the 100-grain load and 1,400 fps muzzle velocity, energy figures reach only 1,371 foot-pounds with the 315-grain Minie. A 460-grain Minie with 100 grains volume GOEX FFg produced a little less than 1,300 fps for an improved 1,727 foot-pounds of muzzle energy. Coupled with the big bore 58-caliber bullet and well over three-fourths of a short ton of muzzle energy, the Zouave is clearly big-game worthy.

The Zouave in History

The Zouaves were fighting men noted for their special uniforms as well as their military ability. They wore what began as North African-style apparel, which became altered considerably over time. French fighters made up companies of Zouaves. Capt. George B. McClellan, a U.S. Army observer in the Crimea, held the Zouave in great esteem. He influenced others to similar thinking, and a Zouave-like soldier emerged in Eastern America. Eventually, there were several Zouave-type fighting groups in middle 19th-century America, and both the North and South had Zouave units during the Civil War. To this day, the colorful outfits remain before the public, because teams of Civil War re-enactors still wear Zouave-like uniforms. Historian Joe Bilby noted one Zouave uniform as "red fezzes with blue tassels, blue jackets trimmed in red, red shirts and sashes, blue and white pillow ticking baggy pants, blue and white horizontally striped hose and white gaiters." He also said, in his article "Zou-Zou-Zou-T I G R R R" for the Dixie Gun Works Black-

powder Annual 1995, that "guns carried by Zouaves did not differ from those of other volunteer regiments." Therefore, the Zouave name, generally attached to the Remington rifled musket of 1863, goes somewhat unfounded and mysterious. A 69-caliber smoothbore was more likely found among the Zouaves. "There is no evidence that any of the Zouaves were issued the colorful Remington Model 1863 or 'Zouave' rifle," Bilby states. So when the modern blackpowder shooter speaks of the Zouave, he means the rifle style described above, and not the soldier.

45-Caliber VS 58

The two major calibers for rifled muskets are very different, not only in size, but also configuration, sectional density, and ballistic coefficient. The latter two have little meaning, however, at close range. Val Forgett, CEO of the Navy Arms Co., managed to take all manner of African game, including elephants, with a 58-caliber rifled musket, the bullet penetrating well in spite of its comparatively low sectional density. In timber and brush country, where shots are close on deer, wild boar, even elk and moose, the 58 by shear virtue of bullet mass will get the job done, especially with decent powder charges pushing the bullets in the 1,400 fps to 1,500 fps zone. A 58-caliber missile makes an impressive wound channel. Many completely penetrated Sam's Bullet Box from one end to the other, pushing through water balloons, clay blocks, even wet newspapers and large catalogs. The 45-caliber rifled musket, on the other hand,

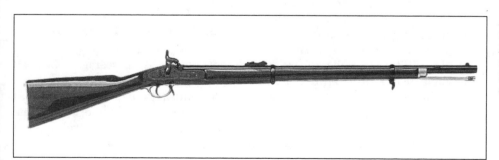

Rifled muskets like this one from the Navy Arms Co., an Enfield Model of 1858, were military in nature, but can serve the big game hunter today, especially in wooded and brushy areas.

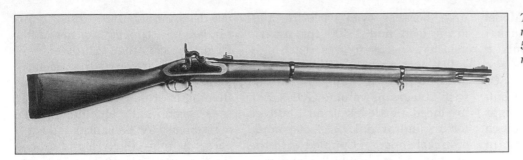

This particular model of Colt's rifled musket is modernized in 50-caliber with conical-shooting rate of twist and a peep sight.

marches to a different drumbeat. These rifled muskets are generally a little more refined than their larger-bore counterparts and are more accurate for longer-range shooting. The Volunteer Rifle and Whitworth Military Target Rifle are the two best examples of 45-caliber rifled muskets that we have readily available today. Either is a magnum in its own right, with apologies for that over-used word. Lyman's latest tests of the Volunteer rifled musket provided the same ballistics appearing in The Gun Digest Blackpowder Loading Manual. Loading the allowed 130 grains of blackpowder behind a bullet in the 475-grain to 490-grain range, muzzle velocity is around 1,500 fps, which certainly overpowers the 45-70 Government, the 45-90 Winchester, and even the impressive Sharps blackpowder cartridges.

The Whitworth Rifled Musket

The Volunteer is interesting ballistically, but the Whitworth is more intriguing historically. It's called a target rifle because it was devised as a long-range instrument. Both the Blue and the Gray used Whitworths during our own Civil War to pick each other off at great distances. The Whitworth also achieved fame as a 1,000-yard match rifle in its time and the replica version can still slap bullets through the bull's-eye at great range. Sir Joseph Whitworth, father of the rifle, was a master toolmaker. He was born in 1803 and died in 1887, in between creating his special shoot-far rifle. Whitworth's claim to fame was a bore of hexagonal configuration, supposedly the voodoo that made bullets group close together. Bullets were cast to match the esoteric bore style. My personal belief is that Sir Joseph's oddball rifling system had precious little to do with its penchant for shooting with admirable accuracy. The Whitworth rifle clustered its bullets so well because the firearm was carefully made and its missiles were properly stabilized in the Whitworth 1:20 rate of twist. Bullets of high sectional density flew point-on all the way to a thousand yards because they had enough initial spin to keep them rotating on their axes. As noted earlier, forward velocity is lost fairly rapidly due to the ravages of the atmosphere, but rotational velocity holds up quite well over long range. So once the Whitworth bullet was stabilized, there was sufficient spin to keep it rotating on its axis at long range, rather than yawing (wobbling) or keyholing (flying sideways) before it reaches a long-range target. Something else that made the Whitworth rifled musket shoot true: good bullets. This factor is not often mentioned in the Whitworth story, but if bullets are not well-cast, accuracy is nothing more than wishful thinking. Rotation or spin overcomes some bullet eccentricity, but when a missile is lopsided, or its base is at the oblique, chances of good groups fall into the slim-to-none category. Without a doubt, Whitworth bullets were well-created in the 19th century, just as they are today.

Ned Roberts, one of the principals behind the 257 Roberts cartridge, was a fan of the Whitworth. He tried various bullets, including a 530-grain design that provided excellent results at the target range. My replica Whitworth test rifle with .451-inch bore and 34-inch barrel weighed in at 9 1/2 pounds. It produced good accuracy with a number of well-cast bullets ranging from 480 to 550 grains. The Volunteer was also tested, providing excellent results in both power and accuracy. Both rifles used musket caps for ignition — English top-hat caps. Mine were RWS brand from Germany. Now we also have musket caps from CCI made in the United States. Musket caps produce good fire and positive ignition, as do all good percussion caps. In the hunting field, Whitworth and Volunteer rifles proved their mettle. Val Forgett took a Wyoming antelope with a Whitworth from his Navy Arms Co., making a good shot at long range. Long sight radius and refined iron sights encouraged solid bullet placement on deer-sized targets out to about 200 yards. While getting close is much preferred, the Whitworth and Volunteer were both accurate and powerful at the 200-yard mark. They also proved field worthy with integral swivels for mounting a sling, plus small-diameter steel ramrods with built-in muzzle protectors and good balance in the hand.

Big Game Effectiveness

Bullet placement is once again on center stage. After seeing a few head of game dropped with 45-caliber rifled muskets, it became clear that the big, solid-lead bullets were capable of tremendous penetration, but not a lot of mushrooming on the target. And so the correct placement of these long lead missiles was more into the shoulder than behind it, especially on thin-skinned, deer-sized animals. Having no direct experience with the 45-caliber rifled musket on moose, bears, or elk, logic suggests that the big lead bullets would be ideal for such game, once again going into the shoulder area. Hunters such as Elmer Keith did quite well on elk, moose, and bears with 45-caliber bullets from blackpowder cartridges that were traveling no faster than projectiles fired from 45-caliber rifled muskets. If anything, the nod goes to the musket, with the exception, of course, of smokeless powder loads in cartridges such as the 45-70 that produce higher velocity than the blackpowder musket can. I did find that shoulder-struck antelope and deer dropped like sacks of spuds. Perhaps a little more meat is lost by a bullet in the shoulder, rather than the chest region, but on the other hand, the game is down swiftly. Good accuracy coupled with good sights made directing bullets a matter of getting a solid stance, taking a clean sight picture with heavy concentration between front sight and target, and then squeezing the trigger.

Legality of the Rifled Musket

Rifled muskets are replicas of old-time guns, and as such should be allowed for any blackpowder-only primitive season. A problem with 45-caliber bullets, however, arises in Colorado, where the projectile cannot be more than twice the length of its diameter. Bullets in the 400- to 600-grain weight range in 45-caliber are definitely more than twice as long as their diameter. These bullets would have to be no more than .9-inches long to qualify for Colorado's strange ruling for blackpowder-only hunts. It's not a safety measure, by the way, because 300 Magnum rifles are legal in the same territory on hunts for the same animals, and they certainly have a longer extreme range than the rifled blackpowder musket. Furthermore, the rifled musket is a front loader in every regard, firing only blackpowder, Pyrodex or other blackpowder substitute, loaded from the front one bullet at a time.

Rifled Musket Triggers

Partly because of its military heritage, the rifled musket is a single-trigger firearm. A proper multiple-lever (double set) trigger breaks

The front sight of the Whitworth is a globe—a perfect little ball of metal.

The rear sight on the Whitworth is capable of long-range adjustment.

Rifled Musket Big Game Hunting Loads

Specifications
Rifle: Navy Arms Whitworth Rifled Musket
Caliber: 45 (.451-inch)
Barrel: 36 inches
Twist: 1:20
Bullet: 490-grain Lyman cast, No. 457121
Load: 90 grains volume FFg (manufacturer's maximum recommendation)
Muzzle Velocity: 1,306 fps
Muzzle Energy: 1,856 foot-pounds
100-yard Velocity: 1,112 fps
100-yard Energy: 1,346 foot-pounds

Specifications
Rifle: Navy Arms Volunteer Rifled Musket
Caliber: 45 (.451-inch)
Barrel: 32 inches
Twist: 1:20
Bullet: 490-grain Lyman cast, No. 457121
Load: 130 grains volume FFg (manufacturer's maximum recommendation)
Muzzle Velocity: 1,474 fps
Muzzle Energy: 2,365 foot-pounds
100-yard Velocity: 1,254 fps
100-yard Energy: 1,711 foot-pounds
Load: 130 grains volume Pyrodex RS
Muzzle Velocity: 1,514 fps
Muzzle Energy: 2,495 foot-pounds
100-yard Velocity: 1,290 fps
100-yard Energy: 1,811 foot-pounds

Specifications
Rifle: Navy Arms Zouave Rifled Musket
Caliber: 58
Barrel: 32 1/2 inches
Twist: 1:48
Bullet: 530-grain .577-inch Minie, Lyman No. 577611
Load: 80 grains volume FFg (manufacturer's maximum recommendation)
Muzzle Velocity: 1,095 fps
Muzzle Energy: 1,411 foot-pounds
100-yard Velocity: 953 fps
100-yard Energy: 1,069 foot-pounds

Specifications
Rifle: Navy Arms Model 1841 Mississippi Rifled Musket
Caliber: 58
Barrel: 33 inches
Twist: 1:48
Bullet: 530-grain .577-inch Minie, No. 577611
Load: 80 grains volume FFg (manufacturer's maximum recommendation)
Muzzle Velocity: 1,102 fps
Muzzle Energy: 1,430 foot-pounds
100-yard Velocity: 959 fps
100-yard Energy: 1,083 foot-pounds

Specifications
Rifle: Navy Arms J.P. Murray Artillery Carbine Rifled Musket
Caliber: 58
Barrel: 23 1/2 inches
Twist: 1:48
Bullet: 530-grain .577-inch Minie, Lyman No. 577611
Load: 70 grains volume FFg (manufacturer's maximum recommendation)
Muzzle Velocity: 980 fps
Muzzle Energy: 1,131 foot-pounds
100-yard Velocity: 882 fps
100-yard Energy: 916 foot-pounds

Specifications
Rifle: Navy Arms 1853 3-Band Enfield Rifled Musket
Caliber: 58
Barrel: 39 inches
Twist: 1:48
Bullet: 505-grain Buffalo Bullet Co.
Load: 100 grains volume Pyrodex RS
Muzzle Velocity: 1,274 fps
Muzzle Energy: 1,820 foot-pounds
100-yard Velocity: 1,101 fps
100-yard Energy: 1,360 foot-pounds

Specifications
Rifle: Navy Arms Parker-Hale Musketoon Rifled Musket
Caliber: 58
Barrel: 24 inches
Twist: 1:48
Bullet: 505-grain Buffalo Bullet Co.
Load: 100 grains volume Pyrodex RS (71.0 grains weight, manufacturer's maximum recommendation)
Muzzle Velocity: 1,226 fps
Muzzle Energy: 1,686 foot-pounds
100-yard Velocity: 1,043 fps
100-yard Energy: 1,220 foot-pounds

Specifications
Rifle: Dixie 1861 Springfield Musket
Caliber: 58
Barrel: 40 inches
Twist: 1:48
Bullet: 505-grain .577-inch cast bullet, Lyman No. 575213 (**Note:** although mold read 505 grains, actual bullet weight was 517 grains)
Load: 60 grains volume FFg (from literature; Dixie offered no maximum recommendation)
Muzzle Velocity: 753 fps
Muzzle Energy: 651 foot-pounds
100-yard Velocity: 676 fps
100-yard Energy: 525 foot-pounds

Specifications
Rifle: Dixie Zouave Carbine
Caliber: 58
Barrel: 26 inches
Twist: 1:56
Bullet: 460-grain Minie, Lyman No. 575213-OS (Old Style)
Load: 100 grains volume Pyrodex RS
Muzzle Velocity: 1,064 fps
Muzzle Energy: 1,157 foot-pounds
100-yard Velocity: 883 fps
100-yard Energy: 797 foot-pounds

Specifications (for comparison purposes only)
Rifle: Dixie Brown Bess Musket
Caliber: 75 (actually 74-caliber bore)
Barrel: 41 3/4 inches
Twist: Smoothbore
Bullet: 494-grain .690-inch round ball
Load: 80 grains volume FFg (from literature; Dixie offered no manufacturer's maximum recommendation)
Muzzle Velocity: 809 fps
Muzzle Energy: 718 foot-pounds
100-yard Velocity: 680 fps
100-yard Energy: 507 foot-pounds

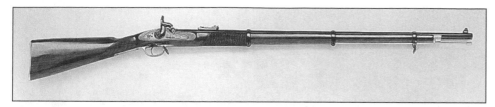

The Whitworth rifle, here in replica form from the Navy Arms Co., was accurate in its day and remains so. It was the choice of certain Confederate snipers during the American Civil War.

cleaner than either the Whitworth or Volunteer triggers. Both of these single-stage (non-set) triggers are acceptable for hunting, and can be tuned for fine target shooting. One example broke at 3 1/2 pounds with minimal creep. Other rifled musket triggers were not that good. These triggers can be improved by a gunsmith, but tampering by the rest of us is not recommended. Judicious filing is needed, and it would be easy to overdo metal removal, creating an unsafe situation.

Loads and Accuracy with Rifled Muskets

Since manufacturers and importers are responsible for the maximum allowable powder charges for the guns they make or sell, shooters must abide by their rulings. Because of large bore size and the consequent volume needed for powder gases to work in 58-caliber rifled muskets, pressures are generally modest, but this does not remove the shooter's responsibility to follow the rules. Rifled 45-caliber muskets do not enjoy quite the same leeway as the 58s when it comes to pressures. Once again, maximum loads must be honored. Powder charges are, as always with blackpowder and its safe substitutes, such as Pyrodex and Clear Shot, created volumetrically with an adjustable powder measure. Accuracy variation between 70-, 80-, and 90-grain powder charges were impossible to detect with either the Whitworth or Volunteer rifles, as well as other rifled muskets that were range tested. A 200-yard maximum range for taking thin-skinned game animals like deer and antelope seems prudent with the Volunteer and Whitworth, while the 58s are much more at

home in brush and timber, where shots are much closer. The trajectory of heavy, ballistically inefficient 58-caliber bullets at modest velocities does not make for a 200-yard big-game hunting range. Even with the Whitworth, off-the-bench groups averaged 4 to 6 inches center-to-center for three-shot strings at 200 yards. This wasn't because the rifle wasn't capable of doing better, but even good iron sights are still no match for scopes.

The Whitworth definitely competed at 1,000 yards, so its inherent accuracy is not deniable. It also claimed the lives of Civil War soldiers at incredible distances. Regardless of these facts, however, the hunter should always stalk for the best possible shot, rather than shooting from afar. Also, gaining a good rest in the field is recommended, if only across a log using a hat or other garment for a forend pad. Accuracy with standard conical bullets was good in both rifles. No hexagonal projectiles were fired in the Whitworth. Following benchrest tests with these guns, several standard rifled muskets were tried, along with a smoothbore Brown Bess, mainly for the sake of curiosity. Actually, I learned more than a little bit about smoothbore shooting from shooting the Brown Bess. The 75-caliber smoothbore was capable of placing its big round ball into a 6-inch bull's eye at 50 yards, but that was it. I never got good enough with the gun to fill me with big-game hunting confidence. Up close, however, there is no doubt that it could do the job on big game with proper ball placement.

Light vs. Heavy Powder Charges

Light powder charges were OK for fooling around with rifled mus-

kets, and they did prove accurate, but definitely not powerful. For example, the 1861 Springfield rifle was not given a maximum powder charge recommendation by the manufacturer, and the only sanctioned load I found was 60 grains of FFg, which reduced the rifle's ballistic effectiveness to popgun status, even with a 58-caliber bullet. If the Springfield can truly handle no greater powder charge, I'd eliminate it from the field as a big-game taker. On the other hand, light powder charges provided decent close-range deer hunting ballistics in 58-caliber rifled muskets. For example, the Musketoon with a 505-grain Buffalo Bullet projectile and 100 grains of powder for more than 1,100 fps MV, or the same volume Pyrodex for 1,226 fps MV and a muzzle energy close to 1,700 foot-pounds, produced enough remaining energy to top half a short ton at 100 yards -- more than sufficient for deer.

Conclusions

The Murray Carbine with 70 grains of FFg puts out enough power for close range on deer-sized game with a 58-caliber missile, but the Zouave certainly provided more potency. The Musketoon, with its handy 24-inch barrel, would make a good choice for brush and timber deer hunting loaded with 100 grains of Pyrodex RS and a 505-grain 58-caliber Buffalo Bullet leaving the muzzle at 1,226 fps MV for a muzzle energy rated at 1,686 foot-pounds. While the energy figure is nothing to shout about, a thumb-sized missile topping 1,200 fps will ventilate a broadside whitetail buck cleanly. A factory-recommended charge of 80 grains FFg gave the Mississippi Rifles enough power for game up to moose and elk

The Whitworth rifled musket was accurate in its own time frame, winning 1,000-yard matches, a choice of certain Confederate snipers. Today, it remains accurate in replica form, this one from the Navy Arms Co.

size at close range with proper bullet placement. The test bullet was a 530-grain Lyman cast from mold No. 577611. I found the long-barreled Zouave on par with its shorter brother because the former was given a 100-grain FFg maximum load, while the latter was allowed 80 grains of the same fuel for no apparent reason other than the manufacturer's decision. The 32 1/2-inch Zouave with 80 grains of FFg was a ballistic twin to the Zouave Carbine with 100 grains of FFg for hunting.

Final Choices

The rifled musket is one more viable choice for the blackpowder shooter, not only for big-game hunting, but also for target work. While the blackpowder silhouette game is officially restricted to breechloaders, the Whitworth would hold its own in such a match, while shorter rifled muskets are workable in any setting where shots are close, as hunting wild boar or whitetails in thick cover. The Volunteer rifle and Whitworth are both overall winners in brush, timber, or the open with their long bullets at decent muzzle velocities. The military-developed, rifled musket is blue collar all the way, honest and hard-working, at home in briar, bramble, cat-claw jungle, black timber, and thick brush, reliable and unlikely to fail after a minor conflict with the terrain. These long guns will never threaten the tremendous popularity of the modern muzzleloader as in-lines continue developing more and more momentum, but for some hunters in certain environments, these rugged rifles could be just about ideal.

Chapter 34

THE BLACKPOWDER CARTRIDGE RIFLE

TWO BLACKPOWDER cartridge rifles have enjoyed a serious comeback upon the modern scene: the single-shot breechloader, to the forefront for the challenging silhouette game, and the lever-action repeater, pushed onward by Cowboy Action Shooting (read more about both games in another chapter). The concern here centers upon the guns, beginning with the breechloader, a rifle style made famous by the buffalo runners of the late 19th century who are credited with downing as many as 60 million bison over the vast western half of America. That, of course, never happened, being a mathematical impossibility, as touched on below. Yet the number killed was shamefully high and the breech-loading gun was definitely deadly on the beleaguered shaggy. The single-shot rifle was made possible by self-contained ammunition, the metallic cartridge, which combined in one unit the three essentials present in the muzzleloader: a bullet, powder to drive the bullet, and some form of igniter to set off that powder charge. Instead of the breech of the firearm containing the powder and bullet, with a source of ignition leading from cap or priming powder into the breech, the breech was now replaced with a metal case holding all three elements: bullet, powder, and a primer seated in the head, which was nothing more than an altered percussion cap. The obvious beauty of the cartridge was convenience in carrying pre-loaded ammunition ready for use and the speed in which repeat shots could be made. Today, along with playing the silhouette game, a number of hunters carry single-shot blackpowder breechloaders into the field, not always loaded with blackpowder, however.

The Blackpowder Single-Shot Cartridge Rifle

Dozens of different blackpowder single-shot cartridge rifles found their way into the 19th century. This is not the forum for discussing each one, because that would take a book of its own. The two that stand boldest against the backdrop of current American shooting are the Sharps falling block and Remington rolling block. Other wonderful single-shot designs are also offered, and will be touched on, such as the fine Winchester High Wall and the Ballard. But the Sharps and Remington get the most play because, according to record, they were the most popular during the latter part of the 19th century when buffalo runners, as they preferred to be called, roamed the vast plains in search of shaggies. A little bit of history about the sad bison slaughter is in order also.

Blackpowder Cartridge Rifles and the Bison

The Gun that Shaped American Destiny. That's what Martin Rywell called the Sharps rifle in his 1979 Pioneer Press book. Rywell's title is right on the money. The Sharps rifle did help to shape American destiny, filling the hands of countless pioneers trekking westward. According to Rywell, an Indian gentleman by the name of American Horse said, "Emigrants passing up the South Platte River to Colorado between 1858 and 1865 were largely armed with Sharps

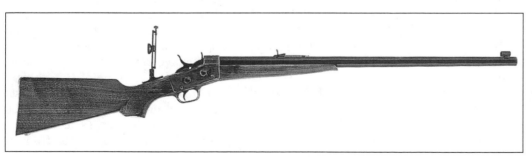

The Remington Rolling Block was made by the thousands, including in smokeless powder cartridges, such as the 7mm Mauser. This copy is from Cabela's. It's chambered for the 45-70 Government round.

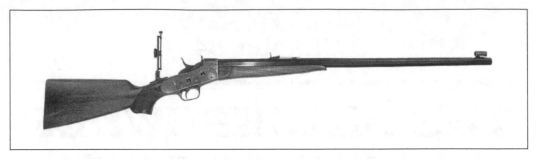

With Vernier tang sight installed, this Black Hills Rolling Block rifle from Dixie Gun Works is ready for some long-range shooting. It comes in calibers 40-65 Winchester or 45-70 Government. Dixie calls it a faithful reproduction of the original rifle used in 1874 during the famous shooting match between the Irish and Americans.

military rifles." The Sharps found its way all over the west, and of course played a role in the American Civil War, where almost 100,000 rifles and carbines served Union troops, according to Rywell. Col. Hiram Berdan's Sharpshooters finally got their Sharps rifles in 1862, using them during the Seven Days Battles of June and July of that same year with devastating effect.

The Sharps rifle, along with the Remington rolling block, is also credited with wiping out up to 60 million bison over an area that covers half of the United States -- a place so vast that even today with vehicle travel it would take months to see only a particle of it. Of course, the few hundred to as many as 10,000 hunters (nobody knows the figure) could not slay even 12 million bison (low figure) in only a few years, let alone 60 million (high figure), which some say roamed the plains.

Picture the professional buffalo hunter traveling in mule-drawn wagons and on foot killing that many animals, plus taking time out while skinners removed the hides. Regardless of this falsehood, it is true that many factions did want the bison out of the way. The Army did, because the Plains Indian warrior depended on the shaggy for meat and even shelter. The railroad did, because running a train through a buffalo herd was no way to cross America. Settlers did, because bison were all over the land they wanted to build on.

So the shoot was on, which was a lousy thing to do. But think about it. If you turned a pack of full-time modern hunters loose today with four-wheel drive trucks, let alone mules and wagons, they wouldn't stand a chance of killing up to 60 million breeding bison over countless acres of U.S. landscape, not to mention British Columbia, Alberta, and Saskatchewan, additional bison ranges in the 1800s. The United States Congress of 1870, according to one author, debated giving up on the Far West because many of the members felt a war with the Plains Indian could not be won. But if the bison were wiped out, then what? No bison, no Plains Indian. So shooting buffs was encouraged by the government.

But buffalo runners, "sportsmen," settlers, soldiers, and travelers west didn't come close to killing up to 60 million bison in the few years the animal was hunted without mercy on his home ground. Something a lot smaller than a bullet finally did the trick. It happened when cattle were introduced into the west. Anyone who underestimates the power of a tiny microbe or virus should consider that the black plague wiped out one-third of the entire population of Europe in the 1500s, while Spanish influenza dropped more people shortly after World War I than all the bombs and bullets spent in that conflict. But all of this is beside the point, although important to understanding an important piece of American history. The present interest is the fact that the Sharps was one of the two rifles that many buff runners carried on their mission impossible — to rid the west of the shaggy.

The Greatness of the Sharps Rifle

Shooting the Sharps cartridge rifle was challenging, of course. The rifle provided only one shot at a time with blackpowder demanding regular cleanup after shooting, not only of the rifle, but also the cartridge cases. But the rifle was still fired much faster than a muzzleloader and the Sharps really wasn't that hard to take care of. It cleaned from the breech end, after all. Col. Frank Mayer, a buff runner, wrote of flushing the bore with cold water, followed by urine, supposedly to introduce a touch of acidity, with a hot water rinse afterward. Also to its credit, the Sharps rifle was offered in a huge array of worthy cartridges, far too many to list here. And it was truly a long-range rifle, capable of winning 1,000-yard shooting matches, as well as dropping buffalo at several hundred yards, especially when topped off with German-made target scopes. It also came in many styles, including a special Creedmoor version for long-range target work (and hunting). A clue to some of the Sharps' great blackpowder cartridges exists in a catalog that shows 40-100 through 50-100 "brass, centre fire re-loading shells" running from 1-

11/16 inches through 2-1/2 inches in length, costing from $22 to $30 per thousand. Low blackpowder pressure was easy on brass, too, and the Sharps Co. promised that "with proper care in re-loading" a cartridge case could be reloaded up to 500 times, provided that each case was cleaned after use to prevent deterioration. The Sharps was great, all right, so good that it can still get the job done today, not only at the silhouette match or ringing gongs in the distance, but also on big game.

Replica Sharps Rifles

There are a number of replica Sharps rifles on the market today. Montana Armory (C. Sharps) Co. of Big Timber, Mont., (see Directory) continues to make Sharps rifles in numerous styles and a variety of chamberings, such as the venerable 45-70 Government, as well as the 40-65 Winchester and 45-120 Sharps round. John Schofftstall, a blackpowder single-shot rifle expert, got the ball rolling. He was far more than a mere fan of the firearm. His dedication to making superb single-shot breechloaders, mostly Sharps models, but also a New Model 1885 High Wall, gives the modern shooter an opportunity to enjoy old-time single-shot blackpowder cartridge breechloaders that shoot well. He and his men accomplished a great deal of worthwhile testing of blackpowder cartridges, too, and his data pamphlet is a fine source of information on the subject. Sharps imports include

Italian-made models from Dixie Gun Works, Cabela's, Navy Arms, and other sources. Cimarron has a Billy Dixon 1874 Sharps rifle in calibers 40-65 and 45-70.

The Remington Rolling Block

Many buffalo hunters preferred the Sharps, but others leaned toward the Remington rolling block breechloader. Joseph Rider is credited with the rolling-block design built by Remington. In fact, some models were called Remington-Riders. The rolling-block principle itself was hardly new, but Rider saw its full potential. Flobert's rolling-block design came very early in gun history with its pivoting breechblock. Rather than a breech sliding up and down (the falling block), the rolling block's breech did just that — it rotated. The action was quite strong for its time, as proved by the fact that it later held smokeless powder rounds such as the 7mm Mauser. W.W. Greener wrote about the Remington-Rider in his revised 1910 edition of The Gun and its Development. He said:

"The rifle was tried at Wimbledon as long ago as 1866, and attracted considerable attention at that time, in consequence of the extraordinary rapidity with which it was loaded and fired; as many as fifty-one shots were discharged within three minutes. . . . The mechanism consists essentially of two pieces, being the breech-piece and extractor, and the other the hammer breech-bolt. This breech-

piece and hammer-bolt each work upon a strong centre pin."

In function, the breechblock rolls back; a cartridge is inserted directly into the breech, and then the breechblock is rolled forward again to lock the action. The significant factor here is the hammer, which falls down into a slot within the breechblock itself. The Remington rolling block remains available to this day, just like the Sharps. Navy Arms has long championed the continuance of the design with several well-constructed replicas. Furthermore, Remington brought the rifle back in two models, a No. 1 Rolling Block Mid-Range Sporter, and a No. 1 Rolling Block Silhouette rifle. Also highly worthy of note is a special Remington rolling block rifle from the Schuetzen Gun Co. This rifle is custom built by R.P. (Richard) McKinney, who was once the top gunsmith for the U.S. Army Marksmanship Unit Custom Shop, Montana Armory, etc. The model tested had wood that goes beyond handsome to another realm, and workmanship was impeccable. Chambered for 45-70 Government, the McKinney Remington Rolling Block -- with a 28-inch, straight-octagon, Douglas barrel -- shot as good as it looked. Considering iron sights, plus trajectory of the 45-70 Government round, this rifle would take big game out to 150 yards with practice. My own shooting with the rifle clanged bullets off a 2-foot-square gong at 300 meters. McKinney's custom rolling block is the J.P. Gemmer model, incidentally.

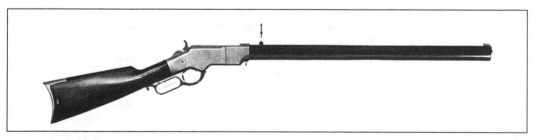

The Henry rifle, patented by B. Tyler Henry of the New Haven Arms Co. when Oliver Winchester was president, came along in 1860. It made considerable impact because of its fast action and large capacity magazine. Today it's offered by several companies in 44-40 Winchester and 45 Colt.

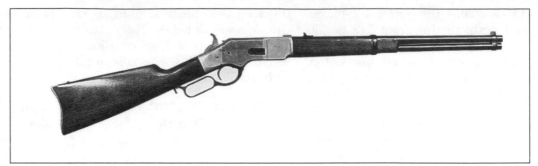

Another famous rifle in its day, the Winchester 1866 remains popular today. Available in replica from several companies.

McKinney's rolling block is proof of the design's continued worth, for no one would build so fine a piece on a poor action. Harris Gunworks has an Antietam Sharps Rifle in 40-65 Winchester or 45-70 Government, made in the United States and offered with special long-range sights. Cimarron also has a Rolling Block Creedmoor.

The Model 1885 High Wall

This is another fine single-shot blackpowder cartridge breech loading rifle in replica form with all the old-time nostalgia left intact. It deserves mention because it's a handy-toting rifle worthy of the big game field as well as the target range. Today, there are several models available. Browning has a Model 1885 High Wall Single-Shot Rifle offered in modern calibers as well as the 45-70 Government round. The same company has its BPCR (Black Powder Cartridge Rifle), similar to the High Wall, except the ejector system and shell deflector have been removed. This rifle is chambered for the 40-65 and the 45-70, also offered in a special Creedmoor model with 34-inch barrel and wind gauge, caliber 45-90. Another Browning 1885 single-shot is the Traditional Hunter with modern calibers, plus the once very popular 38-55 Winchester. Cimarron's 1885 High Wall Rifle is prepared in four chamberings as this is written: 38-55 Winchester, 40-65 Winchester, 45-70 Government, and 45-90 Winchester. This is a replica of the Winchester High Wall of 1885 rifle, a John Moses Browning creation. The Navy Arms version of the Model 1885 single-shot rifle comes in 45-70 with barrels either round or octagon, and target sights optional.

Modern Ballards

Also worthy of mention are the Ballard rifles of current manufacture. These nice rifles are fully machined and carbon case-colored like the originals. Furthermore, they're legal for official blackpowder cartridge silhouette matches because of the time period of the Ballard and its single-shot blackpowder cartridge design. The company, in fact, builds rifles for specific matches, not only blackpowder silhouette, but others such as the Montana Long Range match. Modern-made Ballards are available from Ballard Rifle & Cartridges LLC in Cody, Wyo. The rifle is now provided in a wide variety of chamberings and configurations. Models include the Ballard No. 5 Pacific Single-Shot, the No. 7 Long Range Rifle, and the No. 8 Union Hill Rifle. Among cartridge choices are the 32-40 Winchester, 38-55 Winchester, 40-65 Winchester, 40-70 Single Shot, 45-70 Government, 45-90, 45-110, and others. The No. 5 has double-set triggers and an underbarrel wiping rod. Special long-range tang sights are available from the company, along with various cartridges. The firm specializes in obsolete brass, and carries a complete line of sights to match the rifles.

The Lever Guns

A wide range of lever-action blackpowder cartridge rifles graces the marketplace today. Uberti's 1860 Henry replica brings back the first truly successful lever gun on the market, partly because it shot a "real" cartridge, not the caseless ammo design of the Volcanic. The cartridge was no great shakes: the 44 Henry Rimfire with a case under an inch long. Depending upon the literature, the powder charge is recorded as 24, 25, or 26 grains (blackpowder of course). The bullet weighed 215 grains (216 grains in some sources). This was the rifle you "loaded on Sunday and shot all week," because it had a capacity of 15 rounds. While the Henry rimfire is today considered a pipsqueak, it was a lot better than a sharp stick. Its bullet moving at about the speed of sound was not terribly bettered by the 44-40 Winchester cartridge that followed, although at least the 44-40 could be reloaded. Winchester liked the cartridge designer well enough to put an H on the back of 22 rimfire ammo for ages — H for Henry. Uberti's copy is chambered for the 44-40 or 45 Colt. Cabela's has an 1866 Winchester replica, the first lever-action repeater to bear the company name.

The list goes on and on. Many Model 1892 Winchester copies are on the market from a number of sources. The one tested for this work was the Navy Arms version with a 24-inch barrel. Offered in 44-40 Winchester and 45 Colt, the latter was chosen to match a 45 Colt Navy Arms replica of the Bisley revolver, providing two firearms using the same cartridge. An array of commercial ammunition was fired for chronograph results in the Model 1892. Federal Classic ammo with a 225-grain bullet got 984 fps in the rifle, 620 fps in the revolver. The same bullet weight in one Winchester load delivered 912 fps in the rifle, 663 fps in the Colt Bisley. Winchester's 225-grain Silvertip bullet did likewise in the rifle, but right at 700 fps in the revolver. All loads were terrifically low in standard deviation, including the above, plus Hornady's Cowboy Action, CCI Blazer, Remington, and Cor-Bon. Standard deviations as low as a couple feet per second occurred many times. A handload from Hornady brought a bit more power in the rifle, pushing a 255-grain lead bullet at 1,100 fps MV. This rifle was absolutely enjoyable to shoot.

Navy Arms Co., Cabela's, Cimarron, E.M.F., and other companies import lever-action repeaters that started their careers shooting blackpowder cartridges loaded with blackpowder. The 1873 Winchester has enjoyed a significant return to stardom in replication, along with several Henry models. Cimarron sells a Long Range Model 1873 chambered for the 44-40 Winchester and the 45 Colt. The octagonal

barrel runs a full 30 inches, bringing overall length to 48 inches. Interestingly, this rifle is offered also in 38-40 Winchester. A tang sight is optional.

The good news is that in spite of companies changing what they may sell among the lever-action replicas from the past, these blackpowder cartridge rifles will continue for a very long time to come. What one company drops, another seems to pick up. For example, Navy Arms came along with several models of the Henry rifle, including iron frames, color case-hardened iron frames, brass frames, a military model, a carbine, a trapper version with 16 1/2-inch barrel, even a custom engraved Henry in four grades (A with about 25 percent coverage of the receiver, B with 35 percent coverage and C with 50 percent coverage).

Blackpowder Cartridge Power

Obvious from the above report, there are plenty of single-shot blackpowder cartridge rifles on the market today, so it makes sense to glance at a few of the cartridges available, especially for the single-

shot breechloader fan. There are dozens of rounds offered, from the little blackpowder 25-20 to the big 50-140 Sharps. Old Western Scrounger (see Directory) offers many loaded and ready to fire. While this large number does not compare with the hundreds of different cartridges available in the 19th century, it is sufficient. The following list is a mere wedge out of the pie. Cartridge history is not included in this brief roundup because there are many books devoted to this subject, including loading manuals. Cartridges of the World, available from Krause Publications, is an excellent source of information (see Blackpowder Library).

The 32-40 Winchester

Actually, this was more a Bullard, Ballard, Remington round in the 19th century, but the Winchester 32-40 configuration survived and is still fired. Cases can be formed from 30-30 brass, which gives the round an edge for reloaders. Some marksmen consider this a match/target cartridge. The round was well liked by the old-time Schuetzen shooter, especially

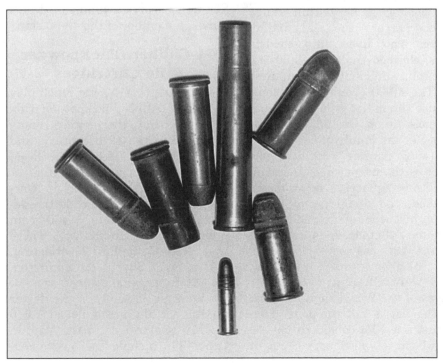

There were many dozens of different blackpowder cartridges on the scene, including rimfires, as well as centerfires. These are a few examples, with a 22 Long Rifle rimfire tossed in for comparison (bottom).

with 190- to 200-grain bullets. Although not a powerhouse, the 32-40 is definitely capable of cleanly harvesting deer-sized game, especially in the hands of an expert rifleman/hunter. A 165-grain bullet achieves 1,360 fps MV with 35 grains of FFFg blackpowder, and about 100 fps less with a 190-grain bullet and 35 grains of FFg. Fine accuracy is the byword for the 32-40 along with mild recoil. Its shortcoming is lack of bullet weight compared with the cartridges that follow. But that's of importance mainly to big-game hunters.

38-55 Winchester

This round fires bullets in the 300-grain class at about 1,250 to 1,300 fps using 45 grains of FFg or FFFg blackpowder. The 38-55 Winchester was popular for many years. It was considered by some a better round than the 30-30 for deer and even larger game. Today, the 38-55, loaded with blackpowder, is applied as a fine target round, as well as a hunting number. No hunter need hesitate about going into the brush with a 38-55 for deer, especially when loaded with a good lead projectile, such as the 305-grain bullet from a SAECO mold. Hunting yes, but the 38-55's claim to fame today remains its penchant for accuracy. It's also mild compared with larger-bore blackpowder cartridges that burn more powder behind heavier projectiles.

40-65 Winchester

This is a dandy cartridge that I became acquainted with when testing a prototype of a new Sharps rifle, the Antietam, that at the time was not yet on the market. The test bullet was a 390-grain lead conical. It took off at 1,300 fps MV in front of 60 grains of GOEX Cartridge grade blackpowder. The 40-65 Winchester is pleasant to shoot and has become a strong candidate for silhouette games. It is also, as revealed above, now offered in many single-shot rifles. The near

400-grain bullet will knock the ram silhouette over at long range with proper hits. Within reasonable range, a hunter has no reason to lack confidence in this cartridge for big game. Although the round is rather mild-mannered, it delivers a good-sized bullet with high penetration potential. An added bonus: Cases can be formed from 45-70 brass. Old Western Scrounger carries newly loaded ammo for the 40-65 with a 260-grain, flat-nose bullet and designated as a blackpowder load.

40-70 Sharps BN (Bottleneck)

This is simply another nice blackpowder cartridge. Tests show no clear advantage over the 40-65 Winchester in terms of muzzle velocity, bullet for bullet, but obviously a few grains more powder push the bullet a little faster. The test rifle put a 330-grain bullet downrange at 1,350 fps MV with 70 grains FFg.

The 40-90s

The 40-90s are excellent blackpowder cartridges, and while currently not as popular as the 45-70 or the 40-65, they make good silhouette shooters and would be reliable on big game within range. Frank Mayer, the old buffalo hunter who lived into modern times, claimed that his 40-90 was more than sufficient for bison hunting. The 40-90 group makes sense because the bullet is heavy enough for most work, including silhouettes. Yet the family of 40s with 90 grains of powder provides good power with modest recoil. Facing the issue squarely, no romance included, the 40-90 group is not magic, just a bit more fuel behind the same bullets loaded into the 40-65. The 19th century was packed with blackpowder rounds, and many were different 40-90s. Cartridges of the World shows several, but the list is not complete. Here are just a few for consideration: 40-90 Bullard, 40-90 Sharps Straight,

40-90 Sharps Bottleneck, 40-90 Ideal, and the 40-90 Ballard, not to be confused with the Bullard.

Bullet weights vary quite a bit in the 40-caliber blackpowder cartridge category. The lightweights weigh around 260 grains, as loaded in Old Western Scrounger 40-65 ammo, while the heavier missiles are in the 500-grain class. Incidentally, the 40-90 Bullard and 40-90 Ballard are about opposites in design. The Ballard is long and lean, while the Bullard is bottle-necked and squat. A velocity of 1,427 fps with a 370-grain bullet is noted for the Ballard, while the Bullard shows a 300-grain bullet at 1,569 fps MV. A 400-grain bullet shoved by a case full of Fg blackpowder puts the 40-90-class cartridge solidly into the world of silhouette shooting and big game hunting, all without undue recoil. For example, chronograph tests with a 40-90 Sharps Bottleneck measured more than 1,300 fps MV with 85 grains Fg blackpowder and a 425-grain bullet. Again, energy figures as normally computed don't praise this load (less than 1,600 foot-pounds at the muzzle), but the big lead bullet packs the mail all the same. There was also a 40-82 Winchester -- Old Western Scrounger carries ammo -- that's almost a member of the 40-90 clan.

44-Caliber Blackpowder Rifle Cartridges

Currently, there's not much play on the 44-caliber blackpowder rifle cartridge, but there were many available in the 19th century, and they were well liked. The 44-60 Sharps fired a 396-grain bullet at 1,250 fps MV, according to Cartridges of the World, while the 44-70 Maynard pushed a 430-grain projectile at 1,310 fps MV. There was a 44-75 Ballard Everlasting, plus a 44-77 Sharps & Remington, a 44-90 Remington, as well as a 44-90 Sharps Bottleneck, the latter driving a 520-grain bullet at 1,270 fps MV (Cartridges of the World). Other 44s include the 44-95 Pea-

Although it arrived too late on the scene to be used in the buffalo hunt, the 50-140-700 Sharps is with us today. Its history may be confused, but there is no question of its power. Here it's shown with a 30-06 Springfield round for comparison.

body "What Cheer" and the 44-100 by Remington and Ballard. The former is historically interesting because it was chambered in the Remington-Hepburn, or No. 3 Long-Range Creedmoor rifle (Remington rolling block), so the 44-100 Remington was designed as a match round from the start.

The 45-70 Government

There were many 45-caliber, single-shot blackpowder cartridge rifles around in the 19th century. These included, among others, the 45-75 Winchester, 45-75 Sharps Straight, 45-100 Ballard, 45-100 Remington, and others. But of the 45s, only the 45-70 Government remains on the standard factory list to this very hour. The round is so important to blackpowder silhouette shooting, as well as hunting, that I've given it its own story. See Chapter 45 for more on this amazing cartridge.

The 45-90 Winchester

This is, for all practical purposes, a longer 45-70. It was introduced in 1886. Claims were made that the extra 20 grains of powder did great things for the 45-90 over the 45-70.

More powerful, yes, but in tests, the 45-90 did not blow the 45-70 away. Nonetheless, it's a good cartridge, able to push 500-grain bullets at about the same muzzle velocity as 400-grain bullets in the 45-70.

The 45-90 2 4/10 Sharps

This 45-caliber blackpowder cartridge is commonly called a 45-90 today. Montana Armory shows the date of introduction as June 8, 1877, by the Sharps Rifle Co. It was touted as a fine long-range target round, credited with winning 1,000-yard matches as late as 1900. A target load is listed as 85 grains of Fg blackpowder with a 500-grain bullet at 1,226 fps MV.

The 45-110 Sharps

This cartridge, also known as the 45-110-2 7/8 Sharps, is credited as being the largest 45-caliber cartridge originally designed for the Sharps rifle. It was chambered in the Sharps 1874 model for the buffalo hunter who wanted plenty of long-range power. Montana Armory shows the cartridge developing 1,360 fps MV with a 500-grain bullet and plenty of accuracy. A lighter 430-grain bullet is listed at 1,430

fps MV, with a lighter-yet 325-grain missile at 1,596 fps MV, all burning 110 grains of Fg blackpowder.

The 45-120 Sharps

This fine cartridge remains well received today, although it is not the round of choice among serious blackpowder cartridge silhouette shooters. The 45-70 Government holds that honor. Nonetheless, the 45-120 remains a good cartridge. There is a problem, however, not with the round itself, but with its history. Students of the Sharps who have studied the company's rounds as well as its rifles insist that Mayer and others who touted the 45-120 as an important cartridge among bison slayers were incorrect. These individuals say -- and feel they can prove -- that this cartridge was not widely in use until after the era of the bison hunt in America. Cartridges of the World notes that the 45-120 was introduced in 1878-79 for the Sharps-Borchardt rifle, "though there is no documentary evidence that the Sharps factory offered rifles in this caliber." John Schoffstall of Montana Armory states that, "Although never offered in the original Sharps rifles, the 45-120-3 1/4 Sharps is the big 45-caliber of the New Sharps line." He confirms his own statement with the clear remark, "The 45-120-3 1/4 was never chambered in an original Sharps rifle."

In spite of lineage problems and historical pitfalls, the 45-120 is a good one. Also known as the 45-120-550, it's a powerful number. The latter nomenclature, from blackpowder days, means 45 caliber with 120 grains of blackpowder and a 550-grain bullet. My own test of the 45-120 in a modern-made Sharps rifle was entirely satisfactory.

I tested the cartridge under the name 45-120-3 1/4, which was another blackpowder designation, this one meaning 45 caliber, 120 grains of blackpowder, with a case length of 3 1/4 inches. A 480-grain Lyman bullet from Lyman mold No. 457121 listed as 490 grains weighed 480 grains in No. 2 alloy. A charge of 110 grains GOEX Fg blackpowder propelled this 480-grain bullet at 1,482 fps MV for a muzzle energy of 2,341 foot-pounds. Remaining velocity at 100 yards was 1,230 fps for an energy of 1,613 foot-pounds.

This sort of ballistic authority is obviously strong enough for any big game on the continent, considering the heft of the bullet. Furthermore, the fine Sharps replica rifle was accurate.

On calm days, putting five shots into a 6-inch bull's eye at 200 yards from the bench posed no problem. Mayer claimed that, "At distances above 500 and up to 1,000 yards, the 45-120-550 Sharps with patched bullets is absolutely unsurpassed by any weapon known to man."

Overstatement, of course, but not an entirely outlandish claim. Its only problem was that if the Sharps was never chambered for the 45-120, which rifle was Mayer speaking of concerning the use of the round on buffalo?

The 50-70-1 1/3 Sharps

This round was also known as the 50-70 Government and it apparently saw much use for hunting in the 1800s. Tested in a New Model 1875 Sharps Sporting Rifle, the cartridge delivered 1,071 fps MV with a 500-grain bullet and 70 grains GOEX Fg blackpowder.

While this is not a lot of bullet speed, it does amount to almost 1,300 foot-pounds of energy. A 528-grain lead bullet left the muzzle at 1,051 fps MV for 1,320 foot-pounds of muzzle energy.

The 50-70 Government was a popular cartridge in the 1870s and 1880s.

The 50-140 Sharps

There were many 50s in use in the 19th century. Passing over the rest, the 50-140 commands attention. This was a truly big round, and it was not an original Sharps chambering. In fact, the cartridge appeared circa 1884, three years after the Sharps company no longer manufactured rifles. This was also the last year of widespread buffalo hunting.

The cartridge was known as the 50-140-3 1/4, as well as the 50-140-700, the latter for a 700-grain bullet. Tested with various 50-caliber bullets, the Big Fifty drove a 638-grain NEI-cast lead projectile at 1,413 fps MV with 140 grains of Pyrodex CTG grade powder (no longer available) for a muzzle energy of 2,829 foot-pounds — in the realm with muzzle energies associated with big-game rifle cartridges.

Today, the 50-140 Sharps is chambered in a currently-manufactured Sharps rifle, the Model 1874 Long Range Express from Montana Armory.

Handloading the Blackpowder Cartridge

This in-depth topic is best handled in books written for the sole purpose of loading blackpowder cartridge ammunition. For present purposes, only a few skeletal notes are provided. For in-depth information, books dealing directly with blackpowder cartridge handloading are a must, such as *SPG Lubricants BP Cartridge Reloading Primer* by Mike Venturino and Steve Garb, a 1992 publication from Cal-Graf, POB 885, Big Timber, Mont., 59011.

This book, only 116 pages long, is packed with worthwhile information, such as Mike Venturino's introduction, which explains the merits of single-shot blackpowder cartridge rifles.

Chapter 1 provides the basics in loading technique, dealing with bullets, lead alloys, bullet sizing, custom bullet molds, primers, powders, wads, the cartridge case, drop tubes, bullet seating, and cartridge case cleanup (with hot soapy water). Steve Garb tells about "Reloading the Match Cartridge" in one chapter.

A number of loads are explained for many cartridges, beginning with the 32-40 — introduced in 1884 by Ballard as a Schuetzen round. Later the 32-40 saw action in lever-action Marlins and Winchesters. Interesting information, but of more importance are all the specifications noted for the cartridge, as well as a good sample load. The 38-55 is treated to two sample loads in this text. The 38-56 has one.

Particulars are interesting. The 38-56, for example, is shown with a 310-grain Hoch custom bullet, 1:30 ratio tin/lead alloy, bullet sized to .377-inch diameter, 55 grains FFg blackpowder, Federal 215 Magnum primer, and a wad made from a waxed milk carton. Velocity came out at 1,308 fps. The test rifle was a Winchester High Wall with 30-inch barrel, 1:18 rate of twist.

FIVE SIMPLE NOTES ON BLACKPOWDER CARTRIDGE HANDLOADING

1. A Case Full of Powder

It is common practice to load large blackpowder cartridges such as the 45-70 Government with very small charges of smokeless powder. While it is just as difficult to prove as the short-started bullet warning sounded often in this book, the fact is, some rifles have been destroyed with light smokeless powder charges in large old-time cartridges. In one case, a shooter experienced a catastrophic failure with a Sharps replica in 45-70, with the rifle blowing up and the shooter suffering a badly injured left hand. While approved smokeless powder loads should cause no problem, shooting the blackpowder cartridge with a case full of blackpowder or Pyrodex leaves no air space. This 100 percent load density condition also produces good accuracy.

2. The Blackpowder Powder Measure

A regular powder measure must not be used to meter out blackpowder or any blackpowder substitute. That's because static electricity or the simple friction of metallic working parts created in these measures (which were developed for smokeless powder, not blackpowder) could possibly result in detonation.

Now there are special metering devices for blackpowder. Lyman's 55 Classic Black Powder Measure is one. It was developed especially for silhouette and cowboy action shooters. The measure features a non-static reservoir and non-sparking internal parts.

Another one is Hornady's special measure, called the Static-Resistant Black Powder Measure with aluminum hopper and cap, plus a brass metering unit calibrated in 5-grain increments to 50 grains and 10-grain increments to 100 grains.

3. How to Get More Blackpowder in the Case

The reason old-time powder charges for certain cartridge cases cannot readily fit into these cases is the change of design through time. The old balloon-head case actually had a greater interior powder capacity than the modern case because the head was thinner. These weaker cases were replaced with new ones having more metal in the head, and therefore stronger and safer.

That's why it's difficult, for example, to get 70-grains of Fg blackpowder into the 45-70 case, which was originally intended to hold that much propellant when the bullet was seated.

More blackpowder or Pyrodex can, however, be settled into a case through the use of a drop-tube, an old and widespread practice. The drop tube is just that: a long tube. Powder is funneled in from the top, and by allowing the charge to slowly trickle down the tube and into the case, the charge is distributed evenly into a compact column.

An example of a commercial drop tube is Lyman's 24-inch Powder Drop Tube. It ties in with the Lyman 55 Classic Black Powder Measure noted above.

4. Use Magnum Primers

Shooters who live and breathe blackpowder cartridge loading, such as Mike Venturino, taught the rest of us that magnum primers do a better job in larger blackpowder cartridge than milder ones. I have since enjoyed success with the Federal 215 large rifle primer and similar magnum primers. The exact reason for this fact is slippery, since blackpowder ignites readily, with the usual No. 11 percussion cap providing plenty of spark to get the show on the road. But magnum primers it is.

5. Paper-Patched Bullets

Paper-patched bullets have shown good accuracy in personal tests, and I understand why others have recommended them in the past. However, this factor does not necessarily show up across the board with every cartridge, and testing of each rifle is needed, because fine accuracy can also be proven with plain lead bullets. The blackpowder cartridge fan, however, should consider paper-patched bullets as viable and worth trying, because they are both.

No wonder the blackpowder rifle has made a comeback. Each one is interesting, from the historically significant Henry rifle to the long-range Sharps. So far, the rifles are seeing action in silhouette shooting (single-shots) and Cowboy Action Shooting (lever-action repeaters).

A person has to wonder when hunters will catch on in a big way to the enjoyment the old-time rifle provides in the game field. Many have, of course, but many more will.

Chapter 35

THE BLACKPOWDER SHOTGUN

A QUESTION often posed goes: "If you had to spend six months in the woods with only one gun to get food, which gun would it be?" The answer is usually a shotgun, although in some parts of the high-mountain west, a rifle might serve the hunter better — more big game, fewer small animals and birds for campfire fare. The blackpowder shotgun is not on par with the top-rated commercial shotgun ammunition of the day. That's because Winchester, Remington, Federal, and other companies produce such great shells, including the 12-gauge 3 1/2 inch magnum with a full 2 1/4 ounces of shot, so it's tough to match modern shotshell ballistic results in a soot-burning shotgun. I tested a Winchester 3 1/2 inch magnum shotshell loaded with 54 No. 4 buckshot. The pattern at 30 yards from a Super-X2 shotgun was one tight cluster. A called-in coyote would have taken several pellets with this load. On the other hand, the in-line Knight TK-2000™ 12-gauge blackpowder shotgun proves that smoke-pole scatterguns can also pack the mail. This interesting modern muzzleloader shotgun comes with a 26 inch barrel, is 45 nches overall and weighs 7 pounds, 9 ounces. Sights are fully adjustable Tru-Glo® fiber optic. Trigger is adjustable for creep and pull weight.

Sling swivels are standard. So is a good recoil pad, necessary considering allowable powder and shot charges. The company's own patterning trial was conducted with 120 grains GOEX FFg blackpowder behind a 2 1/2-ounce shot charge! No. 4 Knight® Red Hot® lead shot was loaded in a 2 1/2-ounce shot cup. The TK2000™ has screw-in chokes (called "advanced jug-choked"), just like so many modern shotguns. Knight supplies an extra-full choke "for your turkey hunting needs," but this choke has much wider application than wild turkeys, such as ducks, geese, and upland birds when "scare radius" increases and longer shots are needed. Improved cylinder and modified chokes are also available from Knight. A 2 1/2-ounce charge of No. 4 shot has 338 pellets — Knight calls it 340 pellets for patterning purposes. At 25 yards, 330 pellets landed inside a 30 inch circle for a 97 percent pattern. At 30 yards, 328 pellets poked holes in the patterning paper's 30 inch circle for a 96 percent pattern. And at 40 yards, 289 pellets were counted inside a 30 inch circle for an 85 percent pattern. The upcoming choke chart shows 80 percent as extra-full choke.

The blackpowder shotgun is a highly versatile firearm, receiving not nearly the attention it deserves. It can be made to deliver fairly

The blackpowder shotgun can often be loaded to closely approach the ballistics of the modern shotgun shell. A well-made double gun in 12 gauge may be allowed as high as 1 1/2 ounces of shot by its maker, while at least one modern muzzleloader in 12 gauge can be loaded safely with more than 2 ounces of shot, according to Knight, the manufacturer.

This side-by-side 12-gauge blackpowder shotgun will not produce the ballistics obtainable with the Winchester Super-X II shown with it, but it will definitely take all game cleanly at normal shotgun ranges.

close to modern shotgun shell ballistics, and as the Knight 12-gauge proves, more than sufficient pellet delivery at 40-yards to bring home the Thanksgiving dinner, Christmas goose, or any upland bird requiring a heavily concentrated pattern of shot. A muzzleloading scattergun can just about do it all, harvesting small game and waterfowl to at least deer-sized big game animals. That's because this gun exists in all colors of the rainbow. Rabbits, wild turkey, grouse, pheasants, sage hens, and many other wild edibles can be brought to bag with a dose of medium-sized shot, such as No. 5 or No. 6. Dove and quail are better served with No. 7 1/2 or No. 8 shot. A good coyote/fox load is a heavy charge of No. 4 buckshot when these varmints are called in close. The patient brush or woods hunter, willing pass up the long shot for the close one, can bring a buck deer down with a single 494-grain round ball fired from a 12-gauge blackpowder shotgun. Because of this versatility, pioneers were well served with their

blackpowder shotguns, protecting home and hearth by filling the air with a mass of lead killer bees, as well as gathering good food. The breed has returned today, not for making a living, but rather enjoying a great time whacking clay pigeons out of the air in a shooting match, or in the game field with appropriate powder and charge, wad system and shot — from lead to bismuth, plus percussion caps, or No. 209 primers being an option in the case of the Knight. Because of its large smooth bores, the muzzleloading shotgun is also easy to clean and maintain, another bonus.

Shooting the Blackpowder Shotgun Today

The blackpowder shotgun in the popular double barrel, field-worthy single-barrel, as well as powerful inline version, delivers top performance at the skeet or trap club as well as the hunting field. This means the modern shooter can rely on it at rendezvous, special shooting matches, and hunting upland birds, wild turkeys, geese, and ducks,

even big game. The only drawback to hunting with the scattergun smokepole is having to reload with care and deliberation as partners with modern shell-shuckers continue hiking ahead. But that's little more than a matter of education and communication.

The Fowler

A fowler is a flintlock shotgun. It lifts the challenge one more notch with its slower lock time (elapsed span from trigger pull to ignition), but it can also be a handsome and good-pointing gun, and as with so many other tools, efficient in the hands of a practiced shooter who masters the flame from the pan with smooth follow-through. The percussion shotgun is far more popular today, but fowling guns like the 20-gauge Trade Fowler from Mountain State Muzzleloading, or the Navy Arms Mortimer 12-gauge can fill the game bag, and have been known to smoke a number of flying targets; however, most shooters choose the caplock as a matter of practicality. Hunters more interested in the experience than a full bag, on the other hand, may enjoy a fowler better than a caplock shotgun.

Single or Double Barrel?

The Knight 12-gauge shotgun featured earlier is obviously a single-barrel gun with top credentials for the field. There are other single-guns that work hard, such as CVA's Trapper single-barrel 12-gauge with chrome-lined barrel and steel shot capability. This gun is not cylinder bored. Rather, the Trapper comes with a fixed modified choke. It only weighs 6 pounds. In some instances, the single is actually the better choice, because it's light and fast, and where no more than one shot is normally needed, as in rabbit hunting under certain conditions, the one-shot shotgun is definitely OK. Regardless, the side-by-side blackpowder percussion shotgun in 12 gauge is the most popular choice today. The 10 gauge is also excellent, especially for waterfowling or any shotgun work demanding a heavy shot charge. Navy Arms has a 10-gauge blackpowder shotgun called the Steel Shot Magnum, "designed for the hunter that is required to use steel shot." The same company has an Upland Shotgun interestingly bore cylinder and modified, the idea being to fire the open barrel first when the covey is on the rise, then go to the other barrel when the birds are farther. Powder/shot charge ratio can be juggled to produce a heavy cloud of pellets out of the open bore at modest velocity, the tighter bore throwing a faster cargo. Higher velocity is not necessary up close, but more pellets increase the odds of a good hit from the first barrel, while the second barrel delivers more energy per pellet for the farther shot.

Bore Sizes

Shooting on the Wing, an 1873 publication by "An Old Gamekeeper," (the author's actual name is not provided) contains a rundown of shotgun bore sizes. Gauge/caliber relationships, according to the Old Gamekeeper, were as follows:

Shotgun Bore Sizes

Gauge	Caliber (inches)
1 gauge	1.669
4 gauge	1.052
8 gauge	.835
10 gauge	.775
11 gauge	.751
12 gauge	.729
13 gauge	.710
16 gauge	.662
20 gauge	.615
24 gauge	.579
28 gauge	.550
32 gauge	.526
36 gauge	.506

So the 10 gauge is a 78-caliber firearm; the 12 gauge is 73 caliber; the 16 gauge is 67 caliber; the 20 gauge is 62 caliber; and the 28 gauge is 55 caliber. This information is useful and instructional, but gauges varied over the years. That fact remains true today.

True Gauge

Certain modern 12-gauge blackpowder shotguns are actually 13 gauge, while some 10 gauges are truly 11 gauge. There's a good reason for this. A 13-gauge blackpowder shotgun handles loading components normally intended for a 12-gauge shotgun shell, while an 11-gauge frontloader handles components sized for a 10-gauge shotshell. Since the wad column fits inside the shotshell, wads are smaller than the inside diameter of the modern shotgun bore. Meanwhile, the blackpowder shotgun has no shell, so dimensioning the bore to accept components intended for the shotgun shell makes a perfect fit. It's vital to test components to ensure that they are sized correctly for a given blackpowder shotgun. Forcing too-large wads downbore can be dangerous, because pressures rise when a load is hampered as gas from the burning powder charge begins to push it. Wads that are too large, but forced downbore anyway, can create this situation. If a wad of any type cannot be seated without undue force, it is wrong for that gun.

Choke

Years went by before importers and manufacturers of blackpowder shotguns listened to those of us who cried out for decent choke systems. Instead, these guns were provided with no choke at all — cylinder bored, in other words. That was not all bad; neither was it all good. For jump-shooting quail when the birds were sitting tight, the no-choke scattergun was all right. It spread its pattern, and if enough small pellets were loaded, the bird was hit solidly. Even then, however, holes in patterns left a lot to be desired. I wrote letters and called regularly asking for choke, finally having jug chokes installed on a couple of my own blackpowder shotguns, as explained below. At last, the message got through. Today, choked blackpowder shotguns are common, as they should be. My own Navy Arms T&T (Turkey & Trap) shotgun carries full and full bores.

Other blackpowder shotguns have screw-in choke tubes offering immediate pattern alteration by inserting different tubes. Some professional gunsmiths install choke tubes in blackpowder shotguns, but not all shotguns are right

One way to carry blackpowder shotgun loads is with 35mm plastic film canisters. They are non-sparking and hold both shot and powder securely.

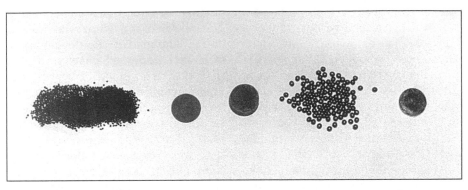

Here is the blackpowder shotgun load laid out in review—powder, over-powder wad, fiber wad, shot charge and over-shot wad.

for this, because there must be sufficient barrel-wall thickness to accept the screw-in tube. As a general rule, a 10-gauge shotgun with an outside barrel diameter of .900 inch and an inside bore diameter of .781 inch (leaving a wall thickness in the muzzle region of .0595 inch), is sufficient for installing choke tubes, according to one gunsmith. The key, of course, is not outside-barrel diameter or inside-bore diameter, but rather the resulting thickness of metal at the muzzle. A 12 gauge with a minimum outside diameter at the muzzle of .825 inch and a maximum bore diameter of .736 inch results in a barrel wall .089 inch thick divided by two, leaving .0445 inch thickness before the tube can be satisfactorily installed. A 20-gauge barrel with an outside minimum diameter of .700 inch plus a maximum bore diameter in the muzzle region of .626 inch leaves a barrel wall thickness of .037 inch, which is, according to the gunsmith questioned, sufficient for choke tube installation.

The Jug Choke

Jug chokes, also known as recessed chokes, were cut from the 19th century into the 20th, and are still being installed today. Cylinder bores have been rendered full choke with this system. When the great blackpowder gunsmith, V.M. Starr, installed recessed chokes, he used a constriction of .021 inch for full choke, .015 inch for modified, and

.010 for skeet choke. These required the use of cardboard wads only, he explained. These numbers compare with standard chokes according to one set of specifications: the 10-gauge shotgun with a .775 inch bore diameter will be choked (constricted) .035 inch for full choke, .017 inch for modified and .007 inch for improved cylinder. The 12-gauge with a .729-inch bore diameter will be choked .035 inch for full, .019 inch for modified and .009 inch for improved cylinder. The 20-gauge with a bore diameter of .617 inch calls for a constriction of .025 inch for full, .014 inch for modified and .006 inch for improved cylinder. The aforementioned variations are shown here, as the Old Gamekeeper's data gave the 20-gauge a bore size of .615 inch, not .617 inch.

Art Belding, a dedicated blackpowder shotgun enthusiast, reported that the jug choke did wonders for his 12-gauge shotgun. Joe Ehlinger of Addision, Mich., accomplished the work. The gun patterned about 45 percent before the jug-choke job. Afterwards, using No. 5 copper-plated shot with a pellet count of 185, and 90 grains volume GOEX FFg blackpowder with the V.M. Starr wad method described below, here is what happened: For eight shots on the pattern board, the shotgun delivered 88, 92, 82, 91, 87, 81, 77 and 83 percent patterns. That's an average of 85 percent, or extra-full choke. If a

blackpowder shotgun does not have sufficient "meat" at the muzzle to be fitted with choke tubes, it can usually be jug-choked.

One-Piece Plastic Wad Columns

One type of blackpowder wad column is the one-piece plastic unit, as found in modern shotgun shells. The one-piece plastic wad can tighten patterns. Residual plastic fouling is removable with Venco's Shooter's Choice solvent, Butch's Bore Shine, or similar solvent, as described in the chapter on blackpowder chemicals. It's important to work on a shotgun's pattern, and wads can make all the difference. Holes, as they are called, not only cause misses, but worse, they may deliver too few pellets on target for effectiveness on game. Choking the gun is the best way to go, but plastic wads in cylinder-bore guns can help, not only by tightening patterns, but also dispersing shot more evenly. The use of a one-piece plastic wad system acts somewhat like a choke, helping to create a denser pattern. Unfortunately, one-piece plastic wads do not correct bad patterns all the time, or completely. In some instances, one-piece plastic wads can hang onto a shot charge, delivering it as a mass of pellets, not a pattern. The only sure way to know is by checking the individual shotgun with a patterning board, as explained below. One-piece standard plastic wads work in blackpowder shotguns because of the aforementioned actual gauge, where a 10 is in fact an 11 and a 12 is really a 13, thereby sizing out just right for plastic wads intended to fit inside of shotgun shells.

Other Wad Columns

Along with one-piece plastic wads, numerous other wad types can be used with the blackpowder shotgun. The simple cardboard wad, associated with the late V.M. Starr, has worked well since the beginning of shotgunning, and it still does. Heavy-grade cardboard wads 3/32-inch thick may be cut from display signs with a punch. These heavy wads are used over the powder charge, two of them, one atop the other. No further wads are placed downbore. The shot charge goes down next with a thin cardboard wad on top to hold the shot firmly in place. That's all there is to the cardboard wad column. As Starr pointed out, "You can put in more wads on the powder if you wish, or if you enjoy cutting them, but my experience tells me that you are just wasting your time." Starr did not use felt wads. He did, however, win several shotgun matches against good shooters using modern shotguns, suggesting that his simple cardboard wad system had to be effective. The blackpowder charge, composed of Fg or FFg, does not tend to destroy wads, which is part of the reason for these simple cardboard cutouts holding up so well in the old-style scattergun. That the wads would be ruined with faster-burning powder is a moot point, because there is no reason to use FFFg in the shotgun. Fg and FFg and equivalent granulations are just right.

The long-preferred wad column consisting of thick-cushion fiber wad over the powder, followed by the shot charge, then one thin over-powder wad remains practical. Luckily, there are many good sources for blackpowder wads, including Circle Fly, Dixie, and Ballistic Products Inc., to name only three.

Choke and Pattern Density

As usual, standardization is hard to come by; however, the following choke designations with pattern percentages provide a reasonable guide. Other sources will present different figures, but not so far off the board as to create a problem. Application of various chokes is guided by common sense and field experience. Common sense dictates that tighter choke is neces-

sary to concentrate more shot on a tough target like a wild turkey or a Canada goose, while more open shot patterns are right for smaller birds on the wing, difficult to hit at all with fist-tight clumps of shot, not to mention destroying edible meat with such tight patterns. Field experience comes in handy, too. One time in Nebraska, I was advised to use the tightest choke available to me, because "these birds take off at quite a distance," that distance known as the scare radius. The advice was on the money. The birds were wild.

Choke Values

Extra-Full = 80 percent or tighter
Full Choke = 70 to 79 percent
Improved Modified = 65 to 69 percent
Modified = 55 to 64 percent
Improved Cylinder I = 50 to 54 percent
Improved Cylinder II = 45 to 49 percent
Cylinder = Less than 45 percent

Patterning

The pattern is the key to performance. Of course, pellet velocity and energy are important, too, but it's no trouble getting good shotgun velocities with the old-time shotgun. In spite of the fact that blackpowder loads are not on par with modern shotgun shells, shot at medium speed is effective. However, obtaining the best possible pattern often requires a little research, which in this case means patterning the blackpowder shotgun to discover what the gun is doing. The goal is the development of a well-dispersed pattern of shot free of holes. In other words, the blackpowder shotgun requires patterning just like its modern counterpart if the shooter is to know for certain, and with confidence, what his gun provides in shot distribution. The process is not difficult. A large sheet of paper is pinned up at 40 yards. The shotgun load is fired dead center into that large sheet of paper. Using a cardboard cutout 30 inches in diameter, a circle is drawn around the concentration of shot on the paper. The holes within that 30-inch circle are counted, and that total is then divided by the number of pellets in the load. If the shotgun fired 100 pellets and fifty of them were in that 30-inch circle, the pattern would be 50 percent, or improved cylinder choke.

Also important is the way the shot are distributed on the paper. Although the above shotgun put half of its charge within the 30-inch circle, were there large holes in the pattern, or were the pellets well distributed? A few shots are required to tell the story. The serious shooter should pattern his shotgun several times until he has a very good picture of the average pattern that gun develops. It's not unusual for a shotgun to pattern 75 percent, but with gaps, known simply as holes. If this situation occurs, a cure is juggling load components. Sometimes a simple change in shot size does the trick.

CVA's Trapper Shotgun is 12-gauge with fixed modified choke, total weight about 6 pounds, chrome-lined barrel, a single-shot ready for action.

For example, if No. 8 shot produces what's called a "blown pattern," which is one with holes in it, No. 6 shot may cure the problem, or vice versa. Another good trick is altering the balance (ratio) of shot to powder by reducing the powder charge rather than adding more shot. This does not always provide a denser pattern, but quite often holes in patterns disappear by simply reducing the powder charge by 10 grains. Components are never to be juggled haphazardly. Nor must the shotgun be loaded with either more shot or powder than allowed by the shotgun manufacturer. Before pattern density can be measured, the number of pellets in a shot charge must be known by consulting the chart below. Only by knowing the number of pellets in the load can the shooter determine the percentage that landed inside the standardized 30-inch circle, using the choke values provided above. Recall that the Knight 12-gauge was credited with delivering an extra-full choke pattern. This was determined by knowing first how many pellets were in the load fired at the patterning board.

Number of Pellets in a Shot Charge

Shot Size	Diameter in Inches	Pellets Per Oz.
No. 12	.05	2,385
No. 9	.08	588
No. 8	.09	410
No. 7	.095	350
No. 6	.11	225
No. 5	.12	170
No. 4	.13	135
No. 2	.15	90
BB	.18	50

The Powder Charge

Fine-granulation powder, such as FFFg, is not recommended. This long-standing rule has been a good one, although not for the reason so often stated, that FFFg in a blackpowder shotgun will cause blown patterns because it creates too much pellet speed. Rather than

FFFg blowing the pattern because it's pushing the shot charge too fast, it is more likely to burn the wads. Even that assessment is open to question. Having picked up a number of spent wads fired from shotguns loaded with FFFg for the sake of testing, some did show probable flame damage of the over-powder wad. Others did not, and of course, the one-piece plastic wad is impervious to the ravages of blackpowder, since it is designed to stand up to smokeless. On the other hand, if the wad on the shot charge was damaged, the pattern would be ruined, because that wad is responsible for driving the shot through the bore. Gas may even bleed through a damaged wad right into the shot itself. The best reason, however, to avoid faster-burning FFFg in the muzzleloading shotgun is the fact that larger granulation Fg, FFg and Pyrodex RS do the job well with very low pressures. Lyman's tests show only 2,500 psi with an ounce of shot and 3 3/4 drams (102.5 grains) of GOEX FFg blackpowder in a 12-gauge shotgun.

The same powder charge with 1 1/8 ounces of shot produces 4,400 psi. The same powder charge with 1 1/4 ounces of shot showed a psi rating of 4,600. Pyrodex RS with a 3 3/4-dram equivalent charge ran 3,600 psi, using 1 1/4 ounces of shot. Going to 1 1/2 ounces of shot, but using the same GOEX FFg powder

and 3 3/4-dram charge, the pressure reading was 5,000 psi. All wad columns were comprised of a cushion-fiber wad and one over-shot cardboard wad. As always, powder charge/shot charge maximums are in the hands of the gunmaker. If no information is supplied, the shooter must write the manufacturer for data. Sometimes allowable loads are pitiful, known as a "lawyer's dream," to avoid lawsuits if a gun does fail -- in spite of the fact that it failed because of something other than an overcharge of power or shot. One manufacturer, for example, held his 10-gauge muzzleloading shotgun to 1 1/4 ounces of shot with a small powder charge. Why bother? Regardless, however, maximum powder and shot charges are not to be exceeded. That is the standing rule, never to be violated.

The Volume-for-Volume Load

A single measure may be used for both shot and powder charge, making loading a cinch. This means that the blackpowder shotgun will handle the same volume of powder and shot. Note the word volume. This has nothing whatsoever to do with the weights of either powder or shot; it is strictly a volumetric proposition. If your shotgun is allowed 90 grains of FFg, set the powder measure at 90, using that same setting for both the shot charge and the powder charge

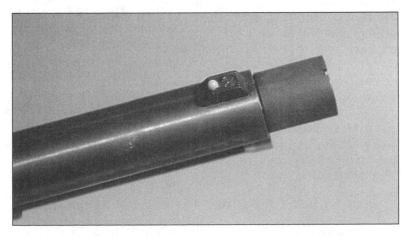

This Knight 12-gauge in-line modern muzzleloader came equipped with an extra full screw-in choke for tight patterning at the 80 percent level.

This is an original 19th century shot flask with a hard leather body. It works as well today as when it was made.

— by bulk. While this is an acceptable way to load as long as a proper wad column is employed, safe juggling of components remains viable. A reduction of powder, while leaving the shot charge the same, often results in marked improvement in pattern density, but the gun must be patterned to learn this. There are too many variables at work to lay down one set of rules for all guns. There is no one powder and shot charge that works in all 12-gauge guns, for example. The wad column itself makes a huge difference in results. One 12-gauge full-and-full shotgun gave its best patterns with the most powerful loads allowed in that gun, a heavy shot charge combined with a heavy powder charge. Another 12-gauge gun gave best patterning when the powder charge was dropped by 20 percent below manufacturer's recommendation. One 12-gauge muzzleloading shotgun that was allowed a full 1 1/2 ounces of shot provided good bird hunting loads with only 1 ounce of small shot and 70 grains of FFg blackpowder.

Improper Shotgun Loading

Blackpowder can create very high pressures, as established earlier. At the same time, we know that the blackpowder shotgun, because of its large bore size, develops low pressures per powder charge as proven with the Lyman data presented above. However, that can be deceiving. True, a 12 gauge loaded with 100 grains of FFg behind a full 1 1/2 ounces of No. 2 steel shot may develop only 4,600 psi, depending upon the wad system, compared with a 50-caliber muzzleloader using the exact same FFg blackpowder with the same 100-grain volume load and a 335-grain Lyman saboted bullet for more than 15,000 psi. However, the blackpowder shotgun can still be overloaded. Loading more shot than allowed by the gunmaker can raise pressures dramatically. A problem with the wad column can also cause pressures to skyrocket, especially when the wad system will not allow upward movement the instant the powder charge is ignited. The separated projectile and powder charge (short-start) warning sounded earlier applies to the shotgun as well. Shotgun barrels are thin, not heavy. They get away with this because of lower generated pressures. At the same time, a bore obstruction can rip a shotgun barrel apart like a thin metal pipe. Finally, while pressures are low with allowable powder charges, this does not mean that the muzzleloading shotgun can stand up to an overload. It cannot. The correct powder in the correct amount must be used.

Lead Shot in the Muzzle-loading Shotgun

Cubed shot was once popular. A sheet of lead was literally chopped into small cubes, sized as desired by the shooter. Talk about fliers! However, while these little cubes of lead were anything but aerodynamic, they apparently worked to some degree, as reported by old-timers who relied on cubed shot to get their supper. At close range on small edibles such as quail and cottontails, the cubes buzzed their way through with considerable effect. Since these and similar game are usually harvested at under 20 paces, cubed lead sufficed. Another lead pellet type from long ago was called swan shot. Warning: Never attempt to make swan shot. It is a dangerous process. A person could be severely burned in the process. Swan shot was created by pouring molten lead through a screen, the drops of hot lead falling into a cooling medium, such as water. The shot hardened when it hit the liquid, often with a tiny tail on each pellet, remindful of the south end of a swan flying north. Although historically interesting, swan shot has been totally outstripped by modern shot and there is no need to make any of it. Proper lead shot is widely available and fairly priced. There is even reclaimed shot for sale from time to time, such as pellets gathered up at skeet and trap club ranges.

Steel Shot in the Muzzle-loading Shotgun

Steel shot is created from soft steel wire, formed into pellets, annealed (heating followed by slow cooling), and finally coated. The process is not unlike the manufacture of steel ball bearings. Initially, shooters had a difficult time with steel shot, often reporting poor patterns and less than spectacular results on game. Much of this has been corrected by learning how to manage steel shot, especially with regard to shotgun choke. Patterns are tighter with steel than lead. Therefore, full-choke guns may deliver fist-tight clumps that are difficult to hit with. Furthermore, pellet size choice is important. Steel pellets lose velocity/energy faster than lead pellets because of differences in mass. Therefore, larger steel pellets are required to deliver more energy downrange.

Negative Aspects of Steel Shot

As stated, steel shot is lighter than lead, pellet for pellet, about 30 percent across the board. Since steel pellets lose velocity faster than lead pellets, larger pellets are relied upon to carry more energy downrange. At the same time, using larger pellets means fewer per shot charge. Taken to an extreme, the steel shot load can carry too few pellets to create a dense pattern downrange, which goes against both hitting the target, and delivering a sufficient number of pellets for good game-taking effect.

Positive Aspect of Steel Shot

While steel shot incorporates negatives, it also has some good properties. Here are a few:

1. No Fliers

Soft lead shot deforms in the bore, creating pellets that look like miniature flying saucers. These are called fliers, and they soon depart the pattern. Of course, up close some of these fliers might actually hit the target, working in effect to broaden a pattern. But fliers are no good. Steel shot is hard so it does not deform into fliers. Each pellet retains its shape, remaining in the pattern.

2. Steel Shot is Round

Lead pellets are quite round, but steel pellets are more round. A round pellet flies more uniformly than an egg-shaped pellet.

3. Steel Shot is Uniform

Steel pellets are uniform, with very little difference in size within a given pellet number. A bag of No. 5s, for example, consists of pellets that uniformly run .120-inch diameter.

4. Steel Shot Creates a Short Shot String

A short shot string means pellets are bunched up in a "cloud" rather than strung out. A string of lead shot may be several feet long at 40 yards, while steel pellets provide a shorter shot string.

Shooting Steel Shot in Muzzleloaders

Steel shot can score a barrel that is not built to withstand the harder metal. In response to this problem, several companies now offer muzzleloading shotguns with steel-shooting capability, such as the Navy Arms Co. 10-gauge double-gun mentioned above. Along with requiring a barrel intended to shoot steel shot without bore damage, the shooter must learn how to manage the harder pellet shot string by first choosing the right shot size. Pellets larger than necessary result in light patterns. For example, No. 6 steel shot (.110 inch diameter) and No. 5 steel shot (.120 inch diameter) provided results not unlike those experienced with lead No. 5 shot on sage hens. BBB steel (.190 inch diameter) is appropriate for large birds, such as geese, with BB steel (.180 inch) more desirable when higher pellet count is desired. Even large ducks can be dropped with No. 1 steel (.160 inch diameter).

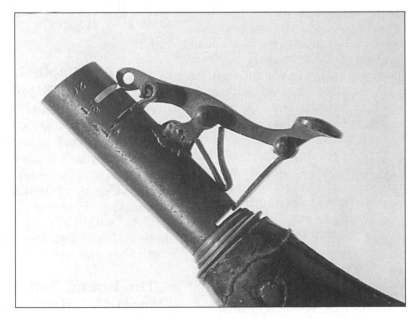

This original 19th century shot flask was, and still is, adjustable for two charges: 1 1/4 ounces and 1 1/2 ounces of shot.

The next step is using less choke. Full choke may have been ideal with lead shot for a certain application, but modified will usually provide better patterns with steel shot.

Bismuth Shot

Bismuth is expensive, which is its greatest drawback. It's also an excellent legal non-toxic shot that meets the law forbidding lead shot in certain areas. Bismuth shot is unique. Ballistic Products Inc. offers a user's guide to Bismuth, detailing its specific characteristics. Bismuth is not quite as heavy as lead, but it is close. Bismuth is certainly much heavier than steel shot pellets of the same size, and only about 8 percent less dense than lead (steel is 27 percent less dense than lead). One dictionary calls it "a lustrous, reddish, white metallic element (symbol Bi)," going on to say that it is used in medicine and cosmetics. It's the "Bis" in Pepto-Bismol®. Pure bismuth is on the brittle side, but making it into an alloy with 3 percent tin greatly improves integrity. It is also harder than lead, except for very hard lead alloys, which are on par with bismuth. We're told that gun barrels intended for lead shot, but not steel, will stand up to bismuth. Since the use of bismuth shot produces higher pressures than lead shot, going by volume is advised. There will be fewer bismuth pellets in a volumetric shot measure compared with lead, but not reduced enough to make a significant difference on game. Bismuth is hard enough to provide good penetration, while being soft enough to upset a little bit in the target, delivering a bit more energy. Bismuth shot for handloading is supplied in various sizes to match intended use.

Tungsten Shot

Tungsten is "a steel gray, brittle, heavy metallic element of the chromium group." Its symbol is W, and at this particular time, with lead working great in the blackpowder muzzleloading shotgun, along with Bismuth and steel shot to handle federal non-toxic regulations, tungsten shot is on the backburner.

Blackpowder Shotgun Ballistics

It's a whole new world now, with Knight's powerful blackpowder shotgun in the running. While velocity is not terribly high in the Knight, even with a 120-grain load of FFg blackpowder, the potency of such a huge shot charge cannot be denied. A 12-gauge shotgun with 1 1/2 ounces of shot (when that much shot is allowed by the gunmaker) and 100 grains volume of FFg blackpowder or Pyrodex RS produces a muzzle velocity of 1,050 to 1,150 fps. That challenges, but doesn't catch, the modern shotshell. While not quite as powerful as a "baby magnum" 12-gauge round with 1 1/2 ounces of shot, this load remains strong all the same. A 1 1/4-ounce shot charge in the same shotgun with 100 grains of Pyrodex RS or FFg blackpowder has produced as high as 1,300 fps muzzle velocity in at least one test gun, but that's on the high side. As a rule, 1,100 to 1,200 fps is about it, which is sufficient if the hunter will apply a liberal dose of sportsmanship, passing up anything resembling a long shot.

The Caplock Shotgun Nipple

The aforementioned "straight-through" nipple — see Chapter 24 — has been found on some blackpowder shotguns. Discarding it in favor of a standard nipple with a small orifice is advised to thwart blowback, which is not much of a problem with the large-volume shotgun bore, but the switch is worthwhile anyway.

The Round Ball in the Muzzle-loading Shotgun

The .690-inch, 12-gauge round ball weighs an average of 494 grains. While it's difficult to achieve much more than 1,000 fps at the muzzle with this ball, close-range authority on deer-sized game is ensured. Loading one barrel with buckshot and the other with a patched round ball is also acceptable, although buckshot is good only at close range.

Extensive tests that anyone can try with buckshot will convince a shooter that patterns are generally less than ideal in the blackpowder shotgun. At 30 yards, firing nine 00 buckshot, only three were in the kill zone with two different shotguns — one with full choke, the other cylinder-bored. Also, each individual pellet carries low power, less than a 36-caliber squirrel rifle, which is hardly ideal for big game. One 00 buckshot weighs only 54 grains, which is lighter than a .350 inch ball. Plus, the little lead pill is lucky to leave the bore at the speed of sound from a muzzleloading shotgun.

Shot Sizes

It's important to understand shot sizes for reference purposes. While shot sizes have never been fully standardized, the following numbers are useful for comparison purposes. They must now, however, be considered the only diameters assigned to certain pellet sizes. There are differences, especially when comparing European shot to Canadian and American shot. Steel shot is included for contrast.

—Lead Shot—			—Steel Shot—		
Size	Dia.	No./Oz.	Size	Dia.	No./Oz.
No. 12	.05	2385	No. 6	.11	315
No. 9	.08	585	No. 4	.13	192
No. 8	.09	410	No. 3	.14	158
No. 7 1/2	.095	350	No. 2	.15	125
No. 6	.11	225	No. 1	.16	103
No. 5	.12	170	BB	.18	72
No. 4	.13	135	T	.20	52
No. 2	.15	90	F	.22	40
BB	.18	50			

Shot Energy

Lead vs. Steel Shot at 40 Yards with the Same Muzzle Velocity

Lead No. 6 = 2.3 foot-pounds
Steel No. 4 = 2.5 foot-pounds
Lead No. 4 = 4.4 foot-pounds
Steel No. 2 = 4.4 foot-pounds
Lead No. 2 = 7.5 foot-pounds
Steel BB = 9.0 foot-pounds
Lead BB = 15.0 foot-pounds
Steel T = 20 foot-pounds
Steel F = 24 foot-pounds

Steel shot sizes show well energy-wise because of their larger diameter. For example, the lead BB is .18-inch diameter, while the steel T is .20-inch diameter, and the steel F is .22-inch. Steel shot in larger sizes carries reasonable energy for clean game harvesting. Of course, loaded properly with a volumetric measure, the weight of the steel charge is less than an equal volume of lead shot.

The Shotgun Ready Load

There are many ways to carry shot, powder and wads for the scattergun. The old flask worked fine. Powder and shot horns are good. So are ready loads, which can be prepared in many ways. Plastic 35mm film containers are also useful, with pre-measured powder charges in one set of containers, pre-measured shot charges in another set. Wads can be carried in a hunting coat pocket. Working with these ready loads is self-explanatory. The gunner pops a top, drops a charge, runs a wad home on top of the powder, drops a shot charge from another plastic can, tops off with an over-shot wad and he's ready to shoot after capping.

Blackpowder Shotgun Recoil

Gone over before, blackpowder is not that efficient, although it burns beautifully in the scattergun and gives nice patterns. Relative inefficiency translates into heavy charges, such as the Knight 12-gauge burning a 120-grain load of FFg or RS. Since the weight of the powder charge is part of the recoil formula, the blackpowder shotgun does come on back to say hello when it's fired, especially with big shot charges. The shooter concentrating on that flying target or big tom turkey strutting out front learns to ignore the comeback of the gun, but there's no getting around the fact that the soot burner can kick. While not necessarily traditional, a recoil pad helps. Of course, the modern muzzleloader comes supplied with one.

Blackpowder Shotgun Safety Reminders

1. After firing one barrel, be certain that the load in the other barrel has remained in place, especially when the same barrel has been shot a few times, the other not at all. A load may creep upbore in the unfired barrel, leaving a space between powder charge and shot charge.

2. Do not use a powder horn to pour powder directly into the shotgun bore. A safer practice is to use ready loads, as with plastic 35mm film containers, or a proper flask system.

3. Uncap a loaded barrel before attempting to load a fired barrel. The danger of loading a fired barrel with the other barrel capped is glaringly evident.

4. Be fully certain that your shotgun bore is clear of plastic fouling if you use modern one-piece wads.

5. Use proper wad column materials only. Don't stuff newspaper, rag-cloth or other foreign bodies downbore in lieu of correct wads.

6. Be certain to cover and/or remove any powder container from the area before shooting. This goes for all muzzleloaders. A spark can fly into a container, be it can or horn, causing an explosion.

7. Watch out for the old ones. There are original muzzleloading shotguns that look to be in good shape, but looks can be deceiving. An original gun must be inspected by a blackpowder gunsmith before firing. The Magna-Glow process can reveal imperfections in the metal. Even after these precautions, consider an old muzzleloader a possible threat. There could be internal wear that cannot be located. Shoot originals with extreme caution. Fire old-time shotguns by remote control before shooting from the shoulder.

8. Use only blackpowder or a safe substitute such as Pyrodex or Clear Shot in the blackpowder shotgun and nothing else.

9. Load by volume only. Do not attempt to load by weights. Steel shot weighs less per volume charge, but this is as it should be. Do not load steel, or any other shot, by weight, nor the powder charge. Remember that a steel shot charge that weighs only 3/4 ounce is recommended for ducks under 35 yards, while a 1-ounce charge of steel shot is recommended for ducks at 35 to 45 yards. Even for geese and wild turkeys, a steel shot charge of only 1 1/4 ounces is considered effective.

10. No load of powder or shot is safe in a gun that is not in perfect repair. Never shoot any gun that is not sound in all respects.

The Versatile Muzzleloading Scattergun

Successful blackpowder shotgunning is an all-encompassing enterprise from choosing the right gun to loading it correctly, patterning, and mastering steel shot. Each shot is a handload, a plus because loads can be altered to match field conditions and game from cottontails in the briar patch to quail in the field, with a possibility for deer on the side with a heavy patched round ball. The old-time blackpowder shotgun is a lot of fun to shoot, but it also offers the modern shooter many options with good power and patterns.

Chapter 36

BLACKPOWDER HANDGUNS

A STROLL through the magazine rack at any newspaper stand or grocery store instantly impresses the viewer with one glaring fact — handguns are "in." Magazine covers prove it. Blackpowder single-shot pistols, cap 'n' ball revolvers, plus blackpowder cartridge revolvers, are interesting, useful sidearms and no blackpowder battery is complete without one or more of these guns. All three gun types have a lot to offer the modern shooter. Collecting, plinking, informal target practice, competition, small-game hunting, big-game hunting, and Cowboy Action Shooting are some of the functions of the one-hand, smoke-making, shootin' iron. Blackpowder handguns fall into several categories, including replica, or at least in-the-spirit copycat, custom, target shooter, small-game hunter and big-game hunter.

Collecting

Serious collectors want originals, but there are a number of excellent blackpowder replica sidearms worthy of show-and-tell, whether or not they are ever fired. Even the pepperbox is available, somewhat a transition firearm between pistol and revolver, resembling an elongated cylinder taken from a revolver, but actually a collection of barrels revolved into position one at a time to line up with the firing mechanism. Not provable, perhaps, but it seems correct that the pepperbox influenced inventors of the revolver. Civil War revolvers were once represented mainly with replicas of the 1860 Colt or 1858 Remington, but today there are numerous models available. They include the Spiller and Burr originally produced in Atlanta between 1862 and 1864, or the Rogers and Spencer Army Model made in Utica, N.Y., toward the end of the Civil War, and the Le Mat revolvers, with the interesting 65-caliber under-barrel. The blackpowder cartridge fan has choices, too. Navy Arms Co. offers the 1851 Navy Conversion from the later 1800s chambered for the 38 Long Colt, the 1872 open top chambered or the 38 Special, Remington's 1890 revolver in 44-40 Winchester or 45 Colt, along with a number of six-guns associated with Colt heritage, including the Bisley model. There's even the New Model Russian revolver shooting the 44 Russian cartridge.

Plinking

No listing of handguns required here — plinking is a great game with any blackpowder handgun, pistol or revolver, replica or not. A few cans placed safely in front of a good backstop and the fun is on, smoke and all.

Informal Target Shooting

That's true, too, for informal target shooting. There are no rules, other than safety guidelines. Any one-hand blackpowder firearm is right for this no-contest shooting. While punching holes in paper is not animated the way plinking is, informal target shooting is a great way to practice, as well as learning new handling and shooting techniques.

Competition

Anything from rendezvous to national matches can include a blackpowder sidearm, single-shot or revolver. Some shooters practice until they excel even with pistols that lack refined sights. At one shoot, a lady pistoleer showed the boys how it was done, taking first place with a "plains pistol" in 50 caliber.

Small Game

Having been trained in recent times to shoot a handgun better than I was previously able, bringing good protein from field to camp will never again be too great a challenge, including mountain grouse,

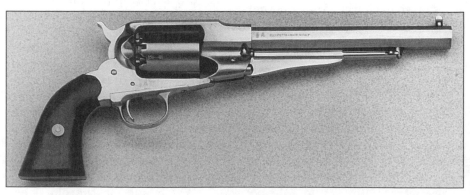

Staying with its original sights, this Navy Arms Co. stainless steel 1858 Remington makes a fine handgun for everyday enjoyment.

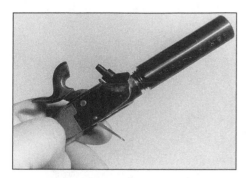

The screw barrel pistol was a unique single-shot percussion. When cocked, the trigger jumped into place for firing. Otherwise, it remained tucked out of the way. Dixie Gun Works offers this one.

which are legally taken by handgun where I go. There are several good guns for small-game hunting, including the Traditions Buckhunter Pro In-line pistol. Too bad this pistol comes only in 50 caliber, because it has adjustable sights and it's easy to hit with. In 36-caliber firing .350-inch round balls, it would be a fine mountain grouse meat-maker. Two good pistols for small-game hunting went down the trail of no return: the Thompson/Center Patriot and Knight Hawkeye. Both can sometimes be located as "previously owned." I'm no pistol marksman, but the day I couldn't deliver three shots into an inch at 25 yards with the Patriot never came, partly due to its double-set trigger system.

Big Game

Taking big game with any pistol requires practice in order to gain confidence as a shooter, plus dedication in getting within range for a nice clean shot. The strongest blackpowder big-game handguns are single-shot pistols, such as the Thompson/Center Encore, and before that the Scout from the same company. The Scout came in 50 and 54 calibers, while the Encore is 50 caliber only at the moment, although the company is working on other calibers. The T/C Encore is a systems pistol offering many different barrels on one frame. Our interest is the 209x50 muzzleloading barrel, a full 15 inches long with adjustable sights, ramrod resting beneath. Rate of twist is 1:28 for conicals. T/C allows up to 150 grains of FFg black powder or Pyrodex RS equivalent. A 110-grain charge of FFg or RS drives a 240-grain bullet in sabot sufficiently for big game from reasonable ranges.

Cowboy Action Shooting

The blackpowder cartridge pistol falls into the rules of this game. There are many available. Ruger's Vaquero with fixed sights fits this picture, along with replicas from several gun companies, such as the Frontier from Cimarron.

Pistol or Revolver?

This is not a difficult choice once the shooter knows which game he wants to play. For example, if big-game hunting with a blackpowder sidearm is the ticket, the obvious handgun is a blackpowder pistol. Nothing in revolver form can touch

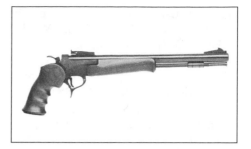

Taking the place of the Thompson/Center Scout powerhouse pistol is another strong handgun, the T/C Encore 209/50 Magnum in 50 caliber. The company allows up to 110 grains volume FFg with a 470-grain Maxi-Hunter bullet for more than 1,175 feet per second muzzle velocity with energy of more than 1,400 foot-pounds.

a muzzle-loading pistol for sheer power, not only with the aforementioned Encore, but also pistols like the Harper's Ferry in 58 caliber, an import from the Navy Arms Co. There are also target pistols capable of good accuracy. These are evident at certain matches. Other matches call for the revolver, and if target sights are allowed, then a gun on the order of the Ruger Old Army is right. If interests center on the Civil War period, a revolver is the choice, especially with the many now available in replication. Which is actually better? The revolver has the firepower — more shots per time. The pistol has the power, especially when allowed big powder charges. Pistols and revolvers simply play different roles. One is not better than the other. But one is usually more correct for a specific application from rounding out a collection to collecting small or big game, or playing at Cowboy Action Shooting, as well as re-enactment of a historical period, rendezvous service, competition, or other use.

The Smallbore Pistol

The smallbore pistol is almost recoilless with the proper load, and simply a lot of fun to shoot. With proper sights, it's also a small-

The Paterson revolver was so-named for its city of manufacture in New Jersey. It came out in 1836 and was known as Sam Colt's five-shooter. This one is a replica from the Navy Arms Co., 36-caliber.

game taker, and it can be used for target work. Dixie Gun Works' Mang Target Pistol in 38 caliber is an example of the latter. It fires a .375-inch round ball with 20 grains of FFFg for a MV of 902 fps — pleasant to shoot. A load of 30 grains of the same powder, same ball, delivers 1,071 fps MV, while 30 grains of Pyrodex P pushes the 80-grain, .375-inch pill at 1,112 fps MV. Energy runs around 200 foot-pounds for the 30-grain charge, plenty for close-range, small-game hunting. There are other smallbore pistols fired mostly for plinking fun or collecting. Pedersoli's Mang pistol in 38 caliber is an example of both in one gun. It is a smallbore, being only 38 caliber, but at the same time it represents the past. Dixie offers the 41-caliber Abilene Derringer, but more notably a true smallbore blackpowder pistol, the Dixie Gold Rush Pepperbox at only 22 caliber made on the style of the Allen and Thurber mid-1800s pistol. The bore really is .220-inch diameter, and this six-shot pepperbox takes No. 11 percussion caps. It fires No. F lead shot with 5 grains of FFFg blackpowder.

The Smallbore Revolver

Surprisingly, the smallbore revolver was seen as a self-defense firearm, and even a military weapon. Many were manufactured in the 19th century — too many to list. Wild Bill Hickok carried a 36-caliber revolver. Several were used during the American Civil War, including the interesting Spiller and Burr 36-caliber revolver. There are many small-caliber blackpowder cap-and-ball revolvers that are handsome little pieces, such as the 36-caliber Colt Pocket Police Revolver. It shoots an 80-grain bullet, .375-inch diameter, at 954 fps MV for a muzzle energy of 162 foot-pounds. While this energy rating is low, apparently some officers considered it sufficient for maintaining law and order. Today, the little Colt Model 1862 Pocket Police, from Colt, makes an enjoyable shooter. Likewise is the New Model Pocket, which was manufactured by Remington between the years 1855 and 1873. This is truly a small handgun, only 31-caliber firing a .321-inch round ball. The barrel on the replica from the Navy Arms Co. is only 3 1/2 inches long. It was considered "very popular during the Civil War and the Old West era," according to the literature. Most of these sub-caliber revolvers wear "point at 'em" sights, not the target-adjustable kind.

The Big-Bore Pistol

Now there are two major branches of big-bore pistols: those of replica persuasion and the modern in-line. The first was sometimes called a horse pistol because it was packed on the old pony instead of in a belt holster. Big is the byword for these guns. The in-the-spirit Lyman Plains Pistol,

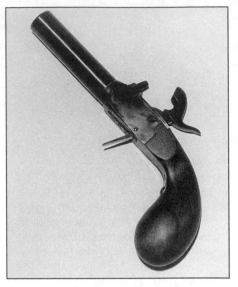

The screw barrel pistol shown here with barrel fully in place, ready to cap and fire.

close to a replica with its old-time lines, comes in calibers 50 or 54. In the latter, a 225-grain round ball leaves the muzzle at more than 900 fps in front of 40 grains volume FFFg for a muzzle velocity of 954 fps. While muzzle energy is only 453 foot-pounds, this pistol remains viable for big game on the order of javelina to deer when carried by an accomplished handgun hunter who gets close for that one good shot. There are other big-bore pistols of bygone days offered by companies today. One is the 58-caliber Harper's Ferry 1806 pistol with a 10-inch barrel. This big flintlock is imported by Dixie and the Navy Arms Co. Once again, muzzle energy is low, but the shear size of a 58-caliber ball is sufficient to make up for some of that. The aforementioned Encore 50-caliber in-line pistol from Thompson/Center, on the other hand, develops impressive muzzle energies on par with the 30-30 cartridge.

The Big-Bore Revolver

Calibers 44 and 45 mark the big-bore revolver. There are many in 44 caliber. The famous Colt Walker is one. Many companies offer this big revolver. However, it's not in the ballistic cards for any of the big-bore revolvers to match up with

The two main types of blackpowder handgun are revolver and pistol.

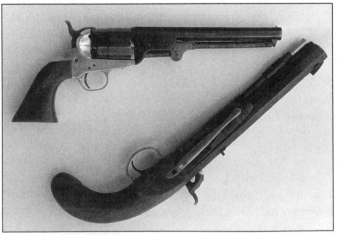

The 1862 Police cap and ball revolver was, by our standards, a smallbore, only 36 caliber firing an 80-grain round ball of .375-inch diameter. But it was effective in its time frame, and remains a lot of fun to shoot today, especially informal targets.

big-bore pistols. Even the big Walker, weighing in at 73 ounces, does not produce the power generated by the bigger bore pistols. Strong medicine in the Walker results in about 1,215 fps MV with a 141-grain, .454-inch round ball for a muzzle energy of 462 foot-pounds — comparable to a 38 Special cartridge.

The 44-caliber Navy Arms LeMat Army revolver fires its .451-inch, 138-grain round ball at 687 fps MV for a muzzle energy of 145 foot-pounds. But there's a little surprise that comes with the LeMat: an under-barrel in caliber 65 that fires a .595-inch cast round ball at 571 fps MV for 230 foot-pounds of muzzle energy. This is not a lot of kinetic energy, number-wise, but a 60-caliber lead round ball remains a formidable missile.

Ruger's Old Army is a 45-caliber, six-shot cap and ball revolver, available with adjustable or fixed sights. It boosts energy ratings to almost 400 foot-pounds with a 146-grain round ball at 1,100 fps MV, burning 40 grains of Pyrodex P powder. The Old Army also shoots the Buffalo Bullet Co. 190-grain conical with 40 grains of Pyrodex P for 1,157 fps MV with a muzzle energy of 565 foot-pounds. A good load in the 38 Special cartridge shows a 140-grain bullet at 1,00 fps MV for a muzzle energy of 311 foot-

pounds. While 565 foot-pounds of delivered energy will definitely take deer-sized game, the Ruger Old Army should not be considered a big-game revolver, except in the hands of a highly proficient handgun marksman and hunter.

On the Trail

A great application for the blackpowder sidearm is on the trail, especially backpacking when small-game season is open. In many areas, mountain grouse and partridge are legally taken with blackpowder handguns, which are also perfectly acceptable for rabbits, squirrels, and other small-game edibles. The type of handgun is entirely subject to individual choice. However, a combination of adjustable target sights from a blackpowder sidearm capable of good accuracy is obviously advantageous. Often, shots are at very close range. Most of my mountain grouse and cottontails come to bag at only 10 to 20 yards distance. Bullet placement, however, is vital, and in spite of close range, good sights and accuracy are necessary for successfully bringing home small edibles.

In the Camp

A camp gun is any firearm that's handy, easy to manage, and reliable. The blackpowder six-gun can be all of those things. Personally, I

have never required a camp gun, and probably never will, but you never know. A friend had a skunk stroll into camp. He didn't want to shoot it for the obvious reason of a gas attack, plus he had no desire to dispatch Mr. Stripes. He didn't know the skunk was rabid, and it ended up biting his 9-year-old son. Quite an unlikely event, but it happened. A camp gun can come in handy.

Self-Defense

On the battlefield, aboard sailing vessels, as well as in saloons and streets all over 19th-century America, the blackpowder sidearm grimly took its toll on the good and the bad. However, in spite of its history, the blackpowder handgun cannot be recommend for self- or family defense. It is simply outdated and outclassed for that purpose.

Completing The Period Outfit

Civil War re-enactments demand proper outfits, including guns, which means handguns as well as long arms. Other period dress, such as 19th-century fur-trapper regalia, also requires a proper handgun to complete the outfit. Study of the period reveals just which guns these are.

Rendezvous

Another worthwhile and important use of the sidearm is at rendezvous. Few mountain-man buckskinner outfits are complete without some sort of period handgun matching up with the rest of the dress.

Blackpowder Revolver Cartridges

The blackpowder cartridge did not develop its full potential until smokeless powder came along. Additionally, these rounds did not achieve full potency until strong handguns were developed to stand up to the pressure. The 45 Colt is a major example of this fact. In a

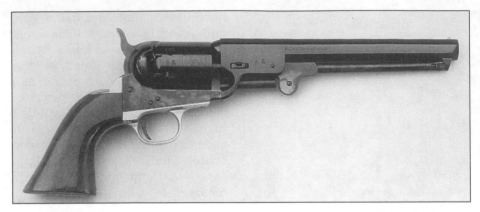

Smallbore revolvers were mainly calibers 31 and 36. This 1851 Colt Navy was chambered in 36 caliber. The Navy Arms Co. replica wears a small bead front sight.

Ruger Blackhawk, which is constructed to withstand the pressure, this old-time round — on board in 1873 — produces magnum punch. Loads allowed in the strong Ruger are not safe in weaker models. However, a big 300-grain Hornady XTP bullet reaches 1,300 fps MV in the Ruger for a muzzle energy of 1,126 foot-pounds. This is far more energy than available with blackpowder. There are several blackpowder cartridges from days gone by that remain viable, not only with modern smokeless powder loads and jacketed bullets, but also blackpowder charges and lead bullets.

32-20 Winchester

This round doubled as a revolver as well as a rifle cartridge. It never generated a lot of power, a fact that in a very real way kept the round alive. The little 32-20 is extremely pleasant to shoot. Yet it will put small game in the pot without a hitch, including the wily wild turkey. It's also a great plinking cartridge. The 32-20 Winchester was introduced in 1882 for chambering in the company's Model 1873 lever-action rifle. Soon, the cartridge was introduced in the revolver. Colt's six-guns chambered for the 32-20 Winchester round were quite popular. Bullets in the 100- to 115-grain category at below the speed of sound did quite a bit of work without undue destruction of tender edibles. Some shooters also relied on the little 32-20 for defense. Today,

the little round is outclassed for that duty. The Lyman Ideal Handbook No. 39, 1953, showed a 115-grain lead bullet doing 925 fps MV from a revolver, with a muzzle energy 219 foot-pounds.

38-40 Winchester

The 38-40 Winchester is interesting because it is so close to the 44-40, right down to actual caliber size, that we wonder why it was

developed in the first place. It came along in 1874, based on the 44-40 case necked down. True caliber was .401, so the 38-40 could have been called the 40-40 Winchester. It fired lead bullets in the 180- to 200-grain class at modest velocities from the handgun, in the area of 900 fps. Nonetheless, it was well liked and some hunters stayed with the 38-40, even with blackpowder, well into the modern era. The 38-40 Winchester fired enough bullet to serve as an effective self-defense round. The Lyman Ideal Handbook No. 39, 1953, showed a smokeless powder hand load with a 180-grain bullet at 1,105 fps MV for a muzzle energy of 488 foot-pounds from a revolver. While not a powerful showing, at the same time, a 40-caliber 180-grain bullet possesses fairly decent penetration potential.

44-40 Winchester

The 44-40 Winchester also remains loaded to this day as another blackpowder cartridge that

Sam Colt's company introduced the world's most famous six-shooter, the single-action cartridge gun. But this revolver did not start that way. The first ones were blackpowder caplocks, every one, including many carried by now-famous shooters, such as Wild Bill Hickok.

won't go away. The squat little cartridge has long been a favorite in the handgun and rifle. It fires a 200-grain bullet at about the same velocity earned by a 180-grain bullet in the 38-40. Lyman's Ideal Handbook No. 39, 1953, gives this round 1,050 fps MV with a 210-grain lead bullet for 514 foot-pounds. The 44-40 was the original chambering for the famous Model 1873 Winchester rifle, and it didn't take long to find its way into a sidearm. Actually, it will handle bullets of 250 grains, but the 200-grain is far more popular. As a sidearm to go along with a blackpowder cartridge rifle, either a single-shot or lever-action repeater, the 44-40 is a good one. It's historically antiquated, yet not truly outdated. Many replica rifles and revolvers are currently chambered for the 44-40 cartridge. Hornady's 5th edition of its fine handbook shows the 44-40 tested in a Cimarron Model P with 4 3/4-inch barrel, the highest velocity with a 200-grain Hornady jacketed bullet showing 1,150 fps MV for an energy rating of 587 foot-pounds.

45 Colt

The 45 ACP (Automatic Colt Pis-

The sash gun was a single-shot pistol with a long bar that slipped into a sash worn around the waist, or as shown here, a belt. Lyman's Plains Pistol is shown.

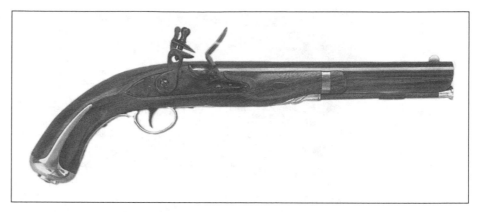

The 1805 Harpers Ferry Pistol, flintlock, does not carry a huge powder charge, but the fact that it fires a 58-caliber bullet makes it formidable at close range.

tol) was developed by John Browning in 1905, becoming the official pistol round of the U.S. Army soon after. The 45 Colt was developed long before that in 1873 by Colt, and did not go by the name of 45 "Long" Colt, as it is so often called today, because there would not be a 45 "short" Colt (45 ACP) on the market for years to come. Notes show original loads with a 255-grain bullet in front of 40 grains FFg blackpowder. This was with the old balloon-head case. New cases hold less powder. Chronograph tests with a 45 Colt in an original Colt Single Action Army revolver carried 37 grains of FFg blackpowder, creating 773 fps with a 255-grain lead bullet for a muzzle energy of only 338 foot-pounds. Of course, smokeless powder loads result in more power for this old round. The Lyman Ideal Handbook No. 39, 1953, showed a 250-grain lead bullet at 1,030 fps MV for a muzzle energy of 589 foot-pounds. The 45 Colt was also noted above with super loads for the Ruger handgun and true magnum performance. But even with the blackpowder load, the big bullet, despite low velocity, proves to penetrate well on test media.

Dangers of Smokeless Powder Loads in Blackpowder Cartridge Handguns

We know that blackpowder handgun cartridges are loaded with modern smokeless powder in some

firearms; however old blackpowder handguns can be blown up with smokeless powder. Heed all information given. An Accurate Arms' loading data book stated that, "The SAAMI maximum average pressure for the .44-40 is 13,000 C.U.P." Accurate Arms went on to say that its smokeless-powder loads in that manual were maximum, running from about 11,000 to 13,000 C.U.P. Within this safety parameter, a 200-grain jacketed Nosler bullet earned 1,008 fps MV with a pressure rating of 13,000 C.U.P. (see glossary) in the 44-40. However, enough cannot be said about playing it safe with the old handguns. Every aspect of the prescribed load must be strictly observed, not only powder and powder charge, but exact bullet, primer, and case.

Muzzleloader Propellants and Blackpowder Handgun Cartridges

FFFg blackpowder and Pyrodex P, along with GOEX Clear Shot, are well-suited to smallbore pistols and the blackpowder revolver. These powders are also safe and workable in blackpowder handgun cartridges. FFg is good in many big-bore pistols, providing good velocity and accuracy. In the powerful Encore, this powder granulation is allowed in a very heavy charge, which is not true whatsoever of other pistols. Occasionally, manufacturers recommend modest charges of FFg in certain big-bore pistols. The Knight Hawkeye, no longer on the market but sometimes located for sale in The Gun List

Conical bullets work in the cap and ball revolver, too.

tition do have the cylinder chamber mouths of their firearms beveled so that the round ball is not shaved upon entry into the chamber. This also, they say, prevents damage to the base of a conical, so the process may be worth considering. Any competent gunsmith can bevel the chamber mouth of a cap and ball revolver. The second point concerns the half-charge, which in most cases in not truly one-half of the usual maximum powder charge held in the chamber of the revolver. If the chamber of the revolver holds 35 grains of powder, for example, 20 to 25 grains of powder seems to enhance accuracy. If the chamber holds 40 grains, 25 to 30 grains of powder may improve accuracy. However, an air space must not be allowed to exist. What would be an air space, due to the smaller powder charge, is filled with an inert material, such as corn meal. A blackpowder revolver with air space in the chambers must not be fired, not only for safety reasons, but also accuracy.

newspaper, proved quite accurate with a light charge of FFFg blackpowder or Pyrodex P.

The Modern Muzzleloading Pistol

Currently, there are only a few modern muzzleloader pistols on the market. The tremendous popularity of the muzzleloading rifle and consequent high sales seems to keep the in-line pistol on the backburner. Yet we know that blackpowder pistols of in-line design can be extremely powerful, stronger than a 44 Magnum handgun. It's impossible to predict the future of

more in-line blackpowder pistols. In the meanwhile, Traditions offers its Buckhunter Pro and Thompson/Center has the Encore.

Blackpowder Handgun Accuracy

Chapter 23 dealt with accuracy. However, two points concerning accuracy in blackpowder cap 'n' ball revolvers are worth considering. The first is chamfering the chamber mouth. A specific test gun did not respond to this treatment. No appreciable improvement was noticed. However, some shooters who compete at the top of cap 'n' ball compe-

Blackpowder Handgun Sights

For Cowboy Action Shooting and other games, sights restrictions may be required. However, those who wish to gain the tightest groups with the most consistency should look into target sights for their guns. Many blackpowder sidearms come with adjustable sights. Sometimes these can be added to other guns.

Typical of Ruger quality, the company's Old Army 45-caliber cap and ball revolver is excellent.

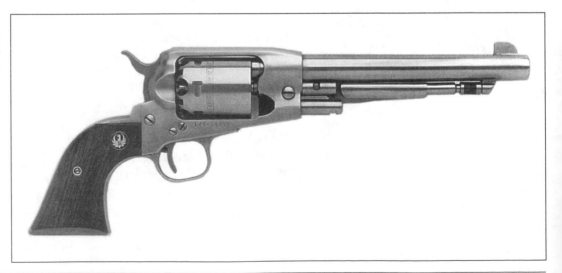

While the blackpowder revolver, shown here in a Navy Arms Co. Bisley, top, was extremely deadly, it is outmoded today for self-defense by guns like the Ruger 45-caliber semi-automatic pistol.

ers. Dirty pistols are not at their most accurate, while dirty revolvers may not even function. Neither, however, is difficult to maintain.

Carrying Blackpowder Handguns

The sash gun was carried about the waist in a sash or belt. This remains the habit of modern-day buckskinners at rendezvous; however, let's hope those guns are not loaded. While a firearm should not go off if it falls to the ground, this unfortunate circumstance has occurred, even with a modern side-arm designed not to fail in that manner. There are a number of holsters, modern and replica, available for blackpowder side-arms.

The blackpowder handgun is not the first choice of today's downwind shooter. The rifle reigns king because of special blackpowder-only big-game hunts. However, this does not detract from the fact that black-powder sidearms in pistol, cap and ball, or cartridge revolver are enjoyable to shoot, with high potential for accuracy, along with power enough for small- to large-game hunting.

Triggers

Everyone in the shooting game knows that triggers can make or break the ability of a shooter to produce good groups with any gun. If a blackpowder handgun has a trigger pull that is too heavy for consistent let-off, or if it's cursed with creep, a competent blackpowder gunsmith can often help the situation. This is a job for a professional. Messing with a trigger can bring the disaster of a gun going off at the wrong time.

Maintaining the Blackpowder Handgun

Cleaning the blackpowder pistol is no problem. The cap 'n' ball revolver requires more attention. Chapter 38 dealt with methods of maintaining both pistols and revolv-

Two good blackpowder cartridge replicas from the Navy Arms Co. go hand in hand—a Model 92 rifle and a Bisley revolver, both chambered for the 45 Colt.

Chapter 37

SMOOTHBORE SUCCESS

THE SMOOTHBORE long arm is not yet defunct, in spite of rifling being around for so long. Blackpowder shooting was dominated by smoothbores for a few centuries, continuing long after rifled arms were widely available. That's because some shooters preferred the fact that smoothbores were, and still are, easy loading and also easy to clean up after shooting, because there are no lands and grooves to capture and imprison fouling. Nineteenth-century ivory hunter William Cotton Oswell, who hunted tuskers as a young man in Africa (see Chapter 46), preferred his smoothbore for elephant hunting because it was faster and easier to reload, especially when he was riding full gallop on his horse in pursuit of pachyderms. At day's end, this professional ivory hunter had an easy time cleaning his smoothbore, too, which was especially welcomed in a camp setting without hot and cold running water. Oswell died in 1893, so his was the era of rifled arms and he did not have to use a smoothbore. S.W. Baker, whose story is also told in Chapter 46, said Oswell was absolutely the first white man to show up in certain parts of South Africa. And when Oswell did show up, he was carrying his favorite "rifle," only it was a smoothbore made by Purdey.

Smoothbores for Really Big Game

Oswell's Purdey was a 10-gauge weighing 10 pounds and charged with "six drachms of fine powder," according to Baker, who borrowed the piece from Oswell for an African hunt. The term drachm was synonymous with dram during this era. A drachm or dram equals 27.34 grains weight, so the load was 164 grains of powder, give or take. Sometimes powder was simply tossed downbore as a "fistful." Baker wrote that he enjoyed great success with Oswell's smoothbore, reporting: "There could not have been a better form of muzzleloader than this No. 10 double-barrel smoothbore. It was very accurate at 50 yards. . ." from Big Game Shooting, 1902. Of course, "very accurate" must be qualified. Baker was hunting the largest four-footed animal in the world, tons and tons big, and at close range. Oswell preferred prepatched round balls for his 10-bore, wrapping them in either "waxed kid" (leather) or linen. The "object of the smooth-bore was easy loading," said Baker. The prepatched ball was rolled tightly in cloth or leather with the excess trimmed close with "metal scissors" so that the wrapping became a part of the projectile. The powder charge was also pre-measured and carried in a paper cylinder, "the end of which could be bitten off," Baker noted. The whole package of powder, paper and all, was thrust downbore after the end was nipped off, followed by the pre-patched ball rammed home with a "powerful loading rod." Later on, Baker cursed smoothbores in print. He had admired his mentor's to begin with, but found smoothbores lacking for long-range shooting compared with a precision-made rifled long arm, which is what Baker carried for his own big-game hunting in Africa and Ceylon. In his book, The Rifle and the Hound in Ceylon, Baker verbally cut the smoothbore to ribbons with an abrupt tongue-lashing. "Smooth bores I count for nothing, although I have frequently used them," he said.

Another well-known hunter of his era, J.H. Walsh, known as "Stonehenge" to his friends, also downplayed smoothbores for hunting. In his book, Modern Sportsman's Gun & Rifle (reprinted by Wolfe Publishing Co.), Walsh warned: "If, however, the six inch circle at 50 yards could be depended on, I should be ready to admit that for large game it [a smoothbore] is a most useful weapon; and with this view I have repeatedly tested smooth-bores by various makers, but the trial has invariably ended in disappointment. Sometimes the first or second, but oftener further on in a short trial, a wild shot occurred, and of course this wild shot may be the one to cost a sportsman his life, when charged by any kind of large game." On the other hand, many military men of the past applauded the smoothbore. Our own General Washington often replaced rifled arms with muskets, believing the smoothbore a better tool for battle, easier to keep in repair, simpler, faster to reload for rapid fire, and it carried a fixed bayonet better than a rifle (Washington believed).

The Brown Bess smoothbore musket remained Britain's first choice of arms, too, for a very long time, firing a .753-inch ball

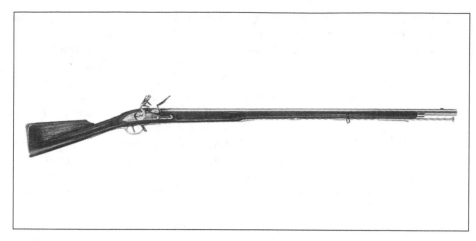

The Brown Bess was a smoothbore musket used by the British and Americans in the Revolutionary War.

(11-bore) with 70 grains of powder. Gen. George Hanger, said to be the best shot in the British Army (he served with Hessian Jaegers during the Revolution) reported that "a soldier's musket, if not exceedingly ill-bored (as many of them are), will strike the figure of a man at eighty yards; it may even at 100. . .," but he concluded that "firing at a man at 200 yards with a common musket, you may just as well fire at the moon" (American Rifleman, August 1947). Notice that Hanger thought smoothbores were more manageable on the battlefield than rifles, but he did not consider them accurate. At the Battle of New Orleans, American rifled arms certainly whipped British smoothbores. But certain American hunters continued to prefer the smoothbore well into the era of rifled long arms. Many traveling with Lewis and Clark into the Far West carried smoothbores. After all, that's what their "fusils" truly were: simply smoothbore arms, the word borrowed from the French meaning either steel or tinderbox. Sometimes, fusils were noted as "trade rifle quality" arms, meaning fairly cheap guns used for bartering. They were mentioned in print as shoulder arms as far back as 1515 in French hunting ordinances, but

were still in use during the 19th century in one form or another.

Then and Now

The historical pull of the smoothbore is magnetic. If these muskets were so ill-firing, so worthless and inaccurate, why did they hang on for so long, even after rifled arms were widely available? Furthermore, their use continued in modern times for a few special blackpowder-only hunts that did not allow rifled arms. But do hunters packing smoothbores have a prayer of cleanly dropping a deer, even at woods ranges of only 50 or 60 yards? After all, this is a much-maligned hunting tool. Even the longbow outshot the common musket back in 1792 in a match on Pac-

ton Green, Cumberland. The range was "over 100 yards" and the bowman placed 16 arrows of 20 shots in the target (size not given). Meanwhile, the best musketeer only hit the target 12 of 20 shots. As Karl Foster (of rifled-slug fame) said in the American Rifleman: "Round balls in smooth barrels have lacked accuracy since guns were first made" (October 1936 issue, p.23). In Scotland, 1803, soldiers practiced to meet Napoleon by firing their muskets. However, they were content when "...every fifth or sixth shot is made to take place in a target of three feet diameter at the distance of 100 yards" (American Rifleman, August 1947, p. 8). When I presented this quote to one of my "buckskinner" friends who had laid out a fat wad of greenbacks for a custom rifle with a smooth bore, he replied, "Must have been damn poor shots." And he went on to tell me that if ever I was in need of venison steaks for supper, just let him get within 75 yards of a buck and "We'll be in meat with my smoothbore." Then he added, "Of course, I stalk for close shots. You do remember stalking, don't you? That's where you get close before you shoot," he said sarcastically. Before turning to tests of my own, I continued turning pages in books and magazines for more information, running across a piece by Harry Root Merklee, a well-

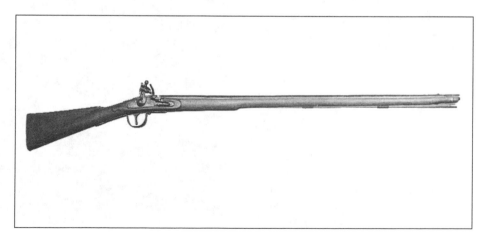

Smoothbore flintlock muskets were not extremely accurate, but were used successfully in battle and in the hunting woods.

known authority on blackpowder arms. His article resided in the April 1961 issue of Muzzle Blasts magazine. Here is what Merklee learned about accuracy with military smoothbore flintlock muskets:

Five men of military age assembled at a local range, each armed with a cal. 69 smoothbore flintlock musket. These were rifles of the Napoleonic wars and were in first class condition. Except for minor details of construction, these muskets were the same as those used during most of the flintlock period, which includes the American Revolution.

The loads for these muskets varied according to their owner's preference but all used the same caliber round ball which would slide down the bore of its own weight; 'fall down' would be a better description, a rattling fit at any rate. No patch was used of any kind. Powder charges ranged from 3 1/2 to 5 drams of FFG powder. Regular shotgun wads of felt 3/8-inch thick were used over both powder and ball.

That was the shootout Merklee described. Note that no patch was used. I doubt that a patch would have made much difference with these muskets in this particular instance. A wad held the ball in place for safety, and while a patch can transfer the impetus of the rifling to the projectile, remember there was no rifling in these smoothbores. Here is what happened: Shooting from a sitting position, the marksmen kept most bullets within a 16-inch circle at 50 yards. Sights on these muskets were too crude to ask for much more in the first place, and trigger pull was referred to as "horrible." Powder charges ranged from 3.5 drams to 5 drams (96 to 137 grains) and recoil proved bothersome with the latter from the sitting position, mainly because of the poorly designed stocks of these guns. The 69-caliber round balls would have weighed 494 grains or so, depending upon exact diameter. A 16-inch

group at 50 yards is a poor showing, but all shooting was done sitting, not from a bench. What could be accomplished under slightly more favorable circumstances? Finding out was one of the more interesting tests of the book.

The Shotgun

A musket is not a shotgun, but first attempts to study accuracy with a smoothbore were made with a double-barreled shotgun shooting patched round balls. Sights were lacking, but sights were also crude on most original muskets. Success and failure came riding on one horse. Power was all right. Accuracy was dismal. The shotgun was a 28-inch-barreled, 12-gauge side-by-side caplock. Eighty grains of GOEX FFg provided a MV of 927 fps. That load was mild, even behind a .695-inch patched ball, which averaged 502 grains weight, so the charge progressed to a flat 100 grains of the same powder for a MV of 1,190 fps. The heavier charge developed 1,579 foot-pounds, which would make a strong showing on deer-sized game in the thicket — more than three-fourths of a short ton of energy at the muzzle. I was interested in close-range shooting, which would be the normal application for such a gun and load. A target a foot across was set up at 40 paces. The 12-gauge round ball had

been tested in Sam's Bullet Box, penetrating a couple feet of media at 50 yards, bettering the "wound channel" I'd gotten from a couple of 30-06 loads. Performance was fine that way, but as admitted, accuracy was in the garbage can. I failed to keep all bullets inside the 12-inch bull, even though I had a solid rest. Of course, sights were not conducive to good bullet placement, but I expected closer clusters from a distance of only 40 yards.

While the gun only wore double shotgun beads for sights, these could be aligned for some semblance of accurate aiming. Nonetheless, no matter how carefully I aimed this double-barrel smoothbore, grouping was poor. The left barrel had a penchant for dropping its projectile into the black at 40 paces with some regularity, while the right often sailed its bullet completely off target, missing everything, including the target frame. I tried the old trick of filing the muzzles to regulate the barrels (make them shoot to the same point of impact). Cutting the inside edge of the right-hand muzzle brought the ball over a little in point of impact, but nothing close to true bore regulation resulted. I gave up after the muzzle looked like a kid with a hacksaw attacked it. I almost concluded that expecting any accuracy from a smoothbore was pointless.

Old double-barrel shotguns like this one make great wallhangers, but don't try to fire one with this much wear.

On the other hand, it seemed that asking for deer-hunting accuracy with a round ball (forget the smooth bore) should be possible at only 40 or maybe 50 yards. A precisely cast round ball has no reason not to fly relatively well for a short distance, even when not spinning on its axis. The round balls used for testing were not lopsided. A perhaps crude, but not altogether worthless test is rolling round balls on a flat surface. High-quality lead pills did not wobble and bounce. They tend to take a fairly straight track. These balls tracked fine, so lousy accuracy from the shotgun at close range remained a mystery. Similar lead pills, but from rifled barrels, easily fell into 1-inch groups at 100 yards when fired from rifled arms, when test guns were outfitted with scope sights. Furthermore, the ball's center of mass rotated on its axis the same as a conical with imperfections in the ball itself, causing the projectile to leave the bore at a different angle of departure each shot. Because matter in motion moves in a straight line, the "heavy" part of the projectile would determine the initial line of flight of the round ball and an imperfect ball would tend to travel on a tangent from the line of the axis. In other words, static imbalance would ruin accuracy.

But the test round balls were uniform, weighing the same from one to the next, and they rolled and spun fine. What if static imbalance (the actual precision of the projectile in terms of mass distribution) was present in those old missiles of the past, when the boys felt lucky to infrequently hit a 3-foot target at 100 paces? Better accuracy potential resided in smoothbores firing good lead spheres, so more work was in order. Lead round balls should do better. A sphere would be less sensitive to rotational stabilization than a conical, a thought worked out a long time ago. W.W. Greener in The Gun said, "Rifling, therefore, is of greater importance when a conical or elongated projec-

tile is used than when the bullet is spherical." The principle of rotating an elongated missile for stabilization was a phenomenon tested hundreds of years ago. There are even relics of crossbow bolts that had been grooved to create a spiral motion. The big ball had mass going for it, too, and the greater the mass, the greater the inertia. The heavier the projectile, the less rotation on its axis necessary to stabilize it, and for big-game hunting with the smoothbore muzzleloader, missiles of at least 1/2-inch diameter prevail. The .690-inch ball that fit the bores of most 12-gauge shotguns, for example, weighed 454 grains. That's a hefty bullet. At the time of the test, Thompson/Center's 56-caliber round ball at 252 grains was for sale at the local blackpowder shop, so I purchased a couple boxes for testing.

Ball Mass and Accuracy

A smaller ball would gain more advantage from rifling than a larger ball, while the larger round ball would be more inherently stable, if made right, as test spheres proved to be. Further research brought Ezekiel Baker's work to light. He was a well-known court ballistician who wrote a gunnery treatise for His Majesty George IV. He said in his 11th edition of the work: "The Honorable Board of Ordnance being anxious to ascertain if rifling a large piece would have the same advantage over smooth barrels which rifles possess over muskets, and would be equally effective in carrying the ball, the experiment was tried at Woolrich [on May 15, 1806] with two wall-piece barrels of equal dimensions, one rifled, the other not rifled." The barrels were 4 feet, 6 inches long, each weighing 20 pounds. The projectiles were 5-gauge round balls. The advantage of the rifled piece was not nearly as pronounced as it had been with smaller round balls of 20-gauge size. What was not tried, however, was very careful sorting of round balls in the 20-

gauge and smaller smoothbore firearms. It was long known that balls "created by pressure," swaged, in other words, were highly uniform; however, I found no old tests in which the smoothbore was fired with very carefully weighed (sorted) round balls. In other words, would balanced spherical missiles make a difference in the smoothbore? Static stability would be improved, for certain, which should improve dynamic stability. So even though the test round balls were uniform, what would happen if they were carefully sorted into specific groups by weight?

Years later, Dr. F.W. Mann concluded, after thousands of experiments, that precision of projectile was the most important single aspect of accuracy. The sphere, if perfect, should in theory fly true, even from a smoothbore. Of course, round ball perfection wasn't possible, but precision was. Rifling vastly improved round-ball accuracy because it "averaged" the imperfections in the ball on a common axis, such as a ball heavier on one side than the other. Rifling twist equalizes lopsidedness on the axis through rotation. In my later tests, round balls were pre-sorted, which improved accuracy in the shotgun to some extent, because the balls were fired in groups. In this way, round balls of the same weight flew together to test group size.

But I still wasn't happy. There was something special about the 56-caliber round balls from Thompson/Center. They were uniform, so sorting was not necessary. The greatest variation in random sampling of 10 balls was only .9-grain. The heaviest in the string was 252.1 grains, the lightest 251.2. The micrometer gave an average diameter of .552-inch. If the T/C ball was pure lead, it would weigh 253 grains. Weighing proved that the T/C ball was precise, and it was not an alloy. Weighing proved the uniformity. What would happen if these good T/C round balls were fired from a well-made smoothbore like the Thompson/Center Renegade in 56-caliber with an adjustable rear sight? This smoothbore was created at the time to give the blackpowder hunter a reliable firearm when law or desire called for a non-rifled bore. Sights at last! Even with a good benchrest, trying to remove extraneous variables while aiming with shotgun beads for sights was an exercise in spinning wheels.

The T/C Renegade proved totally reliable, with 100 percent ignition using CCI No. 11 caps. The test run included firing 80 .550-inch T/C cast 265-grain projectiles. That was the weight written on the box. Actually, these round balls averaged closer to .551 or .552, so they weighed in at 252 grains.

The Renegade with Sights Does Better

Loads selected from the T/C manual, Shooting Thompson/Center Black Powder Guns, which came with the smoothbore Renegade, were shown with T/C patch material, a No. 11 cap, and Maxi-Lube. My tests included three different patch types and three different lubes. The shooting patches were .005-inch, .010-inch, and .013-inch, the first two from Gunther Stifter's German supply house, the last of my own cut, pure Irish linen. The .010-patch proved best of the three, only because it loaded with comparative ease, while still providing a tight bore fit. While a patch is not a true gasket, as we know from Chapter 18 (no cloth patch by itself seals hot, expanding powder gas behind the ball), it is still best to have a tight ball/patch fit to hold the ball on the powder charge and to maintain a consistent load pressure. My direct-load pressure on the ramrod (an N&W steel loading rod) was 45 pounds as maintained by one of the special tools a reader of mine, Chuck French, built for me. This particular regulator provided 45 pounds of uniform pressure upon the powder charge.

The lubes for the test were grease, cream, and liquid: RIG, Young Country Lube 103 and Falkenberry Juice, respectively. All three worked equally in terms of accuracy and many lubes of the day would work equally well. Initially, shooting from the 50-yard bench found the balls striking the black with a 6-inch center-to-center group, good enough for deer in the thicket. Early 100-yard tests were pure singing in the rain. It was a case of sights again — the good sights on the T/C Renegade were fine for hunting, especially in brush and timber country where closer shots are the rule. But for longer-range testing purposes, no iron sight in the land would do what a scope could do. Test-shooting with open iron sights at that moment did not warrant 100-yard shooting. Changing powder charges, incidentally, did not affect accuracy, which remained the same with the three allowed powder charges for the Renegade: 80, 90 and 100 grains of FFg. In light of that fact, and with regard to gaining the highest power, only the 100-grain volume charge was retained. It only developed about 6,000 LUP, with comparatively mild recoil and the muzzle velocity averaged 1,366 fps. In comparison, Thompson/Center tests averaged 1,300 fps, so we were together all the way with chronograph results. The test site was at an altitude of 6,000 feet, with the temperature hovering around 85 degrees Fahrenheit. The muzzle energy of this load was a bit over half a short ton at 1,044 foot-pounds, considering the actual weight of the round ball at 252 grains. At 50 yards, the chronograph showed a retained velocity of 1,101 fps for the 56-caliber ball, with a 50-yard energy of 678 foot-pounds. There is nothing wrong with that energy delivery, considering the size of the ball, and the load easily fell into the deer-hunting range of acceptable power.

Specific Accuracy Steps for Improved Round-Ball Smoothbore Accuracy

1. Sort round balls by weight, discarding those that do not fall within the norm for the batch. Round balls are capable of excellent uniformity in weight, whether commercial or home-cast.

2. Ensure a consistent powder charge by following a set procedure when using the powder measure. The smoothbore needs every break it can get in order to achieve hunting accuracy, and charge-for-charge consistency always promotes accuracy.

3. Use a buffer, such as hornet-nesting material, between the powder charge and the patched ball. This little step provides assurance of good patch condition, which in turn may promote accuracy in some cases.

4. Use good patches that take up the windage in the bore. Although the patch cannot translate the rotational value imparted by rifling because there is no rifling in the smoothbore, the patch is part of the load chain, and it must hold the round ball firmly on the powder charge with good pressure.

5. Be sure to wipe excess lube from the bore after loading. This step ensures the same bore condition from shot to shot, and such consistency never harms accuracy.

6. Review accuracy aspects as outlined in Chapter 23 to be certain that you've done all you can do to upgrade smoothbore accuracy.

7. Choose large calibers. Large round balls have more accuracy potential than small ones because they have more mass and tend to stay "on line" better. In short, they are more stable in flight, while smaller balls also have great accuracy potential with rifling spinning them.

8. If possible, have sights fitted to a smoothbore intended for big-game hunting. No firearm can be expected to shoot well without proper sights.

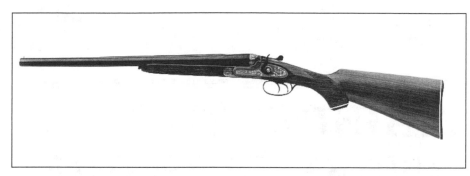

A blackpowder shotgun becomes a formidable deer gun when loaded with round balls.

Vital Consistency

The ball-shooting smoothbore proved amply accurate for deer hunting in woods and timber. Previous shotgun clusters shrank to consistent 8-inch groups at 100 yards with iron sights. A test with a scope sight mounted on the smoothbore could reveal further accuracy potential. At 50 yards, 3-inch center-to-center groups were common, but good groups at any range were possible only after using a careful regimen in the loading process combined with precise missiles, such as those supplied at the time of this test by Thompson/Center. Also, consistency of powder charge was maintained by overfilling the measure, tapping the barrel of the measure 10 times, then swiping off excess kernels of powder by swinging the funnel section of the measure into line with the barrel.

Hornet-nesting material buffer between the patched ball and charge ensured patch integrity. As we know, hornet-nesting material does not catch fire inside the bore, thus saving the patch from burnout. Moreover, a buffer between patch and charge serves to absorb excess lube that might attack the powder charge. Another step in the accuracy process was wiping the bore free of excess lube after the load was seated in the breech of the gun. Firing several groups with the bore untouched (damp) after seating the ball and several groups with the bore wiped with a cleaning patch after seating the ball proved that the latter were always better in the particular test firearm. The point of impact also remained constant with the dry-bore method of loading. Final sight-in was also accomplished with a lube-free bore.

Most interesting were follow-up tests with various smoothbore guns, including a Thompson/Center New Englander single-barrel 12-gauge shotgun with auxiliary rifled 50-caliber barrel. The smoothbore barrel was loaded with one .690-inch round patched ball using the sequence mentioned above with hornet-nest buffer. This test centered on Pyrodex RS powder with a charge of 100-grains volume (70.5 grains weight for the particular lot of powder). Accuracy was more than acceptable, especially considering the shotgun bead as an aiming device instead of true sights with 6-inch center-to-center groups at 50 yards. Carefully loaded, the New Englander could be counted on to strike the chest area of a deer at close range, which was the goal all along. Also interesting was a test run with a Navy Arms Co. Terry Texas Ranger 12-gauge shotgun. This little shotgun was offered with a 12-inch barrel. (*Editor's note: Although considered a blackpowder arm, this model later was ruled to be a destructive device by the Bureau of Alcohol, Tobacco and Firearms, and is no longer made. Federal law generally requires a shotgun to have a minimum 18-inch barrel.*) In the brush, it carried out of the way and came to shoulder rattlesnake fast. Initially, one barrel was loaded with buckshot, the other a single patched .690-inch round ball. The buckshot load was disappointing, so each barrel was consequently loaded with a single patched round ball. Eighty grains of Fg blackpowder provided more than 900-fps muzzle velocity. Not much for energy, but a good wallop at close range on deer-sized game.

While there is no particular reason for a hunter abandoning his rifled muzzleloader for a smoothbore, testing was worthwhile, not only from the historical aspect, but also showing that a smoothbore long arm is capable of hunting accuracy in spite of the fact that it doesn't even come close to the accuracy provided by rifled arms.

Where the law requires, or a blackpowder hunter, for his own reasons, chooses a smoothbore, effective close-range ball placement is totally possible on deer-sized game and larger.

Chapter 38

MAINTAINING THE BLACKPOWDER FIREARM

A TRULY non-corrosive muzzle-loader propellant has not materialized, although there are definitely clean-burning powders available. Non-corrosive powders allow shooting, then putting the firearm away that day without concern for pitting of the bore or discoloration of exterior metal parts, at least for a while. For example, a shooter goes to the range with his 22 rimfire, along with a 308 bolt-action big game rifle. He shoots a hundred rounds through the 22, plus 20 cartridges in the 308. Upon returning home, he puts both firearms into safe lockup and goes about his business. A couple days later, the rifles

are cleaned. Damage? Unless humidity is terrible, no damage occurs. Try that with a muzzle-loader and any blackpowder or blackpowder substitute normally available at the moment and there is definite risk of rust or other invasion of the metalwork, especially in the bore of the gun. Does this suggest that modern cartridge guns do not require after-shooting attention? Not at all. High-velocity jacketed bullets eventually leave copper fouling in the bore, compromising accuracy. A gunsmith I know works on guns that have "lost their accuracy." He tells every customer the same thing. "Take this home and

really clean it. Then come back if accuracy is still off." Most people don't believe him. "If they want to pay me to clean their guns, I'll clean their guns," he says.

The muzzleloader on the other hand, falls prey to the hygroscopic (moisture-attracting) effect of blackpowder. Naturally, the Savage Model 10ML, which is the only muzzleloader allowed smokeless powder as this is written, is an exception when fired with smokeless powder. Furthermore, no muzzleloader suffers from copper fouling because jacketed bullets are encased in plastic sabots. These do leave a little plastic residue behind,

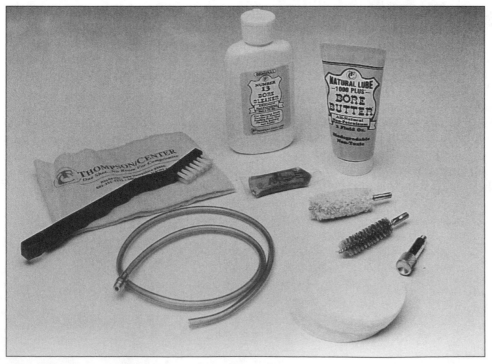

Modern blackpowder shooting maintenance is made easy by new chemicals and tools such as Bore Butter, which keeps blackpowder fouling soft during shooting, to Number 13 Bore Cleaner. Good tools help, too.

Compact cleaning kits like this one from Hoppe's provide a full complement of maintenance products and tools for the gun range.

game would never choose a firearm based upon barrel length for maintenance reasons, shorter tubes are still easier to clean. Deep grooves naturally hold onto fouling a little more than shallower grooves. Once again, this factor is not sufficient for most of us to worry about. But my own custom 54-caliber rifle does not have deep grooves and it shoots a patched round ball with fine accuracy while cleaning up readily. Of much more impact is the removable breech plug. The modern muzzleloader with removable breech plug cleans from the back, easier and faster than from the muzzle. Furthermore, the shooter can look right through the bore to see how clean it looks. Finally, for the shooter who wants to go with a muzzleloader with no more maintenance than a smokeless powder firearm, there's the aforementioned Savage Model 10ML.

Cleaning Before Shooting

Cleaning before shooting means using a modern chemical as a lube. There are many commercial products available today, each one designed to attack blackpowder fouling. These come in various forms of liquid, cream and paste as discussed in Chapter 19. While the all-day shooting promise can be

but that cleans up readily with chemicals described in Chapter 19. There is more good news. Maintaining the muzzleloader today is easier than ever before because of high-tech chemicals that are designed to break down blackpowder fouling so the gunk can be ushered out of the bore and down the drain. So keeping front loaders in top shape today is not that much trouble and blackpowder shooting can be enjoyed without a lot of after-shooting fuss.

Easier-to-Clean Guns

Anyone concerned that firearms maintenance is a stumbling block and unsavory chore should not forsake his or her interest in muzzleloaders. There are blackpowder firearms that tend to clean up easier than others because of barrel length, depth of grooves, removable breech plugs, and smooth bores. A muzzleloader with a 24-inch barrel tends to be a little easier to clean than a rifle with a 34-inch barrel for two simple reasons. The shorter

bore offers reduced surface to clean, and it is also a handier size to fit into the kitchen sink, laundry room wash-tub station, or for that matter, cleaning it with solvent only on the back porch. While most of us deeply involved in the blackpowder

Modern chemicals have come to the aid of muzzleloader fans. Black Off™ from Markesbery is a prime example of a solvent that attacks blackpowder fouling.

overdone, there is no doubt that modern blackpowder chemicals pay off with easier after-shooting maintenance. Anyone doubting this can test for himself, shooting with whale oil, vegetable oil, bear fat, or other substance, then going to the range again with a modern patch or conical lube.

How Clean is Clean?

Using modern chemicals, muzzleloaders can be cleaned very thoroughly. In the past, I was happy when taking a stored muzzleloader out of the gun safe and running a white patch through the bore produced only a little dark stuff. Today, the white patch emerges white, or close to it. This is probably truer of modern in-lines with removable breech plugs than front stuffers that require cleaning from the muzzle, but all front loaders clean up well with the methods described in this chapter, especially with commercial solvents doing the work.

The Evils of Poor After-Shooting Maintenance

The simple water-cleaning method used eons ago got guns clean enough to preserve them, and there is nothing wrong with that method today. However, after-cleaning metal preservers should be used after the water-only cleaning method. The old way of simply pouring water downbore and cleaning with a patch on the end of a ramrod or wiping stick is workable, but there remains a chance, however small, of leaving a trace of moisture in the bore, or for that matter working parts of the gun, such as a trigger or lock. A metal preserving agent can help thwart rust when this happens. When blackpowder guns are not cleaned properly, several bad things can happen. I inspected a muzzleloading rifle once that had completely blown its nipple right out of the nipple seat. The first noticeable aspect of that rifle was the bore. It was caked with fouling. So an unclean muzzleloader can be dangerous. This was certainly true of the old days. In Russell's Journal of a Trapper, "gun accident" accounts were reported. When one man came up missing, "It was then agreed that either his gun had bursted and killed him, or his horse had fallen with him over some tremendous precipice." Why would a gun "burst," as Russell put it? Consider that the bore is filthy and a bullet fails to seat fully in the bore. It's the old short-start problem again.

A poorly maintained gun can also fail in accuracy. When the muzzle, especially the crown itself, becomes corroded or worn, the bullet may not receive sufficient guiding to send it spinning on its way properly. Also, a ring can build up in the bore when a gun is not cleaned efficiently. This ring represents a fouled area that failed to get

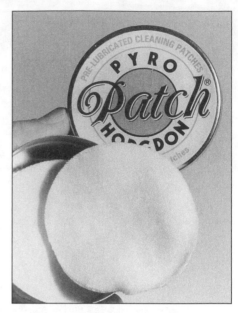

Today's blackpowder shooter has a wealth of special commercial products at his fingertips to make the job of after-shooting maintenance easier, such as these Pyro Patches.

scrubbed clean. It's an etched circle that never goes away. Also, poor cleaning can cause a pitted bore. Pits are rust pockets. Furthermore, the interior of the lock may suffer, failing to work properly if the notches on the tumbler are reduced by corrosion. The firearm could even go off prematurely if the nose of the sear slips out of the full-cock notch or half-cock notch. The nipple seat area may also deteriorate to the point where it fails to transfer the spark from the percussion cap to the breech, causing misfires and hangfires. In a worse case, the nipple may dislodge. The flintlock's touchhole will one day burn out anyway after considerable use, but left unclean, it will suffer damage much sooner. Finally, the stock can suffer damage from fouling.

Blackpowder Corrosiveness

Due to the nature of blackpowder and substitutes, many different salts are left behind following combustion. These salts can cause damage. They are reduced (broken down) with polar solvents, such as water, as well as with many com-

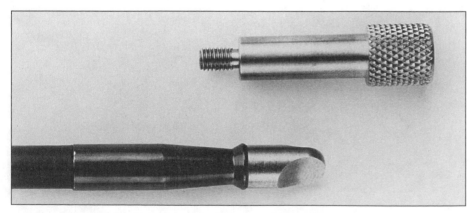

Thompson Center's Super Jag and Breech Plug Scraper are just two more tools designed to make muzzleloader maintenance foolproof and easy to accomplish quickly.

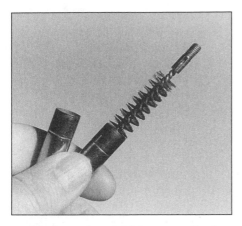

Blackpowder cartridge cases fired with blackpowder require cleaning. A bristle brush like this one dipped in hot soapy water does a good job.

mercial products. At the same time, the corrosive nature of blackpowder can be overstated. Blackpowder does not "eat up" metal on contact. Having tested original muzzleloaders left in a loaded condition perhaps for years, I have yet to find one "eaten up" by blackpowder. True, where the load rested in the bore, there was evidence of damage, but if blackpowder were like a powerful acid, much more harm would have occurred, and it did not. The larger problem is a muzzleloader propellant's tendency to be hygroscopic. Imagine a soda cracker left out in a high-humidity environment. Soon it's soggy. If a muzzleloader is left loaded in a high-humidity environment, the powder will take up moisture and that means rust. A six-month test with several barrels firing Black Canyon, Pyrodex, and GOEX blackpowder, cleaned with two techniques (water only and solvent only), resulted in zero damage to any of the barrels. That included subjecting each barrel to a waiting period before cleaning. However, this would not be wise in a high-humidity area. The test was conducted in a low-humidity setting.

Disassembly Before Cleaning

In all methods of cleaning, the firearm should be broken down before working on it if possible. This is less true of the pinned stock vs. the keyed stock. Pins must be driven out carefully by consulting the gunmaker for directions, ensuring that each pin is driven out from the correct side of the stock, because sometimes pins are tapered. Forcing them out the wrong way can split the stock. Careful observation can usually detect tapered pins, one end being larger than the other. Keyed stocks are simple to "unlatch." The wedge, or key, is forced free and the barrel normally can be lifted out of the barrel channel. For hooked breeches or any firearm that comes apart easily, removing the barrel for cleaning makes the job a lot easier. While the lock need not be removed after every shooting session, it must be checked from time to time, for fouling can get into the workings. The modern muzzleloader with removable breech plug is entirely a different story. The breech plug is removed, normally with a special tool provided with the firearm. Then fouling removal from the bore takes place from the breech end.

Water-Only Cleanup

Ordinary tap water is an acceptable cleaning agent because of its nature as a universal solvent. A cloth should be wrapped around the muzzle of a firearm not taken apart. If not, water can seep between the barrel and the stock. Water breaks down and dissolves most blackpowder residue. It works not only on salts, but also carbon and sulfur. Water is cheap, so a shooter can afford to flush the bore thoroughly to get rid of fouling.

STEPS FOR WATER-ONLY CLEANUP

1. Make certain that the firearm is unloaded with no cap or primer in place. "The gun went off when he was cleaning it" may be an old story, but it has happened. See Chapter 8 for checking for a load using a ramrod, remembering to insert the ramrod to see if it bottoms out, or if it falls short of the bottom of the breech, indicating a load is present.

2. Disassemble the firearm appropriately, removing the barrel if possible. Take out the remov-

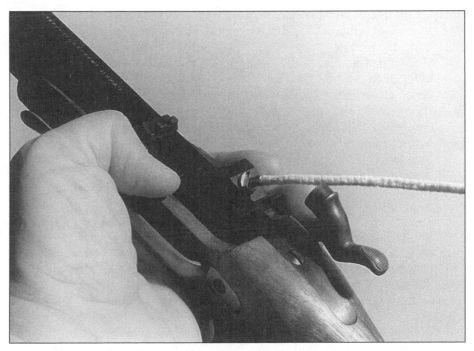

The simple pipe cleaner sold in smoking shops and grocery stores turns into a fine cleaning tool, shown here attacking fouling within the channel of a nipple.

able breech plug on a modern muzzleloader.

3. Flush the bore with cool water. The theory, and no more than a theory, is that cool water will not "set" fouling in the bore. This step gets the process under way, breaking down and flushing out major fouling.

4. Flush the bore with hot water. This is important. Hot water heats the barrel, which in turn aids the drying process. It is impossible with some firearms to reach every little corner with a cleaning patch or pipe cleaner, but if the bore is hot, traces of trapped water evaporate.

5. Use a bristle brush to scrub residue from rifling grooves.

6. Remove the nipple. If the firearm has a cleanout screw, remove it now. The screw allows a flow of water through the breech section. While the nipple seat also affords this passageway, the cleanout screw opens a direct port from the breech. Flushing with the cleanout screw removed helps clear powder residue directly from the breech. Water squirts out vigorously through the cleanout screw hole when poured directly down the muzzle.

7. Leaving the cleanout screw hole open, work the bristle brush through the bore several times with hot water, being careful to guide the stream of water from the cleanout screw hole away from the lock and stock of the firearm. If dirty water invades the lock, lock mortise, or barrel channel, it can promote rust and/or wood decay, especially if the mortises and channels are not well-finished.

8. Douse a toothbrush with hot water and scrub the hammer nose, snail area, metal parts around the lock, nipple seat, nipple threads and other exposed metal parts. A toothbrush does for the outer parts of the gun what a bristle brush does for the bore.

9. Dip a pipe cleaner in hot water and swab the vent of the nipple, as well as the nipple seat of the firearm. Use the same treatment to clean the touchhole of the flintlock.

10. Now it's time to sop up moisture left in the bore. Cleaning patches pick up debris that has been knocked loose by the bristle brush, but not carried off by the water flush.

11. Repeat Step 10 with more dry patches. The first patches out of the bore may be quite wet. Since hot water was used, it won't take long to dry the bore. Continue wiping the bore with dry patches until one emerges white or very close to white.

12. Wipe all channels, cracks, and crevices dry with pipe cleaners.

13. Dry outer metal surfaces. In the process of cleaning the muzzleloader, some moisture and even blackpowder residue may have been transferred to the barrel and lock of the firearm, generally caused by pouring water downbore. Dry with a clean cloth.

14. Wipe the wood to clear off water and residue, then rub the stock with a clean cloth plus a few drops of pure boiled linseed oil.

15. Go over the entire firearm one last time with a soft clean cloth, free of solvent, oil, or any other product. This step picks up traces of residue, extra solvent or linseed oil from the surface of the gun.

16. Run a cleaning patch dampened with a little metal preserver through the bore (be certain to run a dry patch downbore before shooting the firearm next time so that preserver is removed).

17. Apply a light coating of metal-preserving chemical to the outside of the barrel and lock.

18. Occasionally, the lock requires special cleaning. Remove it from its mortise in the stock. Blow dirt out of the workings with canned air or an air hose. Use a toothbrush to flick away stubborn dirt. Wipe all exposed parts clean. Oil lightly.

19. Bright work, such as brass fittings, may be cleaned with a little Flitz on a cloth. Follow with a clean, soft, dry cloth.

Tip: An oily bore may shoot wide of the mark or may produce overly large groups. Sight-in with an oil-free bore and maintain an oil-free bore during shooting. As noted elsewhere, running the cleaning patch down here is no different from loading the bullet downbore, which was just accomplished. The clean patch sops up any excess oil or lube left in the bore from the ball patch or from grease on the conical. After storing a muzzleloader with a little preserving oil in the bore, remove that oil before firing the muzzleloader again. Oil in any bore can cause a hydraulic effect with possible bore damage, as the oil comes between the projectile and walls of the bore, possibly forcing a slight bulge in the bore. This little precaution is worth doing even if damage is unlikely.

Solvent-Only Cleanup

No water whatsoever is used in this method of muzzleloader cleaning. William Large, barrel maker for more than 50 years, scolded me with the warning: "Never touch water to barrels." He went on to say that he had been shooting muzzleloaders longer than I'd been alive at the time, and he did not believe in cleaning with water, relying only on solvent to keep his barrels in perfect shooting condition. Since his barrels have won literally hundreds of muzzleloader matches, I'd say Large knew what he was talking about. Nonetheless, the worn cliché "to each his own" prevails, and if a shooter feels more comfortable with an all-water cleaning, he has every right to pursue that method. Furthermore, some shooters report that in regions of high humidity, the hot-water flush does the best job of getting the gunk out, while allowing the bore to dry thoroughly.

STEPS FOR SOLVENT-ONLY CLEANUP

1. Again, ensure that the firearm is unloaded before attempting disassembly or cleanup, with no cap or primer in place.
2. A proper-sized jag is attached to the end of a cleaning rod to hang onto the patch. If the right jag is used with the correct cleaning patch, the patch will not fall off downbore. And if it does, that's where the worm comes into play. The patch is soaked with one of the modern solvents and run through the bore several times in this step to loosen fouling.
3. After swabbing the bore with solvent, remove the nipple and cleanout screw (if the gun has one) and repeat Step 2. The reason for waiting to remove the cleanout screw until this step is to help loosen it. Solvent runs into the threads of the nipple and cleanout screw, making both easier to remove.
4. Scrub the bore with a bristle brush soaked in solvent. Depending upon how much powder was burned in the bore anywhere from only a few passes with the brush to dozens are required. The brush is important to the no-water cleaning method because the bristles fine their way into the grooves of the rifling to scrub out fouling.
5. Now sop up the goop in the bore by running dry patches through. If a lot of powder was fired, and in spite of cleaning between strings of shots, it may take a few patches to soak up all of the dark liquid in the bore after the bristle brush and solvent have gone to work.
6. Repeat Step 4 with more solvent, more bristle brush work.
7. Repeat Step 5 with more soaking-up cleaning patches. At this point, patches should emerge from the bore at least gray

instead of black or dark brown.
8. Now refer to Steps 12 through 19 in the water method, but forget the water. Use only solvent on a rag to clean exterior metal, while solvent on a pipe cleaner reaches into cracks and crevices. Be certain to dry every part well. Don't fail to use the pipe cleaner or toothbrush. These tools work well with any cleaning method.

Water/Solvent Combination

This method incorporates the hot water flush, plus scrubbing the bore with a solvent-soaked bristle brush.

STEPS FOR WATER/SOLVENT METHOD

1. Make sure that the muzzleloader is unloaded before attempting to clean it. After ensuring that it is unloaded, and free of cap or primer, you may take it apart.
2. Flush the bore with cool water.
3. Flush the bore with hot water.
4. Run a solvent-soaked cleaning patch through the bore several strokes.
5. Make several passes with a solvent-soaked bristle brush.
6. Remove the nipple and cleanout screw (if there is one).
7. Run a solvent-soaked bristle brush through the bore several strokes with the nipple and cleanout screw removed.
8. Sop up all liquid from the bore with cleaning patches.
9. Clean the nipple seat and cleanout screw hole with a pipe cleaner dipped in solvent.
10. Wipe all channels with the toothbrush and pipe cleaners using only a little solvent. Overusing solvent on the toothbrush or pipe cleaner causes the solvent to run into mortises and between metal and wood parts.
11. Wipe the outer portion of the firearm, metal and wood, with clean rags, using a little boiled linseed oil on the stock and a little oil on the metal.

12. Protect the bore with a light coating of rust inhibitor or other metal preserving agent.
13. Attend to the lock if necessary, removing it to clean inside with a cloth and solvent. Use pipe cleaners to get into the crevices. Lightly oil all parts of lock.
14. Attend to the bright work with a little Flitz on a cloth.

Markesbery Muzzleloader Cleaning Method

Although this procedure comes from a specific blackpowder company for a specific muzzleloader, the Outer-Line®, it's worth looking into as an alternative.

STEPS FOR MARKESBERY METHOD

1. Ensure that the firearm is unloaded without cap or primer before proceeding.
2. Place all tools and cleaning products on the bench, ready for use.
3. Thread the cleaning jag onto the aluminum ramrod. (The Markesbery comes with a strong ramrod, plus a T-handle extension that turns the ramrod into a true cleaning/wiping stick.)
4. Loosen and remove the receiver/barrel lug screw on the bottom of the barrel and remove the barrel from the receiver.
5. Remove nipple or optional 400 SRP unit (which takes a small rifle primer). The firearm is now ready for cleaning.
6. Unscrew the breech plug with tool provided.
7. Run cleaning patches soaked with solvent through the bore several passes.
8. In the meanwhile, drop the nipple into a small container of Rusty Duck "Black Off" solvent. (This is the company's special cleaning product)
9. Wipe fouling from rear of rifle with solvent cloth where caps or primers were exploded.
10. Wipe receiver clean with solvent cloth.

11. Run a final solvent patch through bore followed by drying patches.
12. A final patch lightly sprayed with Rusty Duck Protective Lubricant is run through the bore.
13. Reassemble the rifle, being sure to use an anti-seize lubricant on the threads of the breech plug.

While the above method seems long, due to the 13 steps, it actually takes less than 10 minutes, and can be done faster, if there is a reason to hurry.

The 8-Minute Pyrodex Cleanup

STEPS FOR THE 8-MINUTE CLEANUP

1. Ensure that the gun is absolutely unloaded with no percussion cap on nipple.
2. Set cleaning tools and supplies in easy reach, these being: Pyrodex EZ-Clean solvent, Pyrodex Cleaning Patches (these contain a special metal treatment), muzzleloading lube, nipple pick or pipe cleaner, cotton cloth, ramrod with jag, large dry cotton patches, such as used for 12-gauge shotgun, and bristle brush, and toothbrush.
3. Spray E-Z Clean down the barrel and all over the rifle where residue exists. Use a toothbrush to loosen stubborn exterior fouling.
4. Spray seven or eight large patches with EZ Clean until saturated.
5. Using jag, run three of the patches through bore five times each.
6. Do the same with two dry patches.
7. Spray E-Z Clean on bristle brush, run through bore five strokes.
8. Run to final saturated patches through bore ten times followed by two drying patches.
9. Using two Pyrodex Cleaning Patches, one at a time, swab the bore five times with each one.
10. Wipe off exterior of gun with two or three Pyrodex Cleaning Patches, leaving a protective coating on the metal.
11. Use pipe cleaner with E-Z Clean, then dry pipe cleaners to clean nipple.
12. If cleaning a muzzleloader with removable breech plug, coat threads with some type of anti-seize agent.

Cleaning Hints

Nipples are easily cleaned by dropping into a small container with solvent, allowing to soak while working on the rest of the gun, then running a pipe cleaner through the nipple vent. Nipple threads clean up with a toothbrush. After drying nipple with pipe cleaners and a rag, replace in nipple seat of the firearm.

Plastic Fouling

Plastic fouling from one-piece plastic wads in the shotgun or sabots in rifles or pistols may be removed with a modern solvent, such as Shooter's Choice or Butch's Bore Shine using a bristle brush, following instructions on the container.

Blackpowder Cartridge Cases

As the blackpowder gun requires cleaning, so do cases firing blackpowder or substitute. Soak in solvent. Scrub interior with bristle brush. Dry thoroughly. Run through vibratory case cleaner for shiny finish.

Long-Term

After several seasons of heavy use, it's a good idea to treat the muzzleloader to a real checkup. If it does not have a removable breech plug, it might be a good idea to have a blackpowder gunsmith to debreech the gun, cleaning thoroughly, and inspecting the bore.

Shotguns, Pistols and Revolvers

Shotguns and pistols are cleaned very much like the muzzle-loading rifle. All in all, the same goal pertains: get rid of fouling. The revolver is different. A few instructions are provided here. A major difference in revolver cleaning is disassembly. Blackpowder fouling can get into the workings of the revolver, binding up the action.

Cleaning a Revolver With Water

STEPS FOR CLEANING CAP AND BALL REVOLVER WITH WATER

1. Ensure that the gun is unloaded and uncapped before cleaning it.
2. Disassemble appropriately, including removal of all nipples from the cylinder. If this is a routine cleaning after firing only a couple cylinders, the revolver may not require full disassembly.
3. Flush the bore and chambers with cool water.
4. Flush the bore and chambers with hot water.
5. Scrub the bore with water on a bristle brush.
6. Scrub the cylinder and chambers with a toothbrush.
7. Run cleaning patches and water through the bore and chambers.
8. Dry the bore and chambers with patches.
9. Use pipe cleaners and water to clean the nipples.
10. Dry all the parts. If the revolver was not fully disassembled, be certain that no water has invaded the workings of the gun. If you suspect that water has gotten into the working parts, the revolver will have to be fully stripped and all moisture removed. Parts may be dried in an oven on low heat.
11. Wipe the revolver down. Metal parts are wiped with an oily rag. Wooden grips may be wiped down with a rag and a touch of linseed oil.
12. For storage purposes, leave a light trace of oil on all metal parts, on the working parts as

Lyman's super cleaning patches are made of a special twill material for super absorbency and toughness.

A slotted jag like this one is perfect for the range to quickly swab a bore between volleys of shots.

well as on the frame, barrel, and bore. Revolvers with brass frames may be brought back to bright with brass cleaner.

Important: The revolver will require full disassembly if several cylinders full of blackpowder or Pyrodex have been fired. If you are not fully versed in the takedown procedure, get help, but be sure to observe the steps so you can do this job yourself next time around.

Cleaning a Revolver With Solvent

STEPS FOR CLEANING CAP AND BALL REVOLVER WITH SOLVENT

Basically, the steps are the same as for the water-only method of cleaning the revolver, with the exception that solvent is used in place of water. Remember that the revolver will demand a full takedown if several cylinders full have been fired. Furthermore, full takedown is necessary from time to time even when the blackpowder revolver is fired only a few times.

Maintenance Means Protecting

Good gun cases, especially hard ones, are a wise investments, especially if the firearm goes by plane or on a horse.

While the steps may seem tedious, cleaning a blackpowder gun today is no big deal. Yes, it takes a little time, but the fun of blackpowder shooting is well worth the small effort required for proper maintenance.

Chapter 39

MUZZLELOADER TROUBLESHOOTING

IF IT'S mechanical, there's a chance that somewhere along the line, something will go wrong, and if Murphy's Law is involved, it will go wrong at the worst possible time. The day of junk imports is over. Today's muzzleloaders, along with accouterments, are supremely well designed and manufactured of the finest materials. This had to happen. Competition would allow nothing else. Modern muzzleloaders fit this niche perfectly —great designs, superb materials. This pertains to non-replicas and replicas alike — for example, the stout rifled muskets available from various companies. Regardless, things can go wrong, be they ever so minute — and sometimes not so little, especially when safety is involved, as with a hangfire. And so this chapter stands tall among its peers in the book. Warning: the following are intended only for minor mishaps. Any major problem must be brought to the attention of a competent gunsmith.

Muzzleloader Fires One or Two Times, then Balks at Another Attempt to Load

A blackpowder shooter of brief acquaintance brought a muzzleloading rifle to my door. He enjoyed shooting blackpowder, but this rifle was driving him batty. Load once, OK. Load twice, yes. Try to push another bullet downbore and it was no-go. Unfortunately, this problem can have several causes. First, overly deep grooves, intended for gripping the round ball, are not necessary, and yet they can be found on some rifles. These little canyons catch and hold gunk. Somewhere in the future, the situation will improve as rifling lands wear. Meanwhile, lubricating the ball

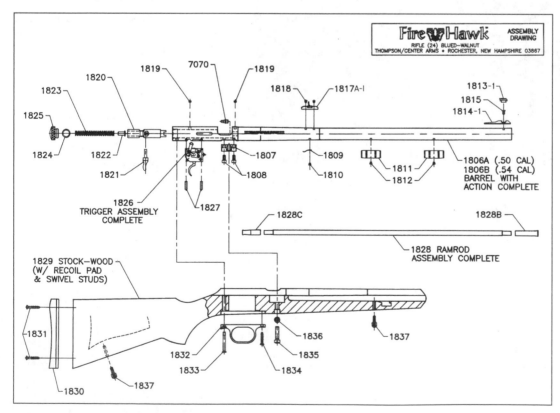

While it is not advisable for the average shooter to perform complicated gunsmithing tasks best left to an expert, knowing the structure of a muzzleloader is useful in troubleshooting, because to know its structure helps to understand its function.

patch thoroughly will help. In this way, the ball patch serves the function of a cleaning patch, up to a point. Total saturation is not advised; however, a well-dampened patch with a high-grade modern liquid lube will help, as will some of the so-called all-day lubes. Second, when conicals are involved in this loading problem, placing a glob of paste or cream lube directly upon the base of the projectile can help promote further loading.

Third, Pyrodex may be the answer. In fact, the proper shooting of Pyrodex calls for firing a reasonable number of times without cleaning between shots. Fourth, GOEX Clean Shot can help, since it lives up to its name as a clean-burning powder. These powder recommendations are trial and error. Blackpowder in a proper bore loaded with the right charge and bullet should allow several shots in a row without loading difficulty. In a Markesbery 54-caliber Outer-Line® rifle under range conditions, a heavy safe hunting charge of Swiss Black Powder with a Parker bullet allowed several successive firings without cleaning the bore. The bullet was lubed mainly on the base, with a touch of lube on the shank only. Fifth, target shooting and plinking do not require hunting charges of powder. Lighter charges will not foul the bore nearly so extensively. Sixth, a change in bullets can turn the trick. I had a rifle that would not allow more than two or three firings without bore swabbing. The single factor of changing bullets repaired the condition completely.

Lock will not stay on half-cock

Some problems are simply aggravating. This one is downright dangerous. The firearm must be taken to a gunsmith for repairs, because something is gravely wrong. The half-cock notch could be worn. Or there might be a problem in the lock mortise itself, the cutout that retains the lock in the stock. This could be an inletting problem con-

cerning the arm of the sear in the lock mortise. I would not venture a guess. Rather, it's time to bring the gun to an expert, who can explain what is happening.

Scoped Rifle Won't Stay Sighted-In

There remain a few scopes out there that do not climb to the top of the mountain in excellence. The recoil of the firearm may cause the reticle to wander. There is no fix for this, except to get another scope of better manufacture. Today, there are many good ones. Torture tested for this book was a Bushnell Elite 4200 2.5X-10X with 50mm objective bell. The scope earned highest merits for optical resolution, discerning objects set up in shady areas clearly and positively. Then came the torture part — dozens of firings with a big-bore muzzleloader firing a maximum allowable charge in a 54-caliber rifle with a bullet weighing more than 600 grains. After several trips to the range, the scope was tested to see if adjustments remained true. They had. A specific movement to direct the bullet up, down, left, or right, did exactly that, every time.

A checkup on scope reticle movement is easily accomplished by securing it, as in the cutout of a cardboard box, then moving the dials. Sometimes this little test reveals a crosswire that actually jumps, rather than cleanly moving over its allotted distance. Along with the obvious factor of getting a good scope to start — one that holds together not only in its reticle, but also lens mounds — there is the little fiend called loose scope mounts. Checking ring screws for proper tightness is done first, making certain to use a screwdriver that fits the slot in the screw perfectly, or the proper allen wrench. Poor fit of either can deform the head of the screw. Checking for a loose scope mount base requires removing the scope to see if the screws holding the base to the firearm are holding strong. If a rifle "shoots loose," that

is, stays sighted for a short while, then has trouble again, a mount may have to be secured with Loctite. There is a milder formulation of Loctite that is just right for this job. It helps secure the scope mount, both rings and base, while permitting easy removal later.

Accurate Muzzleloader Goes Sour

This problem exists more with modern cartridge guns than front loaders, but an accurate blackpowder gun can begin shooting fatter groups without warning. Modern arms are treated to a good bore cleaning to get rid of copper fouling. Oftentimes, this is all that is required to regain former accuracy. Cleaning the bore of a muzzleloader can also restore accuracy, not from copper fouling, but the possibility of extremely stubborn fouling in the grooves of the rifle, or in some cases, plastic residue buildup. In severe cases, a gunsmith can remove the breech plug from the firearm so that the bore can really be reached with a stout cleaning rod and a series of bristle brush scrubbings. Naturally, modern muzzleloaders with removable breech plugs can be cleaned in the home shop, as long as there is a good padded vise to hold the barrel steady while it receives a strong cleaning. Another problem, along with loose scope mounts, is loose anything. When the gun is reassembled after cleaning, everything must be tight. This does not mean applying sufficient torque to break screws or bolts, but tight enough to hold everything in place where it belongs.

If a good gun goes bad and cleaning does not correct the problem, looking for crown damage is recommended. If rifling in this sensitive region is damaged in any way, accuracy can go astray because the crown of the muzzle is the last control and guidance that the rifling has on a projectile. If the crown is damaged, a gunsmith can recrown the barrel. Another worthwhile investigation, especially if the crown of the muzzle is found to be in perfect shape, is looking into bore wear, especially with a round-ball gun. A cloth patch will not burnish a bore quickly, but in time, it can have an effect. An informal bore inspection can be accomplished with a good bore light. Once again, removable breech plugs makes the operation a lot easier. If the bore is "shot out," the firearm cannot be expected to shoot accurately. Fortunately, this condition rarely exists. Blackpowder guns are long-lasting.

Gun Won't Shoot Accurately out of the Box

Although about as likely as finding a 2-karat diamond in your restaurant soup bowl, now and again a brand new rifle will not perform accurately — or more realistically, it will not shoot with the test loads fired at the range. Two remedies are in order. First, contacting the gunmaker is never a mistake. For example, some shooters wondered why they were not getting super accuracy with their new Savage Model 10ML, a rifle that proved highly accurate in tests. A simple change to a stronger sabot did the trick, and the rifle shot the way it was intended to shoot — clustering bullets closely on the target into tight groups. Second, conducting a somewhat scientific search for the best projectile/powder charge combination often brings terrific results. Some bores simply perform better with certain bullets and charges better than others. This sort of testing is fun, because it requires only simple, safe juggling of components, mainly different bullets with different powder charges up to, but never exceeding, the limit set by the manufacturer as a maximum.

Round Ball Inaccuracy

When Dr. Mann concluded that accuracy was mainly a matter of "good bullets from good barrels," he was right, as simple as the conclusion may sound today. Home-cast round balls can be supremely accu-

rate. However, they must be created with care to reach their high potential. Checking the round ball by scale-weighing is simple and fast. This trick should have been applied when the balls were cast, but it's never too late — until they are shot, of course. Commercial round balls can be scale-tested, too, but if they're swaged, odds are these lead pills will be super at the start. Scale weighing means looking for occlusions within the lead round bullet that creates two problems: underweight missiles that fall away from the necessary consistency that accuracy demands, and lopsidedness. Sometimes, rolling balls on a flat surface will reveal problems as they wander off track, but the bullet/powder scale, accurate to a tenth of one grain and even finer levels, will normally show a problem — unless the ball is out of round. Then rolling on a table will produce a better test than weighing. I came upon a batch of economy-priced round balls sized for a 32-caliber squirrel rifle. The rifle was accurate, but not with those lead pills. Weighing did not reveal great variation from one ball to the next, but rolling showed the problem quickly. Those little lead globes were somewhat egg-shaped, definitely not round. Damage is another factor in round-ball accuracy. While a slightly out-of-round ball may fly pretty straight due to equalization of abnormalities on a common axis, nose damage especially seems to throw the sphere off course, while any damage can be bad for accuracy.

Conical Inaccuracy

Various forms of conical bullet damage can do various degrees of harm to accuracy. Minor aberrations are not serious; however, it's just as well to protect the muzzleloader missile from dents and flat spots. The original box is good for regular storage, but for travel from home to range or hunting field, a metal box is better. Any tin will do, taking up excess space in the container with a

soft cloth or paper towel to prevent the lead missiles from crashing into each other en route to the shooting site. Sealing the box, as with a layer of plastic wrap, is always a good plan if the bullets are going to be stored for a while. So is a slight spray of chemical metal conditioner. Conicals seem to suffer badly from base damage. If the base or skirt of a conical is damaged, chances of best accuracy are slim.

Group Hits Left, Right, High or Low

An oily bore can cause this problem. Troubleshooting it is very simple by wiping the bore free of excessive lube with a single cleaning patch after the gun is loaded.

Percussion Muzzleloader Fails to go off in Damp or Rainy Weather

Take it from a fellow who learned the hard way, forgetting his lessons. My Colorado guide, Steve Pike, called a 6-by-6 bull elk to within 12 paces. I know, because after the incident, I paced the distance so I could kick myself. The big bull stood staring. I aimed. Ftttt! It had been raining, and in my haste to leave town, I forgot waterproofing materials. Worst of all, I know I would have gotten that bull, because when the rifle misfired, the sights were lined up perfectly in the center of the neck and there the sight picture remained after the click. There are three general areas that can cause trouble. The least likely of the three is the lock, but a lock can leak water and the water can find its way into the pan on a flintlock or perhaps into the nipple seat via a circuitous route. Although lock leakage probably won't cause a problem, there is a way to make the lock at least moisture-proof if not waterproof.

Waterproofing and Foul-Proofing the Lock

The lock is unlikely to cause trouble in damp weather; however,

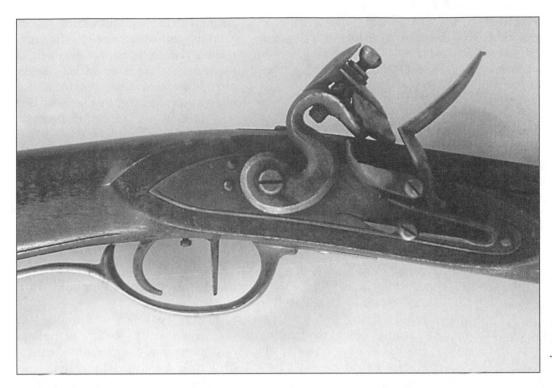

Troubleshooting includes ensuring a good match between flint and frizzen for a flintlock that is not behaving.

water can penetrate the workings, which can never be considered positive. A thin piece of paper, such as onionskin writing paper, is saturated with gun grease. There are many good products on the market. Just make sure it's true grease that will stick, and not runny oil. An alternative is the pre-greased protection paper that comes with new firearms, a possible source being the local gun shop. After the lock is removed from its mortise in the stock, the mortise is used as a pattern, with the greased paper cut to fit the opening with a slight overlap. The assignment of the paper is forming a gasket between the exterior and interior of the lock: a barrier to prevent moisture from passing from the outer stock into the important tumbler area of the lock. The greased paper gasket also discourages blackpowder fouling from attacking inner lock workings. Not to be overdone, one thin piece of greased paper will do. Excess paper could possibly get caught up in the workings of the lock.

Serious Rainproofing

Another area that demands waterproofing is the muzzle of the firearm. This is a very small area for water entry; however, snow falling from a tree, for example, might make its way down the bore, invading the powder charge. While a small rubber balloon stretched over the muzzle will work, there are now specific rubber protectors that slide in place over the muzzle. Either a commercial protector or a balloon will prevent water from entering the bore. The touchhole of the flintlock and vent of the nipple, as well as nipple seat, are real problem areas for the trespass of moisture. The vast majority of failures on rainy days come from these areas, not from the lock itself, or water getting in the muzzle. The flintlock can wear a boot, sometimes referred to a "cow's knee." This boot covering is not entirely handy, but it beats allowing the lock to get wet. The nipple and nipple seat can be waterproofed with specific devices, one being the Kap Kover. If I had my Kap Kover on No. 47, the big bull elk mentioned above would have been mine. Big Bore Express came up with another good nipple-waterproofing device. It's spring-loaded and while hunting, hammer nose pressure keeps the cover down firmly on the device, but when the hammer is cocked, the cover snaps out of the way so the rifle can be fired.

Flintlock Fails to Go Off

A Poor Spark

Ideally, the bevel of the flint is supposed to face downward, but having seen flinters go off like fireworks with reversed bevels, I offer this as advice worth taking, but not provable. One thing is certain, however. The edge of the flint must mate squarely with the face of the frizzen with uniform contact. If the flint is jagged, it's time for a new one, or at least a knapping of the old one. Sometimes allowing a brand new flint to drop against the frizzen a few times helps mate the edge of the flint with the face of the frizzen. An old flint can also be re-angled in the jaws of the hammer, where it may knap itself with a few meetings of flint and frizzen. Sometimes moving the flint sideway slightly in the jaws of the hammer, or a bit forward, also presents a new contact point to the frizzen. And yes, the flint can be turned upside-down (forget the rules) to facilitate a change in mating with the frizzen. The flint can be replaced bevel down after snapping the hammer a few times to chip off any bad spots. Important, yet sometimes overlooked, is the condition of flint and face of the frizzen. Both must be clean and dry, not oily. If the flintlock firearm continues to throw poor sparks with a new well-mated flint that is clean and dry, it's time to check the hammer throw. A spring may have gone weak, failing to provide a good whack of flint against the face of the frizzen. The frizzen itself can eventually wear out, too, demanding replacement. Another problem is setting the flint back into the jaws too far. It should stick out far enough to ensure good contact with the frizzen. See Chapter 28 for more ideas.

Flash in the Pan

There are many reasons for a flash in the pan, but one is not the cause of the flint/frizzen match. After all, the frizzen delivered sufficient hot curls of metal to ignite the pan powder. The problem lies elsewhere. A damp or oily pan can defy proper ignition. Pan powder still goes off, but the flame does enjoy full power. A clogged touchhole is also a possible culprit, whether invaded by a foreign object, or packed full of powder. While blackpowder ignites readily, when it is packed into a small channel, such as a touchhole, a fuse may be created, slowing ignition, or even causing a flash in the pan.

Percussion Cap Fails Under Dry (no rain or snow) Conditions

Modern caps are well-made and reliable. A test of RWS caps from the Navy Arms Co. saw 20 randomly selected from the box and placed in a high-humidity environment on an open piece of paper. After 48 hours of running a humidifier in a closet with these caps, they were tested in a Dixie Screwbarrel Pistol with the barrel removed. All 20 fired. Nonetheless, caps can be inundated by moisture. By firing a cap or two on the nipple prior to loading, damaged caps can usually be detected. If a cap does not give a good bang on the nipple during the clearing process, the shooter should expect ignition trouble. Cap debris can also cause a misfire, and a damaged nipple can be a problem. The wrong nipple can also cause trouble. Naturally, the cap and nipple may not be the root of the misfire at all, if the powder charge got damp.

Brass Furniture Gets Dull

Many shooters prefer the tarnished patina look over the bright appearance, and oxidation won't hurt brass furniture, but for those who prefer the bright look, there is a way to slow the oxidation process. Apply a coat of beeswax to brass furniture, such as nose caps, patch boxes, buttplates, toe plates, and other metalwork. A good product for this is Birchwood Casey Gun Stock Wax. The wax coating forms a modest, but helpful, barrier between the metal and the atmosphere, keeping tarnishing to a minimum.

Lead Bullets Look Powdery or Moldy

Perhaps powdery and moldy are the wrong terms, but lead bullets can get a cloudy appearance, exhibiting a whitish coating that can sometimes be rubbed off as a powder. Although minor surface coating may not harm accuracy, especially with a round ball wrapped in a patch, bullets can be restored to their former dark color, if only for the sake of appearance. A light spray of any of the new products on the market will do the trick, such as Rusty Duck Protective Gun Lubri-

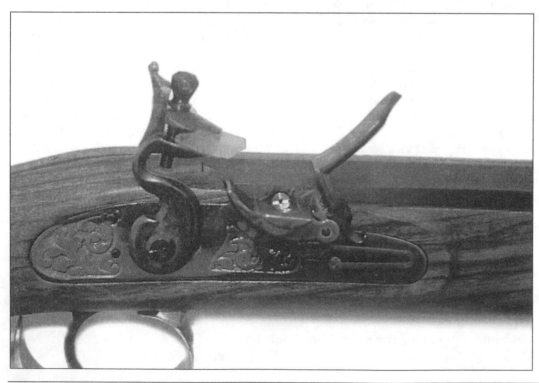

The touchhole shown here on a Lyman flintlock rifle can be replaced when it gets burned out.

Troubleshooting a rifle that has misfired can mean removing the nipple and cleaning it out separately. This can be done at the range with nothing more than a nipple wrench, pipe cleaner, and a little solvent.

cant, which also works in preventing the powdery/moldy coating in the first place. An extremely small amount does the trick: a quick jet of spray, then gently rotating the box to treat all of the bullets to a little of the chemical.

Ramrod Problems

Ramrod Stuck Downbore

A stuck ramrod sometimes occurs during the cleaning process; however, a ramrod can also hang up downbore when seating a bullet. This condition demands very care-ful attention. At all times, ensure that the muzzle of the gun is pointed in a safe direction away from any person or any property. The Kadooty, and other rods with knockers that affect a sliding hammer, don't stay stuck in the first place. But if a rod should get stuck in the bore, especially in the field where professional help may be far away, a leather thong may serve to remove it.

Try this: Tie the thong in a clove hitch around the extended ramrod shaft. Secure the end of the thong to a stationary object, such as a tree. Pull carefully and slowly, but steadily and strongly, on the rifle. If a stuck cleaning patch will not come free, run liquid patch lube down the bore and try again, always maintaining the muzzle in a safe direction. After the rod is pulled free, the bore should be thoroughly swabbed before the next load is run home, because it was probably a dirty bore that caused the problem.

A Wooden Ramrod Can Break

Modern muzzleloaders have modern ramrods. Breaking is

unlikely. But wooden ramrods on traditional front loaders can break. Helpful is a soaking of the ramrod in coal oil, kerosene, or Neat's-foot oil to render it supple, yet not so pliable that a patched ball can't be rammed home. A piece of tubing can be filled with one of the liquids mentioned above, then slid over one end of the ramrod. Ramrods can also be treated with boiled linseed oil to prevent drying and cracking.

Stuck Ball Downbore

Before attempting to remove a stuck ball, the gun must be uncapped or pan powder removed. The Thompson/Center CO2 Magnum Silent Ball Discharger will literally blow a stuck ball free. However, lacking this device, a stuck ball can usually be removed the old-fashioned way, with a screw (not a worm). The screw should be used with a muzzle protector because the protector centers the screw in the bore, preventing contact with the bore walls, and also delivering it to the center of the stuck ball where it belongs. A cleaning rod with a knocker, such as the Kadooty, is excellent for removing a stuck ball. If the rod does not have a knocker, the thong method, noted above for freeing a stuck ramrod, may have to be employed to encourage a stuck ball's removal, with the muzzle always pointed in a safe direction.

Seated Ball, No Powder

Eventually, most of us will do it. We're thinking about that next shot and the patched ball is rammed home without a powder charge in the breech. Now what? The stuck ball method is the best way to get the patched ball back up the bore, using either the CO2 device or the screw attached to the end of a metal loading rod fitted with a muzzle protector. The ball can be safely shot free with a small powder charge, but if it is not driven all the way out of the bore, it should be reseated before once again trying to blow it free. If the gun has a cleanout screw, it is removed. A trickle of powder is poured through the channel, and then the cleanout screw is fully replaced in position

before firing the gun. The muzzle must be aimed in an entirely safe direction so that the expelled projectile will end up in a dirt bank or other proper place. Sometimes a little powder can be trickled into the touchhole of the flintlock rifle for the same purpose. If there is no cleanout screw on the caplock firearm, the nipple can be removed and powder can be introduced through the nipple seat area. Then the nipple is returned fully to its seat before firing the ball into a safe backstop.

Stored Muzzleloader Attracts Rust

This is simply solved with one of the many fine rust inhibitors of the day: any modern metal preservatives that thwart rust.

Patch Lube Good in Summer, But Not in Winter

There are several modern patch lubes that do not harden up in cold weather, at least not enough to cause trouble. These same lubes remain functional in cold weather. The range of temperatures in which the lube functions well is often stated with the product. The vast majority of lubes work well within anything like normal temperature ranges, where most shooters would be operating. Arctic conditions, or the Sahara may pose a different problem.

Troubleshooting the Correctly Seated Load

A witness mark on the ramrod or loading rod after a pet load is found will always tell the shooter when his bullet is fully seated downbore in the breech. The witness mark is made only with a totally clean bore, where the bullet is absolutely seated fully upon the powder charge. After ramming the bullet home, the ramrod or loading rod is left in place, not removed. A mark is made with indelible ink on the rod where it meets the crown of the muzzle. That mark forever indicates when a bullet is fully seated downbore with the specific powder charge decided upon for that

projectile. Perhaps there is heavy fouling in the breech, or a patched ball or conical gets stuck above the powder charge. The marked ramrod instantly indicates the problem, because the line on the rod rides above the muzzle, clearly indicating that the missile has not been completely delivered into the breech of the gun.

Misses Caused by a Moved Sight

A tiny witness mark on sights forever proves where they should rest. This way, if a sight gets bumped, the shooter knows it because the witness mark is no longer matched. Once the front and rear sights are properly aligned in their respective dovetail slots following the sighting of the front loader, a tiny line extending only a fraction of an inch from sight to barrel is made. A gunsmith can make the line with an engraving tool in seconds. Should a sight get nudged out of whack, that condition is readily spotted, because the line extending from sight to barrel is no longer aligned.

Stock Gets Burned from Ignition

The best prevention is a flash cup for the percussion firearm. A flash cup diverts sparks away from the wood. Also, a bit of masking tape around the nipple or lock area of the flintlock will save the wood from getting burned.

Round Ball or Conical is Nose-Damaged When Seated

The nub end of some short starters can put a deep dimple in the round or conical bullet during initial starting into the muzzle of the firearm. The nub of the short starter can be made less offensive to a lead ball by attaching a small piece of electrician's tape to it. Also, there are commercial short starters designed to go easy on the nose of a round or conical bullet. Parker Productions has one (see Directory).

These are a few tricks to keep the muzzleloader making smoke.

Chapter 40

BLACKPOWDER ON THE INTERNET

"THE TIMES, they are a-changin'" go the words of that old saying, and it is true. Today, websites and the Internet serve millions who want information fast. Blackpowder shooters have not been forgotten. There are many websites dedicated to muzzleloaders and blackpowder cartridge guns, along with rendezvous and informational guides. The following are only a few, but they provide a good start for the reader who desires to take one of the many different paths to knowledge available on "the web." Some of these sites are well off the main trail of blackpowder shooting. That is by design, not accident. The front-loading game, along with metallic blackpowder shooting, is wide and varied, with hundreds of interesting side pockets — from building a specific tool in the home shop, to finding out about the overland wagon that brought pioneers from back east to the Rocky Mountains and beyond.

Websites come and go. But once a blackpowder devotee gets in the habit of searching out information on his favorite sport, the habit stays. In spite of the fact that some of the following sites will no doubt fade away in time, many others will stand as long as this edition of The Complete Blackpowder Handbook remains on the shelves of bookstores. In many cases, calling up "blackpowder" or "rendezvous," along with similar generic headings, will put the blackpowder shooter onto interesting websites. However, the following are explicit and ready to go.

Most of these websites were taken from the excellent Muzzle Blasts magazine through the efforts of Alan Garbers, who submitted the information for publication. Belonging to the NMLRA — National Muzzle Loading Rifle Association — brings Muzzle Blasts every month.

www.calcite.rocky.edu/octa/capps.htm
Highly interesting website including many informational guides. Current information included a fantastic review of the overland wagon used to transport people and goods from the east into the great unknown of the American West. Leads on other websites offered. Good advice on buying locally vs. mail order.

www.nps.gov/mima/
Minute Man National Historical Park consists of more than 900 acres of Massachusetts property associated with the Battle Road site of April 1775. A good website for blackpowder shooters interested in history.

www.SASSNET.com/
This is the site of the Single Action Shooting Society (SASS), with weekend shoots listed for every state in the nation throughout the year. A step back in time for the blackpowder shooter.

www.nra.org/
This is the National Rifle Association, which requires no introduction to American shooters.

www.nmlra.org/
The NMLRA, National Muzzle Loading Rifle Association, is dedicated to blackpowder shooters everywhere. with a fine magazine promoting shooting, competition, re-enactments, rendezvous, collecting, and arts, crafts, and history of times associated with the firearms we so much enjoy owning and shooting. Even offers on-line classified advertising.

www.sptddog.com/sotp.html
Interesting website stop for Cowboy Action shooters and other enthusiasts of Old West historical re-enactments. Lots of information.

www.sew-it-seems.com
Blackpowder fans interested in factual information on proper dress from various historical eras will enjoy this stop. Michelle Hoffman has an on-line catalog with pictures of garb from the 1600s to 1890s.

www.wheretoshoot.org
The National Shooting Sports Foundation offers this site for shooters looking for a place to fire their guns. Click on and seek directions.

www.rondylist.com
This site provides a long list of rendezvous held all over the country. Log on and find out where and when the next "doings" are being held.

www.geocities.com/Athens/Acropolis/4756english1.htm
This website brings the history buff into contact with recipes from the 14th-century English feast, all declared authentic and tasty. Might

be a good one for the buckskinner who wants to impress his friends at rendezvous.

www.stitchinscotsman.com
The place for blackpowder shooters interested in attending the rendezvous that requires special clothing. Custom-fit, elk-hide britches, drop-fronts, leggings, shirts, coats and more.

www.users.qwest.net/~cwgrizz/ swroo.html
Another site for anyone seeking to know where and when rendezvous and shooting events will happen in the southwestern United States.

www.thegrid.net/led/bkskn/ flint.html
Dedicated to flintlock shooting, along with many tips and tricks for the blackpowder fan, including recipes.

www.infolink.morris.mn.us/ %7Erbanders/ relic.html
The Town Crier is a forum frequented by anyone interested in Early American history, with thought-provoking discussions among various historians.

www.otmagazine.com/ contents.htm
An on-line Trail Magazine for anyone dedicated to hike the backcountry, interesting for blackpowder hunters who will find sample articles. On-line subscription available.

www.harpweek.com
Harper's Weekly was a well-known periodical, cited in this book for its article on Berdan's Sharpshooters in Chapter 47. Now the famous newspaper is offered on-line from 1857 forward. Mostly for subscribers, but some free information, too.

http://members.aol.com/artgumbus/lithinfo.html
While this site may not seem of interest to blackpowder shooters, the fact is, archery is now part of the rendezvous game, and probably always was in some form or another. This site is about original arrowheads and how to identify them — a fine study for primitive hunters in the front-loading game.

http://dnr.state.il.us/general/ states.htm
The blackpowder hunter can log onto this site for information regarding hunts in many states.

www.theamericanwest.com
This website includes Old West merchandise, some of it sold through auction. Everything from original firearms to Civil War ammo boxes.

www.linecamp.com
Tremendous amount of information on the West. This site leads the shooter to many sources. One search brought up about 40 sources, including "Wagons of the West," of interest to Cowboy Action Shooting fans; hunting and fishing sources; plus a guide to mountain men.

www.warflag.com/shadow/history/firepower.htm
This site is called "Resistance in the Desert," and it deals with firearms used in southeast Morocco. While the topic is narrow — the flintlocks used by native tribes in Africa — it is also of interest to those curious about firearms history.

www.blackhunting.org
Blackpowder Hunting: the official publication of the International Blackpowder Hunting Association with articles, photographs, and a great deal of useful information.

www.ex.ac.uk/%7ejbcalver/cannon.htm
Today, there are cannon shoots held all across the country. This site supplies solid information on different cannons and their applications.

www.palongrifles.com/
About Pennsylvania long rifles, including histories, as well as listings of original museum-quality specimens for purchase.

www.primenet.com/~gullett/
Called The Old Buffalo Ranch, with information about Cowboy Action Shooting, including photographs.

Chapter 41

MODERN CUSTOM BLACKPOWDER GUNMAKERS

EARLY AMERICAN gunmakers created beautiful examples of long rifles and pistols in what has become known as The Golden Age of American Firearms. Nothing has surpassed them in beauty, including the most ornate and well-crafted modern guns of the 21st century. To even think about these elegant firearms passing forever into history is bothersome, but that will never happen. Originals exist in great numbers all over the world in museums as well as personal collections. Moreover, the fine guns, especially of 18th- and 19th-century designs, are still being made today. More surprising is the fact that the artisans building them exhibit the same level of talent associated with the best gunmakers of the past. Their work is just as beautiful, with examples that sometimes replicate the past, but more often show the personal touch of the master who made them, and masters they are. Of course, some gunsmiths build "working muzzleloaders" to accomplish a job, such as hunting or rendezvous games. These guns are functional, and never intended to be pieces of art. Chapter 12 dealt with custom muzzleloaders, plus a list of names and addresses at the end to help the reader locate a gun builder who might make a custom front loader for him to enjoy as a lifetime investment. This chapter is about a few of

their creators: simple profiles to give the reader an idea about the men who continue to keep the Golden Age of Firearms alive in reality as well as memory.

The old-time gunsmith wove his initials into the very fabric of the New World. The gun is so paramount to our history that Tales of the Gun, a national television show on the History Channel, uses the story of the firearm to explain events of the past. The American gunmaker of early days was a responsible businessman dedicated to "making a living," but also created a reputation that survived ages after his passing. These were multi-gifted men (if there were women in the trade, their names and guns have not survived). They had to possess a multitude of talents in order to build firearms.

Even when locks and other parts were purchased, the smith had to meld them into the finished product, sometimes with refinements. Blacksmith, draftsman, woodworker, toolmaker, sculptor, ironworker, carver, inlay artist, and more talents marked the ability of the old-time gunsmith. The community depended upon these men not only in the making of firearms from scratch, but also repairing guns when they needed attention. After all, the firearm was life to the Early American, bringing food to his table, keeping enemies from his door.

Were there space to allow, the biographies of today's professional custom muzzleloader gunmakers would prove riveting. Here are just a few short profiles of interest to the reader, with no offense intended to

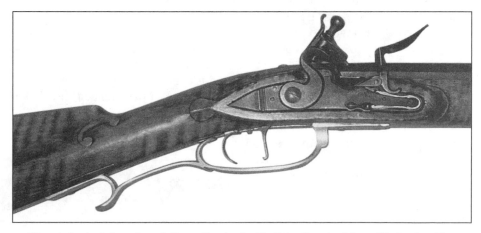

The talented hands of Dan Coats built this fine-looking flintlock rifle. Coats made the rifle for himself.

Fantastic carving by Allen Martin dresses this Kentucky rifle buttstock perfectly.

the many excellent craftsmen excluded, for such was not intended.

K.L. Shelton was taught to build Kentucky rifles by a smith named Taylor Ellington, who lived outside the small hamlet of Moorehead, Ky. At the time of instruction in the mid-1970s, Ellington was in his late 80s. As with so many other talents, Ellington wished to pass his knowledge on, rather than taking it with him. When he recognized the interest Shelton showed in building a fine rifle of the Golden Age, the master faithfully remained with his student. "It took several years before I perfected the art of stock carving and metal engraving," Shelton explained. He also believes that his Kentucky heritage played a major role in the deep interest in rifles of the same name. Both of his parents were raised in western Kentucky near the small town of Sturgis. Shelton graduated from Murray State University in 1965 with a degree in industrial technology, a perfect background for the realization of what he was to become: a professional maker of fine classic muzzleloading rifles. Going on for more schooling, he received a master's degree in higher education from Moorehead State University, perhaps doing what so many of us have done: looking to the more traveled road,

the path leading to more certain employment and security. Three years later, he built his first rifle, the true beginning of a lifetime love affair with the first American art form, the Kentucky rifle. Today, he specializes in the Lancaster School style, recognized by historians as the first truly American rifle. These rifles were built by individual smiths in Lancaster County, Pa., gaining the Kentucky name made famous by Daniel Boone, Simon Kenton, and other explorers of what then was the Kentucky wilderness. Currently, Shelton has an 18-month turnaround period working at his shop in Tucson, Ariz.

A typical K.L. Shelton rifle is exemplified by a tiger-stripe maple stock with octagon barrel ranging from 36 to 42 inches, and calibers ranging from 32 to 58. He prefers Siler locks in either flint or percussion, along with double-set triggers and a brass patch box. German silver inlays, plus incised or relief

carving are included on the finished product, which usually weighs about 9 pounds and measures 52 to 57 inches overall, depending upon barrel length. Left-hand models are available. The customer chooses caliber, barrel length, and specific component parts. He or she also has the option of personalizing the rifle with special carving, metal engraving, and inlays. Shelton believes the Kentucky rifle is superior for hunting and sport shooting, while each one, including those made today, is collectible. There is also authenticity in his rifles, with the shooter stepping back to an earlier time with a rifle very much like the one relied upon by newcomers to his country's shores.

Allen Martin grew up on a farm in Lancaster County, Pa., the very home of the Lancaster-style Kentucky rifle. He was exposed to hunting at a very early age. "I always had a strong desire to own and build Pennsylvania flintlock rifles," he said. The flame of desire erupted into a fire when he was 12 years old and his next-door neighbor showed him an original Lancaster School flintlock rifle. As he put it: "I was hooked!" At 18 years of age, he set out to build his first Pennsylvania rifle, "but it didn't turn out the way it was planned." That was then. This is now. Martin has built 80 rifles to date, with 38 more on order. He is, without a doubt, a true full-time maker of high-grade muzzleloaders. Currently, Martin is recognized as "The Allentown Builder," but in addition to Lehigh County, he also makes Berks-, Lancaster-, and Wommelsdorf-style rifles. Martin tries to keep his rifles

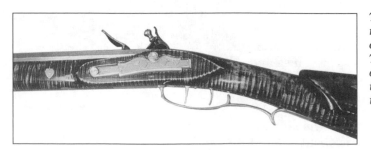

This beautiful rifle is the work of K.L. Shelton. Take notice of the detailed heart inlay forward of the lock plate.

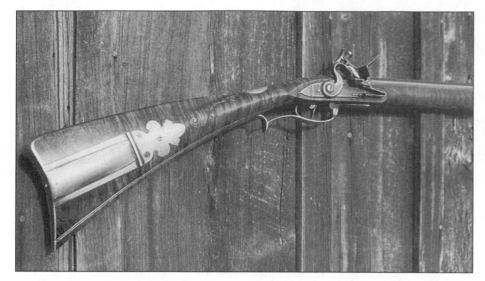

Allen Martin's perfectionist approach shows with this well-fitted patch box and perfect wood finish.

styled after those of southeastern Pennsylvania. Normally, he can finish a rifle in one year; however, he currently is backordered because he won Best of Show at the Dixon Gunmakers Fair in 1999. The winning rifle adorns the cover of the July 2000 issue of *Muzzle Blasts* magazine.

I enjoyed reading Martin's notice informing the public of his art: "(Martin) respectfully informs the Public that he continues to make Flintlock Rifles of high quality, beauty and utility at most reasonable prices. Those individuals who favor Allentown, Lancaster, Wommelsdorf and other Southeastern Schools may now be told that all articles are warranted to be of the finest material and workmanship." Allen Martin has one thing in common with his fellow professional muzzleloader artisans: he makes the guns because he truly admires them, not only for their beauty and accuracy, but also their history. Allen Martin, Der Buchsenmacher, as he's called, is busy today doing what he loves most — making handsome Pennsylvania rifles.

Andrew Fautheree, Andy to his friends, started building muzzleloading rifles in 1960 from his home in Roseburg, Ore. Andy is one of the country's longest continuing custom front-loader makers. He was always interested in making intricate things with his hands, especially from wood, such as model airplanes and railroad cars. As a shooter, however, he was not satisfied with the replica long rifles available at the time. After completing his military obligation, he returned home to excitement about the Civil War Centennial. This sparked his interest in muzzleloading guns of yesteryear, for he was already intrigued with antiques, firearms in particular. His first rifle, as expected, looked nothing like the masterful work he is known for today, but it was a beginning. While it was not perfect to Fautheree's ideals, someone came along who saw the rifle as nice enough to command, as Fautheree puts it, "a very tidy sum of money." He made another rifle, and another, and soon people were asking him to build custom guns.

In only five years, his work gained deserved acclaim, which grew quickly when he made a rifle for a well-known Hollywood stuntman. The stuntman used the gun to bag the Big 5 in Africa, with the story written up in national publications. Today, Fautheree continues making late-period rifles of the Hawken breed, both half-stock and full-stock. However, he builds them all, including Early American and European Jaegers, to Pennsylvania long rifles and even a swivel-breech, double-barrel rifle. He is also commissioned often to duplicate an original rifle illustrated in a book. His vast research library contains almost every antique muzzleloading firearm book ever published, which provides him with visual models that he can replicate in every detail, down to the exact engraving, carving, shape of lock panels, and other features.

One of his big favorites is the target rifle style popular in the New York area in the 1800s, with its fine lines. Although plain when compared with Pennsylvania/Kentucky long rifles, they possess functional locks and triggers, patent breeches, silver inlay work, and above all else, exquisite engraving.

Today, he continues to make both pistols and rifles as an art form, his art being the exacting execution of wood and metal in harmony, balance, and aesthetics culminating in an authentic, artistic custom firearm. While Fautheree remains dedi-

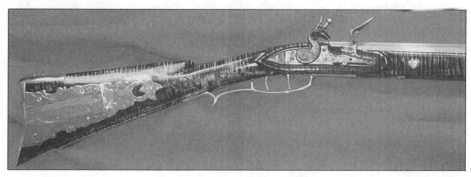

This beautiful rifle is the work of K.L. Shelton. Take notice of the detailed heart inlay forward of the lock plate.

The beautiful lines of this Kentucky long rifle were perfected by gunmaker Allen Martin. Take note of the handsome inlay on the cheekpiece.

cated to rifles and pistols of the past, he was also among the first gunmakers to develop his own website, so that those interested could see his work on the small screen. His turnaround time is one to two years — longer if the customer wants a Pennsylvania rifle with intricate detail and fancy carving.

Homer L. Dangler began collecting, studying, restoring, building, and shooting Kentucky rifles in 1955. He builds near-copies of originals, along with some rifles of his own design, favoring the style of J.P. Beck, an early Lebanon, Pa., gunmaker. Today, Dangler continues to build fine long rifles, while also working on his other passion: restoring, building and flying airplanes. One of his planes appeared on the cover of Sport Pilot maga-

zine, as well as in its 1995 calendar. Dangler, along with building long rifles, helps others interested in the art. He has two videos, for example: Building the American Long Rifle and Carving the American Long Rifle. These are not home videos. Homer had a studio do the shooting, with several cameras for close-up detail. Beginning as a hobby in the 1950s, his work came into such demand that he went professional in 1975 and never looked back. The demand for his work created a living. "The rifles I enjoy building most are the early ones, and having access to them, I am able to duplicate a rifle closely related to the same period and school as the original," he said. Today, the wait for one of his rifles is two years.

Mark Silver is a genius in gun-

making, that title falling short of his actual ability. While perfection is perhaps impossible in the creation of a custom rifle, Silver's work comes close to achieving that level. He began shooting Civil War rifled muskets with a national re-enactment organization in 1963. He was 15 years old. By the time he left the U.S. Navy in 1967, he had restored several pieces. Returning to college in 1971, his interests progressed to building long rifles from blanks as a hobby. Five years later, "hopelessly obsessed with 18th-century gunmaking," as he puts it, he went full time in the trade, having the good luck of working as a journeyman with professional John Bivens. By late 1979, Silver was in his own shop in Northern Michigan. His interest in custom firearms is wide-ranging, including many types of American guns, along with British and continental rifles and fowlers. For the past decade, Mark has focused on researching and redeveloping 18th-century gunmaking techniques, particularly with regard to stock shaping and finishing, such as the use of hand planes, saws, and scrapers. He now specializes in unique recreations of 18th-century American and European style sporting arms using authentic

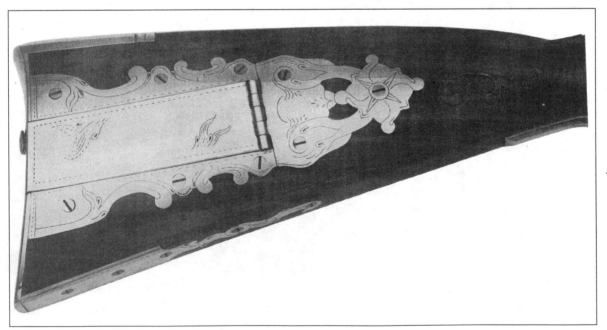

This close-up of a superbly fitted patchbox reveals the details put into place by gunmaker Homer L. Dangler. This sort of works takes a rifle like this beyond the functional to the level of art.

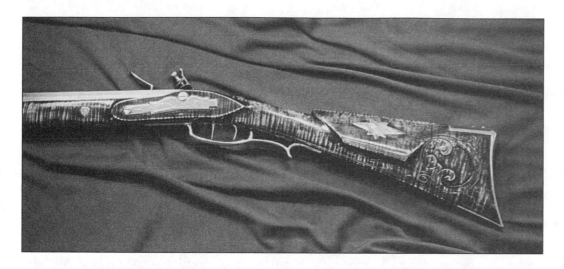

K.L. Shelton's handsome long rifle shown here exhibits perfection not only in metal to wood fit, but also finish.

techniques. Silver also created two kits of his own design, one circa 1750, a Virginia long rifle, the other circa 1730, a Colonial large bore fowler.

Today, his turnaround time on a project is about two years; however, he has recently begun building speculation firearms that, when complete, will be offered for sale. In a way, that plan has backfired, because collectors and shooters who know his work want to be placed on a waiting list so they can be first in line to have one of Mark Silver's fine handmade works of art.

Anyone who appreciates the beauty, history, and function of the firearms that Early American masters created during the Golden Age continues to have a chance owning one associated with the past, but built today by men possessed of the same talent. Their work stands up to the finest quality that yesterday's gunmakers could build.

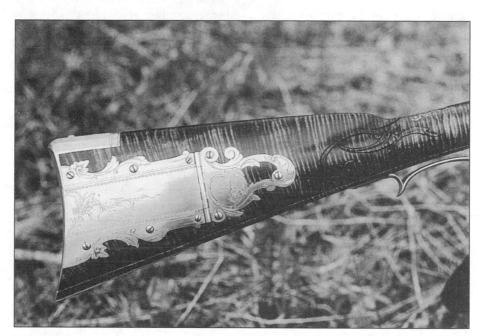

Mark Silver's talent is clearly exhibited here in this exhibition of a perfectly fitted patch box on a 54-caliber York County Pennsylvania long rifle.

Chapter 42

ON THE BIG-GAME TRAIL WITH THE SMOKEPOLE

THE REBIRTH of widespread blackpowder big-game hunting was drawn in a carriage called adventure by the horses of curiosity, historical interest, challenge, and satisfaction. Adventure followed the hunter as he went into woods, mountains, and thickets packing a firearm outdated by at least a century. Curiosity was also satisfied. What was hunting with a single-shot muzzleloader really like? The hunt embodied the special challenge of having to get closer to that buck, bull, or boar, delivering one and only one shot on the mark. And when the tag was canceled, the successful downwind shooter basked in the warmth of true satisfaction.

Before long, however, the rules changed. While there remained a large number of outdoorsmen who continued to enjoy the basic merits of bagging big game with a thunderstick, another, much more powerful reason for using the old-style firearm surfaced. It was the special "primitive" hunt, where modern cartridge-shooting firearms were not allowed. The primitive hunt had at least three major advantages. They were often held in special areas unsuited to long-range rifles, as well as special times of the year, often before or after regular seasons, and where tags were limited to a lottery, odds of drawing a blackpowder hunt were improved

over regular-season hunts. Muzzleloader hunts are still held in special areas during favorable times. The popularity of special blackpowder seasons has decreased drawing odds; however, they're typically still better than regular-season lotteries. One thing is certain: Hunters may get into muzzleloading for that special opportunity, but odds are they'll catch blackpowder fever, forevermore taking the smoky trail.

What Big Game?

There isn't a big game animal in North America that is too much for a muzzleloader. That includes the largest brown bear, otherwise known as coastal grizzly or Kodiak,

Marty Atkinson took this fine record-class caribou with Rabesca's Resources Ltd. of the Northwest Territories, Canada. His rifle was a Knight 50 caliber loaded with 110 grains volume Pyrodex RS and a saboted 240-grain bullet, fired just over 100 yards.

Normally, a 600-grain bullet would be unsuitable for an animal the size of a blackbuck, but the Parker Hydra-Con 600-grain 50-caliber bullet opened up nicely on this one because of its design using hydraulics to cause mushrooming.

that ever caught a salmon in Alaska. Warning: Although there are blackpowder guns that will drop dangerous game, no one should hunt grizzlies or other wild animals that "shoot back" unless backed up by an expert marksman with a powerful repeating firearm. Having only one shot, sometimes two, precludes repeat chances on a charging animal. It's vital that a powerful repeating cartridge gun, especially on the order of a big-bore "stopper," be at the ready for safety. Otherwise, the blackpowder gun is capable of taking any big game animal, including elk and moose. Of course

deer are far and away the number-one big game animal on the continent, whitetails leading by a wide margin with ever-increasing herd numbers. Mule deer are smokepole worthy, too, but their numbers do not match up. Furthermore, while whitetail populations continue to rise, mule- deer numbers are somewhat on the decline as this is written, and no one knows why.

Primary goals of the blackpowder big-game hunter should be pure enjoyment of the chase. There is nothing wrong with having a supreme outdoor experience while in pursuit of filling a big-game tag.

Making meat, as the old-timers sometimes called it, is another worthwhile reason to take big game with the charcoal burner. The Complete Guide to Game Care and Cookery deals with getting game from freezer to field in prime condition, along with listing many fine recipes. There are many other game-recipe books available with hundreds of good meals ready for the making. Along with enjoying an outdoor adventure and taking home good protein, the blackpowder big-game hunt affords that special challenge mentioned earlier, getting a close shot, either by stalking

Using a bullet box or other test device can reveal a good deal about a bullet's forthcoming performance in the field. This 45-caliber Hydra-Con from Parker Productions penetrated all media, creating a long, clean, and prominent wound channel. Performance in the field matched.

The readyload is important to muzzleloader big game hunting, because it provides a relatively fast second shot.

mountain sheep, Coues deer, even the mighty bison.

Big-Game Muzzleloaders

Both rifle and pistol frontstuffers are big-game worthy, the rifle by far heading the pack with the in-line modern version overtaking everything else. The reason for this was stated before: Hunters take up the blackpowder rifle to gain entry into the world of special muzzleloader-only hunts, so they choose the most familiar firearms possible. They often get hooked on smokemakers afterward, but initially the guns are a passport to special seasons held all over North America. Even states that are not extremely devoted to primitive hunts, such as my own Wyoming, offer fine opportunities for the frontloader fan. The rules of the hunt dictate which guns are legal and which are not. But in-lines fare well, even in Colorado, whose game department has struggled for some time with rules governing guns allowed on special blackpowder-only hunts. The in-line modern rifle is to these hunts

or setting up a stand in the right spot. There is also comradeship with special partnering, not only in making a great camp and getting big game out of the field, but also working together to get that good blackpowder shot.

No writer is capable of committing to paper the feelings experienced on the blackpowder path to big game. Going counterclockwise a hundred or more years has its own reward. It's like stepping out of a time machine into the past. The sport has blossomed not only in America and Canada, but also parts of Europe. Italy, for example, through a law placed on the books in 1991, liberalized the ownership of muzzleloaders for hunting in that country. African safaris, once only for the privileged few, are enjoyed by many "working folks" these days, perhaps not for the truly big animals, such as Cape buffalo and lions, but certainly for plains game: greater kudu, impala, gnu, and other interesting quadrupeds. Muzzleloaders were in the hands of the first ivory hunters on the Dark Continent. These huge pachyderms are also taken in modern times by blackpowder hunters such as Val Forgett, president of the Navy Arms Co., who downed the big tuskers with

58-caliber conical-shooters. But the American hunter has sufficient big game to keep him interested, not only fantail and rope-tail deer, but pronghorn antelope, wild boar, javelina, coastal black-tailed deer,

Tree stand safety dictates using a pull rope as shown here to lift all hunting gear upward. Climbing with pack on or firearm in hand can be hazardous.

what the compound is to special bowhunts. No, it does not carry the history or romance of yesteryear, any more than the compound bow speaks of tradition, but it gets hunters into the field with a muzzleloader. It's safe to say that in-line charcoal burners and compound bows have brought more hunters into the field than Kentucky/Pennsylvania long rifles and English longbows ever did. Nevertheless, dedicated hunters with round-ball rifles and traditional tackle do great, especially when they put in that little bit of extra practice and field effort to overcome whatever handicap may be on the path. The pistol is miles behind the rifle in popularity, but a few make the big-game grade, especially the Thompson/Center Encore with the capacity for a big bullet and heavy powder charge. In short, while every general type of muzzleloader is big-game capable (especially some of the rifled muskets), the in-line rifle and non-replicas head the popularity list.

Larry Frasier of Deer Creek Outfitters in Sebree, Ky,, sets up a new tree stand for a hunter. The stand is not placed just anywhere, but rather in a specific spot of high whitetail activity. The author saw 35 deer from this stand the next morning.

Big-Game Blackpowder Cartridge Rifles

Many blackpowder cartridge guns have been reborn in modern arms factories. A whole world of Sharp single-shot breechloaders exists, along with numerous Remington rolling blocks. Lever-actions abound, from repeaters shooting the squat 44-40 cartridge, to rifles chambered for big bores, such as the 45-70 Government. The 45 Colt, a blackpowder round at inception, is also available, as in remakes of the Winchester Model 1892 levergun. Handguns in 38-40, 44-40, 45 Colt, and other large bores are not nearly as powerful as either modern magnums or the Encore, and are generally not correct for today's brand of big game hunting, but in the hands of a great handgun hunter can do the job.

Whence Comes the Power?

Many other places in the book speak of blackpowder potency, including Chapter 32 on big bores. Obviously, blackpowder power comes in launching big bullets at reasonable velocities. Even the smaller pistol bullets — so popular now in sabots, especially for in-line rifles — deal in good bullet weights, such as Fedcral's Bonded Bear Claws in 50- and 54-calibers, 250-grain and 300-grain weights. Meanwhile, the all-lead projectile remains extremely deadly with its ability to punch long wound channels, making way through the large bones of elk and moose. As a crude measure

Preparing a ground blind with interlaced branches. Ideally, cover scent should be added to prevent hunter detection by the keen nose of game animals coming by on the trail.

A hunter in a ground blind—center of photo and to the right of tree— waits with muzzleloader ready for an incoming whitetail. He would be all but invisible but for the blaze orange cap, which had to be worn on this hunt by law.

(because there are many exceptions), it's its safe to say that round balls of 50 caliber and larger pushed near the two century mark are formidable on big game at closer ranges. Truly large round balls don't require 2,000 fps muzzle velocities for power, as the big guns from October Country prove. Pistol bullets are now readily launched at 2,000 fps and faster from muzzleloading rifles due to large allowable powder charges, while lead conicals exit the bore at 1,500 fps and faster for real big boys. The 375-grain Buffalo Bullet SSB escapes the muzzle at 1,700-plus fps in some magnum rifles with 150-grain powder charges.

Every big-game hunter wants the same thing: a fast and clean harvest. Big-bore muzzleloaders allowed a reasonable powder charge and fed the right projectiles will take big game cleanly from close range. That means 100 yards or under, preferably not farther than 125 yards, although certain guns and load prevail at more than 200 yards. There are also a number of special big-game, charcoal-burning rifles intended to give extra power for big-game hunting. The Zephyr is one. From the Pacific Rifle Co., this 62-caliber round-ball shooter is allowed a hefty powder charge for decent muzzle velocity. The big round ball does the rest. Likewise for some of the magnum in-line rifles shooting heavy conicals, such as the Gonic Magnum, which uses 150 grains of blackpowder behind a 486-grain Gonic bullet at 1,610 fps muzzle velocity for an energy rating close to 2,800 foot-pounds. Many other rifles are also allowed super loads: the Markesbery Outer-Line®, Knight Disc Rifle, and Thompson/Center Encore, to name only three. Then there's the Savage Model 10ML, the only muzzleloader allowed to use smokeless powder. Tests showed a 300-grain Hornady .452-inch XTP bullet doing 2,244 fps for 3,360 foot-pounds, more than the 30-06 at the muzzle.

Bullets for Big Game

Placed perfectly, specific bullet design and construction is not a major factor in putting a big-game animal down quickly with one shot. In a perfect world, any hunk of lead capable of producing decent groups downrange would work well, but in the real world, the bullet can make all the difference between a proud

Setting up a drip bag like this one from Wildlife Research Center can provide the hunter with a chance to bag a buck that has gone almost nocturnal, as he may visit the site very early or very late in the day.

moment and a bitter experience. Bullet makers are among the busiest designers in the world. They can never leave well enough alone, and for those of us who hunt with muzzleloaders, that's a blessing. It's impossible to present so much as a partial list of viable blackpowder projectiles. Many pages would be gobbled up in the process. Suffice it that there are literally dozens of excellent big-game projectiles on the market. With a knee-bent apology to the many wonderful missiles left out, the following is an all-but-random selection of specific examples of projectiles that have proven highly effective on big game. Others have worked as well. Round balls, jacketed pistol bullet/sabot combinations, and all-lead projectiles are the three major categories

The author's favorite masking scent is earth, this example from Wildlife Research Center. It can make all the difference in a stalk when the wind changes.

for this all-too-brief encounter with big-game blackpowder bullets.

Commercial or home-cast, round balls of pure lead are, and always will be, extremely effective. It's the same tune played on a different instrument: small for small, big for big. Small round balls, such as the 32-caliber, are supremely good for small game, but should be left out of the big-game scene. Of course, small round balls have taken all manner of big game. The 22 Long Rifle has also accounted for many a whitetail buck, but that does not make it right for deer any more than a 32-, 36-, 40-, or for that matter a 45-caliber round ball is. In the hands of fantastic marksmen/hunters, just about any lead pill will drop big game. For the rest of us, 50s and up are better. As only one sample from a wide world of great jacketed pistol bullets from Speer, Hornady, Sierra, and other companies, the specific jacketed pistol bullet chosen for discussion here is the Nosler .451-inch with sabot. It was selected because it has a frangible front end for quick expansion, especially on deer-sized game; a partition that retains base lead for penetration; and its full 45-caliber size, closer to the 50-bore than 44-caliber pistol bullets. Our conical example is the Hydra-Con™ bullet from Parker Productions with "sealed hydraulic chamber" containing a non-toxic, food-grade lubricant that, upon impact, produces rapid bullet expansion. Along with reliable expansion, the Hydra-Con™ bullet has two, more significant attributes: accuracy and big-time mass. Three-shot groups into an inch at 100 yards from the bench with a scoped muzzleloader are commonplace, with weights ranging up to 650 grains in 50 caliber, 660 grains in the 54 and 670 grains in the 58.

Sam's Bullet Box

A simple wooden box, compartmentalized, with different media in the compartments, may not seem like much of a testing device, but

over the years, Sam's Bullet Box has shown a high correlation between bullet performance in tests and on game. The media used do not truly correspond with bone, body fluids, and muscle structure. While these physiological traits are not simulated by slabs of wood, clay, or water balloons, the end results are reliable because the obstacles in the box challenge bullets to perform. Bullets that blow up in the box blow up on game. Bullets that fly through the box with little telling effect do likewise on game. Bullets that create long, deadly wound channels in the box make similar tunnels in game. Water-filled balloons represent body fluids. Wooden boards take the role of bone. Clay, while in no way similar to actual tissue structure, absorbs energy the way muscle tissue can. The box turns out to be a fairly good working model of a big-game animal. Optional in some compartments of the bullet box are large department-store catalogs. Stacked paper, wet or dry, tortures a bullet, somewhat to an unrealistic degree; however, bullets that survive intact in stacked paper do not come apart on game.

The bullet box tests several aspects of performance: penetration, bullet upset, also known as "mushrooming," wound channel, and retention of original weight. Comparisons between high-energy, jacketed big-game bullets and missiles for muzzleloaders have proven interesting over the years. This is mainly a matter of contrasting what we know to be highly effective against what we want to learn. Walking up to the box and firing into it, however, proves nothing. Hunters do not take big game at the muzzle. Loads must be established to represent downrange velocity/energy figures. This is not difficult to do. Loading manuals provide all the necessary data. For example, the forever-popular 30-06 Springfield cartridge easily starts a 180-grain bullet at 2,700 fps MV. A Hornady manual shows a 180-grain

Cover scents like these can help fool the super noses of bucks, bulls, and boars so the blackpowder hunter can stalk or still-hunt closer to his game.

another full-size catalog, then completely exited the back of the bullet box. This does not mean that a 58-caliber, 625-grain Minie is more effective than a 7mm Magnum. It does show, however, that a big lead bullet possesses a semi-truck load of penetration power. The recovered 625-grain Minie weighed 508 grains — more than 80 percent of its original weight — verifying the fact that lead has high molecular cohesion, because the bullet staying together as a unit rather than fragmenting into pieces. While the bullet box admired lead-bullet effectiveness, it also proved that small round balls, as great as they are on rabbits, squirrels and even wild turkeys, are not right for big game. A .350-inch lead round ball went up against the box. This little pill only made it halfway through the first book. A 50-caliber, .490-inch round ball fared much better in the test box, striking at 1,200 fps. It lost 40 percent of its original weight, but still made it through the first book, the clay, the water, and one-third of the second catalog. A 280-grain, 58-caliber round ball hitting at 1,100 fps lost only 20 percent of its original weight, passing through the first catalog, the clay, the water and completely through a second catalog, finally stopping on the cover of a third catalog.

The Wound Channel

The wound channel is the hole created by a projectile (in this case, in a big-game animal). The process of creating that channel is far more complex than meets the eye. Bullet upset, or mushrooming, dispenses energy, but it also changes the shape of the wound channel. Everyone who has experience harvesting big game with modern cartridges has seen an exit hole far larger than the size of the bullet. This is extremely evident with modern high-speed, mushrooming, big-game bullets. A 2-inch exit hole made by a 30-06 Springfield or similar cartridge is not unusual, but did a 30-caliber bullet really

Spire Point starting at 2,700 fps MV, with a velocity of 2,300 fps at 200 yards. The shooter desiring to find out what his 30-06 bullet does at 200 yards handloads test ammo to about 2,300 fps, give or take a hundred fps or so. A Hornady manual shows the 180-grain 30-06 bullet at 2,300 fps with numerous powders, such as 51 grains weight RL-19. So the handloader prepares a few rounds with the 180-grain test bullet at 2,300 fps. These are fired into the box from point-blank range, simulating actual 200-yard

velocity. For example, a well-made, 175-grain 7mm jacketed bullet fired at about 2,500 fps (representing the arrival velocity at 200 to 225 yards) drove through a Sears catalog, a couple of inches of clay, a water balloon, and three-fourths of a second catalog before coming to rest. The recovered bullet weighed 66 grains.

A 58-caliber, 625-grain Minie bullet striking the same media in the bullet box at 1,200 fps velocity passed through one catalog, the clay compartment, a water balloon, expand to a 2-inch diameter? No, it did not. Double diameter would be only six-tenths of an inch. So what happened? I watched through a 20X spotting scope as a 30-06 bullet struck an antelope buck. The hide flew out and away from the animal as if it were a balloon. There was a 2-inch exit hole, yet the bullet itself was trapped against the hide of the pronghorn. What pushed the hide out? What made the 2-inch exit hole? The bullet did, of course, but not directly. The shock wave in front of the projectile puffed the hide out and made the hole. Black-powder bullets work differently. They do not possess the speed or remaining kinetic energy of the more powerful big-game cartridges, but they do create long wound channels, and they can part bone like a battering ram. Unless the spine or brain is struck, however, the animal is not likely to turn toes-up as it often does when a high-speed bullet hits. Delivered force is nonetheless immense from the more powerful front loaders.

Bullet Placement

Heavy lead bullets not designed to open up readily are best directed into the scapular region (shoulder blades), rather than the chest cavity. When striking the latter, these bullets may pass through with little evidence of a hit. Even if the animal runs only 50 yards or so before falling, it may not be located. I've witnessed bucks dropped in their tracks by a lowly round ball hitting the rib cage from modest range, while similar animals centered likewise with huge conicals walked off after being hit. That's because the ball imparted all its energy in the buck, not the hill behind it. Important: Every hunter owes it to any big-game animal to check out a shot, even if it looks like a complete miss. I took a steenbok in Africa that ran after it was hit squarely behind the shoulder. One onlooker said, "Let's go. He missed." The leader of the safari asked me what I thought. I said I felt the shot was

good. A tracker trotted out into the field and inside of two minutes held up the tiny antelope. Had we not taken time to look, a fine game animal would have fed the hyenas.

Uphill/Downhill Shooting

No one carries a slide rule on a big-game hunt. Figuring exact hold-under for shots at an angle is a wonderful exercise for the desk, but completely impractical in the field. Yet we know that whether shooting at game uphill from the muzzle, or downhill, the bullet in either case strikes high. The best a hunter can do is take this fact into account, holding a little low for shots that are steeply uphill or downhill.

Judging the Range

I was hunting with Bob Hodgdon one afternoon in Wyoming when he put my range-guessing skill to the test. "How far is that boulder?" he asked. I guessed 175 yards. He put his rangefinder on the boulder. It really was about 175 yards away. "How about that one?" he asked. This boulder was steeply uphill from me. I guessed 250 yards. It turned out to be almost exactly the same

distance as the first boulder. I was way off! Today we have access to rangefinders that are compact, light and easy to carry. My Bushnell Yardage Pro Compact 600 only weighs only 12 ounces. It's great for four purposes. First, it improves range estimation. Look, guess, then verify. Second, it tells how to hold on standing game. Third, by pre-testing various spots from a tree stand, the exact distance of an incoming animal is known. Fourth, it totally annihilates "I got that deer at 450 yards!" The rangefinder proves just how far the shot really was.

Knowing Trajectory

Now that the 200-yard muzzle-loader is a reality, knowing the range is more important than ever. Stalking for the close, sure shot is still preferred. But with scoped front loaders of the day, especially shooting more efficient bullets such as the SSB, if a hunter knows the range, he can make that 200-yard strike, but before he can do that, he must also know his bullet's trajectory. Longer-range muzzleloaders can be sighted in from the bench to strike 2 to 3 inches high at 100

The deer lodge is stronger than ever. Hunters find that while the lodge can be expensive, it is also a more certain route to a trophy buck. Here, the author enjoys a meal and conversation with fellow hunters at a deer lodge.

Reading sign is important to the big game blackpowder hunter who enjoys tracking and trailing. This prickly pear pad has been recently worked on by the Southwestern javelina.

yards. Then without moving the sight, the rifle is fired at a target 200 yards away. The center point of the group indicates bullet drop at 200 yards. Now the hunter knows how to hold on a big-game animal from point blank range out to 200-plus yards.

Brush Shooting

One fine afternoon in a particularly splendid patch of Wyoming countryside, I stalked a mule deer buck to only 20 yards. I used a bush to hide my approach. The buck and I were separated by only a rock's throw, the bush still between us. Crack! The buck looked up, then he ambled away. I searched for sign of a hit. There was none. Finally, I hiked over the ridge. There in the view of my binoculars was the very same 4-by-4 buck feeding across a canyon in perfect health. The 54-caliber round ball had undoubtedly struck a branch, which is all it took to go wide of an 18-inch target at only 20 paces. Subsequent tests with all types of guns proved why this happened. Bullets go haywire in brush. Period. That includes heavy slugs from big bores. Even

500-grain 458 Winchester full-metal-jacket bullets veer off course in the brush. The best advice: Get a clear shot. Forget about "brush busting." It's a myth easily tested by anyone. My own little demonstration took place shooting at a target through brush only 50 yards away. A 243 Winchester, 458 Winchester, 54-caliber round ball, and 58-caliber conical all failed to deliver good groups on the target.

Taking the Shot on Big Game

There are several major stances for shooting big game. Offhand is one. This means standing on the hind legs and banging away. It's to be avoided whenever possible. If a shooter must go offhand, and if his rifle has a carrying strap, the hasty sling method helps steady the shot. This amounts to nothing more than wrapping the left arm through the strap for a right-handed shooter. Kneeling is better than offhand and sitting is steadier than kneeling. Prone is good when the lay of the land allows a hunter to go on his belly. I rely often on my walking stick to steady the shot, especially

from offhand, but also sitting. The rules are simple: get into the steadiest possible stance, take a clean sight picture, then squeeze, don't jerk, the trigger.

The Immensely Popular Tree Stand

Take a tip from the modern whitetail bowhunter. Climb a tree. Whitetails pattern pretty well. Set a tree stand up in the right path and chances are a buck will pass by if the hunter spends enough time waiting. Black bears, even elk and moose, are taken by tree stand hunters. I hated the tree stand at first, as well as windmill lookouts, considering them unsporting. But I was wrong. The stand is no less sporting than waiting in a duck blind or goose pit. As for boring, it is not — after I learned to enjoy the wildlife that came to call, from birds to bucks, bulls, and boars. Tree stands are great for blackpowder hunters because they generally afford close shots at slow-moving or standing animals. In the meanwhile, the world goes by. Some of the most amazing wildlife sightings occur from the stand. I once saw a golden eagle kill a mature mule deer doe as I sat perched in a windmill. Another time a coyote and badger parried about a waterhole, neither letting the other come in for a drink.

The Ground Blind

After learning to love tree stands, I tried ground blinds. Kelly Glause, a Wyoming guide stationed in Evansville, set up some great ground blinds. First, he dug pits into the earth near waterholes, then he made rock corrals, and finally little wooden boxes. I also had good luck with simple blinds made of cheesecloth (the material that game bags are made of) draped over a couple of bushes near a game trail or waterhole. Now there's an excellent portable blind from the Game Tracker Co. It's easy to set up, and it works.

Lures

Especially during rut, lures work. There are several ways to use them. Two are fresheningbullet startera deer scrape with the introduction of lure, and lacing a trail. Tree-stand hunters lay out a fine line of lure leading from brush pockets and timber right up to the stand. One afternoon, I had four different bucks come by my stand, nose to the ground as they followed the scent trail I made with artificial musk.

Still-Hunting

I'll be a still-hunter as long as I'm able to hike over distances, which is what the term means — not standing still, but moving quietly through the habitat, wind in the hunter's favor, not haphazardly, but with a plan. This means knowing the lay of the land and how the quarry lives in the niche. Walk a little. Look a lot. It is pursuit hunting at its finest. My way is hiking with walking stick, using the top of the staff as a binocular rest, stopping often to glass for game. This is an ideal method for the blackpowder big-game hunter because it often leads to spotting game that can be stalked for a close shot. Spot and stalk is similar to still-hunting, albeit somewhat less sophisticated, the idea being to cover ground until game is encountered.

Scents

Cover scent is important in stalking close for that one good blackpowder shot. Wildlife Research Center Inc. has come up with superior cover scents in spray bottles. Fresh earth is a good one, as are cedar, acorn and persimmon. While still-hunting through the habitat, a little puff in the air covers human scent. Another way to go is deer or elk lure mixed with water in a spray bottle. If hunters knew how often they were detected by the uncanny noses of big-game animals, they would watch the wind much more carefully, and also rely upon cover scents.

Wind Detectors

I learned the value of a wind detector from the late Elroy French as we stalked the bush veldt in Africa. Elroy had a small bag filled with finely powdered, white campfire coal dust, which he shook from time to time as we still-hunted. The little puff of smoke on the air showed not only wind direction, but how the zephyrs behaved: swirling, circling, changing. There are two major types of commercial wind detector. One is powder contained in a plastic squeeze bottle. The other is a product known as Windfloaters® from AFI Outdoors Co. This stuff is like superfine lamb's wool. A very tiny piece turned loose shows direction and behavior of the breeze. Dropping a little dirt in the air or a leaf is better than nothing, but compares poorly to powders and Windfloaters®.

The Drive

A well-devised drive is deadly on deer, and can work for elk, moose, or other big game. Hunters are posted along a trail or runway while partners hike in their direction, the object being to push game. Wind detectors work again, but this time to ensure that scent goes from drivers to posted hunters. Wind direction is especially vital when only one hunter is driving. The buck or bull scents the hiking hunter, then slips away. If the waiting hunter is in the right spot, a close, clean shot is his.

Does calling work? This Burnham Brothers photograph says yes. Look carefully. That's an African lioness in the center, called in with a Burnham Brothers call.

Scouting

Big-game blackpowder hunters do well to scout an area, searching for signs of game. This sign is generally in the form of tracks and droppings. In time, a hunter learns to determine the age of such sign. By scouting an area before season when possible, hunters don't waste time where the game is not. Of course, it's difficult to scout an area that's far from home. Sometimes, a hunter needs to head for the lodge or get a guide.

The Lodge

The deer lodge was frequented in North America a hundred years ago, and is today more popular than ever. Deer Creek Outfitters in Sebree, Ky., is but one example of a well-run outfit. Manager Tim Stull and staff use professional biologists to manage deer. Only mature bucks, along with a sufficient number of does to keep the herd viable, are taken — no young animals allowed. There is also a scientific feeding program. Stull has only archers and blackpowder hunters on his grounds. Trophies of a lifetime are a possibility. There are lodges in every state now, each one dedicated to a top-flight hunting experience.

Going Guided

As the workaday world grows busier, time becomes more of a premium. That's where the guided hunt comes in. Special blackpow-

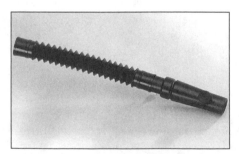

Lohman's Model 1130 Dial-Tone Deer Call operates with a dial that provides the three major types of calls whitetails make: buck grunts, doe bleats, and fawn distress to pull a buck in for a good close blackpowder shot.

der-only seasons are perfect going-guided opportunities. Steve Pike of Tenderfoot Outfitters, Gunnison, Colo., is an example of a guide dedicated to bringing smokepole hunters into the range of trophy elk and mule deer. Pike can talk an elk into slingshot range, let alone the reach-out of a good front loader. Finding a guide is no big trick. Listings on the back pages of magazines prevail. State guide associations are another source. As a test run for this work, I looked into a newly started outfit run by Eric McClenning in Illinois. Typically, McClenning was able to forward complete information on his operation via an address: RR 3 Box 207, Roodhouse, IL 62082-9247. State game departments may also have a list of guides and outfitters, as my home state of Wyoming offers. It's really that simple to get in touch with a guide these days.

Tracking

Having watched black trackers in Africa, I know that a man can follow an animal in the wild. I watched a fantastic tracker follow a single animal through a maze of bush veldt. I did not believe that any man could follow a single animal like that, but he proved that he could, and did. Unfortunately, most of us are not of that caliber, but we can get better through practice. Less skilled trackers do pretty well in snow, for example, and sometimes after a good rain. Dogging steadfastly direct on the trail, however, can be a mistake. Game animals are aware of their back trails. Better to leave the direct trail from time to time, circling ahead, using a wind detector along with spray cover scent or lure.

Calling Big Game

Watching Steve Pike, the Colorado guide, call a bull elk within 12 paces was an unforgettable experience. Pike is an expert, but we can all learn to call game. I got good at calling pronghorn antelope during the rut using a Lohman call. I

This Power Rattle MD-510 can be very effective during rut to draw a buck in for a close blackpowder type opportunity. It works with slap paddles and can be operated with one hand from a tree stand or blind.

learned from the provided audio tape, bringing bucks into close range. One afternoon my daughter Nicole, who had three Wyoming antelope tags, put two does down within 50 yards of each other. I was about to go forward for the duties of field dressing when I saw a buck in the distance. We took cover. I tuned up the Lohman antelope call and drew the buck in to a distance of 100 yards, where she dropped him cleanly with one shot.

Backpack Adventure

Backpacking into undisturbed territory and staying overnight is a prime means of finding that quiet spot perfect for hunting with a charcoal burner. Super packs and pack frames are more abundant than ever. I continue to use several, depending upon the circumstances. A Camp Trails Freighter with shelf is a standby, although I choose a Remington pack and frame for some hunts. I carry a lightweight tent and sleeping bag. The object is to camp with the game instead of heading back in the afternoon. In the morning, you wake up where the wild animals live, usually in a remote spot away from the beaten path.

Hunting Gear

Finally, I latched onto a truly waterproof, yet lightweight, parka from the Woolrich Co. I added Georgia waterproof boots and the wet weather was whipped. A comfortable hunter hunts better. Also important is a good shooting bag. For the traditional long rifle, I like a larger bag with more primitive implements, but for the in-line, the little compact unit from October Country is a beauty, filled with compact-sized tools. Everything necessary is in that little bag, ready to go.

The Blackpowder Hunter's Camp

Good shelter provides good rest and a rested hunter is a safer and better outdoorsman. Sometimes it's the smallest thing that counts. I like a well-lighted camp. Two Coleman North Star Dual-Fuel lanterns provide that, allowing partners and self to enjoy our evenings rather than groping around in half-light. The best camping gear ever is available

right now. Of course, there is nothing wrong with a tipi, either. Not when it's set up correctly. The point is: stay warm, stay healthy, hunt better.

The muzzleloader big-game chase is the lodestone, the crown diamond, the sun's rays of big-game hunting with a firearm, and the well-versed hunter who knows his gun and game has all good chance of success.

Chapter 43

MUZZLELOADER HUNTING FOR SMALL GAME AND VARMINTS

BIG-GAME HUNTING dominates, as sales of blackpowder guns prove; however, small game opportunities abound, along with varmint hunting. Muzzleloaders are wrong for paring numbers in a prairie dog town or lowering the jackrabbit population in an alfalfa field, but they're ideal for taking small game and mountain grouse, as well as coyotes, foxes, and other non-edibles where bag limit means little to nothing. Mainly, the right muzzleloaders include smallbores and the shot-gun, with single-shot pistols plus cap-and-ball revolvers tossed in for good measure. There can be considerable transfer value from small- to big-game arena, especially in the area of marksmanship and gun handling. The shooter consistently able to bring the littler edibles to the pot with head shots is on his way to making that one big boom count on a big buck, bull, or boar. Handling familiarity with front stokers is another advantage gained in the small game/varmint chase.

Small Game

The number-one small game animal in North America, if not the entire world, is the cottontail rabbit or relatives thereof. Powderpuff Tail lives just about everywhere from the sunny deserts of the Southwest to the frigid winter forests of the Northlands, and he's wonderful to hunt. No guide is required, nor expensive license, and normally they are not too far from home. Rabbits make good food, too. The tree squirrel is second on the

The number two small game animal in America, the tree squirrel, is perfect game for the smallbore muzzleloader.

Paul Wait

small-game list and, if anything, even more cherished for the challenge. There are hunters more dedicated to squirrels than they are to deer or ducks. Prepared correctly, the tree-dweller is also a fine dish on the table. Then there are dozens of other small things huntable and edible. The bullfrog comes to mind, along with the raccoon, opossum, porcupine, rattlesnake, turtle, woodchuck, rockchuck, prairie dog, muskrat and beaver. Mainly, we shy from eating these creatures out of upbringing — never ate 'em as a kid, won't eat 'em now. It's cultural and loaded with euphemisms. In other words, what we call a dish is often how we feel about consuming it. Snails are lousy, but escargot is delicious. Embryos sunny-side up sounds terrible, but call it eggs and it's not so bad.

Varmints, Furbearers, and Small Game

There is considerable crossover in categories. The raccoon, for example, is classified as a non-game animal, but may also be sought after for its pelt or tail, and certainly the raccoon has been, and will continue to be, prepared for the supper table. Muskrats fed thousands of trappers and pioneers, but they're generally classified as furbearers, and therefore not considered table fare. The same is true for beavers. Coyotes, foxes, and bobcats are not normally food for man, but they cross over, too, as both varmints and furbearers. Sometimes badgers fall into this dual category as well.

Varmints

In keeping with political correctness, many game departments have moved away from the original and entirely accurate term "varmint" to "non-game species" so as not to offend anyone, but everybody has a varmint. Two across-the-highway neighbors who would probably rather starve to death than shoot an animal are authorized by the state game department to care for injured birds, which they do very well, returning many to the wilds after a stay in "the bird hospital." They've spent many years at this endeavor, having retired from their regular jobs to become full-time caretakers of injured eagles, owls, falcons, hawks, and for that matter, crows, jays and any avian that may have flown into an obstacle or became illegally wounded by a "hunter." One day, I brought an injured kestrel (got caught in a fence) to the pair. As we took the sparrow hawk to its cage, I noticed something. "What's that?" I asked. I had never seen a mousetrap that large. "Oh," the lady told me, "that's our rat trap. Rats come in and eat our bird food, so we trap them."

Varmints, or non-game animals if you prefer, make interesting objects of the chase for blackpowder shooters. Of course, in no way can the muzzleloader control numbers of unwanted damage-causing species. Admittedly, modern arms cannot get that job done, either. I recall a ranch that was infested, the word carefully chosen, with prairie dogs. The pastures were riddled with holes. The area was like the underground of Tombstone, Ariz., where miners tunneled everywhere for precious metals. The rancher called upon hunters to thin prairie dog numbers. Numbers were thinned, but the overall population of rodents remained high until a poisoning program went into effect. That did it. While there has been some repopulation, prairie dogs on that ranch are definitely fewer in number than ever and apt to remain that way, but not from hunting. On the other hand, hunting can reduce overall numbers to some degree.

For hunters who won't consider shooting anything that cannot be eaten, there are animals that go both ways. Young prairie dogs, for example, have been food for man as long as man has lived on the plains. They are still food. Porcupines, while not my idea of tasty fare, have also been eaten, while at the same time these animals in too great of numbers can destroy many valuable trees, making them varmints. I recall a privileged day on a handsome ranch where we were graciously allowed to hunt deer. The rancher bid us good luck, but also voiced a warning. "If I find out that you ran across a porcupine and didn't shoot it, you won't be welcomed back." Trees along his stream were suffering badly, and his little home on the prairie didn't have trees to spare. Porcupines are not good food, but their quills have been prized over the years and still are for decoration on shooting bags and many other items. So the blackpowder hunter goes for varmints because they represent an interesting animal, sometimes providing food or pelts. There is also benefit in thinning varmints. Coyotes, for example, eat many antelope fawns where I live in Wyoming. In their second year, antelope does have twins, usually a male and a female. Two kids often are reduced to one, or none, thanks to coyotes. Bagging coyotes means more pronghorns on the plains, a fact proven by official studies.

Some varmints are just as great a challenge as big game. It takes a good to hunter to consistently bag coyotes with a smokepole, especially in areas where the 300-yard shot is commonplace for the wily wild dogs. The blackpowder hunter cannot bang away at great distance, so he must get close one way or another to make his shot count. Western marmots, also known as rockchucks, are often tough to get to with a muzzleloader. Woodchucks, the eastern version of the marmot, are no pushover, either. That's why long-range varmint rifles firing high-speed bullets found their way into the green fields of the east. Blackpowder hunters can fire from afar with large-bore rifles, where making a hit brings certain results, but the smallbore muzzleloader has to be applied a lot closer, demanding a good stalk. Some of the methods

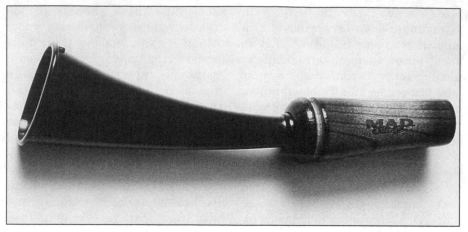

This Custom Cherry Coyote Call form MAD is another way to bring a coyote into blackpowder shooting range.

described below promote that close stalk with the smallbore.

Mountain Grouse

The Rocky Mountain chain has some wonderful bird hunting high up, especially for members of the grouse family, such as the blue or dusky.

The Advantages of Small Game and Varmint Hunting

Small game, and some varmints as well, are often just a little distance down the road. There is no extensive travel involved in hunting them, nor big outlay of cash for hunting tags and licenses. Trespass fees are generally unheard of, too, on private lands where deer, antelope or other game command folding green if you want to hunt private property. In many areas, going for small game or varmints is no more expensive than getting in your car and driving a few miles. And for that, you could come home with several pounds of high-quality food or, on inedibles, an interesting day in the field, and maybe even a little healthful exercise.

There's also economy in the shooting, especially if a smallbore squirrel rifle is put to work. As we know, a 32- or 36-caliber round ball rifle can be fired for less cash outlay than a 22 rimfire, provided the shooter casts his own projectiles and perhaps even makes his own percussion caps with Forster's Tap-O-Cap tool. You'll get about 155 32-caliber round balls, .310-inch diameter, from 1 pound of lead. That's at 45 grains per ball, 7,000 grains to the pound of lead. Find scrap lead, and you're really in business. And at 10 grains volume per shot, count on 700 pops for 1 pound of FFFg blackpowder. The 36-caliber, at 65 grains per ball, does not work out as cheaply, at about 107 balls per pound. But that's still a lot of shooting for 1 pound of metal, and the 36 gets good ballistics with mild powder charges, too.

Cottontail rabbits are so high in protein that a diet of that meat alone would not be wise. However, cooked right, these rabbits are as tasty as chicken, and with the proper accompanying vegetables and other foods, rabbit makes a healthy meal. Par-boiled/fried cottontail is tender and tasty. Squirrels are equally fine, although they require their own cooking style. Many other small edibles can grace the table, delighting the palate. For a whole lot of information on game care, plus dozens of good small game recipes, look into The Complete Guide to Game Care and Cookery, a DBI book.

Both small game and varmint hunting with a muzzleloader have a tremendous amount of transfer value to the big-game field. The hunter practices his finding and stalking techniques, not to mention learning about new gear from boots to coats. He also gains a great deal of field experience with loading and shooting his charcoal burner. One afternoon, I spent four hours in an area terribly overpopulated with ground squirrels. Did I get any practice? I should say so. I loaded and fired my sootburner many times.

The Shotgun for Small Game and Varmints

The muzzle-loading shotgun, flint or percussion, single or double barrel, is a worthy small-game instrument. I think of varmints as rifle candidates, but a shotgun can be a small-game delight and, in some circumstances, better than a rifle. For example, I've hunted cottontails that were wilder than first-grade kids on the last day of school. Jump and run was their game. Under those circumstances, a shotgun turned the trick. I've tried as little as 28-gauge and as large as 10-gauge on small game, and due to the wonderful versatility of the shotgun, every size worked. A mere half-ounce of No. 6 shot can be enough when cottontails are taken almost underfoot, which is sometimes the case. On the other hand, more shot may be the best bet when rabbits are jumping from 30 yards or so, with the target and the shot charge coming together at maybe 40 yards by the time the hunter gets off his shot.

As with quail hunting, I've learned that, for close-range encounters with small-game animals, a shotgun loaded with a sufficient charge of shot and a reduced powder charge can be ideal. One afternoon, I ran across a bunch of truly wild rabbits in a field of heavy brush. I had a 32-caliber round ball rifle with me; spot and stalk just didn't work. I couldn't find sedentary rabbits in the thick brush. The only opportunity to make meat was with the scattergun, and my short-barreled 12 was in the truck, waiting to be put into action. This chokeless double is good for short-range work and, with one-piece plastic wads, puts out a fairly decent pattern out to about 30 yards. I had my favorite rabbit shot along: No 5. I dropped 70 grains of FFg down each bore, followed by one over-powder wad and one cushion fiber wad, then an ounce of No. 5 shot with one over-shot wad. The limit at the time was five cottontails (now boosted to 10 in the same area). I had my five inside of an hour.

The Rifle for Small Game and Varmints

For small game, the 32- or 36-caliber squirrel rifle is ideal. If forced to choose one over the other, the 32 gets the nod, simply because it's large enough with its 45-grain round ball to get the job done. Another reason is because it is even more economical to shoot than the easy-on-the-pocket-book 36. I can't imagine needing anything more than a 32 for small-game hunting. Of course, only head shots count anyway, so this prescription for a 32 or 36 is not chiseled in concrete. If a hunter has a fine 40 or 45 that he shoots well, let him seek small game with it, but I've found that anything larger than 36 is too destructive when other than a perfect head shot is made. For example, I've used a 40 on cottontails, and when the ball hit more neck than head, the shoulder meat was damaged.

However, for varmints, larger-than-36 is OK, although I can't imagine when anything exceeding 40 caliber would be necessary. The largest varmint normally encountered is the coyote, and one 40 ball through the chest region on the desert dog will humanely do the trick.

For comparison purposes, here are a few figures to consider. The ballistics below belong to four different rifles. Remember that a 22 Long Rifle round with a 40-grain bullet at 1,250 fps muzzle velocity gets 139 foot-pounds of muzzle energy. At 100 yards, velocity is around 1,000 fps and energy is 89 foot-pounds.

We can agree that the little 32-caliber, with its 45-grain round ball at close to 1,300 fps muzzle veloc-ity, is just about ideal for rabbits, squirrels and similar small game. Even when barrel length drops from 41 1/2 down to 25 inches, a muzzle velocity of more than 1,100 fps is achieved. Considering that rabbits and squirrels are often taken at 20 yards or so, these velocities, with energies ranging well over 100 foot-pounds, will do the job — and with only a 10-grain powder charge. The 36 is a dandy, too, but admittedly, it does burn more powder. The 40-caliber long rifle is really more than necessary for small game, but on varmints, it's an excellent caliber. For coyotes and foxes, I'd choose the full 50-grain volume FFFg charge for close to 2,000 fps muzzle velocity, giving a 100-yard energy figure more than ample for the largest "prairie wolf."

A Word About Pistols and Revolvers

Nothing said above is meant to downgrade pistols or revolvers for either small game or varmints. The criterion for using either is simple: Can the hunter hit his target? Pistols and revolvers have all the authority necessary to bag small game, as well as varmints. See Chapter 36 for more information.

Sample of Small Game/Varmint Rifle Ballistics

Powder Charge (grs.)	Muzzle Vel. (fps)	Muzzle Energy (fp)	100-Yard Vel. (fps)	100-yd Energy (fp)
Dixie Tennessee Squirrel Rifle, 41.5-inch barrel, 32-caliber, (.310-inch 45-grain round ball)				
10 FFFg	1,263	170	720	55
20 FFFg	1,776	336	852	77
30 FFFg	2,081	462	936	93
Thompson/Center Cherokee, 25-inch barrel, 32-caliber (.310-inch 45-grain round ball)				
10 FFFg	1,120	125	538	29
20 FFFg	1,649	271	775	60
30 FFFg	1,871	350	879	77
Hatfield Squirrel Rifle, 39.5-inch barrel, 36-caliber (.350-inch 65-grain round ball)				
20 FFFg	1,471	312	794	91
30 FFF	1,799	467	882	112
40 FFFg	2,023	591	956	132
Ozark Mountain Arms, 36-inch barrel, 40-caliber (.395-inch 93-grain round ball)				
20	1,294	346	828	142
30	1,584	518	927	177
50	1,993	820	1017	214

In the Field

Once you've decided to hunt small game, then pick the proper gun, you need to know what to do when in the field. There are various methods that work well when toting a smokepole.

Still-Hunting

Small game and varmints can be still-hunted successfully. Slow-motion walking is the ticket, whether in a field for rabbits or a forest for tree squirrels. Still-hunting is perhaps the most interesting way to chase small game or varmints because it keeps a person on the move, seeing things, as well as gaining a little exercise.

Jump and Shoot

Shotgunning for cottontails is really a jump-and-shoot endeavor. It's not very sophisticated, but it works. Walk. Scare something out. Shoot as it runs.

Spot and Stalk

This is very much like still-hunting and, in fact, could be construed as pretty much the same hunting style. If there is a difference, it lies in covering a little more ground a little faster, relying heavily on binoculars for spotting game in the distance and then stalking close for a perfect shot.

"Spot, Dash and Tree" Squirrel Hunting

This manner of squirrel hunting really works, but before going into it, a warning: Do not run with a loaded rifle that is either primed (flintlock) or capped (percussion). There is plenty of time to drop a little pan powder in or fix a cap on the nipple after the dash part of this squirrel-hunting strategy is over. Squirrels do not live in the trees all the time. They work the ground considerably. The hunter hikes a lot with this method, in prime squirrel habitat, looking for a bushytail on the ground. When he spots one, he makes a mad dash straight at the little rodent. Naturally, if the squirrel is close and a good shot is possible, the hunter can ready his rifle and shoot. But what usually happens is this: The hunter slowly approaches and the squirrel dashes off over the ground, quickly getting out of sight.

On the other hand, the mad dash provokes Chatterbox to climb the first tree it sees. Now the squirrel is isolated. True, he may head for his den, but usually that's not what happens. Instead, the squirrel climbs up into the tree, sometimes lying flat on a branch. Squirrels in this setting are very hard to see, so I use binoculars to separate limb from old Umbrella Tail. Once the squirrel is spotted, the hunter maneuvers into shooting position, his rifle recently primed or capped. Now it's time for marksmanship to prevail on a tiny target amidst branches and sometimes leafy foliage.

Calling Squirrels

Contrary to popular notion, and in spite of the squirrel's nickname of Chatterbox, squirrels can be quiet and often are. On the other hand, they have a good voice and love to use it, especially for scolding. Because squirrels do like to talk, a call works well in hunting them. I have a Lohman squirrel call that has brought bushytails from out-of-sight hiding amongst leaves or branches, right out onto a limb in a fighting pose. The squirrel hunter interested in learning more about calling should invest in Lohman's fine video on the subject, called "Squirrel Challenge," and it instructs on aggressive calling, but contains much more than that about squirrels. Calling squirrels is a great way to locate them. It's also a good way to get a squirrel in a tree to show himself.

Calling Varmints

Calling varmints is quite different from calling squirrels. Here, your goal is bringing that fox, coyote or other critter right into small-bore blackpowder range. There are dozens of great varmint calls these days, not to mention the electronic devices available. Whole books have been written on the art of varmint calling. There can be many tricks to this trade. Interested? Do three things: Look for some good books on the subject, certainly, but also head to the video-rental store for some good videos on using varmint calls. And, number three, when you buy your call, insist on an audio tape with it, and listen to that tape several times. Practice!

Calling crows has been a tradition for many decades in America. This MAD Gold Series Crow Call sounds just like the real thing.

Decoying

Snowshoes

There's double meaning here. By "snowshoes" I mean both the hare and the things you wear on your feet to get around in the snow. I've lumped them together because I've had good luck along logging roads in winter for snowshoe rabbits while wearing showshoes on my feet. The snowshoe is not the treat that rabbit is, at least to my taste buds. Snowshoes are hares, like jackrabbits. They are edible, but they can demand some cooking tricks, as noted in The Complete Guide to Game Care and Cookery. But they're also fascinating to hunt, and in many places, seasons are open all winter long. So put snowshoes on your feet and go out for snowshoe rabbits with your muzzleloader. Of course, watch the winter weather and always be prepared to stay safe, warm and fed should a storm come up.

As for the snowshoes themselves, you don't have to look only for snowshoe hares while wearing them. I learned the value of snowshoes during my residence in Fairbanks, Alaska, many years ago. When the snow piled up, I sure didn't want to be housebound, and so my friend Kenn Oberrecht and I donned our snowshoes and took off after cottontail rabbits. Our sandwiches froze into white bricks in our pockets, but we didn't let that deter us from having a good time. While the older-style wooden-frame snowshoe is a dandy, I've turned to Sherpa metal-frame shoes these days. The ones I have are the Lightfoot model, only 31 inches long, and they get me around on those logging roads just fine.

Jack the Rabbit

Jackrabbits are so special that I saved this varmint, non-game ani-

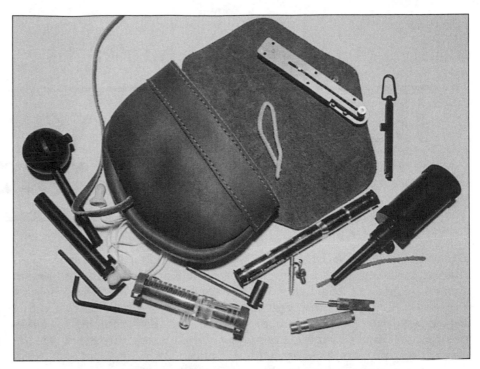

A small shooting bag like this excellent example from October Country, holds all the accessories necessary for the smallbore hunting rifle.

mal or — believe it or not — predator for last. That's right, my state, Wyoming, lists the jackrabbit as a predator. Classify him where you will, but admit that the jackrabbit has done a great deal to get newcomers started in hunting. My first four-footed conquest was at a very tender age in the then-unsettled desert regions outside of Tucson, Ariz. The prize was a jackrabbit taken with a homemade bow. Jacks can be difficult to approach at times, so the 40 round ball is good, with its greater reach than the 36 or 32. But the latter two can be plenty for most jackrabbit hunts.

Reading Sign

Small game and varmint hunting can be taken as seriously as the hunter wishes, right down to learning new areas by studying sign. In wintertime, it's easy to spot rabbit traffic. Trails in the snow, especially along fence lines, give their presence away. Also, crusty snow holds droppings in a starkly contrasting view. Varmint sign can also be studied. After all, just because it's small game or varmints does not mean it isn't full-blown hunting. So use all of your skills and enjoy the small game or varmint hunt as much as your quests for larger game. Small game is good food, and there's something you can do with just about every varmint, from fly-tying materials to pelts. Add a muzzleloader to these hunts, and you've just escalated the experience several notches. Try it and you'll agree.

Chapter 44

BEN'S BIRD AND OTHERS WITH THE SMOKEPOLE

BENJAMIN FRANKLIN wanted the wild turkey as our national symbol instead of the fish-eating bald eagle. He felt the turkey was a better candidate with loftier qualities than the clawed raptor. Thank goodness this great statesmen failed on that one, or we couldn't hunt this fabulous avian for the challenge, outdoor enjoyment, as well as Thanksgiving and Christmas feasts. Now there's even the National Wild Turkey Federation, dedicated to this regal bird's prime continuance as a huntable species. Along with the wild turkey, every upland bird with an open season is legal to the muzzleloading shotgunner. The blackpowder breech-loading shotgun is also legal, but not popular, although blackpowder shells are once again available from Old Western Scrounger (see Directory). They're called "Gamebore" and are sold in 10, 12, 16, and 20 gauges, providing a new lease on life for old-time guns in safe condition. Some states have both fall and spring wild turkey seasons, as does my home state of Wyoming.

That's good, and a little surprising, considering that by the early 1900s, wild turkey populations were in the basement. Indiscriminate year-round hunting, avian diseases gifted to the wild birds by settlers' barnyard fowl, and lost habitat almost spelled doom for the wild turkey. By 1930, only 21 states had a grand total of around 20,000 birds. Now 49 states (all but Alaska) are home to our largest

upland game bird, with more than 2 million of them running around. Far-thinkers decided that one way to preserve the gobbler was transplantation. For example, a number of birds were introduced to the Rockies. Wyoming got some in 1935, when a few sage grouse were traded to New Mexico for fifteen Merriam's turkeys. About a decade later, the flock grew to around a thousand birds. In the early 1950s, 48 turkeys — 15 more from New Mexico plus 33 Wyoming residents — were turned loose in Wyoming's northeastern Black Hills region. They thrived. So did birds in other parts of the Rocky Mountain chain. While Arizona, New Mexico, Colorado, Montana, Idaho and other western states are not considered major wild turkey regions, they now offer thousands of opportunities for hunters.

Wild Turkey Hunting

Wild turkeys live different lives from area to area. A friend owns a little ranch in South Dakota. He can count on seeing wild turkeys at a given waterhole during all but the winter months. These birds must wear wristwatches, because they arrive for a drink about the same time every day, depending on the season of the year. In the Rocky Mountains, where I hunt the birds, seasonal movement is a priceless

Forrest Rhodes took this nice wild turkey with his Knight 12-gauge modern muzzleloader shotgun and a healthy dose of shot.

piece of knowledge. Wild turkeys would be nearly impossible to locate in the vast western reaches that house them if hunters didn't know where to start looking and what to look for. Part of knowing where to look lies in the turkey's daily routine, plus roosting sites, eating habits, food preferences, watering needs, communication calls, and strutting grounds. Sign-finding is highly important, since the birds do move around.

Turkey Lifestyles

I hunt the western gobbler, never having taken a strutter east of the Mississippi, but I have seen the birds while hunting other game, and information handed down here is transferable to a large degree. My birds live a rather simple routine. They get up early in the morning, feed, maybe go to the watering hole, belly up to the table again for a few hours, and then possibly lay up a while during midday. If the mating season isn't under way they dust a little, scratch the ground here and there, feed a bit more, and finally head back to the roost in late afternoon. They perch for the night high above any four-legged predators prowling on the ground. This daily action constitutes a lifestyle: feeding, watering, scratching, dusting, roosting, and mating (in the spring), with plenty of meandering all the while. Knowing these aspects of the wild turkey make them huntable, as is knowledge of their particular habits. Wild turkeys move a lot and eat noisily. Most of the day, the birds are on the roam, which is fortunate for us. If they brushed up like whitetails, turkeys would be even more difficult to find than they already are. A band of birds may move 2 miles or more during a daily feeding romp. Feeding turkeys are noisy, and that's good for hunters. More than once, I've cupped hands around ears to improve my all-too-human sound-sensors as I listened for them. I've also used sound-enhancers to listen for the birds exhibiting

their bad table manners. Now the advantage swings a little bit to the hunter, who may be able to stalk the noise and get a shot.

The wild turkey is omnivorous, eating whatever providence sets in its path, from small beasties to a host of vegetable matter. Three years running I took a tom in northern Arizona because I knew of a special field filled with grasshoppers that time of the fall. Every afternoon several flocks of Merriam's turkeys stepped out of the woods and onto this grassy dinner table. I had my pick of birds and deserve no credit for harvesting them, even with bow and arrow. They were only 20 paces away, busily gobbling up 'hoppers. I never saw another hunter in that particular region, which is too bad. Most of those fine-eating birds fell to winter snows and old age instead of a swift hunter's harvest. Spiders, grubs, snails, crawdads, worms, ticks, millipedes, centipedes, beetles, salamanders, frogs, grasshoppers, and just about anything else that skitters through the grass is fair game for the wild turkey. They also eat grass, berries, and acorns. Leaves of many green plants and numerous cultivated crops are also eaten. Wise hunters hold this image of the western wild turkey: a plucky fellow, unafraid to attack anything not large enough to attack back. It's

fond not only of live food, but if it's green, nutty, seed-like, or smacks of vegetables, the bird will go for it. The turkey gobbles food down whole, snatching it up, pecking at it, picking at it, stripping it away (such as grass seeds), clipping it off, or scratching it out of the earth. Paint this picture of a wild turkey, rather than a barnyard vision of a bird that walks around with its head down pecking for grain all day.

The turkey is a creature of action. it can run like a race horse, but when feeding, walking speed is around 2 mph, except for occasional mad dashes at living things. The flock can easily move 2 miles a day through its outdoor grocery store. I have found most of my birds because of these mobile feeding habits. I climb to a lookout spot, especially a bluff or bank above a waterway. (Note the combination: a high spot coupled with water.) Then I glass, looking for the feeding flock. I listen too, for clucks, gobbles, squawks, and sometimes what sounds like a Chihuahua lap dog lost in the woods. Find. Stalk. Shoot. Of course, it's not that simple, but the spot-and-stalk approach works well for gobblers, especially around water. The birds don't necessarily drink every day, but a hunter may have luck hanging around a watering station for two reasons. First, a flock might

Decoying, especially coupled with good calling, can bring a wild turkey in. Lohman's True Position Breeders decoy set has lured tombirds in close.

This Lohman decoy featuring a bearded tom can be quite effective in bringing a tom into gun range.

just come in to drink. Second, turkeys live near some source of water.

Turkey Sign

Even though I never got a bird at its watering site directly, water is extremely important in turkey hunting. That's not only because they normally live near some form of liquid, but also for sign, such as tracks in mud along ponds, lakes, even streams. The camp-out hunter is smart to park himself not to0 far from a source of water in turkey country. If there's a pond, especially close by, "dusting" it makes sense. This means taking a fallen branch and using it as a broom to clear away all tracks around the water's edge as best as possible. Next morning, the usual hunting plan is followed, but by afternoon, the hunter checks the waterhole to see who came to visit that day. Every track there, turkey and otherwise, will be fresh since all old sign was obliterated. If turkeys are using the water site, hunting the immediate region makes sense, with hopes of finding a flock, of course, but if not, perhaps a roost. What sign to look for? A hunter does not have to be Sherlock Holmes to deduce the meaning of a fresh turkey feather lying a trail, and a turkey track is somewhat more impressive than a sparrow's. It will be the largest bird track in the area.

Droppings are also telltale. The female leaves amorphous blobs. J-shaped rods belong to the male bird. Dusting sites may be found along trails and often along dirt roads. One season, locating a particularly handsome dusting site on an old logging road put me along that dusty artery for two evenings, which resulted in locating a bachelor flock of tom birds. Scratchings also mark turkey activity. Hen scratchings are not always well-defined, but toms may clear a large area under a tree with a V-shaped dugout about a foot and a half long, centralized and well-defined. Sometimes the V-shape loses its form, with the entire base around the tree raked away. It's not rare to find the duff from beneath a pine tree removed. If a deer, elk, or bear did this work, tracks will say so. If the tom bird did it, toe marks prevail, deeply channeled into the ground by the bird's strong feet.

The Roost

The hunter who finds a "hot" roost has an excellent chance of bringing home a holiday bird. Since wild turkeys roost every evening, finding their special tree is like locating his home address. Turkeys fly well. They can lift straight up from the ground to the roosting tree, but some roosting sites are below a dirt bank or cliff. Why, no one can say, but flocks use these high places like a hang glider's take-off strip. The birds hit the tree with the grace of a hippo at a tea party, hopefully clinging to a branch that will be its night's repose. These special trees are not always easy to find, but they are well worth looking for during both scouting sessions and the hunt itself. One afternoon, my hunting partner and I located a hot roost, obvious by the amount of fresh droppings on the ground below. We backed off and waited. Inside of two hours, there was a roaring sound as birds dived from a nearby creek bank, hitting the tree in kamikaze fashion. Filling two tags with a couple of smallbore muzzleloaders was no big trick.

Fall Calling

In the fall of the year, the call serves to locate a flock. Although a gobbler may come in to a call this time of the year, such has never happened to me. However, calling remains worthwhile because the tom may respond, giving away his location. Sometimes a few blasts on a crow call will bring a "gobble-gobble" that can be followed up, too. An owl call has the same effect, eliciting a response. Once the male birds give themselves away, they can be stalked. Although wild turkeys are not terribly smart, they are extremely wary, so stalking means moving slowly, with great care not to announce the approach with the crack of a twig. On the other hand, there is no evidence that wild turkeys sniff the hunter out the way deer do, so watching the wind is mainly for the sake of sound transmission.

Spring Calling

Springtime calling is an entirely different matter. Amour is in the air and a tom bird can be lured into a hunter's lap, provided the hunter has talent as a caller. Those who

Sometimes an owl call like this one will get a tom turkey to gobble and reveal his position.

This MAD Cherry Bomb turkey call sounds just like the real thing.

Blackpowder Turkey Guns

A rifle is excellent for western turkey hunting. A properly loaded 32- or 36-caliber squirrel rifle with patched round ball at about 1,800 fps will take a tom in a heartbeat. The 32 normally achieves this velocity level, depending on barrel length, with about 30 grains of FFFg or Pyrodex P, while the 36 usually gathers this speed with around 40 grains of these same powders. In western woods, such as found in the Black Hills of South Dakota and Wyoming, the opportunity often comes from across a draw, not necessarily a long shot, but sometimes out of shotgun range. With a squirrel rifle, putting a bullet on target is no problem. Called-in birds can also be taken with the muzzleloading rifle. A single 32- or 36-caliber round ball cleanly drops a gobbler with little loss of meat, while at the same time carrying a little more lethality at close range than a 22 WMR (Winchester Magnum Rimfire). The place to aim is the pinion area where the wing joins the body. Another good shot is the lower back with the bird going away. A super marksman can go for the head or neck, of course, but they are very small, and usually moving, targets.

are not expert callers should not overdo it. When the bird responds, the idea is to wait a minute, then answer briefly. Also, at least in some areas, toms won't come in to a call after mid-morning, but they will answer a call all day, and that can be almost as good.

Strutting Grounds

In my state, only toms are legal in the spring, whereas both sexes can be hunted during the fall. So, finding a strutting area in the spring is like an invitation to bagging a bird. These grounds can be traditional, used from season to season, which was the situation for a couple of timbered ridges that lured springtime tom birds to strut for the ladies. One spring, my partner and I slowly worked along one of these ridges. I had already shot a bird, but he still needed his tom. I walked slowly in front, stopping to glass ahead every few steps. The sight that presented itself in my binoculars won first place in my memory that season. As I looked through the glass, it was as if someone had turned

a movie camera on inside of my binoculars. There was a big fan turning from side to side. I signaled my companion and he stalked forward on his own, coming onto several strutting toms ahead. One well-placed shot from his 32-caliber muzzleloader, and he had his prize.

Sound Enhancers

There are now several different sound amplifiers on the market. They're good for turkey hunting, as well as deer stands. The only two I've tried are the Team Super Ear Personal Sound Amplifier by Silencio, with earphones, and the Bracklyn's Gobbler from the archery company of the same name. The latter are tiny in-the-ear hearing aids. Although cupping hands around the ears works well in amplifying sound, these and other commercial units are also good.

Hearing is a sense often overlooked by wild turkey hunters. Blackpowder hunters can take advantage of Walker's Game Ear to pick up the call of a turkey gobbler in the distance.

The Pellet Packer works well in the field for bird hunting. It contains shot, powder, and wad column all in one unit.

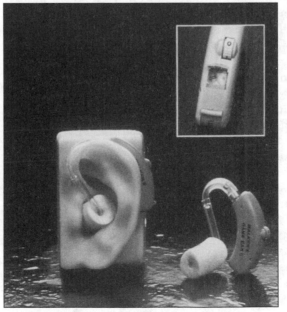

Walker's Game Ear Power Muffs provide the wild turkey hunter with "binoculars for your ears." They have 50 dB of power and a maximum output of 110 dB. In other words, these muffs enhance hearing up to eight times while compressing any noise in excess of 110 dB. The average muzzle blast is 145 dB.

The 32-caliber lead round ball, far right, may seem next to useless compared with the 54-caliber ball, center, and lead conical bullet; however, the little pill can do a great deal of good work in the wild turkey field.

Thompson/Center's Black Mountain Magnum 12 gauge takes a special screw-in "Turkey Choke." It's the T/C Black Mountain Magnum with musket cap ignition with a breech designed for either regular powder or Pyrodex Pellets.

Now that shotgun manufacturers and importers have seen the light, they are offering not only highly powerful guns, which have been around for a long time, but also tight chokes. The blackpowder muzzleloading scattergun is a terrific turkey-taker. Right along, the big Knight 12-gauge has been given its due as a powerhouse with huge shot payload in front of 120 grains maximum of FFg or RS. This gun's extra-full choke pattern is ideal for the task of cleanly taking a wild turkey. That's true, too, for the Navy Arms T&T, also receiving earlier mention, along with the Thompson/Center Black Mountain Magnum 12 gauge with full choke. While guns come and go, and there is no guarantee that these models will always be available, the breed is healthy and will not perish. The strong blackpowder shotgun works too well to lose out entirely, especially with a mix of shot, such as No. 5s and BBs. The smaller pellets help to seal up any possible holes in the pattern, while the larger pellets deliver good energy to the target.

Not to be entirely ignored, the little 25-20 Winchester and sister 32-20 rounds loaded with blackpowder are also good wild turkey-takers. Loaded with FFFg or P, either will put a bird down pronto, and without terrible meat loss. Neither puts out the steam associated with the 36-caliber muzzleloader pumped up with a good powder charge behind a 125-grain lead conical, but both are adequate at close range. The 32-20 develops about 1,300 fps muzzle velocity with 20 grains volume of Pyrodex P.

The successful turkey hunter scouts prospective hunting areas before the season opens, when he can. He looks for sign around streams and ponds and tries to find a roost. The wise turkey hunter also packs a pair of binoculars, using them faithfully. He may also cover plenty of ground, staying in the field all day, since wild turkeys — unlike lazy old whitetail bucks — eat and play by day, sleeping at night.

Turkey Hunting Safety

The wild turkey is perfectly capable of picking out a hunter's face and form from the terrain, and so camouflage is important, especially full camo, meaning a facemask and gloves. At the same time, a hunter hidden by foliage to begin with, plus being fully camouflaged, and calling, can convince another hunter that he, the caller, is a turkey. No one should ever shoot at an uncertain target. That's the safety rule. At the same time, the hidden caller should be on the lookout. If he's stalked by another hunter, it's best to make himself known right away. Don't wave the arms or shout, but instead remain still and speak in a normal tone to avoid prompting a snap shot by the stalking hunter.

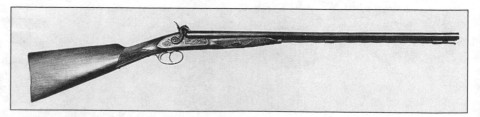

A double-barrel 12-gauge shotgun like this one, which is allowed a full 1 1/2-ounces of shot by the manufacturer, is a good choice for wild turkeys, especially with the fast second shot available. A tight choke adds to its effectiveness.

The blackpowder shotgun is excellent for all upland game, including these Arizona dove taken with a Navy Arms 12-gauge.

Dove are difficult targets, but a properly loaded blackpowder shotgun is up to the task.

Other Birds with Blackpowder

If hunting the wild turkey is a king's sport, which it is, then the rest of the wild birds also qualify for royal status. Here are a few flyers to consider.

Mourning and White-wing Doves

Pass shooting, especially in or near fields or by waterholes, is the usual way to hunt these fine, dark-breasted birds. The action is fast and the target small. Use improved cylinder near waterholes, where birds are slowing down from their high-speed flight. For longer-range shooting at faster birds, a 1 1/4-ounce charge of No. 7 1/2 or No. 8 shot in front of a full complement of black-powder or Pyrodex, plus at least a modified, if not full choke, provides the type of pattern necessary to harvest a limit.

The big trick is lead. One way to get enough lead is pulling well ahead, making certain that the trigger is pulled while the gun is in motion. Leading, then stopping the swing to shoot, means hitting behind on almost every shot. The sustained lead, with the trigger pulled while the gun is still in motion, puts the string out in front of the bird, where it belongs. Leading too much is not usually the problem on fast-flying doves. Since the shot pattern does come as a string, the first part of the

A fast second shot is especially handy on a dove hunt. One barrel is away here, the other ready to fire.

The blackpowder shotgun with cylinder bore (no choke) is at home in situations like this one—a grouse ready to flush at any second and at very close range.

shot charge may miss the bird out front, with the latter part of the string making contact. But if the first part of the string is behind the birds, where else can the remainder of the pattern go but behind the bird?

Quail

All kinds of quail can be hunted with the blackpowder shotgun. Bobwhites, scaled quail, Mearns, California, Gambel's — America has many different kinds of quail. The open-choked, muzzle-loading shotgun does a good job on these birds most of the time, using small size shot as the covey rises close to the hunter. Dogs, of course, add greatly to the hunt by locating the birds, often doing a great job of holding the covey until the hunter arrives.

Waterfowl

All waterfowl from the smallest duck to the largest goose is on the blackpowder shotgun list. Full chokes are the way to go for pass shooting, but ducks on ponds — they call it puddle-jumping — can be taken with more open bores for wider patterns. Again, the latest big-power shotguns rule. However, there's a difference this time. Those guns not suited to steel shot are legally out, or are they? Shooting steel will score the bores of these shotguns, but now there is Bismuth shot, offered through Ballistic Products Inc., to name one source. Bismuth will not

harm "standard bores" originally built for lead shot, the experts say, while at the same time delivering good weight per pellet size.

Shorebirds

Included in this classification is the fantastic sandhill crane, a big bird that stands as high as 4 feet off the ground. Sandhill cranes are now open season on a restricted basis, usually with a permit system in place. Wings on this mighty bird may span 80 inches, with bigger cranes weighing about 12 pounds. Obviously, the 12- or 10-gauge gun is called for here with top loads only: a good parcel of shot pushed by a safe but strong powder charge. Other shorebirds are much smaller, such as the unique rails, snipe, and woodcocks

Blue grouse make a superb camp feast, and are fair upland game for a blackpowder shotgun like this Navy Arms 12-gauge side-by-side caplock.

available in some areas. Of course, these littler birds call for smaller shot sizes and dense patterns.

Pheasants

Pheasants continue to do well in many areas, especially with programs in force to curb "clean-farming," where fields are plucked down to the last segment of vegetation, and hedgerows all but wiped out. Full-choke guns are the ticket for skittish birds jumping at longer distances, but hunting over good dogs can provide much closer shots, with modified choke more practical. Cylinder or even improved-cylinder patterns on pheasants are not the best. These are fairly big birds, and while not necessarily "hard-feathered," as some birds are (especially larger waterfowl), their size does call for good pellet concentration on target. Some hunters prefer larger shot sizes on pheasants, relying on a few hits with more delivered energy; however, smaller shot, such as No. 6, is highly effective where close-jumping is the rule, with No. 7 1/2 ideal and deadly over dogs. The pheasant is a fast-flyer, but making an attempt to deliver the pattern up front into the head/neck region is worth cultivating.

Grouse, Ptarmigan and Partridges

The Rocky Mountain chain is home to some wonderful bird hunting on high, especially for members of the grouse family, such as the dusky and blue. Grouse of various sub-types are also well known, and highly regarded, in other areas. Rifles are allowed for grouse hunting in some parts of the west. These large, delicious birds make fine camp fare for the hunter with a smallbore muzzleloader. They can be fairly tough customers; however, one good 32- or 36-caliber round ball through the lung region puts them in the bag quickly. Where I live in Wyoming, grouse, along with certain partridges, are rifle-huntable in the mountains.

I've also rifle-hunted them in Alaska. The grouse can be an absolute pushover, standing on a limb only a few feet away, inviting the hunter to "please take me for supper." On the other hand, flighty birds are not unusual, sometimes taking wing at the first crack of a twig. The only advise offered for finding blue grouse and their kin is walking the ridges, which the birds seem to use as lanes of travel. Other than that, it seems to be a matter of simply running into these birds, rather than deliberate locating. Ptarmigan, where I

hunted, are strictly shotgun birds. My partner and I did well, however, taking ptarmigan with smaller shot, nothing larger than No. 6, from modified-choke guns.

If a bird is legal and practical to hunt with a shotgun, a smokepole scattergun can do the job. Sometimes a smallbore rifle is even better. Often, it's a matter of the law. Rifles are illegal for most bird hunting in North America. However, either a blackpowder rifle or shotgun can add a big extra dose of pleasure to bird hunting, giving the experience an extra dimension of fulfillment.

Chapter 45

THE 45-70 GOVERNMENT CARTRIDGE — STILL GOING!

AN ENTIRE chapter is devoted to the amazing 45-70 Government cartridge because this old-timer deserves the honor. After all, here in the 21st century, the 45-70 not only is loaded by ammo companies, but it's also the number-one cartridge for silhouette shooters everywhere. Dethroning this king of the silhouette game is unlikely, even though recently threatened by the milder 40-65 Winchester. Furthermore, it's still chambered in modern rifles by Marlin, Ruger, and other companies. The Remington rolling block of the 19th century is back on line, not only with copies from Navy Arms and other importers, but also from the company that put the rifle out in the first place: Remington. More rifles are chambered for the 45-70 than any other cartridge of the blackpowder era. Remember that the 30-30 was a smokeless-powder round from the

beginning, a fact sometimes confused. The round is chambered not only in the Thompson/Center Contender pistol and carbine, but has even found its way into revolvers, as well as a rolling block pistol, plus bolt-action rifles. The 45-70 walks both sides of the street, more than adequate for hunting big game loaded with blackpowder, as well as winning long-range matches, while at the same time delivering even more authority with smokeless powder loads in firearms made to handle smokeless safely, such as Marlin's 1895 lever-action repeater.

One reason for this amazing success story is pure and simple power. While velocity is low because of limited powder capacity in the case, big bullets in the 400-, 500- and even 600-grain range create considerable impact and penetration. Heavy bullets with good momentum also continue downrange with accuracy, as

proven at matches where 1,000-yard targets are hit with 45-70 cartridges loaded with blackpowder. Big bullet lovers credit this old round with more ballistic potential than many of the newer, high-velocity numbers, although that is a point bearing much discussion. Regardless, the 45-70 continues to earn its badge of excellence in spite of its age. After all, it was adopted as the official U.S. Army round chambered in the single-shot Springfield Model of 1873, fondly known as the Trapdoor, because its action was remindful of a door hinge. The barrel wore three-groove rifling with a twist of 1:22. Its acceptance followed an official act approved by Congress on June 6, 1872, authorizing the selection of a breechloader in both musket and carbine form to be carried by soldiers of the U.S. Army. Brigadier General A.H. Terry was senior officer of the deciding board and the Springfield got the nod, the

Modern jacketed bullets in sabots, oftentimes originally intended for smokeless powder handguns, open up well at muzzleloader velocities and are especially potent with boiler room placement.

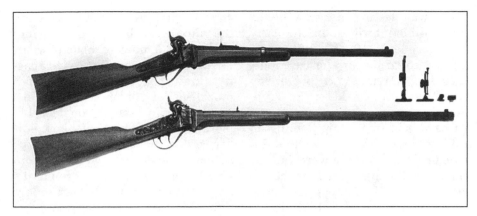

Even Sharps rifle replicas have been chambered for the reliable 45-70 Government cartridge.

45-70 round being its cartridge. Of course, the 45-70 was a blackpowder cartridge through and through, and was christened with blackpowder nomenclature, such as 45-70-405: 45 caliber, 70 grains of blackpowder, with a 405-grain, cast lead bullet. The Trapdoor rifle was capable of withstanding something like 25,000 pounds per square inch of pressure, so 70 grains of Fg blackpowder was perfectly safe in that action with any normal 45-caliber bullet.

The 45-70 saw action as a military cartridge for many years. Not until 1892 did an ordnance board officially declare it finished when the Krag was adopted with its smokeless powder 30 Army round, known today as the 30-40 Krag cartridge. Even for the Spanish-American war, many soldiers were armed with the Springfield Trapdoor, and a few Trapdoors remained in service until World War I. Add it all up, and the 45-70 saw some type of military use for about 45 years, even though many students of military history limit the official life of the cartridge to only two decades. Remember, too, that surplus 45-70s were offered to civilians for prices as low as $1.50 plus shipping. Now add the Numrich conversion kit for under $50, which turned Remington rolling blocks chambered for 43 Egyptian and 7mm Mauser into 45-70s. Navy Arms soon followed with a ready-to-go 45-70 rolling block,

plus the Martini and the Siamese Mauser in 45-70. It is clear why this round never died. Include the re-issue of a Trapdoor by H&R, as noted below.

The Cartridge

The 45-70 Government was, by design or pure chance, a well-balanced cartridge. While the later 45-90 Winchester, for example, was indeed a bit more powerful because of the additional powder charge, it wasn't strong enough to replace the old round. The 45-70 is a straight-walled, rimmed case. Overall maximum case length runs 2.105 inches, including the rim. To give this fact visual meaning, consider the familiar 30-06 Springfield case at 2.494 inches long, but that includes the neck. Take the neck away and the '06 case runs 2.111 inches to the base of the neck and 1.75 inches for the body length minus the head. Compared with some of the old rounds of the same era, the 45-70 was not really that large, certainly nothing like the 50 Sharps, or for that matter the 45-120 Sharps. Across the rim, the round measured .608-inch. Leaving the rim out, the case head of the 45-70 is .505-inch across. The mouth of the case is .480-inch across. That's the 45-70, large enough to contain a good dose of powder, but not an immense case by any means.

Records show that at the outset, the 45-70 was loaded with 70 grains

of Fg blackpowder for the rifle, but only 55 grains of the same powder for the carbine. In either case, the bullet was listed at 405 grains, which remained a popular weight for the 45-70 over many decades. Although the 405-grain projectile worked just fine, the government did load 500-grain bullets in the cartridge in the early 1900s. Many other bullets also found a home with the 45-70, proving that it had more versatility than might be expected. Even a 45-caliber round ball is shown, listed at 140 grains. I found no data to support its construction or exact diameter. But assuming pure lead, the 140-grain round ball would have gone about .450-inch in diameter, since a pure lead ball of .450-inch weighs 137 grains and I imagine the 140-grain notation was rounded off. Also offered was a "collar button." Lyman reintroduced this very short, spire-pointed bullet, but it failed to gain shooter support and was dropped. However, Rapine Bullet Molds (see Directory) continues to offers the collar button two ways with molds for the light spire-point and a heavier, but still short, round nose. The same company also has molds for the 40-65 Winchester and many Sharps rounds, as well as numerous Minie bullets, plus a large number of special 45-70 configurations, including a government-Issue bullet and several variations in exact bullet diameter. Rapine obviously respects the popularity of the 45-70 Government cartridge.

Keeping It Alive

In 1931, amidst the writhing of that financial reptile called the Great Depression, Winchester was the last company to chamber the 45-70 in a lever-action rifle in that time frame — the excellent Model 1886. That should have done it for the old girl, but it was not to be, because while chambering was discontinued, ammunition manufacture was not and a shooter could still purchase 45-70 fodder and fire away. It's difficult to say why the round didn't perish. After all, it was totally outmoded by many new smokeless-powder cartridges. In truth, velocities were maintained at about 1,200 to 1,300 fps for the 405-grain bullet, even with smokeless powder. Why so modest? Because there were plenty of Trapdoor rifles out there, and manufacturers did not want to risk hotter ammo in the actions of these rifles, which were intended for blackpowder pressures by design.

There was also, among many of us, a burning desire to hunt with a rifle chambered for the old 45-70 round. There was no clear reason why, with so many shiny new cartridges to choose from, but I ended up with a Model 1886 Winchester lever-action in a trade. The beautiful old rifle shot well enough, although nothing like my then-new Model 70 Winchester. I landed a couple of deer with it and can safely say that the 405-grain Winchester or Remington bullet from factory ammo whistled through game of this size like a draft through an open window. While my experience with the 45-70 on game is limited, add to it a number of notes compiled from friends who also tried the old blackpowder cartridge in the hunting field, usually for deer. All reports bore the same findings: bullets in the chest region zipped through. Sometimes it was impossible to tell if a hit or miss was registered; however, the deer never got away, running 50 to 100 yards, perhaps, but always folding up. Hit through the shoulder instead of in the chest cavity, the same-size buck collapsed on the spot like an imploded high-rise building. The lure of the 45-70 is far from tarnished. I was not surprised when friend Ron Cox, retired SWAT officer and devoted rifleman, as well as top-rated handgunner, announced that he was building a 45-70 single-shot rifle. He said it was for silhouette competitions, but, "I also intend to hunt with it."

Although there were no major companies chambering the 45-70 after the Great Depression, the old-timer was destined for new life in many different rifles. In the early 1970s, about 10 manufacturers offered firearms for the cartridge, including Harrington & Richardson (H&R) with a remake of the Trapdoor, as mentioned earlier. Navy Arms was busy offering Remington rolling block actions as well as finished rifles, and there were various Sharps rifles chambered for the 45-70 as well. Marlin got on board with its fine Model 1895 lever-action rifle chambered for the 45-70; Clerke Co. had one, too. Ruger chambered both its No. 1 and its No. 3 single-shot falling blocks for the old cartridge, while H&R offered it in a Shikari, which was essentially that company's break-top Topper action. Browning got on board with the 45-70 in a handsome single-shot rifle, as well as in a remake of the Model 1886 lever-action rifle. All the while, Numrich offered kits to convert original Remington rolling blocks that were not in caliber 45-70 to that round.

45-70 Ballistics

Records show that 45-70 factory ammo with 405-grain bullets was loaded to an advertised 1,310 fps. Chronographing samples of the old ammo proved velocities ranging from 1,200 to 1,300 fps that from old ammo picked up at gun shows in Winchester and Remington brands. So while the 45-70 is not ballistically fabulous compared with modern smokeless rounds, as proven by loading data, at the same time there is nothing to pity about

400- to 600-grain bullets leaving the muzzle at the speed of sound, pushed by a dose of blackpowder. Noted earlier was the case-capacity limitation. While 45-caliber muzzleloaders, such as the Whitworth, could burn considerably more than 70 grains of blackpowder, no more than that (even less, as explained below) would fit into 45-70 brass. On the other hand, it's imperative to acknowledge the fact that the 45-70 in rifles manufactured for smokeless powder could develop considerably more velocity than old-time loads allowed. In order to compare the ballistic potential of the 45-70 with modern rounds, which we do because the cartridge continues to find its way into the hunting field as well as long-range competition, smokeless loads must be considered. After all, it's entirely unfair to the old girl to suggest that she's on par in some respects with a round on the order of the 30-06 Springfield when the latter is loaded with smokeless, the former with blackpowder. That's comparing oranges with bananas. Smokeless loads in the 45-70 intended only for rifles that can handle them, push the old round right into the 21st century, especially considering the powerful ammunition loaded by Garrett Cartridges Inc. Garrett continues to update loads, so the ones noted here may no longer be available, while new ones will be. The company is always upgrading its ammo. Regardless of current availability of the specific loads listed

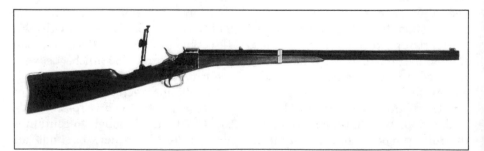

This Navy Arms replica of a Remington Rolling Block rifle is chambered for the 45-70 cartridge. It's a popular choice for blackpowder cartridge silhouette competition shooting.

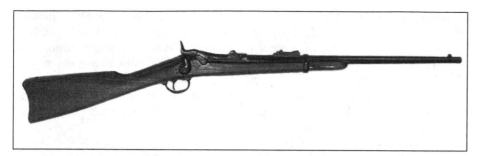

The Trap Door single-shot rifle saw years of service. This replica of the 1873 rifle in carbine form is from Dixie Gun Works. Caliber is the same as the original—45-70 Government.

here, the point is proven that with smokeless powder, the 45-70 is capable of big power. How about a 415-grain bullet at 1,730 fps for more than 2,700 foot-pounds of muzzle energy? Of course, this ammo is not for every 45-70 rifle. In fact, there is a clear warning written on the box: "Garrett's 45-70 Government cartridges safe only in modern rifles & T/C Contenders." The chronograph verified this Garrett 45-70 load at more than 1,700 fps with a hard 415-grain, silver-enriched bullet from a 22-inch barrel. The company recommends this ammo for big game including elk, moose, grizzly, buffalo, even African lions. Another Garrett 45-70 load fired a 400-grain Barnes X bullet at 2,020 fps for more than 3,600 foot-pounds of energy, but also with a warning: "These are safe ONLY in Ruger and Browning single-shots." This is special ammo for specific firearms only, but it's included as reference to the potential power of the 45-70 when loaded with smokeless powder. Meanwhile, Winchester offers an accurate factory load firing a 300-grain, jacketed hollow-point bullet. Chronographed from a short 16-inch barrel, velocity was close to 1,800 fps for more than 2,100 foot-pounds of muzzle energy.

Blackpowder Power

The 45-70 is capable of freight-train performance when loaded with smokeless powder, but for silhouette matches, only blackpowder or a safe substitute is allowed, so what can be expected? Winchester and Remington were forced to sell reduced 45-70 loads, just in case the cartridges found their way into an old Trapdoor rifle or some other action of low-pressure capability. In fact, factory 45-70 ammo is rated at about 16,000 psi, even as loaded with smokeless powder. Data from *The Gun Digest Black Powder Loading Manual,* a DBI book from Krause Publications, shows a Sharps rifle with 28-inch barrel gaining 1,301 fps with a 420-grain cast bullet and 70 grains of GOEX cartridge-grade blackpowder. The actual weight of this charge was 70.8 grains. Muzzle energy for this load registered at 1,579 foot-pounds. Browning's replica Model 1886 lever-action 45-70 was tested with a 322-grain cast bullet and 60 grains of Pyrodex CTG (cartridge granulation no longer available) for a muzzle velocity of 1,437 fps. The same rifle produced 1,205 fps with 65 grains of Pyrodex CTG and a 420-grain cast bullet; or 1,103 fps with a 490-grain cast bullet and 60 grains of CTG. Muzzle energies for the three loads are 1,477, 1,355, and 1,324 foot-pounds, respectively.

A Sharps Model 1855 High Wall in 45-70 with 28-inch barrel earned 1,313 fps with a 405-grain cast bullet and 70 grains of GOEX FFg blackpowder (69.5-grains by weight) for 1,551 foot-pounds of energy. These figures prove that blackpowder ballistics are very much on par with the light smokeless-powder loads offered for years by the ammo companies. The 45-70 with a 500-grain bullet and a full dose of blackpowder or Pyrodex to this day remains big-game worthy, even for elk and moose, for those willing to stalk for a decent close shot.

Kinetic Energy

It's the same song with identical lyrics. The kinetic energy formula does not put a pretty face on the old 45-70 — there's simply not sufficient bullet velocity to create big figures. For example, a 243 Winchester with a 100-grain bullet at 3,100 fps delivers 2,134 foot-pounds of muzzle energy, while a 45-70 with a 500-grain bullet driven by a blackpowder charge shows 1,200 fps for only 1,599 foot-pounds. The old round comes up short on paper, but what about field experience? This is no jab at the Newton formula, for it remains the only accepted mathematical way to measure bullet energy, but a big lead bullet from the 45-70 penetrates well on big game and has proven itself effective for years. In Sam's Bullet Box, the 45-70 with heavy lead bullet penetrates well. In the past, pine boards were accepted as a standard test for penetration. These figures often were listed in catalogs, such as those provided by the Winchester Co. In these tests, a 26-inch-barrel rifle firing a 500-grain bullet at only 1,170 fps penetrated 18 soft pine boards, each 7/8-inch thick, placed 15 feet away. While pine boards may not be the same construction as an elk or moose rib cage, it's inevitable that the same bullet will go far in game.

Getting the Range

The 45-70 cartridge loaded with blackpowder should be confined to short-range shooting because of its comparatively low velocity and high trajectory. Yet, shooters all over the country consistently hit various silhouettes at great distances. One club places a buffalo metallic cutout at 900 yards, and members consistently whack it with single-shot, breech-loading 45-70 (or other caliber) cartridge rifles with open sights. Furthermore, all cartridges are loaded only with blackpowder or a safe substitute, never smokeless. Smokeless powder is not allowed at these events. In spite of low velocity, the old round is capable of hitting at long range, but only when the shooter has a good idea of the distance and knows not only his sight picture, but also how to adjust his sights during the match to change the point of bullet impact. Some of the shots are amazing.

The 45-70 loaded with blackpowder, and wearing only iron sights, provides hits at 1,000 yards that are actually commonplace on various targets, in spite of the fact that it can take between 3 and 4 seconds for the bullet to reach from muzzle to that distance! A 45-70 shooting a 500-grain, round-nose bullet starting out at 1,200 fps was sighted dead-on at 100, 200, and 300 yards. In order to get the bullet on target at 100 yards, the group had to strike almost 4 inches high at 50 yards. For a 200-yard sight-in, the group struck over 13 inches high at 100 yards. To get bullets on target at 300 yards, the group was 34 inches high at 150 yards. These are crude approximations only, because group size is part of the factor. In other words, noting that the 500-grain bullet struck 4 inches high at 50 yards for a 100-yard sight-in includes the size of the group, not solely the trajectory. These figures give an idea of the rather looping trajectory of the 45-70 with its comparatively low muzzle velocity. At the same time, shooting out to a thousand yards, and even farther, can be accomplished with Vernier tang sights possessing a high degree of extremely fine adjustment.

Accuracy

Obviously, the 45-70 is not a choice for modern benchrest competition, where groups are now single holes on the paper. On the other hand, the accuracy potential of the old round is high. If it were not, long-range shooting would be nothing more than wishful thinking. Accuracy, after all, remains mainly a matter of precision-made bullets fired from precision-made barrels, as experimenter Dr. Mann pointed out so long ago, along with proper powder and powder charges from good cases. A single-shot breechloader rifle fitted with a scope for test purposes produced cloverleaf three-shot groups at 50 yards, with sub-inch groups at 100 yards firing 500-grain cast bullets. Accuracy varied widely with other test rifles and iron sights, not to mention different bullets and powder charges. The bullet must be concentric and precise, of course. Ideally, the shooter interested in gaining the highest accuracy from his 45-70 experiments with many different bullets, powders and powder charges.

He also wisely gets help from the experts. Authors like Mike Venturino, Dave Scovill, Paul Matthews, and Steve Garbe have accomplished invaluable testing and the work of these experts should be consulted. Two examples of good 45-70 accuracy study to get the reader started are Handloader's Bullet Making Annual, Vol. I, from Wolfe Publishing Co. of Prescott, Ariz., and Handloader No. 173 for February 1995 from the same publisher. The first contains many articles on making accurate bullets, including Paul A. Matthews' "Best Cast Bullets for the 45-70" and "Lubrication" by Dave Scovill. Mathews and Scovill are both highly-regarded in blackpowder cartridge shooting. The second resource has an article by Steve Garbe, another noted expert, entitled "45-70 Black Powder Target Loads." There are many other sources dealing with 45-70 accuracy. Garbe points out that the 45-70 is to BPCR (Black Powder Cartridge Rifle) silhouette shooting what the 308 Winchester is to high-power target shooting. He writes, "Rifles chambered for the 45-70 have a well-deserved reputation for shooting decently with nearly any intelligently assembled handload." It's the "intelligently assembled" part of that statement that carries weight, meaning learning from research and personal testing. Garbe further points out that even the great barrelmaker Harry Pope considered the 45-70 an inaccurate cartridge, but that was in the old days before the accuracy potential of the round was discovered. Today, we know better.

Accuracy and Bullet Base Integrity

Recovered bullets captured by various media downrange may show base deterioration caused by hot gases from the powder charge. If a base is damaged, accuracy can suffer badly. Experienced blackpowder cartridge shooters safeguard their bullets in proper containers so bases remain intact.

Wads

Wads can be used between the powder charge and the bullet to safeguard the powder charge from the invasion of bullet lube. Some shooters make wads from cardboard milk containers, ensuring that the wad does not adhere to the base of the bullet by matching the wax side of the carton against the base. This way, the wad flies free. Other shooters use gasket material purchased from auto parts houses. This comes in different thicknesses, with .0002-inch and .0003-inch dimensions prominent.

Wax Cookies in Place of Wads

Dedicated blackpowder cartridge shooters investigate many avenues to improve accuracy with their old-time guns. Some go with the "wax cookie" in place of a cardboard wad in between the bullet and the powder charge. These are cut from wax sheets available at beekeeper supply houses in various thicknesses.

Standard Deviation

Standard deviation is a good measure of a load's potential for accuracy. This is a gauge of consistency, with a low standard deviation from the average velocity indicating a good balance between bullet, powder, and other factors, including the primer and the case itself. The 45-70 shows low standard deviations with both blackpowder and safe blackpowder substitutes — often as low as 10 fps, even less. Part of the reason for low figures rests with the powder itself, since it is less sensitive than smokeless with regard to exact tenth-of-a-grain variations from one load to the next. However, the standard-deviation figures registered in my own testing were on line with results compiled by other testers. Garbe, for example, had loads giving standard deviations as low as 4 fps, and in one series of tests, his poorest standard deviation was only 8 fps.

Loading the 45-70

Old vs. New Cases

As noted before, old-time cartridge cases were not constructed the same as modern cases. These 19th-century, balloon-head cases had less "meat" in the head section than modern brass. That is why it can be difficult to get a full 70 grains of blackpowder into a 45-70 case today, especially without a drop tube, because the modern case has more metal in the head area, which cuts down on case capacity. This is not a problem to the shooter. A charge of only 60 grains volume of FFg blackpowder (actual weight 59.3 grains) drove a 405-grain bullet at 1,211 fps muzzle velocity, while a full 70 grains volume of FFg (weighing 69.5 grains on the scale) pushed the same bullet at 1,313

fps. This does not suggest that 100 fps is meaningless, but on the other hand, the lesser powder charge did all right.

Load Density

Best accuracy coupled with safety asks for 100 percent load density in a blackpowder cartridge. A 100 percent load density simply means that the case is full of blackpowder or safe substitute, with no air space. Paul Matthews, one of the country's leading 45-70 cast-bullet shooters, uses the word "never" in considering air space in the case. He feels that in the name of safety, the case should be filled with powder. This factor relates to our frequent discussion of the short-started load in the muzzle-loader with consequent unwanted air space. The bullet determines how much powder can be installed in the 45-70 case, while still maintaining proper overall loaded length of the cartridge. For example, a full 70 grains by volume can be loaded with bullets in the 405-grain class, especially with the use of a drop tube, but that much powder may not fit with heavier bullets. In loading a 500-grain bullet to 100 percent load density in one particular case, a drop tube was required to drop in 67 grains volume of FFg.

The Best Bullet

Properly cast lead bullets shoot extremely well in the 45-70, and also are the rule for the BPCR match, which does not allow the

use of jacketed bullets. There are literally dozens of different bullet styles and weights available from the various companies that offer 45-caliber molds, such as NEI, Lyman, Hoch, Redding-SAECO, RCBS and others, including Rapine, mentioned earlier.

Proper Lubing

In all of the loading data presented by today's experts on the blackpowder cartridge, special attention is given to the type of lube used on the bullet. Dave Scovill pointed out in the Handloader's Bullet Making Annual noted above that lubrication "bears a close scrutiny. Without its protection, cast bullets are nearly useless. Even with it, accuracy and velocity can vary considerably, depending on the type or brand of lube used." This is not the forum for a full-blown discussion on lubes for the 45-70; however, it is important for the shooter to recognize how important lubes are and to study the subject fully for the best accuracy when using cast-bullet loads. A local shooter who enjoys fine results on the range makes his own lube, consisting of one part Toilet Bowl Ring™, two parts beeswax, and two parts lard.

The Primer

The magnum primer, not the standard rifle primer, is preferred for best overall results in the 45-70 loaded with blackpowder.

Crimping Bullets

Bullets for 45-70 ammo used in lever-action rifles must be crimped into the cartridge case, or recoil

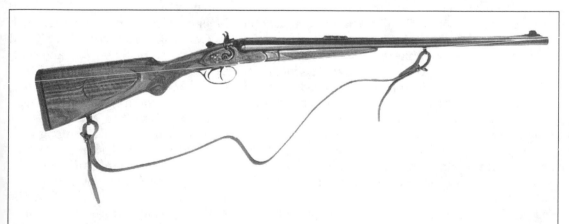

The 45-70 Government cartridge has been offered in many different firearms over the years, repeaters and single-shots. Here is the Kodiak Mark IV Double Rifle chambered in the great old cartridge.

The old-time 45-70 Government, shown here with a cast bullet loaded, next to a 308 Winchester for comparison.

drives the bullet back into the case, because one round is loaded in line with another in the tubular magazine. Also, blunt-nosed bullets are used in tubular magazines to prevent the possibility of the point of one bullet detonating the primer of the round in front of it.

Correct Seating Depth

Bullets must be correctly seated for proper depth in order to create the right overall cartridge length. Some experts feel that with cast bullets in the 45-70, seating so that the bullet just barely engages the rifling is best if that option is available. Some rifles may have too much lead in the chamber to allow this. A successful shooter said that he disagreed with this assessment, insisting that the best results occur when the bullet is seated to leave about a tenth of an inch space between the nose and the rifling, with no contact made.

Recoil

Big-bore rifles like those from October Country, as well as muzzleloaders such as the Zephyr, allow far greater powder charges than those of the 45-70. Compared that way, the old Government cartridge is mild. However, many silhouette shooters who fire 80 to 100 times in the course of a match consider the 45-70 a

"kicker." Recoil can cause two big problems in such a match: fatigue and reduction in concentration. Fatigue is simply tiring through thump after thump on the shoulder and into the cheekbone. Lack of concentration may follow, with possible flinching. One way to work with recoil is developing a mindset. It does not work for everyone, nor all the time, but the shooter reminds himself before firing that he may as well remain in full control, squeezing, not yanking, that trigger, because recoil is identical either way. Jerk the trigger or squeeze it under control, and the gun comes back with the same force every time. In other words, flinch and feel the recoil, or don't flinch and feel the recoil, the latter much preferred.

Recoil in the 45-70 is no different from recoil in any other rifle or round. Powder charge weight and bullet weight account for some of the kick, while the weight of the rifle helps thwart rearward motion. Subloads in the 45-70 will reduce recoil by cutting back on the blackpowder powder charge. But lesser powder charges are wrong in the blackpowder cartridge case, so that option is out — recall 100 percent load density. Going down in bullet weight also reduces recoil, but when a 500-grain bullet, for example, delivers

great accuracy, the smart shooter sticks with it, learning to manage recoil. One good option is increasing rifle weight. The more the gun weighs, the less severe the thump on the shoulder is. Even this choice, however, is not open to everyone, especially with regard to match regulations. NRA Silhouette rules do allow the use of a recoil pad on blackpowder breechloaders, as well as a shoulder pad for the shooter. Both pads help reduce the effects of felt recoil. Finally, shooting from crosssticks rather than prone also helps reduce felt recoil, since cross-sticks allow the body to roll with the punch.

The 45-70 continues its surprisingly long life with no end in sight. New rifles for the round are still appearing. There is no shortage of components for reloading, including fine new brass, superb primers, and blackpowder in many forms, such as Cartridge grade from GOEX and 1 1/2 Fg from Swiss blackpowder, along with Pyrodex RS and Clean Shot. Ready to go bullets abound, such as Lyman's long-range lead conicals. There are also molds for numerous 45-70 bullets. Along with handloaded cartridges, factory ammo is abundant all over the country. Add good accuracy and power, and it's no wonder that the 45-70 Government is still with us.

Chapter 46

IVORY HUNTERS OF THE DARK CONTINENT

HOW MUCH a part of the black-powder shooting world were those 19th-century ivory hunters of the Dark Continent? They lived by the gun, and in the beginning the gun was a muzzleloader. There is a parallel between these Occidental men — British mostly — and the mountain man of America's Far West. Both explored new territory. Both faced untold dangers. Both were in it more for the adventure than the riches, although the ivory hunters certainly made out better on that score than the hapless trappers who made money for others, but precious little for themselves, being traded out of their plews of beaver for goods brought on wagons from the east to the rendezvous. It is impossible, and even wrong, to judge the elephant slayers of the distant past by modern standards. That was then. This is now. It's all in the attitude. The ivory believed, and he was right, that in no way could elephant numbers be seriously reduced, regardless of the number taken, for there were too few hunters dotted over thousands of acres to make inroads on any population of any game. And so they hunted on.

In their time they were applauded as explorers, adventurers, businessmen, and most of all, daring hunters. They shot pachyderms for the ivory, and they did it in the beginning with what they had: soot-belching, big-bore rifles, mostly muzzleloaders. Without the guns, their story would be of little interest in this book. But throw in

The early ivory hunters used big-bore blackpowder rifles — first muzzleloaders and later breechloaders — as shown in this illustration. They were hunting the world's largest four-footed animal. Living dangerously was a way of life for them.

The 19th-century ivory hunter relied on massive lead bullets propelled by heavy charges of blackpowder. Early on, they were blackpowder hunters, for there were no smokeless-powder firearms. Theirs are interesting stories, for they lived interesting lives. They also had much to say about the guns they used. Some of their firearms are seldom exceeded in power to this day with the most modern, bolt-action smokeless powder cartridge rifles.

the firearms and their tale is just as valid as the mountain man's, their guns as interesting — perhaps even more interesting, for they were hunting the largest animal on four feet, not only huge, but intelligent and deadly. In an Africa bush camp during recent times a client, warned not to strike out on his own, disobeyed, taking the track of an elephant. He wanted to take the animal on his own. Instead, the elephant, apparently realizing there was danger on his trail, circled around, caught the hunter, and thrashed him against the trees. This is the animal the early ivory hunters were after with their muzzleloading rifles.

It's been said that the English in India and the Dutch in Africa turned to big-bore, single-shot blackpowder rifles in the early 1800s. That assessment is too general in nature; however, it is true that muzzleloading 4-, 6-, and 8-bore guns were relied upon to stop the charge of the lion or bring down a fortune in ivory. Fortune? Few true fortunes were made by the time the smoke cleared, literally as well as figuratively. But most certainly the ivory hunter made his mark. Some say it was a blemish. Others realistically consider it within the context of history. Who were they? They came out of Europe, as their names imply. There was Major Shakespear

(spelled differently than the famed author of Romeo and Juliet) and S.W. Baker, Harris, Oswell, Roualeyn Gordon-Cumming, and G.P. Sanderson. They were a brave bunch, like the fur trappers who left their safe homes "back East" to roam among grizzlies and Blackfoot out West. These men lived among animals that could kill a human in a second, as well as native peoples who were not always friendly.

Three only of these hardy souls are featured here: William Cotton Oswell, Sir Samuel White Baker, better known as S.W. Baker to his readers, and Frederick Courteney Selous, who signed his name F.C. Selous (pronounced Sell-ooo). But before their brief story, a few words about Gordon-Cumming, Major Shakespear, and the lesser known hunter, George P. Sanderson, are in order. In his book, Five Years Hunting Adventures in Africa, covering 1843 to 1848, Gordon-Cumming wrote about his guns. We learn that he used a Dickson double-barrel 12-bore that eventually "burst from too much fouling," and that he also carried a Dutch-made 6-bore with six balls to the pound, meaning that each bullet weighed close to 1,200 grains. The 6-bore was said to be loaded with 10 to 15 drams of powder. If so, that would be about 270 to more than 400 grains of blackpowder. Even in a rifle weighing 15 pounds, free recoil

was tremendous with so much powder behind such a large missile.

Major Shakespear, from his book, Wild Sports of India, dealing with the period from 1834 to 1859, noted that: "My own battery consists of two heavy double rifles and a double gun; the heaviest is a Westley Richards weighing twelve and a quarter pounds, length of barrel, twenty-six inches, poly-grooved, carrying bullets ten to the pound [a 10-gauge or 10-bore]. It is a splendid weapon, bearing a large charge of powder without recoil; that is to say, its own bullet mould full of the strongest rifle powder." Shakespear's notes are especially interesting because of his reference to a powder charge generated from his bullet mold. In other words, it appears that he used the mold as a powder measure. But even a 10-bore mold, conical as well as round ball, would not produce a very large powder charge. Perhaps that is why the hunter didn't consider recoil fierce. Shakespear also complained about a high trajectory with his 10-bore, the bullet rising about 5 inches at 50 yards in order to strike dead on at about 100 yards. At the same time, the Westley Richards rifle was fitted with two rear sights, one for 150-yard shooting and the other for 250 yards. The entire story is slightly puzzling, but also interesting: a looping trajectory coupled with long-range sights. Furthermore, the venerable elephant hunter considered the powder charge for his 10-bore "heavy." Perhaps something was lost in the translation concerning a powder charge that matched the bullet mold.

Shakespear spoke of a second 10-bore rifle with two-groove rifling instead of poly-grooved, but this one, according to the author, shot "point blank from muzzle up to ninety yards." See below for remarks about the meaning of "point blank." The folding sights on this particular rifle, built by Wilkinson of Pall Mall, were set for 150, 250, and 400 yards. This 10.5-pound rifle with 30-inch barrel was a favorite of Shakespear's, but it leaves a modern shooter wondering about actual ballistics, which is important for any study of a 19th-century shooter's work. Why did Shakespear feel that his Wilkinson shot flatter than his Westley Richards? That is a mystery, but stranger is the famous hunter's remark about recoil being light. At 10 balls to the pound, his 10-bore fired a 700-grain projectile, and if he used the reported 8 drams of powder (more than 200 grains), velocity had to be around the speed of sound, or a bit faster, probably 1,200 fps. Shakespear noted that his rifle fired "without recoil," but it probably developed around 80 foot-pounds of free recoil, even in a heavy rifle, while a contemporary 30-06 sporter may show around 18 foot-pounds of free recoil.

To clear the record on "point blank" is in order. The term did not mean that Shakespear's rifle "shot flat" from muzzle to 90 yards. Point blank comes from a French term. The bull's eye was a white, or blanc mark, and the rifle shot "point blank" when its bullet did not stray either above or below that white circle at a given range. The details of this practice are mainly lost to history, but it seems to have something to do with the parabola of the projectile. For our purpose, all we need to know is that the old-time shooter was not suggesting that his rifle "shot flat," but rather it could be counted on to keep its projectiles within a certain verti-cal limit at a specific distance.

George P. Sanderson deserves a brief mention before we continue on the path toward our three major players. Sanderson wrote a book called Thirteen Years Among the Wild Beasts of India. Comments on his first rifle, a 12-bore, are interesting. They go like this:" I at first killed several elephants with a No. 12 spherical ball rifle, with hard bullets and six drams of powder, but I found it insufficient for many occasions. I then had a single-barreled, center-fire No. 4 bore rifle, weighing sixteen and one-half pounds and firing ten drams, made to order by Lang and Sons, Cockspur Street. A cartridge of this single barrel, however, missed fire on one occasion, and nearly brought me to grief, so I gave it up and had a center-fire No. 4 smoothbore, weighing nineteen and one-half pounds, built by W.W. Greener. This I have used ever since. I ordinarily fire twelve drams of powder with it. Without something of the cannon kind, game of the ponderous class cannot be brought to fighting quarters with even a moderate degree of safety or effect."

Several points of interest are generated from Sanderson's remarks, not the least of which is the W.W. Greener smoothbore, first because it was made by that famous gunsmith and writer, whose works continue to this day, and second because it was a smoothbore, which offered certain advantages: namely ease of cleaning with no rifling to hold fouling, plus facility of loading for the same reason. Also, Sanderson rightly points out that an elephant hunter needed a big bore — a true big bore — to feel the slightest tinge of safety in the work of elephant hunting during blackpowder days. As we know from Chapter 32, big bore was not to the African hunter what it represents to the North American hunter, something that remains true today. A 12-gauge, for example, with its round ball under 500 grains weight, was simply too small for dangerous game. Compare with the Greener 4-bore firing a round ball weighing 1,750 grains! As an aside, consider price. A custom big-bore rifle of the 19th century could run from $750 to $1,000, so states the literature. That's a heap of wampum considering the times, a sum that could constitute the bulk of a year's wages for an ordinary workman.

William Cotton Oswell

The average modern hunter or shooter does not recognize Oswell's name; however, in his own day he was only a rock's throw from famous. Sir Samuel W. Baker, whose own brief mini-bio appears below, said of Oswell, "His name will be remembered with tears of sorrow and profound respect." Oswell was one of the first professional ivory hunters in South Africa. His name is linked with David Livingstone, and it appears that Oswell, along with a partner named Murray, financed a Livingstone expedition that was recognized with a medal given by the French Geographical Society for the first mapping of Africa's lake systems. Oswell hunted often on horseback, and was noted as a great rider. He took to the saddle, gave chase, and then dismounted for the shot when he was within range, "range" being something in the area of about 20 or 30 paces. Short shooting distance made Oswell's smoothbore rifle perfectly adequate. Supreme accuracy was not necessary on a target the size of an elephant's temple at such close range.

Oswell began his hunting career in Africa with a 12-bore double rifle built by Westley Richards, along with a single-barrel 8-bore that fired belted round balls weighing around 875 grains, known in everyday parlance as a "two-ounce ball." Oswell's favorite firearm, however, was a Purdey smoothbore double that, according to S.W. Baker, weighed an even 10 pounds. How did Baker know so much about Oswell's 10-bore? He borrowed the firearm from Oswell in 1861 for an expedition to the Nile. Oswell was retired at the time. Baker at first

William Cotton Oswell was known in England as the "Pioneer of Civilisation." He was a friend and interpreter of Dr. Livingstone, who applauded Oswell in Livingstone's "Zambesi and its Tributaries." Oswell was born in 1818, died in 1893, and was remembered by S.W. Baker as a man "without a rival; and certainly without an enemy; the greatest hunter ever known in modern times."

heaped great praise on the 10-gauge smoothbore, but in later writings, put smoothbores down as too inaccurate to be counted on in the field. That's understandable, because unlike Oswell, Baker took long shots. As for power, Oswell's favorite 10-bore was loaded with "six drachms of fine-grained powder," which we know meant six drams, or 164 grains. It was, of course, a muzzleloader. There were no breechloaders when Oswell acquired the gun. He wrapped his 10-gauge round balls in fine leather or linen, tightly, cutting off excess material. Then he built a paper cartridge containing both powder charge and patched ball. To reload, the hunter nipped the end of the paper cartridge off with his teeth, dropping the powder charge, along with the paper, downbore. Then he put the pre-patched ball on the muzzle and, with a loading rod noted as "powerful," pushed the bullet firmly into the breech upon the powder charge.

Baker pointed out that Oswell's smoothbore "exhibited in an unmistakable degree the style of hunting which distinguished its determined owner. The hard walnut stock was completely eaten away for an inch of surface; the loss of wood suggested that rats had gnawed it, as there were minor traces of apparent teeth." Actually, the stock had been "chewed on" by the wait-a-bit thorn bushes common to Oswell's hunting grounds as he galloped his horse in hot pursuit of elephants. Baker reported that he returned Oswell's smoothbore in good condition, but minus the ramrod, which had been lost when one of Baker's native bearers was attacked by a group of marauders. The frightened man loaded the smoothbore just in time to save his own life, but he did not have time to withdraw the ramrod, which he fired completely through the body of one of his as sailants.

Oswell hunted hard. He wrote of some of his adventures in "African Game Rifles" as part of the Badminton Library, Big Game Shooting, published by Longmans Green & Co. of London, 1902. He said, "I spent five years in Africa. I was never ill for a single day — laid up occasionally by accident, but that was all. I had the best of companions — Murray, Vardon, Livingstone — and several capital servants, who stuck to me throughout. I never had occasion to raise a hand against a native, and my foot only once, when I found a long lazy fellow poking his paw into my sugar tin." He also noted that he "filled their stomachs," speaking of his native helpers. Baker was much more a commander than Oswell, and certainly not above dealing out punishment to people he considered inferior, since he saw himself in the superior role.

Sir Samuel White Baker

If we viewed blackpowder-shooting ivory hunters of the 19th century through the window of our own time, we would dislike most of them. Baker, we would probably classify as an arrogant bigot. But his time was not ours, and so we view him through colored glass looking into the distant past. Baker was an English gentleman, knighted by the Queen herself, and so he considered natives of foreign soils beneath his station. He was known to thrash a servant who didn't do the "right thing." He also shot game at will, unlike Oswell, who spared female elephants and harvested only enough game to feed his followers. This is not a blemish on the person of Baker alone, for some American hunters disrespected wildlife just as much in the same era. While he hunted Africa, Baker is better known for his adventures in Ceylon, and for the book that told about those times, The Rifle and the Hound in Ceylon, reprinted in modern times and still available through interlibrary loan. The book can also be purchased through the Internet. Baker was only 24 years old when he arrived in Ceylon, where he hunted so heavily, and before his career was over, he also hunted the United States as well as Africa. He made two around-the-world hunting trips that included America, these taken between 1879 and 1888. His travels took him also to hunts in Asia Minor and India.

Credited with being the first English-speaking person to travel the Nile, Baker's history is easier to locate than either Cotton Oswell's life story or Selous' biography. After all, in some texts he is known as the "discoverer" of the Nile, just

Sir Samuel White Baker, an English knight, explored the Nile from 1861 to 1865 and was a big man at 6 feet, 6 inches tall and 250 pounds. He was born in London in 1821, married a Hungarian noblewoman when he was 41, and died in England in 1893. He authored Ismalia *and* Eight Years' Wandering in Ceylon.

as Balboa is credited with "discovering" the Pacific Ocean. But our interest is in Baker's firearms and his shooting theories more than his geographical wanderings. His firearms were custom made, as money was no stumbling block for Baker. By his own claim, his first good rifle was also the first firearm to see action in Ceylon in 1845. That "good rifle" was a 4-bore muzzleloader weighing in at a trifling 21 pounds. The single-barrel rifle was two-grooved, made by Gibbs of Bristol. It was noted to shoot a "four-ounce" ball, which makes sense, as there are 16 ounces in pound, making four 4-gauge balls. Looking at it another way, each ball weighed 1,750 grains. The cannon-like rifle was loaded with 16 drams of blackpowder, or more than 430 grains. Muzzle energy was in the neighborhood of 6,000 to 7,000 foot-pounds at the muzzle.

Baker was a big man, and he apparently stood up to his 4-bore with impunity, for he was known to make hits with it, and other ponderous rifles, at very long range — 300 yards and farther. His backup rifle was "only" an 8-gauge single barrel, built by Blisset, with poly-grooved bore and a 2-ounce ball, also loaded with 16 drams of blackpowder. While in Ceylon, Baker put down a great number of elephants, along with considerable water buffalo and other game. His two single-shot rifles were not enough for him, however, so he ordered four more rifles, all 10-gauge muzzleloaders weighing about 15 pounds each. These rifles, made by Holland, became his elephant-hunting battery. He carried them in Africa as well as Ceylon, but when the British army adopted the Snider breechloader, Baker had Holland build him a double-barrel 577 that fired a 648-grain conical bullet at a reported 1,650 fps for a muzzle energy of about 4,000 foot-pounds, well under his previous muzzleloading 4-bore. He carried this rifle to America for deer, bear, elk and bison.

While it's difficult to say exactly how fast Baker's 4-bore round bullets were taking off at the muzzle, with 16 drams of the best black-powder of the day a velocity of 1,200 fps to 1,300 fps is not an overly generous assessment. That would be 6,000 to 7,000 foot-pounds of muzzle energy for 1,300 fps, which may be undercutting Baker's rifle, considering the fact that it could have produced about 1,600 fps or a bit more. Calling it 1,400 fps instead of 1,300 fps, the rifle would have generated more than 7,500 foot-pounds of muzzle energy. If 1,600 fps were achieved, the energy rating would be close to 10,000 foot-pounds, surpassing the 577 breechloader and its 648-grain bullet at 1,650 fps for 3,918 foot-pounds. The point is, Baker's breechloader was a step down from his front loaders in ballistic force, even though it fired a conical with better retention of downrange energy.

Baker eventually gravitated to smaller firearms, owning and shooting a double-barrel 400 Holland Express rifle, which he used for deer-sized game in England and Scotland. However, when he wrote his 1891 book, Wild Beasts and Their Ways, two years before his death, he concluded that for the largest game he would have nothing smaller than an 8-bore rifle firing a 3-ounce projectile in front of 14 drams of blackpowder (about 380 grains). Also interesting is Baker's respect for the round ball. He actually considered the lead sphere more efficient against pachyderms than even the heaviest conical. One of his reasons, and certainly not a scientific one, was explained as the "conical making too neat a wound," sort of like a rapier sliding through something without imparting much energy in the target, whereas the round ball smacked hard, delivering its blow in the target instead of behind it. Some of today's round-ball fans cite Baker's work when their beloved lead spheres are downgraded. In fact, we do know that

when a hunter gets close enough, round lead bullets are lethal.

Frederick Courteney Selous

Selous was a gentleman we probably would have liked, which cannot necessarily be said of Baker. Selous was a man among men. He died a soldier, although he was not truly a professional military man. On January 4, 1917, during World War I, Selous was killed in action as he fought the Germans in Tanganyika as a volunteer. He was born in Regents Park, London, in 1851, making him 66 years old in 1917 when he was shot to death as he led his men against an enemy four times greater in strength. He was educated mainly as a naturalist schooled in England, but finished his education in Switzerland and Germany. He was a good student and could have made a high mark in society, but he read too much of Africa, and there he simply had to go. On September 4, 1871, he arrived on the Dark Continent. He was 19 years old and in possession of only 400 English pounds to launch his career as an ivory hunter. He made his way into wild territory, often straying far afield from his wagons so that he could hunt on foot undisturbed. Tracking elephants with a Hottentot native known as Cigar, F.C. lived off the land. Cigar, by the way, became a friend and partner in the chase and was far more than a "hired man." Wandering afar with only a blanket against the night and his 4-bore muzzleloader over his shoulder, Selous was a genius in the art of what we call woodsmanship today. As for his 4-bore, Selous packed along a bag filled with powder and 24, 4-ounce "round bullets," to use his words. He admitted that sometimes he did not measure his charge, simply dropping a fistful of blackpowder downbore.

Anyone interested in more of the Selous story should read the man's book, A Hunter's Wanderings in Africa, a title still available, especially from bookstores with their quick ability to search the Internet

Frederick Courteney Selous was a professional ivory hunter at 19 years of age in 1871. He was known to grab a handful of powder in the heat of the chase and pour it downbore to reload. Born in London in 1851, he died a hero in 1917 during World War I. Selous spanned the gap between blackpowder and smokeless, going from huge, 4-bore muzzleloaders to a little 6.5mm rifle.

for titles. Luckily, Selous's biography was set down by J.G. Millais, in a book entitled The Life of Frederick Courtenay Selous, D.S.O., written in 1918 (the spelling of his middle name today is Courteney, not Courtenay). Naturalist, writer, settler, guide, explorer, even soldier, Selous' life as an ivory hunter began most interestingly when his double 12-bore Reilly rifle was stolen from a wagon on his first trip out. He ended up taking 78 elephants with a pair of Dutch-made Roer two-groove 4-bores. These were not the finest rifles of the era, but they were powerful. Selous loaded these with 16 to 18 drams of blackpowder, or 437 to 500 grains. So much powder behind the huge 1,750-grain lead ball created recoil that was dreadful. Selous

reported: "They kicked most frightfully and in my case the punishment I received from these guns has affected my nerves to such an extent as to have materially influenced my shooting ever since, and I am heartily sorry I ever had anything to do with them." He went on to shoot much smaller firearms, and is remembered today as the elephant hunter who used a .256-caliber rifle for big game, even elephants.

Although Selous complained that those big Dutch 4-bores harmed his shooting ability, in fact he was known as a superior marksman all his life, using the tiny 256, which is a 6.5mm rifle firing a 160-grain round-nose bullet at only 2,300 fps MV, even for elephants. With a muzzle energy of only 1,880 foot-pounds,

about like a 30-30, Selous usually downed his elephant with one perfectly placed shot. He also liked the ordinary 303 British round with a 215-grain bullet at 2,000 fps MV for 1,910 foot-pounds of muzzle energy. Selous loved to hunt. He hunted not only in Africa as a professional, but also in America as a sportsman. He hiked the Rocky Mountains, also ending up in Alaska with Charles Sheldon, famous naturalist of the day. He also hunted Canada for moose and other game. F.C. Selous traveled the road from muzzleloader to breechloader, and from blackpowder to smokeless. He used them all, from the most hellish big-bore blackpowder muzzleloader to the neat little Mannlicher-type, smokeless-powder smallbore.

Chapter 47

AMERICAN SHARPSHOOTERS FROM BYGONE DAYS

IT'S SAD but true that some of the finest marksmanship displayed came not in the game field harvesting wild animals to the table, but rather the battlefield, including brother shooting brother in our own American Civil War. Being acquainted with a present-day SWAT sniper, I'm aware that the breed is still with us. Snipers were also on hand for the Seven Years War, the American Revolution, the War of 1812, and, of course, long-range shooting was accomplished when the white man and Native American crossed paths in anger. Some of the stories of super-long-range shooting are just that — long-winded tales born of campfire smoke. Others are solid historical fact. Mark Twain had it right when he said, "Of course truth is stranger than fiction. Fiction has to make sense." Certain seemingly unbelievable shooting feats that sound like fiction truly happened. Many accounts of long-range sniping by buffalo runners are probably true. After all, these marksmen were well practiced through daily shooting, and they had accurate, long-range rifles often topped off with target-type telescopic sights of high magnification. Give them a clear target, even at several hundred yards, and the buffalo boys could "dope out" wind drift and bullet drop, delivering a bullet spot-on, especially when the target was a human figure standing upright with plenty of vertical latitude. Shooters who preceded them could also hit the mark at incredible distances.

The First American Snipers

Shooters along the eastern seaboard of North America were probably the first to register long-range hits with their Kentucky/Pennsylvania rifles. Certainly, the British soldiers at the Battle of New Orleans felt the sting of this truth. Later, the mountain man with his plains rifle no doubt registered hits at incredible distances, sometimes through pure chance, no doubt, but also by deliberate aim made possible by familiarity with their rifles. Why not believe it? Similar shooting feats continue to this hour at blackpowder matches, where patched round balls ring gongs out to 500 yards, 600 yards and farther. At least one blackpowder-cartridge shooter proved he can hit a target shot-after-shot at more than 1,200 yards. Deliberate long-range shooting from the muzzles of American soldiers called snipers was very much a part of the American Civil War. Soldiers were selected in part because they were gifted marksmen. After that, they were carefully trained to make far-away strikes on the enemy. Col. Hiram Berdan remains in living history, not as the only officer to recruit snipers for long-range shooting on the battlefield, but because he was probably the first to convince military leadership to put a regiment of sharpshooters together. Berdan was an amateur New York rifleman and target shooter before the war. In 1861, he organized and assembled other good marksmen to join the North as snipers.

They were called Berdan's Sharpshooters, and they wreaked considerable havoc upon the enemy. Other Union U.S. Sharpshooters under the command of Col. Henry A.V. Post, also a New York resident, were also successful in making long-range hits on the enemy. Only those who could pass a shooting test were allowed into these two elite regiments of riflemen. The exact test may have been lost in time, while some stories are almost preposterous, if not entirely false. But a simple set of rules from the literature does seem plausible: 10 shots into a 10-inch bull's eye at 200 yards from any shooting position, including prone, with apparently any rifle. That included target rifles with telescopic or any other sights. Given a good, heavy target rifle of the day with a scope, 10 shots into a 10-inch bull at 200 yards is entirely reasonable.

The Sharpshooter could bring his own rifle, research shows, for which the government reimbursed him up to $60 for its use. It's reasonable to assume that some men brought their best target-shooting guns complete with 19th-century, barrel-

The Civil War saw limited use of the Sharps rifle, mainly in the hands of snipers.

length scope sights. The scopes noted here were not tube sights, but true telescopes, often of high magnification, albeit very limited field of view. Malcolm and Vollmer scopes were quite well known by the time of the American Civil War. Looking like tube sights, these metal tubes were actually precision instruments containing glass lenses, and there is no doubt that they could turn a deadly long-range rifle into a deadlier long-range rifle. As we know from history, Buffalo hunters later in the same century often mounted scopes on their breechloaders that were very much like the ones used in the Civil War.

Claims Factual and Otherwise

An exhibition to show President Abraham Lincoln just how good the Sharpshooters were was supposed to include a hundred men firing at a man-sized target a full 600 yards in the distance. This event supposedly occurred in 1861. Berdan himself was said to be among the marksmen. Out of 100 shooters, all placed bullets in the kill zone, Berdan fired a five-shot group that was about 10 inches in spread. While it is noted that the rifles did wear scope sights, all 100 men hitting the target with all of their shots may seem hard to believe, but stranger things have happened. To top it off, someone asked Berdan to hit one of the targets, a figure of Jefferson Davis, in the eye. Berdan fired his rifle and a neat round hole appeared where once there had been a pupil. Maybe this happened, and maybe not. Lincoln was supposed to have remarked something

about the shot being the luckiest he'd ever seen, or something like that. This story is related in a somewhat different version, printed in a 19th-century Harper's magazine article.

Another possibly overstated claim concerns the one-mile hit credited to a Northern sharpshooter by the name of John H. Metcalf. Supposedly, the event took place in 1864 during the Red River Campaign, specifically the battle of Pleasant Hill in Louisiana. Metcalf took aim on a Confederate general named Lainhart, the distance being over one mile, according to the story. Boom! The bullet struck home. There are many possibilities. One is that the Union sharpshooter fired and someone in the distance fell, at which point he was credited with a one-mile hit. Perhaps the distance could have been over-estimated. Or, the shot truly did occur (stranger things have happened). That the bullet could travel so far and remain deadly is no problem. It could have. That anyone could judge a shot at a mile is on the incredible side. So if the shot were made, fluke would be a good name for it.

Documented Claims

Then there are documented claims. In The Battle of Gettysburg, a scholarly work by Francis Marshal printed in 1914 by the Neale Publishing Co. of New York, the death of Confederate Maj.Gen. John Sedgewick is related. Sedgewick was well known to the North as well as to the South, with his reputation as a gentleman and soldier highly regarded on both sides of the skirmish. In fact, it was said after his

death that Sedgewick had two mourners, "friends and his foe." His soldiers of the Sixth Corps considered Sedgewick their father more than their commander. Professor Marshal related the story this way:

"The numerical sacrifice of human life, however, terrible as it is, does not equal the loss to the Federal army of one life, which has issued from its ranks on its long furlough. Major-General John Sedgewick, one of its main bulwarks for years, the loved commander and father of the old reliable Sixth Corps, is among the dead. Smiling encouragement to some of his men new to battle, whom he saw dodging the bullets that whizzed past, he had just remarked, jokingly: 'Soldiers, don't dodge bullets. Why, they can't hit an elephant at this distance.' At that instant a veteran officer at his side heard the familiar thud of a bullet, and turned to remark it to Sedgewick, who at that moment gave him a smile and fell dead into his arms, shot through the head."

Whitworths and Sharps Rifles

Due to the timing of the Sedgewick episode, the best bet is that the rifle used to fell the great soldier was a Whitworth rifled musket (see Chapter 33). The Whitworth did see action in the hands of sharpshooters on both sides of the fray. And why not? The rifle was accurate, firing long bullets capable of retaining velocity/energy at great distance. But while the Whitworth was without doubt worthy of the sharpshooters, the Sharps rifle seems to have caught considerable favor with army personnel at the time. This would be the blackpowder breech-loading Sharps. It was a breech-loading rifle, yes, but not a cartridge rifle. This Sharps, noted as the New Model 1859 Military Rifle, used paper or linen cartridges. Paper cartridges were nothing new at the time. The soldier nipped off the end and poured the powder downbore, followed by the bullet, or he could ram the whole cartridge, paper and all, down after exposing the powder charge. This was not, however, the case with the Sharps rifle in question.

This Sharps rifle worked quite differently. Its paper or linen cartridge was inserted into the chamber, bullet forward, of course, with the rearmost of the paper or linen cartridge sticking out just a bit beyond the chamber. When the rifle was put into the battery position, the breechblock, which had a very sharp end, cut off the back of the paper or linen cartridge, thus exposing the powder charge to the flash of the percussion cap. This rifle is listed as 52-caliber with a barrel length of 30 inches and a total weight of 9 pounds. The Sharps New Model 1859 Military Rifle is offered in replica form as this is written. Dixie's historical study shows that the rifle was first used by the First Connecticut Volunteers of Hartford, but it was mostly associated with the First United States (Berdan's) Sharpshooters. Two thousand were furnished to the Sharpshooters, with the U.S. Navy receiving 2,780. The balance of the 6,689 rifles built was spread among various army units. The Dixie model of this rifle has a 30-inch, tapered, round barrel with six-groove rifling, and is 54-caliber, not 52. It has a 1:48-inch rate of twist. The 54-caliber part seems quite a bit more reasonable if indeed the Sharps bullet was 56-caliber, as noted in some sources. Asking a lead bullet to swage itself in the bore by two calibers is one thing, while four calibers is quite another. Sights, by the way, are flip-up style with a rear elevator that is adjustable for elevation to 800 yards, and a blade front.

This percussion replica takes musket caps. There is also a Sharps New Model 1859 Carbine, of which approximately 115,000 were made during the Civil War. It was a favorite of cavalrymen. This could make an interesting brush rifle for whitetails and wild boars; however, it would not qualify as a muzzleloader for blackpowder-only hunts — because, it isn't one.

The Confederate Sharpshooter

Berdan's Sharpshooters touched a nerve during their own era and the name has come to us through history. Besides, they were on the winning side, which no doubt elevated their reputation. However, the Confederate Army did have its snipers, and everything suggests that they were at least as good as their Northern brothers. Gen. Patrick Cleburne was in charge of these soldiers. The South apparently put its sharpshooters to work in 1862, but not officially until 1864 did these snipers get their Whitworth rifles. In February of that year, Whitworths were issued to

each man, who heretofore apparently had been armed with their own personal guns. Notes show a 530-grain, 45-caliber conical bullet for these Confederate Whitworths with 2.5 drams of blackpowder, a dram, as noted before, being 27.34 grains weight. So the charge would have been 68 grains of powder, a mild target load.

Was Lincoln Fired Upon?

History says yes, Abraham Lincoln was fired upon in 1864 by Confederate sharpshooters during an attack on Washington. The Southern sharpshooters were apparently several hundred yards from the Union trenches, hidden in farm buildings, when a tall man in a black top hat was spotted behind the Yankee lines. The Rebel sharpshooters lost no time sighting in on the figure, who was there to get a first-hand look at the battle. Apparently Honest Abe had forgotten the marksmanship of his own sharpshooters, or did he not believe that there were any Confederate snipers in the area? Whichever, the Rebs fired a few rounds before Lincoln

Hiram Berdan remains the best-known of the sharpshooter leaders, probably because he seems to be the first man to recognize how deadly a regiment of snipers would be.

was dragged to cover by Gen. Wright. The story goes that the shots were so close that wood near the President was struck, with splinters actually embedded in his clothing. But no cigar for the Rebs. They missed! Some historians wonder if the course of the war may have been altered if Lincoln was killed. We'll never know.

They Shot at Each Other, Too

There were apparently a number of duels between Yankee and Rebel snipers. There is no doubt such meetings occurred, and in some case may have been deliberately invoked by officers hoping to drop a sharpshooter in the other army. Some of these duels were historically recorded. One includes a Private Ide, one of Berdan's sharpshooters, who engaged in a shootout with a Southern marksman in 1862. The bout became a show as soldiers from both sides watched the two men fire at each other from long range. The fight ended when the unnamed Confederate marksman put a bullet through the head of the unfortunate Yankee. Another duel had Rebel sharpshooters firing on Northern soldiers who were pinned down in a ditch, just their knapsacks showing above the trench. Bullets from the Rebs shot the knapsacks to pieces, and when one soldier exposed himself, he himself toppled over. There's also a colorful, if sad, account of a duel between one James Ragin, a Berdan sharpshooter, and a Southern sniper that ended for both when the two men fired simultaneously. The Reb's bullet clipped Ragin in the head, creating a furrow in his hair to the scalp. The Confederate marksman did not fare so well. Ragin's bullet ended the man's shooting for that day and evermore.

Ned Roberts and His Uncle Alvaro

Ned Roberts, in his book *The Muzzle-Loading Cap Lock Rifle*,

Gen. Patrick Cleburne can be thought of as the counterpart of Colonel Hiram Berdan. Berdan led sharpshooters of the Union Army, while Cleburne was responsible for putting a sniper corps together for the Confederate side.

credits his uncle Alvaro (Alvaro F. Annis) with teaching him how to shoot. Roberts said that Annis was one of Berdan's Sharpshooters in the Civil War. Roberts was very proud of that, and he applauded the Sharpshooters, citing an account from Harper's Weekly magazine dated August 7, 1861. The item read, in part: "We illustrate herewith the exploits of Colonel Berdan and his famous sharpshooting regiment, which will shortly be heard of at the war."

On Aug. 7, the colonel gave an exhibition of his skill at Weehawken, N.J., in the presence of a large crowd of spectators. The 'man target' christened Jefferson Davis was set up at a distance of a little more than 200 yards. Col. Berdan inaugurated the firing.

Balancing his rifle for a moment, he fired at the head of the figure. When the smoke had cleared away, the hole made by the bullet was observed by the aid of a telescope, in the cheek, near the nose." The Harper's story went on to say that Berdan hit the target several times,

calling one shot in the eye, with the bullet striking "near enough to that organ to destroy its use had it been a real one." This is another version of the right-eye hit mentioned earlier, incidentally, in which someone called out to hit that spot and Berdan did. The article continues that no man could enter the Sharpshooter regiment without proving that he could shoot at 600 feet (feet, not yards in this version) 10 consecutive shots "at an average of five inches from the bull's eye."

But Was Uncle Alvaro Really a Berdan Sharpshooter?

Roberts mentioned his Uncle Alvaro so often that certain people decided to check the facts. On the one hand, what they learned was damaging to the story. On the other hand, there could be a reason for the discrepancy. The name Alvaro F. Annis does not appear on the roster of Berdan's Sharpshooters Regiment at all, which makes Robert's claims a problem. Nor does the War Department in Washington

Gen. John Sedgewick was a well-loved leader in the Confederate Army; however, he had very little respect for the long-range shooting ability of the Yankees in the distance, and for this he paid the supreme price, as history clearly records.

under the name of the other soldier and Alvaro answered to that man's name. We'll never know if Uncle Alvaro made himself a Berdan Sharpshooter to impress his nephew, or if indeed he truly did take the place of another soldier, whose name has floated down the stream of history, lost forever.

They Were Great Marksmen

Regardless of overstatements and historical flaws, the American sniper was a remarkable marksman with his blackpowder rifle. Of that there is no doubt. Of course, many Americans were great shooters in the 19th century because shooting was nearly a daily way of life at the time. Interestingly, as alluded to above, the shooting prowess of our forebears lives once again with a muzzleloader as well as blackpowder cartridge rifle in all manner of shooting games and serious matches. While a few of the feats credited to both Northern and Southern snipers may have been exaggerated, they probably were not that far-fetched, as proven by the fact that good shooters today can repeat the marksmanship with rifle types from the past.

show Uncle Alvaro listed. What does appear is an attempt to enlist by Alvaro, which proved negative due to failing the physical exam. A year later, Alvaro Annis entered the army anyway, so the story goes, taking the place of a man who had passed the physical exam, but apparently did not relish going to war. After learning of his skilled marksmanship, the Union admitted Annis to the Sharpshooters

Chapter 48

SAM'S AND JAKE'S SPECIAL RIFLE — THE HAWKEN

A PRODUCT that becomes so famous that its trademark name goes generic deserves the fame that it achieves. Kleenex™, Jell-O™, Xerox™, and many other for-sale items gained such widespread acceptance that we often forget to credit them with their rightful ™ mark. The Hawken name falls directly into this circle, except that it never had a trademark. Hawken was more accurately the name of two gunmaking brothers, Sam and Jake, although that's no excuse for taking their name into public domain without permission. After all, Oliver Winchester's "handle"

remains to this day a trademark of a specific firearms company, leaving off the Oliver part. The question is: why did this specific rifle weave so bold a pattern upon the fabric of shooting, not only in its day, but also into our own era? Father Time's racing steeds have once again trampled the facts with relentless hooves. And so we have no absolutely clear and complete story of the Hawken firearm in all its glory. But we do have facts enough to tell an interesting and relatively accurate tale, because Hawken history was recorded in its own time, with more details later

unearthed by men like James Serven, John Baird, John Barsotti, Charles Hanson and other careful students of gun history.

How Special was the Hawken?

I recall asking Dennis Mulford, the gifted custom arms maker, to build a Hawken rifle for me. Dennis was polite, but also slightly insulted. His genre was the beautiful Pennsylvania/Kentucky long rifle, or at least a sister or brother of the ilk, such as the Jaeger with its historical significance. No, Mulford would not build a Hawken

The Hawken breed of rugged rifle was much better suited to the Rocky Mountains and environs than the beautiful slender-wristed Kentucky rifle. Its larger caliber was also more ideal for the Far West.

rifle; however, he obliged with a modified Pennsylvania rifle that bore similar traits, a not-too-long rifle of large caliber suitable for carrying into the wilds for the pursuit of big game. Mulford balked because the Hawken rifle never was a showpiece. It was a work piece, blue collar as the steel mills that poured out the iron for its metal parts. The Hawken was, however, special, not because it was the most accurate rifle of its era, and certainly not for handsome lines, but because it served a specific purpose for a heroic westward traveler, the fur trapper of the Far West known as the mountain man.

The Plains Rifle

The Hawken rifle carried a generic name, along with other firearms, such as those bearing the name of rifle builder H.E. Dimick. Although the specific traits do not always fit every plains rifle, these were generally percussion guns, not flintlocks. They were half-stock rifles on the heavy side, with short barrels when compared to the long tubes adorning the Pennsylvania/Kentucky long rifle (short being in the 34- or 36-inch class). Caliber was large, 50 caliber and over as a rule, as opposed to the 45 caliber and even smaller-bored eastern rifles. Yes, the plains rifle was associated with the west, bearing a ruggedness that matched the tough conditions of an entirely untamed land. The plains rifle generally was adorned with iron mountings, rather than brass or silver. Shiny was not the goal of this rifle. While pistol grips were exceedingly rare, the wrist area was thick enough to withstand significant recoil, while also withstanding a blow to an antagonist, using the heavy iron buttplate as a weapon, some said.

Did Every Mountain Man Carry a Hawken?

Numbers represent gross exaggeration in the Hawken saga. Charles E. Hanson Jr., being the professional researcher that he is,

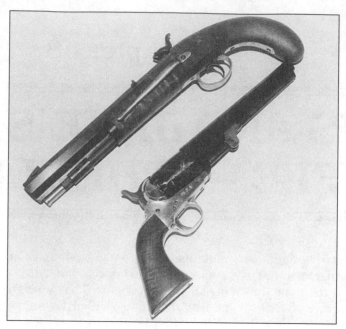

Although the Hawken Brothers were noted for their rifle, they did make pistols as well. They looked very much like the Lyman Plains Pistol, here compared with a cap and ball six-gun.

came up with many rational conclusions about the Hawken rifle. His book, The Hawken Rifle: Its Place in History, is bravely told, not only with facts, but also with personal conclusions. In short, Hanson was not afraid to say what he learned and believed after examining the evidence. "Estimates of enormous Hawken production have been put forth for years by implication," Hanson points out. "Many have assured us that every Mountain Man, including Ashley's crew, had one." Where are the examples? Hanson wants to know that. Yes, Hawkens led a rough life, but guns survive comparatively well, even for a few hundred years, let alone a mere part of a century.

Why weren't Hawkens dug up all over the place in the early 1900s, for example, only three-quarters of a century after the fur-trade era? Because they were never there to begin with, Hanson believes. The author also points out that there are very few Hawken mentions in 19th-century literature, which include diaries and daily logs directly out of the fur-trade era. In addition, very little mention of Hawken rifles is found in the work of 19th-century authors. On the other hand, writers of the period

were not known for detailing particulars about their firearms, any more than we would put down the exact brand name of a shovel we used to plant the garden. The gun was so much a tool that it often received little to no mention in print. Details about guns apparently were not important to most authors of the fur-trade era. Tales of the chase in which great deeds were done seldom make mention of the guns used.

Osborne Russell, in his Journal of a Trapper, never noted the maker of his rifle, unless I missed it. For example, this believable author relates a grizzly bear attack as follows: "I discovered a large grizzly bear sitting at the mouth of its den I approached within about 180 paces shot and missed it. He looked round and crept slowly into his den I reloaded my rifle went up to the hole and threw down a stone weighing 5 or 6 lbs which soon rattled to the bottom and I heard no more I then rolled a stone weighing 3 or 400 lbs into the den stepped back to or three steps and prepared myself for the out come. The Stone had scarcely reached the bottom when the Bear came rushing out with his mouth wide open and was on the point of making a spring at me when I pulled the trigger and Shot him thro. the left shoulder which sent him rolling down the mountain. It being near night I butchered him and left the Meat lying and returned to Camp. The next day I took the meat to camp where we salted it and smoked it ready for winters use." A modern author would tell the reader the make of the firearm, caliber, load, and how the bullet performed.

Furthermore, Hawken shop records simply do not show a multitude of guns manufactured. Also, it's farfetched to believe that the first wave of trappers west had Hawkens with them. They came to the fur trade carrying what they owned, and it was unlikely that their guns were marked "Hawken" because the Fur Trade era begins with the return of Lewis and Clark from their westward exploration. Hanson concludes: "In summary, our research indicates that there were no J&S Hawken rifles before 1825 and does not conclusively document any rifle before 1831." On the other hand, Lewis and Clark were back home

long before that. "Wednesday 24th of September 1806—I slept but little last night however we rose early and commenc[e]d wrighting our letters Capt Lewis wrote one to the presidend and I wrote Govr. Harrison & my friends in Kentucky and Sent of[f] George Drewyer with those letters. . . . Thursday 25th]of Septr. 1806—had all our skins &c suned and stored away in a storeroom of Mr. Caddy Choteau. Payed some visits of form, to the gentlemen of St. Louis in the evening a dinner & Ball."

Stealing the Hawken Name

Some "Hawkens" may not have been Hawkens at all. Hanson believes that many "Hawken" pistols were not. He located several of these guns marked "J&S Hawken," but proofmarks proved that at least parts of the guns were not even of American manufacture. "One that I examined had Belgian proofs under the barrel," he said. Hanson believes that at least some of these pistols were simply marked "J&S Hawken"

when that "brand" became well-known to shooters. There were also Hawken shotguns that may or may not have been the real thing. The Hawken shop did produce shotguns and pistols, to be sure, but the point is, not all guns so marked are true Hawkens. On the other hand, those who believe that all flintlocks marked "Hawken" are phony "because everyone knows that the Hawken was a percussion firearm" are wrong, because this is not the case. While rare, there were a few early flintlock Hawkens.

Other Makers of Plains Rifles

Easy to forget is the fact that a number of gunmakers answered the call for rifles suitable for the challenge of the west. One rather prominent name associated with stout firearms of the plains rifle family was George Tryon. To this hour, a shooter can find a replica of the Tryon rifle. The specific model I tested was built on a back-action lock. It came to these shores through Armsport of Miami. This

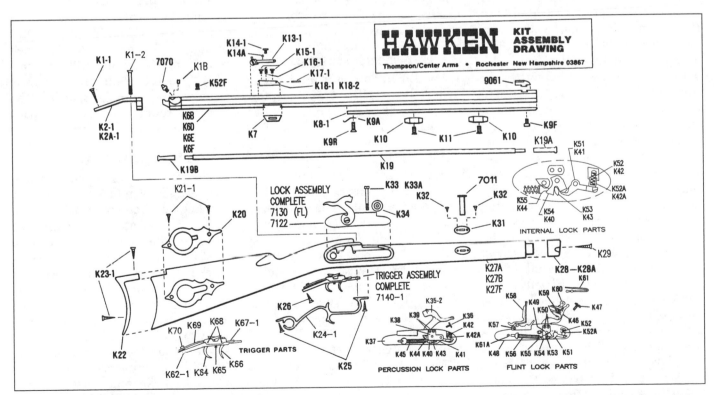

Although the Thompson/Center Hawken is not a replica of the original, many of the parts remain the same and therefore this schematic is useful for anyone interested in how the Hawken was built.

The Hawken rifle had such impact on the shooting world that the breed never died. This young shooter at rendezvous tries his hand with a Hawken-like rifle.

54-caliber percussion rifle was called the Tryon Trailblazer, 32-inch barrel, 1:63 rate of twist. Henry Leman, J.J. Henry, Dreppards, Jacob Dickert, Henry Gibbs, and Henry Deringer represent only some of the names associated with rifles designed for heavy-duty service west of the Mississippi. However, that others built plains rifles does not take away from the fact that the Hawken brand burned itself into the hearts and minds of 19th-century shooters, the rifle deservedly achieving great fame. That is why the name lives on to this day representing a rifle, sometimes a pistol a well. But the point here is: There were other plains rifles. General traits attached to these guns include the warning that there were many variations. However, it's safe to say that a typical plains rifle was usually half-stock, not full-stock. Ithaca built a percussion replica several years ago, appropriately named the Ithaca Hawken, with a stout barrel and large bore. Meanwhile, Hanson, in his book on page 49, reveals a full-stock plains rifle that appears to be damaged in the forepart of the stock. The lock is marked "R. Ashmore & Son." The barrel is 31 1/4-inches long, but evidence of shortening is clear. The barrel is 1 1/16-inch across the flats. It is a percussion rifle with a walnut stock and shortened barrel, weighing 8 pounds, 7 ounces.

Surviving Hawkens

The Colorado State Museum in Denver has a Hawken on display. The rifle belonged to the noted trapper Mariano Modena of fur-trade fame. This is a bona fide Hawken. The rifle is 58 caliber, weighs 12 1/2 pounds, and has a barrel 34 3/4 inches long. It has double keys (two wedges holding stock and barrel together), a large patchbox and nine silver-star inlays. The top barrel flat is stamped "S. Hawken, St. Louis." The lock is stamped "A. Meyer & Co., St. Louis." A silver plate is inlaid into the cheekpiece, recording the purchase in 1833, St. Louis, and presented to Gen. A.H. Jones in 1837. This rifle shows how wide calibers could range in Hawken rifles, the largest on record apparently 66 or 68. A retired Hawken employee remarked, "I made a rifle for his, Ashley's, special use. The barrel was 3 feet and 6 inches long and carried an ounce ball." If indeed this Ashley Hawken fired a 1-ounce round ball, it had to be around 66 caliber. A pure lead round ball .650-inch in diameter weighs 413 grains. A .660-inch round ball weighs 433 grains. There are 420 grains in one ounce. Considering windage (space) in the bore, the round ball would be about one caliber smaller than the bore.

The Kephart Hawken

The famous Kephart Hawken has caused as much trouble as it has helped. Kephart was a historian and a shooter. He bought his Hawken rifle in 1896. It had been in storage for years. He loaded it with 204 grains of blackpowder, a lot for a 53-caliber bore. That powder charge is bothersome for two reasons clearly pointed out in our study of ballistics. First, that much powder would be in the grip of the law of diminishing returns, making a lot of smoke and noise, but not necessarily gaining full benefit in velocity. Second, why 204 grains?

The four grains would be a meaningless gesture, when there would be no discernible difference between 200 and 204 grains of powder. To be fair to Kephart, who wrote much on his Hawken into the middle 1920s and later, he pointed out that best accuracy occurred with much less powder: "82 grains of FFg Deadshot." Some sources show FFFg, by the way. Kephart spoke of the "double charge," which was passed down to us in later times. This mistaken idea had some shooters believing that you could pour as much blackpowder as you pleased downbore for more and more power. We know today that such a practice is unsafe.

The Hawken Shop

Before going on with the Hawken brothers, J.P. Gemmer deserves mention. He, along with a dozen or so other gunsmiths, worked for the Hawken brothers. More importantly, records show that Gemmer bought the Hawken operation in 1862.

This is the story of the rifle, not the men; however, the brothers were treated as one because they acted together in making the Hawken stamp synonymous with the plains rifle. They had impact on an important time in America, the era of westward expansion. Oddly enough, they impacted our era, too. The Hawken name is stamped on contemporary firearms: some dedicated replicas, others looking no more like the original than Olive Oyl resembles a beauty-contest winner. The Hawken came about because the opening of the west did not begin with pioneer wagon trains creaking over the Oregon Trail. It began with the beaver trapper, the mountain man, the hell-for-adventure boys who boldly headed into a territory unknown by the White Eyes. And these lads required a strong rifle.

Their story was touched on earlier and shall not be repeated here. But for the sake of understanding the rifle, recall that the first mountain men to strike out for beaver country followed the Lewis and Clark Expedition of the early 1800s. Thomas Jefferson knew that the western half of America was up for grabs. The French were the first to see many parts of the territory west of the Mississippi River. Coming down from Canada to trap, they got an eyeful of a vast land under the control of no government at the time. The English were also working the region. But it was Jefferson's band, led by Lewis and Clark, who drove a stake marked "America" into the western earth. Some men from the expedition explored on their own, as well as with the group. Although French and English trappers traveled the region, the area was so vast that no stakes were driven. In fact, boots of the European trapper made very few tracks over the unexplored landscape of the Far West in the early 1800s. The mountain-man era was on, and the movement would bring fame to the brothers Hawken, for a new rifle was needed.

The transition from the European Jaeger large-bore rifle — with a big ball but smallish powder charge and low velocity — to the sleek Pennsylvania long rifle — with comparatively fast, but lightweight patched ball — would be continued with another kind of rifle. It was a big bore with a large powder charge driving a heavy lead sphere with superior killing force. Wild animals were bigger out west. It wasn't that bison didn't roam east of the Mississippi, but the real herds were out west. The buffalo, as it was called, was the largest four-footed animal on the North American continent. The smallbore rifle was no more than a gnat-killer against a shaggy. The black bear of the east was well represented out west, but so was his fierce cousin, the much larger grizzly. The rifle that was right back east was wrong out west. The Hawken brothers were not the first, nor hardly the only, gunsmiths to answer the call for a new rifle. However, they were good at what they did, which was manufacturing a working rifle that could be relied on under harsh conditions in the Rocky Mountains, a land explorers called the "marrow of the earth."

The Brothers Hawken

The brothers came by their gunmaking expertise naturally. Grandfather Henry Hawken was a smith of no small ability. His surname was Wee Hawken, but as was common with immigrants to America, the family name was changed. Wee Hawken became Hawkins. Finding that there were a number of Hawkins around, Grandpapa apparently altered the name back to Hawken. However, the Hawkins handle was not lost immediately. Years later, Hawken rifles would often be referred to as Hawkins. Serven notes that a court reference found in a Lancaster, Pa., paper makes reference to a Henry Hawkins. "In November of 1724 Henry Hawkins petitioned the Court — then in Chester County — for redress against John Burt to whom he had apprenticed himself for five years to learn the trade of a gunsmith. . . Henry Hawkins was probably an ancestor of the later Hawkins who made the famous Hawkins rifle in St. Louis, Missouri." Another source, Bruell's Sir William Johnson, noted that "Henry Hawkins was not only a great riflemaker himself but his sons and grandsons succeeded him in later years, establishing shops at Rochester, Louisville, Detroit and St. Louis, until during the last quarter of the 18th and first half of the 19th century, the 'Hawkins' rifle was famous all through the West."

The Hawken story is fairly complete as biographies go, but it does have many gaps, with the branches of the family tree probably taking this form: Henry Hawkins, who would later be Henry Hawken, had a son named Henry Hawken who, with a wife named Julienne, had two sons, Jacob and Samuel. Jacob was born in 1783; Samuel in 1796.

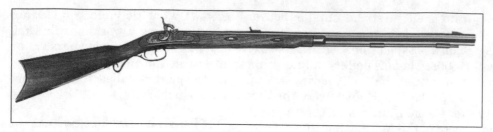

The impact of the Hawken remains with us today. This Lyman Great Plains rifle is reminiscent of the original Hawken rifle, while not being a replica.

Both entered this world at Hagerstown, Md. The Hawken boys' grandfather had been a gunsmith of note, as already stated above. Their father, Henry, was also a gunsmith. Of their youth and growing-up years, I could find nothing substantial. Father Time's horse churned these facts into the clay. But we do know that Jacob, or "Jake," Hawken went to St. Louis in 1807. Hanson believes that Jacob worked at some mechanical enterprise until 1815, when he was able to turn his savings into a gun shop. Timing was right. The beginning of the fur-trade era is considered 1815, with its heyday starting around 1822, per Ashley's advertisement for trappers in that year. Meanwhile, Sam Hawken had a shop in Xenia, Ohio. When his first wife died, he closed that shop in 1822, following his brother Jake to St. Louis to become his full partner. Note the timing: 1822, the very year of Ashley's advertisement. Sam was a great asset to Jake's gunmaking operation.

Another particle of history ties in perfectly with the development of the famous Hawken rifle, this being the percussion cap. Joshua Shaw, an Englishman residing in Philadelphia, had his version of a "copper detonating cap" in 1816, but it was not entirely reliable. If subjected to moisture, it might not fire. There was no reason to switch from the tried-and-true flintlock system to an ignition mode that was less than foolproof. Furthermore, the Shaw cap was highly corrosive. The resulting spark damaged both metal and wood. But there would be an important change in the percussion cap. In 1824, English fulminate of mercury replaced the oxymuriate of potash that Shaw used in his percussion cap. The new cap was not totally clean, but it was not terribly corrosive, either. Furthermore, it could be waterproofed (to a degree) by treatment with sealing wax and spirits of wine. By 1830, the new cap was readily available in America. Sam and Jake were enterprising. Their Rocky Mountain Rifle would be a caplock, with very few flintlocks made by the brothers.

The fur trade was not the only event that brought work into the Hawken shop. Serven's details of a Sam Hawken interview for the newspaper contained these facts: "From Hagerstown I went to Xenia, Ohio, and kept a gun store there, and on June 3, 1822, I arrived in St. Louis. Our first shop was on the levee near Cherry Street. I didn't stop at the first place long; soon we had a new shop on the levee near Olive Street...when the California gold fever broke, I had a bigger demand for guns than I could meet. But I did not raise my prices. From $22.50 to $25.00 was all I asked. Might just as well have got $50.00. Folks wanted me to raise my price, but I said no, those that bought would send back for more, and so they did...." Gold had its impact. But beavers had an even greater effect upon the Hawken gun business. "Every man going West wanted one," said Sam. "William Ashley's men were the next lot to go out; they started for the Rocky Mountains and were driven back by the Indians. The boys had a terrible hard time on that trip. . . . Fremont's company that went to California had my rifles." The Hawken Shop furnished all of the guns for the Missouri Fur Trade Co.

We know that every man going west may have wanted a Hawken, but far from every man had one. The very idea that Hawken was the rifle to own made an impact and the Hawken shop was a big success. The famous Hawken rifle was a reality, and the name survived into modern times, when any blackpowder rifle that carried even similar traits was called a Hawken. History, right or wrong, put Hawkens in famous hands, which may have furthered the mystique that lives on: Mariano Modena, Jim Baker, Jim Bridger, Kit Carson, and others. Bridger owned several Hawken rifles, according to rumor.

The Hawken Story Ends

The story of Jake Hawken ends in 1849. Cholera was rampant and the disease struck him down on May 8. His body may have been cremated along with other victims of the tragedy. But Samuel Hawken lived on, a man of great character. Serven portrays him as a civic-minded, one-time candidate for mayor of St. Louis who also was instrumental in forming one of the first volunteer fire companies in the city. Samuel had never seen the Rocky Mountains, the great territory in which the Hawken rifle was made famous. It was time to go to the marrow of the earth, and so he did. In 1859, ten years after Jacob's passing, Sam took the trail west at 67 years of age. His health was at low ebb, and he wanted to change climates. He walked most of the distance from St. Louis to Denver, on the trail for several weeks, leaving St. Louis April 20 and arriving in Denver June 30. Some report that the Hawken shop was left in the hands of trusted individuals. Instead, it was probably sold. Apparently, Samuel was interested in the Pike's Peak gold strike, but after looking around that area, he returned to Denver to do what he did best: making firearms. He worked out of a log cabin for a while, reporting, "Here I am once more at my old trade, putting guns and pistols in order 'how to shoot'." An advertisement in the Rocky Mountain News, January 25, 1860, read: "S. Hawken, for the last thirty-seven years engaged in the manufacture of the Rocky Mountain rifle in St. Louis, would respectfully say to the citizens of Denver, Auraria, and his old mountain friends, that he has established himself in the gun business on Ferry Street, between Fourth and Fifth, next door to Jones and Cartwright's, Auraria, and is now prepared to manufacture his style of rifles to order."

The change of residence proved to be what Sam Hawken needed. The Rocky Mountain News reported that "Our venerable friend, S. Hawken, whose rifle for years has had an unequaled celebrity among hunters, trappers and voyageurs of the plains and mountains, has raised a tall pole in front of his shop on Ferry Street, on the top of which a mammoth rifle is swung on a pivot. The big gun can be seen from all parts of the city — now pointing at the mountains, now away from them, as it is swayed by the breeze."

The newspaper story went on to say that "Mr. Hawkens (sic) is an old resident of St. Louis, having made guns there for thirty-seven years, and came to this country [Colorado] about a year ago for the benefit of his health, which he informs us has been completely restored."

Colorado was good to Sam Hawken, but home was St. Louis. Sam returned to that city in 1861. He seems to have left a son, William S. Hawken, who had come to Denver, in charge of the new gun shop. The story goes that Sam sold the Hawken shop to J.P. Gemmer. We know that Gemmer did buy the shop, but it appears more likely that he purchased it from William L. Watt and Joseph Eterle. These two men bought it from Sam Hawken, then decided they did not want to run it. A St. Louis directory lists an advertisement that says "William L Watt, Successor to W.S. Hawken, Rifle and Shotgun Manufacturer, 21 Washington Ave., Hawken Rifles always on hand." That advertisement, plus the remarks of Gemmer, indicates that Gemmer did not buy the shop directly from Hawken.

What is important to the Hawken brothers' story is the fact that the rifle they made famous did not die with Jacob in 1849, nor after the selling of the Hawken enterprise. Watt, by the way, no doubt sold some Hawken rifles. John Baird believes that these rifles may have been marked simply "Hawken," and not "S. Hawken," as Sam would do. Perhaps Watt did not have the right to use the full "S. Hawken" stamp. Baird studied an authentic Hawken rifle of the Watt period. It was marked "Hawken" and nothing more. Gemmer, on the other hand, was not restricted concerning the Hawken stamp.

Sam Hawken built rifles until he was 70 years old. He lived with his daughter, Mrs. Fred Colburn, after the passing of his second wife, Martha Richey Hawken. Retired, yes, but Samuel could not stay away from the gun shop. Gemmer reports that the old gentleman visited every day. He still believed in rifles the way he made them, the right way. Apparently, the cartridge gun never won him over completely. He passed up, for example, a chance to sell Colt revolvers.

On May 9, 1884, Sam Hawken went to his final reward. Born on October 26, 1792, that made the great old gunmaker 91 years old.

The authors named above, as well as many others, worked diligently to uncover as many Hawken facts as possible. The reader interested in a deeper knowledge of the rifle and its makers is urged to

The Hawken Brothers were famous for their rifles, not their pistols, but they did make single-shot muzzleloading pistols. This CVA is not a Hawken replica, but it provides the same shooting spirit.

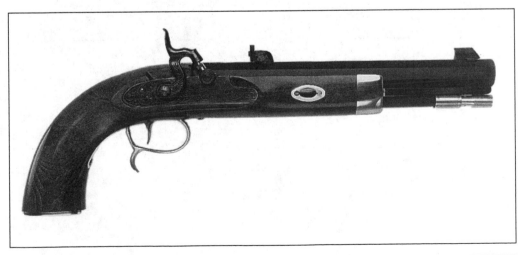

The rugged nature of the original Hawken was born again in half-stock plains rifles like this one fired by a young buckskinner at rendezvous.

locate and digest their writings and others. Muzzle Blasts, the fine magazine of the National Muzzle Loading Rifle Association, has carried a number of stories on the Hawken saga. Sam and Jake Hawken made more than rifles. They made history that continues to this day in the sincerest form of flattery — imitation — not only with replicas, but dozens of non-replica muzzleloaders bearing the name Hawken.

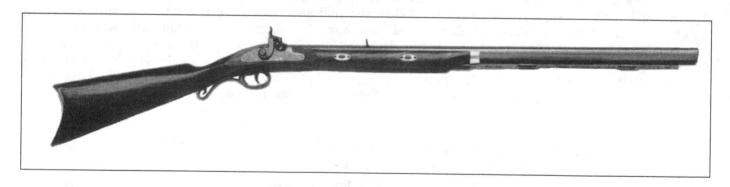

No longer available, the Ithaca Hawken rifle was a true copy of an original, halfstock, percussion, plain iron furniture, open fixed sights, double keys.

Chapter 49

SHOOTING GAMES AT THE RENDEZVOUS

THE ORIGINAL rendezvous was a matter of business enterprise and Yankee Trader ingenuity, luring a gang of devil-may-care adventurers to wander the few-trails region of the Far West in search of beaver streams. With the beaver hat a hot item in the world of fashion, the wise paper-pushers back east had a perfect market. The plan was simple and effective. Let the mountain men, as they would be known, trap flat-tails, bringing the pelts to a central location in summer. Meet them there with wagons loaded with things they enjoyed once, but had no more, and mark everything up many-fold. Trade dollar values for beaver blankets. A trapper could have a thousand, even two showing for his season's labor — good money in an era where a skilled worker might make a buck and a half a day. Whiskey at 30 cents a gallon in St. Louis was cut with water and sold for $2 a pint at rendezvous. Coffee and sugar at a dime a pound back east clipped the mountain men at two greenbacks a pound out west. But that was OK. One mountain man traded the sum value of two grand for the hand of a chief's daughter, they say. She must have been a beauty.

William Ashley was one of the principals in the plan, advertising in the Missouri Gazette, a St. Louis newspaper, on Feb. 13, 1822. He asked for, and got, "enterprising young men." That most of these stalwart lads would never see home again was either an unknown, or not an issue at all. Trapping beaver was hard work, the least damage coming from icy streams that brought on rheumatism, the worst luck running into Bugs' Boys, the Blackfoot Indian, landlord of the territory and one fine warrior whose arrows found the mark all too often. They made their mark,

One enjoyable shooting game at rendezvous is pistol competition. This woman did a great job on the range with high scores.

many places west taking their names: Jackson Hole, Wyo.; Bridger National Forest, Bridger, Mont.; Henry's Fork of the Snake River; Bonneville Pass, Laramie, Wyo., named for the slain mountain man Jaques LaRamie; and many more. Fall came and went. Winter set in. Finally, summer arrived. Off to rendezvous to see old friends and trade beaver pelts for whiskey, tobacco and pretty things to lure a young Indian maiden.

The first rendezvous was held in 1825 when Gen. Ashley gathered his trappers on what is now known as Henry's Fork of the Green River. The actual site is two miles from the present town site of Daniel, Wyo., which in turn is not far from the larger city of Pinedale, Wyo. Every year, there is a pageant held in honor of the mountain men. There also is a museum in his honor. Although the original rendezvous was a business venture, it turned out to be much more than that. Those meetings in the summer brought together white trappers and Indians in a way nothing else had ever done before. Although there were disputes, there was also comradeship. The rendezvous was a time for renewing old acquaintances and making new ones. Along with fur trading, there was story telling, knife and tomahawk throwing, swapping, new and used wares for sale, many games and shooting matches, the grist for this mill. Some shooting matches are as exciting as watching grass grow. Competitions set up by buckskinners, however, have flare, are often creative, fun to do and fun to watch. Some are taken from history, but many others were cooked up by modern buckskinners.

A Few Shooting Tips

Cleaning During a Match

There are generally no rules pertaining to the use of original cleaning chemicals. This means that all-day lubes, as described in Chapter 19, are OK. Also, most matches allow blackpowder substitutes. Pyrodex, as

Modern rendezvous shooting games often include metallic targets of one shape or another at different distances. This one not only rings when struck, but also rotates.

explained in Chapter 15, does not require cleaning between shots for a reasonable number, and there is still the smoke that helps to give these matches an aura of old times.

The Fouling Shot

A fresh bore may shoot slightly off the mark, even if it has been dried with a cleaning patch before and after loading. That first round

Rendezvous shooting games come in all types. In this one, the shooter with flintlock smoothbore only had to move swiftly from one target to the next, reloading and firing at each target.

ball or conical flying wide of the mark can be critical for many matches, opening up an otherwise tight group, missing the blade of the ax, or flying alongside that charcoal briquette. Firing one fouling shot before the match begins is normally allowed and it makes sense for blackpowder, Pyrodex or Clear Shot.

Leftover Lube in the Bore

We've crossed this creek before — an oily, wet, or greasy bore may throw a projectile off course. Where the accuracy of the shot is absolutely vital, it's wise to sight in with a dry bore and maintain a dry bore during a match. This is easily accomplished by running a cleaning patch down-bore after loading. Dangerous? No more so than running the patched ball or conical down on the powder charge, which was necessary to load the gun. The gun must first be sighted in with a dry bore.

Altering Loads for a Match

The idea is to sight in for a match with a specific load, sticking to every aspect of that load chain for the match. A rifle sighted in with a heavy hunting load, then changing that load for the match, is not going to shoot in the same

place. Powder, bullet, patch, lube: Every detail should remain the same. My no. 47 custom 54-caliber round-ball rifle is an especially accurate rifle, and because its rear sight has two notches, no special sighting is required, not even for the 25-yard offhand match. The front sight matches up with the lower rear sight notch picture, and with a 70-grain charge of powder, the round balls chop right into the bull's eye 25 yards away.

A New Flint

A modified Seneca Run was under way, with flintlocks only allowed. Fire, run, stop, aim, fire, run, stop, aim — reloading, of course, for each new target. One of the participants walked up to me during the match and said, "I read what you said about a new flint. It pays off." Naturally, if a flint is doing its job perfectly, it's not changed, but if there is any question about surefire sparks, the old rock has to go, replaced with a new one. That's likewise for all other aspects of flintlock fire — as noted in Chapter 39 on troubleshooting.

Consistency

It's the same song with the same words: consistency or nothing at all

in every respect. While most matches do not require the kind of accuracy that demands a pressure regulator — which places the same force on the bullet, hence the powder charge, for each and every shot — it is worthwhile to seat projectiles with as close to the same force as possible for each load. Some shooters prefer slamming the ramrod down several strokes against the seated bullet. While this may compact the charge to some degree, it is not a necessary step. Good sustained force on the ramrod will seat a bullet fully upon the powder charge. The ramrod should be marked to show that the round ball or conical is all the way home on the powder charge for every shot. Consistency with the powder measure also makes sense, rather than haphazardly dropping powder home. A routine pays off. Sometimes it's a matter of fractions of inches that makes the difference between a hit and a miss, a win or a loss.

Revolver Lock-Up

An improperly lubed revolver can lock up like a rusted hinge, and Murphy's Law says it will happen in the middle of a match. An all-day type of cream on top of the ball just before shooting can help keep the cylinder turning on your cap 'n' ball revolver. Also, after cleaning, a modern high-grade, grease-type lubricant on the interior moving parts of the revolver is helpful.

Check Sights and/or Sight In Before a Shoot

Amazingly, there are shooters who reach the rendezvous with broken or bent sights. Almost as sur-prising is the marksman who arrives for the shoot without knowing where his rifle, pistol, or revolver shoots. If sighs are fully intact, and the blackpowder gun was sighted in for the last shoot, concern is nil to minimal. Other-wise, the shooter must repair or replace sights, while ensuring that his smokepole is sighted in before heading to the rendezvous.

The Games

Knockdown Targets

There are all kinds of targets that fall when struck. Cowboy Action Shooting, for example, has hinged metal plates that tip over from a shotgun blast. It doesn't take much at close range to smack these plates over. A shooter at one event described his handload as 7/8

Rendezvous shooting can be entirely informal — any safe game set up by the shooting club. Here, the shooter has to put a bullet hole through a card.

ounce of No. 5 shot. Silhouettes are, of course, intended to keel over when hit. It's the only thing that counts for score. Pinging and ringing mean nothing, nor does seeing a bullet smack the silhouette through a spotting scope. The important aspect of this game is providing sufficient energy to knock a target over. For long-range shooting with round balls (some events are patched round ball only), with targets as far away as 500 yards (or farther, depending upon the game), the larger-caliber ball makes the difference. Furthermore, in spite of the fact that heavy powder charges are not as efficient as smaller charges, the round ball should be given a pretty good start, not only for energy, but also for the trajectory pattern.

The Silhouette Shoot

The silhouette game is played nationally, and seriously, with single-shot blackpowder cartridge rifles; however, informal silhouettes not associated with the national organization that makes the rules can be rendezvous events for muzzleloaders. A shoot in Nebraska saw an entire series of metallic cutouts set up at various ranges for patched round ball only. Everyone loved the match — those watching as well as participating. Once again, the larger round ball wins out, retaining more of its initial energy than a lighter lead pill, which is vital to knocking the metal animal profile over with one hit.

Splitting the Ball on the Ax Blade

This continues to be one of the most enjoyable matches at rendezvous for shooters and onlookers alike, and it seems to have come from out of the past. The idea is cutting a lead round ball into two pieces on the exposed blade of an ax. A double-bit ax is buried into the center of a large piece of tree stump, one sharp edge protruding outward. A good hit on the exposed blade slices the single bullet into two missiles. Balloons, clay pigeons, anything that will break, are set up

alongside the ax blade. If only one breaks, that's not good. Both are supposed to get thumped as the ball divides into two parts. This is an off-hand event, and as such, rifles of good weight with long sight radius help steadiness and ball placement. Also, a larger-caliber ball makes mathematical good sense. A near miss with a 40-caliber ball may have been a hit with a 50-caliber ball. It also helps to sight in for this event with horizontal grouping considered absolutely critical. The exposed ax blade affords several inches of vertical latitude, but horizontal latitude is confined to the mere width of the ax blade.

The Ricochet Target

Not popular, but interesting, is the ricochet match, where a chunk of heavy metal, such as boilerplate, is placed so that a ball can be skipped from its surface into a safety bank. Situated at the backstop is a breakable target, such as a balloon, clay pigeon, or other object, which is ideal for shooters and spectators. The shooter must skillfully glance the round ball off the boilerplate so that it strikes the target.

The Distant Gong

Rendezvous shooting games play on the senses. Watching a silhouette tip over is more fun for shooter and bystander than a hole in a paper target that no one can even see until the target is brought closer, or the shooter goes up range to take a look. The sense of hearing is treated to a show when the bullet cracks into something that makes a noise. Even with earplugs in place, a metal gong sends back a distinct clang when struck. These are often set up at long range, sometimes so far that the shooter has to pick out an aiming point well above the target. At one rendezvous gong event, the shooter had to aim his rifle to strike a metal gong 500 yards away. Considering the looping trajectory of a round ball, even from a large-bore rifle, it's no simple trick to guide a lead sphere out to 500 yards with accuracy. Successful shooters

hit the 500-yard gong because they used a consistent aiming point far above the target — a visible white spot on the mountain in the background in this particular case. Once again, the larger round ball is better than the smaller one, not only for retained energy, but also trajectory, especially with a safe but strong powder charge behind it.

The Stakebuster Match

The stakebuster match incorporates a wooden plank usually about 6 inches wide, but any other size will work. Two shooters generally team up for this one. The idea is to cut the plank in half with rifle fire. Again, larger calibers are best for mathematical reasons. Fewer hits are required with bigger bullets. Calibers 58 and larger are ideal. Also helpful is sighting in carefully for this close-range event. It takes skill to draw a line across the wood with successive bullet strikes in order to cut the stake in two.

Swinging Charcoal Briquettes

Briquettes swinging on strings suspended from a horizontal wire make interesting targets, with a puff of smoke denoting a solid hit. A good-holding offhand rifle, preferably with a long barrel for muzzle weight and an extended sight radius, helps the shooter in this event.

Playing Cards

Playing cards set up to face the shooter edge-wise are great targets. These are normally arranged at close range, so spectators can witness bullets hitting the cards. Many times, the bullet will make only a slice across the face of the card. It takes a direct hit to cut the card in two.

The Seneca Run

The Seneca Run can be played in different ways. Above, a run with smoothbore flintlocks only was the rule, but rifles are certainly at home in this fast-paced event, which reminds one a little of the Olympic Biathlon. The shooter must successfully accomplish a series of tasks, running from station to station. He must run the course at good speed, because he is up against the clock as well as the targets placed along the way. The marksman with the highest score in the least time is the winner. Rules can vary greatly, not only with the allowed firearm — flintlock, flintlock smoothbore, pistol, revolver — but also the tasks. In one Seneca Run, the shooter had to score on several targets arranged along a path, and after the last target, he was obliged to run back to the starting point to make a fire with tinder, flint, and steel. The tomahawk may be included as part of the run, as may the knife. Running from one target to the next requires reloading safely. Shooting is usually offhand, but one match allowed any stance, even prone. This is a shoot for the athletic. Good shooters who are slow on their feet do not normally claim first place. Ideally, the shooter uses a firearm he is highly familiar with so that he can not only hit the target readily, but also reload without a hitch.

Since most Seneca Runs are conducted with offhand shooting, that longer-barreled, steady-holding rifle with good sight radius is right for the job. It should also hang well, meaning a little front-heavy.

The Log Rest

This event simulates hunting conditions. It can be operated in many different ways. One is to have a walking path, strictly regulated. The contestant strolls along the path, encountering targets at inter-

Another game played at some rendezvous is shooting simple self-bows, that is, bows made of only one material, such as wood, rather than composite.

vals, and always at varying distances. Some are half-hidden by brush. Some are close, some far. Targets can be metallic silhouettes, paper targets with a dirt backstop, cutouts of animals, clay pigeons, and just about anything else. At each station, the shooter is provided with a log. The shooter may take the prone position, or sometimes sits and rests the forend of the rifle on the log. Although heavy-barrel rifles seem to do OK when the barrel itself is rested, as proved by many blackpowder-cartridge rifle shooters, consistency is best maintained by resting the forend of the muzzleloader over the log, rather than the barrel. Also, a heavy rifle, 9 pounds or more, rests more solidly in place than a lighter rifle, which is always the case regardless of rifle type.

Regulation Targets

There are many regulation target matches at rendezvous. They are not, perhaps, as interesting as the novelty shoots, but they are valuable, and, in fact, show off the shooter and his equipment very well. Offhand shooting at regulation targets can be held at 25, 50, 100, 200 yards, even farther. Clearly, the more accurate the firearm the better, be it rifle, pistol, or revolver. As always, the stable firearm is at an advantage. With a rifle, that generally means the heavier model with longer barrel that has forward weight for steady holding and a long sight radius. Practice for the match should involve the same targets, as well as the same firearm and loads, to will be used at rendezvous. Learning to put bullet holes in a specific target face does not always transfer to another style target.

Shotgun Competition

The shotgun is an obvious tool of competition at any rendezvous. Events can range from trap to skeet and anything in between, the only limitation being the range of the shotgun and the imagination of the event designers.

The Primitive Bow at Rendezvous

Mountain men were interested in bows and arrows. Osborne Russell in his Journal of a Trapper reports on running across a group of Snake Indians, as he called them. Editor Haines suggests that these were probably Sheepeater Indians, the only aboriginal peoples known to inhabit the Yellowstone Plateau. "They will well armed with bows and arrows with obsidian. The bows were beautifully wrought from Sheep, Buffaloe and Elk secured with Deer and Elk sinews and ornamented with porcupine quills and generally about 3 feet long," Russell reported. The author also saw an Indian buffalo hunt first-hand. "At length an Indian pursued a Cow close to me running alongside of her he let slip an arrow and she fell." There would be nothing wrong with a mountain man using the bow and arrow to procure a little camp food, especially in a region where a gunshot might be heard by "the wrong people." At rendezvous, primitive type bows are definitely at home, and shooting matches may be held. The bows are made by different artisans. See Traditional Bowyers guide in Traditional Archery, a Stackpole Books publication of 1999 for bowmakers dealing in primitive-style archery tackle.

Anything Safe Goes

As long as it's safe, rendezvous shooting matches can range from moving targets on a taut wire — a great event, usually a boar sliding from right to left, then left to right — to multiple-skill competitions, where rifle, handgun, and even shotgun are put into play in a single match, similar to Cowboy Action Shooting. Most events have spectator interest. Something goes clang like a gong in the distance, or poof, when a charcoal briquette blows up, or pop as balloons are riddled with split-in-two round balls. Meanwhile, silhouettes and many other types of targets topple over when struck. This is good, because it promotes interest in the great sport of blackpowder shooting. Unlike the blackpowder-cartridge silhouette shooting and Cowboy Action Shooting, which are both nationally organized, rendezvous games are designed more for entertainment than score, with fun for shooter and spectator alike.

Chapter 50

BLACKPOWDER CARTRIDGE SILHOUETTE AND COWBOY ACTION SHOOTING

TWO BIG-TIME games played with blackpowder cartridges are silhouette and Cowboy Action Shooting. Both are national shooting sports. Each has its own official organization, along with individual clubs dotting the entire United States and Canada. The blackpowder cartridge came of age — again — with hunters desiring to find out what it was like to pack a single-shot breechloader or lever-action repeater loaded up with cartridges born before smokeless powder. But it's been the two games that brought the cartridges to the height of popularity now enjoyed: silhouette for the single-shot rifle, Cowboy Action Shooting for lever-action repeaters, along with blackpowder cartridge revolvers and older-style shotguns. Replica guns abound for both games, along with every kind of accouterment anyone could imagine, as well as special books on the subjects, including loading manuals. There is no end in sight. Both events continue to grow in membership.

THE BLACKPOWDER SINGLE-SHOT SILHOUETTE GAME
Informal and Local Shoots

While national, if not global, rules and regulations hover over the sport of silhouette shooting with blackpowder cartridge single-shot, breech-loading rifles, clubs all over North America continue to fashion their own special blackpowder cartridge games. Rules vary with each group. For example, how about a "Buffalo Gong Shoot," in which "any single shot breech-loading cartridge rifle or replica in the spirit of the era of the late 1800s to early 1900s" is acceptable? Blackpowder or Pyrodex are allowed in this contest, with duplex loads (smokeless mixed with blackpowder) or smokeless powder forbidden. Only metallic sights are admissible, no scopes. Cast lead bullets were legal projectiles, nothing else, and these had to be without gas checks. The major

competition was a metal gong at 200 yards, offhand shooting only, but as it turned out, the most watched and enjoyed aspect of this particular shoot was the buffalo (American bison) metallic cutout placed at 900 yards. Boom! Wait a bit. Clang! Everybody loved it, shooter and spectator alike.

The buffalo metallic silhouette was not an offhand event. All shooters used crossed sticks. The range was opened one day ahead of the match so that shooters could visit with each other, have some fun, and practice a little before the real thing got under way. This local shootout was typical with plenty of rules, but nothing as stringent as national competition requires. The local shoot is always geared for a good time, even when prizes are offered. Oftentimes muzzleloading events are included along with the blackpowder cartridge games. While gongs and metallic silhouettes are the usual targets, the home club is not bound to regula-

The 1874 Sharps rifle, shown here in the No. 3 Sporter, with Vernier tang sight is a fine rifle for long-range silhouette shooting.

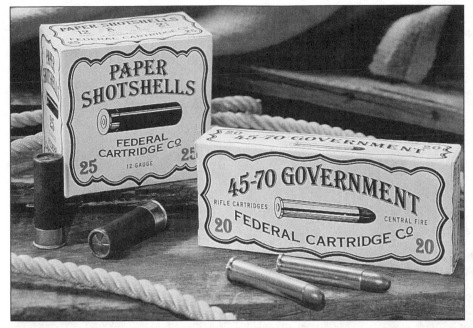

Major ammunition companies like Federal Cartridge Co. have come forth with products of interest to single-shot rifle fans as well as Cowboy Action shooters.

tions, types or sizes of targets, or shooting distances. They make the rules. After all, the shoot has nothing to do with national competition, which is a whole different world.

Shooting Far – Really Far

Perhaps the biggest draw in shooting single-shot blackpowder cartridge rifles is not the rifles — although they are immensely interesting, especially with regard to history — but how far away those targets are! Anyone who has shot long-range competition, or for that matter, informal distance gunnery, has the utmost respect for a shooter who can hit a target at several hundred yards with a high-power scope and super cartridge firing a high-

Cowboy Action Shooting is so big that companies like Cabela's even offer badges that go along with the sport.

velocity, ballistically efficient bullet. Shooters who actually go to a range where distance from muzzle to target is several hundred yards quickly learn that the shot made on that deer across the canyon that seemed to be that far wasn't — at least most of the time. One of the greatest long-range marksmen of all time is Dave Gullo. Gullo demonstrated his ability with an original breech-loading, single-shot, blackpowder cartridge rifle, a piece 120-years old wearing vernier tang sights. The target was a gong placed on a white buffalo cutout. The distance was — wait for It — 1,123-yards. That is two-thirds of a mile.

Gullo believes that it took 3.5 seconds for the bullet to span the distance from muzzle to that dis-

tant target. This could be right, because he could shoot, set the rifle aside, peek in his spotting scope, and see the bullet hit the gong, where it arrives with a clang! and clearly visible splash of lead. Dave casts his own bullets, ensuring that none of these projectiles suffers an occlusion of any kind. An air pocket would drift the bullet off course by a wide margin. Gullo reports that in order for the projectile to hit on target at more than 1,000 yards, he must, as he put it, "aim 50 feet high." He shoots from a benchrest, right? Wrong. This marksman uses crossed sticks only, no bench. That anyone can do this with any sort of repetition lends credence to some of the old buffalo-runner tales, with claims of strikes out to several hundred yards. It also proves that single-shot blackpowder cartridge rifles of yesteryear were capable of high marks in accuracy, resulting in long-range hits on modest-sized targets. Because of the ability of both guns and shooters to hit targets time after time at long range with blackpowder cartridge rifles, a new game was born. Actually, that's not true. Adding the single-shot, soot-burning rifle was new, but the game came to life some time ago in another country.

Longer range projectiles are especially important for blackpowder cartridge silhouette shooting. Lyman produced these LRHP (Long Range High Performance) bullets for better retention of velocity and a flatter trajectory.

Carts on wheels are the ticket for Cowboy Action Shooting. They retain the guns safely, while storing ammo, supplies, and gear.

The Silueta Game is Born

The roots of blackpowder-cartridge silhouette shooting reach down into the rich soil of a sport that began in Mexico. It's difficult to say just when, nor do I have information on exactly who came up with the original idea for the formal silueta match. I do know that in the late 1950s and early 1960s, Victor Ruiz, a well-known marksman from Nogales, Sonora, Mexico, along with several of his shooting companions, such as Milo Martinez, another fine marksman, were firing away at metal cutouts at long range from the offhand position only. Interest grew in the sport, partly because Mexican shooters invited north-of-the-border riflemen to join them. The silueta match soon became a hands-across-the-border friendly competition, and from that point, an international game with literally hundreds of participants that continues to thrive today. Typically, U.S. shooters had to organize silueta into a match with specific rules and regulations, from that point creating an organization to watch over the new sport with rule-making authority.

Modern Rifle Silhouette Shoot

The original silhouette match was built around the centerfire sporting rifle. Rules called for a rifle that a hunter would likely carry into the field for big game. The rifle was to weigh no more

Women are well-represented at Cowboy Action Shooting. This woman fires a Model 1897 pump-action shotgun, which is extremely popular.

than 8 pounds with scope, as I recall. In the beginning, shooters played the game with the same rifles they used for deer and other big game hunting. As the shoot became more sophisticated, however, many rules were designed to keep the sport from deteriorating. As with every sport, special equipment was soon available, which is always the case from pole-vaulting to ping pong. A unique scope-sighted silhouette rifle came along, most-often chambered for the 308 Winchester cartridge. Of course, there were official standards established for the size of the metallic cutouts and the distances at which they were placed.

As part of the package, Cowboy Action Shooting members get a badge with their own number on it.

Blackpowder Cartridge Silhouette

The formal blackpowder-cartridge metallic-silhouette game is definitely an offshoot of the original smokeless powder cartridge match. It is NRA sponsored, with the first official shoot held near Raton, N.M., at the NRA Whittington Center in 1985. The event has been run annually ever since, with ever-increasing interest. Canada has joined in with its own national competition. Australians also shoot blackpowder cartridge silhouette matches, although the game may be in jeopardy in that country because of firearms legislation enacted in the late 20th century.

The Rifles

The rules have changed, and may change again, so it is unwise to set anything down in concrete. The only sure way to find out exactly what is allowed currently is to contact the parent organization, which is not a problem. A cutoff date for rifle manufacture was mandated in the beginning and remains vital to the sport. After all, the competition is for 19th-century, single-shot blackpowder cartridge rifles. The year 1892 was established as a cutoff manufacturing date for legal blackpowder silhouette rifles for formal competition. Before that ruling, 1895 and 1896 were the rifle manufacturing-date limits. Official rulings exist within the parameters of the NRA Blackpowder Cartridge Rifle (BPCR) Silhouette matches. However, the organization found that inclusion or exclusion of specific rifles was not entirely simple. For example, the Stevens 44-1/2, with its falling-block action and exposed hammer, would seem to be disallowed because the 44-1/2 dates from 1903. But the rifle followed a design matching the spirit, inten-

This modern-day cowboy fires away through a window setup at a club meeting. Various targets are used at local clubs, just as long as they are safe to shoot at.

While one Cowboy Action Shooter fires away, another times him.

tion, and even mechanics of the 19th-century, single-shot, breech-loading blackpowder cartridge rifle, and so it was let in the door. The sport still has growing pains, and further changes in allowable rifles may be seen.

Browning, noting the great interest generated in the BPCR Silhouette sport, introduced its version of the 1885 single shot, calling it, appropriately, the Browning Model 1885 BPCR (Black Powder Cartridge Rifle). It even has a long-range metallic sight suited to the game. A few original and rebuilt Sharps rifles, especially the model of 1874, became quite popular in silhouette shooting. But it's mainly the modern replica of this rifle that dominates. Currently, the Winchester Model 1885 High Wall is also popular. Add to these a number of Remington rolling blocks, most of them modern-made replicas, with a few originals, as well as customs built on original or replica actions. There are also Hepburns and Ballards, and even Trapdoor Springfields.

The Cartridge

Since the legal rifle for the sport is a single-shot breechloader of American design, military or sporting, with an exposed hammer, it only makes sense that the cartridge must follow.

These metallic targets took many a direct hit during this Cowboy Action Shooting event.

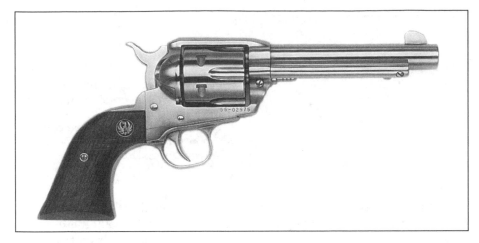

Cowboy Action Shooting has created sufficient impact to interest companies like Ruger in offering guns that meet the challenge, like this handsome six-gun.

The two rifles most carried by the buffalo runner of the latter part of the 19th century qualified immediately, these being the Remington Rolling Block and the Sharps, not to exclude the original Winchester single-shot breechloader, or for that matter the Trapdoor mentioned in Chapter 45. What were the cartridges for these rifles? There were many, but the rules call for only original 19th-century rounds, and they must be of American origin. For example, a great number of Remington rolling blocks were chambered for the 43 Egyptian, but that cartridge is not allowed in formal silhouette competition, at least at the time this work was under way.

While the 45-70 Government cartridge continues as number one in the game, 40-65 Winchester popularity is on the rise. The reason is quite simple: Many rounds are fired during a match. The 45-70 with a 400- or 500-grain bullet in front of a full package of fuel delivers a fairly strong blow to the shoulder. The 40-65 is milder, while still providing enough punch to knock over a metallic silhouette. Actually, there are dozens of rounds that qualify for this sport. The Sharps line alone includes a multitude of them. One shoot had the following cartridges: 40-70, 40-50, 45-100, 44-100, just to mention a few. The list also included, by the way, the huge 50-140 Sharps. While the accurate and mild 38-55 Winchester cartridge has shown up at some matches, it's just a touch shy of striking power to knock down the big ram target, as is the nice little 32-40 Winchester round, which simply does not pack enough bullet weight for the task.

Sights

Only iron sights are allowed. Open sights are approved, but they would create an insurmountable handicap. The vernier tang sight is the rule in this game because it mounts on the tang close enough to the eye to provide a long sight radius, and it is, after all, a peep sight. Furthermore, it can be adjusted for great distances with quick and accurate sighting changes. It is not, however, the only sight used. There are other allowable designs. But no scopes.

The Targets, Distances, and Rules

The targets are the same as those used in the modern rifle silhouette match: chicken, pig, turkey, and sheep. The chicken is placed at 200 meters, the pig at 300, the turkey at 385, and the sheep at a full 500 meters. Cross-sticks (also called crossed sticks) are allowed for the pig, turkey, and sheep, but the chicken is shot offhand and is con-

Marlin's Model 1894 is a handsome rifle that fits the era of Cowboy Action Shooting.

Famous in its day and still going strong, Marlin's lever-action repeater of 1895 has a following in Cowboy Action Shooting in what some call the pot shoots as long as it does not have an integral muzzle brake.

sidered the toughest target to hit, even though it's the closest. The sport is amazingly difficult. Every target looks like a fly speck on a window "away out there," and remember that only iron sights are allowed so there is no magnification! Even the sheep, the largest target, is a mere 13 inches high and 32 inches long. The turkey is taller — 23 inches — but that includes the head and neck. The body itself is only 11 by 13 inches in size; picture that at 385 meters.

Shooters simply have to be highly skilled in order to have a chance at competing in this competition. While heavy rifles are allowed, and heavy rifles do sit well from offhand and rest steady on the cross-sticks, maximum legal weight is 12 pounds, 2 ounces as this is written. That is a far cry from a blackpowder bench gun, for exam-

ple, that can weigh much more. Once again, contact with the parent organization is vital for the latest rules of the silhouette game.

Allowable Powder and Ballistics

Ballistics plays a strong role in the difficulty of this fascinating shooting sport. Velocities range from around 1,100 fps to about 1,300 fps. With only Pyrodex and blackpowder allowed, hopes for higher velocities are eliminated. This means delivered energies at long range are relatively low. A hit target counts for nothing. It must fall over. That's why the larger calibers are imperative. The sheep weighs about 50 pounds, and it's a full 500 meters from the muzzle. Bullets much under 40 caliber simply don't have the remaining punch to always knock the sheep off its

feet, so to speak. It's difficult trying to hit the target at 500 meters with iron sights and a high-trajectory firearm. But hitting it and getting no score is very discouraging. The 45-caliber bullet, weighing around 400 or 500 grains, has enough punch left, even at long range, to knock over the target when the bullet hits. Big lead bullets in the 40-caliber league also qualify.

Drop-Tube Powder Loading

Consider a hole in the ground to be filled with a bunch of rocks. Rocks can be haphazardly dumped into the hole or tossed in a few at a time. Dropping all the rocks in at once will not allow them to settle evenly, which means there will be air gaps between the rocks. Settling them in a few at a time reduces space between the rocks, creating

The lever-action blackpowder cartridge repeater has been born again because of Cowboy Action Shooting.

Cowboy Action Shooting has provided hours of good shooting and good times for literally thousands of club members across North America.

greater uniformity. The same is true of powder. If a charge of black-powder or Pyrodex is dumped into the case all at once, it will not settle nearly as well as trickling in a few grains at a time. The shape of the kernel, being irregular, has something to do with this. Now lengthen the fall of the kernels and a firmly packed charge is much more likely. That's where the drop tube comes in. It allows powder to enter the case from as high as 30 inches or so, but it also introduces the powder a few granules at a time. It can take several seconds to drop a powder charge into a case. For competition, and even for good hunting loads,

the drop tube method comes highly recommended. There is nothing new about it. Drop tubes have been around for a very long time. It's simply an old trick that works very well in producing an evenly packed powder charge. Now there are commercial blackpowder measures offered with drop tubes available. These are safe for use with blackpowder because of their design, construction and materials.

The Primer

After packing the powder into the case via the drop-tube method, the usual condition is 100 percent load density, or very close to it. While

many gun writers, including this one, recommended mild primers in the past because blackpowder ignites readily, that position had to be reversed. Today, magnum primers are recommended for blackpowder cartridges, at least the larger-capacity rounds.

The Bullet

The typical bullet for the 19th-century blackpowder cartridge did not have a rocket-like profile. Therefore, it did not possess a high ballistic coefficient. Velocities are already quite low in the blackpowder cartridge, which means a looping trajectory. Adding blunt-nosed bullets promotes even greater drop. Of course, the tubular magazine of the blackpowder lever-action rifle demanded, and still demands, the blunt-nosed bullet. But the single-shot breechloader does not. That's why serious silhouette shooters have gravitated to projectiles with a higher ballistic coefficient. Lyman even came along with spitzer-shaped bullets in both 40- and 45-caliber, especially aimed toward long-range shooting with the 40-65 Winchester and similar rounds, plus the 45-70 Government and other cartridges of that class.

The Wind and the Sun

Both wind and sun play prominent rolls in blackpowder cartridge competitive shooting. The wind can drift bullets completely off target. Part of the reason is the time of flight, which is very long. With bullets leaving the muzzle at 1,100 to 1,300 fps, and ranges up to 500 meters and more, it takes quite a while for a bullet to go from muzzle to target. The wind has all that time to play on the projectile, so it is common for a breeze to blow a big blackpowder projectile way off the mark. A mere 10-mph zephyr can drift a bullet off course by several feet from muzzle to sheep silhouette at 500 meters. The sun also

plays a role. Light striking the sights can greatly alter bullet placement. That's why covered front sights are prominent.

The Spotter

Because of severe bullet drop, the use of iron sights, wind and light problems, and a host of other gremlins, the spotter becomes a tremendous asset. He's allowed to sit behind the shooter and watch through a telescope to see where the bullets hit. If he's good, he'll be able to tell the marksman where his missile landed, which prompts a sight or hold adjustment for the next shot.

Minimum Accuracy

Mike Venturino, an avid blackpowder cartridge fan for years and well-known writer on the subject, concluded that a 4-inch group at 200 yards constituted minimum accuracy for competition in the silhouette game.

Triggers

Double-set triggers are common. While the rule of hold and squeeze always pertains, being able to touch off a shot at just the right moment is invaluable. The set-trigger, with a very light breaking point, allows that. It's not a trigger jerk, but a

clean, controlled touch-off made possible by that set trigger.

Growing Sport

The blackpowder cartridge and single-shot rifle are back in full force. Blackpowder silhouette shooting on a formal level will probably undergo a few more changes in the future, but that's healthy. Hopefully, the usual tendency to upgrade that prevails in any sport will be carefully regulated. Those steering the sport recognize that if they allow the rules to grow lax, the game will lose a great deal of its appeal.

COWBOY ACTION SHOOTING

America has had a love affair with the cowboy since the 19th century, with dime novels making outlandish claims of fast-drawing and straight-shooting rivaled only by the comics, cheap-paper books, and B-movies that showed Tim McCoy, Tom Mix, Tex Ritter, Lash LaRue, Gene Autry, Roy Rogers, and many others doing the impossible with six-guns and lever-action rifles. It's no wonder that the Cowboy Action Shooting game caught on. Although B-western films faded away some time ago, they were replaced by movies that continued to herald the American gun-toting cowboy. Any-

Cowboy Action Shooting is conducted from various stations both for the interest and for safety reasons.

Getting ready to participate, Cowboy Action Shooters wheel their carts with guns, ammo, and gear toward the shooting area.

one interested in this game should contact SASS: the Single Action Shooting Society currently reachable at (714) 694-1800 by phone, or by e-mail at sasseot@aol.com, or http://www.sassnet.com on the Internet. SASS offers a wealth of information on the sport, plus information on clubs nationwide. Members of SASS receive a permanent alias registration. That's right, the shooter gets to name himself, such as Deadeye Dick or Straight Shot Sue, and that handle is registered, almost like a trademark. There is also a permanent member number assigned to each person, the SASS star badge with that number impressed on it, SASS Marshal lapel pin, membership certificate, subscription to The Cowboy Chronicle, a bi-monthly journal for the organization, the SASS Shooters Handbook or SASS Mounted Shooters Handbook, and a SASS membership card. Life Members receive a Gold Collector's Badge.

There is also a SASS RO Course — Range Operation Safety — given by a person known as the Territorial Governor at the home club, or at the End of Trail Winter Range, and at all SASS regional events. There's a study booklet available for the course. Safety is, of course, of main importance in all Cowboy Action

Shooting events. SASS also keeps shooters abreast of legalities, such as California's passage of a bill excluding firearms capable of holding more than 10 rounds, which affects some of the lever-action rifles popular with Cowboy Action Shooters. "Legislature readily agreed that our cowboy guns were not the intended subject of this legislation," SASS News reported. "Although technically illegal, the Department of Justice wrote a letter to SASS and communicated with the Riverside County (site of END of TRAIL) District Attorney's Office and Sheriff's Office assuring us the law would not be enforced." This is the kind of service SASS is known for, along with a tight rein on rules and regulations. There is also a SASS Mercantile, where members can purchase casual wear bearing the SASS logo, collectible pocket and lapel pins, the SASS Colt Single-Action Revolver, custom orders, deluxe collectibles, log items, and much more, including a video and book collection to choose from.

How the Game is Played

Although Cowboy Action Shooting is not strictly a blackpowder sport, the spirit of the guns is definitely old-time. Furthermore, many fans do load their shootin' irons with blackpowder, which is entirely legal for the

competitions. Three general firearms play a role in cowboy action shooting: revolver, rifle, and shotgun. The revolver is single-action and very much a part of the blackpowder scene. The rifle is usually the same, but the Model 1894, which originally came along in blackpowder-only cartridges, was later chambered to a number of smokeless rounds. Shotguns are generally seen in two major styles: side-by-side double barrel and the Winchester Model 1897 pump-action with exposed hammer. This great old gun continues to please a lot of shooters, including this one, mine being a refurbished '97 in 12 gauge with modified choke. Since some of the events call for three rounds with the shotgun, the pump is a good choice. Rate of feeding three rounds into the '97 is remarkably fast, starting with an empty gun, which is the rule. John Taffin in his fine book, Action Shooting Cowboy Style, a 1999 Krause Publications title, runs through the range of revolvers, rifles, and shotguns mainly used in the events. Part I, the Introduction, includes photos of many legendary B-western cowboy heroes, such as Buck Jones, who proved he was truly a hero when he died in 1942 trying to rescue people from a burning building. My hero, Tim McCoy, with his big cowboy hat, is shown, along with

Gordon "Wild Bill" Elliott and William Boyd, better known as Hopalong Cassidy. And, of course, Roy Rogers, the King of the Cowboys.

Taffin goes into clothing for the game, as well as the intended spirit. There are various stages for shooting, with the clock running to time contestants, but the local club has wide latitude in cooking up its own rules, as long as all safety tenets are observed. Local levels often use four or five individual shooting stages, while a dozen or more are the rule for national matches. Shooting positions may be offhand standing, sitting or prone. Targets can be paper or metal, but at one local club match, bowling pins were used. Under SASS rules, there are five shooting categories. These are Blackpowder, Traditional, Modern, Dualist, and Frontiersman. Blackpowder includes single-action percussion revolvers or cartridge revolvers loaded with blackpowder. Fixed-sight Ruger Vaquero or Old Army handguns are allowed. Lever-action guns must also be blackpowder style. Pump-actions, such as Colt made in the 19th century, are also legal. Traditional is the most popular, according to Taffin. The guns are similar, but may be loaded with smokeless powder. It's not all black-powder cartridges, as the 357 Magnum is allowed. Duelist is an optional category with all shooting accomplished one-handed only. Frontiersman is also an optional category. It requires two early frontier revolvers, original or replica, or the Ruger Old Army with fixed sights.

Guns and Ammo

Cap and ball revolvers are allowed, such as the Colt Model 1860 of American Civil War fame. Many others are also used. Smith & Wesson single-action revolvers are also part of the game, including the Schofield model. Remington single-action cartridge revolvers are also included. Of course, Colts in many styles, including the Bisley, are all right. Ruger revolvers also play a role. Taffin supplies a multitude of good loads for Cowboy Action Shooting in many of the handguns, including data on the popular 44-40 Winchester. This round with Winchester factory ammo will group inside an inch at 50 feet — this distance is used because most Cowboy Action Shooting is close. The 44 Colt is back with factory loads from Black Hills Ammunition. Many other rounds are discussed, including the 32-20 Winchester and what Taffin calls turn-of-the-century cartridges, such as the 38 Special. Lever-action rifles are well represented, with the Winchester Model 1892 very popular, along with the 1894 Winchester. Of course, Models 1866 and 1873 are also in the game. So are Marlins, such as that company's 1894 Cowboy model in 44-40 Winchester. Ammo for these rifles includes many 44-40s, along with 45 Colt, but many other rounds are also legal. Shotguns, as mentioned, include double-barrel side-by-sides and the Winchester Model 97 with appropriate shells.

Typical Local Club Match

A match held in Arizona included several stages. One stage went: "Start standing at middle window of fort both hands on flag rope, one pistol holstered. Rifle with nine rounds staged at left portal and shotgun staged at middle window." At the buzzer, the shooter gets moving, shooting the different targets from the specific positions stated in the rules. At another stage, rules were entirely different for the shooting match. It went like this: "Start standing at a bar holding bottle with strong hand, rifle with six rounds and open empty shotgun staged on bar, two pistols holstered. At buzzer, drop bottle and with rifle shoot the rifle targets twice each, stage rifle with shotgun, shoot S1, S2 and S3. Mandatory: pick up bottle and move to table and set bottle on table, then sweep the pistol targets twice with pistols staging or holstering after each pistol is emptied."

Range Safety Rules

Twenty-two rules were outlined in the brochure for the above Cowboy Action Shooting local club meeting. The first was that every shooter would act as a safety officer, responsible for his own conduct, while alerting others to any possibly unsafe activity. Eye protection is mandatory for everyone, including spectators standing nearby. All firearms must be unloaded at all times except when on the course. All guns must be properly stored. No alcoholic beverages may be carried. Foul language or unsportsmanlike conduct may result in disqualification.

The blackpowder cartridge, not always loaded with blackpowder, is far from dead, as popular single-shot breach loading rifle silhouette and Cowboy Action Shooting prove. Old-time blackpowder cartridge guns and loads are also growing in hunting popularity.

DIRECTORY

American Western Arms
1450 Southwest 10th St.
Suite 3-4
Delray Beach, FL 33444-1264
561-330-0556 (Phone)
877-292-4867 (Phone Orders)
(Email)
(Website)

Supplies the Cowboy Action shooter with leather holsters from 1800s style, along with boots, pants, shirts, and other accessories. Also has a custom Single Action Army revolver.

Arrow Moccasin Co.
P.O. Box 699
Hudson, MA 01749
978-562-7870 (Phone)
(Email)
(Website)

Beautiful *Soulier de Boeuf*, the French Canadian Moccasin "boot" of the past with good looks as well as fine construction, also comes lined.

Ashley Outdoors, Inc.
2401 Ludelle St.
Forth Worth, TX 76105
888-774-4880 (Phone)
800-734-7939 (Fax)
(Email)
(Website)

Produces Ashley Ghost Ring Hunting Sights, especially good under low light conditions, a fully adjustable peep with a large orifice, very compact, available for many different muzzleloaders. Also the Ashley Power Rod and Backup Rod, the former storing like a regular ramrod, but working like a loading rod.

Badlands
1414 South 700 West
Salt Lake City, UT 84104
801-978-2207 (Phone)
801-978-2249 (Fax)

State of the art backpacks with molded foam, Kevlar reinforcement, polycarbonate frames, high-tech packs to help the blackpowder hunter reach that quiet niche where game is muzzleloader-huntable.

Ballistic Products, Inc.
POB 293
Hamel, MN 55340
763-494-9237 (Phone)
888-273-5623 (Phone Orders)
763-494-9236 (Fax)
Website)

This company made great inroads in all shotgun shooting, and today offers a complete line of blackpowder wads, along with shot and many interesting products, such as X-Stream spreaders for 10, 12, 16, and 20 gauge loads. Worth getting the catalog and data sheets for knowledge alone.

Barnes Bullets, Inc.
POB 215
American Fork, UT 84003
385-756-4222 (Phone)
800-574-9200 (Phone Orders)
385-756-2465 (Fax)
(Email)
(Website)

Barnes Bullets has the Expander MZ Muzzleloader Bullet in solid copper with larger hollow-point nose.

Big Bore Express, Ltd.
16345 Midway Road
Nampa, ID 83651
208-466-9975 (Phone)
800-376-4010 (Phone Orders)
208-466-6927 (Fax)

Makes the Black Belt bullet, along with the Copper Magnum bullet for muzzleloaders. Free freight on Black Belt bullet orders.

Birchwood Casey
7900 Fuller Road
Eden Prairie, MN 55344
952-937-7933 (Phone)
800-328-6156 (Phone Orders)
952-937-7979 (Fax)

(Email)
(Website)

Numerous products of interest to the blackpowder shooter, including solvents and other chemicals, plus the Shoot-N-C high visibility target and World of Targets metallic targets.

Bismuth Cartridge Co.
11650 Riverside Drive
Hollywood, CA 91602
818-763-9011 (Phone)
800-759-3333 (Toll Free)

(Email)
(Website)

Non-toxic bismuth shot for the blackpowder shotgun in numbers 7 , 6, 5, 4, 2, and BB.

Blomquist Percussion Works, Ltd.
17406 Tiller Court
Westfield, IN 46074
800-337-1243

Manufactures top quality nipples and nipple wrench in many different sizes for musket caps as well as all standard percussion caps. Ron Blomquist says "Call us with any questions." Ideal contact for shooters having a problem finding a nipple for a special firearm.

Buck Stop Lure Co., Inc.
POB 636
Stanton, MI 48888-0636
(Email)
(Website)

Lures and scents to aid the black-powder hunting in getting close for that one sure shot. Also food lures.

Buffalo Bullet Co.
12637 Los Nietos Road, Unit A
Santa Fe Springs, CA 90670
800-423-8069 (Phone)
310-944-5054 (Fax)

Complete line of muzzleloader bullets in numerous calibers and configurations, from heavy conicals to round balls ranging from 32-caliber to 58-caliber. Makes an interesting 125-grain 36-caliber bullet for fast-twist rifles in this caliber. Conical revolver bullets, too, in calibers 36, 44, and 45. Also a T.C.P. bullet (Total Copper Plated), 50-caliber with sabot.

Burris Co., Inc.
331 East 8th Street
Greeley, CO 80631-9559
970-356-1670 (Phone)
888-228-7747 (Toll Free)
(Website)

Scopes for modern muzzleloaders, such as the handsome and compact 2.5X-8X Whitetail, along with bases and rings, plus binoculars and spotting scopes for the blackpowder hunter.

Bushnell Performance Optics
9200 Cody
Overland Park, KS 66214
913-752-3400 (Phone)
913-752-3350 (Fax)
(Website)

Super high resolution telescopic rifle sights, such as the Bushnell Elite 4200 series, especially the exceptional 2.5X-10X with 50mm objective lens and precise click adjustments, along with a special reverse porro prism binocular, the 12x50 Elite Waterproof, for blackpowder hunters who excel in the spot and stalk method of finding and getting close to big game.

Butler Creek
290 Arden Drive
Belgrade, MT 59714
503-722-5790 (Phone)
503-655-4310 (Fax)
(Website)

Long time in the business of supplying excellent blackpowder accouterments by Michaels of Oregon Co., including the Lightning Loader®, Hot Shot® nipple, touchhole liners, and much more.

CCI/Speer-Blount, Inc.
2299 Snake River Avenue
Lewiston, ID 83501
208-746-2351 (Phone)
208-798-3392 (Fax)

Well-known for excellent CCI percussion caps, now also in musket size, along with Speer high-precision swaged round balls.

Cimarron Firearms Co.
POB 906
Fredericksburg, TX 78624-0906
830-997-9090 (Phone)
830-997-0802 (Fax)
(Email)

(Website)

Full line of Cowboy Action firearms, including Sheriff's Model Colt replica, the Frontier with 7 -inch barrel, custom engraved models, special handles, cap and ball revolvers—a factory engraved Paterson 36-caliber—the big Walker model, also Henry rifle, 1873 Winchester copy, and more.

C. Sharps Arms. Co., Inc.
POB 885
Big Timber, MT 59011
406-932-4353 (Phone)
406-932-4443 (Fax)
(Website)
(Email)

Makers of a multitude of single-shot breechloading rifles in numerous calibers, not only Sharps replicas, but also the 1885 Highwall Sporting Rifle. Also an 1885 Highwall Classic Rifle available in 18-inch to 24-inch barrel lengths. Cartridges for these rifles include the 40-50 Sharps, 45-70 Government, 45-120 Sharps, and many others.

Cabin Creek Muzzleloading
50 West Beaver Street
Hellam, PA 17406
717-757-5841 (Phone)

This Co. boasts "all manner of repair work," and could be a choice for the shooter who has a firearm in need of fixing, or an original requiring repairs for show and tell purposes, and not for shooting.

Cape Outfitters, Inc.
599 Co. Rd. 206
Cape Girardeau, MO 63701
573-335-6260 (Phone)
573-335-1555 (Fax)

Makes of beautiful deluxe Vernier silhouette long-range or mid-range tang sights with two different windage adjustments, one for gross adjustment, the other for fine tuning adjustment. Also a Beach Front Sight reproduction of the original with both globe and blade in one unit.

Cash Manufacturing Co.
POB 130
Waunakee, WI 53597-0130
608-849-5664 (Phone)
(Website)

Beautifully crafted muzzleloader accouterments in a wide variety, including in-line and magazine style cappers for regular percussion caps as well as musket size and 209 primers. One model is good for in-line rifles. Dozens of old-time pieces, including handsome cap and tinder boxes, flash cups, including a flash guard for musket-size nipples. Sights, barrel wedges, the list runs long.

Circle Fly Shotgun Wads
4314 Dale Williamson Road
Union, KY 41091
859-689-5100 (Phone)
(Website)

Circle Fly Shotgun Wads provides a complete line for the black-powder shotgun, including excellent over-powder sealers at reasonable prices. Orders can be taken directly by phone or through regular mail. Wads for shotgun gauges 6, 7, 8, 9, 10, 11, 12, 13, 14, 15, 16, 17, 18, 19, 20, 24, 28 and .410 are available, along with rifle/pistol wads in calibers 32, 38, 40, 45, and 50.

Connecticut Valley Arms
5988 Peachtree Corners East
Norcross, GA 30071
800-320-8767 (Phone)
770-242-8546 (Fax)
(Email)
(Website)

Powerful magnum in-line muzzleloaders in various models with bullet guiding recessed muzzle to properly align conical projectiles, plus popular non-replica St. Louis Hawken 50- or 54-caliber sidelock, along with a Mountain Rifle 50-caliber with 1:66 rate of twist for accurate patched ball shooting. Shotguns, too, with accessories, including shot/powder pouch, shotgun measure, and wads. Long line of useful accessories.

Crazy Crow Trading Post
POB 847 D-5
Pottsboro, TX 75076-0847
800-786-6210 (Phone orders)
903-786-0847 (Fax)
(Email)
(Website)

The rendezvous fan will find a wealth of supplies here, such as a brazier made of sheet iron patterned after a cooking tool used from the Revolution to the 19th century. Iron skillet with a rolled handle to accept "any length of stick," as well as knives, blankets, and many other items for the buckskinner's kit.

Deer Creek Products
POB 246
Waldron, IN 46182
765-525-6181 (Phone)
765-525-9595 (Fax)

Items for Civil War reenactment to hunting, including firearms from the major players as well as muzzleloader supplies and accessories. Still Mowrey Gun Works, with its interesting design. Rifles and shotguns available.

Dixie Gun Works
POB 130
Gunpowder Lane
Union City, TN 38281
731-885-0700 (Phone)
731-885-0440 (Fax)

800-238-6785 (Phone Orders Only)
(Website)

Wonderfully overwhelming catalog of just about anything a blackpowder shooter/hunter, re-enactor, buckskinner, or for that matter, casual plinker could ask for, including a long-barreled 32-caliber squirrel rifle, as well as The Early American Jaeger, a 54-caliber flintlock patterned after the German rifle that made its way to America.

Don Eades Muzzleloader Builder's Supply
HCR 62 – Box 125
Ozone, AR 72854
501-292-8868 (Phone)
501-292-8867 (Fax)

Rifle building parts including barrels, locks, triggers, stocks, browning solutions, wood stains, and much more. Huge parts list. Barrels from 32- through 62-caliber in lengths from 36 to 42 inches. Visa/MasterCard okay.

Dynamit Nobel
81 Ruckman Road
Closter, NJ 07624
201-767-1995 (Phone)
201-767-1589 (Fax)

Several different types of percussion caps, including ribbed and "smooth, no flanges," plus four-flanges with the musket cap.

E.M.F. Co.
1900 East Warner Avenue 1-D
Santa Ana, CA 92705
714-261-6611 (Phone)
714-756-0133 (Fax)

Hartford and Dakota single-action revolvers for the Cowboy Action fan or hunter, along with Premier 1892 rifles, specializing in imported guns from various manufacturers.

Gibbs Rifle Co., Inc.
211 Lawn Street
Martinsburg, WV 25401
304-262-1651 (Phone)
304-262-1658 (Fax)
(Email)
(Website)

Valmore Forgett III calls his Co. the place to find "quality collectible firearms, historic replicas,

and more." Offers information through the Gibbs Military Collectibles Club, along with a *Gibbs Military Journal.*

GOEX Black Powder Co.
POB 659
Doyline, LA 71023-0659
318-382-9300 (Phone)
318-382-9303 (Fax)
(Website)

Long-time producers of GOEX blackpowder in many grades, including Cartridge, as well as Fg, FFg, FFFg, and FFFFg. Also makers of Clear Shot, a blackpowder substitute known for clean its burning properties. Importing economical blackpowder also.

Golden Age Arms Co.
POB 366
Ashley, OH 43003
740-747-2488 (Phone)

The Golden Age Custom Vincent Percussion Full Stock Rifle Kit contains pre-carved curly maple stock, rifle barrel in calibers 32, 36, 40, or 45, breech plug, L&R Durs Egg lock, double set Davis triggers, and other parts, along with instruction book. Co. also has muzzleloader supplies and books.

Hawgs Limited
POB 279
Manton, MI 49663
231-824-6040 (Phone)
800-282-4294 (Phone Orders)
231-824-6205 (Fax)
(Website)

Complete line of synthetic lures and scents especially for deer hunting, along with an interesting video, "Make Whitetails Hunt You," 50 minutes of new ways to create "scent magnets" for deer.

Euroarms of America
P.O. Box 3277
Winchester, VA 22604
540-662-1863

Enfield military rifles in many different models, including the 1853 Enfield 3 Band musket, 58-caliber,

1858 Enfield 2 Band, also 58-caliber, and the 58-caliber Enfield 1861 Musketoon. Also Mississippi Rifle, 1803 Harper's Ferry, CS Richards, and others.

Green Mountain
Rifle Barrel Co., Inc.
POB 2670
Conway, NH 03818
603-447-1095 (Phone)

Makers of barrels found on many commercial muzzleloaders, along with upgrade replacement barrels that convert a round ball rifle to conical-shooter with faster rate of twist.

Hodgdon Powder Co.
POB 2932
Shawnee Mission, KS 66201
913-362-9455 (Phone)
913-362-1307 (Fax)
(Email)
(Website)

Hodgdon Powder Co. is famous for Pyrodex, a blackpowder substitute with a well-earned reputation for its clean-burning characteristics requiring no swabbing between shots at the range for a reasonable number of loads. Also the Pyrodex Pellet in various dimensions and volume-equivalent charges.

Hoppe's
A Brunswick Co.
Airport Industrial Mall
Coatesville, PA 19320
610-384-6000 (Phone)
610-857-5980 (Fax)
(Email)
(Website)

Special blackpowder cleaning kits convenient, complete, and ready to go to work on muzzleloaders. Also numerous solvents, plus excellent bristle brushes and other blackpowder accessories. Ear and eye protection products, plus cases to safeguard the muzzleloader on trips to the range or hunting field.

Hornady Manufacturing Co.
POB 1848
Grand Island, NE 68803
308-382-1390 (Phone)
308-382-5761 (Fax)
(Website)

Superb swaged round balls in many sizes, including a 45-grain 32-caliber sphere for squirrel rifles. Also a special powder measure safe with blackpowder. Many other items for the interested shooter, as this Co.'s website shows.

Kadooty Mfg. LLC
842 S. Tamela Drive
Lake Charles, LA 70605
337-477-7502 (Phone)
337-477-0213 (Fax)
(Email)

The Kadooty is a multi-use loading rod that provides the same pressure upon the projectile, and therefore the powder charge, from shot to shot for highest uniformity. Used in test laboratories, for instruction, competition, hunting, on-the-range shooting. Made of finest materials for indefinite service.

Log Cabin Shop
POB 275
Lodi, OH 44254
330-948-1082 (Phone)
800-837-1082 (Phone Orders)
330-948-4307 (Fax)
(Website)

This Co. has been around for a long time with a good reputation for delivering good products, with a large catalog showing hundreds of items from blackpowder firearms kits, barrels, stocks, over 800 book titles, and much more.

Lyman Products Corporation
475 Smith Street
Middletown, CT 06457
860-632-2020 (Phone)
800-225-9626 (Phone Orders)
(Email)
(Website)

Long-lived American Co. providing the blackpowder shooter with numerous dies for casting bullets, along with a special powder measure safe with blackpowder, plus muzzleloaders, such as the Great Plains Rifle and the Plains Pistol, along with chemicals, such as Butch's Bore Shine and super cleaning patches

Marlin Firearms Co.
100 Kenna Drive
North Haven, CT 06473
203-239-5621 (Phone)
203-234-7991 (Fax)
(Website)

Lever-action firearms representing days gone by from this old and well-established American Co..

Millennium Designed
Muzzleloaders, Ltd.
RR1 – Box 405
Maidstone, VT 05905
802-676-3311 (Phone)
802-676-3322 (Fax)
(Email)

(Website)

Modern in-line muzzleloaders, including the Buckwacka and M2K series with No. 209 shotgun primer ignition, along with a line of accessories. The Buckwacka is a break-open design, calibers 50 or 12 gauge, with closed breech. The M2K series is bolt-action, 50-caliber.

Morrison Precision
6719 Calle Mango
Hereford, AZ 85615
520-378-6207

Makers of high precision barrels using the cut-rifling process. Morrison barrels are noted for supreme accuracy.

Mountain State Muzzleloading
Supplies, Inc.
Route 2 - Box 154-1
Williamstown, WV 26187
304-375-7842 (Phone)
800-445-1776 (Phone – Orders Only)
304-375-3737 (Fax)

(Website)

Rich catalog filled with fine guns and tools for the blackpowder shooter, including hundreds of accouterments, along with mountain man rendezvous supplies and many pre-carved stocks for the builder. Home of the Spitfire Magnum Musket Nipple for both in-line and sidelock firearms in several thread sizes.

Muzzleload Magnum Products
518 Buck Hollow Lane
Harrison, AR 72601
870-741-5019 (Phone)
870-741-3104 (Fax)
(Website)

Muzzleload Magnum Products has the MMP Sabot in many variations to suit different bullets and even different loads. The Co. also boasts a "vast selection of jacketed, cast or swaged pistol and specialty bullets."

Muzzleloading Technologies, Inc.
POB 696
Tooele, UT 84074
435-843-4200 (Phone)
435-843-4210 (Fax)

(Email)
(Website)

New line of White muzzleloading rifles along with special bullets and accessories. Custom shop produces White muzzleloading rifles, sidelocks, and flintlocks.

Naval Ordnance Works and Foundry
Route 2, Box 919
Shepherdstown, WV 25443
304-876-0998 (Phone)

Naval Ordnance Works manufactures an amazing number of projectiles in calibers ranging from .228 through .998, including Minie balls, along with simply huge bullets in monster bore sizes. L.E. Hull, the proprietor, knows his business and exhibits a great deal of interest in creating special bullets for special guns, including muzzleloaders and blackpowder cartridges.

Navy Arms Co.
689 Bergen Blvd.
Ridgefield, NJ 07657-1499
201-945-2500 (Phone)
201-945-6895 (Fax)
(Email)
(Website)

The Navy Arms Co. is home to a multitude of excellent replica firearms, not only regard to several Sharps models, but also an 1873 Springfield Cavalry Carbine Trap-door, along with the Infantry version of the same rifle, plus several Remington Rolling Blocks, the Henry rifle in different styles, along with numerous blackpowder cartridge rifles and revolvers, the top break Schofield among them. Also the 1892 lever-action rifle in 44-40 Winchester or 45 Colt chambering. Accouterments and Navy Arms musket caps.

Nosler, Inc.
POB 671
Bend, OR 97709
541-382-3921 (Phone)
541-388-4667 (Fax)
(Website)

The famous Nosler Partition Bullet is now available in .451-inch diameter in sabot, 260-grain weight, accurate and totally reliable in muzzleloaders with certain expansion of the front half, while the shank section remains intact for penetration.

October Country Muzzleloading, Inc.
P.O. Box 969
Hayden, ID 83835
800-735-6348 (Phone)
(Email)
(Website)

Makers of some of the finest leather shooting bags available anywhere, with a large supply of powder horns and shooting supplies, including the Kap Kover to beat the rain. And Ol' Thunder Patch Lube & Bore Solvent, plus several very large bore round bore rifles of high power for big game hunting, such as the Co.'s 8-bore!

Oehler Research, Inc.
POB 9135
Austin, TX 78766
512-327-6900 (Phone)
800-531-5125 (Toll Free)
(Email)
(Website)

State if the art chronographs for the serious blackpowder shooter who wants to test not only the performance of his firearm, but also the law of diminishing returns. Also exterior ballistics software.

Old Western Scrounger, Inc.
12924 Highway A-12
Montague, CA 96064
530-459-5445 (Phone)
800-UPS-AMMO (Phone Orders)
530-459-3944 (Fax)
(Website)

The word for this Co. is "wild," with a huge line of "obsolete" cartridges now brought back to life, such as the 32-40 Winchester, or how about a 38-56 Winchester, or 40-82 Winchester? Also 45-120 Sharps loaded and ready to fire, as well as the 50-140. Gamebore blackpowder shotgun shells. Many other items in this Co.'s interesting catalog.

Oregon Trail Bullet Co.
2850 Myrtle St.
P.O. Box 529
Baker City, OR 97814-0529
800-811-0584 (Phone)
(Email)
(Website)

Home of the Laser-Cast® Silver Bullet, Oregon Trail produces a number of accurate missiles, such as bullets for Cowboy Action Shooting. One rifleman, shooting an Oregon Trail Laser-Cast® 170-grain, .309-inch bullet in an original Winchester Model 1894 rifle produced inch-size, three-shot groups at 50 yards — with iron sights. There are several good bullets for blackpowder handgun cartridges.

Orion Rifle Barrel Co.
137 Cobbler Village Road
Kalispell, MT 59901
406-257-5649 (Phone)

Jerry K. Cunningham has been long-known in the muzzleloader world as an expert in blackpowder barrel metallurgy. His Orion Co. now offers octagon barrels, especially in round ball twists, cut rifling, 1:72 rate for 50-, 54-, 58-, and 62-calibers, 1:48 for 40- and 45-calibers.

Ox-Yoke Originals, Inc.
34 West Main Street
Milo, ME 04463
800-231-8313 (Phone)
(Website)

A premium bullet lube for black-powder cartridge shooters only touches on the many shooting items from this long-standing Co.. Well-known for Wonder Lube, along with numerous maintenance tools.

Outers-Blount, Inc.
POB 38
Onalaska, WI 54650
608-781-5800 (Phone)
608-781-0368 (Fax)

Numerous firearms cleaning and maintenance products in Outers Gunslick and brand and Outers brand chemicals, also blackpowder kits and accessories, along with a terrific lineup of special targets that provide clean and clear sight pictures.

P West Enterprises
POB 2051
Owensboro, KY 43202-2051
(Website)

Makers of the Pellet Packer, three-compartment pre-loader for the blackpowder shotgun with shot compartment, lid clip to hold percussion cap (weatherproof), powder compartment, and wad/shot cup center compartment.

Pacific Rifle Co.
POB 1473
Lake Oswego, OR 97035
503-620-5154 (Phone)
(Website)

The Zephyr muzzleloading under-hammer rifle in calibers 62, 72, and 8-bore, with Genuine Forsyth Rifling™ is available from this Co., shooting large patched round balls of high weight for big game.

Parker Productions
Custom Hydraulic Conicals
691 Bluegrass Drive
Spring Creek, NV 89815
775-753-2195 (Phone)
775-753-6817 (Fax)

(Email orders)

Bullets in two designs, the Traditional Hunter™ and the Hydra-Con™, the latter unique in that it's a pure lead conical designed for muzzleloaders and Sharps-type rifles has a sealed hydraulic chamber just beneath the nose of the projectile. Upon striking the target, the medium-filled chamber causes certain expansion every time. Made in heavy weights for 45-, 50-, and 54-caliber rifles, including "Colorado Legal" bullets for that state's unique demand that a bullet for blackpowder-only hunts cannot be twice as long as its diameter.

Petro-Explo, Inc.
Elephant Black Powder
7650 US Highway 287
No. 100
Arlington, TX 76001
800-588-8282 (phone)
817-478-88891 (Fax)

(Website)

Imports high-grade blackpowder from Brazil and Switzerland. Brazil's Elephant Black Powder is offered in granulations as fine as FFFFGg (5F), while Swiss includes a special 1 Fg powder in typical hard kernel with clean-burning characteristics and high energy yield.

Prairie River Arms
1180 North Sixth Street
Princeton, IL 61356
800-445-1541 (Phone)
(Website)

Manufactures the Prairie River Bullpup modern muzzleloader, extremely compact 50-caliber in-line with "competition quality sighting" and a patented ignition system.

Rapine Bullet Moulds Mfg.
9503 Landis Lane
East Greenville, PA 18041
(Website)

Manufacturers of numerous moulds useful for muzzleloaders and blackpowder cartridge guns, including several bullets for cap 'n' ball revolvers.

Remington Arms Co., Inc.
POB 700
Madison, NC 27025-0700
800-243-9700 (Phone)
336-548-7731 (Fax)
(Website)

Boasting a thousand pages on the web, Remington has a lot to offer the blackpowder shooter, beginning with the Model 700 ML and MLS, the latter in stainless steel, camo or black composite stocks, 50-caliber bolt-action built on modified Model 700 action. Musket nipple now available. The 19th century Remington Rolling block is offered by Remington again in two models. Also muzzleloader bullets and supplies.

Ruger
Sturm, Ruger & Co.
200 Ruger Road
Prescott, AZ 86301
520-541-8820 (Phone)
520-541-8850 (Fax)
(Website)

Dedicated to blackpowder shooting with its Ruger Model 77/50 bolt-action muzzleloader based upon the excellent Model 77 Ruger bolt-action cartridge rifle, this Co. also continues with the Ruger Old Army, a cap and ball revolver in 45-caliber offered with or without target sights. Now there is also a handgun designed with Cowboy Action Shooting in mind—the Vaquero.

Savage Arms, Inc.
100 Springdale Road
Westfield, MA 01085
413-568-7001 (Phone)
413-562-7764 (Fax)
(Website)

Savage surprised the blackpowder world by bringing outs Model 10ML with smokeless powder capability based upon an entirely different system using the standard big game rifle bolt with locking lugs remaining in normal position for strength, and a special hard steel module serving to hold a No. 209 shotgun primer.

Shiloh Rifle Manufacturing
POB 279
Big Timber, MT
See C. Sharps

Spring Valley Lodges
N3515 Highway F
Brodhead, WI 53520
608-897-8474

The modern muzzleloader and all of the super hunts associated with it lead blackpowder shooter interest at the moment, but many who come to the game via an in-line front loader soon grow interested in "doing it the old way." This Co. makes tepees, wall tents, Baker tents, and lean-tos of the period.

Tentsmiths
POB 1748
Conway, NH 03818
603-447-1777 (Phone)
(Email)
(Website)

In their own words, this Co. takes "the pursuit of living history very seriously" with authentic shelters of a specific time period.

Thompson/Center Arms Co.
POB 5002
Rochester, NH 03867
603-332-2394 (Phone)
603-332-5133 (Fax)
(Website)

Makers of the powerful T/C Encore, a 50-caliber break-open modern muzzleloader fired by No. 209 shotgun primers. Also an Encore big game hunting pistol, along with a multitude of supplies from transparent powder flasks to a strong line of bullets.

Track of the Wolf, Inc.
POB 6
Osseo, MN 55369-0006
612-424-2500 (Phone)
612-424-9860 (Fax)

Parts for builders explains this Co. with its 434-page catalog. Boasts "low prices, same day shipment."

Traditions Performance Firearms
POB 776
Old Saybrook, CT 06475-0776
860-388-4656 (Phone)
860-388-4657 (Fax)

(Email)

(Website)

Long line of muzzleloading rifles both in-line and sidelock, rifles, pistols, and shotguns, cannons, too, plus many interesting and useful accessories, some in compact form ideal for the smaller shooting bag on the trail.

Venco, Inc.
15050 Berkshire Ind. Pkwy
Middlefield, OH 44062
440-834-8888 (Phone)
440-834-3388 (Fax)

(Email)

Venco's Shooter's Choice works against leftover plastic residue in the bore resulting from one-piece plastic wads in the shotgun and sabots. The Co. also offers Black Powder Cleaning Gel Bore Cleaner, as well as a lead remover. This Co. also goes under the name "Shooter's Choice."

Wildlife Research Center, Inc.
1050 McKinley Street
Anoka, MN 55303
612-427-3350 (Phone)
800-USE-LURE (Phone Orders)
612-427-8335 (Fax)

Effective cover scents in many different aromas, including oak and earth, ideal for blackpowder hunters mounting stalks on big game for a certain shot. Also a good video entitled "Hunting Scents and Scent Elimination," explaining the use of scents and lures. A Co. true to its name, with research a top priority.

WANO Schwarzpulver GmbH Black Powder
Luna Tech, Inc.
148 Moon Drive
Owens Cross Roads, AL 35763
256-725-4224 (Phone)
256-725-4811 (Fax)
(Email)

Luna Tech imports high-grade WANO blackpowder from Germany in many granulations, noted for good energy and clean burning.

BOOKS FOR
BLACKPOWDER SHOOTERS

Bookstores remain wonderful places where readers can do hands-on exploration of titles for in-print and out-of-print books. But book searching and book buying have changed immensely in recent times, especially in two ways. First, finding and purchasing a title on the Internet is now commonplace, and for the reader who does not wish to make his own search, most bookstores will perform the service for him. Even the smallest bookstores are now computer-ready to find a title for an interested buyer. Second, libraries everywhere are equipped for interlibrary loans — when a title not in their holdings is located elsewhere, even far across the country. It can be borrowed, generally for a modest fee.

The books presented here are no more than a small beginning for the interested blackpowder fan. No prices are given, as that changes in time. Furthermore, it was once difficult to find a book without knowing the publisher and the published date, today's title searches in the library, on the Internet, or bookstores are usually successful, even if only the book's name or author is known. In some cases, full information was not available, such as date or even publisher. However, because of modern book search engines on the Internet and other sources, these books are quite likely to be located now.

Action Shooting Cowboy Style, by John Taffin, Krause Publications 1999, 320 pp. Slick pages with many photos to illustrate this in-depth coverage of this American shooting game by an author dedicated to the sport.

Advanced Muzzleloader's Guide, by Toby Bridges, Stoeger Publishing Co. NJ, 1985. 256 pp., illus. A guide to muzzleloading rifles, pistols, and shotguns, both flintlock and percussion.

Advanced Black Powder Hunting, by Toby Bridges, Stoeger Publishing Co., NJ. 1998, 276 pp. Guns for the muzzleloader hunter, along with tips on hunting antelope, whitetails, and other game.

The African Adventures: A Return to the Silent Places, by Peter Hathaway Capstick, St. Martin's Press, NY, 1992. 220 pp. This book brings to life four turn-of-the-century adventurers and the savage frontier they braved, including Frederick Selous (see Chapter 46).

African Hunting and Adventure, by William Charles Baldwin, Books of Zimbabwe, Bulawayo, 1981. 451 pp. Facsimile reprint of the scarce 1863 London edition. African hunting and adventure from Natal to the Zambezi.

After Big Game in Central Africa, by Edouard Foa, St. Martin's Press, NY 1989, 400 pp. Reprint of the scarce 1899 edition. This sportsman covered 7,200 miles, mostly on foot from the Zambezi delta on the east coast to the mouth of the Congo on the west.

America's Great Gunmakers, by Wayne van Zwoll, Stoeger Publishing Co. NJ, 1992, 288 pp. This book traces in detail the evolution of guns and ammunition in America and the men who formed the companies that produced them.

American Military Shoulder Arms: Volume 1, Colonial and Revolutionary War Arms, by George D. Moller, University Press of Colorado, CO. 1993. 538 pp., illus. In-depth study of the shoulder arms of the United States. This volume covers the pre-colonial period to the end of the American Revolution.

American Military Shoulder Arms: Volume 2, From the 1790s to the End of the Flintlock Period, by George D. Moller, University Press of Colorado, CO. 1994. 496 pp., illus.
Describes rifles, muskets, carbines, and other shoulder arms used by the armed forces of the United States from the 1790s to the end of the flintlock period in the 1840s.

Antique Guns, the Collector's Guide, 2nd Edition, edited by John Traister, Stoeger Publishing Co. NJ, 1994. 320 pp. Covers vast spectrum of pre-1900 firearms manufactured by U.S. gunmakers as well as Canadian, French, German, Belgian, Spanish and other foreign firms.

Arms Makers of Maryland, by Daniel D. Hartzler, George Shumway Press, PA, 1975. 200 pp. A thorough study of the gunsmiths of Maryland who worked during the late 18th and early 19th centuries.

Baker's Remarks on the Rifle, by Ezekiel Baker, Standard Publications, Inc. (no date provided). Reproduction of his 1835 work, dealing his views on blackpowder shooting.

Black Powder Cartridge Rifle Magazine, edited by John D. Baird, Spider Hill Press, 1995.

Articles excerpted from *Black Powder Cartridge Rifles* magazine from 1980 to 1983.

Black Powder Guide, 2nd Edition, by George C. Nonte, Jr., Stoeger Publishing Co. NJ, 1991. 288 pp. How-to instructions for selection, repair, and maintenance of muzzleloaders, making your own bullets, restoring and refinishing, shooting techniques.

Blackpowder Hobby Gunsmithing, by Sam Fadala and Dale Storey, DBI Books, Inc. IL., 1994. 256 pp. A how-to-guide for gunsmithing blackpowder pistols, rifles, and shotguns.

Blackpowder Loading Manual, 3rd Edition, edited by Sam Fadala, DBI Books, Inc IL, 1995. 368 pp. Revised and expanded edition of this landmark blackpowder loading book. Covers hundreds of loads for many blackpowder rifles, handguns and shotguns.

The Blackpowder Notebook, by Sam Fadala, Wolfe Publishing Co., AZ, 1994. 212 pp.

For anyone interested in shooting muzzleloaders, this book will help improve scores and obtain accuracy and reliability.

Blue Book of Modern Black Powder Values, by Dennis Adler, Blue Book Publications, Inc., 8009 84th Avenue South, Suite 175, Minneapolis, MN 55425. 1998 A 120-page book devoted to values of blackpowder guns, including color photos.

The Blunderbuss 1500-1900, by James D. Forman, Museum Restoration Services. Ont., Canada, 1995.About the guns employed as anti-personal weapons throughout the flintlock era.

Boarders Away, Volume II: Firearms of the Age of Fighting Sail, by William Gilkerson, Andrew Mowbray, Inc. Publishers, RI, 1993. 331 pp. Covers pistols, muskets, combustibles, and small cannons used aboard American and European fighting ships, 1626-1826.

Boss & Co. Builders of Best Guns Only, by Donald Dallas, Safari Press, CA, 1996. 336 pp.

The famous London gunmaker Boss & Company is chronicled from founding by Thomas Boss (1790 - 1857) to the present day.

Breech-Loading Carbines of the United States Civil War Period, by Brig. Gen. John Pitman, Armory Publi-cations, WA, 1987. The first in a series of previously unpublished manuscripts originated by the late Brigadier General John Putnam. Exploded drawings showing parts actual size follow each sectioned illustration.

The Breech-Loading Single-Shot Rifle, by Maj. Ned H. Roberts and Kenneth L. Waters, Wolfe Publishing Co., AZ, 1995. 333 pp. A comprehensive and complete history of the evolution of the Schuetzen and single-shot rifle.

British Military Firearms 1650-1850, by Howard L. Blackmore, Stackpole Books, PA, 1994. 224 pp. Another definitive work on British military firearms.

The British Shotgun, Volume 1, 1850-1870, by I.M. Crudington and D.J. Baker, Barrie & Jenkins, London 1979. 256 pp. An attempt to trace, as accurately as possible, the evolution of the shotgun during its formative years in Great Britain.

The British Shotgun, Volume 2, 1871-1890, by I.M. Crudginton and D.J. Baker, Ashford Press, Southampton, 1989. 250 pp. The second volume of a definitive work on the evolution and manufacture of the British shotgun.

The British Soldier's Firearms from Smoothbore to Rifled Arms, 1850-1864, by Dr. C.H. Roads, R&R Books, Livonia, NY, 1994. 332 pp., illus. A reprint of the classic text covering the development of British military hand and shoulder firearms in the crucial years between 1850 and 1864.

Carbines of the Civil War, by John D. McAulay, Pioneer Press, Union City, TN, 1981. 123 pp. A guide for the student and collector of the colorful arms used by the Federal cavalry.

Cartridges of the World, 9th Edition, by Frank Barnes, edited by M. L. McPherson, Krause Publications, Iola, WI. 512 pp, illus. General-purpose reference work for collectors, police, scientists and laymen for answers to cartridge identification and ballistics questions.

Civil War Breech Loading Rifles, by John D. McAulay, Andrew Mowbray, Inc., Lincoln, RI, 1991. 144 pp., illus. Paper covers. All the major breech-loading rifles of the Civil War and most, if not all, of the obscure types are detailed, illustrated and set in their historical context.

Civil War Carbines Volume 2: The Early Years, by John D. McAulay, Andrew Mowbray, Inc., Lincoln, RI, 1991. 144 pp., illus. Paper covers. Covers the carbines made during the exciting years leading up to the outbreak of war and used by the North and South in the conflict.

Civil War Pistols, by John D. McAulay, Andrew Mowbray Inc., Lincoln, RI, 1992. 166 pp., illus. A survey of the handguns used during the American Civil War.

Collector's Illustrated Encyclopedia of the American Revolution, by George C. Neumann and Frank J. Kravic, Rebel Publishing Co., Inc., Texarkana, TX, 1989. 286 pp. A showcase of more than 2,300 artifacts made, worn, and used by those who fought in the War for Independence.

Colonial Frontier Guns, by T.M. Hamilton, Pioneer Press, Union City, TN, 1988. 176 pp., illus. Paper covers. A complete study of early flint muskets of this country.

The Colt Armory, by Ellsworth Grant, Man-at-Arms Bookshelf, Lincoln, RI, 1996. 232 pp. About the manufacturing house that built Colts.

Colt Heritage, by R.L. Wilson, Simon & Schuster, 1979. 358 pp. illus. The official history of Colt firearms, 1836 to the present.

Colt Blackpowder Reproductions & Replicas, by Dennis Adler, Blue Book Publications, Inc., 8009 34th Ave. So. Suite 175, Minneapolis, MN 55425. As the title promises, a look at collector valued Colt firearms, originals and replicas.

Colt Peacemaker British Model, by Keith Cochran, Cochran Publishing Co., Rapid City, SD, 1989. 160 pp. Covers those revolvers Colt squeezed in while completing a large order of revolvers for the U.S. Cavalry in early 1874, to those magnificent cased target revolvers used in the pistol competitions at Bisley Commons in the 1890s.

Colt Peacemaker Encyclopedia, by Keith Cochran, Keith Cochran, Rapid City, SD, 1986. 434 pp. A must-have book for the Peacemaker collector.

Colt Peacemaker Encyclopedia, Volume 2, by Keith Cochran, Cochran Publishing Co., SD, 1992. 416 pp. Included in this volume are extensive notes on engraved, inscribed, historical and noted revolvers, as well as those revolvers used by outlaws, lawmen, movie and television stars.

Colt Percussion Accoutrements 1834-1873, by Robin Rapley, Robin Rapley, Newport Beach, CA, 1994. 432 pp. The complete collector's guide to the identification of Colt percussion accoutrements; including Colt conversions and their values.

Colt Revolvers and the U.S. Navy 1865-1889, by C. Kenneth Moore, Dorrance and Co., Bryn Mawr, PA, 1987, 140 pp. The Navy's use of Colt handguns and other revolvers during this era of change.

Colt Rifles and Muskets from 1847-1870, by Herbert Houze, Krause Publications, Iola, WI, 1996. 192 pp. Discover previously unknown Colt models along with an extensive list of production figures for all models.

Colt's Dates of Manufacture 1837-1978, by R.L. Wilson, published by Maurie Albert, Coburg, Australia; N.A. distributor I.D.S.A. Books, Hamilton, OH, 1983. 61 pp.

Valuable pocket guide to the dates of manufacture of Colt firearms up to 1978.

Colt's 100th Anniversary Firearms Manual 1836-1936: A Century of Achievement, Wolfe Publishing Co., Prescott, AZ, 1992. 100 pp. Originally published by the Colt Patent Firearms Co., this booklet covers the history, manufacturing procedures and the guns of the first 100 years of the genius of Samuel Colt.

The Colt Whitneyville-Walker Pistol, by Lt. Col. Robert D. Whittington, Brownlee Books, Hooks, TX, 1984. 96 pp., illus. Limited edition. A study of the pistol and associated characters 1846-1851.

The Complete Blackpowder Handbook, 3rd Edition, by Sam Fadala, Krause Publications, WI. 1996. 416 pp. Expanded and refreshed edition of the definitive book on the subject of blackpowder.

The Complete Guide to Game Care and Cookery, 3rd Edition, by Sam and Nancy Fadala, Krause Publications, WI. 1994. 320 pp Over 500 photos illustrating the care of wild game in the field and at home with a separate recipe section providing over 400 tested recipes. A must for the blackpowder hunter who wants the best from his game.

Confederate Revolvers, by William A. Gary, Taylor Publishing Co., Dallas, TX, 1987. 174 pp. Comprehensive work on the rarest of Confederate weapons.

Cowboy Action Shooting, by Charly Gullett, Wolfe Publishing Co., Prescott, AZ, 1995. 400 pp. Comprehensive covered of the guns, loads, tactics, fun and flavor of this Old West era competition.

Development of the Henry Cartridge and Self-Contained Cartridges for the Toggle-Link Winchesters, by R. Bruce McDowell, A.M.B., Metuchen, NJ, 1984. 69 pp. From powder and ball to the self-contained metallic cartridge.

Early American Waterfowling, 1700s-1930, by Stephen Miller, Winchester Press, NJ, 1986. 256 pp. Two centuries of literature and art devoted to the nation's beloved hunting sport of waterfowling.

Early Indian Trade Guns: 1625-1775, by T.M. Hamilton, Museum of the Great Plains, Lawton, OK, 1968. 34 pp. Detailed descriptions of subject arms, compiled from early records and from the study of remnants found in Indian country.

East Africa and its Big Game, by Captain Sir John C. Willowghby, Wolfe Publishing Co., Prescott, AZ, 1999, 312 pp. A deluxe limited edition reprint of the scarce 1889 edition of a narrative of a sporting trip from Zanzibar to the borders of the Masai.

English Pistols: The Armories of H.M. Tower of London Collection, by Howard L. Blackmore, Arms and

Armour Press, London, England, 1985. 64 pp. All the pistols described and pictured are from this famed collection by this expert on the subject.

European Firearms in Swedish Castles, by Kaa Wennberg, Bohuslaningens Boktryckeri AB, Uddevalla, Sweden, 1986. 156 pp. The famous collection of Count Keller, the Ettersburg Castle collection, and others. English text.

Fifteen Years in the Hawken Lode, by John D. Baird, The Gun Room Press, Highland Park, NJ, 1976. 120 pp. A collection of thoughts and observations gained from many years of intensive study of the guns from the shop of the Hawken brothers.

1851 Colt Navies, by Nathan L. Swayze, The Gun Room Press, Highland Park, NJ, 1993. 243 pp. A study of the different 1851 Colt Navy models.

Flayderman's Guide to Antique American Firearms and Their Values, 7th Edition, by Norm Flayderman, Krause Publications, WI, 1998, 656pp. Updated edition of this bible of the antique gun field.

Frank and George Freund and the Sharps Rifle, by Gerald O. Kelver, Gerald O. Kelver, Brighton, CO, 1986. 60 pp. A guide to the Sharps rifle.

French Military Weapons, 1717-1938, Major James E. Hicks, N. Flayderman & Co., Publishers, New Milford, CT, 1973. 281 pp. Firearms, swords, bayonets, ammunition, artillery, ordnance equipment of the French army.

The Frontier Rifleman, by H.B. LaCrosse Jr., Pioneer Press, Union City, TN, 1989. 183 pp. Dealing with the subject promised by the title, riflemen of the frontier era in America.

Game Guns & Rifles: Percussion to Hammerless Ejector in Britain, by Richard Akehurst, Trafalgar Square, N. Pomfret, VT, 1993. 192 pp. Long considered a classic, this important reprint covers the period of British gunmaking between 1830-1900.

George Schreyer, Sr. and Jr., Gunmakers of Hanover, Pennsylvania, by George Shumway, George Shumway Publishers, York, PA, 1990. 160pp. This monograph is a detailed photographic study of almost all known surviving long rifles and smoothbore guns made by highly regarded gunsmiths George Schreyer, Sr. and Jr.

The Golden Age of Remington, by Robert W.D. Ball, Krause Publications, WI, 1995. 208 pp. For Remington collectors or firearms historians, this book provides a pictorial history of Remington through World War I. Includes value guide.

Grand Old Shotguns, by Don Zutz, Shotgun Sports Magazine, Auburn, CA, 1955, 136 pp. Don Zutz is one of the country's most recognized authorities on shotguns. This is a study of the great smoothbores, their history and how and why they were discontinued. Find out the most sought-after and which were the best shooters.

Great British Gunmakers: The Mantons 1782-1878, by D.H.L. Back, Historical Firearms, Norwich, England, 1994. 218 pp. Contains detailed descriptions of all the firearms made by members of this famous family.

Great Irish Gunmakers: Messrs. Rigby 1760-1869, by D.H.L. Back, Historical Firearms, Norwich, England, 1993. 196 pp. The history of this famous firm of Irish gunmakers illustrated with a wide selection of Rigby arms.

Great Shooters of the World, by Sam Fadala, Stoeger Publishing Co., NJ . 288 pp. Book offers gun enthusiasts an overview of the men and women who have forged the history of firearms over the past 150 years.

A Guide to the Maynard Breechloader, by George J. Layman, George J. Layman, Ayer, MA, 1993, 125 pp. Dedicated entirely to the Maynard family of breechloading firearms. Coverage of the arms is given from the 1850s through the 1880s.

Gun and Camera in Southern Africa, by H. Anderson Bryden, Wolfe Publishing Co., AZ, 1989. 201 pp. A limited edition reprint. The year was 1893 and author Bryden wandered for a year in Bechuanaland and the Kalahari Desert hunting the white rhino, lechwe, eland, and more.

The Gun and Its Development, by W.W. Greener, Bonanza Books reprint, no date. 807 pp. Greener's classic on firearms through the ages. A must-have book.

Gun Collecting, by Geoffrey Boothroyd, Sportsman's Press, London, 1989. 208 pp. Comprehensive list of 19th-century British gunmakers and gunsmiths.

Gun Digest 2002, 56th Annual Edition, edited by Ken Ramage, Krause Publications, WI 2001. 560 pp. Full-scale catalog of firearms, including blackpowder guns, plus articles of interest for any shooter.

Gun Tools, Their History and Identification by James B. Shaffer, Lee A. Rutledge and R. Stephen Dorsey, Collector's Library, Eugene, OR, 1992. 375 pp. Written history of foreign and domestic gun tools from the flintlock period to WWII.

Gunmakers of London 1350-1850, by Howard L. Blackmore, George Shumway Publisher, York, PA, 1986. 222 pp. A listing of all the known workmen of gun making in the first 500 years, plus a history of the guilds, cutlers, armourers, founders, blacksmiths, etc. 260 gunmarks are illustrated.

Guns and Gunmaking Tools of Southern Appalachia, by John Rice Irwin, Schiffer Publishing Ltd.,

1983. 118 pp. An illustrated guide to firearms from this unique American setting.

The story of the Kentucky Rifle. Guns of the Wild West, by George Markham, Sterling Publishing Co., New York, NY, 1993. 160 pp. As the title promises, information on this great rifle of the Golden Age of American firearms.

Firearms of the American Frontier, 1849-1917. Gunsmiths of Illinois, by Curtis L. Johnson, George Shumway Publishers, York, PA, 1995. 160 pp. Genealogical information provided for nearly one thousand gunsmiths. Contains hundreds of illustrations of rifles and other guns, of handmade origin, from Illinois.

The Gunsmiths of Manhattan, 1625-1900: A Checklist of Tradesmen, by Michael H. Lewis, Museum Restoration Service, Bloomfield, Ont., Canada, 1991. 40 pp. This listing of more than 700 men in the arms trade in New York City prior to about the end of the 19th century will provide a guide for identification and further research.

The Handgun, by Geoffrey Boothroyd, David and Charles, North Pomfret, VT, 1989. 566 pp. Every chapter deals with an important period in handgun history from the 14th century to the present.

The Hawken Rifle: Its Place in History, by Charles E. Hanson, Jr., The Fur Press, Chadron, NE, 1979. 104 pp. A definitive work on this famous rifle.

Hawken Rifles, The Mountain Man's Choice, by John D. Baird, The Gun Room Press, Highland Park, NJ, 1976. 95 pp. Covers the rifles developed for the Western fur trade. Numerous specimens described and shown photographically.

Historic Pistols: The American Martial Flintlock 1760-1845, by Samuel E. Smith and Edwin W. Bitter, The Gun Room Press, Highland Park, NJ, 1986. 353 pp. Covers over 70 makers and 163 models of American martial arms.

Historical Hartford Hardware, by William W. Dalrymple, Colt Collector Press, Rapid City, SD, 1976. 42 pp. Guns of the Hartford factory.

The History and Development of Small Arms Ammunition, Volume 1, by George A. Hoyem, Armory Publications, Oceanside, CA, 1991. 230 pp. Historical treatise on ammunition, including military musket, rifle, carbine and primitive machine gun cartridges of the 18th and 19th centuries, together with the firearms that chambered them.

The History and Development of Small Arms Ammunition, Volume 2, by George A. Hoyem, Armory Publications, Oceanside, CA, 1991. 303 pp. Covers the blackpowder military centerfire rifle, carbine, machine gun and volley gun ammunition used in 28 nations and dominions, together with the firearms that chambered them.

The History of Winchester Firearms 1866-1992, sixth edition, updated, expanded, and revised by Thomas Henshaw, New Win Publishing, NJ, 1993. 280 pp. This pathos classic is the standard reference for all collectors and others seeking the facts about any Winchester firearm, old or new.

History of Winchester Repeating Arms Company, by Herbert G. Houze, Krause Publications, Iola, WI, 1994. 800 pp. The complete Winchester history from 1856-1981.

Hodgdon Data Manual No. 26, Hodgdon Powder Co., Shawnee Mission, KS, 1993. 797 pp. Includes Hercules, Winchester and Dupont powders; data on cartridge cases; loads; silhouette; shotshell; Pyrodex and blackpowder; conversion factors; weight equivalents, etc.

Home Gunsmithing the Colt Single Action Revolvers, by Loren W. Smith, Ray Riling Arms Books, Co., Philadelphia, PA, 1995, 119 pp. Affords the Colt Single Action owner detailed, pertinent information on the operating and servicing of this famous and historic handgun.

How-To's for the Black Powder Cartridge Rifle Shooter, by Paul A. Matthews, Wolfe Publishing Co., Prescott, AZ, 1995. 45 pp. Covers lube recipes, good bore cleaners and over-powder wads. Tips include compressing powder charges, combating wind resistance, improving ignition and much more from a highly knowledgeable shooter.

Hunting in Many Lands, by Theodore Roosevelt and George Bird Grinnell, The Boone and Crockett Club, Dumfries, VA, 1987. 447 pp. Limited edition reprint of this 1895 classic work on hunting in Africa, India, Mongolia, etc.

Illustrations of United States Military Arms 1776-1903 and Their Inspector's Marks, compiled by Turner Kirkland, Pioneer Press, Union City, TN. 367pp. Reprinted from the 1949 Bannerman catalog. Valuable information for both the advanced and beginning collector.

Indian Hunts and Indian Hunters of the Old West, by Dr. Frank C. Hibben, Safari Press, Long Beach, CA, 1989. 228 pp. Tales of some of the most famous American Indian hunters of the Old West as told to the author by an old Navajo hunter.

Indian War Cartridge Pouches, Boxes and Carbine Boots, by R. Stephen Dorsey, Collector's Library, Eugene, OR, 1993. 156 pp. The key reference work to the cartridge pouches, boxes, carbine sockets and boots of the Indian War period 1865-1890.

An Introduction to the Civil War Small Arms, by Earl J. Coates and Dean S. Thomas, Thomas Publishing Co., Gettysburg, PA, 1990. 96 pp. The small arms carried by the individual soldier during the Civil War.

Jaeger Rifles, by George Shumway, George Shumway Publisher, York, PA, 1994. 108 pp. Thirty-six articles previously published in Muzzle Blasts are reproduced here. They deal with late17th- and 18th-century rifles from Vienna, Carlsbad, Bavaria, Saxony, Brandenburg, Suhl, North-Central Germany, and the Rhine Valley.

Journals of Lewis & Clark, by Bernard DeVoto, Houghton Mifflin, Boston, 1953, 506 pp, author presents the *Journals* intact, with studious and well-researched comments on the adventures of Lewis & Clark.

Journal of a Trapper, by Osborne Russell, Edited by Aubrey L. Haines, University of Nebraska Press, Lincoln, 1965, 191 pp. Haines leaves intact the fascinating report of this real life mountain man. Included: good index and notes by the author, with considerable sources listed.

The Kentucky Rifle, by Captain John G.W. Dillin, George Shumway Publisher, York, PA, 1993. 221 pp. Well-known book was the first attempt to tell the story of the American long rifle. This edition retains the original text and illustrations with supplemental footnotes provided by Dr. George Shumway.

Loading the Black Powder Rifle Cartridge, by Paul A Matthews, Wolfe Publishing Co., Prescott, AZ, 1993. 121 pp. Author Matthews brings the blackpowder cartridge shooter valuable information on the basics, including cartridge care, lubes and moulds, powder charges and developing and testing loads in his usual authoritative style.

Loading the Peacemaker, by Dave Scovill, Wolfe Publishing Co., Prescott, AZ, 1995, 227 pp. A comprehensive work about the most famous revolver ever made, including extensive load data by a trusted expert on the subject.

Longrifles of North Carolina, by John Bivens, George Shumway Publisher, York, PA, 1988. 256 pp. Covers art and evolution of the rifle, immigration and trade movements. Committee of Safety gunsmiths, characteristics of the North Carolina rifle.

Longrifles of Pennsylvania, Jefferson, Clarion & Elk Counties, by Russel H. Harringer, George Shumway Publisher, York, PA, 1984. 200 pp. Treatment in great detail of specific long rifles and gunsmiths of Pennsylvania by a dedicated student of the guns, the period, and the geographical area.

Lyman Cast Bullet Handbook, 3rd Edition, edited by C. Kenneth Ramage, Lyman Publications, Middlefield, CT, 1980. 416 pp. Information on more than 5,000 tested cast-bullet loads and 19 pages of trajectory and wind-drift tables for cast bullets.

Lyman Black Powder Handbook, ed. by Sam Fadala, Lyman Products for Shooters, Middlefield, CT, 2001, 336 pp. Comprehensive load information for the modern blackpowder shooter, with hundreds of loads for a long range of calibers.

The Manufacture of Gunflints, by Sydney B.J. Skertchly, facsimile reprint with new introduction by Seymour de Lotbiniere, Museum Restoration Service, Ontario, Canada, 1984. 90 pp. Limited edition reprinting of the very scarce London edition of 1879.

Massachusetts Military Shoulder Arms 1784-1877, by George D. Moller, Andrew Mowbray Publisher, Lincoln, RI, 1989. 250 pp. A scholarly and heavily researched study of the military shoulder arms used by Massachusetts during the 90-year period following the Revolutionary War.

Military Bolt Action Rifles, 1841-1918, by Donald B. Webster, Museum Restoration Service, Alexander Bay, NY, 1993. 150 pp. A photographic survey of the principal rifles and carbines of the European and Asiatic powers of the last half of the 19th century and the first years of the 20th century.

Military Handguns of France 1858-1958, by Eugene Medlin and Jean Huon, Excalibur Publications, Latham, NY, 1994. 124 pp. The first book written in English that provides students of arms with a thorough history of French military handguns.

The More Complete Cannoneer, by M.C. Switlik, Museum & Collectors Specialties Co., Monroe, MI, 1990. 199 pp. Compiled agreeably to the regulations for the U.S. War Department, 1861, and containing current observations on the use of antique cannon.

More Single Shot Rifles, by James C. Grant, The Gun Room Press, Highland Park, NJ, 1976. 324 pp. Details the guns made by Frank Wesson, Milt Farrow, Holden, Borchardt, Stevens, Remington, Winchester, Ballard and Peabody-Martini.

Mortimer, the Gunmakers, 1753-1923, by H. Lee Munson, Andrew Mowbray Inc., Lincoln, RI, 1992. 320 pp. Seen through a single, dominant, English gunmaking dynasty this fascinating study provides a window into the classical era of firearms artistry.

The Muzzle-Loading Cap Lock Rifle, by Ned H. Roberts, reprinted by Wolfe Publishing Co., Prescott, AZ, 1991. Originally published in 1940, this fascinating study of the muzzle-loading cap lock rifle covers rifles on the frontier to hunting rifles, including the famous Hawken.

The Muzzle-Loading Rifle...Then and Now, by Walter M. Cline, National Muzzle Loading Rifle Association, Friendship, IN, 1991. 161 pp. This extensive compilation of the muzzleloading rifle exhibits accumulative preserved data concerning the development of the hallowed old arms of the Southern highlands.

Naval Percussion Locks and Primers, by Lt. J. A. Dahlgren, Museum Restoration Service, Bloomfield, Canada, 1996. 140 pp. First published as an Ordnance Memoranda in 1853, this is the finest existing study of percussion locks and primers origin and development.

Ned H. Roberts and the Schuetzen Rifle, edited by Gerald O. Kelver, Brighton, CO, 1982. 99 pp. A compilation of the writings of Major Ned H. Roberts which appeared in various gun magazines.

The Paper Jacket, by Paul Matthews, Wolfe Publishing Co., Prescott, AZ, 1991. Paper covers. Up-to-date and accurate information about paper-patched bullets by an author highly regarded in the field of blackpowder cartridge shooting.

The Paper Patched Bullet, by Randolph S. Wright, C. Sharps Arms Publishers, 1985.
A 19-page booklet concerning paper patches, bullets and swaging.

Patents for Inventions, Class 119 (Small Arms), 1855-1930. British Patent Office, Armory Publications, Oceanside, CA, 1993. 7 volume set. Contains 7,980 abridged patent descriptions and their sectioned line drawings, plus a 37-page alphabetical index of the patentees.

Paterson Colt Pistol Variations, by R.L. Wilson and R. Phillips, Jackson Arms Co., Dallas, TX, 1979. 250 pp. A book about the different models and barrel lengths in the Paterson Colt story.

Pennsylvania Longrifles of Note, by George Shumway, George Shumway, Publisher, York, PA, 1977. 63 pp. Illustrates and describes rifles from a number of Pennsylvania rifle-making schools.

The Pennsylvania Rifle, by Samuel E. Dyke, Sutter House, Lititz, PA, 1975. 61 pp., illus. Paper covers. $5.00.
History and development, from the hunting rifle of the Germans who settled the area. Contains a full listing of all known Lancaster, PA, gunsmiths from 1729 through 1815.

The Pennsylvania-Kentucky Rifle, by Henry J. Kaufman, Stackpole Books, 1950.
The development and use of the rifle in Pennsylvania in early America.

The Pitman Notes on U.S. Martial Small Arms and Ammunition, 1776-1933, Volume 2.

Revolvers and Automatic Pistols, by Brig. Gen. John Pitman, Thomas Publications, Gettysburg, PA, 1990. 192 pp., illus. $29.95.
A most important primary source of information on United States military small arms and ammunition.

The Plains Rifle, by Charles Hanson, Gun Room Press, Highland Park, NJ, 1989. 169 pp., illus. $29.95.

All rifles that were made with the plainsman in mind, including pistols.

The Powder Flask Book, by Ray Riling, R&R Books, Livonia, NY, 1993. 514 pp., illus. $70.00.
The complete book on flasks of the 19th century. Exactly scaled pictures of 1,600 flasks are illustrated.

Purdey's, the Guns and the Family, by Richard Beaumont, David and Charles, Pomfert, VT, 1984. 248 pp., illus. $39.95.
Records the history of the Purdey family from 1814 to today, how the guns were and are built and daily functioning of the factory.

The Rare and Valuable Antique Arms, by James E. Serven, Pioneer Press, Union City, TN, 1976. 106 pp., illus. Paper covers. $4.95.
A guide to the collector in deciding which direction his collecting should go, investment value, historic interest, mechanical ingenuity, high art or personal preference.

The Recollections of an Elephant Hunter 1864-1875, by William Finaughty, Books of Zimbabwe, Bulawayo, Zimbabwe, 1980. 244 pp., illus. $85.00.
Reprint of the scarce 1916 privately published edition. The early game-hunting exploits of William Finaughty in Matabeleland and Nashonaland.

Recreating the American Longrifle, by William Buchele, et al., George Shumway, Publisher, York, PA, 1983. 175 pp., illus. $30.00.
Includes full-scale plans for building a Kentucky rifle.

Revolvers of the British Services 1854-1954, by W.H.J. Chamberlain and A.W.F. Taylerson, Museum Restoration Service, Ottawa, Canada, 1989. 80 pp., illus. $27.50.
Covers the types issued among many of the United Kingdom's naval, land or air services.

The Revolving Rifles, by Edsall James, Pioneer Press, Union City, TN, 1975. 23 pp., Valuable information on revolving cylinder rifles, from the earliest matchlock forms to the latest models of Colt and Remington.

Rhode Island Arms Makers & Gunsmiths, by William O. Archibald, Andrew Mowbray, Inc., Lincoln, RI, 1990. 108 pp., illus. A serious and informative study of an important area of American arms making.

The Rifle and the Hound in Ceylon, by S.W. Baker, Arno Press, 1967. Reprint of 19th-century work, a classic by an ivory hunter.

Sam Colt's Own Record 1847, by John Parsons, Wolfe Publishing Co., Prescott, AZ, 1992. 167 pp. Chronologically presented, the correspondence published here completes the account of the manufacture, in 1847, of the Walker Model Colt revolver.

Schuetzen Rifles, History and Loading, by Gerald O. Kelver, Gerald O. Kelver, Publisher, Brighton, CO, 1972.Reference work on these rifles, their bullets, loading, telescopic sights, accuracy, etc. A limited, numbered ed.

Scottish Firearms, by Claude Blair and Robert Woosnam-Savage, Museum Restoration Service, Bloomfield, Ont., Canada, 1995. 52 pathos revision of the first book devoted entirely to Scottish firearms is supplemented by a register of surviving Scottish long guns.

Sharps Firearms, by Frank Seller, Frank M. Seller, Denver, CO. 1982, 358 pp. Traces the development of Sharps firearms with full range of guns made including all martial variations.

Sharps Rifle The Gun That Shaped American Destiny, by Martin Rywell, Pioneer Press, 1979. The history, use and functioning of the Sharps rifle.

Shooting the Blackpowder Cartridge Rifle, by Paul A. Matthews, Wolfe Publishing Co., Prescott, AZ, 1994. 129 pp. A general discourse on shooting the blackpowder cartridge rifle and the procedure required to make a particular rifle perform. Written by an expert.

The Shotgun: History and Development, by Geoffrey Boothroyd, Safari Press, Huntington Beach, CA, 1995. 240 pp. The first volume in a series that traces the development of the British shotgun from the 17th century onward.

Sidelocks & Boxlocks, by Geoffrey Boothroyd, Sand Lake Press, Amity, OR, 1991. 271 pp. The story of the classic British shotgun.

Pistol Simeon North: First Official Maker of the United States, by S. North and R. North, The Gun Room Press, Highland Park, NJ, 1972, 207 pp. Reprint of the rare first edition.

Sixgun Cartridges and Loads, by Elmer Keith, The Gun Room Press, Highland Park, NJ, 1986. 151 pp. A manual covering the selection, uses and loading of the most suitable and popular revolver cartridges. Originally published in 1936. Reprint.

Spencer Firearms, by Roy Marcot, R&R Books, Livonia, NY, 1995. 237 pp. The definitive work on one of the most famous Civil War firearms.

The Sporting Rifle and Its Projectiles, by James Forsyth, Buckskin Press, 1978.
This reprint of an 1863 text is a study in early ballistic data.

SPG Lubricants BP Cartridge Reloading Primer, by Mike Venturino & Steve Garbe, SPG Lubricant, MT 1992. 116-pages. This book is filled with topflight information on the subject of blackpowder cartridge reloading.

Springfield Shoulder Arms 1795-1865, by Claud E. Fuller, S. & S. Firearms, Glendale, NY, 1986. 76 pp. Exact reprint of the scarce 1930 edition of one of the most definitive works on Springfield flintlock and percussion muskets ever published.

Standard Catalog of Firearms, by Ned Schwing, Krause Publications, Iola, WI, 2001. 1,334 pp. Huge pricing guide with 6,000 photos and 12,000 models covered. Includes a color gallery and 80,000 "real world" prices.

The Steel Canvas: Art of American Arms, by R. L. Wilson, Random House, NY, 1995, 384 pp., illus. Presented here for the first time is the breathtaking panorama of America's extraordinary engravers and embellishers of arms, from the 1700s to modern times.

The Sumptuous Flaske, by Herbert G. Houze, Andrew Mowbray, Inc., Lincoln, RI, 1989. 158 pp. Catalog of a recent show at the Buffalo Bill Historical Center bringing together some of the finest European and American powder flasks of the 16th to 19th centuries.

Tales of the Big Game Hunters, selected and introduced by Kenneth Kemp, The Sportsman's Press, London, 1986. 209 pp. Writings by some of the best-known hunters and explorers, among them: Frederick

United States Martial Flintlocks, by Robert M. Reilly, Andrew Mowbray, Inc., Lincoln, RI, 1986. 263 pp. A comprehensive illustrated history of the flintlock in America from the Revolution to the demise of the system.

U.S. Military Arms Dates of Manufacture from 1795, by George Madis, David Madis, Dallas, TX, 1989. 64 pp. Lists all U.S. military arms of collector interest alphabetically, covering about 250 models.

U.S. Military Small Arms 1816-1865, by Robert M. Reilly, The Gun Room Press, Highland Park, NJ, 1983. 270 pp. Covers every known type of primary and secondary martial firearms used by Federal forces.

Weapons of the Highland Regiments 1740-1780, by Anthony D. Darling, Museum Restoration Service, Bloomfield, Canada, 1996. 28 pp. This study deals with the formation and arming of the famous Highland regiments.

The Whitney Firearms, by Claud Fuller, Standard Publications, Huntington, WV, 1946, 334 pp. An authoritative history of all Whitney arms and their maker. Highly recommended. An exclusive with Ray Riling Arms Books Co.

Winchester: An American Legend, by R.L. Wilson, Random House, New York, NY, 1991. 403 pp. The official history of Winchester firearms from 1849 to the present.

The Winchester Book, by George Madis, David Madis Gun Book Distributor, Dallas, TX, 1986. 650 pp. A new, revised 25th anniversary edition of this classic book on Winchester firearms. Complete serial ranges have been added.

Winchester Dates of Manufacture 1849-1984, by George Madis, Art & Reference House, Brownsboro, TX, 1984. 59 pp. A most useful work, compiled from records of the Winchester factory.

The Winchester Era, by David Madis, Art & Reference House, Brownsville, TX, 1984. 100 pp. Story of the Winchester company, management, employees, etc

The Winchester Handbook, by George Madis, Art & Reference House, Lancaster, TX, 1982. 287 pp. The complete line of Winchester guns, with dates of manufacture, serial numbers, etc.

Winchester Lever Action Repeating Firearms, Vol. 1, The Models of 1866, 1873 and 1876, by Arthur Pirkie, North Cape Publications, Tustin, CA, 1995. 112 pp. Complete, part-by-part description, including dimensions, finishes, markings and variations throughout the production run of these fine, collectible guns.

The Winchester Single-Shot, by John Cambell, Andrew Mowbray, Inc., Lincoln RI, 1995. 272 pp. Covers every important aspect of this highly-collectible firearm.

PERIODICALS OF INTEREST FOR THE BLACKPOWDER SHOOTER

American Hunter

National Rifle Association, 11250 Waples Mill Rd., Fairfax, VA 22030. Publications Div. $35.00 yr. Wide scope of hunting articles, including muzzleloader outings.

American Rifleman

National Rifle Assn., 11250 Waples Mill Rd., Fairfax, VA 22030. Publications Div. $35.00 yr. Firearms articles of all kinds, including blackpowder guns.

The Backwoodsman

P.O. Box 627, Westcliffe, CO 81252. $16.00 for 6 issues per yr.; $30.00 for 2 yrs.; sample copy $2.75. Subjects include muzzleloading, woodsmanship, primitive survival, trapping, homesteading, blackpowder cartridge guns, 19th century how-to.

Black Powder Cartridge News

SPG, Inc., P.O. Box 1625, Cody, WY 82414/307-587-7621. $20 yr. (4 issues). For the blackpowder cartridge enthusiast; features gun profiles, match results, product reviews, collector's corner.

Black Powder Times

P.O. Box 234, Lake Stevens, WA 98258. $20.00 yr.; add $5 per year for Canada, $10 per year other foreign. Tabloid newspaper for blackpowder activities; test reports.

Blackpowder Hunting

Bradbury Communications, 570 Boxelder Road, Glenrock, WY 82637. $20 yr. (4 issues). For those who enjoy blackpowder hunting this magazine carries articles on small and big game, plus reviews of new products on the market.

The Cast Bullet Journal

Official journal of The Cast Bullet Association. Director of Membership, 4103 Foxcraft Dr., Traverse City, MI 49684. Annual membership dues $14, includes 6 issues. Learn about cast bullet shooting from experts.

Fur-Fish-Game

A.R. Harding Publishing. Co., 2878 E. Main St., Columbus, OH 43209. $15.95 yr. A mainstay magazine for many years, filled with hunting and woodsmanship.

Gun List

700 E. State St., Iola, WI 54990. $29.95 yr. (26 issues); $54.95 2 yrs. (52 issues). Indexed market publication for firearms collectors and active shooters; guns, supplies and services.

Gun World

Gallant/Charger Publications, Inc., 34249 Camino Capistrano, Capistrano Beach, CA 92624. $22.50 yr. For the hunting, reloading, and shooting enthusiast.

Guns

P.O. Box 85201, San Diego, CA 92138. $19.95 yr.; $34.95 2 yrs.; $46.95 3 yrs. In-depth articles on a wide range of guns, shooting equipment and related accessories for gun collectors, hunters and shooters.

Muzzle Blasts

National Muzzle Loading Rifle Association, P.O. Box 67, Friendship, IN 47021. $30.00 yr. annual membership. This official publication of the NMLRA is all blackpowder, with many articles on fascinating subjects.

Muzzleloader

Scurlock Publishing Co., Inc., Dept. Gun, Route 5, Box 347-M, Texarkana, TX 75501. $18.00 U.S. yr.; $22.50 U.S. for foreign subscribers. The publication for blackpowder shooters who appreciate the history as well as the shooting aspect of the sport; noted for beautiful covers.

Outdoor Life

Times Mirror Magazines, Two Park Ave., New York, NY 10016. Special 1-yr. subscription, $11.97. Extensive coverage of hunting and shooting. Shooting column by Jim Carmichel.

Rifle

Wolfe Publishing Co., 6471 Airpark Dr., Prescott, AZ 86301. $19.00 yr. The sporting firearms journal filled with carefully researched articles on all manner of shooting, including blackpowder guns.

The Shotgun News

Snell Publishing Co., Box 669, Hastings, NE 68902/800-345-6923.

$29.00 yr.; foreign subscription — call for rates. Sample copy $4.00. Gun ads of all kinds.

The Single Shot Exchange

P.O. Box 1055, York, SC 29745 or 803-628-5326. $31.50 for 12 issues. Blackpowder cartridge, Schuetzen, Cowboy Action, collecting, buying, selling, informational articles.

The Tomahawk & Long Rifle

3483 Squires, Conklin, MI 49403. $20.00 yr.; foreign $27.00. About mountain men by mountain men since 1972; the official publication of the American Mountain Men Association.

Sports Afield

P.O. Box 7166, Red Oak, IA 51591 for subscription services or 800-234-3537. $13.97 for 12 issues. Informational format with many hunting stories; also an almanac section with tips for outdoorsmen.

BLACKPOWDER ASSOCIATIONS

American Custom Gunmakers Guild
Jan Billeb, Exec. Director
P.O. Box 812
Burlington, IA 52601-0812
319-752-6114 (Phone or Fax)

American Single Shot Rifle Association
Gary Staup, Secretary
POB 362
Delphos, OH 45833

American Society of Arms Collectors
George E. Weatherly
P.O. Box 2567
Waxahachie, TX 75165

Browning Collector's Association
Secretary: Scherrie L. Brennac
2749 Keith Dr.
Villa Ridge, MO 63089
314-742-0571

The Cast Bullet Association Inc.
Ralland J. Fortier
Membership Director
4103 Foxcraft Dr.
Traverse City, MI 49684

Colt Collectors Association
25000 Highland Way
Los Gatos, CA 95030

Contemporary Longrifle Association
POB 2097
Staunton, VA 24402

Hopkins & Allen Arms & Memorabilia Society (HAAMS)
1309 Pamela Circle
Delphos, OH 45833

International Blackpowder Hunting Association
P.O. Box 1180
Glenrock, WY 82637
307-436-9817

National Muzzle Loading Rifle Association
Box 67
Friendship, IN 47021

National Rifle Association of America
11250 Waples Mill Rd.
Fairfax, VA 22030

North-South Skirmish Association Inc.
Stevan F. Meserve
Exec. Secretary
507 N. Brighton Court
Sterling, VA 20164-3919

Remington Society of America
Leon W. Wier Jr., President
8268 Lone Feather Ln.
Las Vegas, NV 89123

Single Action Shooting Society
1938 North Batavia St., Suite C
Orange, CA 92665
714-998-0209
Fax: 714-998-1992

Southern California Schuetzen Society
Dean Lillard
34657 Ave. E.
Yucaipa, CA 92399

U.S. Revolver Association
Brian J. Barer
40 Larchmont Ave.
Taunton, MA 02780
508-824-4836

Winchester Arms Collectors Association
Richard Berg
Exec. Secretary
P.O. Box 6754
Great Falls, MT 59406

OUTFITTERS FOR BLACKPOWDER HUNTERS

TODAY'S BUSY hunter is often well-advised to "go guided," saving a great deal of scouting time. Competent guides know the area and the game, raising a hunter's odds for success measurably. Furthermore, game is packed by guides from field to camp. Today, there are a number of outfitters dedicated to muzzleloader hunting. They understand that the blackpowder shooter must get closer to his game, and they're good at stalking, as well as calling game in. Naturally, there are fees for services. The hunter must weigh the fees against his personal odds of taking the game he wants on his own, without help. For each outfitter, a contact person and telephone number are supplied. The prospective hunter should call for brochures, prices and seasons.

Deer Creek Outfitters
POB 39
Sebree, KY 42455
270-835-2424

Contact Person: Tim Stull
Specialty: Muzzleloader hunts for trophy whitetails on private grounds. Facilities include room and board in a modern building. Tree stands are the rule. Also waterfowl, upland game, wild turkey. The lands are in a game management program.

Tenderfoot Outfitters
POB 85
Gunnison, CO 81230
800-880-2970

Contact Person: Steve Pike
Specialty: Horse and mule pack trips into wilderness territory during Colorado's special blackpowder-only elk and deer season. Large wall tents

with stoves; food prepared by cook in the mess tent. Some hunting on horseback; elk and deer field dressed and packed in by guides.

Coal Creek Outfitters
POB 797
Evansville, WY 82636
307-234-8940

Contact Person: Kelly Glause
Specialty: Unique hunts on the high desert of Wyoming for prairie mule deer and antelope. Hunters can elect to stay on the grounds or in Casper, which is about one hour away. Food is camp-cooked with packed lunches for hunters taking stands in ground blinds and windmills. High rate of success because of the strong number of game animals with good blinds arranged at frequently visited waterholes.

Copeau Creek Outfitters
POB 460
Porcupine Plain, Saskatchewan
Canada S0E 1H0
306-278-3023

Contact Person: David N. Osecki
Specialty: Black bear, whitetail deer, Canada geese, and other game. Focuses on large whitetail bucks. Licensed outfitter and guides.

Moose Valley Outfitters
POB 124
Lark Harbour, Newfoundland
A0L 1H0
709-681-2115

Contact Person: Dean MacDonald
Specialty: Fly-in hunts only with one-on-one service (one hunter, one guide) for moose, caribou, and bear.

Pacific Rim Guide Outfitters, Ltd.
No. 340 185-911 Yates Street
British Columbia, Canada V8V 4Y9
888-826-1011

Contact Person: Jim Shockey
Specialty: Extremely large black bears hunted on Vancouver Island; trophy whitetails and color-phase black bears in Saskatchewan.

Blue Ridge Guide Service
4638 Blue Ridge Drive
Springville, CA 93265
559-539-5102

Contact Person: Bill Sweetser
Specialty: Located only three hours from Los Angeles, this outfitter guides for black bear, wild turkey, bobcat, coyote, deer, wood ducks, band-tailed pigeons and other game along the western slope of the Sierras.

Circle K Ranch, Inc.
27758 Highway 145
Dolores, CO 81323
970-562-3808

Contact Person: Allen Cannon
Specialty: Drop-camps available; also pack-in elk and deer hunts in Colorado's San Juan Mountains. Promises spacious lodge and cabins. Also horse rental for freelance hunters.

Elmer Trophy Outfitters
36 Table Butte Road
Silver City, NM 88601
505-535-4200

Contact Person: Bill Elmer
Specialty: Wide range of game, including Coues deer, mule deer, elk,

bear, turkey, and javelina. Hunts both Arizona and New Mexico.

G.W. Petersen Outfitting
Old Glendevey Ranch, Ltd.
City Road 190
Jelm, WY 82063
970-435-5701

Contact Person: Garth Petersen
Specialty: Registered guides take hunters to big game on what this outfitter calls "a quality experience" in game-rich Wyoming. Horses available. Trained staff to help the hunter find and take game.

Triple O Outfitters
POB 99
Hamilton, CO 81638
970-824-6758

Contact Person: Larry Osborn
Specialty: Full-service operation, including hunts for small game, elk, deer, bear, and antelope. Cabins for family and guided hunts. Tents for drop camps. Uses pack horses to reach areas closed to motorized vehicles.

Flying B Ranch
Route 2 – Box 123C
Kamiah, ID 83536-9553
208-935-0755

Contact Person: Joseph Petersen
Specialty: Horse pack-in hunts for deer and elk from "deluxe back country camps;" also cougars, as well as bear and whitetails from "luxurious lodge." Elk and deer muzzleloader-only seasons. Free video and brochures for serious inquiries.

Sunny Brook Camp and Ranch
Outfitters
HC – Box 36C
Sparks, NE 69220

Contact Person: Steve Breuklander
Specialty: Either lodge or well-stocked camps located along the Niobrara National Scenic River, with guided hunts for whitetails or mule deer with muzzleloaders. Spring and fall turkey hunts. All on private grounds.

Neal Adventures
709 W. Park St.
Belgrade, MT 59714
406-388-2733

Contact Person: Craig Neal
Specialty: Although located in Montana, the outfitting is in Nebraska's Sandhills country. Family-operated guiding on 18,000 acres exclusively reserved for muzzleloader or archery hunters only. Whitetails and mule deer. Also spike camps for do-it-yourself hunters.

Orion Outfitters and
Guide Service
6 Page Road
Londonderry, NH 03053
603-434-7437

Contact Person: Paul M. McCarthy
Specialty: Guided trophy moose and black bear hunts for blackpowder or bow only, along with whitetail deer and wild turkeys. All hunts set up individually. Families welcome.

Southwest New Mexico Trophy
Outfitters
POB 9
Quemado, NM 87829
505-773-4729
505-773-4545

Contact Person: Carlton Armstrong
Specialty: Hunt the Gila wilderness with this outfitter for elk with a muzzleloader. Also, pronghorn antelope, wild turkey, mule deer, lions, and ibex. This outfitter guarantees license.

Bear-One Guide Service
245 Park Street
Milo, ME 04463
207-943-0954

Contact Person: Brent Bailey
Specialty: Dedicated bear hunter Brent Bailey offers prime black bear hunts in pristine Maine woods territory. Bailey guided one hunter to the state record for blackpowder at the time, currently still No. 4 in the listings. He scouts areas all year long. Moose also for those who draw a license.

Headwaters Guide Service, Inc.
341 Southline Road
Galaway, NY 12074
518-882-6855

Contact Person: Marty Eisenbraun
Specialty: Guided blackpowder hunts for deer and bear in the southern part of the interesting Adirondack Mountains. Accommodations for all four seasons in "comfortable camps," with "hearty meals in yurts (round tents)." Private camp is adjacent to state domain.

Elk Song Ranch
59653 Morgan Lake Road
LaGrande, OR 59653
541-963-6711

Contact Person: Ross Seyfried
Specialty: Fully guided muzzleloader hunts into pristine territory in an area described as one of the most dense populations of elk in the United States. Hunters have seen "several hundred elk daily" during certain times of the year.

Southern Oregon Game Busters
POB 1576
Medford, OR 97501
541-770-5050

Contact Person: Doug Gattis
Specialty: Boasting 100 percent success on the elusive blacktail deer. Elk and bear hunts are also available from this guide service.

Triple Creek Hunts
HC 72 – Box 421
Fort Laramie, WY 82212
307-837-3023

Contact Person: Jim Freeburn
Specialty: Guided trophy muzzleloader hunts for mule deer and whitetails, antelope and elk, on private ranches in Wyoming and northwest Nebraska. High rate of success for quality bucks noted.

Moose Valley Outfitters
POB 124
Lark Harbour, Newfoundland
Canada AOL 1H0
709-681-2115

Specialty: Fly-in hunts only for moose, caribou, and bear with a one-on-one guide-to-hunter ratio.

TABLES

7,000 grains weight = 1 pound

437.5 grains weight = 1 ounce

15.43 grains weight = 1 gram

453.6 grams = 1 pound

25.4 mm = 1 inch

Conversions

Pounds times 7,000 = grains weight

Ounces times 437.5 = grains weight

Grains times .00229 = ounces

Grams times 15.4324 = grains weight

Inches times 25.4 = millimeters

Millimeters times .03937 = inches

One meter = 39.37 inches

One yard = .914 meters

27.34 grains = 1 dram

16 drams = 1 ounce

2,000 pounds = 1 short ton

2,240 pounds = 1 long ton

Round Balls to the Pound

The following are not exact but useful in figuring how many balls can be cast per pound of lead.

2 bore = 2 balls to the pound

4 bore = 4 balls to the pound

8 bore = 8 balls to the pound

10 bore = 10 balls to the pound

12 bore = 12 balls to the pound

20 bore = 20 balls to the pound

58 caliber = 25 balls to the pound

54 caliber = 30 balls to the pound

50 caliber = 40 balls to the pound

45 caliber = 53 balls to the pound

40 caliber = 75 balls to the pound

36 caliber = 108 balls to the pound

32 caliber = 155 to the pound

WEIGHT IN GRAINS PER VOLUME FOR SELECTED MUZZLELOADER PROPELLANTS

VOLUME OF POWDER/ACTUAL WEIGHT IN GRAINS

(Adjustable Powder Measure)/(RCBS Electronic Scale)

CLEAR SHOT FFg
100 grains volume/100.0 grains weight

CLEAR SHOT FFFg
100 grains volume/112.0 grains weight

GOEX FFg
100 grains volume/100.0 grains weight

GOEX FFFg
100 grains volume/102.0 grains weight

GOEX CARTRIDGE GRADE
100 grains volume/102.5 grains weight

WANO FFg
100 grains volume/103.0 grains weight

WANO FFFg
100 grains volume/105.0 grains weight

WANO 7FA
100 grains volume/105.0 grains weight

SWISS BLACK POWDER Fg
100 grains volume/108.0 grains weight

SWISS BLACK POWDER 1 1/2 Fg Schuetzen
100 grains volume/109.0 grains weight

SWISS BLACK POWDER FFg
100 grains volume/111.5 grains weight

SWISS BLACK POWDER FFFg
100 grains volume/107.5 grains weight

SWISS BLACK POWDER FFFFg
100 grains volume/103.0 grains weight

ELEPHANT BLACK POWDER FFg
100 grains volume/108.5 grains weight

ELEPHANT BLACK POWDER FFFg
100 grains volume/110.5 grains weight

PYRODEX RS
100 grains volume/70.0 grains weight

PYRODEX RS SELECT
100 grains volume/67.0 grains weight

PYRODEX P
100 grains volume/73.5 grains weight

PYRODEX 50/50 PELLET
Each 50-grain volume pellet = 37.0 grains weight

EXPLANATION: The volume/weight figures presented here will **not** repeat exactly because of variables. An Uncle Mike's adjustable powder measure was used for this evaluation. A different brand powder measure, or for that matter another powder measure of the same brand, may not produce identical results. Furthermore, powder lots (specific runs) differ. The data above are valuable, however, to show the general concept of volume/weight relationships for the brands and granulations represented.

INDEX

T

Thimble 59, 77

Touchhole 49, 56, 59, 60, 64, 81, 146, 150-152, 191-194, 220, 296, 298, 305, 306, 308

Trajectory 31, 66, 80, 124, 164, 165, 170, 227, 230, 231, 238, 242, 249, 250, 259, 263, 323, 345, 346, 350, 373, 378, 382

Trigger 31, 32

Twain 14, 63, 356

Twist 39, 40, 72, 75, 77, 79, 82, 83, 87, 126, 131, 158, 159, 162, 166, 170, 173, 175, 176, 180, 183, 233, 242, 243, 245, 250, 251, 254, 256, 258, 268, 281, 291, 342, 358, 364

V

Vent pick 49, 59, 60, 150

Venturino, Mike 268, 269, 346, 383

Volumetric charge 49, 57, 105, 109, 112, 113, 115-117, 174, 175

W

Wad 54, 64, 65, 67, 121, 143, 144, 147, 153-157, 268, 271, 273-276, 279, 289, 290, 300, 331, 337, 346

Wad column 67, 155, 156, 191, 272, 279, 337

War of 1812 356

Wax cookie 346

Wedge 125, 191, 196, 265, 297, 364

Whale oil 139, 142, 296

Whitworth, Sir Joseph 71, 97, 101, 126, 127, 129, 182, 253, 257, 260

Winchester 27, 55, 73-75, 83, 85, 90, 97-100, 111, 126-128, 143, 165, 166, 171, 179, 182, 197, 199, 205, 207, 220, 242, 245-248, 256, 261-268, 270, 271, 280, 284, 285, 319, 324, 337, 338, 342-346, 348, 361, 379-381, 383-385

Wind drift 130, 233, 234, 356

Windage 59, 73, 77, 164, 186, 225-227, 231-234, 254, 255, 292, 364

Wiping stick 54, 59, 296, 299

Wound channel 61, 167, 246, 248, 249, 255, 290, 317, 319, 321-323

Z

Zouave 71, 254, 255, 258-260

Be the Fastest Gun in the West

Colt's Single Action Army Revolver
by "Doc" O'Meara
Learn more about the *Colt Single Action Army Revolver* as "Doc" O'Meara guides you through a historical look at the world's most famous revolver. With production figures and serial number ranges for early versions of the gun, this book is a must for any collector. O'Meara also mixes in stories about rare Colts and their owners that will both inform and entertain anyone interested in the gun that has come to symbolize the American cowboy.
Hardcover • 8-1/2 x 11
160 pages
250 b&w photos
16-page color section
Item# CSAAR • $34.95

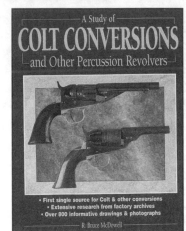

A Study of Colt Conversions and Other Percussion Revolvers
by R. Bruce McDowell
This ultimate reference details Colt revolvers converted from percussion (cap and ball) to cartridge. Includes technical specifications, exceptional photos and accurate drawings plus historical information gleaned from government files, manufacturers, museums and private collections.
Hardcover • 8-1/2 x 11
464 pages
792 b&w photos
Item# FCOL • $39.95

Action Shooting Cowboy Style
by John Taffin
Feel the rich gun leather and taste the smoke of America's fastest-growing shooting game. Every aspect is explained for shooters of all levels. Join the fun of cowboy-style shooting. Let John Taffin take you from the general store where he'll show you the latest in old western garb, to the firing line where some of the fastest guns around drop the hammer in search of a winning score.
Hardcover • 8-1/2 x 11
320 pages
300 b&w photos
8-page color section
Item# COWAS • $39.95

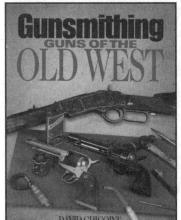

Gunsmithing: Guns of the Old West
by David Chicoine
Learn to repair, improve and upgrade your antique and replica firearms from the Old West. This gunsmithing manual provides step-by-step detailed illustrations for more than 40 popular original and replica Old West guns. You'll be able to keep your favorite cowboy action shooting guns functioning properly, and you'll know when to have an experienced gunsmith perform the repairs.
Softcover • 8-1/2 x 11
352 pages
300 b&w photos
Item# GUWS • $27.95

The Top Shooter's Guide to Cowboy Action Shooting
by Hunter Scott Anderson
Become a better cowboy action shooter. As a veteran of hundreds of these mock gun battles, Hunter Scott Anderson teaches shooters of all skill levels how to improve their shooting and their ranking among competitors. This book teaches you how to move effortlessly through a course of fire, while maintaining the accuracy needed to score well. This is the cowboy action-shooting book that will take you to the next level.
Softcover • 8-1/2 x11
216 pages
200 b&w photos
Item# TSCA • $21.95

Classic Colt Peacemakers
by "Doc" O'Meara
Colt's Single Action Army revolver, the Peacemaker, is arguably one of the most recognizable handguns in the world. As the "gun that won the West," it is also one of the most revered, adorned and collected. Now, you can admire some of the greatest examples of this fine revolver and read the stories behind them. With photography so striking and revolvers so beautiful you can almost feel the quality of these wonderful guns, *Classic Colt Peacemakers* brings the finest guns in the world to your finger tips.
Softcover • 8-1/4 x 10-7/8 • 128 pages
150 color photos
Item# CCPM • $21.95

To place a credit card order or for a FREE all-product catalog call

800-258-0929 Offer GNB1

M-F 7am - 8pm • Sat 8am - 2pm, CST

DBI BOOKS
a division of Krause Publications

Krause Publications, Offer GNB1
P.O. Box 5009, Iola WI 54945-5009 • www.krausebooks.com

Shipping & Handling: $4.00 first book, $2.00 each additional. Non-US addresses $20.95 first book, $5.95 each additional.

Sales Tax: CA, IA, IL, PA, TN, VA, WI residents please add appropriate sales tax.

Satisfaction Guarantee: If for any reason you are not completely satisfied with your purchase, simply return it within 14 days of receipt and receive a full refund, less shipping charges.

Top References for Top Shooters

The Gun Digest® Blackpowder Loading Manual
3rd Edition
by Sam Fadala
Worth its price just for the load data on 158 firearms alone. Sam Fadala crafts instructive articles and a loading tutorial into the must-have book blackpowder shooters have been craving. All-new information with expanded sections.
Softcover
8-1/4 x 10-11/16
368 pages
390 b&w photos
Item# BPL3 • $19.95

Modern Muzzleloading for Today's Whitetails
by Ian McMurchy
Edited by Patrick Durkin
Muzzleloading expert Ian McMurchy reveals what hunters should seek when buying an in-line rifle, and then offers insights on their use from the shooting range to the deer woods. In-line rifles revolutionized muzzleloader deer hunting in much the same way the compound bow propelled bow-hunting into a pastime for the hunting masses. McMurchy also offers detailed advice on developing straight-shooting, hard-hitting loads for deer hunting, and how to discover each gun's long-range capabilities.
Hardcover • 8-1/4 x 10-7/8 • 208 pages • 100 color photos
Item# MODMZ • $34.95

Black Powder Hobby Gunsmithing
by Sam Fadala and Dale Storey
Keep busy with projects for all levels of competence, from kitchen table through home workshop, all the way to the academic. Step-by-step tutorials on building from kits and a resource directory make the grade.
Softcover
8-1/4 x 10-11/16
256 pages
440 b&w photos
Item# BHG • $18.95

UPDATED ANNUALLY

Gun Digest® 2002
The World's Greatest Gun Book, 56th Annual Edition
edited by Ken Ramage
Keep up-to-date on the latest collecting and accessory information the gun industry offers. This 56th edition showcases a new full-color section on engraved and custom guns, all-new feature articles, fresh new product reports and a completely updated catalog and reference section. Don't miss the expanded and updated Directory of the Arms Trade including directories of products, services and manufacturers.
Softcover • 8-1/2 x 11
560 pages
2,000 b&w photos
16-page color section
Item# GD2002 • $27.95

Flayderman's Guide to Antique American Firearms and Their Values
The Complete Handbook of Antique American Gun Collecting, 8th Edition
by Norm Flayderman
Norm Flayderman is today's foremost authority on U.S. antique arms history. His book is the bible for antique American arms and a must-have historical reference and price guide for collectors, shooters, and hunters. Identify and evaluate market prices for more than 4,000 firearms manufactured between 1850 and 1900.
Softcover • 8-1/2 x 11
672 pages
1,700+ b&w photos
Item# FLA8 • $34.95

Mauser Military Rifles of the World
2nd Edition
by Robert W. D. Ball
Learn how to identify every Mauser model from 1871 to 1945 while looking over production figures and the relative rarity of each model. This updated edition of a collector's classic unveils 100 new photos of rare guns and the men who used them. Whether your interest is in collecting or military history, this book gives you all the details you won't find anywhere else.
Hardcover • 8-1/2 x 11
304 pages
1,000 b&w photos
48-page color section
Item# FCM02 • $44.95

To place a credit card order or for a FREE all-product catalog call

800-258-0929 Offer GNB1

M-F 7am - 8pm • Sat 8am - 2pm, CST

DBI BOOKS
a division of Krause Publications

Krause Publications, Offer GNB1
P.O. Box 5009, Iola WI 54945-5009 • www.krausebooks.com

Shipping & Handling: $4.00 first book, $2.00 each additional. Non-US addresses $20.95 first book, $5.95 each additional.
Sales Tax: CA, IA, IL, PA, TN, VA, WI residents please add appropriate sales tax.
Satisfaction Guarantee: If for any reason you are not completely satisfied with your purchase, simply return it within 14 days of receipt and receive a full refund, less shipping charges.

Two Great Offers from the Hobby's Best

Get more than 20,000 guns in every issue of *GUN LIST*. You'll find it easy to locate the guns you want, or buyers for those you want to sell. Just use the easy index to find what you want. It's alphabetized, for your convenience. Plus, checking prices in each alphabetized category can give you a quick fix on what similar guns would sell for in your area. Pure and simple, *GUN LIST* is the gun buyers' friend.

BLADE brings you the latest information on knives, knife-makers and knife-making. From the finest hand-mades to factory workhorses, you'll stay on the cutting edge in *BLADE*. More than 120 pages in every issue means you'll get more articles and knife info than other knife magazines provide in a year!

Act Now!

Order Form

( ) 6 issues (one-half year) of *BLADE* Magazine . . . . Just $9.99
( ) 13 issues (one-half year) of *GUN LIST* . . . . Just $15.00

( ) Check or money order (to **Krause Publications**)
( ) MasterCard ( ) VISA ( ) Discover/Novus ( ) American Express

Credit Card No._____

Expires: Mo_____ Yr_____

Signature_____

Name_____

Address_____

City_____ State_____ Zip_____

Phone No._____

Email address (optional)_____

Mail with payment to Krause Publications
Dept. ABA6WV, 700 E. State St., Iola, WI 54990-0001

Charge Card Orders Dial Toll-Free **800-258-0929** Dept. ABA6WV
7 am - 8 pm, M-F and 8 am - 2 pm, Sat., CDT